THE UTAH GUIDE

THE UTAH GUIDE

Allan Kent Powell

Fulcrum Publishing
Golden, Colorado

The information in *The Utah Guide* is accurate as of January 1995. Prices, hours of operation, telephone numbers, and other items change rapidly. If something in the book is incorrect or if you have ideas for the next edition, please write to the author at Fulcrum Publishing, 350 Indiana Street, Suite 350, Golden, CO 80401-5093.

The Utah Guide provides many safety tips about weather and travel, but good decision making and sound judgment are the responsibility of the individual.

Library of Congress Cataloging-in-Publication Data
Powell, Allan Kent.
    The Utah guide / Allan Kent Powell.
        p.   cm.
    Includes index.
    ISBN 1-55591-130-7
    1. Utah—Guidebooks. I. Title.
F824.3.P68   1995
917.9204'33—dc20   94–41333
                                                                    CIP

Printed in the United States of America

0 9 8 7 6 5 4 3 2 1

Fulcrum Publishing
350 Indiana Street, Suite 350
Golden, Colorado 80401-5093
800/992-2908

CONTENTS

ACKNOWLEDGMENTS

My parents, Leland and Luella Powell, have been a constant support and have instilled in me a deep love for Utah. Both have contributed in important ways to my view of Utah and its people. My father, who has spent many years traveling the state, knows it as well as anyone of his generation and is my bridge between the past and the present. My mother has helped me see that people are at the heart of any endeavor.

This guide book is really a Powell family production. My wife Brenda and children Lee, Liesel, and Adrianna have accompanied me during much of the research and have provided their own perspective of what is important and worth including in the book. Having the opportunity to involve them made the project all the more rewarding and worthwhile. I appreciate both their help and their patience.

Bob Baron and the staff at Fulcrum Publishing deserve special thanks. I appreciate Bob asking me to write the Utah Guide, and I especially appreciate his good advice, when the project seemed overwhelming, simply to go out and have fun with the assignment. Carmel Huestis and Tammy Ferris have been a delight to work with during the writing and editing stages. Thanks also to Patty Maher in the production department. Richard Firmage, a fellow Utahn and colleague, has provided a book design that deserves special praise. Leslie Jorgensen of Jorgensen Design has created functional maps that add to the artistic quality of the book.

It is impossible to list the hundreds of people who have provided information, read chapters, shared secrets about their favorite places, and guided me as I learned more about this special state. I am indebted especially to regional and local travel directors; to staffs of the National Park Service, National Forest Service, and Bureau of Land Management; to city, county and state employees throughout Utah; and to the owners, managers, and staffs of the hundreds of businesses and facilities who made my work in compiling this guide book so easy and enjoyable. To each of you, I extend my heartfelt thanks.

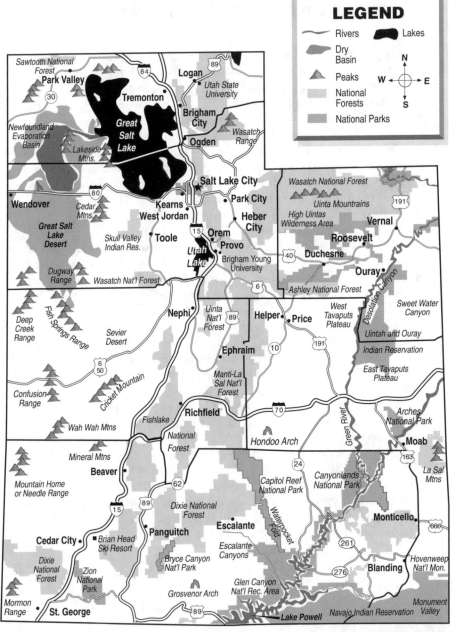

LEGEND

Rivers		Lakes	
Dry Basin			
Peaks			
National Forests			
National Parks			

N
W ← → E
S

Sawtooth National Forest
Park Valley
30
Tremonton
Logan
89
84
Utah State University
Brigham City
Great Salt Lake
Newfoundland Evaporation Basin
Wasatch Range
Lakeside Mtns.
Ogden
Salt Lake City
Wendover
Cedar Mtns.
80
Kearns
West Jordan
Park City
Heber City
Wasatch National Forest
Uinta Mountrains
191
Great Salt Lake Desert
Skull Valley Indian Res.
Toole
15
Orem
Provo
High Uintas Wilderness Area
Vernal
Roosevelt
Dugway Range
Utah Lake
Brigham Young University
40
Duchesne
Ouray
Wasatch Nat'l Forest
6
Ashley National Forest
Desolation Canyon
Deep Creek Range
Fish Springs Range
Sevier Desert
Nephi
Uinta Nat'l Forest
89
Helper
Price
West Tavaputs Plateau
Sweet Water Canyon
Uintah and Ouray
6
50
Cricket Mountain
Ephraim
10
191
Indian Reservation
Confusion Range
Wah Wah Mtns
Fishlake
Richfield
National Forest
70
Hondoo Arch
Green River
East Tavaputs Plateau
Arches National Park
Moab
163
Mineral Mtns
Beaver
62
Capitol Reef National Park
24
Canyonlands National Park
La Sal Mtns
Mountain Home or Needle Range
15
89
Dixie National Forest
Escalante
Waterpocket Fold
Monticello
666
Cedar City
Brian Head Ski Resort
Panguitch
261
Dixie National Forest
Zion National Park
Bryce Canyon Nat'l Park
Escalante Canyons
276
Blanding
Hovenweep Nat'l Mon.
Mormon Range
St. George
89
Grosvenor Arch
Glen Canyon Nat'l Rec. Area
Lake Powell
Navajo Indian Reservation
Monument Valley

Utah

INTRODUCTION

BACKGROUND INFORMATION

In 1846, a year before the first Mormon pioneers arrived in Utah, a visitor from Switzerland en route to California named Heinrich Lienhardt stopped at the Great Salt Lake after a laborious and difficult wagon journey through the mountains. In one of the first written descriptions of the land now known as Utah, the 24-year-old Lienhardt captured the essence of what is still the Utah experience for visitors and residents alike: "The clear, sky-blue water, the warm sunny air, the nearby high mountains…made an unusually friendly impression. I could have whistled and sung the entire day."

One hundred fifty years after Lienhardt's visit to Utah, this place and its 2 million people still make a good impression. The scenery is as beautiful and varied as you will find anywhere. As the 15 million annual visitors to Utah will attest, it offers something for everyone. Within a few hours' drive you can find 12,000-foot mountain ranges with alpine forests, meadows, lakes, streams, ski slopes, and hiking trails. Monuments of stone cut and shaped by the forces of nature have been left in the galleries of an outdoor museum laid out over thousands of square miles of deserts, plateaus, and canyons. The Wasatch Front mountain range, which includes the greater Salt Lake City area, offers a wealth of cultural, educational, and recreational opportunities.

For the last three years, much of my spare time has been spent researching and writing this guidebook. In working on this task, I have tried to describe and explain things as if I were writing for my personal friends—those who, like me, have lived most of their lives in the state, and those who travel from other parts of the country and the world to see my home state. By looking at Utah with an eye to sharing it with others, I have seen it in even more varied and exciting ways than in the past. My love and appreciation for Utah has grown in ways I had not anticipated when the project was first proposed. I have met hundreds of people who also love the state and love to share it with others.

Whether you are a longtime resident or are preparing to spend your first day in Utah, you will find that history, scenery, activities, and people

1

are the basic ingredients of your Utah experience. I hope this book helps add a measure of enjoyment and understanding to that experience.

HISTORY

The human habitation of what is now called Utah stretches back at least 12,000 years to a people archaeologists call the Paleo-Indians, that included the Clovis and Folsom cultures. These people, who appeared after North America's last ice age, were essentially hunters of large game. As the Paleo-Indians began to gather plants and seeds to supplement their diet, they moved into what is known as the Archaic stage, a period that lasted from about 7,000 to 1,500 years ago. Two cultures, the Anasazi and the Fremont, began to plant corn and squash crops and to raise animals, such as turkeys, for food. They left behind an abundant treasure of rock art, artifacts, and structures. The Anasazi culture existed in southern and southeastern Utah from 2,000 until 700 years ago. The Fremont culture was roughly contemporaneous, beginning about 1,500 years ago and located to the north and west of the Anasazi. Like the Anasazi, the Fremont culture disappeared about AD 1300, although it is uncertain whether the Fremont people were absorbed by the Ute and Shoshoni Indians who wandered into the state in search of game. The Anasazi moved southeast into New Mexico and Arizona, as an apparent combination of long-term drought and incoming Navajo and Ute Indians forced them to leave.

The first known European to enter Utah was Juan Maria Antonio De Rivera, a Spaniard who journeyed northwest from Abiquiu, New Mexico, and reached the Colorado River at present-day Moab in the fall of 1765. Eleven years later, in 1776, an expedition led by two Franciscan friars, Francisco Atanasio Dominguez and Francisco Velez de Escalante, left Santa Fe in search of an overland route to Monterey, California. Forced to swing far to the north because of the impassable canyons of northern New Mexico and southern Utah, the group entered Utah from Colorado near the present route of Hwy. 40 and continued westward to Utah Valley, where they encountered friendly Ute Indians who seemed anxious for them to return and establish a Catholic mission. Early snows blocked the route to California, and the expedition returned to Santa Fe after an arduous journey through the rugged canyons of southern Utah. The expedition left a fascinating diary of its travels that has provided historians and anthropologists with a wealth of information.

Traders traveled into Utah from New Mexico until well into the next century. In the early 1800s, Utah became the focus of fur trappers. From New Mexico, men like Etienne Provost and Anton Robidioux brought both a French-Canadian and Mexican element. From Canada, Peter Skene Ogden represented the British Hudson's Bay Company in search of pelts. The beaver population was already declining by the time American trappers like Jedediah Smith, William Ashley, and James Bridger, coming from St. Louis, could claim Utah for American interests. All three groups met in Utah in 1825, leaving a legacy of adventure tales and place names that still stirs the imagination.

The Mormon pioneers reached the Salt Lake Valley on July 24, 1847. Their arrival followed a remarkable series of events that began in western New York State in 1820, when Joseph Smith, caught up in the fervor of religious revivals that swept the region, prayed for guidance about which church he should join. An angel appeared, telling Smith not to join any existing church; instead, through him, the pristine Church of Christ would be restored. In subsequent visitations, he was instructed about where to find inscribed golden plates that provided an account of early Christians in the Americas and recounted a visit by Jesus Christ to the American continent following his crucifixion and resurrection. The new scripture was translated by Joseph Smith and published as the Book of Mormon in 1830. That year Joseph Smith also established the Church of Jesus Christ of Latter-day Saints which was based on the Bible, the Book of Mormon and the doctrine that Joseph Smith and subsequent leaders of the church were prophets chosen by God to provide ongoing revelation for the church. The nickname "Mormons" was quickly applied to members of the church, and while it is not an official name it is recognized and used by Mormons and non-Mormons alike. LDS is also a popular short form for the Church of Jesus Christ of Latter-day Saints.

Under Smith's charismatic leadership and an aggressive missionary program, the church grew rapidly and moved from its New York location first to Kirtland, Ohio, then Missouri, and finally Nauvoo, Illinois. Conflicts developed with neighbors in each location, and Mormons were forced to leave Missouri; and then, after Joseph Smith was assassinated by a mob in 1844, Brigham Young organized the exodus which brought Mormons to Utah in 1847.

Young had a vision of the region as a beehive of industry and activity, thus explaining Utah's nickname as the Beehive State. The Mormon leader used the beehive image in his choice of the word "Deseret" as the name for the provisional state. Deseret is a Book of Mormon word which means "honey bee." You will see the bee, the beehive and the word Deseret used as highway road signs and historic markers; even the name of Salt Lake City's baseball team, the Buzz, traces its roots back to the pioneer symbol. The word Deseret is still used in names and titles in everything from newspapers to banks and livestock companies.

One of the attractions of Utah was that it was not inhabited by other Americans and under Brigham Young's leadership more than 300 settlements were made throughout Utah and much of Idaho, Wyoming,

Arizona, and Nevada. A number of these settlements, such as Nephi, Lehi, Manti, and Moroni, took their names from places and individuals in the Book of Mormon. Others, such as Brigham City, Heber City, and St. George, for example, are named for early Mormon leaders. These settlements were populated by an influx of Mormon converts from the East, Great Britain, and the Scandinavian countries as well as through the practice of polygamy instituted by Joseph Smith in Illinois. Young's dream of statehood for Deseret, which would have included all of Utah and Nevada, southwestern Wyoming, western Colorado, northwestern New Mexico, the northern two-thirds of Arizona, and southern California, including San Diego, did not come to pass. Politicians in Washington burst the bubble of the unrealistic dream and created the Utah Territory as part of the Compromise of 1850. The name Deseret was dropped, but the boundaries of the Utah Territory, a name taken from the Ute Indians, still included all of Utah, most of Nevada, western Colorado, and southwestern Wyoming. By 1868, Utah was reduced to its present size.

Abhorrence of polygamy and the conviction that the Mormon authoritarian system clashed with the American ideals of democracy led to nearly a half century of conflict and contention with both mainstream America and the federal government. A federal army was sent to Utah in 1857 and 1861, and federal laws were passed that greatly curtailed the activities and businesses of the Church. Utah was denied statehood until 1896. Statehood came after the Mormon Church agreed to abandon the practice of polygamy in 1890 and to disband its Church-directed political party in favor of participation with the national political parties.

Meanwhile, other individuals and forces had a significant impact on Utah. Mormons saw all Native Americans (including the Shoshoni, Utes, Paiutes, Goshutes, and Navajo in Utah) as descendants of the ancient people who left the Book of Mormon and undertook measures to convert, civilize, and control the Indians. Despite generally good relations, conflicts broke out in the 1850s and 1860s, which eventually led to the placement of Utah Indians on reservations by the US government. Prospectors discovered rich mineral deposits and mining boom towns sprang up all over the state. The completion of the transcontinental railroad at Promontory Summit on May 10, 1869, not only had a tremendous impact on Utah but on the rest of the nation as well. That same year, Major John Wesley Powell made his first voyage down the Green and Colorado rivers and initiated an ongoing era of water reclamation and recreation that was crowned with the construction of Lake Powell and Flaming Gorge Reservoir in the 1960s. By the turn of the century the railroads, coal mines, and copper mines of Utah were drawing non-Mormon immigrants from southern and eastern Europe creating a much more diverse and interesting population.

With the abandonment of polygamy (although not by all residents of Utah—an underground polygamy movement continues) and the granting of statehood, Utah seemed to abandon its peculiar course and to become more integrated with the rest of the US. Utahns rushed off to fight in the Spanish-American War and World War I, feared that communists and their agents were deceiving their fellow citizens, consumed illegal alcohol during the Prohibition Era, and suffered as much as the rest of the country during the Great Depression of the 1930s.

World War II brought about the expansion of military installations in Utah and left a defense industry that continues to be an important part of the state's economy. The postwar period led to a boom in recreation and tourism, which continues to focus on the ski industry, travel to Utah's national parks and monuments, historic sites, wilderness areas, and the wild rivers within the state.

Today Utah remains an interesting and diverse state. Utah is still the headquarters for the worldwide Church of Jesus Christ of Latter-day Saints, and the Mormon religion does affect much of what happens in the state and the attitudes that shape key decisions. But Utah has also tied its future to high-tech industry and recreation and tourism. Utah expects to launch an even greater future by hosting the 2002 Winter Olympics.

Suggested Reading—
Dean L. May, *Utah: A People's History* (University of Utah Press, 1987). This well-written, nicely illustrated, 200-page history of Utah provides an excellent overview of the state's history from prehistoric times to the present. Edward Geary's *Goodbye to Poplar Haven* and *The Proper Edge of the Sky* (University of Utah Press, 1985 and 1992) are two remarkable books that get to the heart of the Utah experience. The first is a collection of stories from his and my small hometown of Huntington, while the second examines, through history, travel narrative, and personal essay, Utah's high plateau country. *The Story of the Latter-day Saints* (Deseret Books, 1976), by Mormon historians James B. Allen and Glen M. Leonard, is the most comprehensive one-volume chronological history of the LDS Church.

GEOGRAPHY AND GEOLOGY

Utah's 84,916 square miles makes it the 13th largest state in the US. The state has one of the largest elevation differentials in the nation with Beaver Dam Wash, in the extreme southwestern corner of the state, the lowest point at 2,350 feet and Kings Peak, in the northeastern part of the state, the highest point at 13,528 feet. Kings Peak is one of 24 peaks in the Uinta Mountains with an elevation greater than 13,000 feet. Although the Uintas are Utah's highest mountains—and there are three other mountain ranges with peaks over 12,000 feet: the LaSals, Deep Creeks, and Tushars—it is the Wasatch Mountains where all the world-famous ski resorts are located. The tallest mountain in the Wasatch Range is Mt. Nebo, at 11,877 feet.

Three major physiographic provinces are found within the state. The Rocky Mountain province is the smallest and consists of the Wasatch and Uinta mountains. The Great Basin includes most of the western half of the state. Named by John C. Fremont in the 1840s, the Great Basin has no outlet to the sea, and much of the Utah portion was beneath the waters of ancient Lake Bonneville which covered roughly the western two-thirds of Utah until about 12,000 years ago. The eastern half and extreme southern part of Utah is on the Colorado Plateau. All the rivers and streams on the Colorado Plateau eventually drain into the Colorado River, which makes its way to the Gulf of California and thence to the Pacific Ocean. The Colorado Plateau has some of the most spectacular scenery in the world. Five national parks, four national monuments, Lake Powell, the Glen Canyon National Recreation Area (including Lake Powell), several wilderness areas, wild and scenic rivers, the northern portion of the Navajo Indian Reservation, and smaller Indian reservations are located within Utah's Plateau country.

The geologic history of Utah can be summed up in four words: diverse, complex, spectacular, and ongoing. Geologists have identified more than 600 rock units, which they have consolidated into eight phases, to tell Utah's geological story.

The first phase (3,000 million to 1,000 million years ago), the basement for Utah's geologic structure, saw the formation of metamorphic rocks by extreme heat and pressure.

During the second phase (1,000 million to 360 million years ago), warm, shallow-water conditions deposited thick accumulations of sediments. These gray, limestone rocks contain many fossils, such as trilobites, that record the habitat and life in these seas.

During the third phase (360 million to 250 million years ago), sedimentary rocks continued to be deposited at varying thicknesses. This phase also saw the sinking of the Paradox Basin in the Four Corners area and the uplift of the Uncompahgre Highland north of the basin. Contemporary with the Paradox Basin was the Oquirrh Basin in which shallow sea deposits formed layers of sandstone, shale, and limestone as much as 3 miles thick.

During the fourth phase (250 million to 100 million years ago) warm seas and extensive sand dunes filled deserts developed during Sahara-like conditions. These deposits became the colorful conglomerates, shales, and sandstones found in southern Utah's national parks. Rocks of this phase also contain the remains of dinosaurs and uranium deposits.

The fifth phase (100 million to 60 million years ago) occurred when the North American continental plate collided with the Pacific continen-

tal plate, just off present-day California. The impact caused reverbera-
tions in the earth's crust and produced the series of mountain ranges that
stretch across the Great Basin like an accordion. To the east, extensive
swamps were covered by sedimentary rocks over time and hardened to
produce Utah's rich coal deposits.

During the sixth phase (60 million to 37 million years ago), the uplifts
that created the Uinta Mountains, San Rafael Swell, Waterpocket Fold,
and Circle Cliffs anticline occurred, as a result of the creation of the Rocky
Mountains.

The seventh phase (37 million to 15 million years ago) was a period
of tremendous volcanic activity, the evidence of which is most visible in
the high areas of central and southwestern Utah. Some of the heated rock
was not spewn from the ground but congealed with mineral-bearing
fluids to form the ore-bearing rock that was extracted at Alta, Park City,
and Bingham Canyon. In southeastern Utah, the Henry, Blue, and La Sal
mountains were formed.

The eighth and last phase (15 million years ago to the present) saw
most of the western North American continent lifted to its present
elevation and tremendous erosion forces unleashed which carved the
spectacular canyons of the Colorado Plateau. In many of the mountain
ranges, glaciers cut canyons such as Little Cottonwood Canyon, in which
are located the ski resorts of Alta and Snowbird. In the western half of
Utah, the mountain ranges appeared like chains of islands amid Lake
Bonneville, which, at its crest approximately 25,000 years ago, stretched
over more than 20,000 square miles and reached a depth of more than
1,000 feet. About 15,000 years ago, the lake spilled over into the Snake
River. The remnant of the lake evaporated, leaving Utah's geological
marvel, the Great Salt Lake.

Suggested Reading—
These books offer more information on the geology and geography
of Utah: *Geologic History of Utah* (Brigham Young University Press, 1988)
by Lehi F. Hintze; *Geology of Utah* (Utah Museum of Natural History,
1986) by William Lee Stokes; *Roadside Geology of Utah* (Mountain Press
Publishing, 1990) by Halka Chronic; and *Utah Atlas* (Brigham Young
University Press, 1981) by Wayne Walquist et al.

FLORA AND FAUNA
Utah's deserts, benchlands, and mountains and the marshlands
around the Great Salt Lake provide a diverse habitat for a wide range of
plant and animal life. Wildlife observation areas have been noted in the
Seeing and Doing sections of this book. The Utah Division of Wildlife
Resources is the wildlife authority for the state. It has a number of

programs to promote the protection and enjoyment of wildlife and works closely with other state and federal agencies. The division has an extensive education program. Call or write the **Utah Division of Wildlife Resources, 1596 West North Temple, Salt Lake City, UT 84116; (801) 596-8660.**

Suggested Reading—
Utah Wildlife Viewing Guide (Falcon Press, 1990) by Jim Cole, a wildlife biologist with the Wasatch-Cache National Forest, is a handy and inexpensive guide to some of the best and most easily accessible wildlife viewing sites in Utah.

CLIMATE

The mountains and deserts are responsible for a wonderful variety in Utah's climate. You can be skiing in a snowstorm in the mountains above Salt Lake City and the next hour be on the first tee at one of the valley golf courses in a light sweater ready for a pleasant round of golf. Generally the ski season runs from mid-Nov.–Apr., although the ski season often ends before the snow does! The Utah Department of Transportation keeps the roads to the ski areas plowed and sanded, but there are usually several days during the year when the roads are closed due to avalanches or avalanche danger. Because automobile travel throughout Utah usually involves going over high mountain passes, it is always a good idea to check on **road conditions** by calling **(801) 964-6000.** Utah weather patterns are tricky and snowstorms do not always cover the entire state. Often while northern Utah is being covered by snow out of the Pacific Northwest, southern Utah is enjoying sunny skies. Occasionally storms will move in from southern California to inundate the southern part of the state while the northern half remains dry. Utah temperatures are quite mild, especially compared to the cold extremes in Wyoming and Montana to the north or the searing summer heat in Arizona to the south and Nevada to the west. Areas of the state do get very hot, however, especially the St. George area, the Mojave Desert, southern Utah canyons, and deserts of the Great Basin. In the Salt Lake Valley, winter daytime temperatures are usually between 20 and 45 degrees Fahrenheit, with nighttime temperatures dropping into the single digits and below zero for some nights but usually in the teens and twenties. In the summer, temperatures reach above 100, but the humidity is usually very low, making the heat much more tolerable than in moister climates. Summer evening temperatures are usually in the 60s and 70s. The St. George area within the Mojave Desert in extreme southwestern Utah is known for its mild winter temperatures and is a favorite destination of "snowbirds." The summer temperatures, however, can soar well above 100 degrees, making air-conditioned buildings and cars a must.

During the summer months, afternoon thunderstorms can develop quite unexpectedly, especially over the mountains, so be prepared. The thin mountain air causes temperatures to cool off considerably at night, so if you are going to be in the mountains after dark be sure to have a coat or warm sweater. Whether hiking the mountain trails or boating on the many reservoirs in the summer, skiing the well-groomed slopes in the winter, or sightseeing in the state and national parks, you will get plenty of exposure to sun, so be prepared with hats, sunscreen, and lots of drinking water.

——————— VISITOR INFORMATION ———————
GENERAL INFORMATION

In Salt Lake City, visit the **Utah Travel Council,** located in historic Council Hall, across the street from the State Capitol. You may also write for information to **Utah Travel Council, Council Hall/Capitol Hill, Salt Lake City, UT 84114-7420;** or call **(801) 538-1030.** One of the council's best publications of the Travel Council is its annual "Utah Travel Guide," which is available at no cost. The council also sponsors welcome centers on Interstate 15 near the Utah-Arizona border, outside St. George; in northern Utah on Interstate 15 near Brigham City; along Interstate 70 at Thompson near the Colorado-Utah border; near Echo Junction on Interstate 80; and in Vernal on US Hwy. 40. Multiagency visitor centers are located in Ogden, Hanksville, Moab, Monticello, and Escalante. In Salt Lake City, the **Visitors and Convention Bureau** at the corner of **West Temple and 200 South** is an excellent source of information. The bureau also operates a center at the Salt Lake International Airport.

Utah is divided into 10 travel regions. The travel regions are funded with local room taxes and some money from the Utah Travel Council. Each region has its own travel office with full-time staff and is an excellent source of information for their particular areas. The 10 regions are:

1. Bridgerland. 160 North Main, Logan, UT 84321; (801) 752-2161 or 1-800-657-5353.

2. Canyonlands. Center and Main Streets, Moab, UT 84532; (801) 259-8825 or 1-800-635-6622.

3. San Juan. 117 South Main, PO Box 490, Monticello, UT 84535; (801) 587-3235 or 1-800-575-4FUN.

4. Castle Country. 155 East Main, PO Box 1037, Price, UT 84501; (801) 637-3009 or 1-800-464-3790.

5. Color Country. 906 North 1400 West, PO Box 1550, St. George, UT 84771-1550, (801) 628-4171 or 1-800-233-8824.

6. Dinosaur Land. 235 East Main, Vernal, UT 84078; (801) 789-6932 or 1-800-477-5558.

7. Golden Spike Empire. 2501 Wall Ave., Ogden, UT 84401; (801) 627-8288 or 1-800-255-8824.

8. Great Salt Lake Country. 180 South West Temple, Salt Lake City, UT 84101-1493; (801) 521-2822.

9. Mountainland. 2545 North Canyon Rd., Provo, UT 84604; (801) 377-2262.

10. Panoramaland. 250 North Main, PO Box 820, Richfield, UT 84701; (801) 896-9222 or 1-800-748-4361.

TIPS FOR VISITORS

The Mormons—If you like to experience different cultures, Utah is a good place to visit. For many outsiders, Utah and Mormons are often considered synonymous. While the majority of Utahns are members of the Church of Jesus Christ of Latter-day Saints, there is, however, a rich diversity of other religions and ethnic groups. This is especially true along Utah's Wasatch Front, the urban corridor that lies generally between the west slope of the Wasatch Mountains and the eastern side of the Great Salt Lake. But to understand the Mormon culture and its people, here are a few facts to keep in mind.

• Mormons practiced polygamy for nearly a half century from the early 1840s until the leader of the Mormon faith issued the "Manifesto" in 1890, which ended any new "plural marriages," as they were called. From 1890 to the present there have been followers of the Mormon faith who did not accept this. These people practice polygamy, and consequently, they are not considered members of the official church.

• Most Mormons do not use tobacco, alcohol, coffee, or tea (although herbal tea is acceptable).

• Mormons are encouraged to tell others about their faith. Some of the more zealous will take the opportunity to inform you of the church and its doctrine, but this is more the exception than the rule.

• The Mormon Sabbath is on Sunday. Most members attend a three-hour block of meetings that begin at 9 or 10 am, although they may begin as late as 3 or 4 pm if several congregations (called wards) share the same church building. Visitors are welcome at these meetings.

• Members of the Mormon faith range from those who are antagonistic or apathetic, to those who are sometimes called "cultural Mormons," that is, those who remain Mormons because of tradition and family, those who are totally committed, or those who are the most extreme and are sometimes considered zealots or "iron-rods" by the rest.

Drinking Laws—Contrary to popular belief (both inside and outside the state), alcoholic beverages are available in Utah. Prohibition was repealed in Utah in February 1933. In fact, Utah takes credit as the state that ended national prohibition, since it was the 36th and final state to ratify the 21st Amendment. Alcoholic beverages are served with meals in many restaurants and hotels after 1 pm. Bottled liquor can only be purchased at state-operated liquor stores, easily identifiable by their gold-and-brown logos and letters. Mixed drinks are served in nonexclusive private clubs, but visitors are welcome at these clubs, with temporary memberships available for a nominal fee.

Driving—Car rentals are easily arranged at the Salt Lake International Airport. You need a national driver's license or an International Driver's Permit. Utah law requires that seatbelts be worn. A right turn is permissible on a red light, after you come to a complete stop and traffic is clear.

Money—
Credit Cards—Major credit cards are accepted nearly everywhere. Cards are useful for putting a security deposit on a rental car or guaranteeing room reservations.

Travelers Checks—Credit cards seem to be used much more than travelers checks, but travelers checks can be replaced almost immediately if they are lost or stolen. Foreign visitors should get checks in US dollar denominations, as most banks are unable to exchange foreign currencies. If you need to exchange foreign currency, the most convenient location in Salt Lake City is at the **American Express Travel Service Office** at **175 South West Temple, (801) 328-9733,** located west of the Salt Lake Travel and Convention Bureau Visitors Center.

Student and Senior Discounts—Seniors can find discounts at many movies, motels, restaurants, golf courses, and ski resorts. Student discounts are much more difficult to find, but carry your student identification with you just in case. A college or high school activity card or International Student Identification Card (ISIC) will do.

Telephones—The entire state of Utah is served by the long-distance prefix 801. If you are calling from outside the state, you must use the prefix. Long distance calls within the state also require using the 801 prefix before the number. For long-distance directory assistance outside and within Utah, call 1-801-555-1212. For emergency assistance, dial 911.

Time—Utah is on Mountain Standard Time, which is two hours earlier than Eastern Standard Time (New York) and one hour later than Pacific Standard Time (California). Utah is either seven or eight hours earlier than Western Europe, depending on the time of year.

Tipping—Fifteen percent is considered a generous tip in most Utah restaurants. Taxi drivers, barbers, hairdressers, and bartenders expect tips in the 15 percent range. A dollar for one or two bags is adequate for porters and bellboys.

GETTING THERE

Since pioneer days, Salt Lake City has been known as the "Crossroads of the West," and with the establishment of Delta Airlines' western hub in Salt Lake City, the city will continue as a crossroads into the 21st century. Air travelers to Utah can be in Salt Lake City from most parts of the United States in less than half a day. Once you arrive at the airport it is easy to get to downtown Salt Lake City or the nearby ski resorts. Travelers to the canyons of southern Utah may want to consider flying into Las Vegas, Nevada. There are good air connections in Las Vegas, and, from there, it is only a two-hour drive to St. George. Salt Lake City and Las Vegas are both located along Interstate 15, about seven hours' driving time apart.

From Salt Lake City, you can catch connecting flights to Cedar City and St. George, but most people rent a car in Salt Lake City and drive to their destinations in Utah and the surrounding states. The major car rental agencies have counters at the **Salt Lake City Airport,** which are conveniently located in the parking terrace adjacent to the terminals. Depending on the time of year, sometimes you can get excellent weekend and weekly rates. During the winter, rentals come equipped with ski racks; four-wheel-drive vehicles are especially popular. Agencies at or near the airport include **Advantage, (801) 531-1199; Agency, (801) 534-1622; Alamo, (801) 575-2211; Avis, (801) 575-AVIS; Budget, (801) 298-1460; Dollar, (801) 575-1580; Hertz, (801) 575-1683; National (801) 575-2277; Payless, (801) 695-2596; Snappy, (801) 363-1003; and Thrifty, (801) 595-6677.**

The Greyhound bus terminal is located in the downtown Salt Lake area, less than a block west of Temple Square, at **160 West Temple.** For routes and schedules, call **(801) 355-9579.** Limited train service is available on **Amtrak,** with stations located in Salt Lake City in the historic **Denver and Rio Grande Railroad Station, 450 West and 320 South, (801) 364-8562,** and in Ogden at the **Historic Union Station at 25th St. and Wall Ave., (801) 627-3330.** The nationwide toll-free number is **1-800-421-8420.** Trains arrive or leave only once or twice each day, often at inconvenient hours. The Amtrak stations are not open all the time and, more often than Amtrak officials care to admit, trains are delayed and passengers are transported by chartered bus to the next destination. Nevertheless, the Amtrak trains that serve Utah pass through some of the most memorable scenery in the world. Everyone should take the train between Salt Lake City and Denver at least once.

INFORMATION FOR DISABLED VISITORS

Each year Utah becomes more conscientious about providing better facilities, access, and activities for those with disabilities. Parks, museums, and other attractions have designated handicapped parking and handicap access to buildings. Excellent **disabled ski programs** have been established at **Snowbird, Alta,** and **Park City.** River guide outfits are expanding their float trips to accommodate people with disabilities. Mountain trails at **Snowbird** and **Brighton** have been made handicapped accessible, as have a number of trails in Utah's national parks. Campgrounds in national and state parks are improving their handicapped facilities. Handicapped fishing areas have been established at **Brighton's Silver Lake** and at **Payson Lake.** Utah has made a concerted effort to comply with all provisions of the Americans with Disabilities Act passed by Congress in 1992.

Suggested Reading—

A useful source of information is the *National Park Access Guide for the Handicapped* available from the US Government Printing Office, Washington, DC 20402.

—————— HOW THE BOOK ——————
IS ORGANIZED

The Utah Guide is arranged into six geographic regions: Northern, Northeastern, Wasatch Range, Central, Southern, and Southeastern. Within these six regions are 33 sections or "destinations," including cities, areas, and national parks. The first sections provide the necessary background to each section. Major Attractions and Other Attractions are described, as are Festivals and Events, Outdoor Activities, Seeing and Doing, Where to Stay, Where to Eat, and Services.

FESTIVALS AND EVENTS

Utahns celebrate all of the major national holidays and a few of their own. The most important state holiday is Pioneer Day celebrated annually on July 24, which commemorates the arrival of the first Mormon pioneers in Utah. Celebrations and activities are held in many communities throughout the state, but the largest is in Salt Lake City with the Days of '47 parade, rodeo, fireworks, races, and other activities. Communities have their own special celebrations, and most of these have been indicated in the appropriate sections. For an events calendar, contact the **Utah Travel Council, Council Hall/Capitol Hill, Salt Lake City, UT 84114-7420; (801) 538-1030 or 1-800-200-1160.**

OUTDOOR ACTIVITIES

You will find the possibilities for outdoor activities in Utah almost endless. Bicycling, hiking and backpacking, skiing, snowmobiling, river floating, golfing, tennis, fishing, and horseback riding are some of the most popular.

BIKING

Mountain biking has taken Utah by storm and at least two locations, **Moab** with its unique slickrock and **Brian Head** with its high mountain trails, have developed national and international reputations. Fat-tire festivals are held in numerous locations (including Flaming Gorge, Bryce Canyon, Park City, and Brian Head) during the summer months. Many local travel offices have published biking guides to their areas. Local bike shops are a good source for rentals, repairs, equipment, and information about other possibilities.

Suggested Reading—

Dennis Coello, *Bicycle Touring Utah* (Northland Publishing, 1988); Greg Bromka, *Mountain Biking the Wasatch and Uintas* (self-published, 1989) and *Mountain Biking Utah's Canyon and Plateau Country* (self-published, 1990). Elliott R. Mott has published three volumes under the title of *Cycling Possibilities.* They include Salt Lake City, Northern Utah, and the Wasatch Front. In addition, Bicycle Utah Inc. publishes an annual *Utah Bicycle Vacation Guide* (as well as nine guidebooks that cover each of Utah's travel regions) with 20 rides that includes maps, elevation charts, and written descriptions. The vacation guide is free. It is available from **Bicycle Utah, PO Box 738, Park City, UT 84060; (801) 649-5806.**

FISHING

A favorite pastime of Utahns, the fishing in Utah ranks as high as anywhere in the West and includes well-stocked lakes and reservoirs and rapid-flowing trout streams. The **Utah Division of Wildlife Resources, 1596 West North Temple, Salt Lake City, UT 84114; (801) 596-8660.**

Suggested Reading—

For a detailed introduction to fishing in Utah, Hartt Wixom's *Fishing and Hunting Guide to Utah* (Wasatch, 1990) is the best book on the subject.

GOLF

There are nearly 100 golf courses in Utah and new ones are under construction all the time. Most of Utah's courses are municipal or county owned and greens fees are reasonable. There are a number of fine courses in the Salt Lake and Park City areas. The St. George area, with its seven courses, is a golfer's mecca during the winter when snow closes Utah's other courses and the warm St. George winters draw thousands. The Utah Travel Council offers a free annual Utah Golf Directory upon request. The Utah Golf Association publishes *Fairways*, four times a year, with news about tournaments, courses and the Utah golf scene. For more information about golf in Utah, contact the **Utah Golf Association, 110 East Eaglewood Dr., North Salt Lake, UT 84054; (801)299-8421.**

HIKING AND BACKPACKING

Whether you are a life-long resident or this is your first day in Utah, you can't spend your time better than on Utah's unforgettable hiking trails. Less traveled than national park trails are those in the national forests and on BLM land. If you want to sever contact with the outside world for a few days, there are over a dozen designated wilderness areas from the Paria Canyon and Pine Valley Mountain areas in the south to the Mount Naomi and Wellsville Mountain areas in the north. There are also a number of wilderness study areas that are open to backpackers.

Suggested Reading—

Dave Hall's *The Hiker's Guide to Utah* (Falcon Press, 1991) describes 60 hikes throughout Utah. In *Hiking the Wasatch*, John Veranth (Wasatch Mountain Club, 1988) covers the possibilities in the Salt Lake area.

HORSEBACK RIDING

Riding clubs, rodeos, and horseback rides are a part of the cowboy tradition that still flourishes in the West. There are a number of riding stables and trail rides available throughout the state, and I have tried to cover as many as possible. New stables are being established all the time, so check with local tourist officials. You can also request the *Outfitters and Guides* book from the Utah Travel Council. Published annually, it includes listings for horseback rides.

RIVER FLOATING

The eastern half of Utah is cut by three rivers—the **Colorado,** the **Green,** and the **San Juan**—that provide excellent opportunities for river floats. The rapids don't get any bigger or more violent than through Cataract Canyon below the confluence of the Green and Colorado rivers. There are plenty of outfitters in the Moab area to provide any kind of trip you can imagine. Flaming Gorge, Vernal, and Green River are locations for float trips on the Green River, and you can retrace the route of the historic 1869 John Wesley Powell expedition. Bluff provides access to the San Juan River for an interesting float to Mexican Hat or beyond through the Goosenecks of the San Juan and on to Lake Powell. If you don't have time for a multiday river adventure, there are day and half-day tours that introduce you to Utah's rivers and awaken a desire for more. Not all trips are through roaring rapids. Some are a nice leisurely float that gives you time to relax and enjoy Utah's canyon country from a whole new perspective. The Utah Travel Council can provide you with literature about river trips.

Suggested Reading—

Gary C. Nichols, *River Runners' Guide to Utah and Adjacent Areas* (University of Utah Press, 1986).

SKIING

Utah has an international reputation for some of the best powder skiing on earth. As moisture-laden clouds moves eastward from the Pacific Coast, part of the moisture is combed out of the clouds by the mountains over which they pass. As the snows reach the Utah mountains, they become light and powdery. The mountains of powder provide a challenge and unequaled thrill to ski through the waist deep substance that is even lighter than feathers. The majority of Utah ski resorts, located in the **Park City** area and **Big and Little Cottonwood canyons,** east of Salt Lake City, are all within an hour's drive time from the Salt Lake City Airport. Skiing is big business in Utah, and the possibility of hosting the 2002 Winter Olympics has already marked Utah as one of the world's premier ski areas.

Suggested Reading—

Claire Walter's *Rocky Mountain Skiing* (Fulcrum, 1992) has excellent chapters on the Park City area, Sundance and the Little Cottonwood Canyon resorts of Alta and Snowbird. In *Wasatch Tours,* Alexis Kelner and David Hanscom (Wasatch, 1976) cover the cross-country and backcountry tour possibilities in the Salt Lake area canyons. The Utah Travel Council also publishes a free annual "Winter Vacation Planner," which gives up-to-date information on Utah's ski areas.

SNOWMOBILING

Snowmobiling is one of Utah's favorite winter pastimes, and trail systems can be found throughout most Utah mountains. The Utah Division of Parks and Recreation offers trail maps, *The Utah Snowmobile Directory*, and other information about snowmobiling possibilities. Contact the Utah Division of Parks and Recreation, 1636 West North Temple #116, Salt Lake City, UT 84116; (801) 538-7220.

SEEING AND DOING

The seeing and doing section covers a variety of activities including cultural activities, museums, historic sites, ghost towns, scenic drives, wildlife, nightlife, and shopping.

ARCHAEOLOGICAL SITES

You're never very far from archaeological sites in Utah. Most are from the Fremont and Anasazi cultures, which reached their high point in Utah about 1250 A.D. Government agencies, including the Utah Division of Parks and Recreation, the National Park Service, the Bureau of Land Management and the Forest Service have given archaeological resources a high priority at places like **Edge of the Cedars, Anasazi State Park, Fremont State Park, Grand Gulch, Hovenweep National Monument,** and various locations in Utah's national parks. The rock paintings (pictographs) and chiseled inscriptions (petroglyphs) of the ancient inhabitants are of special interest as Utah has some of the best preserved rock art in the world at places like Barrier Canyon in Canyonlands National Park and Nine Mile Canyon in the Price area. For more information about sites that are open to the public, contact the **Antiquities Office, Division of State History, 300 Rio Grande, Salt Lake City, UT 84101-1182; (801) 533-3500.**

Suggested Reading—

Polly Shaafsma, *The Rock Art of Utah* (University of Utah, 1993); Kenneth B. Castleton, *Petroglyphs and Pictographs of Utah,* (Utah Museum of Natural History, 1979 and 1984); and David B. Madsen, *Exploring the Fremont* (Utah Museum of Natural History, 1989).

CULTURAL EVENTS

The Utah Travel Council as well as regional and local travel councils keep a calendar of events that includes concerts, theater, art festivals, folk festivals, and other cultural activities. The Utah Arts Council, established in 1899, was the first state arts agency in the nation and it continues to support and encourage endeavors in all areas of the fine arts and folk arts. The Council, also known as the Division of Fine Arts, is located at **617 South Temple, Salt Lake City, UT 84102; (801) 533-5895**

Suggested Reading—
Vern G. Swanson, Robert S. Olpin and William C. Seifrit, *Utah Art* (Gibbs Smith, 1991). *Utah State of the Arts* (Meredian, 1993) contains 15 essays on all aspects of the arts in Utah including painting, sculpture, architecture, dance, crafts, film and video, theater, music, opera, photography, folk and ethnic arts and literary arts.

DINOSAURS

Children and adults alike have always been fascinated with dinosaurs and Utah is dinosaur country. More dinosaur bones have been excavated in Utah than any other place in the US, and you could plan a week-long trip to visit the quarry sites and museums that interpret the 100-million-year-old bones. **Dinosaur National Monument** is the first place to start, along with a visit to the **Museum of Natural History** in Vernal. The **Cleveland-Lloyd Quarry Site** in Emery County is open to visitors in the summer, and nearby museums in Price—the **College of Eastern Utah Museum** and Castle Dale—the **Museum of the San Rafael,** have dinosaur skeletons taken from the quarry. While at these places, ask about the Long Walk Site, which promises to add even more information about the prehistoric dinosaurs. You can also see dinosaur skeletons at the **Brigham Young University Physical Science Museum** and the University of Utah's **Museum of Natural History.** In Ogden, a **Dinosaur Park** has been established with replicas of 44 dinosaurs.

GHOST TOWNS

Throughout the state you can find a good sprinkling of mining, railroad, and agricultural ghost towns. Some places labeled ghost towns are still inhabited, and locals take offense to that designation. I have noted a number of these places and hope that those who still live in these towns will forgive the designation.

Suggested Reading—
The Historical Guide to Utah Ghost Towns (Western Epics, 1972) by Stephen L. Carr is the best ghost town guide for the state.

HISTORIC SITES

A number of local historical societies have worked with their travel offices to produce in brochure and pamphlet format guides to local historic sites. I have tried to mention these in the appropriate chapters. For specific questions about historic sites in the state, contact the **Utah Historic Preservation Office, Division of State History, 300 Rio Grande, Salt Lake City, UT 84101-1182; (801) 533-3500.**

Suggested Reading—

Thomas Carter and Peter Goss, *Utah's Historic Architecture, 1847–1940* (University of Utah Press, 1988). Two of the state's foremost architectural historians have compiled an interesting, well-illustrated introduction to Utah's historic architecture.

Peter H. DeLafosse, *Trailing the Pioneers: A Guide to Utah's Emigrant Trails 1829–1869* (Utah State University Press, 1994). This handy guide provides historical background and automobile tour directions for five important early trails through Utah—the Spanish Trail, the Bidwell-Bartleson Trail, the Mormon Pioneer Trail, the Hastings Cutoff and Hensley's Salt Lake Cutoff. Mark Angus' *Salt Lake City Underfoot: Self-Guided Tours of Historic Neighborhoods* (Signature Books, 1993) is the first citywide historic sites guidebook and is divided into 11 tours, 5 designed for walking and 6 for biking. The book gives information on historic buildings in the downtown area, Capitol Hill, Avenues, University of Utah, and other neighborhoods in the city.

MUSEUMS

There are a variety of museums in Utah, but the most museum-oriented organization has been the **Daughters of Utah Pioneers (DUP).** Since its founding in 1901, the Daughters has established an impressive museum on Salt Lake City's Capitol Hill, three blocks north of Temple Square, and dozens of local museums, often called "relic halls," throughout the towns and cities of the state. Many of these museums are included in this book, and they offer an interesting glimpse at the past and at the way Utahns interpret and cherish their past. You will also want to visit the **LDS Church Museum of Art and History,** located across the street west of Temple Square. Other museums range from a fine prehistoric museum in Price and interesting mining and railroad museum in Helper to a superb Greek ethnic museum in Salt Lake City and museums of fine art and natural history at the University of Utah. For more information and a free booklet listing all of Utah's museums, contact the **Utah Office of Museum Services, 324 South State St., Salt Lake City, UT 84114-7910; 1-800-533-4235.**

SCENIC DRIVES

Some 27 byways and 58 backways have been given official designation. Most of these have been described in the appropriate sections. If you notice one of the road signs designating a scenic byway, you can assume you are in for some spectacular sites.

Suggested Reading—

Utah Scenic Byways and Backways, a joint publication of local, state, and federal agencies, has full-page sections with color photographs and descriptions of all the designated byways and shorter descriptions of the backways throughout Utah. Ward J. Roylance's *Utah: A Guide to the State* is a 1982 revision of the original 1940 Utah Writers' Project Guide and includes 11 detailed driving tours that cover the entire state. John W. Van Cott's *Utah Place Names* (University of Utah Press, 1990) is a handy paperback arranged alphabetically with brief explanations for the names of several thousand place names throughout the state. In 1993, Vivienne and Jim Bailey began publication of *Utah Highways Magazine.* Lavishly illustrated with color photographs by Utah's best professional photographers, the magazine has short articles about special places to visit in Utah. It is highly recommended both as an introduction to Utah, a quarterly reminder of your visit to Utah, and an invitation to return to the Beehive State. You can order a six-issue subscription. Contact **Utah Highways Magazine, PO Box 639, Draper, UT 84020-0639; (801) 571-1471.**

WHERE TO STAY
ACCOMMODATIONS

The selection of places to include has been based on personal experience, local recommendations, and availability. Since most people know what to expect at hotel and motel chains, these are generally not included unless they are the only accommodations available, or because the high demand for lodging merited listing a larger number of choices. If you would like a complete listing of all lodging facilities in a particular area, contact the regional travel offices, listed at the end of each chapter under Services. For toll-free reservation numbers for the chain hotels and motels, call **1-800-555-1212** and ask for the number of the specific chain.

Bed and breakfast inns are given high priority in this section because of the personal attention they provide and the unforgettable facilities they offer. If you've never stayed at one, treat yourself to this memorable experience. Contact the Utah Travel Council for information on the bed and breakfast directory it publishes annually. **Bed and Breakfast Inns of Utah, PO Box 3066, Park City, UT 84060; (801) 645-8068,** can also provide up-to-date information about its members.

Only two youth hostels can be found in Utah—in Salt Lake City and Moab—but an attempt has been made to include inexpensive lodging in each of the sections. Prices vary depending on the season and room type. The following approximate price range, based on double occupancy, has been used throughout this guidebook.

$	less than $25
$$	$25 to $50
$$$	$50 to $100
$$$$	$100 and up

CAMPING

Perhaps because of Utah's pioneer heritage, there is a long tradition of camping in Utah. Camping opportunities range from backpacking into wilderness areas, to basic campground facilities in the national forests and national parks, to the most luxurious private RV parks. In the national forests, you can camp anywhere unless it is posted otherwise. In those national parks where camping is permitted, you may only use designated areas with the exception of some backcountry primitive sites. Review the sections on the individual national parks and inquire about camping regulations at the various park headquarters. Most campgrounds on public and state land with such amenities as showers, restrooms, and drinking water charge fees for camping. For wilderness and backcountry camping there is no charge. Without exception, all private campgrounds charge fees. Each section lists both public and private campgrounds. The **Utah State Campground Owners Association** publishes an annual directory to Utah's private campgrounds and RV service centers. It is available free of charge at most visitor centers, or by writing to **UCOA, 9160 South 300 West, Suite 6, Sandy, UT 84070.**

Despite the rugged-looking mountains and scenic wonders, Utah is a very fragile state. The impact of more and more visitors and residents requires that everyone follow a few basic practices that will enhance the quality of the outdoor experience for others and help preserve the land for future generations. Remember to leave each campsite cleaner than you found it and for backcountry camping, be sure to practice minimum-impact camping techniques.

1. Tread lightly when traveling and leave no trace of your camping. Drive and ride only on roads and trails where such travel is allowed; hike only on established trails, on rock or in washes. Camp at designated sites, or where allowed, at previously used sites. Avoid placing tents on top of vegetation. Unless signs indicate otherwise, leave gates open or closed as you find them.

2. Pack out your trash and recycle it; clean up after less thoughtful visitors and dispose of human waste properly. Carry a small shovel or trowel to bury human waste 6 to 8 inches below the ground. Select a site well away from water sources. Pack out all toilet paper in a plastic bag with your other trash. Do not bury any trash.

3. Camp at least 300 feet from isolated water sources to allow for wildlife access. Where possible, carry your own drinking water. Leave potholes undisturbed and wash well away from pools and springs (at least 100 feet) using biodegradable soap.

4. Minimize your use of campfires by using a portable stove or self-contained charcoal fire for all your cooking. If you must have a campfire, keep it very small and avoid building new fire rings. Collect only dead and down wood and gather it from seldom-used areas well away from popular campsites. Do not build fires in alcoves or underneath cliff faces and keep all cans, bottles, aluminum foil and other items that do not burn out of the fire ring. Burn the logs down to ashes then douse with water. Don't smother a campfire with soil and always make sure the fire is dead out before you leave.

5. If you encounter wildlife, maintain your distance and remain quiet. Teach children not to chase or pick up animals. Leave pets at home if possible—if not, keep them under control.

6. Leave historic sites, Native American rock art, ruins, and artifacts untouched for the future. Admire rock art from a distance and never touch it. Stay out of ruins, leave artifacts in place and report violations.

WHERE TO EAT

Listings for Where to Eat were determined by my own experience and favorites, recommendations by locals, an aversion to chain restaurants and availability. I have personally visited nearly everyone of the restaurants listed in the guide. Those I was not able to visit but which had good local recommendations or those that met my fourth criteria of availability without anything special to mention have been listed in the guide without much elaboration. I've tried to include restaurants to fit all budgets. Remember that changes in hours and ownership makes it impossible to guarantee that all information is up-to-date. So use the material provided as a guide only.

Anyone who has traveled the backways of Utah knows that of the four factors just mentioned, availability is often the most important factor. After a full day of travel and sightseeing, you are just happy to find a place that is open and that will cook for you.

A general price guide, based on the price of an entrée per person, is provided under the following system:

$	Under $5
$$	$5 to $10
$$$	$10 to $20
$$$$	$20 and up

THE UTAH GUIDE

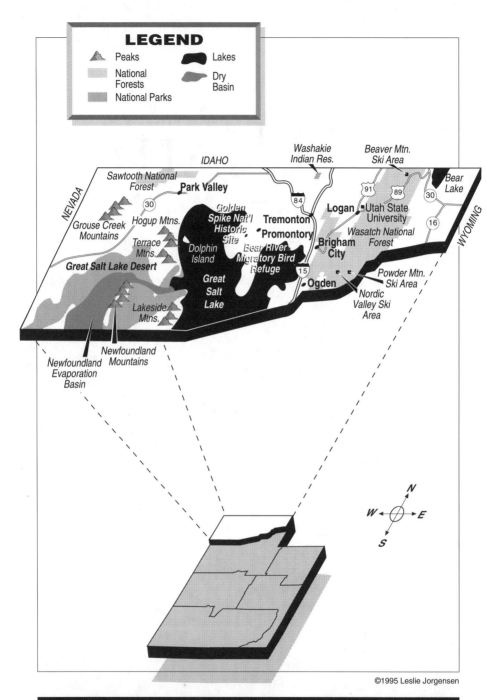

Northern Region

NORTHERN REGION

Bear Lake

Surrounded by mountains, Bear Lake—Utah's second largest natural freshwater lake—is like a drop of turquoise. The lake has 71,000 surface acres and 48 miles of shoreline; it is shared by both Utah and Idaho as their borders divide the lake roughly in half. Geologists postulate that, until about 10,000 years ago, the Bear River ran into and out of the northern end of the lake. A series of upheavals that created the Bear River Plateau along the eastern side of the lake, however, changed the course of the river bypassing the lake. Since then, the level of the lake has remained relatively constant, with the inflow from a half-dozen small streams and precipitation equaling the outflow from evaporation and percolation. In addition, canals have been constructed to bring excess water into the lake from the Bear River and to discharge water through the lake when needed downstream. Since the establishment of Bear Lake State Park in the early 1960s, recreation at the lake has continued to expand. The Utah side has undergone more extensive development than the Idaho side, particularly along the western and southern shores.

HISTORY

Shoshone Indian campsites dotted the shores of Bear Lake for many decades before Donald Mackenzie, a red-haired Scottish fur trapper for the North West Company of Canada, discovered the lake in 1819. He named it Black Bears Lake, which was later changed to Bear Lake. Fur trappers also called it Weaver's Lake, apparently for John Weber, who led a group of American trappers to the lake in 1824, or Sweet Lake, for its contrast to the Great Salt Lake located 70 miles to the southwest. As the western fur trade developed during the 1820s, Bear Lake became a central location for the third and fourth annual fur trapper rendezvous, which were held at the southern end of Bear Lake in 1827 and 1828. Because of the lack of navigable rivers into the West, annual trading caravans made their way overland each year, bringing goods and equipment to a designated location where they would be exchanged for the beaver pelts taken by fur trappers during the past year. Held for a couple of weeks during the month of July, the annual rendezvous was much more than a business convention. American trappers, Native Americans, and others from throughout the West came together to renew acquaintances, to socialize, to drink, and to catch up on events back East and throughout the world. Of the 16 rendezvous held between 1824 and 1840, the two held at the southern end of Bear Lake were among the most memorable. William Ashley, organizer of the Rocky Mountain Fur Company, sent west a group of 46 men with $22,500 worth of supplies and a cannon mounted on wheels, which became the first wheeled vehicle to cross the Rocky Mountains. While waiting for the caravan, 20 Blackfeet Indians killed a Snake Indian and his squaw. The assembled Indians and some 300 trappers responded and killed several of the Blackfeet during a six-hour fight. A few days after the battle, Jedediah Smith reached the rendezvous, having spent the past year traveling to California and returning across the Sierra Nevada and the Great Salt Lake Desert to reach Bear Lake on July 3.

Thirty-six years after the fur trappers broke camp, at the conclusion of the 1828 rendezvous, Charles C. Rich built cabins on the western shore of the lake, at what is now Garden City. Early residents reported seeing on several occasions a huge creature swimming in the lake at speeds faster than a horse could run on land. Earlier, the Shoshone Indians had also reported that a great beast lived in the lake that preyed on buffalo when they came to the edge of the lake to drink. The buffalo vanished in the 1830s and, according to the Indians, the monster as well.

GETTING THERE

Bear Lake is located 125 miles north of Salt Lake City and 40 miles north of Logan. Take Interstate 15 north from Salt Lake City for 56 miles and exit at Brigham City (exit 364), then turn east onto US Hwy. 89, which skirts south of Brigham City, then heads northeast for 25 miles to Logan. Continue on Hwy. 89 for 40 miles, through Logan Canyon, to Garden City on the western side of Bear Lake.

——— OUTDOOR ACTIVITIES ———

BIKING

Bear Lake Loop—
You can circumnavigate Bear Lake in a fairly easy 45-mile loop that offers a spectacular view of the lake and the national wildlife preserve at the north end of the lake. Most riders begin at Garden City and ride south on Utah Hwy. 30 to Laketown.

Outside Laketown, watch for a country road that heads north around the eastern side of the lake, the road to Cisco Bay, and continue on this road around the lake until it joins US Hwy. 89 at Saint Charles, Idaho. Follow US 89 back to Garden City. A new paved trail from Ideal Beach to the Bear Lake Marina will be completed in 1995.

Bear Lake Summit to Meadowville (Garden City-Summit Meadowville Loop)—

If you want to make this a loop ride you can, but it requires a leg-burning climb from Garden City to the Bear Lake Summit. Most bikers will want to catch a ride to the summit and begin the bike ride here. Follow the dirt road south to Temple Canyon, where it heads northeast to Meadowville. From the summit to Meadowville is 15.5 miles; it is an easy-to-moderate ride. If you are making a loop to Garden City, continue from Meadowville down to Utah Hwy. 30 and ride north along the western side of the lake for about 8 miles to Garden City.

BOATING

Boating, sailing, fishing, water-skiing, and windsurfing are all popular activities on the lake. The Bear Lake Marina has an 80-foot-wide launching ramp and dock spaces for 200 boats. Rendezvous Beach, at the south end of the lake, also has a boat launching ramp as well as First Point and Rainbow Cove on the east side. Boat and other water sport rentals are available at several locations around the lake.

FISHING

When you talk about lake fishing in Utah, Bear Lake usually comes to mind first. Fifteen species of fish inhabit the lake, although the cutthroat trout is the only true native. Cutthroats up to 15 pounds in weight have been taken; however, lake trout twice as large have been caught! Half a million cutthroat trout are planted in the lake each year. Rainbow trout, whitefish, and cisco are also popular to catch. Each

year for a week or so in late January, the cisco run occurs as thousands of 7-inch-long Bonneville cisco come to the surface to spawn along the lake's eastern shore. The fish are scooped up in nets through holes chopped in the ice or by wading in the icy water. Some claim the fish are good eating, while others use them only for bait. Ice fishing occurs during the winter along the western side of the lake; and protective "sheds on sleds" can be rented at the Bear Lake Marina.

GOLF

Bear Lake Golf Course—

This 9-hole golf course is located at the south end of Bear Lake on the hills above the lake. The course offers beautiful views of the lake and the southern end of Bear Lake Valley. For reservations, call **(801) 946-8742.**

HIKING

Limber Pine Trail—

If you drive to Bear Lake via US Hwy. 89, or if you drive up the mountain west of Garden City for a panoramic view of Bear Lake, take time for the 1-mile-round-trip hike to Limber Pine. For years it was thought that the limber pine growing here was a single tree 25 feet in circumference and more than 2,000 years old. Closer study, however, indicates that the tree is actually five trees that have grown together; it is less than 600 years old. A free nature trail guide is available at the trail head which provides a fascinating insight into the flora, fauna and geography of the area. The trail is located at the Bear Lake Summit, approximately 5 miles west of Garden City.

SNOWMOBILING

Garden City—

A groomed snowmobile trail begins at Garden City and climbs into the mountains west of Bear Lake providing access to more than 100 miles of groomed trails. The trailhead is at the junction of US Hwy. 89 and Utah Hwy. 30 with parking available north of the **Bear Lake Motor Lodge.**

SEEING AND DOING

CAVES

Minnetonka Cave—

Located 10 miles up St. Charles Canyon just across the Utah-Idaho border. The cave was discovered in 1907 by Edward Arnell of St. Charles, Idaho, when he felt a draft coming from a small hole near a cliff. The reason the cave was named Minnetonka is not entirely clear, but old-timers indicate that it is an Indian word meaning "falling waters." The entrance was enlarged and steps installed as one of the government's New Deal projects in 1936. Visitors must be able to climb stairs since you go down and then back up a total of 896 stairs inside the cave. This nine-room half-mile long limestone cavern contains remarkable stalactites, stalagmites and banded travertine. The largest of the nine rooms is the 90-foot-high 300-foot-diameter Ballroom. The cave is open daily mid-June–Labor Day from 10 am–5:30 pm. Ninety-minute tours of the cave depart every half hour. Be sure and take a warm jacket with you since the temperature inside the cave remains a constant 40 degrees Fahrenheit. For information call **(208) 847-0375.**

HISTORIC BUILDINGS

Paris Tabernacle—

Located 14 miles north of Bear Lake in Idaho, the 1889 Paris Tabernacle is a must for anyone traveling in the area. This magnificent building, constructed of local fieldstone, is the primary religious building in the Bear Lake Valley. It was designed by Don Carlos Young, a son of Brigham Young, with the stone cutting and carving carried out by Jacob Tueller and his three sons. The Tuellers were immigrant stonemasons from Switzerland who spent years working on the project. The stone was quarried in Indian Creek Canyon, 18 miles away, and hauled around Bear Lake by horse and ox teams; in the winter it was sledded across the ice of Bear Lake. To reach the Tabernacle continue north on US Hwy. 89.

You can't miss it on the east side of the highway as it passes through Paris.

Wilford Woodruff Cabin—

Built in 1872 as a home for Wilford Woodruff, who became the fourth president of the LDS Church in 1887, this log cabin has been restored by volunteer labor and is now used as the Randolph Tourist Information Center. The house was an early "duplex": one side for Sarah Brown Woodruff, one of Wilford Woodruff's plural wives; the other side was the home of Woodruff's eldest son and his family. **85 South Main** in Woodruff.

NIGHTLIFE

Pickleville Playhouse—

The name Pickleville raises a smile when most people hear it spoken, and that smile will continue if you enjoy the humor offered at the Pickleville Summer Theater. From late June–Labor Day, the Pickleville Playhouse Summer Theater presents an old-fashioned musical melodrama that is fun for any age. A western cookout featuring rib-eye steaks, beans, salad, rolls, and brownies, with cowboys serenading while you eat begins at 6:30 pm; the show starts at 8 pm. The early residents of this community were so grateful to Charles C. Pickel, who supervised the improvement of the town's water supply, that they named their hamlet Pickleville. For information and reservations call **(801) 946-2918, 563-5225, or 753-1944.**

SCENIC DRIVES

Laketown Scenic Byway—

The Laketown Scenic Byway is really an extension of the Logan Canyon Scenic Byway (see the **Logan and Cache Valley** chapter). It follows around the southwestern end of Bear Lake between Garden City and Laketown along state Hwy. 30. The 15 mile byway provides access to Rendezvous Beach and offers spectacular views of the lake and plenty of photo opportunities. (See also Logan and Cache Valley, pp. 39–40.)

WILDLIFE

Bear Lake National Wildlife Refuge—
The 17,600-acre National Wildlife Refuge is located in the marsh and grass-lands north of Bear Lake. There are observation sites where you can watch for the wide variety of birds—the Canada goose, mallard, pintail, canvasback ducks, hill cranes, herons, egrets, and white pelicans.

WHERE TO STAY

ACCOMMODATIONS

Bear Lake Bed and Breakfast— $$$–$$$$
Just across the Utah-Idaho border in Fish Haven, Allen and Esther Harrison operate a four-room bed and breakfast. All rooms are nonsmoking. One room has a private bath, the others share a bath. **500 Loveland Ln., Fish Haven, ID 83287; (208) 945-2688.**

Bear Lake Motor Lodge—$$$
Nineteen rooms. **50 South Bear Lake Blvd., Garden City; (801) 946-3271.**

Ideal Beach Condominiums—$$$
Thirty-six condos. Two heated outdoor pools, saunas, hot tub, tennis courts, and miniature golf. **2176 South Bear Lake Blvd., Garden City; (801) 946-3364 or 1-800-634-1018.**

The Inn at Harbor Village—$$$
Fifty one-bedroom condominiums and several two- and three-bedroom townhomes. **1900 Bear Lake Blvd., Garden City; 1-800-866-0935.**

Inn of the Three Bears at Bear Lake— $$$–$$$$
Located in a turn-of-the-century Victorian house and operated by Jeanne and Gerry Groll, Inn of the Three Bears is a five-minute walk from Bear Lake. The three rooms each have separate private baths with an outdoor hot tub available. Breakfast features homemade breads and fruits in season. In late summer and early fall, count on the raspberries which are a Garden City delicacy. **135 South Bear Lake Blvd., Garden City, UT 84028; (801) 946-8590.**

CAMPING

PRIVATE

Bear Lake KOA Kamp—
This 250-site campground has 100 full hookups. All the usual KOA amenities. Open from mid-April–Oct. On Hwy. 89 in Garden City, on the western side of Bear Lake; **(801) 946-3454.**

Bluewater Beach Campground—
Another large campground in Garden City, Bluewater Beach offers 152 sites, 55 of which are full hookups. Equipped with toilets, showers, laundry, disabled facilities, and group sites. Open mid-May–mid-Sept. **(801) 946-3333.**

Sweetwater RV Park & Marina—
This small fully equipped campground offers 20 sites, nearly all of which have full hookups. **2176 South Bear Lake Blvd.; (801) 946-8735.**

PUBLIC

Bear Lake State Park—
With 138 sites, 46 with full hookups, toilets, showers, laundry facilities, and nearby boating and swimming opportunities, Bear Lake State Park is a popular campground with visitors. Located at the southern end of Bear Lake 2 miles west of Laketown on Hwy. 30. An additional 15 trailer sites and 22 tent sites are available at the Bear Lake Marina, 2 miles north of Garden City on US Hwy. 89. (Showers, toilets, boating, and swimming also

available.) One hundred primitive camp sites may be found on the eastern side of the lake at Cisco Beach. For information about camping within Bear Lake State Park, call **(801) 946-3343.**

Sunrise Campground—
Located in the Cache National Forest, 8.2 miles southwest of Garden City on US Hwy. 89, there are 26 RV trailer and tent sites. Open mid-June–mid-Sept.

WHERE TO EAT

There is not an abundance of places to eat around Bear Lake, especially if you get there in the off season, which is anytime but summer.

Bear Lake Motor Lodge—$–$$
The most reliable of the Bear Lake eateries for being open when you want to eat. Open daily 7 am–8 pm. **50 South Bear Lake Blvd., Garden City; (801) 946-8892.**

LeBeau's Drive In—$
There is an ongoing debate about whether LeBeau's or the Quick 'N' Tasty (see next entry) have more fruit in their raspberry shakes. Summer hours Mon.–Sat., 10:30 am–10:30 pm. **69 North Bear Lake Blvd.; (801) 946-8821.**

Quick 'N' Tasty Drive-In—$
This is my favorite drive-in in Garden City. It features home-cut fries, family-grown beef burgers, and raspberry shakes made from freshly picked berries from the berry patch just outside town. Summer hours Mon.–Sat., 10:30 am–10 pm. **28 North Bear Lake Blvd.; (801) 946-3489**

South Shore Grill—$$–$$$
The grill features fresh trout. Open 10 am–2 pm; Tues.–Sat. for dinner, 5:30 pm–10 pm; Sun. brunch from 10 am–2 pm. **2176 Bear Lake Blvd.; (801) 946-3421.**

SERVICES

Bridgerland Travel and Tourism Office—
160 North Main St., Logan, UT 84321; (801) 752-2161 or 1-800-882-4433.

J. GOLDEN KIMBALL

A legend and folk hero in Utah because of the stories about his imperfections in a society that seemed to demand perfection, especially of its leaders, J. Golden Kimball is one of the most colorful individuals to come out of the Bear Lake Country. J. Golden was one of 65 children fathered by Heber C. Kimball, Brigham Young's right-hand man until the elder Kimball's death in 1868. After his father's death, J. Golden became a mule skinner, moved to Meadowville near Bear Lake, and learned the profanity that continued as part of his vocabulary after he was called to be one of the LDS Church general authorities in 1894. His humor, wit, sprinkling of "damns" and "hells" in his speeches, and unsanctimonious common touch made Kimball one of the most beloved leaders in the history of the Mormon Church. The essence of J. Golden Kimball is captured by Thomas Cheney in his book *The Golden Legacy: A Folk History of J. Golden Kimball* (Peregrine Smith, Salt Lake City, 1974).

Logan and Cache Valley

Logan is one of Utah's most popular cities. Many Utah residents have attended school at Utah State University in Logan where the lush green Cache Valley offers a welcome relief from the deserts and red rock of much of the state. Many people also feel that the Logan area combines the best of small-town, rural America with the intellectual and cultural atmosphere of an 18,000-student university. Logan has also been something of a regional religious center for northern Utah and southern Idaho for more than a century since the construction of the Logan Temple, which began in 1877 and was completed in 1884. The Logan Temple is one of four historic temples constructed by the LDS Church in Utah during the 19th century. The other three are located in St. George, Manti, and Salt Lake City.

HISTORY

Like much of northern Utah, Logan and the surrounding Cache Valley were home to fur trappers in the 1820s, who wintered in what is now called Willow Valley. During the summer of 1826, a trapper was accidentally buried alive while excavating a cave in which to store or "cache" furs. The unlucky trapper's body was left buried; ever afterward, the valley was known as Cache Valley. That same year, another fur trapper, Ephraim Logan, was killed by Indians and his body buried in the mountains east of Cache Valley, leading the canyon to be called Logan Canyon. During the Mormon trek westward in 1847, Brigham Young met several fur trappers who advised the Mormon leader to forego the Salt Lake Valley because of the scarcity of timber and to settle in Cache Valley. Although Young opted for the Salt Lake Valley, Mormons began settling the Cache Valley in 1856, when Maughn's Fort, known today as Wellsville, was established in the southern end of the valley. Three years later, five additional settlements were established: Providence, Mendon, Logan, Richmond, and Smithfield. Prosperity came with the arrival in Logan of the Utah Northern Railroad in 1873, which opened markets for the valley's grain and dairy products. Much of the valley's 20th-century prosperity came from the 1888 decision to establish Utah's land grant agricultural college in Logan. Known today as Utah State University, the institution is the valley's largest single employer.

GETTING THERE

Logan is located 81 miles north of Salt Lake City and can be reached by taking Interstate 15 north for 56 miles to the Brigham City exit, then following US Hwy. 89 east-northeast for 25 miles through the Wasatch Mountains, by way of Wellsville (Sardine) Canyon into Cache Valley.

MAJOR ATTRACTIONS

Utah State University

Utah State University was established in 1888 as Utah State Agricultural College; in 1957, the institution became known as Utah State University. Although the sports teams are known as the Aggies, and agricultural studies continue to be one of the school's leading areas of study, the university has a strong diversity of programs—from the humanities to the sciences. The university's landmark building, "Old Main," dates from 1889 and sits on the brow of the hill overlooking Cache Valley. The university has a full schedule of **concerts, programs, and sporting activities.** For information about upcoming events, call **(801) 797-1158**; for ticket information call **(801) 797-0305.** Don't miss USU's famous Traditional Aggie Ice Cream, which is available at the student union building or at the Food Science Building at the east end of the campus.

FESTIVALS AND EVENTS

Festival of the American West

last week of July and beginning of August

One of Utah's most popular summer festivals, the Festival of the American West is held on the Utah State University campus the last week of July and first days of Aug. At the festival artisans demonstrate traditional crafts, including woodcarving, leather carving, blacksmithing, wheelwrighting, quilting, Indian jewelry, and beadwork. You will also find historic games and contests; western dancers and music; Dutch-oven potatoes, buffalo stew, Mormon johnnycakes, and Navajo tacos, as well as a two-hour theatrical production called "The West: America's Odyssey," with a cast of more than 200. Other popular events associated with the festival include the Dutch-oven cook-off and the American Heritage Quilt Festival. For more information, call **(801) 797-1143** or **1-800-225-3378.**

Cache County Fair and the American West Rodeo

second weekend in August

Usually held the 2nd weekend in Aug., the fair and rodeo are long-time Cache Valley traditions.

Martin Harris Pageant

mid-August

Martin Harris is one of Mormondom's most important figures. In 1830 Harris, along with Oliver Cowdery and David Whitmer, gave their solemn witness that an Angel of God showed them the golden plates from which Joseph Smith translated the Book of Mormon. After many years away from the church he helped found, Martin Harris journeyed to Utah to spend the last years of his life among the Mormons. He settled in Clarkston and died there in 1875. The Martin Harris Pageant, held in mid-Aug. under the sponsorship of the LDS Church, depicts Harris' life and the early history of the Mormon Church. A 2,500-seat outdoor theater has been constructed for the yearly event. There is no admission charge; however, because of the pageant's popularity, tickets should be obtained beforehand from the **Book Table, 29 South Main** in **Logan,** or by writing the **Martin Harris Pageant, PO Box 151, Clarkston, UT 84305.**

OUTDOOR ACTIVITIES

BIKING

The mountains surrounding Cache Valley provide plenty of opportunities for mountain bikers. The "Bridgerland Mountain and Roadbike Trails" guide describes 23 routes, ranging from easy to moderate rides, around Cache Valley to 50-mile-loop mountain rides to steep, technically demanding up-and-back climbs. The guide is free and available at the **Bridgerland Travel Region Office, 160 North Main St.** in **Logan.**

Green Canyon—

The 12-mile up and back ride through Green Canyon is an easily accessible mountain ride along a well-maintained dirt-and-gravel road that is especially pretty in the spring and fall. Take 1900 North to reach the trailhead which begins about a mile east of 1600 East in North Logan at the Cache National Forest Boundary. Green Canyon is the location for the quarry that produced the granite used in the construction of the Logan Temple and Tabernacle and numerous pioneer homes in and near Logan.

Hyde Park Route—

This easy, 9-mile loop begins at the Utah State University campus at 700 North and heads east to 1500 East, then turns north, passing through the town of North Logan to 2300 North where it drops back to the west, to 1200 East and continues on north to the end of 1200 East in Hyde Park. There, it heads west to 800 East (Hwy. 237), where it turns back to the south all the way into Logan to 700 North, then back to the beginning point. Although North Logan and Hyde Park have become "bedroom communities" for USU faculty and staff, there is still enough of rural Cache Valley left to make this an enjoyable ride.

Little Pyrenees Route—

This moderate, rolling hill route gives you a good view of south Cache Valley as you head south out of Logan on Hwy. 165, past Providence, Millville, and Nibley for about 7 miles to Hyrum. After turning west through Hyrum, the route passes around the northern end of Hyrum Reservoir and continues west to US Hwy. 89/91. After crossing the highway, turn north and follow Hwy. 23 through Wellsville and on to Mendon. Take 100 East through Mendon and, just north of town, turn east for the last leg back into Logan at 600 South. The 24-mile loop offers an excellent view of the farmland and communities along the east side of the valley, a close-up view of the towering Wellsville Mountains and interesting ride alongside the marshes of the Little Bear River, before the road crosses the Logan River just west of Logan.

Richmond/Cornish Route—

If you want to see the northern end of Cache Valley, this 28-mile loop takes you through beautiful farmland and the towns of Richmond, Cove, Lewiston, Cornish, and Trenton. Start the ride in Richmond, at the intersection of state Hwy. 142 and US Hwy. 91. Head east to 3000 East in Richmond, then turn north and follow the route as it moves up and down the hills for about 3 miles to 11800 North. Turn west and ride through Cove to Hwy. 91, then follow the highway north to its intersection with state Hwy. 61. Turn west on Hwy. 61, passing through Lewiston and on to Cornish. In Cornish turn south on Hwy. 23 to its intersection with state Hwy. 142. Turn east and follow Hwy. 23 through Trenton and back to the starting point in Richmond.

Riverside Trail—

This is an easy-to-moderate 6-mile round-trip ride in Logan Canyon that parallels the Logan River and follows along the Logan City waterline right of way. Some parking is available at the trailhead, above the first dam in the canyon, but most riders follow US Hwy. 91 up the Canyon for a short distance before turning off at the trailhead.

BOATING

Bear Lake—
See Outdoor Activities in the **Bear Lake** chapter.

Hyrum State Park—
The most popular motor boat and water-skiing location in Cache Valley is Hyrum Reservoir located 8 miles south of Logan, southwest of Hyrum on state Hwy. 165.

Newton Reservoir—
Located northwest of Logan, the Newton Reservoir was one of the first reservoirs constructed by Mormon pioneers in Utah. Today it is popular for water-skiing.

BUNGEE JUMPING

Sports Tower—
This place qualifies as Utah's first bungee jumping center. In addition to the bungee jumping tower, you will find other contraptions for thrill-seekers. **1900 South 1000 West.** For prices and schedules, call **(801) 750-0822.**

CANOEING

Although Utah is not noted for its canoeing opportunities, the Cache Valley area offers the best locations in a state known more for its deserts than its waterways. The Bear River can be navigated from below the Oneida Dam in Idaho across the border into Utah as far as Cutler Reservoir. With the exception of a 4-mile-long section of moderate whitewater below the Oneida Dam, the Bear River is a placid river that offers good opportunities for bird watching. For local canoers, the most popular stretch of the river is the 11-mile section between Trenton and Amalga. Access to the river is still quite primitive, but boaters on this section can put in at the bridge across the Bear River on Utah Hwy. 142 and take out at the bridge on Utah 218.

Canoe rentals are available at **Trailhead Sports, 117 North Main, Logan; (801)753-1541.**

FISHING

Blacksmith Fork River—
Another excellent fly-fishing stream is Blacksmith Fork River, which can be reached by following state Hwy. 101 east out of Hyrum toward the Hardware Ranch Game Management Area.

Hyrum Reservoir—
In addition to being a popular boating and water-skiing area, Hyrum Reservoir is also stocked with rainbow trout and bass.

Logan River—
One of the most popular fly-fishing streams in Utah, the Logan River in scenic Logan Canyon is stocked primarily with rainbow trout, but some cutthroat and brown trout are also found in the river.

Newton Reservoir—
One of the first reservoirs constructed by Mormon settlers in Utah, Newton Reservoir is stocked with trout, bass, bluegill, and catfish.

GOLF

Birch Creek Golf Course—
As Cache Valley's oldest 18-hole public golf course, Birch Creek is popular with local residents. Located in Smithfield, 7 miles north of Logan. Take US Hwy. 91 north out of Logan to Center St. in Smithfield—the views of Cache Valley are spectacular. Turn east for six blocks to the course; **(801) 683-6825.**

Logan Golf and Country Club—
Although this is a country club course, it is open to the public on a space-available basis. So, if you are a member of the club you can call for a tee time; if you aren't, you can show up and hope that you get one. Usually you can. Recently nonmembers have been able to make reservations up to a week in advance. The inconvenience and extra cost are well worth it, for this is one of the best courses in the state. Built during the early 1930s, it started as a 3-hole course, and then evolved to 9, then 18. It is located

east of Utah State University campus at **710 North 1500 East; (801)753-6050.**

Logan River Golf Course—

Opened in 1993, the Logan River Golf Course is one of Utah's newest courses and a radical change from the more parklike, open, and easier courses that the majority of Utah golfers are accustomed to. In a word, most duffers find this a fairly difficult course, with narrow fairways and small, difficult-to-hit greens. Through it all, you are surrounded by near-century-old trees, the Logan River and a half dozen beautiful ponds. **550 West 1000 South, Logan; (801) 750-0123.**

Sherwood Hills Golf Course—

Situated in picturesque Wellsville Canyon and visible from US Hwy. 89/91, this 9-hole course is part of the Sherwood Hills Resort. While the course does not look very appealing from the highway, don't let that deceive you; most of the holes are hidden in the maples and quaking aspens. The overlooking mountains, the solitude, and the squirrels and birds make this a memorable course. Uncrowded, with tee times usually easy to arrange, the resort and course are located 12 miles southwest of Logan; **(801) 245-6055.**

HIKING

If you are an avid hiker and are going to spend any time in the Cache Valley area, you will want to buy *Cache Trails*, a 78-page book that provides descriptions of 40 trails in the surrounding mountains. A smaller guide, "Bridgerland Hiking Trails," describes 15 trails and is available at no cost from the Bridgerland Travel Region or the Logan Ranger District Wasatch/Cache National Forest. The trails range from short, easy rambles, like the Riverside Nature Trail described below, to strenuous climbs, like those in the Wellsville Mountains, that challenge the most fit of hikers.

Crimson Trail—

For a bird's-eye view of lower Logan Canyon, the Crimson Trail takes you above the rugged limestone China Wall Formation, where you can look down into the canyon. The trail begins at the Guinavah-Malibu Campground and follows the Riverside Nature Trail for the first couple of hundred yards before it climbs steeply along switchbacks up the mountain for an elevation gain of about 800 feet in the first mile, requiring plenty of rest stops to catch your breath. Once you have the climb out of the way, it becomes an easy hike with a total distance of approximately 4 miles to the Spring Hollow Campground. It's another mile back along US Hwy. 89 to the Guinavah-Malibu Campground or the Riverside Nature Trail. This is an especially pretty hike in the fall, as the trail takes its name from the crimson-colored maple leaves along the route.

Riverside Nature Trail—

This easy 3-mile round-trip trail follows the Logan River between Spring Hollow and the Guinavah-Malibu Campground–Picnic Area in Logan Canyon. The trail is a favorite of bird watchers, and the Bridgerland Audubon Society in cooperation with the Forest Service has prepared an excellent brief guide to the flora and fauna along the trail. The brochure, "Riverside Nature Trail," is available at the trailheads and local tourist offices. To reach the trailhead, follow US Hwy. 89 up Logan Canyon for about 4 miles and watch for the Spring Hollow Turnout, where parking and restrooms are located across the river.

Wellsville Mountains—

It is said that the Wellsville Mountains in the southern end of Cache Valley are the steepest mountains in the US. Within a couple of miles, the mountains rise nearly 5,000 feet over the communities of Wellsville and Mendon. The mountains are a designated wilderness area, with three trails that lead to the summits for a spectacular view of Cache Valley to the east and the Great Salt Lake and Bear River to the west. Hikers can go up and back on the same trail or make a loop using the Stewart Pass Trail and Deep Canyon Trail, leaving a shuttle vehicle at the other trailhead.

Box Elder Peak Trail—This is a steep, 4-mile-long trail, with an elevation gain of 4,000 feet. The trailhead begins south of Wellsville, off US Hwy. 89/91. Follow the highway south, past Wellsville, to the first big turn, then look for an unpaved road just north of the turn, which is the beginning of the trail. Plan at least 5 hours to make the 8-mile round-trip.

Deep Canyon Trail—If you take the Stewart Pass Trail to the summit of the Wellsville Mountains, you can continue northwest along the ridgeline for 1.75 miles past Mendon Peak and Scout Peak then descend using the Deep Canyon Trail. If you make this loop, you will want to leave a car at the Deep Canyon Trailhead, which is reached by driving west out of Mendon on Third North for about 2 miles. The total hiking distance up the Stewart Pass Trail and back along the Deep Canyon Trail is approximately 8 miles, with the steep climb making it a strenuous undertaking requiring the better part of a day. The long-distance views and surprisingly thick foilage are a just reward. Take plenty of water and protection against the winds and colder temperatures that can be expected along the ridgeline.

Stewart Pass Trail—This 3-mile-long trail climbs past Coldwater Lake and Hughes Peak to Stewart Pass. The trailhead begins southwest of Mendon and is reached by turning west off the Mendon Main St., south of the stop sign, onto a gravel road. Drive along the gravel road for about 3.5 miles, until it ends near a watering trough, then look for the trailhead. The trail heads south for .75 mile toward Coldwater Lake; past the lake, it turns west for about 2 miles as it makes a steep climb to Stewart Pass. Allow at least 3 hours to the summit and back.

High Creek Trail—

Heading up the mountain east from Richmond, the 12-mile round-trip High Creek Trail climbs 2,600 feet, passing mountain wildflowers and waterfalls to reach a snow-fed lake at the base of Naomi Peak. To reach the trailhead drive north past Richmond on US Hwy. 91, then watch for a marked turnoff on the eastern side of the road about a mile past the **Pepperidge Farm factory** where you might want to stock up on cookies for the hike. (The factory thrift store is open at various hours Tues.–Sat.) Drive east for 5 miles to the end of the road.

Wind Cave Trail—

One of the most interesting features in Logan Canyon is Wind Cave located in the China Wall Formation on the north slope of Logan Canyon. It is actually a series of three openings that resemble a triple arch. The largest opening is about 40 feet wide and 20 feet wide. It is a strenuous 2-mile hike to the cave as the trail climbs nearly 1,000 feet. There are exposed cliffs near the cave. The parking area at the trailhead has space for a dozen or so cars and is located 5.3 miles up Logan Canyon from the Lady Bird rest stop. A sign indicates Wind Cave.

HORSEBACK RIDING

Beaver Creek—

Bryan Lundahl operates a horseback riding facility in Logan Canyon, 25 miles northeast of the city and .25 mile east of the turnoff to the Beaver Mountain Ski Resort. Rides are from one hour to two and a half hours, and you will be taken through the mountains covered with aspens, pine trees, and wildflowers, and past a beautiful mountain stream. Open during summer, Mon.–Sat, 10:30 am–7:30 pm; **(801) 753-1076.**

SKIING
CROSS-COUNTRY SKIING

Cross-country skiing has become particularly popular with USU students and other residents of Cache Valley. "Cache Tours" lists 30 cross-country ski areas in the Cache Valley area of interest to serious cross-country skiers.

Backcountry Yurts—

If you want a unique cross-country skiing experience in the forests and meadows of the Wasatch Mountains coupled with accommodations right out of Mongolia, the Powder Ridge Ski Touring Company offers the Steam Mill Yurt and the Bunch Grass Yurt. Yurts are portable, round, skin- or canvas-covered shelters, supported by a wood-frame structure. They have been used for centuries by nomadic peoples in Central Asia. The yurts are located between 3.5 and 4 miles skiing distance from the trailhead with elevation gains of 1,500 and 2,100 feet that require between three and five hours skiing time to reach them. The yurts are equipped with wood-burning stoves, bunkbeds with foam mattresses, propane cook stoves, gas lanterns, and complete kitchens. Most skiers enjoy not only the trails to the yurts but also the nearby bowls, meadows, and woods, which offer plenty of options for skiers of all abilities. Guides can be hired and are recommended for first-timers. For information and rates, contact **Powder Ridge Ski Touring, 7124 West Hwy. 30, Petersboro, UT 84325; (801) 752-9610.**

Sherwood Hills Resort—

This resort, located 12 miles southwest of Logan on US 89/91, has over 11 miles of groomed trails. Ski rentals are available; **(801) 245-5054.**

DOWNHILL SKIING
Beaver Mountain Ski Area—

The only downhill ski area in northern Utah, Beaver Mountain has been a family-operated ski area since 1939. It has three double chairlifts to serve the 22 runs on 364 skiable acres. The longest lift is the 4,600-foot Harry's Dream (named for owner Harold Seeholzer), which climbs to an elevation of 8,800 feet and is within a few feet of the summit of Beaver Mountain. The capacity of all three chairlifts is 2,600 skiers an hour. Located 30 miles northeast of Logan off US Hwy. 89. With day passes the cheapest in the state, Beaver Mountain is popular with Utah State University students. Seventy-five percent of its terrain is for beginning and intermediate skiers. Beaver Mountain averages 450 inches a year. There is a ski school, ski rental shop and a lodge with a cafeteria and short-order homestyle food. For information and ticket prices write **1045 1/2 North Main, Suite # 4, Box 3455, Logan, UT 84321;** or call **(801) 753-0921.**

SNOWMOBILING

Snowmobiling is popular in northern Utah, known as America's Snowmobile Playground. "The Snowmobile Trail Guide," available free from the Bridgerland Travel Council, lists 16 trailheads in northern Utah and 3 in southern Idaho.

SWIMMING
Logan Municipal Pool—

This indoor pool is open year-round. **114 East 1000 North; (801) 752-9323.**

TENNIS
Community Recreation Center—

Except for the 12 tennis courts on the Utah State University campus, the Community Recreation Center is the best place for tennis. With four outdoor courts, but no lights, and two indoor courts available for by the hour (fee charged in addition to admission to the Recreation Center), die-hard tennis players can be accommodated. You cannot reserve the outdoor courts, but the indoor courts can be booked. Call **(801) 752-3221.** The center is located at **195 South 100 West** in **Logan.**

Logan Muncipal Pool—

Four outdoor, lighted courts are available at the Logan Municipal Pool. **114 East 1000 North; (801) 752-9323.**

———— SEEING AND DOING ————

ART GALLERIES

Logan is home to several art galleries that exhibit local artists and, on occasion, traveling exhibits. These galleries include:

Alliance for the Varied Arts Gallery—
Bullen Center, 43 South Main; (801) 753-2970.

Barkers White Pine Gallery—
855 South Main; (801) 752-3657.

Fuhriman's Framing and Fine Art—
75 South Main; (801) 752-0370.

Greystone Gallery—
55 North Main in the Emporium; (801) 752-9440.

Mountain Place Gallery—
In the **Sportsman, 129 North Main;** (801) 752-0211.

HISTORIC SITES AND BUILDINGS

Logan has an abundance of historic homes and buildings. Available at no charge is the booklet "A Self-Guided Walking Tour of Logan's Historic Main Street," which provides information on **14 Main St. buildings,** most of which were constructed at the turn of the century.

Bear River Massacre Site—

For more than a century it was known as the Battle of Bear River. Historian Brigham D. Madsen, in his study *The Shoshoni Frontier and the Bear River Massacre,* has put the events of January 29, 1863, into perspective and leaves little question that the deaths of 250 Shoshoni (most of whom were women and children) were a massacre. More Native Americans were killed by whites in a single day at Bear River than even at the 1864 Sand Creek Massacre or in 1890 at Wounded Knee. Twenty-three soldiers, under the command of Colonel Patrick Connor, stationed at Fort Douglas in the Salt Lake Valley, died in the encounter. The site, located a few miles north of Lewiston just across the Utah-Idaho border along US Hwy. 89, has been designated a National Historic Landmark.

Logan Tabernacle—

One Mormon building that visitors can enter is the historic Logan Tabernacle, located between **Center and 100 North** on Main St. in downtown **Logan.** The tabernacle is used for community meetings and is open to LDS members and nonmembers alike. Construction commenced in 1864, but the building was not completed until 1891—partly because subsequent work on the Logan Temple took a higher priority. Built of gray granite trimmed in white, the Logan Tabernacle is one of the oldest remaining tabernacles in the Mormon West. The building is open for tours, and the green space surrounding the building offers a parklike atmosphere in the heart of Logan.

Logan Temple—

Mormon leaders had a good eye for the proper location of their most important religious buildings. The Logan Temple and the Manti Temple in Sanpete County, are the most dramatically situated of the eight Mormon temples in Utah. Constructed on a hill overlooking downtown Logan, the temple can be seen from nearly every part of Cache Valley. Since its completion in 1884, the Gothic-style gray stone edifice, with its towers, buttresses and battlements, has seemed to preside over affairs much like the castles and fortresses of medieval Europe. In 1979, amidst great controversy from both within and outside the Mormon church, the interior was extensively remodeled and most of the historical interior was lost. But, unless you are a Mormon yourself with proper credentials, you will not be allowed inside the temple to see it. Still, the exterior of the building is well worth a look, and the view of Cache Valley from Temple Hill is glorious. The temple is located between **200 and 300 North** and **200 and 300 East** in **Logan**.

MUSEUMS

Daughters of Utah Pioneers Museum—

This museum houses pioneer artifacts from the Logan and Cache Valley area. Open during the summer Tues.–Sat., 10 am–4 pm. The museum is located in the same building as the **Bridgerland Travel Region Office, 160 North Main**.

Nora Eccles Harrison Museum of Art—

Located on the Utah State University Campus, this museum features permanent exhibits of the art museum's own collections as well as new exhibits every six to eight weeks. Workshops and gallery talks are featured. Open Tues., Thurs., and Fri. 10:30 am–4:30 pm; Wed. 10:30 am–9 pm; Sat. and Sun. 2–5 pm. Closed Mon. and holidays. Admission is free. For information call **(801) 750-1412**.

Ronald V. Jenson Living Historical Farm—

Under the management of Jay Anderson, one of the world's foremost authorities on the varied aspects of "living history," the Jenson farm is a unique interpretation of a typical 1917 Mormon family farm. The farm is located on 120 acres 6 miles southwest of Logan on US Hwy. 89/91 and comprises 10 historic buildings, vintage farm equipment, and livestock of the World War I era. The farm is operated as part of Utah State University and is staffed by volunteers, a small professional staff, and graduate students earning degrees in outdoor museum studies, folklore, and history. Because the primary mission of the farm is to train graduate students and to preserve agricultural life of a bygone era, this is one museum that has not been overcommercialized or compromised for the convenience of modern-day

visitors. Admission fees are modest, and events such as sheep shearing, haymaking, grain harvesting, threshing, canning, cider pressing, and meat processing are scheduled to coincide with the natural cycles of farm life. Other events reflect how such events as Easter, Arbor Day, a wedding reception, Old Folks Day, the 4th of July, Pioneer Day, Halloween, and Christmas would have been commemorated in 1917. A free self-guided tour brochure is provided to visitors. For schedules and further information, write **Ronald V. Jenson Living Historical Farm, Wellsville, UT 84339; (801) 245-4064**.

SCENIC DRIVES

Hardware Ranch Road Backway—

If you don't mind traveling on a single-lane dirt road, you can make a nice loop combining the Logan Canyon road with the Hardware Ranch Rd., otherwise the more commonly used route up Blacksmith Fork Canyon to Hardware Ranch is a worthwhile trip in itself. The road follows state Hwy. 101 east from Hyrum for 18 miles to Hardware Ranch, a popular winter wildlife viewing area. The road to Hardware Ranch is paved and takes you past steep canyon walls into broad meadows. If you combine the drive with a return via Logan Canyon, continue along the dirt road that heads north from the ranch for approximately 25 miles to its junction with state Hwy. 30 at the southern end of Bear Lake at Laketown.

Logan Canyon Scenic Byway—

The 41-mile drive from Logan to Bear Lake through Logan Canyon is not only the most often used route to the resort area, but it is also one of the most scenic drives in the state. The limestone cliffs in the lower end of the canyon, the swift-flowing Logan River, and the groves of quaking aspen and pine trees show off Utah's mountains at their best. Logan Canyon offers several interesting stopping points. The **Old Jardine Juniper** is located on a limestone ridge 1,500 feet above the road and can be reached by a steep 1.5-mile climb from

Cottonwood Campground, located about 15 miles from Logan. The juniper is the largest known Rocky Mountain "red cedar" and is estimated to be more than 3,000 years old. The tree, discovered in 1923, is 45 feet high and 27 feet in circumference. Another historic event occurred in 1923 when an **11-foot grizzly bear known as Old Ephraim** was killed. An 11-foot-high granite shaft marks the site. It is located 6 miles from the highway and can be reached by heading southeast about a mile up the highway from the Cottonwood Campground using an unpaved forest road along Temple Fork. The bear's skull, a relic owned by the Smithsonian Museum, is on display at the **Bridgerland Travel Region Office, 160 North Main** in **Logan.**

Tony Grove Lake is a beautiful body of water that is popular with fishermen. It is located 5 miles off the highway 20 miles up the canyon from Logan. At the summit of Logan Canyon, an easy mile-long trail can be taken to the Limber Pine (see Outdoor Activities in the **Bear Lake** chapter, p. 27). The gradual 30-mile assent to the summit of Logan Canyon is contrasted with a steep 11-mile descent over switchbacks to Garden City in Rich County. Along the road are several pullouts, where you can stop and admire the breathtaking view of turquoise-colored Bear Lake that takes up most of the valley below. Logan Canyon is another favorite place to view autumn colors.

Wellsville Canyon—

The primary access to Cache Valley is via Hwy. 89/91 from Brigham City. The 12-mile drive between Brigham City and Wellsville in the southern end of Cache Valley is picturesque year-round, but it's particularly beautiful in the fall.

THEATER AND OPERA

Old Lyric Theater Repertory Company—

Housed in the historic Lyric theater in downtown Logan, this theater company is operated by the Utah State University department of theater arts. During June, July and Aug., it offers a variety of comedies,

drama and musicals in repertory. The 1913 building is also reported to house a friendly ghost who is a fan of Shakespeare. The ghost has been spotted at the edge of the balcony wearing a fool's cap and Elizabethan-era clothing, and laughing during rehearsals. **28 West Center; (801) 750-1657.** For more information, write to the **Old Lyric Repertory Company, Theater Arts Department, Utah State University, Logan, UT 84322-4035.**

Utah Festival Opera Company—

Thanks to Cache Valley native Michael Ballam, July has become Opera Month in Logan as the Utah Festival Opera Company, which launched its first season in 1993, performs three operas in repertory throughout the month. Look for this well-endowed musical endeavor to expand in the future with possibly a longer season with even more productions. Ballam, who has had an outstanding international opera career as a tenor, is taking as his model the highly successful Utah Shakespearean Festival in Cedar City and is committed to a traditional approach to opera. The Company has an excellent facility, the recently restored Ellen Eccles Theatre (formerly the historic Capitol Theater which was built in the early 1900s), involvement from the Utah State University Music Department, support of a large all-volunteer guild, and encouragement from the community. Look for this undertaking to become a nationally recognized opera festival. For information write or call **Utah Festival Opera Company, Ellen Eccles Theatre, 43 South Main, Logan, UT 84321; (801) 752-0026.**

TOURS

Cache Valley Cheese Factory—

Cache Valley cheese is known throughout Utah and the Intermountain West and the Cache Valley Cheese Factory in Smithfield offers a unique opportunity to watch cheese-making in progress. You can sample the cheese and make purchases at the chalet. Tours can be arranged 10 am–noon, Mon.–Fri. by calling **(801) 563-3550.** Open Mon.–Sat., 8 am–5 pm. **6350 North 2150 West.** Take state Hwy. 218 west from

Smithfield for 3 miles. Similar arrangements can be made at **Gossner Foods Cheese Factory, 1000 West 1000 North, Logan; (801) 752-9365.**

WILDLIFE

Bird Watching—
The Bear River meanders through Cache Valley forming marshes and wetlands, which offer a variety of locations for bird watching. Over 250 species of birds have been sighted along the river.

Hardware Ranch—
Originally homesteaded in 1868, Hardware Ranch is one of the most popular winter wildlife viewing locations in the state. Owned and operated by the Utah Division of Wildlife Resources since 1946, the ranch produces wild meadow hay, which is used to feed huge herds of elk during the winter. Visitors ride sleighs across the snow into the meadows where hundreds of elk are fed. The elk have become very tame, and some will come right up to eat hay off the sleigh. To reach the ranch, take state Hwy. 101 east out of Hyrum up Blacksmith Fork Canyon for 18 miles. The road can be snow-packed in the winter but is usually well sanded. Winter days are cold; temperatures with the wind chill factor can drop well below zero, so dress accordingly. Some elk stay year-round, and the visitor center/restaurant is open all year. You can take covered wagon and horseback overnight trips that include BBQ dinner, western games, and a Dutch oven breakfast. For information and reservations call **(801) 245-3131** or **245-3329.**

ZOO

Willow Park Zoo—
If you are looking for an inexpensive—or free—outing for children, the Willow Park Zoo is worth an hour or two of your time. The zoo is located in a section of Logan City's 15-acre Willow Park. Most of the animals are birds such as ducks, swans, wild turkeys, peacocks, and bald eagles; but there are also pygmy goats, monkeys, two black bears and a family of wallabies. The zoo is open year-round, except Thanksgiving, Christmas, and New Year's Day, 8 am–dusk. **419 West 700 South; (801) 752-3060.**

WHERE TO STAY

ACCOMMODATIONS
BED AND BREAKFASTS
AND INNS
Alta Manor Suites—$$$
This newly constructed facility is built with a strong Tudor flavor and offers eight elegant one- and two-bedroom nonsmoking suites. Each suite has a natural gas fireplace, full kitchen with microwave oven, a bath with whirlpool tub, and separate shower. A light continental breakfast is included. **45 East 500 North; (801) 752-0808.**

Center Street Bed and Breakfast—$$ to $$$
Operated by Clyne and Ann Long. There are 13 rooms available in three buildings: a 114-year-old mansion, a carriage house, and the smaller White House. Several of the rooms have private hot tubs and are furnished with VCRs. Private breakfasts are served in each room. **169 East Center St., Logan, UT 84321; (801) 752-3443.**

Logan House—$$
Rod and Marion Vaughn have done a fine job in converting this historic Logan house into a six-room bed and breakfast inn. Each room has a private bath each equipped with a whirlpool. For families, there's The Family Room with two double beds, a hide-a-way sofa and portable crib. The Master Suite has an adjoining balcony and sitting porch. The Logan House also hosts receptions and small conferences. **168 North 100 East; (801) 752-7727.**

Sherwood Hills—$$ to $$$

Fifty-seven rooms and a restaurant. Off US Hwy. 89 in Sardine Canyon, approximately 12 miles south of Logan. There is a golf course (see the Golfing section) and cross-country skiing in the winter; **(801) 245-6424.**

University Inn—$$

Seventy-four rooms. Located in the center of the Utah State University campus, adjacent to the Student Center and within walking distance of the football stadium, basketball arena, and library. **(801) 797-1153.**

Zanavoo Restaurant, Lodge, Bed and Breakfast Lodge—$$ to $$$

Located a five-minute drive up Logan Canyon along Hwy 89, Zanavoo (an Indian word for" beautiful") was constructed in 1948. The eleven rooms include private baths with hot tubs for each room. The lodge is situated along the Logan River, and the pine and oak-clad mountains make this a beautiful site year-round. The restaurant offers American dishes, with prime rib being a weekend favorite; **(801) 752-0084** or **752-5052.**

MOTELS

Best Western Baugh Motel—$$

Seventy-seven rooms, heated pool. **153 South Main; (801) 752-5220.**

Best Western Weston Inn—$$

Ninety rooms. The heated indoor swimming pool is a favorite for children. **250 North Main; (801) 752-5700.**

Comfort Inn—$$

Eighty-three rooms. Heated indoor pool and whirlpool. **447 North Main; (801) 752-9141.**

Logan Days Inn—$$

Forty-eight rooms. **364 South Main; (801) 753-5623** or **1-800-325-2525.**

Super 8 Motel—$$

Sixty-one rooms. **865 South Main, Hwy. 89/91; (801) 753-8883.**

CAMPING

PRIVATE

There are three small private campgrounds in the Logan vicinity. **Western Park Campground** has 21 sites with 15 complete hookups. **350 West 800 South; (801) 752-6424. Bandits Cove** has 12 complete hookups at **590 South Main St. (801) 753-0508;** and 1.5 miles south of Logan, on Hwy. 89, the **Riverside RV Park and Campground** has 14 sites with 10 complete hookups. All three campgrounds are open year-round.

PUBLIC

Hyrum—

Three forest service campgrounds within a distance of 3.5 miles in Blacksmith Fork Canyon along state Hwy. 242 offer a total of 27 camping spots. **Pioneer Campground,** 9 miles from Hyrum has 18 sites; **Friendship Campground** 1.5 miles farther up the canyon has 6 sites; and **Spring Campground,** another 2 miles up Hwy. 242 has 8 sites. Only the Pioneer Campground has drinking water; it is the only campground where a fee is charged.

Logan Canyon—

Within a 23-mile stretch along Hwy. 89 through Logan Canyon, there are 10 public campgrounds. All campgrounds include both tent and trailer sites, but there are no hookups. Most campgrounds have fewer than a dozen sites, although the **Tony Grove Lake Campground** and the **Guinavah-Malibu Campground** have 37 and 40 sites, respectively. Beginning with those closest to Logan, the campgrounds and their distances from Logan are: **Bridger,** 10 sites, 5.8 miles; **Spring Hollow,** 12 sites, 6.5 miles; **Guinavah-Malibu,** 40 sites, 8 miles; **Preston Valley,** 3 sites, 10.7 miles; **Wood Camp,** 6 sites, 12.4 miles; **Lewis M. Turner** 10 sites, 22.2 miles; **Red Banks,** 12 sites, 22.7 miles; and **Tony Grove Lake,** 37 sites, 28.7 miles. Fees are charged for most campgrounds; most have drinking water and restrooms.

WHERE TO EAT

Bluebird—$$

This restaurant has been on Logan's Main St. longer than anyone can remember, and its interior takes you back at least 40 or 50 years. Under the same ownership of the Copper Mill, the Bluebird continues to serve traditional American dishes such as roast beef, baked ham, roast turkey and fish. Open daily 7:30 am–9 pm. **19 North Main; (801) 752-3155.**

Copper Mill—$$ to $$$

The Copper Mill is owned by John Booth, who also owns the Bluebird (see above). The Copper Mill specializes in prime beef. Open 11 am–9:30 pm weekdays, and until 10:30 pm on Fri. and Sat. Closed Sun. **55 North Main; (801) 752-0647.**

DeVerl's Juniper Inn—$ to $$

When DeVerl Hoth opened his restaurant nearly 40 years ago, he wanted it to survive for a long time, so he named it for the juniper tree in Logan Canyon that has been around for about 3,500 years. The restaurant is now run by his son, Kelly, and seems well on its way to attaining the longevity of its namesake. It specializes in steak, chicken and fish. Open Tues.–Sat., 11:30 am–10 pm. **4088 North Main, Hyde Park; (801) 563-3491.**

Gia's Restaurant—$$

The place for Italian food in Logan, with homemade pastas, seafood, and steaks, and separate dinner dining rooms, delicatessen, and pizzeria offering homemade Sicilian-style pizza. The pizzeria, located in the basement of the building, has a big-screen TV, sawdust on the floor and initials and other carvings in the wooden tables. It's a favorite of USU students and those with fond memories of such places in other university towns. Dominic Catalano, who opened the restaurant in 1973, named it Gia's in honor of his youngest daughter. Open Tues.–Sun. for lunch 11 am–2 pm; dinner 5 pm–10 pm. **119 South Main; (801) 752-6384.**

Grapevine—$$ to $$$

Although it has only been in Logan since 1992, the Grapevine has quickly developed a reputation as one of Utah's finest restaurants with a diverse and unique menu with such items as pork tamales and fish sausage. Open Wed.–Sat,. 6 pm–10 p.m. **129 North 100 East; (801) 752-1977.**

Mandarin Garden—$ to $$

The Mandarin Garden offers Mandarin and Szechuan Chinese cuisine. It has been rated as the best Chinese Restaurant in northern Utah by *Utah Holiday* magazine. Open Mon.–Fri., 11:30 am–10 pm; Sat., noon–11 pm; Sun. noon–9:30 pm. **432 North Main; (801) 753-5789.**

Mendon Station—$$ to $$$

Mendon is located 8 miles west of Logan. The historic Mendon Railroad Station, which once served travelers on the Utah Northern Railroad, is now a popular restaurant featuring homemade soups and breads, steaks, and fresh fish, as well as prime rib on weekends. Open Tues.–Sat., 4 pm–10 pm. **95 North Main; (801) 752-2570.**

SERVICES

Bridgerland Travel and Tourism Office—

160 North Main St., Logan, UT 84321; (801) 752-2161 or 1-800-882-4433

Brigham City

For many Utahns, Brigham City means peaches, and it is unfortunate for many visitors that with the completion of Interstate 15 many are unaware of the 12-mile stretch of US 89/91 that runs south from Brigham City through Perry and Willard with its string of fruit stands. Located near the Great Salt Lake, Brigham City has long been an access point for observing the rich variety of waterfowl that inhabit or visit the marshes along the lake. Since the establishment of the Golden Spike National Historic Site in the 1960s, Brigham City has hosted thousands of railroad buffs who have made their pilgrimage from all over the world to the Promontory.

HISTORY

The prehistoric inhabitants of the region found the marshes at the mouth of the Bear River where it enters the Great Salt Lake offered a rich supply of food, and archaeologists have studied their lakeside camps with great interest. West of the lake, in places like Hogup Cave, archaeologists trace the Desert Archaic culture back 10,000 years. Mormon settlers moved to what they called Box Elder in 1851. The settlement was renamed Brigham City for Mormon leader Brigham Young in 1854, when he sent his trusted friend Lorenzo Snow to direct affairs. Snow encouraged Scandinavian immigrants to come to Brigham City and worked with them to establish the Brigham City Mercantile and Manufacturing Association, a cooperative that employed more than 500 people in a variety of economic endeavors, including a store, a woolen mill, a planing mill, a sheep herd, a dairy herd, a hat and cap factory, and other ventures designed to make Brigham City completely self-sufficient. The Brigham City Cooperative encouraged Brigham Young to push for the establishment of other cooperatives throughout the state under what was known as the United Order Movement. The completion of the transcontinental railroad at Promontory, 30 miles west of Brigham City, on May 10, 1869, marked not only a new phase of American history, but a new era for Utah. A non-Mormon city, named Corrine, was established in 1869 on the Bear River, just 5 miles west of Brigham City. The pretentious city of 1,500 people quickly overshadowed Brigham City. It pushed to become the western terminus for the Union Pacific Railroad and the eastern terminus for the Central Pacific Railroad and seemed destined, at least in the minds of Corinnethians, to become the new capital of the Territory of Utah. Merchants, speculators, and camp followers moved into the town as the railroad was completed. Within a few years, though, the dreams vanished, people moved on, and Corinne, despite its still-standing historic 1870 Methodist church, became another Mormon village. By the turn of the century, the cooperative movement had died and Brigham City moved placidly through the first half of the 20th century until World War II led to the opening of Bushnell Hospital where over 13,000 wounded veterans of the battlefields were treated. In the postwar era, Brigham City's economy has depended heavily on the defense industry, with Morton-Thiokol being the largest employer. With a primary emphasis on the manufacture of rockets and rocket motors, Morton-Thiokol faced cutbacks in the post–cold war era. Today, many of Brigham City's 17,000 or so residents are employed at Morton-Thiokol, west of the city.

GETTING THERE

Brigham City is located about 60 miles north of Salt Lake City, off Interstate 15 at exit 364.

———— MAJOR ATTRACTIONS ————

Golden Spike National Historic Site

HISTORY

Some say it was the most significant accomplishment of the 19th century: linking the Atlantic coast with the Pacific coast by rail. That event took place at Promontory Summit on May 10, 1869, as dignitaries and officials of the Central Pacific Railroad and the Union Pacific Railroad met to drive the last spike to join the two railroads. Four symbolic spikes—two gold, one silver and one a combination of iron, silver, and gold—and a laurel rail were used in the ceremony. Then, the actual last spike, an ordinary iron spike, was hammered home at 12:47 pm, and the Union Pacific's "Engine No. 119" and the Central Pacific's "Jupiter" pulled forward. Men on both locomotives shook hands marking the completion of the railroad.

It is fortunate that the driving of the last spike took place in an isolated part of Utah where the original site and much of the original grade has been preserved from the impacts of development. The transcontinental railroad was built by Chinese laborers, the main workforce for the Central Pacific; and Irish and German immigrants, many of them veterans of the Civil War, were employed by the Union Pacific in constructing the line west from Omaha, Nebraska. Once in Utah, Mormon workers augmented the efforts of both companies. Lucrative federal land grants and subsidies were awarded for each mile of track completed. Another incentive was the promise of Mormon trade to whichever company reached Ogden first. The competition saw miles of parallel grades constructed within Utah at a frenzied pace, until Congress acted to set the meeting point for the two railroads at Promontory. The Promontory route remained the primary transcontinental route until 1904, when the Lucin Cutoff, a trestle constructed across the Great Salt Lake west from Ogden, was completed. Finally, in 1942, the original 123-mile-long Promontory track was salvaged for the war effort.

After World War II, local people began commemorating the driving of the golden spike with a ceremony and a reenactment of the event. In 1957, Congress set aside 7 acres at Promontory as a National

Historic Site, which was enlarged to 2,176 acres in 1965. That year, a road was constructed to the site and plans developed for a huge centennial celebration. A visitor center and working replicas of the original steam engines were built in 1980.

GETTING THERE

Take exit 368 from Interstate 15 and drive west on Utah Hwy. 83, approximately 30 miles to the visitor center. The Golden Spike National Historic Site is administered by the National Park Service. For more information, write **Superintendent, Golden Spike National Historic Site, Box W, Brigham City, UT 84302; or call (801) 471-2209.**

DRIVING TOURS

At the visitor center pick up a booklet describing the driving route past the parallel grades built by the two companies, cuts and fills, rock culverts, and other remnants of the original construction work. Numbered signs along the route correspond to interpretive information in the booklet.

For a more extensive tour, requiring most of the day and a four-wheel-drive vehicle, see the Central Pacific Railroad Trail Backway in the Scenic Drives section.

EVENTS

Each year on the **anniversary of the driving of the last spike,** local actors dress up in period costumes and take the roles of the participants at the first driving of the last spike. Based on historical documentation, the event is reenacted as accurately as possible at 12:47 pm using the speeches of the day and two reconstructed steam engines. There is usually a large crowd for this event, so plan to come early. Be prepared for any kind of weather from warm summer days to a winter snowstorm.

Held the second Sat. in Aug., the annual **Railroaders Festival** draws more than 3,000 attendees. The festival features a reenactment of the driving of the last spike, demonstrations, music and a number of contests, including buffalo chip throwing, railwalking, boiler stoking, greased pole climb, hand car races, and amateur spike driving. A world champion spike driving contest, sanctioned by the *Guinness Book of World Records,* is also held. The world record of 16.4 seconds for driving six spikes was set in 1984 by Union Pacific employee Dale Jones, a regular annual participant in the contest. For baseball purists, the festival also includes a three-day baseball tournament played with rules, uniforms, and equipment from the 1880s.

Held the week between Christmas and New Year's at the visitor center, the **Golden Spike Annual Railroaders Film Festival and Winter Steam Engine Demonstration** is an excellent opportunity to watch the steam engines at work in the cold of winter and to rub shoulders with other railroad buffs.

HIKING

At the eastern end of the driving tour, you can take the **Big Fill Hike,** an easy .75-mile walk down the railroad grade to the Big Fill and Big Trestle sites. Here, the difficult terrain forced the Central Pacific Railroad to spend two months building a massive fill 170 feet deep and 500 feet long to get across the deep ravine. The effort required 500 men and 250 teams of animals. The Union Pacific did not have two months to make a fill, so its workers constructed an elaborate but temporary wooden trestle, parallel to the Central Pacific's Big Fill.

VISITOR CENTER

The center provides an excellent orientation, with a 20-minute introductory slide presentation, films, and talks given by National Park Service rangers. Books on railroading and Utah history books, maps, souvenirs, and film are available for purchase. Inquire about times for the steam engine demonstrations. The visitor center is open daily 8 am–6 pm in summer and 8 am–4:30 pm the rest of the year.

———— FESTIVALS AND EVENTS ————

Box Elder County Fair and Rodeo
late August

Held in Tremonton, the fair features a variety of exhibits, livestock judging, and other events, with the rodeo and parade the main attraction for many. **(801) 257-3874.**

Peach Days Festival
weekend after Labor Day

Brigham City peaches and its Peach Days Festival are known throughout Utah as one of the state's oldest community celebrations. Held the weekend after Labor Day, usually just at the conclusion of the peach harvest, the festival features a parade, a carnival, the Peach Queen pageant, an art show, and bicycle and foot races.

———— OUTDOOR ACTIVITIES ————

BIKING

Bear River Migratory Bird Refuge—
One of the most enjoyable ways to see the Bear River refuge is on a bicycle. If you ride from Pioneer Park in Brigham City, the round-trip loop is a total of 44 miles. For a shorter ride, you can begin at the refuge headquarters and ride the 12-mile gravel loop through the refuge.

Central Pacific Railroad Trail Backway—
See the Scenic Drives section.

East Box Elder County Loop—
This 50-mile loop is relatively flat and goes over paved roads. It begins in Pioneer Park in Brigham City and follows Hwy. 83 to Corinne then continues to the junction with Utah Hwy. 102. Turn north and ride through Penrose and Thatcher and follow the highway as it turns east to Tremonton. East of Tremonton, turn south on Utah Hwy. 84, which passes through Elwood and Bear River City, before rejoining Hwy. 83 at Corinne. Follow Hwy. 83 east back into Brigham City.

East Promontory—
A couple of miles after the turnoff from Hwy. 83 to the Golden Spike National Historic Site and before the road starts up the mountain to Promontory Sum-mit, a paved road heads south along the eastern side of the Promontory Mountains and the western side of the Bear River arm of the Great Salt Lake. You can follow the road to Promontory Point for a round-trip ride of 50 miles. As you ride, watch for pelicans and other birds.

BOATING

Willard Bay State Park—
From Interstate 15 it looks like it is part of the Great Salt Lake, but Willard Bay is a fresh-water, manmade reservoir constructed between 1958 and 1964. Fed by waters from the Ogden and Weber rivers, the 14-mile-long Arthur V. Watkins Dam separates the fresh water from the salt-laden waters of the Great Salt Lake. Because of its easy access from Interstate 15 and its close proximity to Brigham City and the Ogden metropolitan area, Willard Bay hosts more than a half million boaters, water-skiers and sailboaters a year. Willard Bay contains 16 different species of fish, including carp, and it is stocked with wall-eyes, catfish, and trout. There are two marinas with boat launching ramps. The North Marina has an excellent sandy beach, ideal for swimming. To reach it, head west on 300 North St. out of the town of Willard. (Take exit 360 off Interstate 15.) The South Marina is primarily a day-use area for boaters and is less crowded than the North Marina. Reach it by taking exit 354 off the

interstate at Pleasant View, then heading west 3 miles on 4000 North St.

FISHING

Mantua Reservoir—

Located on the east side of the town of Mantua, the 554-acre reservoir is just off US Hwy. 89, 4 miles north of Brigham City.

GOLF

Belmont Springs Park Golf Course—

Two partners purchased this land to grow tomatoes, but after they started to play golf they decided to build a golf course instead of a farm. They laid out the course themselves and opened it about 1975. You be the judge of how well they did, but if you like the challenge of hills and slopes that leave your ball a hundred yards from where you thought it should be, this is the course for you. There is a swimming pool adjacent to the clubhouse and RV camping nearby. Located 1 mile south of Plymouth, off Interstate 15; **(801) 458-3200.**

Brigham Willows Golf Course—

When Brigham City built the Eagle Mountain Course, it sold the original city course, still known locally as the Brigham City Golf Course, to private parties. While the course has not received the level of maintenance that it deserves, this is a delightful course to play. Located at the northern end of Brigham City, the half-century growth of a variety of trees—huge cottonwoods, weeping willows, majestic poplars, and pine trees—gives this course a parklike feeling. The course is flat, although the craggy mountains loom to the east. The rural location, the music of songbirds, and the lack of any crowds give you the feeling that you are playing on your own private course. This is only a 9-hole course, but if you are looking for a quiet, pleasant, shady course with the cheapest greens fees around, Brigham Willows is highly recommended. **900 North Main; (801) 723-5301.**

Eagle Mountain Golf Course—

This course was opened in 1989 and is located on land that was part of the Bushnell Military Hospital during World War II. Later, the hospital buildings were used for the Intermountain Indian School. Some of the structures are still standing, considered eyesores by some, but historic sites by others. The course runs along US Hwy. 89 from Brigham City to Logan. The course is not considered difficult. **780 East 700 South, Brigham City; (801) 723-3212.**

Skyway Golf Course—

You can usually get on this 9-hole course without much delay. The course is flat, with straight and narrow fairways and elevated greens. The course is located next to the Tremonton Municipal Airport. Drive west on Main St. and turn right on the first road immediately west of the Rodeo Grounds; **(801) 257-5706.**

HOT SPRINGS

Belmont Springs—

Located on a campground once used by Shoshone Indians, and astride the Salt Lake Cutoff, which pioneers used to travel northwest from Salt Lake City to join the California Trail near City of the Rocks, this historic site was first developed as a resort in the 1920s. After a couple of decades of nonuse, it was redeveloped in the 1970s. There are six main springs from which 4,000 gallons flow every minute into the adjacent Malad River. The water averages between 90 and 100 degrees Fahrenheit and has a slight salt content, which makes it possible to swim with your eyes open without the irritation of treated water. There is a swimming pool, three hot tubs, and a well-maintained dressing room. The 9-hole golf course is described above. Tropical fish and a species of Australian lobster are grown in ponds on the grounds and sold commercially. The swimming pool and hot tubs are open daily Apr.–mid-Oct. Admission fee charged. There is also a 4,000-foot-long **Scuba Diving Park,** where certified divers with their own equipment can dive into a 50-foot-wide channel that ranges from 10 to 35 feet in depth. The warm water and large sized tropical fish, which seem to flourish here, make this an ideal location for winter scuba diving. Located a mile south of Plymouth, off Interstate 15; **(801) 458-3200.**

Crystal Springs Resort—

There are hot mineral baths, a freshwater swimming pool, and water slides at this year-round water park. Located in Honeyville, 10 miles north of Brigham City on Utah Hwy. 69, you can also take exit 375 off Interstate 15 to get there. Summer hours are 10 am–10 pm, daily; winter, noon–9 pm, but 10 am–10 pm Fri. and Sat. and noon–7 pm Sun. Admission fee, with additional charges for the water slide.

———— SEEING AND DOING ————

HISTORIC SITES

Brigham City Tabernacle—

With its 16 brick buttresses and steeples, imposing front tower, and varying colors of field stone, the Brigham City Tabernacle is one of the most picturesque neo-Gothic church buildings constructed by 19th-century Mormons. Originally built between 1865 and 1890, it burned down in 1896 and was rebuilt within a year with the addition of the 16 buttresses and towers. **251 South Main St.** Open daily for tours May–Oct., 9 am–9 pm; **(801) 723-5376.**

Willard Houses—

Situated on a narrow neck of land between the mountains and the Great Salt Lake, Willard is one of the most beautiful communities in the entire state. Much of its beauty comes from the wonderful collection of 19th-century stone homes that have been preserved here. Willard was one of the first historic districts in Utah listed in the National Register of Historic Places. The houses were constructed during a 20-year period (1862–1883) by Shadrach Jones, a stonemason from Wales, who came to Utah in 1854 at the age of 17. Jones died of pneumonia in 1883, when he returned to Wales as a Mormon missionary, and, with one exception, no stone houses were built in Willard after that date. The houses—all located within a 12-block area—are said to reflect styles and construction methods of the stone houses in Wales. It is easy to shoot a whole roll of film either walking or driving around the town. None of the homes is open for tours, but the owners are proud of their houses and don't mind picture taking.

MUSEUMS AND GALLERIES

Brigham City Museum and Art Gallery—

This unique combination of community museum and art gallery features regional and national art exhibits, as well as Brigham City history. Under the able direction of curator Larry Douglass, it is well worth a visit. Admission is free. Open Tues.–Fri., 11 am–6 pm; Sat., 1 pm–5 pm. Closed Sun. Located on the lower floor of the building at **24 North 300 West; (801) 723-6769.**

SCENIC DRIVES

Central Pacific Railroad Trail Backway—

If, after your visit to the Golden Spike National Historic Site, you want to experience part of the distance covered by the transcontinental railroad through the vastness of the West, you can continue west to Promontory, where the road bends to the northwest to get around the north end of the Great Salt Lake. At the north end of the lake is Locomotive Springs National Waterfowl Management Area. (You can also reach it by driving southwest from Snowville; exit 7 off Interstate 84.) From Locomotive Springs, follow the old Central Pacific Railroad Grade along the northern extension of the Great Salt Lake Desert for 80 miles to Lucin near the Utah-Nevada border. About half of the road is maintained as a county road; the unmaintained portion requires a four-wheel-drive vehicle and is best traveled during dry

The transcontinental railroad was completed at Promontory, Utah on May 10, 1869, shown here in this modern day reenactment. Photo by Allan Kent Powell.

weather. Take plenty of time to stop and view the rockwork and trestles that remain. You can return to Snowville and Brigham City by driving 5 miles north from Lucin to Utah Hwy. 30. But if you have time, you can continue north 20 miles to Grouse Creek, an isolated ranching community that time seems to have forgotten. From the junction with Utah Hwy. 30, it is an 80-mile drive back to Snowville.

Willard Peak Road Backway—
High-clearance vehicles are required for this climb up Willard Peak. The road begins in Mantua off US Hwy. 89 and heads south to Willard Basin before it ascends to Inspiration Point near Willard Peak. During the 14-mile drive, the elevation gain is nearly a mile, from 4,200 feet in Mantua to 9,400 at Inspiration Point. The view of the Great Salt Lake and the valley below from Inspiration Point is worth the journey. The road winds through forests of aspen, spruce and fir, past Perry Reservoir and close to terracing done by Civilian Conservation Corp (CCC) crews during the 1930s. Plan at least three hours for the trip, with extra time for sightseeing, hiking, and picnicking.

THEATER

Stagestop Theatre—
Located in the small town of Collinston, popular plays and musicals are offered year-round on Mon., Thurs., Fri., and Sat. evenings. Reservations requested. **3585 West Bigler Road, Collinston, UT 84306; (801) 458-3967** or **1-800-248-2530.**

TOURS

A mile or so north of the turnoff from state Hwy. 93 to the Golden Spike National Historic Site is the main office for **Morton-Thiokol Corporation,** one of Utah's larg-

est employers. The company manufacturers solid propellant rockets, which are the rocket and booster shells for a number of the nation's spacecraft, including the space shuttle. An open-air (rocket garden) display of a dozen or so rockets stands in front of the building. Signs provide a brief explanation of the rockets and their use.

WILDLIFE

Bear River Bird Refuge—
The sign that spans Main St. in downtown Brigham City carries the name of the city and underneath, "home of the Bear River Bird Refuge." The dikes, dams, and roads that comprised the historic Bear River Refuge were largely destroyed by the rising waters of the Great Salt Lake in the early 1980s, but the 65,000-acre refuge located at the mouth of the Bear River is making a comeback. Located at the crossroads of two of North America's major migratory waterfowl flyways, the refuge provides an excellent opportunity to view more than 200 species of birds. The refuge is located 15 miles west of Brigham City.

Willard Bay Harold S. Crane Waterfowl Management Area—
Another excellent place to view the Great Salt Lake birds is at Willard Bay. During the high migratory periods in the spring and fall a great variety of birds can be seen. The area is part of the Willard Bay State Park and is best reached from Interstate 15 by taking exit 354, then turning west onto 4000 North and driving to the South Marina of Willard Bay to walk in, or continue west on 4000 North onto the gravel road for vehicle access into the area. Managed by the **Utah Division of Wildlife Resources; (801) 479-5143.** Bird lists, maps, and the free "Nature Guide to Willard Bay" brochure are available at the Willard Bay State Park.

——— WHERE TO STAY ———

ACCOMMODATIONS

HoJo Inn—$$
Year-round swimming pool and therapy pool; 44 units. Restaurant. **1167 South Main, Brigham City, UT 84302; (801) 723-8511.**

Sandman Motel—$$
Thirty-six units. **585 West Main, Tremonton; (801) 257-5675.**

Western Inn—$$
Forty-six units. Located just east of Interstate 84 exit 40 and Interstate 15 exit 382. **2301 West Main, Tremonton; (801) 257-3399.**

CAMPING
PRIVATE

Belmont Springs—
Seventy sites with full hookups. Open Apr.–Oct. Located 1 mile south of Plymouth on Hwy. 80; **(801) 458-3200.**

Brigham City KOA—
This is a smaller KOA campground, with 50 sites, 25 with full hookups. Open Mar–mid-Nov. The campground is located in Perry, south of Brigham City, on US Hwy. 89; **(801) 723-5503.**

Crystal Springs Campground—
Part of the Crystal Springs Resort in Honeyville; 124 RV trailer sites, half of which have full hookups. Open year-round. Toilets and showers; swimming at the resort. **8215 North Hwy. 69; (801) 279-8104.**

Golden Spike RV Park—
Equipped with 60 full hookups, tent spaces, Laundromat, restrooms, private showers, game room, playground, horseshoe and volleyball area, picnic area, and hot tub. **1025 West 975 South, Brigham City; (801) 723-8858.**

Mountain Haven Campground—
Fifty-four RV sites with complete hookups. Open mid-Apr.–mid-Oct. Located in **Mantua** at **130 North Main; (801) 723-7615.**

PUBLIC

Box Elder Campground—
There are 80 RV trailer sites and 49 tent sites. Open mid-May–Sept. Located off US Hwy. 89, 3 miles north of Brigham City and 2 miles south of Mantua, just west of Mantua Reservoir. Fee charged.

——— WHERE TO EAT ———

Idle Isle Restaurant—$ to $$
The Idle Isle is one of my favorite historical restaurants in Utah. During World War II, Bushnell Hospital was located just south of Brigham City. A large percentage of the 13,000 patients were amputees. The Idle Isle Restaurant announced that as soon as any patient who was being outfitted with artificial legs could walk through the door on their own, he would be given a free steak dinner. Needless to say, that kind of offer encouraged many men in their recovery and rehabilitation. As one of Utah's oldest continuously operating restaurants, the Idle Isle was established in 1921 by PC and Verabel Knudson, as an ice cream and candy store. It evolved into a full-service restaurant and survived the Great Depression, sometimes staying open as long as necessary to take in enough money to pay the daily bills. Although a modern sign graces the exterior, the interior is little changed from the 1920s. A marble-and-onyx fountain, handcrafted wooden booths, old-fashioned candy cases, and coffee urns all give the feeling of stepping back a half century or more in time. Dinners include a three-course meal, including homemade rolls with apricot preserves and pie for dessert. For lunch you

might want to try a bowl of their home-made soup along with rolls and preserves. You will also want to try the chocolates made in the basement of the restaurant. **24 South Main, Brigham City; (801) 734-9062.**

Maddox—$ to $$

This steak house on old Hwy. 89, just south of Brigham City, is a northern Utah institution. Since 1949, several generations have made Maddox a destination for burgers and steaks. Founded by Irvin Maddox, who developed a legendary ability to judge cattle, the restaurant has a reputation for serving the very best beef at very reasonable prices. Irvin has passed that tradition on to his son Steve, and Maddox remains one of Utah's most popular restaurants. It used to be that you could see the feedlot right from the restaurant so that, according to more than one observer, "you could watch the cattle and eat one at the same time." If you don't want to go inside to the restaurant, an old-fashioned drive-up area is located on the northern end. Open Tues.–Sat., 11:00 am–9:30 pm; closed Sun. and Mon. **1900 South Hwy. 89; (801) 723-8845** or **1-800-544-5474.**

SERVICES

Brigham City Area Chamber of Commerce Visitor Center—

6 North Main St., Brigham City, UT 84302; (801) 723-3937.

Golden Spike Empire Travel Region—

2501 Wall Ave., Ogden, UT 84401; (801) 627-8291 or 1-800-ALL-UTAH.

Tremonton Visitor Center—

Located in the old McKinley School, which now serves as the Tremonton Community Center. **130 South Tremont St.; Tremonton, UT 84337; (801) 257-3371.**

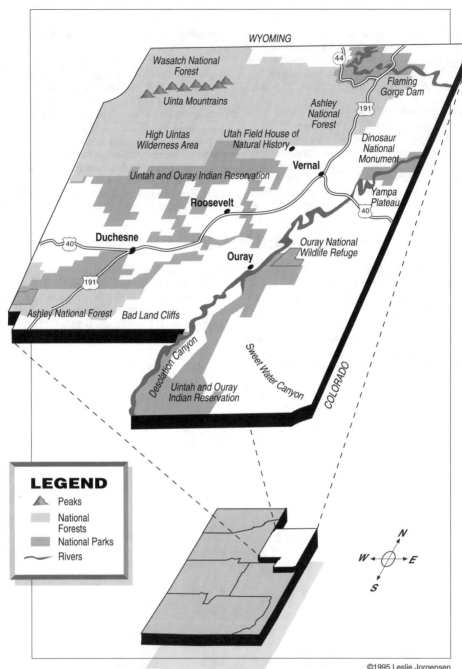

Northeast Region

NORTHEASTERN REGION

Roosevelt and Vernal

Utahns call it the Uinta Basin, or simply the Basin. While it is not a basin in the strictest sense because the Green River cuts its course southward through the badland cliffs out of the basin into Desolation Canyon, it does look like a gigantic, elongated dish running west to east. The most dominant feature is the Uinta Mountains, which form the northern rim of the basin. The rounded summit of Kings Peak at 13,528 feet is the highest point in the state. The towns of Roosevelt and Vernal are at 5,280 feet, making for pleasant summers in the basin and cooler temperatures in the mountains. In winter an inversion layer often sits over the basin, keeping temperatures at or below 0 degrees Fahrenheit for days. Early spring, summer, and early fall are the best times to visit the area. Vernal is the county seat for Uintah County. Roosevelt is located in Duchesne County whose county seat is at Duchesne 28 miles to the west. Roosevelt's high school is named Union High School because it was built exactly on the county line to allow students from both counties to attend the school without any complications. Roosevelt, named for Theodore Roosevelt, who was president of the US when the community was established in 1905 to 1906, is surrounded by the Ute Indians' Uintah and Ouray Reservation. Contention, primarily over water rights and legal jurisdiction, continues to characterize relations between the Utes and the descendants of the Anglo settlers who arrived in the Uinta Basin after portions of the reservation were opened to settlement in 1905. Ute Tribal Headquarters is located at Fort Duchesne, about 8 miles east of Roosevelt.

HISTORY

Millions of years before human arrival in the Uinta Basin, dinosaurs lived in a completely different environment than that of today. The discovery of a rich deposit of dinosaur fossils by Earl Douglass in 1909 led to the establishment of Dinosaur National Monument in 1915. The

55

Fremont people lived in the Uinta Basin from about AD 200 to 1300 and have left rock art and other remains that have attracted the interest of archaeologists. The Fremont culture seems to have died out around AD 1300 just as Ute Indians arrived in the area. The Utes were here when the first Euro-Americans arrived in 1776. The Dominguez-Escalante Expedition crossed the Green River near the southern boundary of present-day Dinosaur National Monument, just north of the town of Jensen on September 16, 1776. They followed a Ute Indian trail westward through the basin to the Uinta and Duchesne rivers. Fur trapper William Ashley and company floated down the Green River in 1825 and were glad to escape the adventure with their lives. French-Canadian trapper Etienne Provost, working out of New Mexico, also reached the basin in the mid-1820s, followed by Antoine Robidioux who established a trading post in the area by 1832.

Perhaps the most important event in the history of the Uinta Basin was the establishment of the Uinta Indian Reservation by President Abraham Lincoln in 1861. The original reservation included more than 2 million acres of land and was to be the home of the Uintah Utes, who already occupied the basin, as well as other Ute tribes throughout the territory of Utah. In 1881, the White River Utes were forced to move from Colorado to the Uintah Reservation. A second reservation of nearly 2 million acres was established in 1882, immediately south of the Uintah Reservation. The Ouray Reservation was to be home to the Uncomphagre Utes who, under their Chief Ouray, were pressured to leave their homeland in Colorado. In time, the two reservations merged, to become known as the Uintah and Ouray Indian Reservation. It is now the largest Indian reservation within the state. The population is approximately 3,000.

Anglos began to arrive in Ashley Valley in the early 1870s. By 1880, the settlement of Vernal had been established and Uintah County was formed. During the 1880s and 1890s, and even into the 20th century, the Uinta Basin developed a rough-and-tumble tradition. Vernal lay astride the "Outlaw Trail," which connected the Brown's Park area north of the basin and the Robbers Roost region to the south—two isolated places of refuge from the long arm of the law. Matt Warner, Elza Lay, Butch Cassidy, Harry Longabaugh (alias the Sundance Kid), Harvey Logan (alias Kid Curry), and other members of the Wild Bunch were no strangers to Vernal. The town's Outlaw Trail Festival, held during the summer, commemorates the region's outlaw legacy.

Roosevelt and other communities were established after the Uintah Reservation was opened for settlement in 1905. The Dawes Act of 1887 allowed for each adult Indian married male to be granted homesteads of 160 acres (lesser amounts of land were granted to women, single males, and orphaned children) and for the remaining land to be opened for settlement by non-Indians. The opening of the Reservation created a "land rush" in the area, as Anglo settlers poured in from Utah and Colorado to take advantage of the new lands.

The agricultural development of the area coincided with the discovery of gilsonite and other asphaltums. Later, oil was discovered, with commercial production beginning in 1948. The region boomed during the energy crisis of the 1970s, then became depressed during most of the 1980s. Crucial to the present economy and future of the Uinta Basin is the Central Utah Project, which was started in 1959 with the construction of the Steinaker Reservoir, part of the Vernal unit, and followed by Red Fleet Reservoir, part of the Jensen unit of the project. The Central Utah Water Project, a multimillion dollar Bureau of Reclamation project that impacts much of the state, including the urbanized Wasatch Front, is still under construction, and the completion of the early projects at Steinaker and Red Fleet have helped sustain the long-term project.

GETTING THERE

Roosevelt is 145 miles east of Salt Lake City; Vernal is another 30 miles east of Roosevelt on US Hwy. 40. Driving from Salt Lake, take Interstate 80 east to its junction with US Hwy. 40, as it heads south to Heber City. From Heber City, US 40 heads southeast up Daniels Canyon, past Strawberry Reservoir, where it turns back to the east and enters the Uinta Basin at Duchesne. Travelers coming west through Wyoming can exit Interstate 80 just west of Rock Springs onto US Hwy. 191, which heads south, crossing into Utah near Flaming Gorge Reservoir, across the dam, and continuing south to Vernal. From Colorado, most travelers enter Utah on US Hwy. 40 heading west. A road has been proposed connecting Vernal and Interstate 70 through the scenic Book Cliffs, but it will be many years before the road is built—if at all.

———— FESTIVALS AND EVENTS ————

Outlaw Trail Festival
mid-June through mid-July

Famous outlaws from the past have been named honorary citizens in the Uinta Basin, where a host of summer activities are sponsored as part of the Outlaw Trail Festival. The festival dates from 1985 and has grown steadily from a weekend activity to a festival that runs from mid-June–mid-July. The festival has something for just about everyone: art exhibits and competitions, a multiday trail ride, a women's .22 shooting competition, a folk arts festival, a rodeo, and a musical production based on the legends of Butch Cassidy and the Wild Bunch; **(801) 789-6932 or 1-800-477-5558.**

Northern Ute Pow Wow
early July

This event includes a rodeo, dancing, singing and drumming competitions, arts and crafts. Held at **Fort Duchesne** the weekend closest to the 4th of July, this is an excellent chance to learn more about contemporary and traditional Ute culture; **(801) 722-5141.**

Dinosaur Roundup Rodeo
mid-July
Held in mid-July at the **Western Park, 300 East 200 North,** this rodeo ranks among the top 50 rodeos nationally; **(801) 789-1352.**

Dina-soar
Hot Air Balloon Festival
late September
Held the third weekend in Sept. This hot air balloon festival attracts participants from all over the West; **(801) 789-5816.**

——— OUTDOOR ACTIVITIES ———

BIKING

The **Dinosaurland Travel Office** has published a pamphlet, "Dinosaurland Area Bike Routes," which describes eight different routes in the area, ranging from the 4-mile **Bassett Springs Loop** to the 50-mile **Vernal/Lapoint Loop.** Both of these routes are rated for advanced riders. The former because of its length and the moderate-to-steep grades and the latter because steep ascents and descents through rough and sharp rocks require great skill in handling the bike.

Less-than-advanced riders will find two routes, the **Asphalt Ridge Loop** and the **Range Study Loop,** more to their liking. The Asphalt Ridge Loop begins at the scenic viewpoint on US Hwy. 40, 5 miles southwest of Vernal. The 7-mile loop is along graded and paved roads with no major grades and is considered an easy ride. From the scenic viewpoint, the route follows Hwy. 40 for 2 miles to where the powerlines cross the highway. Here you turn left onto a dirt road that follows the power lines for 1.7 miles. After you cross a low pass, you stay on the dirt road as it turns to the left and heads in a northwesterly direction along the base of Asphalt Ridge for 2.5 miles back to the beginning point. As you ride along Asphalt Ridge, look for outcroppings of natural black asphalt. Vernal residents took advantage of this resource to become one of the first Utah towns to have paved streets.

The **Range Study Loop** is located in Ashley National Forest, 24 miles north of Vernal on Hwy. 191. The 10-mile loop is suitable for intermediate riders. While it offers an excellent view of Diamond Mountain to the east, the route does violate the natural law of biking: it goes downhill first. The loop makes a gradual descent to the bottom of the draw for the first 4 miles, then the route turns sharply to the right and begins a steep, but short (a third of a mile), climb, followed by 5 miles of a steady but gradual ascent.

For a copy of "Dinosaurland Area Bike Routes," write or call **Dinosaurland Travel Board, 25 East Main, Vernal, UT 84078; (801) 789-6932** or **1-800-477-5558.** The guide can also be obtained at the **Vernal Welcome Center, 235 East Main, Vernal.**

FISHING
Big Sand Wash Reservoir State Park—

One of Utah's undeveloped state parks, the 400-acre Big Sand Wash offers fishing (rainbow trout), **sailing,** and **water-skiing.** The lake was created in 1967 and is located 14 miles west of Roosevelt, between Blue Bell and Upalco.

Hill Creek—

This stream is quite isolated and is located on the Hill Creek extension of the Uintah and Ouray Reservation, which means you need a tribal fishing permit. To reach Hill Creek, take state Hwy. 88 south from US Hwy. 40, about 14 miles northeast of Vernal. Follow Hwy. 88 south to Ouray, then continue south on the dirt and gravel roads that follow Hill Creek to the top of the **Tavaputs Plateau.** The **Towave and Weaver reservoirs,** located along Hill Creek, are 35 miles up Hill Creek. Before going into these areas, however, check with the **Ute Tribe Fish and Game Department** at Fort Duchesne for permits, maps, and road conditions. Roads in the Hill Creek area usually require a four-wheel-drive vehicle and can be very treacherous when wet. Both reservoirs are stocked with fish; Towave is especially good for brown, where they may weigh up to two or three pounds. Due to a recent US Supreme Court decision concerning tribal boundaries and jurisdiction, persons traveling to Hill Creek may be denied access or charged a fee to cross Indian lands.

Jones Hole Creek—

The 4-mile stretch of Jones Hole Creek from the fish hatchery to the Green River is considered one of the most productive sections of trout stream in the state. It is also one of the most popular, and wildlife managers are concerned about its ability to handle more pressure. For directions see the **Jones Hole Backway** in the Scenic Drives section.

Moon Lake—

There are a thousand or so natural lakes in the High Uinta Mountains and, of those lakes, Moon Lake is the largest. The lake was enlarged by the construction of a dam by homesteaders in the Uinta Basin (my grandfather was one of the leaders in the undertaking and, as a young man, my father hauled supplies by pack train from their home in Altonah). Today, the lake is 32 miles in length and is located 32 miles north of Duchesne, at the southern edge of the High Uintas Wilderness Area. The road to Moon Lake is paved, except for 8 miles of road across the **Uintah and Ouray Indian Reservation.** Moon Lake is home to eastern brook trout, cutthroat, rainbow trout, splake, and Kokanee salmon. The edge of the lake also serves as the main trailhead to lakes and streams located

within the adjacent wilderness area. **Moon Lake Resort** provides basic accommodations; **(801) 454-3142.**

South Slope Streams—

The streams coming down the slope of the Uinta Mountains offer some of the best trout fishing in the state. Beginning on the west and moving eastward are the **Duchesne River, Rock Creek, Lake Fork, Uinta River,** and **Whiterocks River.** They all yield a good number of stocked rainbow and small cutthroat and brook trout. All the streams flow through the **Uintah and Ouray Indian Reservation,** where fees are charged for fishing; the fewer number of fishermen you encounter might make it worth purchasing a day or seasonal permit, available in **Mountain Home,** at the **Bottle Hollow Resort,** and other **sporting good stores in the Uinta Basin.** North of the reservation boundary there is also plenty of good fishing. The streams are reached by a network of roads north of US Hwy. 40. State Hwy. 35, which begins 6 miles north of Duchesne off state Hwy. 87, follows the Duchesne River for much of its course. Rock Creek and Lake Fork are best reached by taking state Hwy. 87 north from Duchesne, then following the road north to Mountain Home. The Uinta and Whiterocks rivers are located north of Roosevelt. The county road to Whiterocks is located east of Roosevelt, off Hwy. 40.

Starvation Reservoir State Park—

Located off US Hwy. 40, 4 miles west of Duchesne, 3,310-acre **Starvation Reservoir,** completed in 1972, is one of the major components of the Central Utah Project. The origins of the name "Starvation" are difficult to trace. One version holds that fur trappers caught in the winter snows robbed an Indian food cache and survived while their victims starved. A counter version reports that the fur trappers were victims of Indians who stole food from a cache of food hidden in a group of caves along the southwestern shore of the reservoir. Despite its name, the reservoir offers excellent walleye, smallmouth bass, and a few browns. Administered as a state park, there are fish-cleaning facilities and 31 camp sites, open year-round, with showers, modern restrooms that are wheelchair accessible, drinking water, and picnic tables are available during the summer.

Steinaker State Park—

Named for a pioneer ranching family in the Vernal area, Steinaker Reservoir was begun in 1961 as one of the first units of the Central Utah Project. The reservoir is filled by waters diverted from Ashley Creek several miles to the west. The reservoir, also a state park, is popular with boaters and fishermen, and, during the cold Uinta Basin winters, offers excellent ice fishing. Rainbow trout and largemouth bass have been successfully planted in the reservoir. There are 31 camp sites equipped with drinking water, sewage disposal, and restrooms.

Red Fleet State Park—

As the fourth, and newest, state park in the Uinta Basin, the 650-acre **Red Fleet Reservoir** was completed in 1980 and is named for the red sandstone formations, which resemble a fleet of ships, that rise above the western shore of the lake. Rainbow trout, bluegill, and largemouth bass are sought year-round by fishermen. Twenty-nine campsites with drinking water and modern restrooms are located within the park.

GOLF

Dinaland Golf Course—

Constructed in the early 1950s, Dinaland Golf Course, with smiling little dinosaurs for its tee markers and 150-yard markers, expanded to 9 holes in 1994. The expansion included new greens for all the holes, new directions for some of the old fairways, new ponds and marshlands, and more effective use of a tributary of Ashley Creek that meanders through the course. Before its expansion, the course was often crowded, but the expansion to 9 holes makes it possible to get on just about any time. Usually open mid-Mar.–mid-Nov.

Located east of town at **675 South 2000 East** in **Vernal; (801) 781-1428.**

Roosevelt Golf Course—

Unless you happen to land at the Roosevelt Golf Course on a Wed., when the women's league plays, or during one of the infrequent tournaments, there is usually no waiting to get on the course, and reservations are not necessary. A 9-hole course that was first opened in 1973, the course has been expanded to 18 holes. The fairways are lined with large poplar and cottonwood trees, giving a parklike feeling to the course. One of the most memorable holes is the 16th, with the green located in a box canyon with a manmade waterfall that drops over the wall into four ponds that cut across the front of the green. The course is located just north of Roosevelt. **1155 Clubhouse Dr.; (801) 722-9644.**

HIKING

Outside the Wasatch Front, the Uintas make up Utah's most popular mountain hiking region. The mountains are especially noted for the wilderness hiking opportunities, and most native Utahns have made at least one multiday backpacking trek into the mountains with scout groups, church groups, families, or friends. If you want the most comprehensive guide to Hiking the Uintas, pick up a copy of Mel Davis and John Veranth's *High Uinta Trails* (Wasatch, 1993). One trail of special note is the .25-mile-long **Yellow Pine Trail,** a self-guided trail that has been constructed to provide the physically challenged an opportunity to enjoy the outdoors. Cassette tape tours are available from the campground host during the season. **Guided tours for the physically challenged** can be arranged by calling the **Duchesne District Office; (801) 738-2482.** There is also a **5-mile-long trail** that follows Rock Creek from Upper Stillwater Reservoir down to the Yellowpine Campground. Most hikers will catch a ride to the reservoir, then walk back along the trail, hoping to see forest birds, mule deer, elk, moose, marmots, and other small animals. To reach the **Rock**

Creek Trail, drive from Roosevelt or Duchesne to Mountain Home, then turn west onto Forest Rd. 134, the Rock Creek Rd., and follow it for 21 miles to the Yellow Pine Campground.

HORSEBACK RIDING

All 'Round Ranch—
Not far from Dinosaur National Monument, All 'Round Ranch offers half-day scenic rides and four- to six-day range riding. **PO Box 153, Jensen, UT 84035; (801) 789-8972 or 1-800-603-8069.**

Flying J Outfitters—
This is a working cattle ranch that offers guided day rides. **PO Box 284, Myton, UT 84052; (801) 646-3208.**

J/L Ranch Horseback Rides—
Located near Whiterocks Canyon, the J/L Ranch offers horseback rides of two or three hours, half-day and full-day trips, or week-long trips into Ashley National Forest. The J/L Ranch is located 23 miles northwest of Vernal, but you will need precise directions if you are not a native of the area. Call **(801) 353-4049** for information and directions.

Western Livery, Inc.—
Provides horse-drawn carriage rides and a narrative historical tour of Vernal. **1934 North 500 East, Vernal, UT 84078; (801) 789-0971.**

RIVER RUNNING

Within the region, rafting is also done in Desolation Canyon on the Green River by Chapoose River and Trails, PO Box 141, Ft. Duchesne, UT 84023; 1-800-854-4364.

See also the **Dinosaur National Monument** chapter.

SKIING
CROSS-COUNTRY SKIING
The **Dinosaurland Travel Region** publishes a brochure "Dinosaurland Eastern Uintas Cross-Country Ski Trails," which describes eight different trails and loops off US Hwy. 191, beginning with the 2.5-mile-long Little Brush Creek Loop Trail, 22 miles north of Vernal. For copies of the brochure write or call, **Dinosaurland Travel Board, 25 East Main, Vernal, UT 84078; (801) 789-6932 or 1-800-477-5558.** The brochure can also be obtained at the **Vernal Welcome Center, 235 East Main, Vernal.**

SNOWMOBILING

There are more than 75 miles of groomed trails in the **Uinta Basin Snowmobile Complex.** The main trailhead is at the turnoff to the Red Cloud Loop, off Hwy. 191, 14 miles north of Vernal. A snowmobile corridor has been developed to connect Flaming Gorge Lodge and Red Canyon Lodge on the north side of the Uinta Mountains with the Red Cloud Loop, providing access from the trailhead to the Flaming Gorge area. Other trailheads are at **Taylor Mountain Rd.** and **Brownie Canyon Rd.** A map for the Uinta Basin Snowmobile Complex can be obtained for a modest charge from the **Dinosaurland Travel Board, 25 East Main, Vernal, UT 84078; 1-800-477-5558.**

SEEING AND DOING

HISTORIC SITES

Parcel Post Bank—

Architecturally, it's not exactly a masterpiece: a two-story brick building built in 1916 on the corner of Vernal Ave. and Main St.; but its method of construction shows the kind of ingenuity that was necessary for survival in the isolated Uinta Basin of premotorized vehicle days. Bank President William H. Coltharp wanted to build an impressive building that would reflect the prosperity of the first decade of the 20th century. While "ordinary" red bricks were available from a local brickmaker, Coltharp opted for fancy textured bricks that were available only in Salt Lake City, 175 miles away. But the freight cost from Salt Lake City was four times the price of the bricks, so Coltharp hit on the idea of mailing the 80,000 bricks—individually wrapped, from Salt Lake City to Vernal. At 7 cents a brick, the total cost was approximately $5,600 and, since postal regulations prohibited one person from receiving more than 5,000 pounds of parcel, the bricks were sent to several addresses in Vernal. The bricks were sent by the Denver and Rio Grande Railroad to Mack, Colorado, where they were loaded on a narrow gauge railroad and sent to Watson, Utah, and then hauled by wagon to Vernal, a total distance of 407 miles including the last 65 miles by wagon. Shortly after Vernal got its "mail-order" building, postal regulations were changed. The building, constructed in 1916, is still used as a bank.

Uinta Stake Tabernacle—

Constructed from 1900 to 1907, the Vernal Tabernacle is one of only a few Mormon tabernacles constructed in Utah to serve as the religious centers for cities and outlying areas. The Uinta Stake Tabernacle was used for a number of years as a local arts and culture center; then, in 1994 Mormon church officials announced that the historic building would be renovated for use as a temple. This marks the first time in the history of the Mormon Church that a building has been renovated to serve as a temple. All others have been originally constructed for that purpose. **500 West and 200 South.**

MUSEUMS

Daughters of Utah Pioneer Museum—

Just across the street from the historic Uintah Stake Tabernacle, the DUP Museum is housed in an 1887 stone tithing office. The building once served as a collection and distribution center for the produce and livestock that made up the 10 percent of income tithe that members of the Mormon Church are required to donate to the church. Built during the first decade of Mormon settlement in this area, it is one of the oldest surviving structures in eastern Utah. The original tithing office was expanded and the complex now houses an impressive collection of artifacts. Open daily 1 pm–7 pm from Memorial Day–Labor Day, or at other times by special request. Corner of **200 South and 500 West.**

Utah Field House of Natural History—

If you come to Dinosaurland, the name for this travel region, it is almost impossible to escape dinosaurs—whether you find them as tee box markers on the local golf course, on billboards, or as life-size replicas at the Utah Field House of Natural History, a state park. Fifteen dinosaurs including the 8-ton horned triceratops, the 6-ton stegosaurus, the 12-ton, 80 foot-long diplodocus, and the ferocious tyrannosaurus rex, along with other prehistoric animals, inhabit a garden just west of the Field House and are an irresistible attraction for young and old alike. Inside the Field House, exhibits and paintings introduce the area's geology, natural history, paleontology, and anthropology. Open summers, 8 am–9 pm; after Labor Day, 9 am–5 pm. Also located within the

Field House is the **Vernal Welcome Center,** making this an ideal "first stop" for visitors to the area. The Field House is located at **235 East Main St.; (801) 789-3799.**

Western Heritage Museum—

This private museum features the Leo C. Thorne Fremont and Ute Indian Collections, plus western carriages, saddles, and rifles. There is also a **western art gallery** that features a variety of western artists. Open Mon.–Sat. 10 am–6 pm Memorial Day–Labor Day; open Mon.–Fri. 10 am–5 pm the rest of the year. The museum is located near the rodeo and fairgrounds at **300 East 200 South; (801) 789-7399.**

SCENIC DRIVES

Flaming Gorge/Uintas Scenic Byway—

This section of Hwy 191 north of Vernal is also known as the "Drive Through the Ages" a road that climbs through 19 geologic formations during the 30-mile ascent of the Uinta Mountains toward Flaming Gorge Reservoir. Signs indicate the geologic formations for both directions of travel. The Uinta Mountains are a huge anticline, which runs east and west. As you drive out of Vernal, the layers read from youngest to oldest, with the gray Mancos shale being the youngest. The oldest rocks, nearly a billion years old, are Precambrian sedimentary rocks of sandstone and siltstone which make up the core of the Uinta Mountains. A brochure with additional information is available at the Vernal Visitor Center. In the next few years, this road will be reinterpreted under a new theme: "Wildlife Through the Ages."

Jones Hole Road Scenic Backway—

This 80-mile-long out-and-back road is paved for its entire length. It begins 4 miles east of Vernal, where it leaves 500 North and heads in a northeasterly direction to climb out of Ashley Valley, 2,600 feet up Diamond Mountain, before it turns east, terminating at **Jones Hole National**

Fish Hatchery. Travelers can visit the hatchery, which produces trout for streams, lakes, and reservoirs in Utah, Colorado, and Wyoming. The hatchery is open daily 7 am–4 pm. From the hatchery, visitors can take a 4-mile hike down to the Green River in **Dinosaur National Monument.** The paved road is quite narrow, especially as it follows the narrow and rugged canyon into Jones Hole. Diamond Mountain, over which the road passes, was the site of a scandalous swindle in the 1870s, when Phillip Arnold and John Slack salted the area with industrial diamonds, and then sold their claim for a fortune. The well-known geologist Clarence King uncovered the fraud, when he found partially cut and polished diamonds on the mountain which, it was learned, were smuggled into the US from South Africa. Arnold and Slack had deceived a group of San Francisco investors that the discovery was genuine by allowing two men to examine the discovery with the condition that they be blindfolded as they entered and left the area. The two swindlers netted $150,000 each; but Phil Arnold was caught while John Slack escaped with his share.

Nine Mile Canyon Drive—

See the **Price** chapter.

Red Cloud/Dry Fork Loop Backway—

Designated as an official Utah Scenic Backway, this 45-mile-long drive begins 14 miles north of Vernal off US Hwy. 191. The drive consists of paved, gravel, and dirt sections. The road is closed by snow in winter. During late spring, summer, and early fall, though, it makes a beautiful drive, as it winds past fishing streams and through the aspen groves, open meadows, and lodgepole pine forests of the Uinta Mountains. The latter are rough and sometimes impassable when wet. The road heads west off Hwy. 191 until it reaches the North Folk of Ashley Creek, where it swings south toward Dry Fork Canyon then southeastward back toward Vernal.

WILDLIFE

Ouray National Wildlife Refuge—

The refuge extends along 12 miles of the Green River and provides excellent habitat for some 209 different species of migratory birds in the spring and fall. Golden eagles are found year-round, and bald eagles will gather in the refuge during early winter. Mule deer are visible year-round. The refuge is owned by the US Fish and Wildlife Service and has an information kiosk and an observation tower. Interpretive brochures are available, including a 10-mile automobile tour. Open sunrise to sunset year-round. To reach the refuge, take US 40 west from Vernal for 14 miles, then turn south onto Utah 88. The refuge is located 16 miles to the south. For information write or call **Ouray National Wildlife Refuge, 266 West 100 North, Vernal, UT 84078; (801) 789-0351.**

Pariette Wetlands—

Another good location for observing migrating birds is the Pariette Wetlands. Surrounded by miles of desert, the wetlands provide freshwater feeding grounds for a variety of birds, including mallards, pintail, Canadian geese, herons, egrets, white-faced ibises, and American bitterns. To reach the wetlands, drive to Fort Duchesne and head south for 5 miles, crossing the Duchesne River. At the intersection, turn west and drive 16 miles across Leland Bench to Pariette Wash, where you follow the signs to the overlook. These roads are all gravel and difficult to travel when wet. The wetlands are on BLM land. For information, contact the **Vernal District Bureau of Land Management, 170 South 500 East, Vernal, UT 84078; (801) 789-1362.**

WHERE TO STAY

ACCOMMODATIONS

Hillhouse Bed and Breakfast—$$

Operated by Linda Young, this is the only bed and breakfast in the Uinta Basin. Now that Linda's children are grown and have left home, she has turned the family house into a five-room bed and breakfast. Two of the rooms have private baths and TV; one has a private patio and entrance. Three of the rooms are equipped with two beds and children are welcome. There is even a playroom just off the dining area with plenty of toys for children. Parents can sit at the table to eat and visit while the children play close by. The family room has a good supply of videos and Linda, a lifelong resident of the Vernal area, can provide plenty of information and recreational tips. There is a hiking and biking trail across the street which leads to a spectacular overlook of Steinacker Reservoir. Linda's breakfasts include fresh fruit and juices, pancakes, and rolls. **75 West 3300 North, Vernal, UT 84078; (801) 789-0700.**

Stillwater Canyon-Falcon's Ledge—$$$$

Jim Bills, co-owner of the Falcon's Ledge, describes it as "a world class lodge, designed to provide a quality refuge for those seeking personal and private outdoor experiences." Bills, a successful financier, combined his money and dream of an outdoors retreat with the fishing and guide skills of partner Howard Brinkerhoff to undertake a unique enterprise for the Uinta Basin. With only eight units, the personal touch is emphasized at Falcon's Ledge. Even if you don't stay there, you can arrange guided fishing and wilderness trips through the lodge, as well as courses in backpacking, mountain biking, and falconry. Falcon's Ledge is located 17 miles north of Duchesne, off state Hwy. 87, on the southern slope of the Uinta Mountains. For information, write or call **Stillwater Canyon-Falcon's Ledge, Box 67, Altamont, UT 84001; (801) 454-3737.**

ROOSEVELT

Best Western Inn—$$
Heated pool and adjacent coffee shop; 40 units. Three miles east of Roosevelt, on **US Hwy. 40; (801) 722-4644** or **1-800-354-7803.**

Frontier Motel—$$
Fifty-four rooms. **75 South 200 East; (801) 722-2201** or **1-800-248-1014.** The **Frontier Grill** is located adjacent to the motel and is open from 6 am–9 pm.

VERNAL

Best Western Antlers Motel—$$
Fifty-three rooms. Heated pool, wading pool, and playground. **423 West Main; (801) 789-1202** or **1-800-528-1234.**

Best Western Dinosaur Inn—$$
Fifty-nine rooms. Heated pool, whirlpool, playground, and adjacent coffeeshop open 6 am–10 pm. Located adjacent to the Vernal Welcome Center and Utah Field House of Natural History. **251 East Main; (801) 789-2660** or **1-800-528-1234.**

Days Inn—$$
Forty rooms. **260 West Main; (801) 789-1011** or **1-800-382-1011.**

Econo Lodge—$$
Fifty-one rooms. **311 East Main; (801) 789-2000** or **1-800-424-4777.**

Split Mountain Motel—$$
Forty rooms. **1015 East Hwy. 40; (801) 789-9020.**

Weston Lamplighter Inn—$$
One hundred sixty-five rooms. **120 East Main; (801) 789-0312** .

Weston Plaza Hotel—$$ to $$$
This is one of Vernal's newest hotels with 102 rooms. Indoor heated pool, whirlpool, and restaurant. **1684 West Hwy. 40; (801) 789-9550.**

GUEST AND DUDE RANCHES

Defa's Dude Ranch—$$$
Located on the north fork of the Duchesne River, with good access into the Uinta Mountain Wilderness area, the ranch has 17 rustic cabins, public showers, RV hookups, and a cafe. **5491 South State St., #20, Salt Lake City, UT 84107; (801) 848-5590.**

Flying J Outfitters—$$$
This working cattle ranch has three cabins and offers fishing and horseback trips. **Box 284, Myton, UT 84052; (801) 646-3208.**

J/L Ranch—$$$
Two nonsmoking cabins are available at the J/L Ranch near Whiterocks. Guided fishing trips and trail raids can be arranged. **PO Box 129, Whiterocks, UT 84085; (801) 353-4049.**

Quarter Circle E Guest Ranch—$$$
Located near Vernal, with cabins, a cafe, a bar, horseback riding, guided trips. **PO Box 318, Lapoint, UT 84039; (801) 247-2749.**

CAMPING
PRIVATE

Campground Dina—
Dina has 115 trailer sites, 82 of which have full hookups, and 300 tent sites. Toilets, showers, laundry, and a dump site are available. Open year-round (winter fees are paid on the honor system). **930 North Vernal Ave.; (801) 789-2148.**

Country Village Trailer Park—
Twenty trailer sites, half of which have full hookups. It does not have toilet or shower facilities. Located 8 miles east of Roosevelt, on Hwy. 40; **(801) 722-2890.**

Fossil Valley RV Park—
All 45 trailer sites have complete hookups, 10 tent sites, and the park is equipped with toilets, showers, a laundry, and a dump site. Open Apr.–Oct. **999 West Hwy. 40; (801) 789-6450.**

Vernal KOA—
All 55 trailer sites have complete hook-ups, and the campground is equipped to KOA standards. There are also 4 camping cabins. Open May–Sept., **1800 West Sheraton Ave.; (801) 789-8935.**

PUBLIC

The Uinta Mountains offer many camping opportunities in the Ashley National Forest. Most campgrounds are open from mid- and late May–mid-Sept., and fees are charged at most campgrounds. The following are grouped according to the closest community, starting with Hanna on the west and concluding with Vernal on the east.

Altamont—North of Altamont, there are five campgrounds within a 5-mile radius, located along the Yellowstone River and Swift Creek: **Yellowstone, Bridge, Reservoir, Riverview,** and **Swift Creek.** Riverview is the largest with 19 tent sites. There are no showers or toilets. Yellowstone is located 17.5 miles, and Swift Creek (the farthest north) 22 miles north of Altamont.

Duchesne—Yellow Pine Campground, located 29 miles north of Duchesne, has 29 tent sites, drinking water, and toilets. A smaller campground 1 mile to the north is **Miners Gulch** with 5 tent sites.

Hanna—Four campgrounds located northwest of Hanna off Hwy. 35: **Aspen Grove** (33 sites); **Hades** (17 sites); **Iron Mine** (27 sites); and **South Fork** (5 sites). Aspen Grove is the largest and the closest to Hanna, 8 miles away. The other three are 11, 12.5, and 15.8 miles from Hanna, respectively. There are no toilet or shower facilities in the campgrounds, but all are equipped with drinking water.

Moon Lake—A popular fishing and recreation location, the Moon Lake Campground has 19 trailer and 37 tent sites. Drinking water and toilets are available. There is a group site that has 25 RV and tent sites.

Roosevelt—About 25 miles north of Roosevelt, there are three campgrounds located within 1.5 miles of each other, along the Uinta River. **Uinta Canyon** has 24 trailer and 24 tent sites, **Uinta River** has 20 tent sites, and **Wandin** has 4 trailer sites and 3 tent sites.

Vernal—Five campgrounds are located along a 5-mile stretch of Hwy. 191, about 30 miles north of Vernal. The largest, **Lodgepole,** has 25 trailer and tent sites and drinking water and toilets; **Red Springs** has 13 trailer and tent sites; **East Park** has 21 sites; and **Kaler Hollow** has 4 tent sites.

See also the Outdoor Activities section.

—————— WHERE TO EAT ——————

ROOSEVELT

Cow Palace—$ to $$$
Specializes in steaks and hamburgers. Has a charming Old West atmosphere. There's a self-order section, or you can eat in the "saloon" where you can get full service and daily specials. Open Mon.–Thurs. 11 am–9 pm.; Fri. and Sat. 11 am–10 pm. Closed Sun. Located east of the Best Western Inn, on Hwy. 40 2 miles east of Roosevelt; **(801) 722-2717.**

Greenbriar—$ to $$
Greenbriar offers family style faire with prime rib Friday and Saturday evenings.

Daily specials. This is a good place to get an early morning breakfast. Open daily 5:30 am-10 pm. Located just west of the Best Western Inn on Hwy. 40 east of Roosevelt; **(801) 722-2236.**

Frontier Grill—$ to $$
Located next to the Frontier Motel, the Grill is Roosevelt's most popular eating establishment. Open daily 6 am–9 pm. **65 South 200 East; (801) 722-3669.**

Sorry Nag—$ to $$
This restaurant wins the award for the best atmosphere of any restaurant in the

Uinta Basin. The interior is designed as a humble hacienda; seating outdoors is under some quaint but pleasant bowries. The food is western and Mexican. Steaks, fried chicken, charbroiled chicken breast, grilled halibut with Dutch-oven potatoes on the western side of the menu, and fajitas, taco salads, and combination plates on the Mexican side. Open Mon.–Thurs.. 11 am–9 pm; 11 am–10 pm on Fri. and Sat. Located on the north side of Hwy. 40 as it passes through Roosevelt. **133 North 200 East; (801) 722-3610.**

VERNAL

Casa Rios—$ to $$

This Mexican restaurant serves lunch and dinner. Open Tues.–Sat. 11 am–2:30 pm and 5 pm–8:30 pm. **2015 West Hwy. 40; (801) 789-0103.**

H. R. Weston's Restaurant—$$

Located in the Weston Hotel. Open Tues.–Sat. for breakfast from 7 am–10:30 am and for dinner from 5 pm–9 pm. **1684 West Hwy. 40, (801) 789-9550.**

Skillet and Car 19—$ to $$

Traditional breakfasts. Sandwiches and burgers for lunch, and steaks, filets, shish kebabs, halibut, catfish, and other entrées for dinner. Open daily 6 am–10 pm. Located in the Dinosaur Inn Best Western at **363 West Main; (801) 789-3641.**

—— SERVICES ——

Ashley National Forest, Roosevelt Ranger District—

The Roosevelt district office also has information and maps and publications for sale. Open Mon.–Fri. 8 am–5 pm. Located on the western edge of town. **244 West Hwy. 40; (801) 722-5018.**

Ashley National Forest, Supervisor's Office and Vernal Ranger District—

The district office provides information about recreation and activities on the national forest and has books and maps for sale. Open Mon.–Fri. 8 am–5 pm. **355 North Vernal Ave., Vernal, UT 84078; (801) 789-1181.**

Bureau of Land Management, Vernal District—

For information about recreation on BLM lands, check in at the district office; **170 South 500 East** in Vernal. Open Mon.–Fri. 7:45 am–4:30 pm; **(801) 789-1362.**

Dinosaurland Regional Travel Office—

Although this office is not set up to handle walk-in visitors you can obtain tour information, brochures, from the Dinosaurland Regional Travel Office. **25 East Main St.** in Vernal; **(801) 789-6932** or **1-800-477-5558.**

State Welcome Center—

Located in the eastern end of the **Utah Field House of Natural History** at **235 East Main St.** in Vernal; **(801) 789-4002.** (Plans are to build a new welcome center in Jensen, at the turnoff to Dinosaur National Monument, which should be open in late 1995.)

Dinosaur National Monument

Dinosaur National Monument spreads out over the mountains, plateaus, and deserts in the northeastern corner of Utah and northwestern corner of Colorado, with enough river running, hiking, scenic drives, and geology to occupy days and days. Mountains, narrow-cut canyons, raging rapids in the bowels of river gorges, majestic walls of sandstone, broad expanses of bench land, and broken vistas of the upper Colorado Plateau are the setting for a treasure house of dinosaur bones nearly 150 million years in age.

The 300-square-mile Dinosaur National Monument is really two parks in one. It started out as just the Dinosaur Quarry in 1915 and was later expanded to include the fabulous scenery and recreation potential of the Green and Yampa rivers, which merge inside the monument at Echo Park. The national monument is not a 300-square-mile dinosaur graveyard. There are a number of dinosaur sites known within the monument, many of which have not been fully evaluated. But these sites constitute only a very small part of the park. The best-known site is the Quarry site and for most visitors, an hour is sufficient time to see it. There are two paved scenic roads in Dinosaur National Monument: the Split Mountain and Green River Campground Rd., which leads east from the Dinosaur Quarry Visitor Center, and Harper's Corner Rd., which goes north from the Monument headquarters just east of Dinosaur, Colorado. A third road, accessed off Harper's Corner Rd., is a 13-mile-long dirt road that drops into Echo Park for a view of Steamboat Rock and the confluence of the Green and Yampa rivers. There are three other dirt roads: Cub Creek Rd., Island Park Rd., and Yampa Bench Rd.

HISTORY

Just as Dinosaur National Monument is really two parks, it also has two histories: the geologic history and the history of its evolution as a national monument. Geologically, the area gained its significance 150 million years ago, during more tropical times, when extensive floodplain deposits were laid down over a widespread area of what is now Colorado, Wyoming, eastern Utah, northern New Mexico, parts of Montana and South Dakota, and the panhandle of Oklahoma. Dinosaurs inhabited the swamps around the shallow river that meandered over this flood plain. As they died, their remains settled into the deposits, and over time were preserved in what is now known in Utah and Colorado as the

Morrison Formation. The formation is named for Morrison, Colorado, where the first major discovery of dinosaurs from this formation was made in 1877. A "dinosaur rush" developed from the Morrison discoveries, as paleontologists competed to see who could discover the most dinosaurs. By 1900, dinosaurs remains had been found in Colorado in Morrison and Cañon City, and in Wyoming in Como Bluff, Bone Cabin Quarry, and Howe Quarry. The Utah discovery occurred in August 1909, when Earl Douglass, a paleontologist from the Carnegie Museum in Pittsburgh, Pennsylvania, came upon a hogback, or ridge that had been formed by the earth tilting steeply upward. In this hogback, Douglass found eight large dinosaur vertebrae weathering out of the sandstone. The bones were from the tails of a sauropod, an apatosaurus or a brontosaurus, which proved to be the most complete skeletons ever discovered. The skeletons had come to rest in a sandbar along an ancient river and were covered over by sand and mud. They were brought near the surface when violent uplifts reshaped the land, creating the Uinta Mountains. Erosion had completed their exposure.

Douglass dug the site for the next 15 years, sending dinosaur bones to the Smithsonian Institution in Washington, DC, to the University of Utah, and more than 350 tons of fossils to the Carnegie Museum. The quarry proved to be the most prolific dinosaur quarry in the Morrison Formation. In addition to the apatosaurus or brontosaurus, Douglass uncovered a plant-eating camarasaurus, a diplodocus, a barosaurus, a camptosaurus, a dryosaurus, and a stegosaurus, as well as meat-eating dinosaurs such as allosaurus, ceratosaurus, and torvosaurus. Researchers have found the tracks of more than 200 individual animals in various parts of the monument. Some scientists postulate that the accumulation of dinosaur bones in one place resulted from a terrible drought that hit the area forcing large numbers of dinosaurs to congregate at ancient river channels to obtain water. As they died, their bodies lay in the dry river channels. Later flash floods picked up the dinosaur remains and carried them down the river channels, leaving them in a logjam of dinosaur bones that became the quarry.

The 80-acre quarry site was designated a national monument in 1915, while Douglass was still excavating, often using dynamite to blast through the overlying rock layers. During the 1930s, a Works Progress Administration Project expanded the quarry face, but no new fossils were exposed or excavated.

The park was greatly expanded in 1938, when President Franklin D. Roosevelt recognized the scenic and recreational value of 328 square miles east and northeast of the quarry and added it to the monument. During the 1950s, Dinosaur National Monument was embroiled in controversy when the Bureau of Reclamation proposed the construction of a multipurpose dam inside the monument at Echo Park. The proposed dam and reservoir, according to historian Mark W.T. Harvey "... sparked the biggest conservation crusade to date in the twentieth century." Led by the Sierra Club, the Wilderness Society, and the National Parks Association, a host of groups and individuals pressured Congress into deleting the dam from the Colorado River Storage Project in 1956.

A new visitor center replaced the original sheetmetal building in May 1958. The Quarry Visitor Center proved significant in National Park Service history, as it was the first park service facility to employ a modern architectural design instead of the rustic design traditionally favored in national parks.

GETTING THERE

The Dinosaur National Monument's Quarry Visitor Center is located 7 miles north of Jensen, off US Hwy. 40, approximately 200 miles from Salt Lake City and 20 miles from Vernal. From Jensen, it's another 20 miles east on Hwy. 40 to the Dinosaur National Monument Headquarters, located 2 miles east of Dinosaur, Colorado, at the junction of the highway with Harper's Corner Rd. This road takes you into the monument on the east side of the Green River. A fee is charged whether you are in a car, on a bike or motorcycle, or on foot.

DINOSAUR QUARRY VISITOR CENTER

The 1958 Dinosaur Quarry Visitor Center now encloses the quarry. Until recently, visitors could watch paleontologists pecking away at the rock to expose and extract the dinosaur bones. The exposing of new dinosaur bones is generally completed at this location and it is no longer possible to watch the scientists at work. Nevertheless there is plenty to see at the quarry. Interesting displays and knowledgeable park rangers add to the experience, and there is a good selection of books on dinosaurs and natural history for purchase in the bookstore. The quarry is open 8:00 am–7:00 pm daily early June–early Sept., and 8:00 am–4:30 pm the rest of the year. From Memorial Day–Labor Day, you are required to park in the parking lot and take a shuttle bus to the center; the rest of the year you may drive directly to the center. Entrance fee charged.

PARK HEADQUARTERS

Park headquarters is located about 30 miles east of the Quarry Visitor Center, at the junction of US Hwy. 40 and the Harper's Corner Rd. The building is staffed by rangers. and also has. Free backcountry camping permits (required for overnight camping) may be obtained at the headquarters office, as well as from other ranger stations. Exhibits, books for sale, and other information available. A 31-mile-long paved scenic drive along Harper's Corner Rd. heads north from the park headquarters. Park headquarters is open 8 am–4:30 pm daily June–Aug.; Mon.–Fri. the rest of the year. For more information, write to **Superintendent, Dinosaur National Monument, 4545 Hwy. 40, Dinosaur, CO 81610**; or call **(303) 374-2216**.

OUTDOOR ACTIVITIES

BIKING

Dinosaur National Monument
Chew Ranch Rd.—

A good intermediate loop of 24 miles, this ride starts in the lower parking lot of the quarry and follows the main monument road. After 5.4 miles, you cross the Green River and continue another 2.4 miles, before turning right onto a dirt track that winds up the hill. This section of the ride—about 8 miles—is on dirt and takes you out of the monument. Where the dirt road forks, bear to the right, as the loop heads south back to US Hwy. 40. When you reach the pavement, you have a 1.5-mile ride along the highway; this is the most unpleasant part of the ride because of the traffic. At Jensen, turn right onto Hwy. 149 for the 6-mile ride back to the monument. Fees are collected at the entrance station, so make sure you carry your receipt with you for reentry. Most of the loop is on desert terrain, so carry plenty of water. The ride is best made in the spring or fall, or early in the morning during the summer. For further information, check at the **Quarry Visitor Center.**

HIKING AND NATURE TRAILS

Box Canyon and Hog Canyon Trails—

At the Josie Morris cabin site, there are two short, fun hiking trails. The .5-mile Box Canyon Trail heads north from the parking area. An authentic example of a "box canyon"—with steep walls on three sides, and only one way in and out—it was used by Josie Morris, a local rancher, as a corral

for her stock because the vertical walls meant that the entrance and exit were the same. East of the cabin and spring, the 1.5-mile-long Hog Canyon Trail takes you farther into a second box canyon—also used by Josie Morris for her livestock.

Cold Desert Trail—

Located adjacent to the park headquarters, the .25-mile-long nature trail gives an excellent introduction to the Cold Desert Life Zone, which is found around the 6,000-foot elevation. A well-illustrated trail guide, which explains the plants and animals of this zone, is available inside the headquarters building for a small charge.

Desert Voices Trail—

This 2-mile-long trail begins at the northwest end of the parking area at the Split Mountain boat ramp. The trail follows up a stream bed then climbs up and over a ridge before looping back to Split Mountain. The climb is moderately strenuous, but this is a trail that invites you to go at an easy pace and is designed as a teaching tool for children. There are numerous markers along the trail that deal with such topics as plants, animals, geology, soil, history, preservation, multiple use, vandalism, chaining, revegetation, cryptogramic soil, and cattle. Near the beginning of the trail is a garbage pit; items were placed there in 1992 to demonstrate how long it takes for them to disintegrate in the desert environment. Some of the markers have quotes and paintings by children about the environment. Quotes about the sun, wind, animals, and rocks are a delight to read. Near the end of the trail, there is even a message from Dr. Seuss and the Lorax about unrestrained growth for young and old alike.

Echo Park Hiking Trails—

In Echo Park there are a couple of interesting trails that take you along the course of the Green River. You will want to hike the .25 mile or so upriver to the junction of the Green and Yampa rivers. You may continue up the Yampa until the canyon walls close in on you. Check with the ranger in **Echo Park** for trail conditions and information about other possibilities.

Gates of Lodore Trail—

This 1.5-mile round-trip, easy-to-walk nature trail follows the Green River to the Gates of Lodore at the extreme northern end of the monument and at the south end of Brown's Park. The Gates of Lodore was named by Andy Hall, the youngest member of John Wesley Powell's expedition down the Green and Colorado rivers in 1869. Hall recalled the English poet Robert Southey's poem "The Cataract of Lodore," which includes the words: "All at once and all o'er, with a mighty uproar; And this way the water comes down at Lodore." A **trail guide** is available at the headquarters and quarry.

Harper's Corner Trail—

The Green River meanders 2,500 feet below around the knifelike point of Harper's Corner. The narrow ridge that leads to the point allows you to look into the channel on both sides. To the right you can see down to Steamboat Rock and Echo Park; to the left, the river heads in a southern course through Whirlpool Canyon toward Split Mountain. At the end of the trail, the ridge sweeps up to a point to one of the most dramatic vistas in the monument, where you can look into both sides of the canyon. The 2-mile-round-trip trail begins at the terminus of Harper's Corner Rd., 31 miles north of the monument headquarters, and winds back and forth from one side of the ridge to the other. An excellent **trail guide** is available at the headquarters or at the trailhead for a small charge.

Jones Hole Trail—

To reach this trailhead you must take the Jones Hole Scenic Backway (see Scenic Drives in the **Roosevelt and Vernal** chapter, p. 63). The road takes you to the Jones Hole Fish Hatchery just outside the northern boundary of the monument. The 4-mile-long trail heads south through a deep gorge to the Green River in Whirlpool Canyon. Along the trail there are trees and steep rock walls with a few petroglyphs. The trail provides foot access to one of the most remote sections of the Green River, which otherwise could be seen only by boat or raft.

Plug Hat Nature Trail—

A .25-mile-long nature trail that begins 4 miles north of the monument headquarters on the Harpers Corner Road, the trail offers an overview of the Uinta Basin.

Ruple Point Trail—

An 8-mile out and back trail that begins at the Island Park Overlook, just inside the southern boundary of the monument on Harper's Corner Rd. At the end of the trail is a spectacular overlook of the Split Mountain Gorge through which the Green River flows.

Sound of Silence Route—

This 2-mile-long trail, located on the paved road 2 miles from the Dinosaur Quarry, is designed to introduce visitors to minimum-impact desert hiking on undeveloped routes. The route is not a trail and is somewhat difficult to follow, as you must estimate the distance in yards from one point to the next. It is also quite steep in some sections. There are 26 markers along the trail that correspond to information about dinosaurs, plants, animals, geology, soil, and history provided in a **trail guide** available for a small charge at the quarry or park headquarters.

RIVER FLOATING

Both the Green and Yampa rivers are popular with river runners, and because the river takes you to places that are otherwise inaccessible, it is one of the best ways to experience Dinosaur National Monument. A popular trip starts at the north end of the monument, at the **Gates of Lodore,** where the Green River roars through Lodore Canyon for about 20 miles to Echo Park and its junction with the Yampa River. Although few rafters use it, **Echo Park** is another good place to put in for the ride through Whirlpool Canyon and Split Mountain to the southern boundary of the monument. Boaters on the Yampa River start from Deerlodge Park. All trips must have a river permit prior to launching. Information about permits for private rafting trips through the monument can be obtained by writing **Superintendent, Dinosaur National Monument, 4545 Hwy. 40, Dinosaur, CO 81610;** or by calling **(303) 374-2468** between 9 am–noon Mon.–Fri.

Adrift Adventures—

Although it also offers multiday river trips, Adrift Adventures specializes in one-day paddle or oar boat trips from Split Mountain to Jensen. **PO Box 192, Jensen, UT 84035; (801) 789-3600** or **1-800-824-0154.**

Don Hatch River Expeditions—

This outfit offers one- to five-day rafting trips on the Green River, following the route taken by the 1869 historic John Wesley Powell Expedition through Split Mountain into the Uinta Basin. Hatch Expeditions began in the 1920s, under Buzz Hatch, and is the oldest commercial tour expedition company on the Green and Colorado rivers. Hatch also offers longer, three- to five-day trips on the Yampa River, the last remaining free-flowing river in the entire Colorado River system. **PO Box 1150, Dept. S, Vernal, UT 84078; (801) 789-4316** or **1-800-342-8243.**

SEEING AND DOING

SCENIC DRIVES

Cub Creek—

This 12-mile-long scenic drive begins at the Utah entrance to the monument, goes past the Dinosaur Quarry, then on to the Josie Morris Cabin at the foot of Split Mountain. One of the region's most colorful characters, Josie Morris built her cabin in 1914 as her ranch headquarters and lived in it for 50 years. The view of Split Mountain is stunning. Ever since Major John Wesley Powell named it in 1869, geologists seem to have been at a loss to explain how the Green River could, at least so it appears, split the mountain in two. A **road guide** is available for a small charge at the park entrance, at park headquarters, or at the Quarry Visitor Center. The guide points out such features as the impressive Indian petroglyphs located about 10.5 miles from the entrance to the monument.

Echo Park Rd.—

This is a dirt road that leaves Harper's Corner Rd. 25 miles from the monument headquarters. The 13-mile-long road drops down into Echo Park for a close look at Steamboat Rock and the junction of the Yampa and Green rivers. During his 1869 trip down the Green River, Major John Wesley Powell noted the echoes bouncing off Steamboat Rock. Early in the 1900s, Echo Park was better known as Pat's Hole. Pat Lynch was an Irish-born hermit, who lived many years in the caves along the Green River. He died in 1917, at the age of 98. He had a reputation for making pets of wild animals in the area, including one mountain lion that responded from afar when Lynch would screech at it. In dry weather, the road is generally passable for high-clearance passenger vehicles; it is not suitable for trailers, motor homes, or other heavy vehicles. The first 8-mile section begins with a steep descent on a series of switchbacks, then you descend through Sand Canyon onto the Yampa Bench. At the mouth of Sand Canyon, keep to the left (otherwise you will be on the Yampa Bench Rd.). After 2 miles you reach the James and Rial Chew Ranch, an historic ranch established in 1910 that you may view from the road. From the Chew Ranch it's about 3 miles to Echo Park through the narrow Pool Creek Canyon. Two miles beyond the ranch, you will come to a sign that indicates petroglyphs. Park your vehicle, then follow the short trail, keeping a lookout high up on the sandstone wall where the petroglyphs are located. There has been significant erosion since the ancient inhabitants pecked the figures into the sandstone, so they are much higher up on the cliff than you would expect. A half mile down the road is Whispering Cave, a narrow crack in the rock more than 100 feet high that extends back a distance. It's another .5 mile to Echo Park from Whispering Cave.

Harper's Corner Rd.—

This road heads north from US Hwy. 40 and monument headquarters 2 miles east of Dinosaur, Colorado. Pick up a copy of "Journey Through Time," a guide to the 31-mile-long paved scenic road at the park headquarters. The guide explains that Harper's Corner was actually a natural corral used by a rancher named Harper. The steep walls kept his cattle from climbing out, and all he needed to secure them was a short stretch of fence at the mouth of the box canyon. You will want to plan enough time for the 2-mile roundtrip hike to the overlook, 2,500 feet above Echo Park, and the drive down into Echo Park. It is easy to spend an entire day on this road, which measures 62 miles round-trip from park headquarters.

Yampa Bench Rd.—

This is a long, bumpy, dusty road that begins 8 miles from the junction of the Echo Park and Harper's Corner roads. A four-wheel-drive vehicle is recommended, but high-clearance two-wheel vehicles can travel the unpaved road. It heads east for 38 miles, along the Yampa Bench, into some of the most remote parts of the monument. Near the east end of the monument, the road turns southeast and exits the monument, rejoining US Hwy. 40 at Elk Springs. From there it is a 32-mile drive back to the monument headquarters.

WHERE TO STAY

ACCOMMODATIONS

There is no lodging within Dinosaur National Monument. The nearest accommodations are in Vernal. See the **Roosevelt and Vernal** chapter.

CAMPING

PRIVATE

Dinosaur Village—

The closest private campground to Dinosaur National Monument, Dinosaur Village is located 1.5 miles west of Jensen on Hwy. 40. All 50 sites have complete hookups, and the park is equipped with showers and toilets. Open Apr.–Oct; **(801) 789-5552.** For information on other private campgrounds in Vernal see the Services section.

PUBLIC

Two modern campgrounds are located 4 and 5 miles east of the Dinosaur Quarry, off Hwy. 40. **Split Mountain Campground,** with 35 sites, is open spring–fall; **Green River Campground,** with 100 sites, is open Memorial Day–Labor Day. Unlike other National Park Service campgrounds, you can usually find a place. Spaces are available on a first-come, first-served basis, and a fee is charged.

There are four other smaller campgrounds; **Echo Park** (14 sites), the **Gates of Lodore** (17 sites), **Rainbow Park** (4 sites), and **Deerlodge Park** (8 sites), where no fees are charged. Only Echo Park and Lodore have drinking water. All four have limited development, are quite remote, difficult to reach, and are used primarily by river floaters.

Backcountry camping is permitted in roadless sections of the monument. A permit is required. It is best to check with park rangers either at the park headquarters or the Quarry Visitor Center for information.

SERVICES

Dinosaur National Monument Headquarters—

Superintendent, Dinosaur National Monument, **4545 Hwy. 40, Dinosaur, CO 81610; (303) 374-2216.**

Dinosaurland Regional Travel Office—

Tour information, brochures, etc., are available. **25 East Main St.** in **Vernal; (801) 789-4002** or **1-800-477-5558.**

Klething Peak in the Uinta Mountains, located northwest of Dinosaur National Monument. Photo by Allan Kent Powell.

Flaming Gorge
National Recreation Area

Flaming Gorge is many things. The original name was given by Major John Wesley Powell and his men on May 26, 1869, during their epic journey down the Green and Colorado rivers. As they prepared to pass through the Uinta Mountains, Powell recorded in his diary:

> The river is running to the south; the mountains have an easterly and westerly trend directly athwart its course, yet it glides on a quiet way as if it thought a mountain range no formidable obstruction. It enters the range by a flaring, brilliant red gorge, that may be seen from the north a score of miles away. The great mass of the mountain ridge through which the gorge is cut is composed of bright vermilion rocks; but they are surmounted by broad bands of mottled buff and gray, and these bands come down with a gentle curve to the water's edge on the nearer slope of the mountain. This is the head of the first of the canyons we are about to explore—an introductory one to a series made by the river through this range. We name it Flaming Gorge. The cliffs, or walls, we find on measurement to be about 1,200 feet high.

The name Flaming Gorge was originally applied only to where the Green River cuts into the Uinta Mountains; today, however, when people refer to Flaming Gorge they are talking about both the reservoir and the northeastern corner of the state that borders both Wyoming and Colorado. This area includes Brown's Park, a 35-mile-long, 6-mile-wide valley through which the Green River flows. Flaming Gorge Lake, which covers more than 66 square miles with a shoreline of 375 miles, and the surrounding area are included in the Flaming Gorge National Recreation Area administered by the US Forest Service. The recreation area includes the section of the Green River below the dam through Red Canyon to the west end of Brown's Park, part of the north slope of the Uinta Mountains on the south, and extends across the Utah-Wyoming border partway up Blacks Fork and up the main channel of the Green River to a point about 3 miles south of the city of Green River, Wyoming. The **visitor center** for the recreation area is located at the **Flaming Gorge Dam**.

HISTORY

Flaming Gorge had a colorful history before and after Powell named the area. The first recorded travelers through Flaming Gorge were General William H. Ashley and members of his 1825 fur trapping party. Ashley set out in a 16-foot by 7-foot bullboat made of buffalo hides on

April 22, 1825, to look for beaver. He also hoped to ascertain whether the Green River was the fabled Buenaventura River, which misinformed map makers had drawn running southwest from the Rocky Mountains to the Pacific Ocean. Ashley's wild adventure took him through Flaming Gorge and Split Mountain, where his bullboat filled with water and nearly sank, before his men rescued the boat and pulled it to land. Ashley recorded in his diary that his men saved his life, for he could not swim. Ashley continued down the Green River into the Uinta Basin, where he left the Green River at Minnie Maud Creek. After making a circular journey around the Uinta Mountains, he returned to the Flaming Gorge area at the end of June. While floating down the Green River, Ashley designated Henry's Fork as the site of the first Rocky Mountain fur trapper rendezvous. Held 20 miles up Henry's Fork from its junction with the Green River, this first rendezvous established an institution that lasted until the end of the fur trade era in 1840. In describing the first rendezvous, James Beckwourth records:

> When all had come in, he [William Ashley] opened his goods, and there was a general jubilee among all at the rendezvous. We constituted quite a little town, numbering at least eight hundred souls, of whom one half were women and children. There were some among us who had not seen any groceries, such as coffee, sugar &c., for several months. The whisky went off as freely as water, even at the exorbitant price he sold it for. All kinds of sports were indulged in with a heartiness that would astonish more civilized societies.

As the rendezvous system began to wane and was replaced by trading posts, Philip Thompson and William Craig established a trading post in Brown's Hole, known as Fort Davy Crockett, in 1837.

Nearly a quarter of a century after Ashley's trip down the Green River, the next recorded journey down the Green through Flaming Gorge occurred. Several California-bound 49ers concluded that the Green River offered the easiest route to their goal. Using an abandoned ferryboat, then dugout canoes, they set out down the Green River from near the Sweetwater crossing in Wyoming. They got as far as the mouth of the White River in the Uinta Basin, and then met Wakara, the Ute Indian chief, who convinced them they had better abandon their river route and head west to Salt Lake City if they ever wanted to reach California.

More successful in reaching his objective was John Wesley Powell and his 1869 voyage down the Green River to its confluence with the Colorado River and on through the Grand Canyon.

In 1870, the first cattle herds were brought to the Brown's Park–Flaming Gorge area. By the 1880s, cattlemen, cowboys, rustlers, settlers, and outlaws all intermingled in the region. Outlaws like Butch Cassidy, the Sundance Kid (Harry Longabaugh), Matt Warner, Elza Lay, Tom Horn, the Queen of the Cattle Rustlers (Ann Bassett), and many others left their mark on the history of the Brown's Park and Flaming Gorge area. Dirt roads were not completed from Green River, Wyoming, to the north and Vernal, Utah, to the south until the 1920s and 1930s.

When construction of the Flaming Gorge dam began in 1958, the northeastern corner of Utah was still very much a primitive area of scattered ranches. Access into the area from the south was made possible by the construction of the Cart Creek dam in 1959 and connecting traffic made possible in 1963 when construction of the dam was completed and the highway built along the crest of the dam. As the lake filled, it became one of the top fishing and boating sites in Utah.

GETTING THERE

Flaming Gorge is located about 250 miles east of Salt Lake City and can be reached by two major routes. The northern route follows Interstate 80 east into Wyoming, then exits the interstate at Fort Bridger and heads south on Wyoming Hwy. 414 and across the Utah border onto Utah Hwy. 43, which takes you to Manila, near the western shore of the reservoir. The southern route follows Interstate 80 east to the junction with US Hwy. 40, which you follow through Heber City and on to Duchesne, Roosevelt, and Vernal. At Vernal, head north on US Hwy. 191, over the eastern portion of the Uinta Mountains, to Flaming Gorge Dam. Both routes are approximately the same distance, although the southern route is probably a little longer. The southern route offers the opportunity to do some touring in the Uinta Basin and at Dinosaur National Monument; however, the steep climb up US 191 from Vernal makes the northern route the best choice for trailers and RVs. The northern route also offers Fort Bridger as an attraction. It is located approximately two-thirds of the way between Salt Lake City and Manila.

———— FESTIVALS AND EVENTS ————

Bike Tour
of Flaming Gorge
July 24th
Bike races and a bike tour of the Flaming Gorge area are held the weekend of Pioneer Day (July 24th). **(801) 789-6932** or **1-800-477-5550.**

Dinotrax Bicycle Festival
mid-August
Usually held in mid-Aug., this bicycling festival includes several different tours of the area on Sat. and races on Sun. Part of the Cannondale Cup Series. A kid's nature camp is provided. Families are encouraged to attend; **(801) 789-6932** or **1-800-477-5558.**

OUTDOOR ACTIVITIES

BIKING

Bear Canyon–Bootleg—

This easy 3-mile round-trip ride goes west from the Firefighters Memorial Campground, located south of the dam off Hwy. 191, to an overview of Red Canyon and Flaming Gorge Lake.

Canyon Rim Ride—

This trail is 4 miles one way and is a generally flat ride with access from three points: the Red Canyon Visitor Center, Canyon Rim Campground, and Greendale Rest Area. It offers a spectacular view of the 1,400-foot-deep Red Canyon.

Death Valley—

This is a strenuous 15-mile out-and-back ride that begins at milepost 16.5 on Utah Hwy. 44 south of Manila. The route ends at the top of Sheep Creek Hill, with its fine view of Flaming Gorge Lake.

Dowd Mountain—

A 10-mile round-trip ride with moderate grades, which begins at the Dowd Mountain road off Utah Hwy. 44 14 miles south of Manila. The ride is along the dirt road that takes you to the Dowd Mountain Overlook for spectacular views of Flaming Gorge and the western portions of Flaming Gorge Lake.

Flaming Gorge Trails—

A brochure produced by the Flaming Gorge National Recreation Area describes five biking trails. The brochure is available at the Flaming Gorge Visitor Center, at the dam or by writing **Flaming Gorge Ranger District, Flaming Gorge National Recreation Area, PO Box 278, Manila, UT 84046;** or calling **(801) 784-3445.**

Sheep Creek Canyon Loop—

The 20-mile Sheep Creek Canyon Loop offers some magnificent scenery and remarkable geologic formations-at a price. The long, steep, uphill climbs make this a ride for riders who are in excellent physical condition. The road follows the old route of Hwy. 44 and is paved most of the way; however, the pavement has not been maintained and, in several heavily deteriorated sections, the road has been graveled. The road begins 6 miles south of Manila, on Hwy. 44, at Sheep Creek Gap and US Forest Service Rd. 218, where parking is available. The first 5.5 miles are through a broad relatively level valley, past the grave of Cleophas J. Dowd, who was murdered by his partner Charles Reasoner on April 11, 1897. It was reported that Reasoner was upset with Dowd for the chain-beating Dowd gave his son, George Dowd, when a team ran away with him tearing up a harness. South of the Dowd grave, the road enters the narrow confines of Sheep Creek Canyon, where Big Spring gushes from the canyon wall at the rate of 25 cubic feet per second and the northern exposure of the Uinta Fault can be seen. Then the road leaves the bottom of the canyon and climbs for 5 miles, via a series of switchbacks, to the top. Here is where your physical conditioning is tested. Once on top, the ride becomes easy. After 2 miles, you return to Hwy. 44 and turn left to head back to your vehicle. Since Hwy. 44 is the main route between Manila and Dutch John, there can be a fair amount of traffic along the road. After a stop at the scenic viewpoint to take in the spectacular view of Sheep Creek Bay on Flaming Gorge Lake, the road drops along an 8 percent grade and more switchbacks for a couple of miles to the road to Sheep Creek Bay. From the turnoff there is a half-mile climb to Manns Campground, and then a mile of level terrain back to the starting point.

Swett Ranch—

This 6-mile round-trip ride begins at the eastern end of the Greendale Rest Area on Utah Hwy. 44 and takes you to the historic Swett Ranch (see the Seeing and Doing section).

FISHING

Flaming Gorge Reservoir—

If you want to go for the big ones, Flaming Gorge Reservoir is the place. As the lake trout, or Mackinaw, matured during the decade of the 1980s, Flaming Gorge yielded more lake trout over 30 pounds than any other spot in the US—perhaps the world. The Utah record is a 51.5-pound, 46.5-inch lake trout, caught in the Lucerne Bay area by Curt Bilbey of Vernal in July 1988. It goes without saying that Flaming Gorge is one of the most popular fishing spots in Utah. While catching the real big ones requires a boat, know-how, and sophisticated equipment, the lake is also kind to the average fisherman; rainbow trout can be caught from the shore. Smallmouth bass are numerous and, in the upper end of Flaming Gorge, channel catfish flourish. Kokanee salmon up to 5 pounds are also taken in the open water. In early Sept. and late Oct., the Kokanee turn a deep crimson and make their way upstream to spawn. Marinas are located at **Cedar Springs** near **Dutch John** and **Lucerne Valley**, on the west side of the lake near Manila and Buckboard just below the confluence of the Blacks Fork and Green rivers in Wyoming.

Green River—

The Green River, just below Flaming Gorge Dam, is famous as one of America's best fly-fishing locations. The river is well stocked with rainbow, brown and cutthroat trout. Because of its popularity, in 1995 or 1996 the forest service may begin limiting the number of people fishing there.

Guided Fishing Trips—

Flaming Gorge Recreation Services offers guided fishing trips that include transportation to and from the river, lunch, boat, and guide. If you are serious about taking a big lake trout, the use of local guides will increase your chances tremendously. **Flaming Gorge Recreation Services, PO Box 367, Dutch John, UT 84023; (801) 885-3191.** The Collett family at **Flaming Gorge Lodge** can also provide fishing guides for one- to three-day fishing trips; **(801) 889-3773.**

RIVER RUNNING

Flaming Gorge Dam to Little Hole—

The 7-mile stretch of the Green River from just below Flaming Gorge Dam not only offers excellent fly-fishing but is a popular river float trip. The high narrow canyons, wildlife, and sections of small rapids make this a memorable but safe trip for families and groups, even those who do not have much experience with the rubber rafts. Rafts, life jackets, paddles and bail buckets can be rented from **Flaming Gorge Recreation Services, Flaming Gorge Lodge,** and **Flaming Gorge Flying Service,** including transportation to and from the river. If you don't want to make the trip alone and want the services of a qualified guide, half- and full-day trips can be arranged through Flaming Gorge Recreation Services. While most rafters leave the river at Little Hole, you can continue down the river into Brown's Park to Jarvie's Ranch or on to Taylor's Flat, if you want to make a full day's trip. Past Little Hole, the river becomes placid, the going slow and there are fewer boats. The fishing is still good, and you can visit the **John Jarvie Historic Property** (see the Seeing and Doing section). To get back to Flaming Gorge requires a long circular ride through Jesse Ewing Canyon and Clay Basin to Hwy. 191.

SEEING AND DOING

HISTORIC SITES

Flaming Gorge Dam—

Although some might argue that a structure that was completed in 1963 is not old enough to be "historic," the Flaming Gorge Dam has certainly had an impact on northeastern Utah. The dam is 502 feet high and required nearly 1 million cubic yards of concrete. The crest of the dam is approximately 1,200 feet in length and carries two lanes of traffic as part of Hwy. 191. A visitor center is located at the dam, and self-guided tours (8 am–4 pm year-round) can be taken inside the dam to view the generators and turbines. There are also exhibits and a small bookstore. The visitor center is open from 9:30 am–5 pm, year-round.

Oscar Swett Ranch—

For a glimpse of what ranch life was like in the Flaming Gorge area, the Swett Ranch, owned and operated by the Flaming Gorge Ranger District of the US Forest Service, offers a great opportunity. The Swett family began grazing cattle in the region in the early 1900s. In 1912 Oscar and Emma Swett were married, and their first home was an abandoned log cabin which Oscar disassembled and hauled to their homesite. The single-room cabin was only big enough for one bed—a large box filled with straw and covered with blankets in which Oscar, Emma, and three children slept. In 1919 a two-room log cabin was built and then in 1929 the five-room lumber house was built using lumber Oscar had cut in the nearby forests and sawed at his own mill. All three buildings were used by the Swett family, which included seven daughters and two sons. A bathroom was added to the frame house in the 1950s, but after much protest by Oscar, who said, "You're not supposed to have a bathroom in the house." Oscar finally conceded to the bathroom, but he wouldn't let the door open into the house so to make a visit one had to go out on the porch and then enter the bathroom. Horse-powered equipment was used on the ranch from 1909 until 1970; much of the equipment, including hay mowers, hay rakes, bull rakes, wagons, a bobsled, hay stackers, a hay ram, ditchers, road graders, riding plows, and a binder, has been preserved on the ranch. The ranch also includes a cellar—which Emma kept filled with the 500 and 1,000 quarts of fruit and meat she bottled each year, springhouse and other outbuildings, all of which have been listed in the National Register of Historic Places. Oscar died in September 1968, working on the homestead until the day he died. Emma died three years later in May 1971. The ranch is now part of the Flaming Gorge Recreation Area. Volunteer caretakers live at the ranch during the summer months and act as hosts to visitors. The ranch is located 1.5 miles west of the Greendale Campground. For information about access to the ranch, inquire at the **US Forest Service** office in **Dutch John** or at the **Flaming Gorge Visitor Center**.

Ute Mountain Fire Tower—

While fire towers can be found all over the Northwest, there is only one in Utah, and the forest service has done an excellent job of preserving this important structure. Constructed by the Civilian Conservation Corps in 1937, the tower rises high above the forest to give a panoramic view of the surrounding area. It was used by forest service personnel until 1969 to detect forest fires and provide weather data. For Lee Skabelund, who led the effort to preserve, restore, and list the tower in the National Register of Historic Places and open it to visitors, the tower is important for historic and personal reasons. Lee spent his honeymoon at the tower as a brand new forest service employee and claims that every young couple should start their marriage with such beauty and isolation. The tower is located 10 miles south of Manila, off the Sheep Creek Canyon Rd. and west of the Summit Springs Guard Station.

John Jarvie Historic Property—

Obviously Bureau of Land Management officials had a difficult time coming up with a name to describe what is usually called the John Jarvie Ranch. More than a cattle ranch, it was the headquarters for Jarvie's prospecting activities; the location of a general merchandise store and post office, which served the Brown's Park area; a cemetery; and a ferry across the Green River. John Jarvie settled in Brown's Park in 1880 and was well liked by the other residents. A native of Scotland, Jarvie could play the organ and concertina and was in high demand at social functions. But his popularity did not prevent his violent death at the hands of two robbers on July 6, 1909. After shooting Jarvie, the murderers placed his body in a boat and sent it down the Green River, where it was discovered eight days later near the Gates of Lodore, in the eastern end of Brown's Park. The two men were never apprehended. Today the Jarvie Historic Property includes the original two-room dugout in which Jarvie lived; the reconstructed store, which serves as a museum; a stone house built by Jack Bennett, one of Brown's Park's numerous outlaws (but one who was sent to prison where he learned enough masonry skills to erect the house); a blacksmith shop; and a corral built from hand-hewn railroad ties that floated down the Green River from the Union Pacific line. Open every day May–Oct. 10 am–5 pm, with tours available. To reach the property take US Hwy. 191 north to the Utah-Wyoming border, then turn east onto the Clay Basin Rd. and follow it as it heads south through the Jesse Ewing Canyon to the Green River, then follow the road back to the west. The distance from the junction with US Hwy. 191 is 22 miles, including the 2 miles through Jesse Ewing Canyon, where there are steep grades of up to 17 percent.

SCENIC DRIVES

Brown's Park Road Scenic Backway—

The route to the John Jarvie Historic Site via the Clay Basin Rd. is along the Brown's Park Rd. Scenic Backway, which leaves Hwy. 191 5 miles north of Dutch John and descends through the narrow, twisting, winding Jessie Ewing Canyon. After visiting the John Jarvie Historic Site, return to the junction and continue along the road, following the Green River south and eastward into Colorado. A small suspension bridge, which accommodates just one vehicle at a time, allows you to cross the river. You are now in the heart of Brown's Park with all its outlaw lore and history. The road then loops back into Utah and south into Crouse Canyon, as it exits Browns Park. Continuing south up Crouse Canyon, the road passes through vertical cliffs with pine and juniper forests on the side hills before crossing Diamond Mountain and connecting with the Jones Hole Rd. (see the **Roosevelt and Vernal** chapter). Here, you have three options: either follow the Jones Hole Rd. east to its terminus; follow the road southwest into Vernal, where you can return to Dutch John via Hwy. 191; or simply retrace your route back through Brown's Park and on to Dutch John. Throughout your drive, keep an eye out for mule deer, elk, and antelope, which are quite common. The road from Dutch John to the intersection with the Jones Hole Rd. is approximately 50 miles and requires a couple of hours both ways.

Flaming Gorge-Uintas Scenic Byway—

Hwy. 191 is one of two paved roads that bisect the Uinta Mountains. The other route, the Mirror Lake Hwy. (see the **Heber Valley** chapter), covers the western part of the mountains. About 100 miles to the east, Hwy. 191 heads north out of Vernal, across the eastern end of the mountains, to reach Flaming Gorge Reservoir, 45 miles away. The steep climb from Vernal passes through rocks laid down over a billion years ago. A series of 20 interpretive signs point out geological formations along this Drive Through the Ages. The road also offers magnificent views to the south from the switchbacks up the mountain. Once on top, the drive through pine and aspen forests and mountain meadows is an especially refreshing experience in summer. Travelers will want to continue on Hwy. 191 at least to the Flaming Gorge Dam and visitor center before retracing their route back to the junction with Hwy. 44, which skirts Flaming Gorge Reservoir on the east, and then continues north to Manila, 67 miles from Vernal. Along Hwy. 44, stop for a stunning view of Flaming Gorge Reservoir from the Red Canyon Overlook, 4 miles from the junction with Hwy. 191. Eighteen miles from the Red Canyon Overlook is the turnoff to the Sheep Creek Canyon Geologic Area. This 8-mile drive winds its way along a paved road through one of the most scenic canyons of the state.

Sheep Creek/Spirit Lake Loop Backway—

The road through Sheep Creek and the 17-mile drive to Spirit Lake are a designated Scenic Backway, and the 48-mile round-trip drive offers a unique blend of geology and scenery. The Sheep Creek loop is an open book on geology. When volcanic activity along faults beneath the earth's surface created the Uinta Mountains, the northern side of the fault, visible in Sheep Creek Canyon, underwent little vertical movement, but the rock strata were bent up and exposed like ruffled pages of a book. The exposed formations display some primitive marine fossils—trilobites, marine crustaceans, corals, sponges, sea urchins, and other life forms, along with the tracks of crocodilelike reptiles. While the Sheep Creek Loop is across a paved road for the most part, the Spirit Lake portion of the drive is gravel and can become washboarded with heavy use. Nevertheless, this part of the backway is well worth your time, as the beautiful pine and aspen forest and meadows of wildflowers offer a restful contrast to the dramatic geology and sheer walls of Sheep Creek Canyon.

The drive usually takes about 2.5 hours and is located off Hwy. 44, between Manila and the junction with Hwy. 191.

WILDLIFE
Flaming Gorge Lake—

Boaters on the reservoir should keep an eye out for a variety of birds, including ospreys and endangered peregrine falcons. Occasionally bighorn sheep can be seen high in the cliffs around the lake and on Kingfisher Island, which lies between Skull Creek and Hideout Canyon on the northern side of the lake. You might also spot pronghorn antelope, elk, black bears, bobcats, and mountain lions.

Lucerne Peninsula—

The Lucerne Peninsula is located on the northwestern side of Flaming Gorge Reservoir, where there is a high probability for viewing antelope year-round in and near the Lucerne Valley Campground. The wetlands adjacent to the reservoir are home to ducks, geese, herons, egrets, and other waterfowl. Bald eagles can also be seen in the early winter while there is still some open water for them to fish. Lucerne Valley is located about 8 miles from Manila and may be reached by traveling east on Hwy. 43 for 4 miles, then turning southeast onto US Forest Rd. 146 at the Lucerne Valley turnoff and following it 4 miles to the campground.

Sheep Creek—

The Sheep Creek Geological Loop, which may be driven or bicycled, also offers good possibilities for viewing mule deer, elk, moose, and bighorn sheep during the spring, summer, and fall. Sheep Creek itself is a favorite spawning grounds for Kokanee salmon, which can be seen at the mouth of Sheep Creek during Sept. Fishing is prohibited in Sheep Creek during spawning.

WHERE TO STAY

ACCOMMODATIONS

Most people camp at Flaming Gorge, but there are a few motels.

FLAMING GORGE
Flaming Gorge Lodge—$$ to $$$

Flaming Gorge Lodge offers 22 motel rooms and 22 condo units and is the largest motel in the Flaming Gorge area. There is a restaurant at the lodge. Located on Hwy. 191 at Greendale, about 3 miles south of the dam; **(801) 889-3773.**

Red Canyon Lodge—$$ to $$$

Located 3 miles west of the junction of Hwy. 44 and Hwy. 191. The rustic cabins share a central shower house and restroom; deluxe cabins have their own restroom facilities and either a single or double bedroom; and luxury log cabins have two queen beds in a separate bedroom and a pullout couch in the living room. Luxury units also have a kitchenette, vaulted ceilings, and full bathrooms; **(801) 889-3759.**

MANILA
Flaming Gorge Cafe and Bunkhouse—$$ to $$$

Eleven rooms. At the junction of Hwy. 43 and Hwy. 44 in the center of Manila. **Box 220, Manila, UT 84046; (801) 784-3131.**

Niki's—$$

Ten rooms. Located on Hwy. 43 as it enters Manila from the west. **Box 294, Manila, UT 84046; (801) 784-3117.**

Steinakers Motel—$$

Five rooms. On Main St. **Box 194, Manila, UT 84046; (801) 784-3104.**

Vacation Inn—$$

Twenty-two rooms. Located a half mile west of Center St. **Box 306, Manila, UT 84046; (801) 784-3259 or 1-800-662-4327.**

CAMPING
PRIVATE
Flaming Gorge KOA—

With so many public campgrounds, it is not surprising that there is only one private campground in the Flaming Gorge area. Located in Manila, the Flaming Gorge KOA has 40 trailer sites, all with complete hookups, and 25 tent sites. The campground has showers, toilets, a laundry and a dump site. Open mid-April–Nov. Located on Hwy. 42 and 3 West; **(801) 784-3184.**

PUBLIC

Within the Flaming Gorge area there are 22 public campgrounds—13 in the Ashley National Forest and 2 maintained by the Bureau of Land Management in Brown's Park—with a total of more than 800 trailer and tent sites. The two BLM campgrounds, **Bridge Hollow** and **Indian Crossing,** are small, with 12 and 10 trailer and tent sites, respectively. Of the US Forest Service campgrounds, **Arch Dam** is an overflow campground and has no hookups. Water is available as are pit/vault toilets. The largest campground with 147 trailer and tent sites is the **Lucerne Valley Campground,** 8.5 miles east of Manila, off Hwy. 43. Second in size, with 122 sites, is **Antelope Flat,** 11 miles northeast of Dutch John, off Hwy. 191. **Firefighters Memorial,** with 94 tent and 78 trailer sites, is located near Flaming Gorge Dam and provides good access to fishing and boating on the Green River. There are a few small campgrounds. **Greendale** has 7 sites, and **Gooseneck,** on the Flaming Gorge Lake 15 miles southwest of Dutch John, has 6 sites. The public campgrounds usually open some time in May and close during Sept. Because of the 6,000-foot elevation, the recreation season is fairly short, and most campgrounds fill up on summer weekends. During the middle of the week, sites are usually available, but if you want to be sure, reservations for both the **Ashley National Forest** and **Flaming Gorge National Recreation Area** campgrounds can be made by calling **1-800-280-CAMP.**

WHERE TO EAT

Flaming Gorge Lodge—$ to $$
Open for breakfast, lunch, and dinner. Located 3 miles west of the junction of Hwy. 44 and Hwy. 191; **(801) 889-3759.**

Red Canyon Lodge Restaurant—$ to $$
The restaurant is part of the Red Canyon Lodge complex located off Hwy. 44, 3 miles west of the junction of Hwy. 44 and Hwy. 191. Open daily Apr.–Oct. for breakfast, lunch, and dinner; **(801) 889-3759.**

SERVICES

Flaming Gorge Chamber of Commerce—
Box 122, Manila, UT 84046; 784-3483.

Flaming Gorge Dam Visitor Center—
Open daily from Memorial Day–Labor Day, 8 am–6 pm; Labor Day–Oct., 9 am–5 pm; Nov.–Memorial Day, 10 am–4 pm. Closed Thanksgiving, Christmas, and New Years. Books about the area can be purchased at the center.

Red Canyon Visitor Center—
With a spectacular view into Red Canyon, this visitor center is open daily 10 am–5 pm, Memorial Day–Labor Day. A small bookstore is included in the center.

US Forest Service, Flaming Gorge Ranger District—
PO Box 278, Manila, UT 84046; (801) 784-3445.

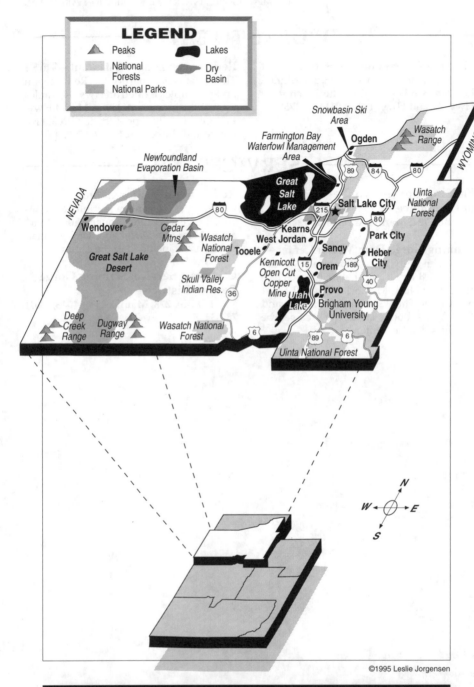

Wasatch Range

WASATCH RANGE

Salt Lake City and Environs

For nearly a century and a half, Salt Lake City boosters have given the title "The Crossroads of the West" to their city. Located in the center of the Intermountain West, Salt Lake City links California and the West with the Great Plains, and the Desert Southwest with the Pacific Northwest. Salt Lake City also sits at the crossroads of the nation's national park system, the hub of a wheel with one Utah national park at the end of each of five spokes as well as spokes that extend to national parks in Nevada, Colorado, Wyoming, and Arizona including Grand Canyon National Park, Great Basin National Park, Mesa Verde National Park, Rocky Mountain National Park, Yellowstone National Park, and Glacier National Park.

Salt Lake City is, however, much more than a place to pass through, as the term "crossroads" may suggest. Since it was founded by Mormon pioneers in 1847, it has been the world headquarters of the Church of Jesus Christ of Latter-day Saints. It is a city that has always known its destiny—to become a religious and spiritual center for people all over the world.

Mormon values have provided a solid foundation for the city and shaped its development in many ways; but Salt Lake City has not grown up in a Mormon vacuum. Many different groups play important roles in the collective life of the city. In addition to the old-world flavor brought by Mormon converts from Great Britain and western Europe, other ethnic groups—Irish-Catholic miners, German-Jewish merchants in the 19th century; Italian, Greek, and Slavic laborers at the beginning of the 20th century; and, more recently, Southeast Asians, Southeast Pacific Islanders, Hispanics, and African-Americans—contribute a richness and vitality.

Salt Lake City serves as the state capital. But long before the capitol was constructed in 1916, the city and the entire valley were laid out from Temple Square in the heart of the downtown area using a grid street system, based on Joseph Smith's plan for the City of Zion. The four streets on each side of the Temple are known as North Temple, West Temple, South Temple, and Main Street—on the east side of the temple. Using the grid system, you can determine where you are in relation to Temple Square by counting the blocks in the address. For example, the University of Utah is located at 1400 East and 200 South, which is 14 blocks east and 2 blocks south of Temple Square. The Wasatch Mountains are to the east, the lower Oquirrh Mountains are to the west, and downtown Salt Lake City is at the north end of the valley. As long as you can see the mountains, you should know in what direction you are headed. In the downtown area there are 6.75 blocks per mile; elsewhere in the valley the ratio is 8 blocks to the mile. The population of the city is approximately 200,000 people, while another 500,000 people live in the valley outside the Salt Lake City limits. The valley is approximately 25 miles long from south to north and 20 miles across from east to west.

The settlement of Salt Lake City has often been compared with the Puritan settlement of Massachusetts two centuries earlier. Both Mormons and Puritans claimed to suffer from unresponsive governments and intolerant circumstances. Responding to God's direction, both fled their familiar homes for the wilderness, where they sought to establish a model society.

Even though today fewer than half the population of the city are active Mormons, the Mormon influence is strongly felt throughout the community and state. As with any community built on religion, tradition, and history, these influences can be both positive and negative. The Mormon foundation, it is argued, helps build close families and good neighborhoods, promotes a positive work ethic, brings economic opportunity, and contributes to a viable community life. On the other hand, Mormons have been criticized as being intolerant and too eager to force their views and lifestyle on others. While both viewpoints are true, Mormons—like all Americans and citizens of the world—are becoming more tolerant. Look for and expect the positive, but be prepared to understand the negative if it arises.

To understand Salt Lake City and its people, a visit to Temple Square is essential. But there is much more to the city than the religious and historic buildings associated with the Mormon faith. Take time to visit the Great Salt Lake. It is a landmark that is still little understood and perhaps under-appreciated by local residents. If you come to Salt Lake City in the winter, chances are you are coming to ski. Utah's majestic mountains, unsurpassed snow conditions, moderately priced lift passes, excellent ski schools, fine accommodations at Snowbird, Alta, and Park City, easy air access, and close proximity of the airport to the ski resorts all make Salt Lake City one of the skiing capitals of the world. But if you come in the summer or fall, the mountains are just as attractive to hikers and sightseers. Enjoy the music and arts of the city. The Utah Symphony performances, free Temple Square concerts, and performances of Ballet West, the Utah Opera Company, and other groups in the restored Capitol Theater are all opportunities to experience the cultural quality of the city.

HISTORY

When Brigham Young and his band of 147 pioneers founded Salt Lake City in July 1847, the area was still Mexican Territory. However, with the end of the Mexican War and the signing of the Treaty of Guadalupe Hidalgo on February 2, 1848, a large area of the Southwest including all of present-day Utah, was ceded to the US. Before the arrival of the Mormons, the Salt Lake Valley had been something of a neutral zone between the Ute Indian tribes living in Utah Valley to the south and the Shoshoni tribe to the north. Before them, the Fremont people had occupied the marshlands around the Great Salt Lake.

Soon after the arrival of the first Mormon group, others quickly followed, as the Mormons completed their exodus from Illinois and Iowa. Converts to the faith also arrived, mostly from Great Britain, Denmark, and Sweden. With Utah as the new Mormon homeland, Salt Lake City became the capital of a region of religious settlements, which ultimately expanded north across the Canadian border and south into Mexico. In directing the settlement of more than 300 town sites in the vast Intermountain West, Brigham Young earned the apt name, "The Great Colonizer." Although Mormons had sought a place of refuge in the wilderness, they were seldom alone. Two years after Salt Lake City was established, the great California gold rush was in full swing. Many 49ers stopped off in Salt Lake City to get supplies and exchange worn-out animals for those that would carry them on to California. A number of them spent the winter in Salt Lake City when it became impossible to complete their journey due to heavy snows. The federal army arrived in 1857 and established a large camp 40 miles south of the city, at Camp Floyd. Although the camp was abandoned at the outbreak of the Civil War in 1861, California Volunteers were sent to Salt Lake City to keep the mail lines open and to keep an eye on the Mormons. These volunteers were veterans of the California gold fields and quickly took up prospecting in Utah's mountains, a practice discouraged by Brigham Young, who wanted to see the Mormons build up their farms and home industry rather than pursue the fickle promises of gold or silver mining. Discoveries were made in the mountains surrounding Salt Lake City, and mining operations were greatly enhanced with the completion of the transcontinental railroad in 1869.

Mining, the railroads, smelting, the military, politics, and merchandising were all factors that brought non-Mormons to Salt Lake City, and they often came into conflict with the Mormon settlers. Following Mormon abandonment of polygamy and separatist politics, statehood was granted to Utah in 1896. Soon after, a public school system was established, and children from all religious backgrounds met on common ground. The communitarian ideas of Joseph Smith and Brigham Young were abandoned and capitalism fully embraced.

Salt Lake City has grown and prospered throughout the 20th century, but like much of the nation, suffered severely during the Great Depression, recovering during World War II, when the defense industry grew. The postwar boom left its mark on a highly urbanized Salt Lake City and suburbanized Salt Lake Valley. Recreation, including the budding ski industry, became more important. New businesses moved into the city. The University of Utah built on its reputation as a research facility and leading medical facility. Technological and environmental issues continued to grow in importance. And Mormons and non-Mormons worked together more effectively for the good of the community.

Today Salt Lake City is a very different city from the one envisioned by the original pioneers. But the seeds they planted have brought forth good fruit and, combined with the contributions of subsequent generations and new arrivals, have made Salt Lake City a special and unforgettable place.

GETTING THERE

Salt Lake City International Airport is only 6 miles from downtown Salt Lake City and is served by nine major airlines and three regional carriers offering more than 500 flights daily. Salt Lake City is a regional hub for Delta airlines, which serves nearly 50 western destinations and connections to most major US cities. The airport has a full range of car rentals, and overnight accommodations are just a few miles away.

Amtrak operates passenger trains out of Salt Lake City. The Amtrak office and station is located in the old Denver and Rio Grande Railroad Station at **300 South 450 West.** For information and schedules call **(801) 364-8562** or **1-800-872-7245.**

Salt Lake City is at the crossroads of Interstate 15, which runs south from Idaho through Utah, Arizona, Nevada and into southern California, and Interstate 80, which runs west from Wyoming through Utah, Nevada, and into northern California.

MAJOR ATTRACTIONS

Great Salt Lake

Award-winning author and naturalist Terry Tempest Williams writes of the Great Salt Lake, "I love this body of water—its paradoxical nature, the way it will not be tamed. ... Great Salt Lake is Trickster. Nothing is as it appears. It is wilderness adjacent to a city; a shifting shoreline that plays havoc with highways; islands too stark, too remote to inhabit; water in the desert that no one can drink. It is the liquid lie of the West." (*Salt Lake Tribune*)

Few Utahns really know the Great Salt Lake. Williams, a descendant of 1847 Mormon pioneers, is one who does. But for most of the million or so people who live within a half hour or less drive to its shores, it is as remote as the most isolated canyons of southern Utah, as distant as the ocean. Although the lake has been visited and admired for nearly two centuries, it remains largely undeveloped. Utahns accept the lake as it is, visitors often wonder why it is so difficult to visit and so unappreciated by locals. Perhaps Williams is right, it will not be tamed, and because it will not be tamed Utahns have learned to live with it by ignoring it. Perhaps the lake is just waiting for a younger generation like Williams' to appreciate, understand, and love it. As urban Utahns look for quality outdoor experiences close to home, the lake seems to beckon with open arms.

The Great Salt Lake is the largest water body between the Great Lakes and the Pacific Ocean. It is also the largest salt lake in the western hemisphere. The lake is a shallow remnant of Lake Bonneville, a large, deep freshwater lake that occupied much of western Utah, but disappeared about 10,000 years ago at the end of the last ice age. The lake is fed by several streams but has no outlet. As a result, the salt content of what was once freshwater has increased over the centuries due to evaporation. The Great Salt Lake is eight times saltier than the ocean and has had a salinity level as high as 27 percent—a level exceeded only by the Dead Sea. Because its dimensions can change drastically as its water rises and falls, it is difficult to give an exact size of the lake. For example, in 1962, the lake elevation was 4,192 feet above sea level, giving it a surface area of 969 square miles. A 20-foot rise in elevation to 4,212 feet above sea level, in the early 1980s, allowed the lake to expand to a surface area of 2,300 square miles. At 4,200 feet above sea level, the lake is approximately 75 miles long and 50 miles wide. Each year two million tons of minerals are added to the lake through erosion and evaporation. In early days, there were rumors of a school of whales living in the lake, but in reality only small brine shrimp and blue-green algae can survive in the lake and a few insects, notably the brine fly, live around the lake. The brine flies are annoying but do not bite. Dead brine shrimp, algae, and vegetation exposed by the ever-changing shoreline are the sources of the sometimes unpleasant odor around the lake, which, when the wind is blowing from the west, spreads across the Salt Lake Valley. The Great Salt Lake supports over 200 different species of birds which use the lake and surrounding land for breeding, migrating, and wintering. A wonderful introduction to the lake and its birdlife is found in Terry Tempest Williams, *Refuge: An Unnatural History of Family and Place,* in which each of the book's 36 chapters is named for a different species of bird associated with the lake.

HISTORY

The freshwater marshes around the lake were used by prehistoric inhabitants as an excellent source of food including ducks and cattails. As early as 1703, reports circulated in Europe about a large body of salt water west of the Mississippi. In 1776 the Dominguez-Escalante Expedition recorded accounts of the lake from the Ute Indians, although they did not journey the 50 miles north from Utah Lake to see it for themselves. Trappers visited the lake in the 1820s, including Jim Bridger, who may have been the first American to see the lake, but was convinced initially that it was an arm of the Pacific Ocean. US Army Captain John C. Fremont explored part of the lake in 1843. Four years later, Mormon pioneers arrived in the uninhabited region. The Mormons initially called their city Great Salt Lake City, but in time it was shortened from four to three words. The lake became a popular recreation spot for early Utahns, and a number of bathing resorts were established along its shores. The largest and most famous was Saltair, which was built in 1893 atop 2,500 piles driven into the lake bed, about three quarters of a mile from the shore. Saltair became known for its roller coaster, wonderful dance floor, and buoyant waters. It closed in 1968, after the receding lake left it high and dry. The beautiful onion-domed pavilion was destroyed by fire two years later. A second Saltair was built, but this time the rising waters of the lake flooded the building. It remained closed until 1993, when it was reopened, a hundred years after the original Saltair was built. The high waters of the 1980s caused by large amounts of snow and rain prompted state government leaders to install a gigantic pump on the west side of the lake to divert water into the desert, away from Interstate 80 around the south end of the lake and the Salt Lake International Airport runways to the east. A few industries have been established along the Great Salt Lake. Each year 400,000 tons of salt, used for everything from table salt to salting icy roads, is harvested from the lake. Also extracted are magnesium, used in structural metal; potash, used as fertilizer; and lithium, used as an alloy in steel.

SEEING AND DOING

Antelope Island—
See the **Ogden** chapter.

Farmington Bay Wildlife Management Area—
Under the administration of the State Division of Wildlife Resources, Farmington Bay is less than a half hour's drive north from downtown Salt Lake City. The marsh was inundated by the Great Salt Lake in the 1980s, but after the lake receded marshlands reestablished themselves and thousands of migrating and resident birds returned. Interpretive activities at the site include identification of and information about the birds, the relationship between the fresh and salt water, and the management of a marsh system. There is an auto tour route you can drive. The area is open daily from 8 am–5 pm. To reach the refuge, take Interstate 15 north to exit 325 and head west across the interstate on State St. to 650 West. Drive south to Glover Ln., then turn west and follow the signs to the Farmington Bay Wildlife Management Area. For information, call **(801) 596-8660.**

South End of the Lake—
To reach the lake from downtown Salt Lake City head west on Interstate 80 about 15 miles and take the Great Salt Lake State Park/Saltair exit (exit 104). At the state park you can wade in the shallow waters, swim, or go for a 20-minute speedboat tour of the lake. The newly reopened **Saltair Resort** hosts concerts, dances, and parties on most weekends. For event information, call **(801) 250-4400.**

Temple Square

Each year Temple Square receives more visitors by far than any other attraction in Utah. Its location in the heart of downtown Salt Lake City makes it easy to get to, and there is plenty to do when you arrive. Temple Square is the Mormon Mecca, and while the religion does not require the faithful to make a pilgrimage to this particular temple, most do. In Mormon theology, the temple serves as the holy place in which sacred ordinances or rituals for individuals, ancestors, and living families are performed. Among these are marriages, and you are likely to see young couples in wedding attire having their pictures taken on the temple steps following their marriage ceremony.

Because of the sacred nature of the temples, only members of the Mormon faith in good standing are permitted inside; however, visitors are welcome inside all the other buildings. Expect to be asked by guides if you would like a tour of the square and a brief explanation of the history and doctrine of the Church of Jesus Christ of Latter-day Saints. These **tours** are well worth the time because they not only provide basic information, but allow you to meet a committed Mormon. Many of the guides are young, former missionaries, whose have been engaged full-time for two years seeking converts in almost every country in the world. Missionaries work together in pairs, are often easily recognizable by their dark suits, white shirts, and short haircuts on the males. The missionaries themselves or their families pay the expenses for the two years they are "in the mission field." In recent years, more and more young women and retired couples have been sent out as missionaries. At times the missionaries and guides are guilty of overzealousness in their efforts to teach non-members the Mormon religion.

The Salt Lake Temple was one of the major reasons so many thousands of Mormon converts came to Utah from England and Europe during the century between 1850 and 1950; but with the construction of temples around the world, members are now encouraged to remain in their homelands to "build up the Kingdom" there rather than emigrate to Utah.

The site for the Salt Lake Temple was selected by Brigham Young four days after the Mormons arrived in the Salt Lake Valley in July 1847. A 10-acre block was set aside for the temple, and construction began in 1853 after plans were prepared by Truman O. Angell, based on a sketch given him by Brigham Young. For various reasons, the temple was not completed until 1893, while three other temples were completed and in use in St. George, Manti, and Logan. Temporary buildings were constructed and used, and the famous tabernacle, used for services and meetings open to everyone, was completed in 1867.

Temple Square itself has five buildings that you will want to visit: the **temple**, the **tabernacle**, the **Assembly Hall**, and the north and south **visitor centers.** In addition there are several monuments on the square: one dedicated to Joseph Smith, another to the handcart pioneers, and yet another to the seagulls, which saved early Mormon crops from infestation by crickets. Just outside the square, to the east, is the **Brigham Young Monument**, which was first erected in 1897 during the 50th anniversary of the Mormon arrival in Utah. It was moved north from the intersection of South Temple and Main Street in 1993 to provide better traffic flow through the intersection.

Plan also to extend your visit to the blocks to the east and west of Temple Square. On the east block is located the **Joseph Smith Memorial Building,** formerly the Hotel Utah; the **Church Administration Building;** the newer 26-story **Church Office Building; Relief Society Building;** and **Brigham Young's Beehive and Lion House.** On the west block, facing Temple Square, is the **Family History Library,** where genealogists come from all over the world to do research; the **Museum of Church History and Art;** and the **Osmyn Deuel Log Cabin.** Since you will need lunch if you are spending the entire day, consider the **Lion House Pantry** (see the Where to Eat section), the **Garden**

Restaurant located on the top floor in the Joseph Smith Memorial Building (see the Buildings section), or one of the food courts in the **Crossroads Mall** and **ZCMI Center,** located across the street, south of Temple Square.

Depending on your schedule, you may want to arrange your visit around one of the following events.

EVENTS AND ACTIVITIES

LDS Church General Conference

Twice a year, the first weekends in Apr. and Oct., church leaders and members of the LDS Church convene in the Salt Lake Tabernacle for the semiannual conference. Sessions are held in the tabernacle on Sat. and Sun. mornings and afternoons. No church services are held in the meeting houses throughout Utah and surrounding states, and members are encouraged to listen to or watch live broadcasts in their own homes. This is an especially busy time on Temple Square, and unless you come with the express purpose of attending the conference (possible, if you are willing to wait in long lines for the limited public seating that is available), these are two weekends during the year that the casual traveler may wish to avoid.

Mormon Tabernacle Choir Broadcast

Perhaps as famous as Temple Square itself is the Mormon Tabernacle Choir, which traces its beginnings back to 1849, when Brigham Young invited John Parry, the leader of a recently arrived group of Welsh converts, to organize a choir for the next general conference. This choir became the nucleus from which developed the Mormon Tabernacle Choir. Today, members of the choir come from all walks of life to volunteer their time and talents. As worldwide ambassadors of the LDS Church, the members are selected on the basis of character and musical competence. The choir made its first recording in 1910. Since then millions of records, tapes, and compact discs have been sold. On July 15, 1929, the choir made its first radio broadcast of what is now the oldest continuous nationwide network broadcast in America. The weekly broadcast is released worldwide to nearly 1,000 radio and television stations. The half-hour broadcast begins at 9:30 am on Sun. mornings. To attend the live performance of the choir in the tabernacle you must be seated by 9:15 am, so plan to arrive early. Babies and small children are not permitted in the tabernacle during the broadcast. In addition to the selections by the choir, a brief "Spoken Word" is given, which touches on universal Christian and humanitarian themes.

Mormon Tabernacle Choir Rehearsal

The choir rehearses on most Thurs. evenings throughout the year and the tabernacle is open to the public from 8 pm–9:30 pm. You can come and go as you please. The rehearsals provide not only a chance to hear the magnificent music but to become better acquainted with the personality of the choir and its conductor. When possible, I like to take guests to Temple Square on a Thurs. evening for the rehearsal and return Sun. morning for the broadcast.

Mormon Tabernacle Organ Recitals

One of the world's magnificent organs, the Mormon Tabernacle Organ, is outfitted with 11,000 pipes, which form a dramatic backdrop at the west end of the hall. They are accessible through the five ranks of keyboards and numerous stops at the organ console. Free organ recitals are offered May–Sept., Mon.–Fri. at noon and at 4 pm. Sat. and Sun. recitals are at 4 pm.

Mormon Youth Symphony and Chorus Rehearsals

On most Tues. evenings, the Mormon Youth Symphony rehearses in the tabernacle, and on Wed. evenings the Mormon Youth Chorus holds forth. These rehearsals are open to the general public from 8 pm–9:30 pm.

Temple Square Christmas Lights

From the Fri. after Thanksgiving through New Year's Day, Temple Square is decorated with thousands of Christmas lights and a nativity scene. It seems like every Utah family makes an evening visit to Temple Square during the Christmas season to see the lights. This is a special time on Temple Square, and if you have the opportunity, don't miss it.

Temple Square Concert Series

On most Fri. and Sat. evenings at 7:30 pm you can attend a free concert in the Assembly Hall. There is a wide variety of instrumental and vocal performances throughout the year with choirs, chamber music, vocal, and instrumental soloists. Call **(801) 240-3318** for information about upcoming concerts and special events.

BUILDINGS

Assembly Hall

This Victorian Gothic–style chapel was designed by Obed Taylor and built on the southwest corner of Temple Square between 1877 and 1882. The spires, though lower, offer a nice balance to the larger temple located on the opposite corner of the square. Smaller in size than the huge tabernacle, the hall is ideal for smaller functions such as the weekend concert series.

Beehive House, Lion House, Brigham Young's Office, and Eagle Gate

This complex along South Temple is what remains of Brigham Young's estate. The earliest building, Brigham Young's small office, was built in 1852 and is located between the larger Beehive House and Lion House. The Beehive House, named for the beehive that adorns the roof as a symbol of

activity and industry, was constructed of adobe between 1853 and 1854. It is open for free **guided tours** daily from 9:30 am–4:30 pm, except Sun., when the hours are 10 am–1 pm. The Lion House, constructed the year after the Beehive House in 1855, housed most of Brigham Young's 26 wives and 56 children. Not open for tours, you can see part of the house if you eat lunch in the **Lion House Pantry**. East of the houses, spanning State Street, is the **Eagle Gate**. The gate has been enlarged several times since my great-grandfather, Ralph Ramsay, a handcart pioneer from England, carved the original eagle atop the gate in 1859. It can be seen in the **Pioneer Memorial Museum** at **200 North Main St.**

Church Administration Building

The gray granite Greek Revival–style Church Administration Building, at 47 East South Temple—an address as famous to

Mormons as 10 Downing St. to the British—was completed in 1917 and houses the offices of the general authorities of the LDS Church. The lobby has walls of polished marble. The building was constructed as an expression of both stability and respectability by early 20th-century church leaders.

Church Office Building

Utah's tallest building, the 26-story Church Office Building was built between 1969 and 1972 and houses most of the auxiliary and departmental organizations of the Mormon Church. The building is not without controversy, as some argue that it overshadows the historic temple too much, leaving the impression of a church more concerned about its bureaucracy than the spiritual needs of the members. Be that as it may, the building offers a wonderful view of the Salt Lake Valley from the **top-floor observation deck** which is open to the public.

Family History Library

The world's largest genealogical library is located in downtown Salt Lake City, on the west side of Temple Square, at **35 North West Temple.** The LDS Family History Library is open to the public. On your first visit to the library, take a few minutes to view the **video presentation**. It will acquaint you with the five-story library's mission and resources. Also pick up the **free booklet** "A Guide to Research" to help you get started. Briefly, Mormons believe that all persons, whether living or dead, will have the opportunity to hear the full Gospel of Jesus Christ and accept or reject Christ as their Savior. Because certain "saving" ordinances (such as baptism) must be performed here on earth even for the deceased, Mormons have identified the names of dead ancestors and have acquired copies (often through a cooperative microfilm programs) of church, civic, and other records from around the world to help identify all those who have and are living on the earth. These records are open to anyone, and genealogists and historians are able to use records in the Family History Library,

which otherwise, would be very difficult to locate and obtain access for personal and scholarly use. Furthermore, trained staff are available on each floor to answer questions and assist in using the collected records. Inquire about the daily classes. Each month features **classes** on a different area of research. The library is open Mon. 7:30 am–6 pm, Tues.–Fri. 7:30 am–10 pm, and Sat. 7:30 am–5 pm. For further information call **(801) 240-2331.** Be sure to ask about the free parking.

Joseph Smith Memorial Building

Constructed as the Hotel Utah in 1911, this building was designed to provide visitors to the city with first-class accommodations, a function it performed admirably until Aug.1987 when it closed to undergo renovation for adaptive reuses. It is now used for offices, banquet, reception and meeting rooms, a chapel, restaurants, and houses the 500-seat Legacy Theater. A **53-minute dramatic film,** "Legacy," is shown in the theater. The film depicts the trials and triumphs of the Mormon people, from the founding of the Church in 1830 to the eve of Utah's statehood in 1896. Admission is free. There are several showings daily, beginning at 9:00 am. The Grand Lobby, which was the most impressive feature of the old hotel, has been restored to its original elegance. During the Hotel Utah days, the **Roof Restaurant** was one of the most popular eating places in Utah for special occasions. It has been reopened for dinner from 5 pm–10 pm and features a gourmet buffet and a panoramic view of Temple Square below. The **Garden Restaurant,** located on the south end of the top floor and more moderately priced, is open from 11 am–10 pm. Both are open daily, except Sun.

Mormon Handicraft Store

Occupying the northwest corner of the intersection, kitty-corner from the Relief Society Building, the original Mormon Handicraft Store was organized by the Relief Society during the Great Depression as a consignment outlet, offering women a means of both supplementing the family income and preserving pioneer arts. That tradition continues, as Mormon Handicraft carries almost 10,000 items made by close to 2,000 women. Craft demonstrations are also held in the store, including weekly quilting classes taught by master quilters. Mormon quilts are famous and are highly desired collector's items. If you are looking for a lasting and meaningful souvenir, pay a visit to Mormon Handicraft at **105 North Main St.**, open Mon.–Fri. from 9 am–10 pm during the summer and 9 am–9 pm the rest of the year. Sat hours are 9 am–6 pm; **(801) 355-2141.**

Museum of Church History and Art

Mormons have always had a sense of history. This has left Utah with a tremendous collection of diaries, artifacts, and works of art, which have been used to great advantage by a professional museum staff in the Museum of Church History and Art. The 1983 museum includes a scale model of Salt Lake City in 1870, covered wagon, an immigrant ship's bunk, and exhibits that focus on events and developments in LDS Church history from Utah and around the world. There is something for everyone in the museum, with free audio tours, multimedia programs, films, puppet shows, and children's activities. Located at **45 North West Temple,** open Mon.–Fri. 9 am–9 pm, Sat., Sun., and holidays from 10 am–7 pm; **(801) 240-3310.**

Relief Society Building

Occupying the southeast corner of the intersection of Main St. and West Temple, the Relief Society Building was built in 1956 and houses one of the most important institutions of the Mormon religion. The Women's Relief Society was organized in 1842 in Nauvoo, Illinois, under the direction of Joseph Smith, as a charitable, educational, and religious sisterhood. Once in Utah, the Relief Society built its own halls and granaries, in which were stored wheat and grain that had been harvested by the women for distribution or sale for charitable purposes. This tradition is symbolized by the ornamental wheat stocks on the front of the Relief Society Building. The Relief Society had its own publication and many of its early leaders, including Eliza R. Snow, were active in the women suffrage movement. The Relief Society continues to be one of the foundations of the Mormon religion, as women look to the needs and welfare of both members and nonmembers in the neighborhoods and communities throughout Utah and other places.

Salt Lake Tabernacle

Built between 1864 and 1867, the Salt Lake Tabernacle is one of the most finely engineered, interesting architectural structures to be found anywhere. The tabernacle was constructed under the direction of Henry Grow, with later modifications to the interior made by temple architect, Truman O. Angell. The long, low-arching dome rests on 44 sandstone pillars. A 10-foot-thick wooden arch rests on each of the 44 pillars. These arches are braced by latticelike cross-members that were originally fastened with wooden pins and rawhide thongs. The lattice truss arch roof system displays a unique engineering system that has been documented as part of the Historic American Engineering Record. The tabernacle is 250 feet long and 150 feet wide, with a seating capacity of approximately 8,000, including both the floor and balcony areas. The original tabernacle organ contained 700 pipes, but it has since been expanded to 11,000—some as small as three-eighths of an inch and the largest 32 feet in length. Be sure to attend one of the musical performances noted previously to experience the wonderful acoustics of this historic building. It has been said, and proven, that you can hear a pin dropped in one end of the hall at the other end.

Salt Lake Temple

The Salt Lake Temple, with its famous six spires, took 40 years to complete (1853–1893) and is a worldwide symbol of the Mormon faith. The east tower rises 210 feet from the ground with the 12.5-foot, gold-leaf-covered statue of the Angel Moroni, (the compiler of the Book of Mormon who returned to earth as an angel to pass the holy scripture on to Joseph Smith) standing atop the center tower. The temple is 186.5 feet long and 118 feet wide. The 167.5-foot-high walls were only 20 feet high when Brigham Young died in 1877. Although access to the interior of the building is restricted, visitors can marvel at the unique design and craftsmanship in this building, especially the native granite of which it is made, which was hauled by ox team from the quarry in Little Cottonwood Canyon, about 15 miles to the southeast. Several books have been published about the temple, the most recent of which include photographs of the interior. They are C.

Mark Hamilton's, *The Salt Lake Temple: Monument to a People*, Richard Neitzel Holzapfel's, *Every Stone a Sermon: The Magnificent Story of the Construction and Dedication of the Salt Lake Temple;* and Nelson B. Wadsworth's, *Set in Stone, Fixed in Glass: The Great Mormon Temple and Its Photographers*. Ask about these books at the museum bookstore, or at Deseret Bookstore, one of the most complete bookstores in the downtown area, located across the street south of the Beehive House in the ZCMI Mall.

Visitors Centers

Located at the north and south entrances to Temple Square, the modern visitors centers offer a good introduction to the religion of the Latter-day Saints through pamphlets, displays, films, and other media. Be sure to visit the north visitor center to see the wonderful replica of the Christus Statue by Danish sculptor Bertel Thorvaldsen.

─── OTHER ATTRACTIONS ───

University of Utah

Utah's largest public institution of higher education, with approximately 27,000 full-time students, the University of Utah was originally established by Mormon pioneers as the University of Deseret in 1850. With the approach of statehood, the name of the institution was changed to the University of Utah in 1894. The federal government gave 60 acres from Fort Douglas as a new campus site on the east bench of Salt Lake City. Classes opened at the new campus in October 1900, and the campus has now expanded to 1,400 acres. Utah's only medical school is located at the University of Utah. The medical center has

received worldwide recognition, especially in the research and development of artificial organs. Two popular museums on the campus are the **Museum of Fine Art** and **the Museum of Natural History** (see the Museum section). Other popular activities include football and basketball games, gymnastics meets featuring the **Lady Ute Gymnastic Team** (perennially one of the top two or three gymnastic programs in the nation), concerts at the University's **Jon Huntsman Special Events Center,** and theatrical productions at the **Pioneer Memorial Theatre, Kingsbury Hall, and Babcock Theatre.** For general information, call **(801) 581-7200.**

FESTIVALS AND EVENTS

Asian Festival
2nd Saturday in May

Since 1978, Utah's Asian communities have united to sponsor one of the most interesting and unique cultural events in Salt Lake City. Usually held the 2nd Sat. in May, the festival includes booths, food, fashions, and music and dance by Utah immigrants from Mongolia, India, China, Tibet, Japan, Korea, Thailand, Vietnam, Laos, the Philippines, and Polynesia. The assortment of foods, the variety of dances, and the opportunity to share it all with neighbors from around the world make this a special event.

Living Traditions Festival
3rd weekend in May

This celebration of Salt Lake City's folk and ethnic arts is a joint project of the Salt Lake City Arts Council and the Folk Arts Program of the Utah Arts Council. Music, dance, crafts, and foods are the ingredients that make this Salt Lake City's most popular spring festival. Nearly 20 different ethnic groups have food booths offering everything from Native American to Palestinian to Vietnamese delicacies. The music and folk dancing performances are even more diverse, with 40 different groups performing on two different stages. The festival is held on the grounds of the historic Salt Lake City and County Building, which make an ideal setting for the event. The stages are located on the south and the north sides of the massive building and are usually staggered just enough to allow festival goers to walk to the other side of the building for the performances. The groups change each year, although some have performed nearly every year since the first festival in 1986. The countries and cultures represented include: the Philippines, Mexico, the Ukraine, Vietnam, Korea, Germany, Tonga, Samoa, Switzerland, Peru, Argentina, India, Greece, Lebanon, Scotland, Thailand, Russia, England, Africa, the Basque area of France/Spain, and the Jewish culture. The festival is usually held the 3rd weekend in May. For information, call **(801) 533-5760.**

Scottish Festival and Highland Games
2nd Saturday in June

Utah has a substantial Scottish population and each year, under the sponsorship of the Utah Scottish Association, Scottish groups and families from all over the state get together at historic Fort Douglas, usually on the 2nd Sat. in June, to celebrate the Scottish heritage with music, dance, lore, booths, and athletic contests. The Utah festival is founded in Scottish antiquity dating back at least to the reign of King Malcolm in the 11th century. Originally the games were competitions among clans. Today they involve individuals and bands, but clans such as McAllisters, McDougal MacDuff, MacFie, McKay, and others occupy the north side of the Fort Douglas parade ground with tents and booths. On the south side vendors offer just about anything you could want from Scotland. Drum and bagpipe bands compete individually and join together for a spectacular march down the parade ground. Usually held at noon, and as part of the closing ceremony at 4:30 pm, this is an event not to be missed. Folk singers and groups perform traditional Scottish and Irish music. Children's dance competitions and games are a joy to watch. Traditional skills of strength and balance are tested with the stone put, hammer toss, weight tosses for distance and height, and the traditional caber toss where contestants balance a 20-foot or longer pole cupped in their hands and then toss the 100- or more pound pole (the "caber" in Gaelic) as far and as straight as they can. It is the next best thing to being in Scotland. For information call **(801) 571-6212** or contact **Richard D. Barnes, Utah Scottish Association, 389 West 100 South, Bountiful, UT 84010, (801) 295-5762.**

Gina Bachauer International Piano Competition

mid-June

For two weeks in mid-June, the Gina Bachauer International Piano Competition is held as pianists from around the world compete for thousands of dollars in prize money, a Steinway grand piano, and recording and concert contracts that could, in the tradition of a Van Cliburn, skyrocket them into worldwide fame. If you are a classical music lover, this is a great opportunity to enjoy performances by pianists who will likely be the stars of tomorrow. The competition involves about 60 pianists selected from several hundred applicants. In the preliminary rounds, pianists play two 15-minute programs and 20 are selected as quarterfinalists and play a concerto with piano accompaniment. The 10 semifinalists play a 50-minute solo recital, and the 6 finalists play a concerto with the Utah Symphony in a two-night event that ends the competition. For information and ticket prices call **(801) 533-NOTE.**

Slavic Festival

3rd weekend of June

Utah has had a small but significant Slavic population for nearly a century, since the first groups of single men from Croatia, Serbia, Slovakia, and Slovenia arrived to work in the smelters at the copper and coal mines. Under the sponsorship of the Zivio Ethnic Arts Ensemble, the Slavic Festival has expanded to include representatives from Russia, the Ukraine, Poland, Bulgaria, the former Czechoslovakia, and the provinces of the former Yugoslavia. The festival has been held annually since 1983 on the 3rd weekend in June, with Sat. designated as Slavic American Heritage Day in Utah. There is plenty of food from the Slavic countries but it is the music that keeps visitors there for hours. With three live performances going on at the same time in separate locations, you could listen to a native of Czechoslovakia accompany himself on the guitar and sing romantic songs of his homeland in an intimate setting; watch the Zivio Ethnic Arts Ensemble perform native dances and play and sing music from the Balkans on ethnic instruments; or dance the polka to the music of one of the best polka bands around, the Rocky Mountain Polka Express. Since 1993, the festival has been held at the Utah Center Plaza in downtown Salt Lake City.

Utah Arts Festival

end of June

Since its establishment in 1976, the Utah Arts Festival has become Utah's largest and longest-running gathering of artists. The festival is held at the west end of South Temple, which is blocked off to automobile traffic between the Union Pacific Railroad Station and 300 West St. and the Triad and Delta centers. The five-day event begins on Wednesday and runs through the last weekend in June. Exhibitions are held in the historic Union Pacific Railroad Station, which highlight the work of new and emerging artists as well as under-exhibited artists. Festival goers will also enjoy the wide variety of entertainment by more than 50 musical groups, artistic demonstrations, an artists marketplace, and food booths. The literary arts are also represented with a book fair and book signings by Utah authors. Separate children's programs are offered, with a special family admission designed to encourage parents to bring their children to the festival. The activities run from noon–midnight each day, except Sun., when the festival ends at 10 pm. For more information, call **(801) 322-2428.**

WestFest International

last week in June

This popular community celebration in West Valley City attracts more than 30,000 people each year. Held at the **Granger Park, 3500 South and 3600 West,** the festival includes, amusement rides, food booths, children's games, a mountain man village, arts and crafts, demonstrations, and entertainment. WestFest is held the last week in June on Thurs., Fri., and Sat. Sat. events include a 6-kilometer run, a parade from the Valley Fair Mall to Granger Park, and fireworks at night. For information, call **(801) 963-3600.**

Days of '47
mid-July

Ask any Utah Mormon what, next to Christmas, is the state's most important holiday and chances are he or she will say the 24th of July. This was the day that the vanguard of Mormon pioneers under the leadership of Brigham Young arrived in the Salt Lake Valley. Also known as Pioneer Day, the event has been celebrated in one way or another since 1848. It is a state holiday, and many Utah communities hold special celebrations. In Salt Lake City, the big event is the 24th of July Pioneer Parade, one of the largest and oldest in the US. The parade includes approximately 300 floats and groups and many parade goers make it a ritual to sleep out the night before to secure a viewing spot. This is not necessary, though, unless you want to join in the all-night festivities. I've been able to go down two or three hours before the parade and find a good spot. Two other parades are held in connection with the Days of '47: a horse parade with more than 1,200 horses is held the week before the 24th, and a children's parade—reportedly the largest children's parade in the country with more than 4,000 children mostly dressed in pioneer costumes— is held the Sat. morning before Pioneer Day. Other activities on Pioneer Day include the 26.2-mile-long Deseret News Marathon and a 10K race. The marathon begins at 5:15 am in the mountains above Salt Lake City and follows part of the original pioneer route down Emigration Canyon. The mountain course takes its toll on runners and is not one on which you should expect to set a personal best time. The last segment of the races follows the parade route, providing a large audience to watch and cheer on the runners. Another morning option is the sunrise service at 7:00 am in the Salt Lake

Tabernacle, which features selections by the Mormon Tabernacle Choir and an address by one of the Elders of the Church. An eight-day World Champion Rodeo concludes on the evening of July 24. Firework displays all over the valley are an appropriate ending to the celebration. For information, contact the **Salt Lake Convention and Visitors Bureau** at **(801) 521-2822.**

Summerfest International Arts and Folk Festival
2nd week in August

Since 1989 the Bountiful/Davis Art Center has sponsored this festival that attracts dance groups and musicians from a dozen or more countries around the world. The festival is usually held the second week in Aug. Throughout the week performances are scheduled from Ogden on the north to Bountiful on the south. A highlight is the Parade of Nations down Bountiful's Main St. on Thurs. evening. Performances are held in the Bountiful Park (**400 North and 200 West**) all day on Fri. and Sat. and from noon–5 pm on Sun. During the day, each group performs for approximately 30 minutes during the day and for 10 minutes in the evening. Utah artists join in the festival with booths and exhibits. Ethnic and American food is also served. Admission to the parade and the opening ceremonies on Thurs. evening is free. Otherwise admission fee charged. For information, call **(801) 292-0367.**

Utah State Fair
beginning of September

Sept. is the fair month in Utah, with the Utah State Fair running for 10 days, usually from the first Fri. in the month through the next Sun. Judging by the crowds at the fair, it seems that every Utahn attends at least one day of the fair and for many reasons. There is plenty to see and do with countless exhibits, contests, shows and demonstrations, livestock auctions, carnival rides, a rodeo, horse show, music competition, and live entertainment nightly. The fairgrounds are located at **1000 West and North Temple** streets. Wonderful turn-of-the-century fair buildings have been restored and are listed in the National Register of Historic Places. For information, call **(801) 538-8440.**

Greek Festival
1st weekend after Labor Day

If you are in Salt Lake City the 1st weekend after Labor Day, don't miss the annual Greek Festival at the historic Holy Trinity Greek Orthodox Church at **300 South and 300 West**. Begun in 1976, it has become one of the most popular of all festivals in Salt Lake City. The festival begins at 11 am on Fri. and runs until Sun. evening. Almost the entire downtown community comes to the festival for lunch on Fri., so expect long lines from about 11:30 am–2 pm. But the *dolmathes, fasolakia, pilafi, pastitsio, spanakopites, stifatho, souvlakia, gyros*, and Greek chicken make any wait worthwhile. Even longer lines seem to form for honey-sweetened Greek pastries, such as *baklava*, made from recipes brought by immigrant Greek women to Utah. The Greek Orthodox community of the Salt Lake Valley spends nearly all year preparing for the festival, and almost as impressive as the food is the cheerful efficiency with which the well-trained volunteers carry out their assignments. In addition to the food, festival visitors can participate in traditional Greek dances, attend cooking demonstrations, listen to a Byzantine choir program, watch a slide presentation on the history of Greek immigration to Utah, visit the first Greek museum in the US, and tour the historic church.

Ceilidh Scottish Festival
last weekend in October

This small weekend festival grows larger every year. It is held at the First Pres-byterian Church on **347 East South Temple** the last weekend in Oct. The Ceilidh (pronounced Kay-lee) is a Scottish festival featuring a traditional Scottish feast, dart tournaments, highland dancing, and other Scottish entertainment, including bagpipes. The Kirkin'o'th' Tartan representatives from the various Scottish clans are present and greetings are brought from the Queen of Britain by the British consul general. Some say the Kirkin' has its roots in Scottish history, when the wearing of the tartan was outlawed in 1745 by the British crown, and some clansmen began to carry swatches of the material concealed under their clothes. During church services, the clergymen would give a blessing, the clansmen would touch the hidden tartan and, with no outward sign, an underground Kirkin' occurred. However, the first modern Kirkin' service was probably held in Washington's New York Avenue Presbyterian Church in 1941. Since that time, Kirkin' ceremonies have been held throughout the US. While attending the festival, plan to tour the English-Scottish Gothic Revival–style building, built from red sandstone quarried in Red Butte Canyon. The cornerstone was laid in 1903. For additional information, call the church office at **(801) 363-3889.**

Dickens Christmas Festival
day after Thanksgiving–Christmas

This Christmas festival began in 1981 and has grown to become one of Utah's most popular Christmas activities. With more than 100 shops, plenty of food, and live continuous entertainment on three stages, the Utah State Fair Park is transformed into a beehive of Christmas activity from the day after Thanksgiving–Christmas. For information, call **(801) 350-7586.**

OUTDOOR ACTIVITIES

FISHING

East Canyon Reservoir and State Park—

Located just 28 miles northeast of Salt Lake City, East Canyon Reservoir is an extremely popular recreation site for fishermen, boaters, and water-skiers from the Salt Lake Valley. The first dam was constructed in 1896 at Red Rock Gorge from rock with a plate steel core to store irrigation water for downstream users in Weber and Davis counties. Between 1915 and 1916, an arched reinforced concrete dam was constructed below the site of the original dam. The third, and present, dam was constructed in 1964 downstream from the other two structures. Built as part of the Weber Basin Reclamation Project, the dam is 260 feet high and 440 feet wide at the crest. The reservoir was formed over about 6 miles of the Mormon Trail, which followed East Canyon Creek south before ascending Big Mountain, where the pioneers had their first glimpse of the Salt Lake Valley. In 1967, East Canyon State Park was established along the shores of the reservoir. Included within the state park are a number of picnic tables and, at the north end of the lake, 31 camping units with showers, modern restrooms, and drinking water. Another 100 tent sites are located within the state park. There are a store, snack bar, and boat rentals at the north end marina. Fees are charged for camping and day use within the state park. Winter activities include ice fishing, cross-country skiing, and snowmobiling. The reservoir is accessible by two all-weather routes, which depart from Interstate 84: state Hwy. 66 southeast from Morgan and state Hwy. 65 south from Henefer. The shortest route from Salt Lake City—state Hwy. 65—heads north from Interstate 80 in Parley's Canyon. The climb over Big Mountain is made by a series of switchbacks; however, the picturesque and historic route along the old Mormon Trail is closed during the winter. Campground reservations can be made by calling locally **(801) 322-3770** or long distance **1-800-322-3770**.

GOLF

Bonneville Golf Course—

Situated on the east bench of Salt Lake City, just south of the University of Utah, and among one of the valley's most exclusive older residential areas, the Bonneville Golf Course has been a long-time favorite for many Salt Lake golfers. The course has a good combination of difficult and easy holes, with most locations offering a beautiful view of the valley. The course is located at **954 Connor St.** and can be reached by turning south onto the first street (Connor St.) after crossing the intersection of Sunnyside Ave. and Foothill Dr. (approximately 850 South and 2100 East), as you head east on Sunnyside Ave.; **(801) 596-5041**.

Bountiful Golf Course—

This beautifully landscaped, well-maintained course, located high up on the west slope of the mountains north of Salt Lake City, offers a spectacular view of the Davis County cities of Bountiful, Centerville, Farmington, and Woodscross, snuggled between the expansive Great Salt Lake and the Wasatch Mountains. While the course is challenging, with plenty of oak brush and trees to claim errant shots, the fairways seem to be wider and more inviting than other mountain courses in the state. With the mountain terrain as a factor, each hole is different. This municipal course is best reached from Salt Lake City by driving north on Interstate 15 to the Woodscross exit 318, where you head east through the intersection to Orchard Dr. Turn north and follow Orchard Dr. to 1800 South. Head east up the mountain, until just before you start into the canyon (Mueller Park) then turn south on Bountiful Blvd. to 2430 South. For reservations, call **(801) 298-6040**.

Forest Dale Golf Course—

There are a lot of reasons to recommend the Forest Dale Course, not the least of which is that it is the oldest existing golf course in Utah. Built in 1906, it was acquired by Salt Lake City in 1924 and has been open to the public ever since. One of the nice features of the course is the historic clubhouse, which is no longer in use, but there is a strong neighborhood movement to have it restored. In 1906, the course was on the outskirts of Salt Lake City, but today the course is located in a well-established neighborhood that has been bisected by Interstate 80. On the south side of the interstate is the golf course, and on the north side is Fairmont Park. But even though the interstate parallels the left side of the first hole, it is located high above the golf course and generally screened by trees, so there is relatively little noise. The course was renovated in the mid-1980s; new tee areas and berms and mounds were added to give more contour to what was formerly a flat and level course. Located at **2375 South and 900 East,** Forest Dale is one of the closest courses to the downtown area. For reservations, call **(801) 483-5420.**

Mountain Dell Golf Course—

The closest mountain golf course to Salt Lake City, Mountain Dell is located off Interstate 80 just 15 minutes up Parley's Canyon. In 1991, Mountain Dell became the only 36-hole course in the state. The Canyon Course has 13 of the original Mountain Dell holes, while the Lake Course has one of the most unforgettable holes you will ever play. Mountain Dell is usually open from mid-Apr.–mid-Nov. and is a special favorite during the hot days of summer when the temperature at Mountain Dell is usually about 10 degrees lower than at the courses in the Salt Lake Valley. Another attraction is the wildlife. Deer are commonly seen and, in the fall, a large herd of elk frequent the course. One day in Oct., when I was at the course, a moose had just left the number one tee box on the Canyon Course. The courses are surrounded by the Wasatch Mountains, with the 5th and 6th holes on the Lake Course located near the last campsite for the 1847 Mormon Pioneers before they ascended Little Mountain and into the Salt Lake Valley. You can make reservations for either course by calling the Salt Lake City automated reservation system at **(801) 972-7888.**

Mountain View Golf Course—

Mountain View is a most appropriate name for this golf course. From anywhere on the course, you can look to the east and see the magnificent Wasatch Mountains 8 miles away. The view of the mountains is unsurpassed anywhere else in the Salt Lake Valley, and it is worth the price of the green fees just to walk around the course gazing at the fortress of mountains across the valley. As a golf course, Mountain View is a flat, easy-to-play course, with few obstacles and wide fairways. Indeed, with the view of the mountains, lush lawn, minimal trees, and fairways the width of alfalfa fields, it is easy to lose one's concentration on golf. For an urban course, noise is at a minimum here, which, along with the breathtaking view of the mountains and ease of play, makes this one of my favorites. Located at **2400 West and 8660 South; (801) 255-9211.**

Wingpointe Golf Course—

This golf course caters to both local golfers and air travelers. If you have a couple hours layover at the airport, walk or take a taxi there and either hit a bucket of balls or play 9 or 18 holes. The clubhouse is well stocked with rental clubs, but if you just want to hit a bucket of balls the accommodating clubhouse personnel will loan you a club or two at no charge. The course is a Scottish links–style course with no trees, but plenty of water. Wingpointe is located at **3600 West and 100 North,** just off Interstate 80 and the north end of the Bangerter Hwy. as it enters the airport. With automobile traffic on three sides and airplanes taking off overhead, Wingpointe is the noisiest course in the state, but it demands enough concentration that you tend to forget about the noise. Single players can usually join a group without much trouble, but if you are from out of town and you want to make a reservation you can do it with a credit card using the Salt Lake City automated reservation system at **(801) 972-7888.**

HIKING

There are hundreds of hiking trails to fit all levels of ability and stamina in the mountains around Salt Lake City. The trails are close, usually within a half-hour's drive of the city and offer wonderful mountain scenery, especially during summer. I have described some of my family's favorites here, but for those who would like to examine all the possibilities I recommend *Hiking the Wasatch*, by John Veranth, which describes more than 200 trails in the Salt Lake area.

Lake Blanche Trail—

Using the Lake Blanche Trail, you can hike to three alpine lakes: Lake Blanche, Lake Florence, and Lake Lillian. If you don't mind some scrambling over boulders and cliffs, you can continue from the lakes to hike one of the three peaks that loom above the lakes: Sundial Peak at 10,320 feet, Dromedary Peak at 11,107 feet, or Mount Superior at 11,132 feet. To Lake Blanche, it is about 3 miles from the trailhead in Big Cottonwood Canyon. It's another .5 mile to take in the other lakes. It is a steady and sometimes steep climb up the trail, with about a 1,000-foot elevation gain per mile. However, the view of the lakes and the feeling of going into the heart of the mountains makes this a rewarding hike. The trailhead is located on a side road off the highway up Big Cottonwood Canyon. The side road is located at the base of an S turn. You can either leave your car along the side of the highway and walk up the service road about a quarter of a mile to where the trail starts, or you might find a parking spot by driving up to the trailhead. The S turn is located about a mile beyond the Storm Mountain picnic area, or about 5 miles up Big Cottonwood Canyon.

Mount Aire Trail—

The 2-mile hike to the top of Mount Aire in Mill Creek Canyon offers a spectacular view of the Salt Lake Valley, Parley's Canyon through which Interstate 80 heads east, Mill Creek Canyon, the Wasatch Mountains, and Oquirrh Mountains from its summit at 8,621 feet. Though not as high as peaks farther south, it does provide a worthwhile hike for a view from the top of a mountain. Because this is a steep trail, hiking times one way can vary between one and two hours, depending on one's condition and how much time is spent admiring the scenery. The trail begins about 6 miles up Mill Creek Canyon, at the Elbow Fork Trail head. Located on the north, or left-hand side of the road going up the canyon, the trail follows straight up Elbow Fork for about .5 mile, where the trail branches with the righthand trail following up for about 1.5 miles to Lambs Canyon Pass. Staying to the left, the Mount Aire trail crosses a stream via a footbridge, then climbs steeply up the canyon to Mount Aire Pass. En route, the trail passes through dense trees and is especially pretty in the fall. From Mount Aire Pass, the trail heads east zigzagging its way up the southern slope through Gambel oak to the top of Mount Aire. From here the sight of quiet, soaring eagles, and the breathtaking view is well worth the effort. Particularly impressive is the view from the summit back into Mill Creek Canyon, where the canyon road far below, surrounded by dense pine and aspen trees, appears like a string in a deep hole, giving an impressive perspective to your efforts in climbing to the top.

Mueller Park Trail—

Although this trail is used by people on motorcycles and all-terrain vehicles, hikers are the most regular users. The destination from Mueller Park is the ridge at Rudy's Flat, 4.5 miles up the mountain, on the City Creek Range. The trail provides spectacular views of the Great Salt Lake and down City Creek Canyon into the Salt

Lake Valley. To reach Mueller Park from Salt Lake City, take exit 318 off Interstate 15. The road heads in a northeasterly direction, then turns north as it becomes Orchard Dr. Stay on Orchard Dr. to 1800 South, then turn east and continue until you enter the mouth of the canyon, ending at Mueller Park.

North Canyon Trail—

An alternative to the 9-mile round-trip on the Mueller Park Trail is to follow the North Canyon Trail up to Rudy's Flat, where it intersects with the Mueller Park Trail. The trail up Rudy's Flat is about 2.5 miles, making the round-trip to Mueller Park 7 miles total. This plan requires leaving a shuttle vehicle at Mueller Park, or arranging to be dropped off and picked up. To reach the North Canyon Trail, follow the same route to Mueller Park to 1800 South and Bountiful Blvd., where you turn right and head back south to 3400 South, then turn east and follow the road to the end of the pavement. Here, the trail begins as a dirt road and narrows as it becomes a series of switchbacks cutting back and forth up to the ridge.

White Pine Trailhead—

Located 5.5 miles up Little Cottonwood Canyon and just under a mile down the road from Snowbird Resort, the White Pine Trailhead offers the most convenient access into the Lone Peak Wilderness Area. A parking area provides off-road parking in the narrow and heavily traveled Little Cottonwood Canyon. From the parking area, hikers cross Little Cottonwood Creek over a footbridge and continue along the White Pine Trail for a mile until the trail branches. Continue up the White Pine Trail as it follows a switchback eastward onto the ridge, or cross the stream over a footbridge about 50 yards upstream from the switchback and follow the Red Pine Trail north and westward around the ridge. This portion of the trail—approximately 1.5 miles from the parking area—is an excellent hike for those wanting to spend a couple of hours in the mountains. The trail

around the ridge offers magnificent views in three directions: east up the canyon to the Snowbird Resort and the head of Little Cottonwood Canyon; north across the canyon to the steep slopes of Twin Peaks and Dromedary Peak; and south, down the canyon with a spectacular vista of the southern end of the Salt Lake Valley. As the trail turns to the south, it follows along the ridge through pine forests to an old mine dump, where a bridge crosses the Red Pine Fork and a trail follows westward up a switchback into Maybird Gulch. This route is not marked by signs, and most hikers continue up the steep Red Pine Trail approximately another mile to Red Pine Lake, one of the most beautiful sites in the Wasatch Mountains. Surrounded by pine trees, the deep emerald waters reflecting the silhouette of the granite ridge to the west, this is a picture-perfect scene. But there's more. Upper Red Pine Lake located above Red Pine Lake to the southeast can be reached by a steep .5-mile trail and scramble across a field of granite boulders. The hike offers a spectacular view of lower Red Pine Lake. The upper route also provides access to the Pfeifferhorn whose summit, at 11,326 feet, exposed slopes, and lingering snow makes this an ascent for well-conditioned and experienced hikers.

DISABLED HIKING ACCESS
Brighton/Silver Lake—

The 1-mile circular route around Silver Lake, at the base of the 10,000-foot Mt. Millicent in Big Cottonwood Canyon, offers a unique opportunity to experience an alpine lake and the wildlife that makes its home around the lake. The trail consists of two sections of boardwalk, which cross the marshy meadows and sections of pathway through wooded sections. The boardwalks also provide access for those in wheelchairs to fishing docks at the lake.

Snowbird—

A barrier-free, .5-mile-long nature trail begins at the Snowbird Center in Little Cottonwood Canyon and winds along the base of the mountain, with 10 interpretive signs introducing the natural history along the way. The 8-foot-wide, asphalt-paved trail has no more than a 6 percent grade. The trail takes visitors through meadows filled with wildflowers and frequented by deer, squirrels, porcupines, and songbirds, and sometimes elk, moose, coyotes, badgers, hawks, and eagles. At the end of the trail, a lookout deck provides a spectacular view of the mountains, as well as down the glaciated Little Cottonwood Canyon to the Salt Lake Valley below.

HORSEBACK RIDING

East Canyon Outfitters—
Located at the foot of Big Mountain, astride the old Mormon Trail approximately 25 miles east of downtown Salt Lake City on state Hwy. 65, you can ride along the old Mormon Trail or explore other areas of the Wasatch Mountains. Information can be obtained and reservations made through the East Canyon Resort; **(801) 355-3460.**

Valley View Riding Stables—
Draper, in the southeastern part of the Salt Lake Valley, still has a strong rural flavor and is a good location for the Valley View Riding Stables. With horses for every level of rider, Valley View is perhaps the finest horseback-riding facility along the Wasatch Front. Unguided rides, which let you go where and when you want, are encouraged for qualified riders, while the less-experienced riders have access to professional assistance. A variety of options are offered. Located at **1300 East 13800 South Draper; (801) 572-9088.**

RUNNING AND JOGGING

Jordan River Parkway—
During the 14 years or so that my running partners and I have been running this route, we figure we have already logged several thousand miles and expect to log at least that many more before our jogging careers are over. This is a flat course that

follows the Jordan River as it heads north toward the Great Salt Lake. It begins at the west end of the Utah State Fair grounds, where the Jordan River crosses North Temple at about 1200 West. There are a couple of places where you have to cross streets, but otherwise it is an automobile-free run, with spots of shade and several foot bridges across the river. You can follow it all the way out to the Rose Park Golf Course; a return run along the trail is the recommended route. The trail begins about 2 miles west of downtown Salt Lake City, but it is easy to find. Just go to the north side of Temple Square and follow the street west to the Jordan River.

Liberty Park—
One of Salt Lake City's largest public parks. This is a favorite with runners because of the shade from the mature trees, the flat terrain, and the lack of automobiles. Joggers can run the inside road, which is about 1.3 miles per lap, or along the outside edge of the park, at about 1.5 miles a lap. The park is located between **900 South and 1300 South** and **500 East and 700 East.** It is about a 2-mile run to the park from downtown Salt Lake City.

Memory Grove and City Creek Canyon—
If you are staying in the downtown area, a great route for running can be found by heading north up Main St., circling around the state capitol, and following Bonneville Rd. into City Creek Canyon. Bonneville Rd. begins just beyond the northeast parking lot of the state capitol complex. Follow Bonneville Rd. until it makes a U turn back to the south and return along the east side of the canyon. Continue up the City Creek Canyon Rd., which is closed to automobile traffic. Follow this road for just over 5 miles to its termination at Rotary Park. It is an especially popular route with lunchtime joggers, especially during the summer, when the trees and stream offer relief from the summer heat. On the return, follow the road as it heads back to the city through

the canyon to Memory Grove. This nice easy downhill run is a good place to put yourself on cruise control and experience that runner's high. The first part of the run, up Main St. and past the Capitol Building, is a strenuous uphill run, which continues, though not as steeply, up City Creek Canyon.

Sugarhouse Park—

This was the site of the Utah Territorial Prison, but now is one of the city's busiest parks. A favorite for joggers, the gentle rolling hills over the 2.3-mile perimeter lap around the park offers distance, variety, and a safe place away from automobiles to run. You can also run the inner circle of the park, which is a little over a mile in distance. Located at **2100 South and 1300 East.**

University of Utah—

There are a number of good running trails in and around the university area. One goes through Fort Douglas into Red Butte Canyon; another goes through Research Park and on to Pioneer Trails State Park. If you are at the university and want to go for a jog, you can check at the Einar Nielsen Field House for suggestions or just head east toward the mountains, keeping in mind the basic rule of jogging: run uphill to start, so that you don't have to at the end.

RACES

July 24th Marathon and 10K Race—

See Days of '47 in the Festivals and Events section.

Salt Lake Classic—

Held Sat. morning on Memorial Day weekend, the Salt Lake Classic is a favorite fun run among runners in the Salt Lake Valley, drawing more than 4,000 entrants for the 5K and 10K runs. Begun in 1977, sponsors initially encouraged professional racers with guarantees and prize money; however, in the last few years, professionals have bypassed the race, giving current and former local university runners a usually uncontested

claim on the prizes. Although it does not draw the same numbers as the Breakers to Bay Race in San Francisco, those who come in costume add much to what is already a festive occasion. The course is ideal for both the serious racer and the sightseeing jogger. It is one of those unusual routes that appear to have no uphill stretches, only a gentle downhill slope for almost all of the course. Starting in the shadow of the Salt Lake Temple, runners have a chance to climb up on the statue of Brigham Young for a quick picture with the Mormon Colonizer before the race begins. The 10-kilometer route heads south down Main St. through Salt Lake's downtown area, to 1700 South, where the course turns east along tree-lined streets, with turn-of-the-century houses and 1920s bungalows, to Liberty Park, where the final mile loops through the historic park.

SKIING
CROSS-COUNTRY SKIING
Solitude Nordic Center—

With 12 miles of machine-worked trails, the Solitude Nordic Center, located at Silver Lake between the Solitude and Brighton ski resorts in Big Cottonwood Canyon, is Utah's oldest cross-country ski area. There are both classic and skating lanes, with two rental shops and a children's trail. Group lessons and private lessons are available. For information and prices call **(801) 272-7613.**

Other popular cross-country ski areas include **Mountain Dell Golf Course** in Parley's Canyon and the **Mill Creek Canyon Rd.**

DOWNHILL SKIING
Alta—

Two slogans capture the essence of Alta: "The best powder on earth," and "Alta is for skiers." With a well-deserved worldwide reputation for its dry powder snow, Alta has consciously kept its focus on skiing since the first chairlift—the Collins Lift—began operation in 1939. The

Alta Lodge was opened for business in 1940. During World War II Alta continued to develop as a recreational haven from the cares of the war, as well as a training center for ski troops. After the war, Alta continued to cultivate its reputation as the destination for serious skiers.

Even before it became Utah's ski center, Alta had a colorful history. In 1863, prospectors discovered silver, and claims were located and mines opened. By 1873, Alta boasted a population of 5,000, with 186 buildings, including 26 saloons. The Emma Mine, which was discovered in 1868, produced more than $3.8 million worth of silver and became the center of an international scandal when British investors were "taken" by unscrupulous promoters after the ore veins played out. A narrow-gauge railroad was constructed up Little Cottonwood Canyon to Alta in 1875. The Panic of 1893 and other economic disasters brought an end to the 19th-century mining town, although a second, but smaller mining boom lasted from 1904 to 1927. Today, skiers glide across old mine dumps, and, in the summer, openings and other evidence of the bygone mining days can be seen.

Alta is located at the end of the Little Cottonwood Canyon road, 8 miles up the canyon and a mile beyond the Snowbird Resort. Alta has six double chair lifts, two triples, and four rope tows, which service 2,000 acres of ski terrain accessed by 39 runs. The average annual snowfall here is more than 500 inches. The terrain is classified as 25 percent beginning, 40 percent intermediate, and 35 percent advanced. The longest run is 3.5 miles with an elevation drop from 10,550 feet to 8,500 feet. If you are an expert skier, you will soon learn about the numerous chutes and powder areas. Beginners might want to stay with the Albion and Sunnyside lifts at the upper or eastern end. In fact you can purchase a reduced price ticket if you are just going to ski these areas. Alta usually has some of the best-priced lift tickets around, offering both full-day and half-day passes. The ski season usually runs from mid-Nov.–mid-Apr.

The **Alf Engen Ski School** caters to all ages and levels of skiers. They say Alf Engen invented dry powder skiing, so if you want a good introduction to Alta's powder, a lesson might just be the ticket. Reservations for classes are recommended. Call **(801) 742-2600**. A nursery and child care are offered in the **Albion Ticket Building.** Call **(801) 742-3042** for reservations and prices.

Accommodations are available in five lodges at Alta, and a number of privately owned condominiums, townhouses, and vacation homes. The **Alta Reservation Service** will give you the whole picture as to what is available and at what price. Call **(801) 942-0404**. The five lodges, listed below, operate on the American plan, which includes two or three meals a day. Some include lift tickets in the lodging price and all five lodges are within easy reach of the ski slopes. A variety of rooms are available, from dormitory rooms with shared baths to two-bedroom suites with private bath, sitting room, and fireplace. All five lodges face the ski slopes to the south and have tremendous views of the mountains.

Alta Lodge—$$$ to $$$$
Heated swimming pool and saunas. **Alta, UT** 84092; **(801)** 742-3500 or 1-800-748-5025.

Alta Peruvian Lodge—$$$ to $$$$
Heated outdoor pool and outdoor therapy pool. **Alta, UT** 84092; **(801)** 742-3000 or **1-800-453-8488.**

Goldminer's Daughter—$$$ to $$$$
Hot tubs, saunas, and exercise room. **Alta, UT** 84092; **(801)** 742-2300 or 1-800-453-4573.

Rustler Lodge—$$$ to $$$$
Fifty-six rooms. Heated outdoor swimming pool, saunas, and Jacuzzi. **Alta, UT** 84092; **(801)** 742-2200 or 1-800-451-5223.

Snow Pine Lodge—$$$ to $$$$
Outdoor hot tub and Scandinavian sauna. **Alta, UT** 84092; **(801)** 742-2000.

These five lodges all have excellent restaurants that are usually open to the public. The only nonlodge restaurant is the **Shallow Shaft**, which offers steak, seafood, and pizza. Cafeteria-style facilities are open near the lifts for a sandwich, soup, or chili lunch.

Brighton—

This is the ski area where I learned to ski—as did my children 20 years later. Brighton has a reputation as Utah's family ski area, and for good reason. With each paying adult, up to two children 10 years and younger, ski for free. A special Intro-Ski program is available for both children and adults, which provides a lift pass, ski rentals, and lesson all for a price equal to the lift pass at some resorts. A further incentive to families and carpoolers is a discount offered whenever five or more skiers ride together. Not only is this a nice gesture, but it cuts down on traffic and pollution in the canyon. The skier capacity at Brighton is 11,000 skiers per hour on two high-speed quads, two triple chairlifts, and three double chairs. There are more than 60 designated runs and trails, and snow-making equipment helps mother nature along on the lower runs. There are four general areas to the resort, Mt. Majestic, the original part of the ski area; Snake Creek Canyon Lift, which takes you to the summit for a glimpse down the other side of the mountain into Heber Valley; Clayton Peak, to which access was provided by construction of the Great Western detachable quad lift in 1992; and on the other side of the parking area, the Mount Millicent lift, first built in 1948, provides access to skiing on the southern side of the mountain. Night skiing is also offered.

Brighton was named for William Stewart Brighton who, with his wife Katherine, emigrated to Utah from Scotland in 1857 as handcart pioneers. In 1870 Brighton took out an 80-acre homestead in the Silver Lake area, and in 1874, built a small hotel to accommodate miners traveling back and forth between Alta and Park City. Recreational skiing began as early as 1915, with excursions from Salt Lake City. The Wasatch Mountain Club, organized in

1920, built a cabin at Brighton in 1928, which stands today, hidden in the pine trees not far from the Mt. Majestic Lift. The first ski lift, a T-bar tow, was put into operation in 1939.

Unlike Alta and Snowbird, there are only a few accommodations in Big Cottonwood Canyon. The **Brighton Lodge** has 20 rooms adjacent to the ski slopes, call **1-800-873-5512** for reservations. The **Brighton Chalets** are individual private cabins with furnished kitchens, call **(801) 942-8824** or **1-800-748-4824**. **Das Alpen Haus** has four suites, all with private bathrooms, a sauna, fireplace, and gourmet breakfasts prepared by hosts Charles and Nola Hobbs; **(801) 649-0565**. Eating facilities at the Brighton Ski Resort include the **Alpine Rose** and the **Millicent Chalet.**

Snowbird—

Opened in 1971, Snowbird is the Salt Lake City area's newest and largest ski resort. With more than 900 rooms in four facilities, Snowbird is designed to accommodate out-of-town skiers. Snowbird receives an average of 500 inches of snow a year (623 inches during the winter of 1992–1993). The ski season usually goes from mid-Nov.–early May. A 120-passenger tram carries skiers from the Snowbird Center, at 8,100 feet elevation, to the top of Hidden Peak, at 11,000 feet. From Hidden Peak, you can ski down through Peruvian Gulch on one of Utah's longest runs: the 3.5-mile Chip's Run, named in honor of the son of a close friend of resort developer Ted Johnson who was killed in the Vietnam War. Six other chairlifts provide access to much of the nearly 2,000 skiable acres along 48 ski trails. The tram and lifts can accommodate up to 9,200 skiers an hour. In 1993, Snowbird established family ski zones for skiers who want to ski with families and friends at a relaxed pace. Skiers can purchase a day or half-day ticket for either the tram and chairlifts or the chairlifts only. Discounts are usually offered for late spring skiing. Skiers age 70 and over ski free.

Snowbird is only 29 miles from the Salt Lake City International Airport, so skiers from anywhere in the US can catch an early-morning flight to Salt Lake City and still have a full afternoon of skiing. You can drive to Snowbird, ride the tram and be skiing down the slopes in less than an hour.

The Snowbird complex is designed for easy walking access, and the compact layout lets you walk from the upper building, **Cliff Lodge,** to the lower building, **Iron Blosam Lodge,** in about five minutes. Cliff Lodge provides ski-out and ski-in access, while for the other lodges, the ski lifts are located a short walk away. Half the terrain is for advanced and expert skiers, but beginning skiers have access to plenty of area, including the Chickadee Lift, which runs from the base of the tram at the Snowbird Center to just above the Cliff Lodge. The Snowbird Ski School, with a full-time staff of 125 qualified instructors, offers private or group lessons for skiers of every ability. Snowbird also provides a Mountain Host Program, which offers free guided skiing tours daily to acquaint newcomers with the lifts and runs that are best suited to their abilities. Snowbird also sponsors a disabled skier program which provides instructors, guides, and equipment to hundreds of individuals who otherwise would never have the chance to ski.

Ski rentals are located in the Cliff Lodge and at the Snowbird Center.

Cliff Lodge is a deluxe hotel with 532 rooms and a wide range of amenities, including an open-air, year-around, roof-top pool and giant whirlpool, sauna, steam room, aerobics and weight training rooms, spa, salon, retail shops, game room, children's center, in-room babysitting, and four eating establishments: the **Mexican Keyhole** (Mexican food), the **Aerie** (continental cuisine, located on the top floor), the **Spa Cafe** (health food, on the 10th floor), and the **Atrium,** where you can eat breakfast, lunch, and dinner at the base of the 11-story Atrium. Rates at the Cliff Lodge during the high ski season range from a dormitory room with four twin beds and a full bath to a two-bedroom suite.

The three other facilities at Snowbird include the **Lodge at Snowbird** with 136 rooms, the **Inn** with 65 rooms, and **Iron Blosam Lodge** with 159 rooms. These condominium accommodations include bedrooms only or units that have completely furnished kitchens. Most units face south and offer open-air balconies with a spectacular view of the mountains and ski slopes. The Iron Blosam Lodge has a fine Italian restaurant, **Wildflower Ristorante and Lounge,** located on the third level.

Other eating facilities are located at the Snowbird Center, where you can dine in the **Steak Pit** or eat at the **Forklift,** a family restaurant that serves traditional American breakfasts, lunches, and dinners. The **Rendezvous** offers cafeteria-style breakfasts and lunches. The **Birdfeeder,** on the outdoor plaza, has burgers and fries. The **Rocky Mountain Chocolate Factory** is a favorite stop for most Snowbird visitors. If you are staying in one of the units with kitchen facilities, it is best to stock up on food and supplies at one of the Salt Lake City supermarkets before you drive up to Snowbird. But if you need a few items, chances are you will find them at the **General Gritts Convenience Store,** located in the Snowbird Center. Other shops at the Snowbird Center include a pharmacy, camera, souvenir, ski clothing, wine, and liquor stores.

Snowbird describes itself as a ski and summer resort, and for many visitors summer and fall are the best times to be at Snowbird. **Tram rides** continue until the end of Oct., when they stop for a two-week maintenance period before the ski season begins. Take the tram up the mountain and enjoy the breathtaking view of the Wasatch Mountains from Hidden Peak. Some visitors like to ride the tram up and hike back down along the 3.5-mile-long service road to the Snowbird Center. Even more practical is to hike up the road from the Snowbird Tram to the top of Hidden Peak, where the ride back down on the tram is free.

One of my favorite outings is to drive up to Snowbird on a Sat. or Sun. morning in Sept. or Oct., hike to the top of Hidden Peak, and return to the Snowbird Center by early afternoon to enjoy the Oktoberfest which is held in a huge tent, that can accommodate up to 2,000 people, adjacent to the Snowbird Center. The Snowbird **Oktoberfest** runs from noon to 6:00 pm on weekends from Labor Day weekend–late Oct. A full program of German folk music by the Bavarians-A German band, the Rocky Mountain Polka Express, and yodeler Kerry Christensen plus the wonderful German food, beer, and members of Salt Lake City's German community dressed in Tyroler hats, lederhosen, and dirndls, is as close to being in Bavaria as you can get.

Other summer attractions include performances by the **Utah Symphony,** including the traditional program featuring Tchaikovsky's 1812 Overture with authentic cannons, remains a perennial favorite. There is also an annual **Utah Jazz and Blues Festival,** mountain biking, wall climbing on the 115-foot climbing wall on the westside of the Cliff Lodge, and five outdoor tennis courts. The Snowbird Institute offers a variety of performances, seminars, and workshops in dance, music, education, and the humanities during the summer. The July 4th weekend is the **Snowbird Outdoor Sports Festival,** with a rock wall climbing competition, mountain bike races, bike clinics, two-person sand volleyball, a sports festival expo, entertainment, and food.

Snowbird is a sister city with Zermatt, Switzerland, and a piece of granite, taken from the top of the Matterhorn and presented by Zermatt to Snowbird as a gesture of friendship, is prominently displayed in the outdoor plaza area of the Snowbird Center.

There are a number of special packages available during the winter and summer. For information about lodging, dining, lift ticket prices, activities, and special events, call **(801) 742-2222** or **521-6040** from Salt Lake City.

Solitude—

Located 12 miles up Big Cottonwood Canyon, Solitude has a reputation for reasonable lift ticket rates, uncrowded skiing, and challenging slopes. It is ranked among the top 40 ski areas in North America. With four double, two triple, and one high-speed detachable quad chairlift, Solitude can service over 10,000 skiers an hour. There are over 1,100 acres of skiing on 63 trails. For powder skiers, **Honeycomb Canyon** offers more than 400 acres of excellent dry powder skiing. Ski lessons are available through the **Solitude Ski School; (801) 649-0000.** Currently there are no lodging facilities at Solitude, but plans are to construct an area called New Village, which will have lodging and restaurants. The **Roundhouse Restaurant,** located at the top of the Moonbeam II Chairlift, is an excellent place for lunch or dinner. Dinner reservations can be made by calling **(801) 649-8400** or **534-1400.** The Solitude ski season usually runs from mid-Nov.–late Apr. For information and lift prices, call **1-800-748-4754**

SWIMMING

There are 14 public pools in the Salt Lake area. For information about the pools located throughout the valley, call the **Salt Lake County Parks and Recreation Office** at **(801) 468-2560,** or the **Salt Lake City Recreation Division** at **(801) 972-7800.**

Deseret Gym—

In downtown Salt Lake City, the Deseret Gym, located a block north of Temple Square at **161 North Main St.,** has an Olympic-size pool and a family pool. The gym also has an indoor jogging track, exercise room, and racquetball and squash courts. Call **(801) 359-3911.**

Steiner Aquatic Center—

This facility was opened in 1990 and has both an outdoor and indoor pool. It is located just south of the University of Utah at **645 South Guardsman Way.** For schedules and information call **(801) 583-9713.**

TENNIS

Liberty Park—

Traditionally Liberty Park has been the place to play tennis in Salt Lake City.

There are 16 tennis courts and a pro shop in the west center area of the public park. Liberty Park is located between **900 and 1300 South and 500 and 700 East.** For tennis information and reservations, call **(801) 596-5036.**

Oquirrh Park Tennis Center—

Located in the southwestern part of the valley, this is one of the best outdoor tennis facilities in the state. There are eight lighted tennis courts and a pro shop with rental equipment, including a tennis ball machine. The facility is open daily Apr.– Oct. Located at **5624 South 4800 West,** across the street from Kearns High School; **(801) 966-4229.**

Salt Lake City and Salt Lake County Parks—

Most of the city and county parks have tennis courts available on a first-come, first-served basis. For the locations of city parks call **(801) 972-7800.** County park information is available at **(801) 468-2299.** I suggest one of the six courts just west of Raging Waters on 1700 South and about 1400 West—they are seldom used.

SEEING AND DOING

AMUSEMENT PARKS

49th Street Galleria—

For an afternoon or evening of arcade games, bowling, miniature golf, batting cages, roller skating, and other family-oriented activities, the 49th Street Galleria is a favorite with Salt Lakers. The Galleria is located just off Interstate 15 at **360 West and 4998 South** in Murray; **(801) 265-3866.**

Lagoon Amusement Park—

For some Utah youngsters, Lagoon is one of the first words they learn. This popular amusement park was opened in 1886 at a site 4 miles west of present-day Lagoon, on the shores of the Great Salt Lake. When the waters of the lake receded, the resort was moved to its present location in 1896 and the name changed from Lakeside to Lagoon. The enterprise was undertaken by Simon Bamberger, a German Jew who became Utah's fourth governor in 1916. Bamberger established the Bamberger Railroad Line between Ogden and Salt Lake City. One of the reasons for building the resort was to encourage riders on the "Bamberger."

Over the years, the resort has undergone extensive changes to provide visitors with something new and more exciting each year. Evolving from the original activities of swimming and dancing, Lagoon is perhaps best characterized as four parks within one: an amusement park, a water recreation park, a pioneer village, and an entertainment center. Two perennially popular rides are a turn-of-the-century carousel and a wooden roller coaster, constructed in 1921. Some rides are geared more to teenagers—or those who think they still are teenagers. There is the Colossus, with its two inverted loops; the Giant Ferris Wheel, a recent attraction, which is now the most visible feature in the park; the Tidal Wave (which is the ride that marked my crossing from youth to middle age); and dozens of other rides for thrillseekers. The water park is known as "Lagoon A Beach" and is included in the all-day ticket.

The nucleus of Lagoon's Pioneer Village was moved to the park in 1974, from a private collection of historical buildings and artifacts in Salt Lake City. The historic buildings include an early drugstore, a schoolhouse from Wanship, a railroad station from Kaysville, a post office from Charleston, and a rock chapel, moved stone by stone from Coalville. The tool and work bench of John Browning, along with some of the early inventor's guns are on display. Rides, gunfight reenactments, a jail where youngsters can be locked up, and a log flume ride provide plenty of action in the village. Entertainment is provided by the All-Star Marching Band that parades throughout the park and by the Music

USA group. The Victorian opera house is an attractive feature of the park, and musicals and melodramas are staged inside. Lagoon is open on weekends mid-Apr.–Memorial Day weekend; then open daily until Labor Day; then weekends only the remainder of Sept. The park opens at 11:00 am and closes at 11:00 pm during the summer months, with earlier closing times in Apr., May, and Sept. Visitors can purchase an entrance pass or an all-day ride pass. For further information and ticket prices, call **(801) 451-0101** or write to **Lagoon, PO Box N, Farmington, UT 84025.**

Raging Waters—

On a hot summer day, there are few places more enjoyable than Utah's premier water park: Raging Waters. Opened in 1979 amid some controversy about putting ocean waves in the middle of the desert, more than a quarter of a million people visit Raging Waters each year. With 11 pools, including the giant wild wave pool, and 19 slides, Raging Waters is Utah's largest water theme park. There are all kinds of slides—from the most gentle to the world's first H_2O Roller Coaster and the 289-foot-long Acapulco Cliff Dive, which has two drops: 40 feet and 20 feet. Other facilities include a popular rope swing, two leveled kiddies pool, and picnic areas. For the young and the young at heart, this is the place to spend a summer day. Located at **1200 West and 1700 South** and open from Memorial Day weekend–Labor Day; **(801) 973-6600.**

HISTORIC BUILDINGS

Bingham Copper Mine—

The world's largest open-cut copper mine is located in Bingham Canyon, in the southwestern corner of Salt Lake Valley. The mine is so massive that it is visible from almost anywhere in the valley and looks like a gigantic amphitheater cut from the mountain. Ore was discovered in Bingham Canyon in the 1860s, but it was not until 1906 that the open pit operations began. The excavated hole is more than .5 mile deep and 2.5 miles across. The mine

itself could seat more than 9 million people and several Rose Bowl or Cotton Bowl stadiums would fill the pit bottom. In excess of 5 billion tons of material have been removed to produce more than 12 million tons of copper-making the mine the world's largest source of the metal. The mine is located 22 miles from downtown Salt Lake City and can be reached by taking Interstate 15 to 7200 South, then heading west to 7800 South, continuing west to the Bingham Hwy. Turn south and follow the highway to Copperton and watch for the signs to the visitor center. Copperton was a company town, built by Kennecott Copper as a home for its managers and workers in the 1920s. It was designed to be a show place for products made from the mine's copper. The Copperton Park as also a nice place to stop for a picnic lunch. The visitor center is open from early Apr.–Oct. For information call **(801) 322-7300.**

Cathedral of the Madeleine—

Constructed in 1909 and completely restored in 1993, the Cathedral of the Madeleine is one of Utah's architectural masterpieces. The Romanesque-style cathedral was built under the direction of Lawrence Scanlan, the first Catholic bishop of Utah, who is buried under the main altar. The interior is in the Gothic Revival–style, with beautiful stained glass windows. The cathedral is open daily from 6:00 am–6:30 pm. Free guided tours, which last approximately one hour, are available by appointment; call **(801) 328-8941.** The cathedral is located at **331 East South Temple.**

Fort Douglas—

Established 3 miles east of downtown Salt Lake City, in 1862, by Civil War volunteers from California under the command of Colonel Patrick Edward Connor, Fort Douglas was named in honor of Illinois Senator Stephan A. Douglas, Lincoln's opponent in the famous Lincoln Douglas Debates. The military force was sent to Utah to keep the mail and stagecoach line open between the east and California during Indian unrest that threatened to cut off the two sections of the country. It was also said that Connor was to keep an eye on the Mormons and that it was no accident that he had his cannons trained on Brigham Young's home in the valley below. The fort was deactivated in 1991 and turned over to the University of Utah. A drive through it reveals some fine officers' quarters dating from the 1870s, built from red sandstone quarried in nearby Red Butte Canyon. There are also stone barracks buildings and administrative buildings, which date from about 1900 to the 1930s. During World War II, Fort Douglas was the headquarters for the Ninth Army Command, whose jurisdiction included all army activities in Washington, Oregon, California, Arizona, Idaho, Montana, and Utah. One of the most interesting areas is the cemetery, where Patrick Connor is buried, along with some of his soldiers, as well as veterans and dependents who have served in the military since the Civil War. In the southeast corner of the cemetery are the graves of German, Italian, and Japanese prisoners of war who died in Utah during World War II. In the southwestern corner is the cemetery's largest monument, which commemorates German prisoners of war who died at Fort Douglas during World War I. The Fort Douglas Military Museum, located on the south side of the parade ground, has exhibits on the history of the fort and the history of the military in Utah. The museum is open Tues.–Sat. from 10:00 am–noon and 1:00 pm–4:00 pm. For information call **(801) 524-4154**.

Utah State Capitol Building—

One of the finest examples of the Renaissance Revival architectural style in the US, the capitol was designed by the German-born architect, Richard K. A. Kletting. I speak for most Utahns when I say this is one of the most stately and magnificent public buildings anywhere. Located on Capitol Hill, at the head of State St., the building stands above downtown Salt Lake City and the rest of the valley like a sentinel. The building was completed in 1915 at a cost of $2.75 million. The copper dome

and colonnade of Corinthian columns remind visitors of the US capitol in Washington, DC. Inside, the ceiling of the dome is 165 feet above the floor and is decorated with seagulls, the state bird, and murals depicting events in Utah's history. Many of the paintings throughout the rotunda were made by Utah artists as part of the 1930s New Deal WPA program, which put unemployed artists to work during the Great Depression. Inside the capitol, be sure to see the Gold Room, which is adorned with 23-karat Utah gold leaf, and the Mormon Meteor Race Car, in which Salt Lake native Ab Jenkins set numerous speed records on the Bonneville Salt Flats located 120 miles west of Salt Lake City. You may view sessions of the Utah state legislature from the fourth-floor balcony. In front of the capitol stands a replica of the sculpture of Chief Massasoit, created by Utah-born Cyrus E. Dallin. There is also a monument to the Mormon Battalion, commemorating its 2,000-mile march to California during the Mexican War, and one remembering Utah's Vietnam War veterans. The Vietnam Memorial, located on the west side of the capitol, has become a sacred spot. A more-than-life-size statue of a soldier returning from a patrol stands in front of a wall that lists the names of all Utahns killed in the Vietnam conflict. Just across the street to the south, in the restored Council Hall, is the Utah Travel Council, an excellent source of information about the state.

MUSEUMS AND GALLERIES

Children's Museum of Utah—

Opened in 1983, the Children's Museum is a wonderful place for children and those who accompany them. It is located in the old Wasatch Springs Plunge swimming facility at **840 North 300 West,** which served as a major recreation area for decades. The building has a charm all its own and seems a perfect meeting place for the city's past and future. Hands-on items, such as an airplane cockpit where children become the pilot, an 18-wheeler cab, a small grocery store, a gas station, and a bank; an exhibit where children can experience what it is like to be blind, a health-care section where children can play doctor on a dummy, and a section where dinosaur bones can be uncovered, are favorites. The museum is open Mon.–Sat. from 9:30 am–5:00 pm. For information about events and admission prices, call **(801) 322-5268.**

Hellenic Cultural Museum—

This jewel of a museum is located in the basement of the Holy Trinity Greek Orthodox Church. The church was constructed in 1924 in what was then the heart of Salt Lake City's Greek town. Curators and volunteers have taken great pains to collect and exhibit artifacts from the Greek immigrant experience in Utah. The museum is actually the first in the US devoted exclusively to Greek immigrants. Many of the items are clothing and artifacts brought to Utah from Greece beginning with the first immigrants who came in the first decade of the 20th century. Others are tools and other items used by the early Greeks in Utah. The museum makes effective use of photographs and documents to illustrate the acculturation process including aspects of the economic, religious, educational, and social life. In 1994, the museum was cited by the American Association for State and Local History as one of the outstanding ethnic museums in the country. The museum has no paid staff, so hours are quite restricted. If you can't make the scheuled hours, call and ask if special arrangements can be made. Bill Drossos, Jim Kastanis, Andy Katsanevas, Chris Metos, and Con Skedros are dedicated volunteers who are often at the church. If you mention how interested you are in seeing the museum, if it is at all possible one of these gentlemen or another volunteer will likely give you a personal tour. Open Wed. 9 am–noon, Sun. 11:30 am–12:30 pm. Tours arranged by appointment. **279 South 300, West, Salt Lake City, UT 84101; (801) 328-9681.**

Pioneer Memorial Museum—

Built by the Daughters of Utah Pioneers in 1950 as a replica of the old 1860s Salt Lake Theater, the Classical Revival–style Pioneer Memorial Museum is located on Capitol Hill at **300 North Main St.,** three blocks north of Temple Square and a block west of the state capitol. The museum displays a wonderful collection of pioneer artifacts, original wagons and handcarts, clothing, furniture, photographs, and other memorabilia. The Daughters of Utah Pioneers was organized in 1901 and throughout the 20th century has been the leading organization in preserving historic buildings and operating "relic halls" in many of the state's communities. The DUP, as they are affectionately called, were preservationists long before the term became popular, and the Pioneer Memorial Museum is the organization's showpiece. Admission is free. Open Mon.–Sat. 9:00 am–5:00 pm. During the summer, the museum is also open Sun. from 1:00 pm–5:00 pm; **(801) 538-1050.**

Salt Lake Art Center—

This city art center features outstanding regional and national exhibitions accompanied by stimulating lectures, films, and discussions. One of my recent favorites was a series of exhibitions under the title "History, Memory, and Media: An Examination of the Internment of Japanese Americans During World War II." The exhibition included over 100 works of art created during the war by more than 30 Japanese-American artists in the internment camps, current photographs from the relocation camps, and a video created from footage commissioned during the internment by the federal government. The accompanying lecture series was held on five evenings over a four-week period. The series included nationally prominent historians, the photographers whose pictures are on exhibit, the showing of a film on Utah's Topaz War Relocation Camp produced by the University of Utah public television station, and a local educator who has carried out several projects with her students to document the Topaz experience. Not all exhibitions reach the level of "History, Memory and Media," but they come close, and the Salt Lake Art Center is a hidden gem still waiting to be discovered by visitors and many locals. Admission is free. Open Tues.–Sat. 10 am–5 pm and Sun. 1 pm–5 pm. Located at **20 South West Temple.** For exhibition and program schedules, call **(801) 328-4201.**

THIS IS THE PLACE STATE PARK

Includes Old Deseret Village, Pioneer Trail State Park, and This is the Place Monument.

Old Deseret Village—

Old Deseret Village is a collection of over a dozen buildings from the early Utah pioneer era with more planned for the future. The first building located in the park, the Brigham Young Forest Farm House, was moved from its original location near 800 East and 2400 South in the valley in 1975. At the time of its construction in 1863, the farm house was about 4 miles outside the city limits on a 600-acre farm, owned by Brigham Young, but on which he spent little time. It was occupied by some of his wives from time to time and provided dairy products for Young's large family. Its new setting at Old Deseret—on the outskirts of the village separated from the other buildings in the village by orchards, pastures, and corrals—maintains a sense of isolation, though on a much smaller scale. Nevertheless, the house seems more like a country manor house and provides an excellent opportunity to tell the story of 19th-century family life and the kind of organization needed to provide for a many-member family.

While you are in the village you will find the buildings spread out in a manner typical of Mormon villages where there were often four houses located on the four corners of a block with the rest of the space used for pastures, barns, corrals, and gardens.

Some of the reconstructed buildings include a blacksmith shop, a pioneer dugout house, and the Social Hall—a two-story Greek Revival–style building built with 2-foot thick walls in downtown Salt Lake City in 1852 to 1853. The other buildings have been moved to the village from

towns throughout Utah and locations in the Salt Lake Valley. They include adobe, log, and frame buildings. The 1858 Milo Andrus house, a large frame structure, was used as the family residence and as an inn for travelers. In the village, it represents a pioneer general store. The oldest building is the 1847 Levi E. Riter cabin, which was originally located in the Old Pioneer Fort and was constructed shortly after the initial settlement. Other favorites include the three-room adobe house built by Charles C. Rich in Centerville during the early 1850s for two of his wives. It depicts how a polygamous family lived in a small house. The small, unpretentious Mary Fielding Smith house was built in 1850 in an isolated area southeast of Salt Lake City as the residence of the widow of Hyrum Smith, who was killed with his brother and Mormon founder, Joseph Smith in 1844. The Manti ZCMI Mercantile building, a two-story commercial building moved to the village when threatened with demolition, depicts the end of the pioneer era as the arrival of the railroad made goods more plentiful and necessitated the establishment of a church mercantile system, known as Zions Cooperative Mercantile Institution (ZCMI), to compete with an influx of non-Mormon businessmen. Guides in period costume are stationed at most of the buildings to explain the history and often to demonstrate pioneer crafts.

Old Deseret Village is open daily from 11 am–5 pm, Memorial Day–Labor Day and on some weekends during the rest of the year. The park grounds are open daily from 8 am–8 pm year-round. Admission fee charged. To reach the park head east on 800 South to the entrance of the park at **2601 East Sunnyside Ave.** (800 South becomes Sunnyside Ave. at about 1400 East). The park is located across Sunnyside Ave. north of Hogle Zoo. For information, upcoming events, and hours call **(801) 584-8391.**

Pioneer Trail State Park—

Next to Temple Square, the most historic spot for Utah Mormons is at the mouth of Emigration Canyon, where Brigham Young and the first band of Mormon pioneers entered the Salt Lake Valley. This is the spot where, after a more than three-month wagon journey from Nebraska, the Mormon leader declared, "This is the place!" The site was commemorated with a small marker until 1947 when, during the centennial celebration, the striking This Is the Place Monument was erected. In 1960, the monument and surrounding grounds became a state park, and in 1970 planning for the "Old Deseret" village began and the first building, the 1863 Brigham Young Forest Farm House was moved to the site in 1975. Since then, the village has continued to expand with the addition of more buildings, activities, and programs as it depicts everyday pioneer Utah from the beginning of settlement in 1847 until 1869 and the coming of the railroad. There is presently a small visitor center near the monument, however a much larger visitor center is planned for completion in 1996. The center will interpret the two main elements of the park, the monument and Old Deseret. The village is located on the sloping hills, atypical of most Utah pioneer villages, and so be prepared for a strenuous uphill hike along dusty roads, or take advantage of the horse-drawn wagons if you want to see all of the village. Throughout the year a number of special activities are planned at the village. As you might expect, Pioneer Day, July 24, is the most popular day of the entire year and there are plenty of activities to justify a visit even on such a crowded day. Pioneer Independence Day, July 4, is also a popular day, when you can experience a 19th-century 4th of July celebration. Other events include Pioneer Spring Days, Old Deseret Days, Pioneer Harvest Days, Pumpkin Harvest Days, and the Christmas Candlelight Tour. Dates for these events vary, so check at the village for the exact days.

This Is the Place Monument—

Utah's largest man-made monument, at 60 feet high and 86 feet long, this monument was dedicated in 1947 to mark the centennial of the arrival of the first group of Mormon pioneers to the Salt Lake Valley. Historians have debated for years just what and where Brigham Young expressed his conviction that the valley was to be the new Mormon homeland. But if it wasn't on the brow of the ridge overlooking the valley and if the exact words were a not a prophetic proclamation, "This is the place!" it should have been. On top of the monument are the three principal Mormon leaders: Brigham Young in the center, flanked by Heber C. Kimball on his right, and Wilford Woodruff on his left. On the lower platforms to the south are members of the 1776 Dominguez-Escalante Expedition and to the north are fur trappers who entered the area in the 1820s. Bas-relief sculptures on the sides depict a variety of events from Utah's early history, including the Donner-Reed Party, many members of which died tragically in California's Sierra Nevada mountains; government explorers such as John C. Fremont and Captain Benjamin L.E. Bonneville; and Shoshone Chief Washaki. The monument was designed by Mahonri M. Young, a grandson of Brigham Young, and is a wonderful visual aid to the early history of Utah.

Utah Museum of Fine Arts—

The Utah Museum of Fine Arts on the University of Utah Campus is Utah's oldest and most diverse art museum. Art objects representing all principle artistic styles and periods of civilization may be found here. The museum has a good collection of European and American art, but attention has also been given to art from the Egyptian, southeast Asian, Japanese, Chinese, Navajo, African, Oceanic, and pre-Columbian cultures. This is a museum for art lovers and for families with children. The African tribal masks fascinate both the young and old. The museum staff has prepared an excellent series of pamphlets called "Passport to the World of Art," which are small workbooks that children can use to develop a greater understanding of the art on display and to make their visit even more enjoyable. I cherish the diversity of art in the museum. There's an English Room, furnished like that of an English country house in the center of which is a large 16th-century oak table with walnut chairs and a 15th-century carved French mantel. There are Buddha heads from 12th-century Cambodia and 13th-century Thailand; figures from Mexico that date back to 200 BC; an Egyptian wall relief from the Old Kingdom 4,500 years ago; beautiful and colorful Flemish oil paintings from the 16th and 17th centuries, including Pieter Brueghel, the Younger's, "The Dance Around the Maypole," one of the museum's most prized possessions. There are nine permanent galleries and three that are used for special exhibitions. There is no charge. The museum is open Mon.–Fri. 10 am–5 pm and Sat. and Sun. 2 pm–5 pm. For information, call **(801) 581-7332.**

Utah Museum of Natural History—

Located at the southern end of University Circle, in the old University of Utah Library Building, the Utah Museum of Natural History is one of Utah's most popular museums because of its excellent collection of artifacts and fine exhibits. The exhibits feature dinosaur skeletons and prehistoric life in Utah. There are two allosaurus, a camptosaurus, and a stegosaurus from the Jurassic Age. Extinct but more recent skeletons include the Huntington Mammoth, a sabre-tooth cat, giant beaver, wolf, bison, and horse. The museum is the official state depository for prehistoric Native American artifacts, and the collection includes items from most of Utah's important archaeological excavations. Other exhibits include a minerals and gems area and exhibits of birds, reptiles, amphibians, and carnivores of Utah. There is the Romney Mine on the second floor, a replica of a hardrock mine from the 19th century. One of my favorite items is the Barrier Canyon Mural that replicates the other worldly anthropomorphic Fremont Rock Art figures. The mural was painted in 1940 as a WPA project under the direction of local artist Lynn Fausett. There

is also a hands-on discovery room for children that includes, among other attractions, a bone yard where children can excavate for dinosaurs. Open Mon.–Sat. from 9:30 am–5:30 pm and Sun. from noon–5:00 pm. Admission fee charged. Call **(801) 581-6927** for more information.

Utah State Historical Society Museum—

The Denver and Rio Grande Railroad donated its historic 1910 Railroad Station to the State of Utah in 1978 to house the Utah State Historical Society. The grand building, which was built in competition with the 1909 Union Pacific Station three blocks to the north, has been an excellent facility for the state's history agency. The lobby area contains an excellent exhibit, covering Utah from prehistory to the present, taking as its theme Utah at the Crossroads. Exhibit items depict Utah's dinosaurs, earliest peoples, pioneers, agriculture, mining, industry, and tourism and recreation. There is a fine bookstore and gift shop near the exhibit where you can purchase books about Utah's past. The Utah State Historical Society's library, with its extensive manuscript and photograph collection, has become a second home to Utah historians. The museum is free and open to the public, Mon.–Fri. 8:00 am–5:00 pm, and Sat. from 10:00 am–2:00 pm. The library operates under a more restricted schedule. For information, call **(801) 533-3500.** The station is at **300 South and 450 West.**

Wheeler Historic Farm—

In 1898, Henry J. Wheeler built his farmhouse of brick and adobe on 75 acres. The house, outbuildings, fields, pastures, and woods are now operated as an historic farm by Salt Lake County. Glenn Humphries has directed the farm since it opened in the mid-1970s. He has given careful attention to making it a special place for today's urban children to learn about life on a turn-of-the-century farm. Children's activities include helping to milk cows, feed chickens, and gather eggs. Other demonstrations and activities vary with the seasons. Located at **6351 South 900 East.** For information, call **(801) 264-2212.**

MUSIC, THEATER, AND BALLET

Ballet West—

One of America's leading ballet companies, Ballet West has its roots in the University of Utah dance program. Willam F. Christiansen, a pioneer in ballet in the US and founder of the San Francisco Ballet Company, returned to his native Utah to found the first university department of ballet in the nation. In 1955, the first of the ongoing performances of Tchaikovsky's Nutcracker Suite was given. It has become an annual Utah Christmas tradition, first performed by the University Ballet, then the Utah Civic Ballet, which was organized in 1963 and renamed Ballet West in 1968. Ballet West also offers a full season of classical, modern, and original works at the historic Capitol Theater. **50 West 200 South; (801) 533-5555.**

Pioneer Theatre Company—

Located on the western edge of the University of Utah campus, Pioneer Theatre Company puts on two musicals and five plays a year. Performances run from Sept.–May. This professional theater company operates under the umbrella of the University of Utah's College of Fine Arts; although independent, it has an ongoing relationship with the university's Theatre Department. The National Endowment for the Arts, the Utah Arts Council, the Salt Lake Arts Council, private businesses, and individuals provide financial assistance for the theatre. For ticket information, call **(801) 581-6961.**

Utah Opera Company—

After a distinguished European and East Coast opera career, Glade Peterson returned to Utah to organize the Utah Opera Company in 1978. The professional opera company offers five or six major operas each season which, like the ballet, are per-

formed in the historic Capitol Theater at 50 West 200 South. Operas are usually sung in the original language with English super titles. For schedules and tickets, call **(801) 533-6494.**

Utah Symphony—

The Utah Symphony is considered a state treasure. Its origins tie in the strong Mormon tradition of music, coupled with Franklin D. Roosevelt's 1930s WPA program, which hired unemployed musicians to perform concerts during the Great Depression. The orchestra was so popular that after federal funding decreased, it continued on its own through World War II and, in 1946, was renamed the Utah Symphony. The following year, Maurice Abravanel was chosen as conductor and, under his talented and untiring leadership until his retirement in 1979, the Utah Symphony became one of the nation's best symphony orchestras. Abravanel received much recognition for his work, but short of renaming the symphony after him, the most fitting memorial was to rename, in 1993, the newly constructed symphony hall for him. Abravanel Hall is located on the southwestern corner of West Temple and South Temple streets, across from Temple Square. The symphony, under the leadership of Joseph Silverstein, performs year-round, with a full schedule from Sept.–Apr., followed by a summer series in July and Aug. Abravanel Hall is a delightful place to listen to a concert, and there are usually some ticket returns available for most performances. For information and tickets, call **(801) 533-6683.**

NIGHTLIFE

D. B. Cooper's—

One of downtown Salt Lake City's oldest night spots, D. B. Cooper's is named for the man who hijacked a Northwest Orient Airlines flight between Portland and Seattle on November 24, 1971, secured a $200,000 ransom, and parachuted from the plane into the Oregon night. Neither Cooper, his body, nor the money were ever found. Many years, later $5,860 in damaged bills was accidentally found along the Columbia River, and two former FBI agents, Bernie Rhodes and Russell Calame, published their conclusion as to Cooper's identity in a 1991 book from the University of Utah Press, *D. B. Cooper: The Real McCoy.* The private club features live music Mon.– Sat. from 8:30 pm–12:45 am. Located at **19 East 200 South; (801) 532-2948.**

Zephyr Club—
Opened in 1983, this private club is considered by many the premier live-entertainment spot in Salt Lake City. With live performances almost nightly, the club features blues, jazz, and rock and roll performed by nationally known as well as regional and local groups. Located at **301 South West Temple** and open daily from 5:00 pm–1:00 am during the winter; and 7:00 pm–1:30 am in the summer. For information, call **(801) 355-CLUB or 355-5646.**

PARKS
International Peace Gardens—
Among all of the public parks in Salt Lake City, this is one of my favorite gardens. The feelings of peace and universal brotherhood make this a special spot. The International Peace Gardens are located in Jordan Park at 1000 South 900 West and are open from mid-May–Nov., from 8:00 am–dusk, at no charge. The idea of a peace garden in Salt Lake City was born in 1939, the year World War II broke out in Europe, but it wasn't until after the war that the project was resurrected. In 1947, Salt Lake City's various ethnic and national groups were approached about developing a section of the park that would reflect the diverse cultures and nationalities living in the city. The International Peace Gardens were dedicated on August 15, 1952. As new groups have come to the Salt Lake Valley, they have added their own sections to the gardens. Cultures and countries that are represented include Brazil, Great Britain, Wales, Ireland, Canada, Mexico, China, Japan, Korea, India, the Philippines, Lebanon, Denmark, Sweden, Norway, Finland, Germany, Switzerland, The Netherlands, Italy, Greece,

Africa, and Russia. The most recent addition is from Salt Lake's Vietnamese community. Each country has developed a unique way of representing its country with flowers and landscape elements. For example, the Dutch have a model windmill and a 12-foot-long wooden shoe holding tulips; the Germans have a linden tree beside a well and gate to the town as described in an old folksong; the Swiss have a scale model of the Matterhorn; and India has a bronze Buddha. This is a wonderful place to come and reflect on the diversity of people that have come to Salt Lake City from all over the world and to teach children about other countries and their cultures.

Liberty Park—
One of Utah's oldest and largest urban parks, Liberty Park was established in 1881 on land that was originally settled by Isaac Chase. Chase's mill and home may be found within the park. Brigham Young bought the land and buildings from Chase in 1860. They were purchased by Salt Lake City from the Brigham Young estate in 1881. The park contains a variety of large mature trees and a circular roadway that is popular with joggers and bicyclists. The interior of the park is a joy for walkers. Children enjoy the amusement area and the Tracy Aviary, which was established in 1938 and is home to more than 240 species of birds. A beautiful fountain, donated by Obert C. Tanner, was constructed a few years ago, depicting the mountains and canyons east of Salt Lake City. The first public tennis courts were built in the park about 1915. Liberty Park has been one of the most popular tennis spots in the city ever since. The park is also the finishing place for the Days of '47 parade, the marathon and the 10-kilometer race, the holiday fireworks displays, and numerous other summer events.

Memory Grove—
The closest park to downtown, this is one of Salt Lake City's unappreciated treasures. A good spot for those who seek a quiet, reflective time away from the urban bustle. Memory Grove is located at the

mouth of City Creek Canyon at **135 East North Temple** just east of Capitol Hill and northeast of the LDS Church office building. The park was built by the Salt Lake Chapter of the Service Star Legion as a memorial to the Utah veterans of World War I. It was dedicated in 1924. Within the park is a French railroad boxcar, which was filled with mementos and treasures and given to each state by France in gratitude for America's support during World War I. Following World War II, a memorial chapel was built in the park. It is surrounded by memorial stones, placed by family members, to veterans who died in service but whose bodies were not returned to Utah. Other artifacts, including cannons, a personnel carrier from the Vietnam era, and a memorial to the Utahns killed at Pearl Harbor are also located in the grove.

Red Butte Garden and Arboretum—

Beautiful Red Butte Canyon, just east of the University of Utah and Fort Douglas, is the setting for one of the real jewels among Salt Lake City's parks and gardens. The garden and arboretum are under the direction of the University of Utah, and waterfalls, tranquil ponds, thousands of beautiful flowers, and sculpted ornamental grass collections provide an idyllic setting. Outside the gardens are 4 miles of hiking trails in a pristine natural area full of wildflowers, native shrubs, and grasses used by native birds and animals. The hiking trails wind through the old stone quarries from which red sandstone was taken to build buildings at Fort Douglas and a number of other buildings in Salt Lake City from the late 1840s until the 1930s. An amphitheater is used for a variety of activities including concerts, lectures, folk dance performances, and classic Greek tragedy productions. A visitor center, named for the late Walter Pace Cottam, a distinquished professor of botany at the University of Utah, opened in Aug. 1994. To reach the garden, drive to Fort Douglas and head east on Stover St. until it becomes Red Butte Canyon Rd., then con-

tinue east to the garden. For information, call **(801) 581-4747** or **581-8936**.

PLANETARIUMS

Hansen Planetarium—

The original Salt Lake City Public Library, built in 1905, has been the home of the Hansen Planetarium since it first opened in 1965. During the past three decades the Hansen Planetarium has become one of the most popular and best-known planetariums because of its innovative star shows that have educated two generations of Utahns about the heavens. The science and star shows are projected onto a 50-foot domed ceiling. Slides, films, 3-D images, sound effects, narration, and music are combined to educate and entertain. Laser light shows choreographed to music are also presented. The Planetarium also has a space science museum, hands-on exhibits, a gift shop, and a bookstore. For hours, show times, and current programs and exhibits, call **(801) 538-2098**. The planetarium is located at **15 South State St.,** just south of the Eagle Gate.

SCENIC DRIVES

Big Cottonwood Canyon Scenic Byway—

State Hwy. 152 is one of Utah's major recreation roads, providing access to the ski resorts of Brighton and Solitude in the winter and a number of hiking trails in the summer. Perhaps the most spectacular point in the canyon is Storm Mountain, located only 4 miles up the canyon. A picnic ground (fee charged) maintained by the US Forest Service offers plenty of picnic tables and a magnificent view of the granite peak, Storm Mountain, which looms high above the road and campground. Farther up the canyon are a number of hiking opportunities such as the Lake Blanche Trail. About a mile below Brighton, is the Guardsman's Pass Rd., a dirt road that takes you up over the pass, where you can drop down into Park City, 14 miles away, or head south into Heber Valley, just over 22 miles away. To reach the canyon, leave Interstate 215 at the 6200 South exit and follow the signs that direct you to the Big and Little Cottonwood Canyon recreation areas. At approximately 7000 South turn east at the light and follow the road to its terminus at the Brighton Ski Resort 15.

Bountiful/Farmington Loop—

This 24-mile-long drive offers panoramic views of Davis County, the Great Salt Lake, the mountain ranges west of the lake, and Morgan Valley to the east. From the valley floor, the road gains nearly a mile in elevation as it reaches Bountiful Peak at 9,000 feet. The gravel road is narrow, rough, and washboarded for much of the way. The switchbacks up the side of the mountain are steep, and the narrow road and precipitous slopes demand caution and attention. Nevertheless, the views are unforgettable and well worth the effort. While the loop can be taken in either direction, most people begin in Bountiful, taking 400 North east to 1300 East, then turning north onto the Ward Canyon Rd. The last segment of the loop descends Farmington Canyon. Passenger cars manage the road in good weather, but the going is slow. Four-wheel-drive vehicles and pickup trucks are preferable.

Little Cottonwood Canyon Scenic Byway—

Serving the ski resorts of Snowbird and Alta, this is the most heavily traveled mountain road along the Wasatch Front. Planners have talked for years about developing a public transportation system that would greatly limit the use of private vehicles in the canyon. Such a system would certainly enhance visitation since it is impossible to drive and take in the canyon's sheer, glaciated, granite walls. Short of driving up the canyon in an open-top convertible or Jeep, the Utah Transit bus is still the best way to reach the ski resorts and to view the canyon. Alternatively, you may

want to join the scores of bicyclists who ascend the nearly 4,000 feet from the canyon's mouth to the highway's end, 7 miles up the road at Alta. In addition to its world famous skiing, Little Cottonwood Canyon offers plenty of hiking opportunities, such as the White Pine and Red Pine trails. To reach Little Cottonwood Canyon, take Interstate 215 to the 6200 South Canyon exit and continue south along Wasatch Blvd., past state Hwy. 152, which turns east up Big Cottonwood Canyon. State Hwy. 210 continues south before turning east up Little Cottonwood Canyon.

Mill Creek Canyon—

This lovely mountain drive is especially pleasant because people who drive up the canyon do so to sightsee and are usually in no big hurry to reach a destination, as is too often the case in other canyons. A modest fee is charged at the entrance to the canyon. There are several picnic areas, some excellent hiking trails, and Log Haven Restaurant (see the Where to Eat section) located in the canyon, which deadends about 12 miles up the canyon. This drive is especially beautiful in the fall because of the stunning autumn foliage, as well as in the summer. You can reach Mill Creek Canyon by driving to Wasatch Blvd. and 3800 South, then heading east toward the mouth of the canyon.

Pioneer Memorial Scenic Backway—

This 34-mile-long scenic backway retraces the route of Mormon pioneers into the Salt Lake Valley through Emigration Canyon. It begins at the This Is the Place Monument across from Hogle Zoo, in the mouth of Emigration Canyon, and heads east up the canyon, over Little Mountain, then swings to the north to ascend Big Mountain. It was from the summit of Big Mountain that the pioneers got their first glimpse of the Salt Lake Valley. The backway continues down Big Mountain, past East Canyon Reservoir, and on to the junction Utah Hwy. 65 with Interstate 84 at Henefer. From Henefer, you can either return along the route you came, take Interstate 84 west toward Ogden, or turn right and join Interstate 80 a few miles southeast of Henefer and follow it through Parley's Canyon back to Salt Lake City. The backway is impassable during the winter.

SHOPPING

Crossroads Mall and ZCMI Center—

These two huge downtown malls are located across the street from one other and, with a combined total of more than 200 stores and shops, you should be able to find anything you are looking for. The Crossroads Mall is on the west side of Main St., between South Temple and 100 South; the ZCMI Center is on the east side. Both malls have covered parking terraces and are good places to park for touring or attending events on Temple Square, which is across the street to the north. ZCMI, which stands for Zions Cooperative Mercantile Institution, was established in 1868 under the direction of Brigham Young as the hub of a network of Mormon-run cooperatives. The aim of these cooperatives was to keep the economic wealth of the Mormon kingdom circulating among its members, instead of allowing it to slip away to the flood of merchants due to arrive with the coming of the transcontinental railroad in 1869. ZCMI was one of the West's first department stores. Today, it still offers excellent quality merchandise. The store's restored cast iron western facade is a downtown landmark. Both malls are open Mon.–Fri. 10 am–9 pm, and Sat. 10 am–6:00 pm. The Crossroads Mall is open Sun. noon–5:00 pm.

Sam Weller's Zion Book Store—

Utah's favorite bookstore is Sam Weller's Zion Book Store at **254 South Main.** Opened in 1929 by Sam's father, an immigrant from Germany, Sam has continued the tradition of operating a fine bookstore and is recognized as the foremost authority on Utah and western books in the state. This is the place to call for rare and out-of-print books and for the best selection of Utah and western history and literature anywhere. The basement used-book department has thousands of copies of books

organized by topic available at bargain prices. Open Mon.–Sat. 10:00 am.–6:00 pm; **(801) 328-2586.**

Trolley Square—

During the early 1970s, the old trolley barns, between **500 South and 600 South** and **600 East and 700 East**, were rehabilitated in one of Salt Lake City's first adaptive reuse projects. They are now a shopping center-a popular attraction with both visitors and long-time residents. A number of specialty shops, restaurants, and movie theaters can be found here. Shops are open Mon.–Sat. 10 am–9 pm and Sun. noon–5 pm.

PROFESSIONAL SPORTS TEAMS

Salt Lake Buzz—

In 1994, Triple A baseball returned to Salt Lake City after having been absent for more than a decade. The Portland franchise moved to Salt Lake City and to a brand new baseball stadium, Franklin Quest Field, built on the site of the old Derks Field. One of the reasons for building the new stadium at the Derks Field location was to preserve what many consider the best stadium backdrop in the world—the towering Wasatch Mountains. The stadium is a modern facility that, coupled with the design and use of traditional green-colored seating, made it seem historic when I attended the inaugural game on Apr. 11, 1994. The expansive natural green grass of the outfield and the majestic mountains rising in the distance beyond the centerfield fence make this a baseball Shangri-la. For tickets and schedules call **(801) 485-3800.**

Utah Jazz—

When the New Orleans Jazz professional basketball team moved to Salt Lake City in 1979, the owners of the team decided to keep the original name, even though most people find Utah and jazz to be quite incongruous. Nevertheless, the Jazz has captured the hearts of Utahns as the state's only major league sport franchise. The 20,000-seat Delta Center was completed in time for the 1991–1992 NBA season for an increase of nearly 8,000 seats from the previous home in the Salt Palace. The Delta Center is located between South Temple and 100 South on 300 West, three blocks west of Temple Square. The changing fortunes of the Jazz and what team they are playing against determine the availability of tickets for home games. Usually you can get tickets, but it is best to get them as early as possible. Call **(801) 355-3865** for tickets and schedules.

ZOOS

Hogle Zoo—
Hogle Zoo is a Salt Lake City and Utah institution. The zoo occupies a 50-acre site at the mouth of Emigration Canyon, just south of the This Is the Place Monument. With more than 1,000 animals at the zoo, there is plenty to see. Favorites include the sea lions, monkeys, apes, polar bears, elephants, giraffes, rhinoceros, hippopotamus, lions, and tigers. There is also a children's petting zoo and miniature railroad rides. Until 1972, the zoo's most popular animal was Shasta the Liger. Born in 1948 of a tigress mother and lion father, Shasta lived 24 years—the equivalent of 120 years for a human. Thanks to the skills of a taxidermist, Shasta has occupied a place of honor in the Tiger House since 1972. Hogle Zoo is open daily year-round, from 9:00 am–6:00 pm in the summer, 9:00 am–5:00 pm in the spring and fall, and 9:00 am–4:30 pm during the winter. The zoo is located at **2600 Sunnyside Ave.; (801) 582-1631.**

Tracy Aviary—
See Liberty Park in the Parks section.

WHERE TO STAY

ACCOMMODATIONS

Anniversary Inn—$$$
While this unusual bed and breakfast caters to couples celebrating anniversaries, under the theme Rediscover the Magic, anyone looking for a unique bed-and-breakfast experience will want to check out the Anniversary Inn. The Inn is the outcome of the fantastic imagination of Tom and Dorothy Heers and their friends. The Heers invited family and friends to sketch their "dream room," each of which has been incorporated into the 13 suites inside the mansion. Each suite is unique, but the most memorable is the Carriage Suite, where guests sleep in a bed built into a carriage and the Lake Powell suite with red rock walls, waterfall, and a raft bed. Each suite has a stereo with surround sound, VCR or video disk player with complimentary movies, a refrigerator full of snacks, a pair of cozy robes, and a continental breakfast. One of the suites allows disabled access. The Inn is located in an historic mansion that was built before 1890 for one of Utah's pioneer Jewish merchants, Emmanuel Kahn. Tours of the Inn conducted Tues. afternoons from 2:30 pm–3:30 pm. **678 East South Temple; (801) 363-4900.**

The Anton Boxrud
Bed and Breakfast—$$ to $$$
Designed by one of Salt Lake City's best-known architects, Walter E. Ware, this house was built in 1901. It was renovated as a bed and breakfast with careful attention to preserving the stained glass, woodwork, hardwood floors, and pocket doors—doors that disappear into the side walls. Of the four rooms, one has a private bath; the other three—with a queen bed, double bed, and twin beds—have a shared bath. All rooms are nonsmoking. Ray and Margaret Fuller are the owners. Located a half block south of the Governor's Mansion at **57 South 600 East; (801) 363-8035.**

Brigham Street Inn—$$$

This grand red-brick Victorian building was constructed in 1898 as the home of Walter Cogswell Lynn, a self-made man who became a success despite being abandoned in Salt Lake by his parents at age 12. The current owners restored the 2.5-story house into what is now a very elegant bed and breakfast. Each of the nine rooms is individually decorated and includes a private bath. A continental breakfast is served in the dining room. **1135 East South Temple; (801) 364-4461.**

Inn at Temple Square—$$$

Constructed in 1930 to provide additional lodging across the street from Temple Square, the Inn was renovated after the Hotel Utah was closed. While not as luxurious as the old grand hotel, the Inn does offer excellent rooms and an other-era ambiance not found in the larger hotels that share the same block. There are 90 spacious and nicely decorated rooms. Guest may use the Inn's library and the Carriage Court Restaurant. Easy access to Temple Square, Symphony Hall, and the Delta Center. **71 West South Temple; (801) 531-1000 or 1-800-843-4668.**

Peery Hotel—$$

The Peery Hotel, established in 1910, is Salt Lake City's oldest hotel. Although it fell into disrepute for a number of years, it was restored in 1985 to an elegance that makes this a favorite stop for visitors who want to combine the best of a hotel and bed-and-breakfast experience. There are 77 guest rooms, each uniquely appointed with antiques and other furnishings. A continental breakfast is provided, along with daily newspapers, shoeshines, and shuttle service to and from the airport. Other amenities include a whirlpool and exercise room, conference rooms, two restaurants, and a state liquor store on the premises. **110 West Broadway (300 South); (801) 521-4300 or 1-800-331-0073.**

Pinecrest Bed and Breakfast Inn— $$ to $$$

Emigration Canyon is the location for this 6-acre estate, which boasts gardens, a stream, and a trout pond. The Inn has six rooms, each with a private bath. Two of the rooms have private Jacuzzi tubs, two others have fireplaces and kitchens. Phil and Donnie Davis are the owners. Pinecrest is about 10 miles—20 minutes—from downtown Salt Lake City, up Emigration Canyon. Follow 800 South past Hogle Zoo as the road enters the canyon. **6211 Emigration Canyon Rd., (801) 583-6663 or 1-800-359-6663.**

Saltair Bed and Breakfast—$$ to $$$

Jan Bartler and Nancy Saxton are the innkeepers at what is the oldest continuously operated bed and breakfast in Utah. The 1920s Mission Revival–style house is listed in the National Register of Historic Places. It has five guest rooms—two with private baths, three with a shared bath. No smoking is allowed in the house. The Saltair is within walking distance of the University of Utah and just over a mile to downtown Salt Lake City. **164 South 900 East; (801) 533-8184.**

Spruces Bed and Breakfast— $$ to $$$

Each of the four suites in this 1903 Gothic Revival–style house has a private entrance, television, telephone, and bath. One of the units has three bedrooms and a living room; two of the units have kitchens. Breakfast is served in the Tree Room, or you can take it to your own room. The Spruces is located in the Cottonwood area of Salt Lake City, just north of the Wheeler Historic Farm. Jane E. Johnson is the owner. **900 East 6151 South; (801) 268-8762.**

Wildflower Bed and Breakfast— $$ to $$$

This 1891 Victorian house, which is listed in the National Register of Historic Places, is located in what was one of Salt Lake City's first streetcar suburbs. The "Perkins Addition" allowed Salt Lake City's affluent to live in a "pure, healthful, invigorating atmosphere free of smoke and dust and only a twelve-minute five-cent fare streetcar ride on the 900 East line to the city center." Since 1891, the city has grown up around the Perkins Addition and 1700 South has become a route for commuters to the nearby Westminster College campus. There are three nonsmoking rooms, the largest of which is the third-floor suite, which has a kitchen, living room, private bath, and entrance. Breakfast is served in the formal dining room. **936 East 1700 South; (801) 466-0600.**

AIRPORT
A large complex of chain hotels and inns has sprung up off Interstate 80, 2 to 3 miles west of the Salt Lake International Airport. All offer good accommodations, heated swimming pools, restaurants, and shuttle service to the airport.

Airport Hilton—$$$ to $$$$
Two hundred ninety-six units; **(801) 539-1515 or 1-800-HILTONS.**

Comfort Inn—$$ to $$$
One hundred sixty units; **(801) 537-7444 or 1-800-535-8742.**

Holiday Inn—$$$
One hundred ninety-one units; **(801) 533-9000.**

Nendels Inn Airport—$$ to $$$
Ninety-one units; **(801) 355-0088.**

Quality Inn—$$ to $$$
One hundred eighty-eight units; **(801) 537-7020 or 1-800-522-5575.**

Radison Hotel—$$ to $$$
One hundred twenty-eight units; **(801) 364-5800 or 1-800-333-3333.**

DOWNTOWN
With the exception of the Peery Hotel and the Inn at Temple Square, described previously, most Salt Lake City visitors who stay in the downtown area do so in one of the following chain hotels. All offer shuttle service to the airport, have restaurants, heated swimming pools, whirlpools, exercise rooms, and are within walking distance of Temple Square and the Delta Center.

Double Tree Hotel—$$$
Three hundred eighty-one units. **215 West South Temple; (801) 531-7500 or 1-800-528-0444.**

Embassy Suites Hotel—$$ to $$$
Two hundred forty-one units. **600 South West Temple; (801) 359-7800.**

Salt Lake Hilton— $$$ to $$$$
Three hundred fifty-one units. **150 West 500 South; (801) 532-3344 or 1-800-HILTONS.**

Holiday Inn—$$$
One hundred sixty units. **230 West 600 South; (801) 532-7000.**

Howard Johnson—$$ to $$$
Two hundred twenty-six units. **122 West South Temple; (801) 521-0130 or 1-800-GO-HOJO.**

Little America—$$$
Eight hundred fifty units. **500 South Main St.; (801) 363-6781 or 1-800-453-9450.**

The Marriott Hotel—$$$ to $$$$
Five hundred sixteen units. **75 South West Temple; (801) 531-800 or 1-800-228-9290.**

Olympus Hotel—Best Western—$$ to $$$
Three hundred ninety-four units. **161 West 600 South; (801) 521-7373.**

Quality Inn—$$ to $$$
Two hundred forty-seven units. **154 West 600 South; (801) 521-2930.**

Red Lion—$$$ to $$$$
Five hundred two units. **255 South West Temple; (801) 328-2000.**

Shilo Inn—$$ to $$$
Two hundred units. **206 South West Temple; (801) 521-9500.**

OTHER
Avenues—$
The Avenues is a member of the American Youth Hostel Association (YHA) and has inexpensive dorm rooms, plus single, double, and triple bedrooms. It is a popular lodging place with young travelers to the city. Guests have access to kitchen and laundry facilities and two lounges with fireplaces and color TVs. The Avenues is located in a large residential area of the same name, just a short walk from downtown. Most of the homes date back to the turn of the century, with a number from the second half of the 19th century. The entire Avenues area has been listed in the National Register of Historic Places. Ed and Cindy Peebles are the proprietors. **107 F Street; (801) 363-8137.**

Residence Inn by Marriott— $$$ to $$$$
With fireplaces, loft bedrooms, and kitchens, this is a place for those who want apartment-style accommodations away from home and are willing to pay for them. Heated pool, whirlpool, sport court, and airport transportation. Located about a mile from the downtown area and a couple of blocks from Trolley Square. **765 East 400 South; (801) 532-5511 or 1-800-228-9290.**

University Park Hotel—$$$
Located south and east of the University of Utah in the University Research Park, not far from historic Fort Douglas, Hogle Zoo, and the This Is the Place Monument, this is a popular hotel for visitors to the university and for those who want to be out of the downtown area. The University of Utah's colorful basketball coach, Rick Majerus, likes the hotel so much that he has made it his permanent residence. Two hundred twenty units, heated indoor pool, whirlpool, exercise room, rental bikes, and airport transportation. **480 Wakara Way; (801) 581-1000.**

SKI AREAS
For Alta and Snowbird, see the Skiing section; for Park City, see the **Park City** chapter.

CAMPING
PUBLIC
Public campgrounds are limited to two US Forest Service campgrounds in Farmington Canyon. **Sunset Campground** is 4 miles up the canyon and offers 32 sites for tents and trailers. Five and a half miles farther up the canyon, and a thousand feet higher in elevation, the **Bountiful Peak Campground** has 79 sites. Picnic tables, drinking water, and primitive toilets are available. Both campgrounds are open from June–Sept. No fees are charged at either campground, but stays are limited to seven days. For information, call the **Wasatch Cache National Forest** at **(801) 524-5030.**

PRIVATE
There are two large RV parks located just 2 miles west of Temple Square and Downtown Salt Lake City on North Temple Street. **CAMP VIP** has 250 sites with 198 pullthrough full hookups and a grass tent area. There are showers, a laundry, grocery story, and outdoor pool open during the summer. **1350 North Temple; (801) 328-0224.**

The **KOA Kampground** has more than 300 sites and a tent area. There are showers, outdoor pool, laundry, a playground, and grocery store. **1400 North Temple; (801) 355-1192.**

North of Salt Lake City—
Cherry Hill Campground—One of the largest and most elaborate private campgrounds in the state, Cherry Hill Campground offers everything from tent camping with no hookups to full hookups with water and electricity. The campground has 250 spaces, including 143 pullthrough spaces. Located 20 minutes from both Salt Lake and Ogden, and just five minutes from Lagoon Amusement Park, this is a popular campground, so reservations are recommended. The campground is adjacent to Cherry Hill Recreation Park, which includes water slides, miniature golf, theater, swimming pool, baseball batting range, game rooms, and an inner-tube river

run. The campground is outfitted with a convenience store, laundry, snack bar, service station, and gift shop. An added bonus for campers is the invitation to pick and eat cherries and peaches from the orchards, as they become ready. To reach the campground from Salt Lake City, take exit 326 off Interstate 15, then go 2 miles north on US Hwy. 89 and watch for the campground on the west side of the highway. **1325 South Main, Kaysville, UT 84037; (801) 451-5379.**

Lagoon's Pioneer Village Campground— Located adjacent to the Lagoon Amusement Park, the Pioneer Village Campground offers 204 RV trailer sites, 91 of which have complete hookups and 57 are

drive throughs. Another 58 tent sites are available, and the campground has plenty of shade trees, picnic tables, drinking water, showers, and a laundry. Opened from Apr.–Oct.; **(801) 451-2812.**

South of Salt Lake City—
Mountain Shadows RV Park—Located in the south end of Salt Lake Valley, just off Interstate 15, Mountain Shadows is a well-maintained campground with 99 full hookup pullthrough spaces. The park has a tenting area, swimming pool, spa, exercise room, game room, big screen TV in the clubhouse, showers, playground, grocery, and laundry facilities. Take exit 294 off Interstate 15 and head east, then take the first road (Minuteman Dr.) south for 2 miles; **(801) 571-4024.**

WHERE TO EAT

There are hundreds of eating establishments in Salt Lake City and surrounding communities. I have chosen to highlight some of my own favorites and those of friends and people I trust. Readers who want a more extensive guide to Salt Lake Area restaurants should obtain a copy of Debbie and R. F. Boehm's *This Is the Place to Dine: A Guide to Salt Lake Area Restaurants*, which has full-page descriptions of 171 restaurants in the Salt Lake City and Park City areas.

AMERICAN
Crown Burgers—$
When John Katzourakas opened the first Crown Burger in 1978, many of us thought that the hamburger had been rediscovered, if not reinvented. The charcoal-grilled burgers are a Salt Lake City favorite, and we owe John a debt of gratitude for leaving his native Crete in 1963 to emigrate to Utah and make his burgers a Salt Lake City institution. Other menu items include pastrami burgers, fish and chicken sandwiches, and salads with a tangy Greek dressing—my personal favorite. With tasty food, low prices, and quick service, this is a good place to grab a quick lunch. Hours

are from 10:00 am–10:30 pm Mon.–Sat. John's place is at **377 East 200 South; (801) 532-1155.** Other family members operate places at **118 North 300 West,** three blocks west of Temple Square, just off North Temple, **(801) 532-5300; 3190 South Highland Dr., (801) 467-6633;** and **2684 South 3200 West, (801) 972-8586.**

Lamb's Restaurant—$ to $$$
One of Salt Lake City's oldest continually operating restaurants, Lamb's was a 20-year-old establishment in Logan before it moved to its present location in Salt Lake City's Herald Building in 1939. The original owner, George P. Lamb, a Greek immigrant, worked his way west, arriving in Utah in 1910. He worked as a waiter until he went into business for himself. In 1941 he took on Ted Speros, born in Bingham Canyon to Greek parents, as a partner, and since his retirement in 1982, Ted's son John Speros has operated Lamb's. The building in which Lamb's is located was constructed in 1905 to house the *Salt Lake Herald* newspaper and is listed in the National Register of Historic Places. Little has changed since 1939, and a visit to Lamb's allows you to step back more than a half-century backward in time.

The booths and table are the same; the menu features most of the traditional items; and the waitresses wear the old-fashioned white uniforms that are seldom seen in Utah anymore. Open for breakfast, lunch, and dinner Mon.–Sat. 7:00 am–9 pm. Lamb's is a Salt Lake City favorite for breakfast. The lunch menu features sandwiches and salads, while long-time dinner favorites include fried large oysters, several selections of seafood, grilled pork chops, and roast leg of lamb. **169 South Main St.; (801) 364-7166.**

The Lion House Pantry—$ to $$

The basement of Brigham Young's 1856 three-story home is the location for this cafeteria-style lunch room. It is popular with employees at the nearby LDS Church offices as well as downtown shoppers. Good, low-priced food, and the historic setting make it an excellent choice for lunch. The pantry is located in rooms that were used by the Brigham Young family not only as a pantry and kitchen but for school classes, and as a fruit cellar and buttery. The lunch menu changes daily but features homemade soups, fresh-from-the-oven desserts, and traditional main courses of beef, fish, and poultry. Vegetarian dishes are also available. Open for lunch only from 11 am–2 pm, Mon.–Fri. A seafood and prime rib buffet is offered Fri. evening, from 5:30–9:00 pm and Sat. from 5:00–9:00 pm. Reservations are accepted for the evening buffet only. **63 East South Temple; (801) 363-5466.**

Log Haven—$$ to $$$

This is my favorite mountain restaurant in Utah. Located up Mill Creek Canyon, just east of Salt Lake City, this twisting and winding road has no ski resorts or large developments at its terminus. There is no greater pleasure than a drive up Mill Creek Canyon, a hike up one of the trails described above, and then Sunday brunch or dinner at Log Haven. The original log cabin was constructed as a summer home by L. F. Raines, a Utah entrepreneur, in 1920. Across the road, a pond and artificial waterfall offer an added element of charm to Log Haven's

setting. The menu includes a variety of American and Continental entrées from pasta to duck, steak, and lobster. The Mill Creek Mud Pie is a house specialty. The Sunday brunch is especially popular for the wide selection of excellent food and the chance to enjoy a Sunday outing in the canyon. Open for dinner Tues.–Sat. 6:00 pm–10:00 pm and for brunch on Sun. 9:30 am–2:30 pm. Closed Mon. Located 4 miles up Mill Creek Canyon (head east on 3800 South off Wasatch Blvd.). Reservations are recommended; **(801) 272-8255.**

Market Street Grill and Market Street Broiler—$$ to $$$

Seafood in Salt Lake City means the Market Street, whether it is the Grill, downtown in the historic 1906 New York Hotel on Post Office Place, or the Broiler, located in old historic Fire Station No. 8 just west of the University of Utah Campus. Both restaurants are operated by Gastronomy, Inc., a restaurant group that prides itself on its national reputation for excellent food, professional service, unique surroundings, and an innovative approach to establishing and operating good eating establishments. The seafood is flown in daily from both coasts. Other menu items include ribs, steak, chops, and chicken, along with a full selection of breakfast items. Both restaurants are open Mon.–Fri. 6:30 am–10:00 pm, and on Sat. 7:30 am–11 pm. The Grill offers Sunday brunch from 11:30 am–3:30 pm. Both are open Sun. for dinner 4 pm–10 pm. The Grill is located at **50 Post Office Pl.; (801) 322-4668;** and the Broiler at **260 South and 1300 East; (801) 583-8803**.

Peery Pub and Cafe—$ to $$

The beautifully restored Peery Hotel makes an excellent setting for this popular lunch and dinner place, and it is a favorite lunch spot. The elegant gray walls with mahogany trim are eye-catching. The Pub serves soups, sandwiches, and salads from 11:00 am–10:30 pm Mon.–Sat. A daily pasta salad special is offered. The cafe is open from 5:00 pm–10:00 pm for dinner Tues.–Sat. The parent of the Peery Pub is the **Pub** at **Trolley Square**. It has the same menu and hours as the Peery, but is open only to those 21 and over. **110 West 300 South; (801) 521-8919.**

Ruth's Diner—$ to $$

Opened in 1946 by Ruth Evans, a former Salt Lake City cabaret singer, and located a short 2-mile drive up Emigration Canyon, Ruth's Diner has become a Salt Lake City institution. Ruth opened her first diner in 1930, but lost her lease in 1946. Undaunted, she bought a Salt Lake trolley car, moved it up Emigration Canyon, and operated it for more than three decades until she sold it to Curtis Oberhansly. Several additions have been made to the original trolley car, and you won't recognize it as such, but Ruth's is perhaps the last of the original diners left in Utah. The menu has also undergone considerable change since Ruth cooked hamburgers in a frying pan and served beer out of a cooler. Curtis and his partner Mike Ray have expanded the menu and offer a variety of sandwiches, salads, burgers, and ethnic specialties. Breakfast is served 9 am–3:30 pm. Open seven days a week from 9 am–10 pm. **2100 Emigation Canyon Rd.; (801) 582-5807.**

ASIAN

Cafe Trang—$ to $$

Like other American cities, Salt Lake City has seen the establishment of several Vietnamese restaurants during the past several years, but the most popular with locals is the Cafe Trang. This is a small family restaurant, and there is something heart-warming about watching the young lady working the cash register busy with her homework whenever she has a spare minute. Other family members are congenial waiters and waitresses. The cafe does not look like much either from the outside or the inside, but the Vietnamese food is excellent and the Chinese food a good alternative for those who still have not discovered the excellence of Vietnamese food. The most popular Vietnamese foods with Americans include the rice noodles, served with vegetables and a special fish sauce, or the delicious soups served with bean sprouts and other vegetables. Open Tues.–Thurs. 11:00 am–9:00 pm; 11:00 am–9:30 pm Fri. and Sat. **818 South Main Street; (801) 539-1638.**

Mandarin—$$ to $$$

The best Chinese restaurant is not located in Salt Lake City, nor is it owned by a Chinese family. The Mandarin is located 10 miles north of Salt Lake City in Bountiful, and the owners are of Greek ancestry. Nevertheless, my Chinese-American friends do agree that the food is excellent, the decor exquisite, and the kimono-clad young American waitresses charming. There is an excellent selection of beef, chicken, duck, lamb, pork, seafood, and vegetarian dishes. You will usually have to wait to get a table, especially on weekends; however, if you have a party of 10 or more, reservations are taken on weekday evenings. Open Mon.–Sat. from 5:00 pm–9:30 pm weekdays; 5 pm–10:30 pm on weekends. **348 East 900 North, Bountiful; (801) 298-2406.**

Mikado—$$ to $$$

Salt Lake City's oldest and most complete Japanese restaurant is the Mikado, located a block south of Temple Square. The Mikado features a sushi menu, plus Japanese dinners either served or prepared and cooked at your table. One of everybody's favorite dishes, which is cooked at your table, is shabu shabu, which are thin slices of prime beef, stir fried with fresh vegetables, mushrooms, and bean cake lightly cooked in a special broth and served with a delicious dipping sauce that comes in a special iron pot. Children's dinners of shrimp tempura and chicken or beef teriyaki are offered. You can eat western style seated at tables or Japanese style in private dining rooms where you take your shoes off and sit on mats around a low table. Open for dinner Mon.–Thurs. from 6:00 pm–9:30 pm; Fri. and Sat. 6:00 pm–10:30 pm. Reservations are recommended. **67 West 100 South; (801) 328-0929.**

Thai House Restaurant—$$

Located just north of the South Campus of the Salt Lake Community College on State St., the Thai House Restaurant looks quite plain on the outside, but the interior is pleasant and the Thai food excellent. If you are a stranger to Thai cuisine, don't be afraid to ask the very pleasant waitresses for suggestions and what you can expect. Thai food has a much fierier, spicier taste than Chinese and Indian foods, and is strongly aromatic with lemongrass and small chiles. My favorites include the paht khing stir-fried chicken with ginger and green onion, which you can also get as a vegetarian dish without the chicken. If you want the hot stuff, try one of the beer or chicken curry dishes. Open Mon.–Thurs. 11:30 am–9:00 pm, Fri. 11:30 pm–10:00 pm, and Sat. noon–10:00 pm. Reservations are recommended for dinner on the weekends. **1499 South State St.; (801) 486-8043.**

CONTINENTAL

Finn's—$$$ to $$$$

Finn and Grete Gurtholt, natives of Norway, opened Finn's in 1952 and, if the Salt Lake Landmark Commission gave out certificates for the city's oldest and most authentic restaurants, Finn's would head the list. Long a favorite of Salt Lakers for its excellent food and lasting elegance, dinner at Finn's is a special experience. The seven-course dinners make eating a full-evening affair. Entrées, such as Wiener schnitzel, broiled steak, lamb, and shrimp, are served on large china platters. Several different kinds of bread are served; all are baked daily in the restaurant's bakery. The Alaskan cream puff, a pastry shell filled with ice cream surrounded by whipped cream and topped with a delicious caramel sauce, is a must for dessert. Finn's is open Mon.–Sat. 6:00 pm–10:00 pm and is closed Sun. Reservations are required. **2675 East Parleys Way; (801) 466-4682.**

Fleur de Lys—$$$ to $$$$

In the summer of 1993, the Fleur de Lys relocated from its 17-year home in Arrow Press Square south a few blocks to Postal Place, next to the old downtown post office. To this a larger facility, the owner Madame Marguerite Gales, brought with her the beautiful tapestries and the little touches that made the original location so special. Chefs Patrick Yves and Jan and Edward Puc prepare a variety of entree selections, including beef, seafood, fowl, veal, and lamb. Veal Napoleon chevre, the rack of lamb, and soups from the French provinces are favorites. Reservations are required, and it be sure to give yourself plenty of time to enjoy the excellent food, pleasant atmosphere, and charm of what many Salt Lakers consider the city's best French restaurant. Open Mon.–Sat. 5:30 pm–10:00 pm. **39 West Market St.; (801) 359-5753.**

La Caille at Quail Run—$$$$

At the turnoff from Wasatch Blvd., a white-and-blue road sign informs you that La Caille is 2 kilometers ahead. This is just one of the small touches that help convince you by the time you leave La Caille you have really spent the evening at a French country estate rather than at the bottom of Little Cottonwood Canyon. The building is a replica of a French château, and the grounds have a brick road, trees, vineyards, flowers, creek, and pond. The menu includes some of the most expensive items to be found in all of Utah, but for the connoisseur and the romantic, it is all worth it. Dinner at La Caille is an unforgettable experience. Some friends of mine have a "La Caille savings bank"—they save a couple of dollars a week for an annual dinner at La Caille. There is a good variety of French and continental dishes of poultry, seafood, veal, beef, and lamb. Favorites include the rack of lamb, broiled and served with marnier glaze and veal medallions served with portabella mushrooms and champaign cream sauce. For dessert don't pass up the flaming baked Alaska. Open daily for dinner from 6:00 pm–9:00 pm and Sun. for brunch from 10:00 am–1:00 pm. Reservations are required. **9565 South Wasatch Blvd.; (801) 942-1751.**

Le Parisien—$$ to $$$

The other favorite French restaurant in the downtown area is the Le Parisien, a restaurant that has been around for over two decades. There are three sections to the restaurant, but I prefer the middle section where the red-and-white-checked tablecloths help establish the atmosphere of a quaint and cozy restaurant. The food is very good and moderately priced. In addition to several basic French dishes—quiche Lorraine, coq au vin, veau Français, châteaubriand béarnaise, rack of lamb Provençale, and my favorite, the tournedo aux champignons—sautéed filet of beef cooked in a red wine and mushroom sauce—there are fish and Italian dishes. The fish dishes include salmon, trout, scallops, sole, and a fish of the day. If you don't want the traditional lasagna, spaghetti, and manicotti dishes, ask about the pasta of the day. The chef likes to experiment with different ways of presenting pasta, and if you like something different, you won't be disappointed. Open Mon.–Sat. 11:00 am–11:00 pm and Sun. 4:30 pm–10:00 pm. **417 South 300 East; (801) 364-5223.**

GERMAN
Marianne's Delicatessen—$ to $$

Klause Rathke, who broadcasts a weekly German hour on a local radio station, claims that the German dishes prepared by cook Sylvia at Marianne's, a four-generation delicatessen, are at least as good as you will find in Germany, if not better. Marianne's parents opened the delicatessen in the 1950s when they immigrated to Utah from Germany after World War II. Marianne and her husband Horst took over the delicatessen in the 1960s, and today their daughter and granddaughter are involved. Horst makes his own sausages, and a lunchtime favorite is the Sausage Sampler, which includes a small bratwurst, knackwurst, and weisswurst. Homemade sandwiches and soup are offered, and each day Sylvia prepares a traditional German dinner special such as sauerbraten, roladen, Kasseler, and Konigsburger Klopse. The restaurant is located in the western half of

the delicatessen, which has a good assortment of imported goods, including a collection of more than 300 German language videos, which are available for rent. Open Tues.–Sat. for lunch, from 11:00 am–3:00 pm. **149 West 200 South; (801) 364-0513.**

Siegfried's Delicatessen—$

Salt Lake City is fortunate to have two fine German delicatessens that complement each other with their lunch service. Where Marianne's is a slower-paced, sit-down-and-be-served establishment, Siegfried's is a faster-paced, pick-up-your-tray, cafeteria-style place, whose main offerings are sandwiches or the bratwurst dinner, with one of Siegfried's own sausages and a choice of two heaping scoops of sauerkraut, red cabbage, coleslaw, hot or cold potato salad, macaroni salad, green salad, or a refreshing cucumber and tomato salad. While you are waiting in line, you will pass a case filled with wonderful German cakes and pastries. Go ahead and order one with your lunch. After all, you only live once. The delicatessen is well stocked with imported items, and Siegfried has his own bakery, which produces delicious German bread, rolls, and pretzels. Siegfried Meyer came to Utah from East Germany at the age of 12 and took over the delicatessen from another German family in the 1970s, when he was in his twenties. His food is popular with downtown businessmen, workers, and German-Americans who come to shop. Open Mon.–Sat. for lunch from 11:00 am–3:00 pm. **69 West 300 South; (801) 355-3891.**

GREEK/MIDDLE EASTERN
Cedars of Lebanon—$ to $$$

Raffi Daghlian, an Armenian Lebanese, opened this restaurant in 1981, after he came to Salt Lake City to study at the University of Utah Medical School. His Lebanese wife, Marlene, and Moroccan chef and dietician, Abdule, are instrumental in the restaurant's success. While most dishes are Lebanese and Armenian, the Cedars of Lebanon also offers food from Israel, Morocco, Greece, and Turkey. This is one of the few places in Salt Lake that serves couscous (crushed wheat). The chicken couscous and couscous plate for vegetarians are both recommended. If you are calorie-conscious, Abdule has put together four specials with chicken, beef, lamb, and a vegetarian combination plate dinner with less than 600 calories. On Fri. and Sat. evenings exotic belly dancers circle around while you eat, making dining at the Cedars of Lebanon a visual as well as a gastronomic delight. Don't let the storefront-like appearance discourage you, and if you are a stranger to Middle Eastern food, be assured that there are plenty of dishes you are guaranteed to like. Open Mon.–Sat. for lunch 11:00 am–3:30 pm and for dinner 5:00 pm–10:00 pm; open until 11 pm on Fri. and Sat. Reservations are required on the weekend. **152 East 200 South; (801) 364-4096.**

Hungry I—$$ to $$$

For years, the best place in Salt Lake City to buy Greek gyros, souvlaki, and other Greek staples was the Hungry I on State St. Unfortunately, that more earthy establishment is now closed. A more elaborate and, alas, pricier restaurant has been opened on Foothill Dr.; fortunately, however, the Greek food is at least as good if not better and more varied than at the original location. My favorite is the Hellenic sampling platter which offers a taste of just about everything. Open Mon.–Fri. 10 am–10 pm; open Sat. to 11 pm and Sun to 8 pm. **1440 South Foothill Dr.; (801) 582-8600.**

Star of India—$$ to $$$

Salt Lake City's Indian restaurant was established in 1990 by Parshotam Singh, who left his northern Indian homeland of Punjab because of the Sikh unrest. Parshotam will explain the intricacies of Indian food and offer recommendations for first-timers. The food is cooked on charcoal in a special custom-made clay oven, just like those used in India. The menu offers a variety of traditional Indian breads, rice, plus lamb, chicken and seafood dishes. There are 10 vegetarian dishes such as saag paneer, a classic Indian vegetable dish with cubes of homemade cottage cheese, cooked with spinach and mild spices; or channa masala—chick peas, fresh tomatoes, and cubes of potatoes cooked in a tangy sauces of spices carefully flavored with herbs. A special lunch buffet allows you to sample several of the dishes, or, for dinner, the chef's special thali offers 12 different items. Open Mon.–Sat. for lunch 11:30 am–2:30 pm and dinner 5:30 pm–10 pm. **177 East 200 South; (801) 363-7555.**

ITALIAN

Baci Trattoria—$$ to $$$

Gastronomy, Inc.'s success with fine restaurants in historic buildings (see the Market Street Grill and Market Street Broiler above) led them to expand their endeavors to the historic buildings on Pierpont Ave. where they operate the Baci Trattoria, which features excellent Italian food, and Cafe Pierpont, which specializes in Mexican food. The Baci Trattoria offers traditional Italian foods, including European-style individual plate pizzas baked in a wood-burning oven, freshly made pastas and lasagna, and veal, chicken, and fish dishes. The interior of the restaurant alone is worth a visit. The huge three-sectioned stained glass pictures behind the bar are magnificent, while the upstairs section has a 50-foot-long mural on the east wall painted by seven Utah artists. Open for lunch Mon.–Fri. 11:30 am–2:30 pm, and for dinner from 5:00 pm–10:00 pm; open until 11:00 pm on Fri. and Sat. nights. **134 West Pierpont Ave.; (801) 328-1500.**

Fresco's—$$ to $$$

This is the only restaurant in Utah for which the entrance is through a bookstore. Fresco's is a small, intimate place, located in the back of the King's English bookstore. Inside there is room for only 46 guests at the 13 tables. The restaurant doubles in size during the summer when patio seating is available. This is a restaurant that locals do not like to tell others about, but good news travels fast. The food is excellent, but the capacity, as noted, is small, and dinner reservations are a must in the winter and often must be made a week in advance. Diners like to come early and browse in the bookstore before enjoying their meal. The menu is primarily northern Italian. The most popular item is the linguini con tutti mari, pasta tossed with prawns, sea scallops, crab, and fresh fish, served in herbed seafood butter sauce with dried tomatoes. Manager Jim Gamble maintains that the hidden jewel of the restaurant is the scalloppine di maiale, broiled tenderloin of pork, served with a raspberry demiglacé. There are usually a half-dozen specials for lunch and dinner and they are excellent. Chef Lane Pellinger has a well-deserved reputation for the excellent main dishes as well as the tasty soups that he prepares. For an appetizer, try the polenta con funghi e fontina, and see why there was a near riot by regulars when it was taken off the menu for a few weeks. The establishment has a full liquor license, and the food is designed to interact with a wide choice of available wines. Servers are well-trained so they can recommend the appropriate wine with any of the selections. Open for lunch Mon.–Fri. 11:30 am–2:30 pm and daily for dinner 5:30 pm–10 pm. **1513 South 1500 East; (801) 486-1300.**

Lupo's Italian Restaurant—$$ to $$$

Marian Lupo, who started Lupo's Restaurant in the railroad and coal mining town of Helper, Utah, in 1966, was born to Frank Bonacci and his wife Filomena, both from the village of Decollatura in Calabria. Frank became committed to the American union movement shortly after his arrival in the US and worked as an organizer for nearly two decades, until the United Mine Workers of America was finally recognized in Utah's coal fields. Mary learned to cook from her mother and became as famous for her Italian cooking as her father for his work in behalf of organized labor. Today Mary's son, Jim Lupo, continues the tradition with his fine Italian restaurant. The food is plentiful and excellent. My favorites include the shrimp scampi and the veal scaloppine served with green peppers, mushrooms, and linguini. In addition to the main dish, dinners include soup, salad, spumoni ice cream, and fresh-brewed cappuccino. Open for lunch Mon.–Sat. 11:00 am–3:00 pm and 4:00 pm–10:00 pm for dinner. **249 East 3300 South; (801) 466-0371.**

Ristorante Della Fontana—$$

Located in an 1892 church, the Della Fontana has been a Salt Lake City favorite for more than a quarter of a century. The large hall, stained glass windows, fountain in the front of the room, and old pews, which are used for seating on the sides, as well as the Mediterranean touch to the furnishings, are unforgettable. The Italian food is excellent, and with a six-course dinner or three-course lunch, you have plenty to eat and need plenty of time to eat it. Lunch includes a pot of minestrone soup, bread, salad, and the main course. Dinners also include fresh fruit, Italian sherbet before the main course, and dessert, fruit or cheese and crackers. Open Mon.–Sat. 11:30 am–10:00 pm. **336 South 400 East; (801) 328-4243.**

MEXICAN
Cafe Pierpont—$$ to $$$

Located next door to the Baci Trattoria and also operated by Gastronomy, Inc., the Cafe Pierpont has the look and feel of an elegant but festive Mexican restaurant. The restaurant is laid out in a long, high-ceiling, two-tiered, hall-like room with large windows and a door that, in summer, leads to the sidewalk dining area. The 15 overhead fans decorated with red, white, and green streamers; tile floors; dark brown wainscoting around the walls; and full windows give a festive palacelike feel that is unique in the Salt Lake area. A popular place with the lunch crowd and when there is a Jazz game or other special event in the downtown area, Cafe Pierpont is also known for its excellent Mexican food. In addition to the regular combination plates and fajitas, there is a strong emphasis on seafood dishes. My favorite is the Baja combo, which includes a crab enchilada with salsa verde, a Mexican prawn skewer, grilled halibut served with a wonderful fruit salsa, and Baja rice. Other favorites include the halibut tacos and rock shrimp chile relleño combination and the jumbo Mexican white shrimp Veracruz in which the shrimp is cooked casserole-style with olives, peppers, onions, tomatoes, chiles, and mangoes. The fresh vegetable enchilada—corn, tomatoes, zucchini, red onion, black olives, carrots, bell pepper, and cheeses rolled in corn tortillas and covered with ranchero sauce is popular with vegetarians. Open Mon.–Fri. 11:30 a.m.–10:00 pm and on Sat. 4:00 pm–11:00 pm Sat. and 4:00 pm–9:30 pm Sun. **134 West Pierpont Ave.; (801) 364-1222.**

Red Iguana—$ to $$

Based on appearance, this is not a place you would think to stop, and if you did you would have second thoughts about entering. But the Red Iguana likes it that way and has a loyal following of customers who claim that the this is the best spot for authentic Mexican food in all of Utah. Don Ramon, from San Luis Potosi, has put together a menu that includes traditional Mexican dishes, American favorites, and new items designed to please the palate of Salt Lakers. Items to consider include the garlic soup and the cheese soup; Ramon's hometown favorite, traditional enchiladas potosinas, which are four small stuffed enchiladas made with thick fresh masa and filled with cheese, green onions and chiles, and served with guacamole; the vegetarian dish made up of two deep-fried tortillas folded into a triangle and soaked in black mole that are stuffed with beans; and via Mexico, a traditional Mexican dish of turkey served in a mole sauce of red chiles, spices, and chocolate. Open Mon.–Sat. from 11:30 am–9:00 pm, until 10:00 pm on Fri. and Sat. **736 West North Temple; (801) 322-1489.**

Rio Grande Cafe—$$

This restaurant shares the historic Denver and Rio Grande Railroad Station with the Utah State Historical Society and has a wide-ranging clientele. The food, perhaps best described as Americanized-Mexican, is tasty. A daily special is offered, along with a full menu of salads, combination plates, and à la carte plates. My favorites include the tostadas, smothered bean burrito, and cheese enchilada. If you are eating alone, the twin-facing counters in the center of the restaurant offer a chance to rub elbows with others, and if you want a corner for two you can find that as well. Open Mon.–Sat. from 11:30 am–2:30 pm and for dinner from 5:00 pm–10:00 pm. **270 South Rio Grande St.; (801) 364-3302.**

Santa Fe Restaurant—$$ to $$$

This is the younger and fancier sibling of Ruth's Diner (see above). Both are located in Emigration Canyon and provide a relaxing getaway from the bustle of the city with a short drive into the canyon. The Santa Fe is a Southwest-Mexican restaurant located in a nicely designed two-story modern building that also houses the Cactus Club—a private club where a visitor's temporary membership can be obtained for a nominal price. (Or ask the hostess about other alternatives.) The attractive thing about the Cactus Club—in addition to more liberal rules about liquor—is that you can sit on the outside terrace where Emigration Creek babbles by just below. Upstairs there is also a very nice outside patio with a spectacular view of the mountains and boxes loaded with flowers. If you choose to eat inside, the spacious room with floor-to ceiling windows, is almost as good as being outdoors and usually more comfortable (but you can't hear the creek inside). Menu items include chicken and fish dishes, steaks, salads, pasta, sandwiches, and burgers. There is a soup of the day, which I have always found very delicious, and an appetizer not to be missed is the corn cakes and chipotle shrimp. A dinner favorite is the chicken roulade and sweet corn tamale. The Santa Fe is located adjacent to Ruth's Diner. Take 800 South, which becomes Sunnyside Ave., east past Hogle Zoo and the This Is the Place Monument into Emigration Canyon. Watch for the two restaurants on the right a couple of miles up the canyon. Open Mon.–Fri. 11:30 am–2:30 pm and 5 pm–10 pm; Sat. 5 pm–10 pm; and Sun 10 am–2:30 pm; **(801) 582-5888.**

Toucan Cantina—$$ to $$$

For my good friends and neighbors, Mike and Shauna Petersen, the Toucan Cantina is their favorite place for an evening out in Salt Lake City. We listened to their glowing descriptions of the food for several months, before joining them for dinner. We were not disappointed. The heaping plates of food are served in a delightful setting with open-beam ceilings, tile floors, and enormous windows, making this an appealing place for Mexican food. The combination plates are the favorites, the most popular being with the Toucan fiesta plate, which includes a beef taco, cheese enchilada, chile relleño, tamale, rice, and beans. Be sure to try one of the delicious desserts. Open weekdays for lunch 11:30 am–2:30 pm and for dinner 5:00 pm–11:00 pm. Sat. hours are 11:30 am–11:00 pm and Sun. 11:30 am–10:00 pm. **4810 South Highland Cir.; (801) 272-1044.**

VEGETARIAN / HEALTH
Park Ivy Garden Cafe—$ to $$

For the health conscious, the Park Ivy is about as pure as it gets. No meat or eggs are used, and those dishes in which dairy products are used are free from rBGH. Organic produce from a small farm in American Fork is used, and all cooking and drinking water is filtered. The cafe is small and does not lend itself well to large groups; most patrons come alone or in pairs. The small tables out front handle only two people, while in the back room, there are a couple of tables that can accommodate up to four people. The breakfast menu includes fresh fruit, fresh juices, organic coffee, and three kinds of breakfast buns with three different toppings. For lunch and dinner there are sandwiches, burgers, and even a vegetarian hot dog and black bean chili cheese dog. There are nine different specials and entrées that make for a delicious meal. My favorites include the Greek artichoke salad, the burrito, pasta, and a lasagna made with a combination of spinach, artichoke hearts, carrots, garbanzo beans, tomato mushroom sauce, and four cheeses. Takeout is available. Open daily 7 am–9 pm. **878 South 900 East; (801) 328-1313.**

Shanghai Cafe—$ to $$

The Shanghai Cafe is a favorite restaurant of many of my vegetarian friends. It offers both dishes that have meat substitutes such as tofu and various combinations of vegetables, noodles, and rice. Owner Long Tang named the restaurant after the city of Shanghai, which was the city he dreamed about seeing while he was a government worker in his native Saigon. Fate brought Long and his family to Salt Lake City instead of Shanghai and for a good purpose. Long Tang and his family understood the physical and spiritual values of vegetarianism long before it became the health trend of today, and it shows in their cooking. Nevertheless nonvegetarians can find plenty of choices that include meat and chicken in the 255-item menu of Chinese and Vietnamese dishes. The combination of vegetarian and nonvegetarian food plus the attractively decorated open rooms bathed in sunlight from the tall south and west windows makes this a popular eating place. Open daily for lunch and dinner 11 am–9:30 pm. Located at **145 East 1300 South; (801) 322-1841.**

See also the **Cedars of Lebanon** restaurant, above, in the Greek/Middle Eastern section of Where to Eat.

SERVICES

Commercial Bus Transportation—

While UTA only offers bus service to the ski areas in Big and Little Cottonwood canyons, two commercial bus companies offer daily morning departures from downtown Salt Lake hotels to Snowbird and Alta as well as to Park West, Park City, and Deer Valley. For information, rates, schedules, and reservations, call **Le Bus (801) 975-0202;** or **Lewis Brothers Stages (801) 359-8347** or **1-800-359-8347.**

Public Transportation—

The **Utah Transit Authority** offers bus service throughout the Salt Lake Valley and north as far as Ogden and south as far as Provo. Visitors can purchase an inexpensive day pass at the downtown visitor center **(180 South West Temple).** For skiers staying in the Salt Lake area, the UTA is one of the best and cheapest ways to get to the ski resorts in Big and Little Cottonwood canyons. You can catch the bus in downtown Salt Lake City, at the mouth of the canyons, or several other valley area locations. The buses are even equipped with special ski racks so you can take your equipment with you. Buses leave every 10 to 15 minutes starting at 7:00 am and ending 9:00 am, seven days a week and make several afternoon departures from the ski areas. For tickets and information, call **(801) 262-5626.**

Salt Lake Convention and Visitors Bureau and Information Center—

Open Mon.–Fri., 8:00 am–7 pm; 8:00 am–5:30 pm in the winter; Saturday 9:00 am–4:00 pm and Sun. 10:00 am–4:00 pm. **180 South West Temple; (801) 521-2868 or 1-800-541-4955.**

Taxis—

Twenty-four-hour service is available from **Yellow Cab, (801) 521-2100; Ute Cab, (801) 359-7788; and City Cab, (801) 363-5550.**

Utah Information Center—

Located at **Salt Lake City International Airport.** Also operated by the Salt Lake Convention and Visitors Bureau, the Information Center in Terminal 2 at the airport has Salt Lake area brochures, visitor information, accommodations, attractions, plus information about the national parks and Utah travel regions. The booth is staffed daily from 9 am–5 pm, but brochures are available 24-hours a day; **(801) 575-2800.**

Utah Travel Council—

Located in the historic Council Hall, which was constructed between 1864 and 1866 and moved to its present site in 1962 across the street south of the State Capitol Building, the Travel Council has brochures and information from all over Utah, plus a bookstore with regional books, maps, and videotapes. Open year-round Mon.–Fri. 8:00 am–5:00 pm, and Sat. and Sun. 9:00 am–5:00 pm; **(801) 538-1030.**

The Beehive House, which gets its name from the beehive constructed on top of the house, was built in 1854 as Brigham Young's official residence. It is located about a block east of Temple Square. Photo courtesy of the Utah State Historical Society.

Ogden

The city of Ogden lies nestled beneath the towering peaks of Ben Lomond and Mt. Ogden, between the Wasatch Mountains and the east side of the Great Salt Lake, at the junction of the Weber and Ogden rivers. With a population of nearly 70,000, Ogden is one of Utah's largest cities, and throughout much of the state's history, ranked second only to Salt Lake City in size. Ogden has been a railroad center since 1869. It is the only major Utah city located directly on the transcontinental railroad route and the closest connecting point to the railroad for Salt Lake City. Ogden also lies at or near the mouth of two major Wasatch Range canyons: Ogden and Weber canyons. Ogden Canyon provides access to three ski resorts—Snowbasin, Nordic Valley, and Powder Mountain—Pineview Reservoir, and the towns of Huntsville, Liberty, and Eden in the Upper Ogden Valley. Weber Canyon—through which the transcontinental railroad was constructed in 1869, followed a century later by Interstate 84 is just south of Ogden and leads to the towns of Mountain Green and Morgan.

Ogden Defense Depot, Clearfield Naval Supply Depot, and Hill Air Force Base were established in and just outside Ogden in the 1930s and 1940s. They have brought both economic prosperity and a considerable influx of military personnel and civilian defense employees and their families from throughout the country. Ogden is home to a regional office of the Internal Revenue Service and the US Forest Service. Weber State University, which celebrated its centennial in 1989, has a student body of approximately 13,000 students. The university maintains a strong liberal arts and technology orientation and offers master's degree programs in education and accounting. Surrounding the city of Ogden are the communities of Pleasant View, North Ogden, Harrisville, South Ogden, Washington Terrace, Riverdale, Roy, Clinton, Sunset, Syracuse, Layton, and Kaysville. With its majestic mountains, recreational opportunities, close access to the Great Salt Lake, some of Utah's best museums and local festivals, university and a cosmopolitan population, Ogden is an attractive destination for all visitors.

HISTORY

If you look at the area's place names, you understand what an important part the early American fur trade played in Ogden's history. Its first settler, Miles Goodyear, was a fur trapper. The city, canyon, and river were named for Peter Skeen Ogden, a fur trapper for the Hudson Bay Company who arrived from the Northwest in 1825. John Henry

Weber, a German-Danish immigrant who became a fur trapper, reached the Wasatch Mountains in 1824. He is immortalized throughout the area, in such places as Weber Canyon, Weber River, Weber County, and Weber State University. Weber Canyon was the site of one of the most famous events during the fur trapper era—an event that had international implications. Peter Skeen Ogden had been sent into Utah to completely trap out beaver in the area to keep American trappers from pushing farther into the Hudson Bay domain, which covered present-day Oregon, Washington, and British Columbia. Ogden and his men took a large number of beaver, but when they came into contact with a group of trappers in Weber Canyon led by Johnson Gardner, (a subordinate of John Weber) Gardner proclaimed that the British trappers were trespassing on American soil (actually both groups were trespassing in Mexican Territory) and invited any of Ogden's men to join the Americans who wanted to. Many of Ogden's men did desert, taking with them their beaver pelts, even though most had been paid in advance by the Hudson Bay Company for the beaver they would trap. Americans called the location in Weber Canyon the Mountain Green Trapper Confrontation Site, while Ogden bitterly marked the location on his map as "Deserter Point."

The failure of the overall Hudson Bay strategy to keep Americans out of the Northwest was apparent in less than a decade. American missionaries journeyed to the Oregon Territory, forerunners of the American migration along the Oregon Trail during the 1840s. One who traveled west in 1836 with Oregon-bound missionaries Marcus and Narcissa Whitman in 1836 was Miles Goodyear, a fur trapper who went on to establish Fort Buenaventura on the Weber River to serve westward-bound emigrants. He finished his trading fort in 1846, the year before the Mormon immigration to Utah. In 1848 his holdings were purchased for $1,950 by James Brown, under the direction of Mormon leaders. Goodyear left for the gold fields of California where he died in 1849. Originally named Brownsville, the name of the settlement was changed to Ogden by the Utah Territorial Legislature in 1850, in honor of Peter Skeen Ogden, even though Ogden did not actually visit the location of his future namesake.

California-bound Swiss-German emigrant, Heinrich Lienhart, traveled through Weber Canyon and around the south end of the Great Salt Lake during the summer of 1846, but did not visit Fort Buenaventura; however, he did leave a record of his favorable impressions of the area: "If there had only been a single family of white people here, I probably would have remained. What a shame that this magnificent region was uninhabited." Lienhart would be surprised to see what changes have been wrought in the century and a half since he passed through the region.

GETTING THERE

Ogden is located 35 miles north of Salt Lake City, off Interstate 15. Railroad service is available to Ogden, with the Amtrak station located in the historic Ogden Union Station.

———— MAJOR ATTRACTIONS ————

Antelope Island State Park

If you were to ask the Utah Division of Parks and Recreation what has been its most frustrating park, I am sure they would say Antelope Island. At 26,000 acres, it is Utah's largest state park. More than a half million people visited Antelope Island in the 1970s, and it became one of Utah's most popular state parks. However, when the waters of the Great Salt Lake started to rise in the early 1980s, the 7-mile causeway road that connects the island with the east shore of the lake was covered by water, along with many of the beaches and newly constructed facilities on the island. In 1987, the Great Salt Lake reached 4,212 feet above sea level, its highest elevation since the Mormon pioneers arrived. Since then, the waters have receded and the road across the causeway has been rebuilt to provide access to the variety of activities on the island. Antelope Island was named by US Army Captain John C. Fremont in 1845, when the low level of the lake allowed him to ride across to the island where he found the island inhabited by a herd of pronghorn antelope. By the 1870s the antelope were gone, and the island was used by Brigham Young and others to graze cattle and horses. Today you can still find a variety of wildlife. Over 350 species of birds have been identified in the Great Salt Lake surrounding Antelope Island. Other animals include include deer, pronghorn an-

telope, coyotes, badgers, bobcats, eagles, rabbits, and buffalo. The present herd of buffalo was started in 1893, when William Glassman brought 12 buffalo from Nebraska to Utah and transported them to Antelope Island on a barge. The herd has grown to approximately 600 head. The free roaming buffalo herd is one of the island's major attractions. Antelope Island is also the burial site for Mrs. George Frary. She and her six children accompanied George Frary to the island in the early 1890s, where she died of a ruptured appendix in 1897 before her husband, fighting storm driven waves, could return from the mainland with a doctor. The island offers plenty of opportunities for hiking, biking, horseback riding, wildlife watching, sunbathing, and swimming. There is also limited access to the historic Garr Ranch House. Built of adobe by Fielding Garr in 1848 or 1849, the house is one of the oldest remaining pioneer buildings in Utah. For information, call **(801) 538-7221.**

Weber State University

Situated on Ogden's eastern bench, Weber State University has been a vital part of Ogden's social and cultural life since Weber Academy was established in 1889. The university's Dee Events Center offers a regular schedule of programs and activities for the community. For information about campus activities and programs, call **(801) 626-6000;** for the Dee Events Center, call **(801) 626-8550.**

FESTIVALS AND EVENTS

Ogden/Hof Sister City Festival and Winterfest

3rd weekend in January

In cooperation with German sister city Hof, Ogden stages one of the best winter festivals in the entire state. The festival usually includes a delegation from Hof, a torchlight parade, a snow-sculpting contest, ice skating, and dog sled demonstrations. A ski hill, built on Ogden's Historic 25th Street using snowmaking and grooming equipment, is the site for demonstrations. The Ogden Union Station makes a good venue for polka bands and German food. A progressive cross-country ski dinner is also held, with stations set up throughout the Mount Ogden Golf Course. Call **(801) 729-8915** for more information.

Railroads, Gems, and Guns

March

Throughout Mar., the Ogden Union Station hosts three shows that attract the general public and hobbyists from around the country. The Utah State Railroad Festival includes displays of dozens of model railroads, which are set up in the lobby. The Gem and Mineral Show is heaven for rock hounds, with the hand-crafted jewelry and stones available for purchase and classes and demonstrations held. The Utah Gun Collector's Show centers around the John M. Browning Collection and lures gun collectors from all over the West. For more information and specific dates, call **(801) 629-8444.**

Juneteenth Day

mid-June

Modestine and John Carpenter instituted a new celebration in Ogden in 1993: Juneteenth Day. The day traces its history back to the Carpenters' native Texas where freed slaves coined the word "Juneteenth" to commemorate June 19, 1865, the day news arrived that President Lincoln had signed the Emancipation Proclamation freeing them from slavery. The news arrived nearly a year and a half after Lincoln signed the document on January 1, 1863, and two months after Lincoln's assassination in Washington, DC. The two-day festival is seen as a way to bring people together to share the traditions and culture of African-Americans. Activities include a parade, food, live music, cultural exhibits, races, a 3-on-3 basketball tournament, and concludes with gospel and jazz music in the MTC Park on Monroe Blvd. Call **(801) 729-8915** for more information.

Ogden City Pioneer Days

July10 through 24

Commemorating the 1847 arrival in Utah of the first Mormon pioneers, Pioneer Days runs for six days Outdoor western concerts, a craft fair, a children's parade, car shows, and the Pioneer Days Rodeo are among the events. For more information call **(801) 629-8214.**

Mountain Men Rendezvous

Easter, Labor Day, and Thanksgiving weekends

Held the Easter, Labor Day, and Thanksgiving weekends at Fort Buenaventura, the era of the mountain men of the 1820s and 1830s is recreated with black-powder rifle demonstrations, tanning, and other arts and crafts. For information, call **(801) 621-4808.**

─────── OUTDOOR ACTIVITIES ───────

BIKING

Antelope Island—

Antelope Island State Park was reopened in the summer of 1993 after high water in the 1980s covered the causeway to the island. From Syracuse, head west on state Hwy. 127 for 7 miles across the causeway to Antelope Island. Once on the island, 6 miles of paved road and 20 miles of graveled roads offer access to much of the island.

Little Mountain—

It is a flat, easy ride from Ogden to Little Mountain, where you have a fine view of the Great Salt Lake from the heights of Little Mountain. Head west on 12th St. A good place to begin is the parking lot at **12th and Wall Ave**.

Mountain Green to Porterville—

A nice 30-mile round-trip ride through Morgan Valley begins at Mountain Green and follows the access road next to the interstate and winds through the towns of Peterson, Porterville, and Morgan.

Ogden Bay Waterfowl Refuge—

This 42-mile round-trip loop is described in the Wildlife section. A good place to begin is from the park in Roy at **1900 West and 4000 South**. The ride is level and automobile traffic is usually light.

Ogden River Parkway—

See the Parks and Recreation section.

Pineview Reservoir Circle Tour—

A pleasant ride around Pineview Reservoir in the upper Ogden Valley is a 15-mile loop that begins off state Hwy. 39 and swings through the towns of Eden and Huntsville. If you want to extend the ride you can continue northwest from Eden to Liberty or ride east of Huntsville to the Trappist Monastery (see the Monasteries section, p. 150).

Powder Mountain—

The Powder Mountain Ski Area encourages mountain bikes with bike rentals and guided tours from the Powder Mountain Sports Shop. There is no charge for access to the ski area, which is open daily from 9 am–4:30 pm, but all bikers must adhere to proper biking etiquette, wear safety helmets, and stay on the established roads and trails. At this time there is no lift service for bikers so be prepared for some strenuous climbing. For more information, call **(801) 745-3772**.

FISHING AND BOATING

Lost Creek Reservoir and State Park—

The waters of Lost Creek Reservoir are held behind a 220-foot earth-filled dam, constructed in the l960s. The reservoir is reached by taking the Devil's Slide/Croydon exit off Interstate 84, 10 miles northeast of Morgan. The road to Lost Creek Reservoir has been recently paved. A boat launching ramp is available. Fifteen tent sites, without any modern conveniences except running water, offer primitive camping at the reservoir.

Ogden River—

Trout and whitefish fishing is possible along Ogden River, below the Pineview Reservoir, but the most popular trout fishing stream in the area is along the south fork of the Ogden River above Pineview Reservoir. This is a very picturesque stream, as it flows through a narrow canyon of the Wasatch Mountains.

Pineview Reservoir—

Located up Ogden Canyon, 12 miles east of the city, Pineview Reservoir is a popular boating and fishing spot. The reservoir is best known as a crappie and tiger muskie-lunge fishery. Bass, bluegill, perch, and black bullhead are also common. Trout are sometimes found, though not in the same abundance as in other lakes.

GOLF

Ben Lomond Golf Course—

If you are looking for a flat, easy-to-walk course, then Ben Lomond might be just the one. Located beneath Ben Lomond Mountain, named by an early Scottish settler, the first 9 holes were built by a group of golfers who considered the only other golf course in the area, El Monte, to be too crowded. The back 9 were opened in 1965. The greens are small, and most are elevated and hard to hit. Although technically it is a private course, Ben Lomond is open to the public. Located north of Ogden, in the town of Harrisville, just off US Hwy. 89 at **1800 North; (801) 782-7754.**

El Monte Golf Course—

Built in 1926, El Monte is one of Utah's oldest golf courses and one of two golf courses run by Ogden City. The course has a wonderful clubhouse, designed by local architect Eber F. Piers and built of stone quarried nearby. The bungalow style building is one of 13 WPA buildings constructed in Ogden during the Great Depression. The clubhouse (built in 1934-1935) is listed in the National Register of Historic Places. The course is located near the mouth of Ogden Canyon, and canyon winds are so blustery that early morning golfers are given an incentive to play before 9:00 am on weekdays with green fees of only $3! (Seniors can play for $4 anytime on weekdays.) The course is a 9-hole par 35, with nice wide fairways, rolling terrain, and a parklike setting. **1300 Valley Dr.; (801) 629-8333.**

Mount Ogden Golf Course—

The second Ogden City golf course, Mount Ogden was constructed in 1985 and is one of the most difficult courses in the state. As Pro Steven Wathen indicates, the course is an extreme challenge for the average golfer. It is not long, playing 5,888 yards from the white tees and 6,294 yards from the blue tees. But the mountainous terrain, narrow, scrub oak-lined fairways, and elevated greens are more than enough to humble most golfers. Almost all of the fairways either run up the mountain or down into gulleys and up the other side, or have sharp doglegs to the left. This is why more than 80 percent of the golfers ride rather than walk. The golf course offers spectacular views of Ogden, the Great Salt Lake, and Weber State University below, especially from the number 5 and 6 holes. Mt. Ogden Golf Course can be reached by turning east off Harrison Blvd. at 29th St., a few blocks north of Weber State University, at the south end of the Ogden High School campus. **3000 Taylor Ave.; (801) 629-8700.**

Round Valley Golf Course—

If you are looking for a pleasant, uncrowded golf course not far from either Salt Lake City or Ogden, Round Valley is a good choice. Located just east of Morgan, the 18-hole course is set on the south side of the Weber River. The modern clubhouse includes a snack bar. Pull carts, electric carts, and golf clubs can be rented in the pro shop. To reach the course take the Morgan exit off Interstate 84 and follow State St. to 100 South. Watch for a sign on the east side of the street that says Round Valley. There is also the usual golf course sign of a bouncing ball headed toward the flag that has been placed on the west side of the street, but it is well hidden by the branches of an overhanging tree. Follow the road as it heads west and then swings north around a hill for a couple of miles into Round Valley. **1870 East Round Valley Rd.; (801) 829-2796.**

Valley View Golf Course—

This beautiful course, opened in 1974, has been recognized by *Golf Digest* as one of the top 75 public golf courses in the US. It is enjoyable for a number of reasons: the variety of holes where no two seem the same, the beautiful view of the mountains to the east and the Great Salt Lake to the west, and the trees, which include pine, cottonwood, Russian olive, scrub oak, and Lombardy poplar. The trees seem almost like participants in the game rather than obstacles. The rows of beautiful poplar trees on the course recall a time when many Utah valleys were marked by rows of poplar trees growing along the edge of ditch banks, which served as boundaries and windbreaks for 19th- and early 20th-century farms. The front nine are easier than the back nine, and good golfers have a possibility at birdies on the last four holes. The course is best reached from US Hwy. 89, which runs along the base of the mountains between Ogden and Far-mington. **2501 East Gentile** in Layton; **(801) 546-1630.**

Wolf Creek Resort—

Situated adjacent to the Wolf Creek Resort (where condos can be rented for the night), in the small town of Eden east of Ogden, this semiprivate golf course is more expensive than the public golf courses in Ogden, but it is still a favorite of local golfers. The front 9 are located across Wolf Creek Dr., east of the clubhouse, and contain a good number of traps and hazards, although the fairways are quite open. The back 9 are located on the sloping hill below the clubhouse, with the tree-lined fairways much tighter than on the front 9. The course's location on the east side of beautiful Weber Valley is a plus. **3900 North Wolf Creek Dr.** in Eden; **(801) 745-3365.**

HIKING

Indian Trail—

This ancient trail took Indians above the bottom of Ogden Canyon and was especially useful in the spring, when the high waters of the Ogden River made it dangerous and nearly impossible to travel along the canyon bottom to reach the Upper Ogden Valley. Local volunteers (who were at work the Saturday we hiked the trail) have labored to reestablish this trail and connect it with the Cold Water Canyon Trail farther up Ogden Canyon. Its close location to the city makes it a popular route with local hikers. The trail is 10 miles round-trip, although many hikers only cover a portion of the trail before returning to their vehicles. For example, a 3.3-mile hike to the Coldwater Canyon Viewpoint requires about two hours one way and takes you past the highest point of the trail, where a small emergency shelter has been

constructed. There are several viewpoints along the trail, with spectacular views into Ogden Valley, Ogden Canyon, and the mountains above Warm Water and Cold Water Canyons. The trail climbs high along the mountains, as it winds out of Ogden Valley into Warm Water and Cold Water canyons. There are places where the trail is very narrow. You should exercise great caution because one misstep could send you on a long and dangerous slide down the slope. A brochure describing the trail is available at local information centers. Park at the western end of the trail (take 22nd St. as far east as you can and look for the parking area with the trail, beginning at the northeast corner of the parking area.) The eastern terminus of the trail is in Ogden Canyon on state Hwy. 39 at the Smokey Bear sign. There is a parking area and interpretive sign here as well.

Skyline Trail—

The road up North Ogden Canyon provides access to the Skyline Trail. At the top of North Ogden Pass you have north and south options. Heading south, you follow the Skyline Trail for 3 miles, then take a western branch, the Lewis Peak Trail, for 2.7 miles to an outstanding overlook that takes in the Ogden Valley from Willard on the north to Antelope Island on the south. The eastern branch continues another 4 miles to the trailhead near the Port Boat Ramp on the northwest side of Pineview Reservoir. If you take the north option, it is a 9-mile hike to Ben Lomond Peak. This is a more difficult hike, with an elevation gain of about 3,500 feet. But the trail offers spectacular views and the possibility of seeing mountain goats and other wildlife.

Snow Basin—

From the Snow Basin Ski Resort, several hiking trails offer a variety of possibilities, ranging from easy to difficult. The Maples Campground to Sardine Ridge Trail begins in the lower Snow Basin parking lot, heads north to the Maples Campground, and continues north up to Sardine Ridge for a 3.1-mile round-trip hike with a

700-foot elevation gain. The Green Pond Loop begins about 30 yards behind the sign, at the entrance to the upper parking lot, and makes a 3.5-mile loop around Green Pond, an active beaver pond. The strenuous and difficult Mount Ogden Trail is an 8-mile roundtrip hike up Mount Ogden that climbs more than 3,000 feet in elevation. It begins by following the ski lift service road west, between the ski school and ski patrol buildings.

Taylor's Canyon—

Another trail with easy access from Ogden is the Taylor Canyon Trail, which climbs nearly 5,000 feet along its 4.5-mile-long precipitous route. There are spectacular views along the trail, which begins at the eastern end of 27th St. and climbs up Malan's Peak to Malan's Basin where there are opportunities for primitive overnight camping.

HORSEBACK RIDING

Pheasant Run Ranch—

1339 North 1200 West, Ogden, UT 84404; (801) 392-3977.

PARKS AND RECREATION

Ogden River Parkway—

One of the most exciting developments in Ogden during the 1990s is the establishment of the Ogden River Parkway. The result of the combined efforts of government, private corporations, and countless hours of donated time by community groups, the parkway stretches for 3.1 miles along the Ogden River from Washington Blvd. to the mouth of Ogden Canyon. Taking the trail out and back makes it a 10-kilometer jogging hiking, or biking ride. The trail passes through the MTC Learning Park, where the Utah State University Botanical Gardens have been relocated; the Big D sports park, with a children's playground and baseball and soccer fields, skirts the north side of the El Monte Golf Course, and passes Dinosaur Park (see the Museums and Galleries section, p. 151). The entire route is black-topped and offers disabled access. The next phase will extend the parkway another 2 miles west, from Washington Blvd. to the confluence of the Weber and Ogden rivers. Later, a parkway will be established along the Weber River and, with the development of other trails on the eastern slope of the Wasatch Mountains, a 21-mile loop around and through Ogden will be available to recreationists.

RUNNING AND JOGGING

Mount Ogden Exercise Trail—

Constructed around the Mount Ogden Golf Course, this 3.1-mile jogging trail is located near Weber State University. You can add an extra mile to the trail by taking the university's par course fitness circuit, at the south end of the loop. Begin the course at the northeastern corner of the loop, at the eastern end of 29th St. behind the high-rise apartments, or on the west side of Taylor Ave., just south of 32nd St.

SKIING
DOWNHILL

The three ski resorts in the Ogden area are usually uncrowded and a good alternative to the Salt Lake City and Park City resorts. Snow Basin with 1,800 skiable acres, and Powder Mountain with 1,600 skiable acres, are among Utah's five largest ski areas, behind Park City (2,200 acres) and Alta and Snowbird, each with 2,000 acres.

Nordic Valley—

Located at an elevation of only 5,500 feet, Nordic Valley usually receives less snow than the other Utah resorts and therefore opens later and closes earlier than other locations. Eighty percent of the 85 skiable acres served by two double chairlifts are beginner and intermediate runs, making this a good area for beginners and families (especially since lift tickets are cheaper than at the other resorts). The area is only open for daytime skiing on Fri. Sat., and Sun., but opens for night skiing Mon.– Sat. 5 pm–10 pm. Nordic Valley is located southwest of Liberty, off state Hwy. 162. For information, call **(801) 745-3511.**

Powder Mountain—

The land on which this private ski resort is located has been in the Cobabe family since 1903, but it wasn't until 1972 that it opened for skiing. Dr. Alvin Cobabe, an Ogden family practitioner, was urged by friends not only to establish the ski area on the family land, but to take up skiing. Dr. Cobabe did that at the age of 54 when the resort was established and still continues to ski nearly every day at the age of 76. Powder Mountain remains a friendly, family-operated ski area with excellent powder skiing and very reasonable rates. As Dr. Cobabe explained, he never planned Powder Mountain to be a big glitzy resort, rather he wanted a more personal family-oriented experience.

The three chairlifts at Powder Mountain provide access to three mountains and a wide variety of skiing, from beginning slopes to powder bowls. One of the things I like about Powder Mountain is that each of the three lifts, including the 6,000-foot-long Hidden Lake lift, offers beginner to expert runs down the mountain. This means that whatever your choice of slopes, you can still meet at the bottom of the lift to ride back to the top with friends and family. Powder Mountain has a well-deserved reputation for good powder skiing—some days the powder is so light you can hold it in your glove and blow it away with a gentle breath—with access to the back-country powder skiing provided by a Snow Cat. There is a 1,900-foot vertical drop on the Hidden Lake side (where a shuttle will pick you up on the highway road) and a 1,700-foot drop on the Timberline side. There is night skiing from 4:30 pm–10 pm on the Sundown Lift—known for its access to unbelievable sunsets.

The ski school serves skiers of all levels. There is a nice beginner ski package with a day-lift pass, ski rental, and group lesson for a very reasonable price.

Powder Mountain is also a favorite area for snowboarders.

Lodging facilities are minimal, with a two- and three-bedroom suite with kitchens and five motel-type rooms with microwaves and small refrigerators. At the mouth of the canyon, the Wolf Creek Condos are popular lodging facilities with Powder Mountain skiers. Eating facilities include the **Powder Keg Restaurant, Powder Mountain Lodge, Hidden Lake Lodge,** and **Sundown Lodge.** Most skiers drive up from the Ogden area through Ogden Canyon on state Hwy. 39 to the Pineview Dam, then turn left (north) onto state Hwy. 162 and follow it north through Eden and Liberty to Powder Mountain. Skiers coming from Salt Lake City (55 miles to the south) can take the Trappers Loop Rd. from Interstate 84, then head north through Huntsville and around the east side of Pineview Reservoir to Eden and state Hwy. 162. For information, call **(801) 745-3772.**

Snow Basin—

If Utah wins the bid to host the 2002 Winter Olympic Games, Snow Basin will be the site of the downhill races. The ski area has five lifts, a double-chair beginners lift, and four triple-chair lifts, which provide access to 39 designated runs and several excellent powder bowls. Snow Basin was opened in the 1940s and is one of Utah's oldest ski areas. During World War II, amputee patients from Bushnell Hospital were taught to ski here. There are no overnight accommodations at Snow Basin, but a day lodge provides full food service, and a ski and rental shop can handle all equipment needs. Children and beginners ski packages are offered through the ski school. Snow Basin is located east of Ogden 17 miles on the other side of Mt. Ogden. Take state Hwy. 39 through Ogden Canyon to state Hwy. 226 on the south shore of Pineview Reservoir. If you are coming from Salt Lake City, you can take Interstate 84 up Weber Canyon, exit onto the Trapper's Loop Rd. (state Hwy. 167) and take it to Huntsville and the intersection with state Hwy. 38, then follow it back west to the junction with state Hwy. 226. Telephone is **(801) 399-1135.**

SWIMMING AND WATER PARKS

Indoor Swimming—

Ogden has three public indoor swimming pools: **Ben Lomond Community Pool** at **800 Jackson Ave.; (801) 399-8690; Ogden Community Pool** at **2875 Tyler Ave., (801) 399-8693;** and **Marshall White Center Pool** at **222 28th St., (801) 399-8346.**

Layton Surf and Swim—

The outdoor **public swimming pool** is only open during the summer, but the **Wild Wave Pool** is open year-round. During cold weather, a bubble is placed over the Wild Wave Pool, and it functions as an indoor swimming pool during the day, except between 6 pm–9 p.m. when the wave machine churns up the water. Summer hours are noon–8 pm. During the winter, the Wild Wave Pool is also used for water aerobics, school classes, and school swim teams. **465 North 275 East** in Layton. For times and prices, call **(801) 546-8588.**

Wild Waters Water Park—

This popular park is located at 1750 South 1350 West, off the Interstate 15 21st St. exit. Open during the summer, for information and ticket prices, call **(801) 629-8801.**

TENNIS

Public Tennis Courts—

There are six public tennis courts located at the entrance to **Mount Ogden Golf Course** at **3000 Taylor,** six courts at **Ben Lomond High School** at **800 Jackson Ave.,** four in **Liberty Park** at **22nd St. and Monroe St.,** and two courts each at **Bonneville Park: Quincy and 2nd St.; Monroe Park** at **30th St. and Monroe;** the **Marshall White Center,** at **1220 23rd St.**

———— SEEING AND DOING ————

BASEBALL

Ogden Raptors—

If you want to see professional baseball at its beginning level, the Ogden Raptors, an independently owned team in the Pioneer League, offers 35 home games between mid-June and the beginning of Sept. The current field seats about 2,500 fans and is located at **3405 A Ave.** Plans are in the works to construct a new stadium for the team. For general information call **(801) 393-2400** or for tickets call **(801) 393-2450.**

HISTORIC BUILDINGS

Historic Downtown Ogden—

The Ogden City Landmarks Commission has prepared an excellent walking tour brochure that includes nine buildings in the downtown Ogden area. A photograph and brief description is included for each of the buildings. The oldest building is the 1845 **Miles Goodyear Cabin** (see the Museums section), built by the trapper two years before the Mormon pioneers arrived in Utah. The other 19th-century building is the **Episcopal Church of the Good Shepherd,** a carpenter Gothic–style church built in 1874 and 1875. Early 19th-century buildings include the 1906 **Masonic Temple;** the **old Post Office,** a classical Revival–style federal building built between 1905 and 1909; the 1913 **Eccles Building;** two 12-story **skyscrapers** built in 1927; the **First Security Bank;** the **Biglow** (now the Radisson) **Hotel;** and the **Ogden Municipal Building,** a wonderful art-deco–style building constructed as a New Deal WPA project in 1939. The guide also includes one of the state's real architectural treasures: the 1924 **Egyptian Theater.** Designed by Utah architects Hodgson & McClenahan, the Egyptian Revival–style theater is one of the few surviving examples of this style of architecture, which was used primarily in movie theaters. The building is covered in Egyptian ornamentation, including two sculpted Egyptian deities seated on the roof and six sculpted pharaohs on the facade.

Historic 25th St.—

Imagine a time when the country's railroad stations bustled with the arrival and departure of America's traveling public—a time before air travel or cross-country automobile jaunts over an elaborate interstate highway system. In those days transcontinental travel took several days. Ogden served as one of the nation's major railroad centers and was the major connecting point on the transcontinental railroad route between Chicago and San Francisco. One of the most famous businesses on historic 25th St. was the London Ice Cream Parlor. Operated by Belle London, an infamous madame, she served her famous cherry pie and ice cream in the main floor parlor, and in the small rooms on the second floor delicacies of another sort. Local wags referred to the London Ice Cream Parlor as the place to get pie on the first floor and tarts on the second floor.

MONASTERIES

Holy Trinity Abbey—

The alpine valley setting for the Holy Trinity Abbey near Huntsville makes you think that you are visiting a centuries-old monastery in Bavaria or Austria, even though the abbey was only founded in 1947. The buildings, grounds, and the 30 or so Cistercians (often called Trappists) monks who live in the abbey convey a feeling of serenity, love, and godliness that makes a visit rewarding to individuals of any faith. The abbey's reception room is open daily (except Sun.) 8 am–noon and 1 pm–5 pm. The monks live in 8-foot by 10-foot rooms in war-surplus quonset huts. They support themselves by raising alfalfa hay, and Angus cattle, and by selling their bread, honey, cereal, peanut butter, and eggs. The abbey consists of 1,878 acres of land, of which about 780 are under cultivation. There are approximately 2,000 chickens and 500 head of cattle. When not working at their assigned tasks, the monks devote themselves to prayer and scriptural reading. Visitors may attend the mass and chants held in the chapel, also a converted quonset hut. For those in search of longer

spiritual refreshment, the abbey also offers one- or two-day retreats to males of all faiths over the age of 20. While no tours are provided, a slide show describes life and work at the monastery. Bread, honey, eggs, and peanut butter can be purchased by visitors at the reception room. To reach the monastery, head east out of Huntsville on Utah state Hwy. 39 and follow the signs. The monastery is located 4 miles southeast of Huntsville. **1250 South 9500 East; (801) 745-3784.**

MUSEUMS AND GALLERIES

Daughters of Utah Pioneers Museum and Miles Goodyear Cabin—

Utah's oldest surviving cabin was constructed by fur trapper Miles Goodyear, some time between 1845 and 1846. Goodyear was born in 1817 in Hamden, Connecticut, orphaned at four, and bound out to families until he was 19. In 1836, he joined the Whitman-Spaulding Missionary Group bound for Oregon, but left the company at Fort Hall on the Snake River and set out on his own. He became a mountain man, marrying Pomona, the daughter of Ute Chief Peteet-neet, in 1839. As the fur trade declined and westward emigration increased, Goodyear followed the example of other trappers like Jim Bridger and erected a fort for trade with the emigrants. After the arrival of the Mormons in 1847, Goodyear sold his cabin and animals to them and moved on to California, where he made a rich gold find on the Yuba River, but became ill and died in Nov. 1849. His cabin was moved to this site in 1928 and has been preserved by the Daughters of Utah Pioneers. The cabin is adjacent to the 1902 Relief Society Building, built for the women's organization of the LDS Church. The building was acquired by the Daughters of Utah Pioneers in 1926 and has been used as a pioneer museum ever since—with the exception of World War II, when it was requisitioned by the federal government to be used as Ogden's first day-care center for children of women working at the defense installations in and around Ogden. The Goodyear Cabin and Relief Society building are located at **2148 Grant Ave.** and open mid-May to mid-Sept., Mon.–Sat. 10 am–5 pm.; **(801) 393-4460.**

Fort Buenaventura—

After the Miles Goodyear Cabin was moved, the location of the original fort was preserved in historical documents and established as a state park in 1979. Following extensive archaeological study of the site, Fort Buenaventura was reconstructed, using wooden pegs and mortise-and-tenon joints instead of nails and cottonwood logs. In 1846 Miles Goodyear used the name Fort Buenaventura for his outpost. Earlier travelers and mapmakers had speculated on the existence of a river that flowed west to the Pacific Ocean, which they called the Rio Buenaventura. Perhaps Goodyear believed in the mythical river, or he was using the Spanish word for good fortune or good journey to welcome the expected California-bound travelers. Mountain men reenacters hold an annual rendezvous at the park and, throughout the year, other activities and programs recall the days when Peter Skeen Ogden, John Weber, Etienne Provost, Jim Bridger, Jedediah Smith, and others camped along the banks of the Ogden and Weber rivers as members of the elite fur trapper fraternity. Guides in mountain man costumes interpret the fort and the lifestyles of the mountain men as well as of the Native Americans of the region. The fort is open 8 am–dark year-round, except winter holidays. To reach the fort, take the Ogden 24th St. exit (exit 347) off Interstate 15, and head east. Watch for the signs directing you to turn south off 24th St. onto A Ave., then almost immediately make a left turn east off the bluff and follow the road south to the parking area. Admittance fee charged per vehicle. For further information, contact: **Fort Buenaventura State Park, 2450 A Ave., Ogden, UT 84401-2203; (801) 621-4808.**

Hill Air-O-Space Museum—

This is a must for any World War II buff or anyone interested in airplanes. Construction of Hill Field began in 1939, and the base played an important role during World War II when it employed more than 22,000 personnel as a center for maintenance and rehabilitation for combat aircraft. Today, Hill Field is home to F-16 squadrons. The combination of modern aircraft flying overhead and historic planes on the ground make this a memorable visit. The main museum building contains small exhibits, a gift shop, and a theater showing a video about Hill Field. The museum hangar houses a dozen aircraft including a P-51D Mustang, a B-17; Flying Fortress, a C-47; Douglas Skytrain, an F-84 Thunderstreak; and a Lockheed Blackbird spy plane. Outside there is a collection of more than three dozen old aircraft. A restored World War II vintage Post Chapel, which has a stained glass window replicating the one placed by members of the US 8th Air Force in the Grafton-Underwood Chapel in England. The museum is free and open Tues.–Fri. 9 am–3 pm, Sat. 9 am–5 pm, and Sun. 11 am–5:00 pm. The museum is located just east of Interstate 15 at the Roy exit, (exit 341). For information, call **(801) 777-7400.**

Ogden Dinosaur Park—

Opened in April 1993, the Dinosaur Park is located on 5 acres of land at the mouth of Ogden Canyon and contains replicas of 44 prehistoric dinosaurs. The dinosaurs range in size from an 18-foot by 45-foot tyrannosaurus rex to smaller replicas of crawling, swimming, and flying reptiles. They are made of concrete mixed with fiberglass, steel rods for reinforcement, and painted with an ultra-violet-resistant paint. Well-placed information signs provide insights into the life and characteristics of the individual dinosaurs, which make this a positive educational experience. For adults, watching children look at the dinosaurs is more than worth the admission fee. **1544 Park Blvd.; (801) 393-3466.**

Ogden Union Station—

The 1924 Ogden Union Station is listed in the National Register of Historic Places and still serves as the Amtrak Station for Ogden. Visitors will find a variety of museums and shops housed in the station, which is something that should not be missed when you are in Ogden. Among the museums are the Browning Firearms Museum, with more than 100 models made by John M. Browning, considered the world's greatest gun inventor; the Browning-Kimball Car Collection with Packards, Pierce Arrows, Lincolns, and Cadillacs on display; the Utah State Railroad Museum with a collection of historic locomotives, a model railroad, and other railroad artifacts; and the Natural History Museum, with gems and minerals from the Intermountain area on display. Other features of the station are a **Japanese House of Peace, the Myra Powell Art Gallery,** a **gift shop,** and an **information center** with books, brochures, and information about activities in the Ogden area. The museums are open Mon.–Sat. 10 am–6 pm and during the summer Sun. afternoons 1 pm–5 pm. Admission fee charged. The station is located at the western end of 25th St. at **2501 Wall Ave.** For information on tours and upcoming events at the station, call **(801) 629-8444.**

NIGHTLIFE

The Shooting Star Saloon—

Even in the West there are few saloons that have lasted more than a century. Huntsville's Shooting Star Saloon, however, is one. Opened in 1879, the saloon has been a second home for generations of Huntsville residents and has earned fame as one of the most hospitable places anywhere. The food is good, too, even if there is only one item on the menu. The Star Burger is made with two quarter-pound beef patties topped with knockwurst, cheese, sautéed onions, tomato, lettuce, and a special sauce—all served on a bun. This is one burger you will not forget. The Shooting Star is also one unforgettable place. Owners John and Heidi Posnien have taken great care to preserve as much of the ambiance of the old saloon as possible. A mounted St. Bernard head, a hitching post out back, dollar bills stuck to the ceiling, and other relics from the past are all sources of yarns that are part of the saloon's character.

A combination of western saloon, English pub, and German kneipe (Heidi after all is *"echte Berlinnerin"*) the saloon has charm, hospitality, and lives by the rule "Enjoy yourself, but don't impose on others." The saloon is open from noon–midnight daily, except Sun., when it opens at 2 pm. Customers must be 21 or over. **7350 East 200 South, Huntsville, (801) 745-2002.**

SCENIC DRIVES

Ogden River Scenic Byway—

Sometimes known as the road over Monte Cristo, this scenic byway actually follows the Ogden River along state Hwy. 39, east to Huntsville in the Ogden Valley, and then up the south fork of the Ogden River through heavily wooded hills that are especially beautiful in the fall. The Monte Cristo Mountains are part of the Cache National Forest and form the boundary between Rich County and Cache County. An unusual place name, even for Utah, John Van Cott, Utah's expert on place names, offers three possible origins for the name Monte Cristo: (1) It is believed that miners returning from the California gold mines thought this range resembled the Monte Cristo mountain range in California. (2) The name could have been given by early French-Canadian trappers in a hybrid form of the literal "Mountain of Christ." (3) One of the early road builders carried the book *The Count of Monte Cristo,* which he read to his coworkers around the camp fire in the evening. While the officially designated Scenic Byway ends 44 miles from Ogden at the eastern boundary of Cache National Forest, it is certainly worth continuing the drive down the canyon to Woodruff. A half day or an entire day could be spent driving over this byway, and then north to Bear Lake and back to Logan over the Logan Canyon Scenic Byway. This route is especially recommended in the fall on a weekday, when there is less traffic.

Trapper's Loop Road Scenic Backway—

This designated Scenic Backway follows what was probably the route of Peter

Skeen Ogden and his Hudson's Bay fur trappers, as they moved south out of Ogden Valley across the mountains to the Weber River in May 1825. The drive across the 9-mile paved road from Mountain Green north to Huntsville gets you thinking about which hills Ogden must have crossed and what ravines he followed before meeting up with Etienne Provost and Johnson Gardner along the Weber River. The all-weather route also offers a spectacular view of Mount Ogden from the west side and provides access to the Weber County ski resorts of Snow Basin, Powder Mountain, and Nordic Valley.

Weber Canyon—

Interstate 80 through Weber Canyon reveals the east side of the Wasatch Mountains, the beautiful Morgan Valley, and two interesting sites—one historical and the other natural. The Mountain Green Trapper's Confrontation took place in the vicinity of the Mountain Green Rest Stop on the westbound side of the interstate. At the rest stop, a monument to Peter Skeen Ogden recalls the events of 1825, when American trappers challenged the British Hudson Bay brigade under the leadership of Ogden. Devil's Slide is one of the most unusual natural formations in Utah. Devil's Slide is an outthrust of a bed of quartzite, with two parallel reefs of Jurassic–era limestone 20 feet apart and 40 feet high stretching up the side of the mountain. The unusual formation is the result of the faster erosion by the softer soil and stone that covered the limestone. Devil's Slide is located just north of Interstate 84 at exit 111, 7 miles north of Morgan.

WILDLIFE

Beus Park—

This natural wetland area was rescued from undesirable elements and cleaned up by neighbors to make it safe for human beings and attractive to birds and migrating waterfowl. A paved trail, a trail brochure, and bird listing containing the 95 different species that have been identified here make this a haven for bird lovers.

To reach the park, drive to 42nd St. and Harrison Blvd. Continue east on 42nd St. as it curves to the north and Beus Park.

North Fork of the Ogden River—

The Wasatch-Cache National Forest has established a series of trails along the North Fork of the Ogden River as it enters Pineview Reservoir. The trail system provides opportunities to view both riparian and wetland wildlife. A large variety of songbirds reside in the trees, willows, and thick underbrush. Along the reservoir edge, waterfowl species include Canadian geese and a wide variety of ducks. Bald eagles, red-tailed hawks, great horned owls, and other raptors also frequent the reserve, along with mule deer and moose. Plans are to make the area disabled accessible by blacktopping the trails. To reach the area, take Utah highway 39 east through Ogden Canyon to Utah 162, where you drive across the Pineview Reservoir Dam. From the junction, drive 3.8 miles to the parking area, just across the bridge on the east side of the North Fork. Look for the binoculars sign indicating a wildlife viewing area.

Ogden Bay Waterfowl Management Area—

This extensive 20,000-acre wetland area on the east side of the Great Salt Lake is an excellent area for viewing such wetland birds as gulls, sandpipers, grebes, herons, ducks, and geese. Hikers have acess to the the dike roads past vehicle gates year-round. A vehicle loop is also open. There are several ways to reach the area. Perhaps the easiest is to take exit 341 (Roy) off Interstate 15 and head west on state Hwy. 97 to its end, then turn north on state Hwy. 108 for 0.1 mile turn west onto state Hwy. 98, which becomes 5500 South in Hooper and continue west to 7500 West. Turn north to the management area headquarters.

Ogden Nature Center—

Some might find it ironic that this 127-acre nature center has the Internal Revenue Service as its western neighbor and the army's Ogden Defense Depot as its eastern neighbor. Executive director Mary Cox points out, though the fact that the nature center lies between these two huge complexes makes it a real oasis in this urban setting. The area along Mill Creek was used as farm land until 1940, when it was acquired by the Ogden Defense Depot and used to store munitions until after World War II. In the 1970s, the Defense Depot donated the property to Ogden City, with the provision it be used for recreation purposes. The nonprofit Ogden Nature Center was set up in 1977 to administer the property and to help restore the area to a natural state. Ponds and marshlands have been established and thousands of trees planted. Bird species include great blue herons, snowy egrets, willets, Canadian geese, wood ducks, red-winged blackbirds, meadow larks, and red-tailed hawks. Mammals include racoons, muskrats, red foxes, porcupines, and mule deer. Admission fee charged. **966 West 12th St.; (801) 621-7595.**

WHERE TO STAY

ACCOMMODATIONS
BED AND BREAKFASTS AND LODGES
Jackson Fork Inn—$$ to $$$

Have you ever wanted to sleep in a barn? Here's your chance. Jackson Fork Inn is an old dairy barn that has been converted into a restaurant and inn with eight rooms, each with a private bath; five rooms have hot tubs large enough to accommodate two adults. A self-serve breakfast is included, and dinner meals can be purchased in the evening. Located on Hwy. 39, **7345 East 900 South, Huntsville, UT 84317; (800) 255-0672** or **(801)745-0051.**

Snowberry Inn—$$ to $$$

Located 15 minutes up Ogden Canyon, the Snowberry Inn overlooks Pineview Reservoir and is an excellent choice for both summer and winter stays. Boating, swimming, hiking, and biking are primary activities in the summer, while close proximity to Ogden's three ski resorts makes this a good location for skiers. Wildlife watching is a popular year-round activity. Roger and Kim Arave offer five nonsmoking rooms, each with its own bath. A full homemade country breakfast and access to the hot tub are included. The inn is wheelchair accessible. **1315 North Hwy. 158, Eden, UT 84310; (801) 745-2634.**

Vue De Valhalla—$$ to $$$

This small bed and breakfast is situated on the second fairway of the Nordic Valley Golf Course. Owners Andy and Marie Cook offer one suite, which includes bedroom, sitting room, dressing room, private deck, TV, and VCR, and one bedroom with a double bed. Both rooms share a bath. A continental breakfast is provided. **2787 Nordic Valley Rd., Liberty, UT 84310; (801) 745-2558.**

Wolf Lodge—$$$

This summer and winter resort has 50 condominiums available for rent. Condominiums range from a one-bed unit to two-bedroom units with four beds that can accommodate up to eight people. All units have fully equipped kitchens. Summer activities include an outdoor heated swimming pool, waterslide, two tennis courts, miniature golf course and the 18 hole championship Wolf Creek golf course. There is a club house with an exercise room, sauna, and Jacuzzi open year-round. In the winter the ski resorts of Powder Mountain, Snow Basin, and Nordic Valley are close by. Located north of Pineview Reservoir on the road to the Powder Mountain Ski Area. **3615 North Wolf Creek Dr., Eden, UT 84310; (801) 745-2621 or 1-800-345-8824.**

HOTELS AND MOTELS
**Best Western High Country Inn—
$$ to $$$**

Heated pool, whirlpool, exercise room, tanning bed, and free VCR; 110 rooms. Restaurant open 6 am–10 pm. **1335 West 12th St.; (801) 394-9474 or 1-800-594-8979.**

**Best Western Ogden Park Hotel—
$$$**

Heated indoor pool, whirlpool, and exercise room; 287 rooms. Restaurant open from 6 am–11 pm. **247 24th St.; (801) 627-1190.**

Flying J—$$ to $$$

Heated pool; coffee shop and dining room open 24 hours; 101 rooms. **1206 West 21st St.; (801) 393-8644.**

Holiday Inn—$$$

Heated indoor pool, whirlpool, exercise room, game room, and restaurant; 109 rooms. **3306 Washington Blvd. (801) 399-5671 or 1-800-939-6841.**

Radisson Suite Hotel—$$$

One hundred twenty-six rooms in the center of downtown Ogden. This is the former historic Ben Lomond Hotel, for many years the best hotel in Ogden. All rooms have been renovated. The dining room and coffee shop are open 6 am–9:30 pm. The Skyroom on the 11th floor has the best view of the city and is well-known for excellent steaks and seafood. **2510 Washington Blvd.; (801) 627-1900.**

CAMPING
PUBLIC

East of Huntsville along state Hwy. 39 (see the Ogden Canyon Scenic Drive section), there is a series of 10 campgrounds on national forest land along a 6-mile stretch that have a combined total of 261 RV trailer sites and nearly 350 tent sites. All have toilets and nearly all have drinking water. The campgrounds are open from mid-May–the end of Sept. or the end of Oct. The largest, with 96 sites, is **Anderson Cove** located 2.5 miles southwest of Huntsville. The other nine are: **Jefferson Hunt,** 25 sites; **Hobble,** 9 sites; **Magpie,** 30 sites; **Botts,** 11 sites; **South Fork,** 32 sites; **Perception Park,** 24 sites; **Lower Meadows,** 15 sites; **Upper Meadows,** 9 sites; and **Willows,** 10 sites.

Within the Ogden city limits, **Fort Buenaventura** has 25 trailer and tent sites (no hookups) available from Mar.–Nov. It is located at **2450 A Ave.; (801) 621-4808.**

PRIVATE
Century RV Park—

This park has 73 pullthroughs with paved sites and full hookups. There is also a heated pool, Laundromat, and showers. Open year-round. Take exit 346 off Interstate 15. **1399 West 2100 South; (801) 731-3800.**

WHERE TO EAT

AMERICAN
**Prairie Schooner Steak House—
$$ to $$$**

In keeping with its namesake, this restaurant offers dinner in covered wagons surrounded by what seems to be a beautiful outdoor prairie under the stars. Steaks, prime rib, and a daily seafood special top the menu. Open for dinner, Mon.–Thur. 5:00 pm–10:00 pm, Fri. and Sat. 5:00 pm–11:00 pm, and Sun. 4–9 pm. **445 Park Blvd.; (801) 392-2712.**

Timber Mine—$$ to $$$

This interesting restaurant, housed in a huge timber building, has been made to look like an old mine on the inside. Antiques and artifacts are on display, and individual booths are constructed like side rooms off the main passageway. The booths have individual dimmer lights, so you can eat in total darkness if you want. (You might want to keep children on the outside of the booth to stop them playing with the switch—a mistake we made.) The fare includes steaks, prime rib, and seafood. Open daily for dinner from 5 pm–10 pm in summer and 5:30 pm–10 pm in winter. **1701 Park, Ogden.; (801) 393-2155.**

CAJUN
Cajun Skillet—$$ to $$$

There aren't many places in Utah where you can get authentic Cajun food and that makes the Cajun Skillet a top choice of those who enjoy authentic New Orleans food. Thomas Jackson, owner and cook, grew up in Baton Rouge, Louisiana, and learned to cook from his grandparents. He claims that some of his recipes, including those for corn bread, jambalaya, gumbo, hush puppies, fried okra, plantation vegetable soup, and sweet potato pie, go back to when his ancestors were slaves. After graduating from culinary school he worked at a variety of places, eventually becoming a chef at the Hotel Utah until its closure in 1989. At the urging of friends, he opened the Cajun Skillet that same year. Thomas is from a family with 17 children. Six of his brothers operate a 175-acre plantation 15 miles outside Baton Rouge, where they raise the catfish, frogs, turtles, and alligators that Thomas has sent to Utah by air express for his customers. The daily fresh fish selections and special dishes, like alligator and frog's legs, are chalked on a large blackboard on the north wall in his restrauant. Thomas is assisted by two of his five children, Greg and Landraux, and his wife Chris. The restaurant is open 9 am–11 pm, so you can also order Cajun-style breakfasts. Located across the street from the Ogden Municipal Building. **2250 Washington Blvd.; (801) 393-7702.**

ENGLISH
Camelot—$$ to $$$

Given the name, you'd expect this to be an English restaurant, but what will surprise you is just how English it is! Outside, an old cart, statuary, and ponds with ducks and geese provide an appropriate setting. The restaurant, owned by Joseph and Stella Vaz from Liverpool, England, is located in a re-created 16th-century estate house, complete with a suit of armor and a tower that you can reserve for a romantic six-course dinner for two. If that is too fancy, or it's too many steps to climb, the main floor is divided into two sections: a more intimate inn-style section, with private booths, or the music room, with open tables, a dance floor, and piano music on Fri. and Sat. evenings. Camelot is the only place I know of in Utah where a formal English afternoon tea is served. In addition to tea, there are finger sandwiches filled with smoked salmon, beef, tomato, or cucumber; and warm-from-the-oven scones served with the traditional Devon clotted cream and preserves, and a selection of cakes. For lunch you can get shepherd's cottage pie, fish and chips (of course), vegetarian quiche, and a variety of sandwiches, soups, salads, fish, and pasta. Dinner items include such traditional English dishes as roast beef and Yorkshire pudding, London broil, Cornish game hen, steamed salmon, gamekeepe's casserole, fisherman's pie, and Camelot's variation on beef Wellington, known as seafood Wellington, which is a pastry stuffed with shrimp, crab, salmon, and halibut and served with a special sauce. Open 11:00 am–10:00 pm weekdays, but until 11:00 pm on Fri. and Sat.; open for Sun. brunch 10:00 am–3:00 pm. The restaurant is located in Layton; take exit 335 off Interstate 15 and head east for about half a mile. Reservations are recommended on weekends. **930 West 2000 North; (801) 773-1000.**

GERMAN
Bavarian Chalet—$$ to $$$

Established in 1983, this is the most authentic German-style dinner restaurant in the state. In 1977 Wolfgang and Heidi Stadelmann visited southern Utah and fell in love with Lake Powell. Heidi, a native of Heidelberg, had graduated from the chef's school at Tegernsee in Bavaria, while Wolfgang, a native of Stuttgart, with a master's in business from the University of Munich, had worked nearly 10 years as the city manager of Fellbach, a town outside Stuttgart. It took them four years to immigrate to Utah, but after a year of traveling around the US they moved to Ogden and opened their restaurant. Their establishment has all the charm of a Bavarian inn, with all kinds of Old World collectibles throughout the restaurant. In fact their daughter, Claudia, operates a small but charming gift shop within the restaurant. The food is traditionally German— schnitzels, sauerbraten, sausage, fish, and chicken, along with made-from-scratch apfelstrudel and kasestrudel. If you don't want a full dinner, you can order one of the specials, which includes soup or salad; however, if you are up to it, Wolfgang recommends the King Ludwig sampler plate. The Stadelmanns had special plates made to hold the Wiener schnitzel, jaeger schnitzel, bratwurst, knackwurst, sauerkraut, red cabbage, spatzle, and vegetables. Open Tues.–Thurs. 5 pm–10 pm; Fri.–Sat. 5 pm–11 pm; closed Sun. and Mon. The Bavaian Chalet is located in a complex of shops and businesses at **4387 Harrison Blvd.** in Ogden; **(801) 479-7561.** Reservations are recommended, especially on weekends.

Restaurant Wolf—$$ to $$$

Ogden's "other' German restaurant was established in 1992 by Catherine Rabbel, a Berlinerinn who brings to Ogden's Historic 25th St. a taste of her native Berlin with such selections as Berliner rostbratwurst, Berliner bouletten, and Berliner sauerbraten along with venison, duck, salmon, and other dishes. Open from 10:30 am–10:30 pm Mon.–Sat.; Sun. 4:30 pm–10 pm. **256-258 25th St.; (801) 394-3717.**

ITALIAN
Berconi's—$ to $$

This Italian restaurant, located just south of the Weber State University campus, features 28 varieties of pasta, deep dish, thick, and thin crust pizza; and veal and chicken dishes. Open Mon.–Thurs. 11 am–10 pm; Fri. and Sat. 11 am–11 pm, and Sun. 4:30–9:30 pm. **4850 Harrison Blvd.; (801) 479-4414.**

La Ferrovia Ristorante—$$

About 10 years ago, sisters Giuseppina and Rita Lodice came to the US from Naples, Italy. Along with their husbands and children, the sisters have worked to establish a good, inexpensive Italian restaurant in one of the restored buildings on Ogden's 25th St. They offer a good selection of pasta, calzones, and soups made from authentic southern Italian recipes, as well as an excellent house dressing. All breads and pizza dough are made in the restaurant. If you have a favorite Italian dish that is not on the menu, you can call in advance and they will make it for you, providing they can obtain the correct ingredients. Daily specials, takeout service, and a children's menu are available. Open 11 am –9 pm and 11 am–10 pm Fri. and Sat.; closed Sun. and Mon. Located just south of the Ogden Park Hotel; **210 25th St.; (801) 394-8628.**

MEXICAN
Chaparros—$ to $$

There are three Chaparros at various locations in the Ogden area. Owner Abel Chapparo, who hails from Sonora, Mexico, has made a great success of his homestyle Mexican food. He spends most of his time at the Wall Ave. restaurant, but the menu at all three establishments is the same. A popular choice is the Sonora Mexi-combo, which features three items from Abel's Sonoran homeland—a tamale, a relleno, and a shredded beef taco. **205 West 29th St., (801) 393-0955; 755 North, Harrisville Rd., (801) 782-2400;** and **3981 Wall Ave., (801) 391-7777.**

--------------------- SERVICES ---------------------

Multiagency Visitor Center—
Golden Spike Travel Region and the
Ogden and Weber Visitors Bureau are
located in the historic Ogden Union Station at **2501 Wall Ave., Ogden, UT 84401;**
(801) 627-8288 or **1-800-ALL-UTAH.**

This Is the Place Monument. Photo by Allan Kent Powell.

Provo and Orem

Provo and Orem lie in the heart of Utah Valley, the first valley south of the Great Salt Lake Valley. Located on the east shore of the state's second largest natural lake, Utah Lake, the two valleys and their two lakes are connected by the 40-mile-long Jordan River. Like its namesake in the Holy Land, the river flows out of the freshwater Utah Lake into the salt waters of the Great Salt Lake, just as the Biblical Jordan River flows from the Sea of Galilee into the Dead Sea, though in opposite directions. Ten major communities and an equal number of smaller settlements were established along the eastern shore of Utah Lake and are now home to more than a quarter of a million people. From north to south the communities are Lehi, American Fork, Pleasant Grove, Orem, Provo, Springville, Spanish Fork, Payson, and Santaquin. The Wasatch Mountain Range forms the eastern boundary of Utah Valley and includes, at the north and south ends, two peaks that approach 12,000 feet in elevation—Mt. Timpanogos (11,750 feet) and Mt. Nebo (11,877 feet). The mountains provide a variety of recreation possibilities and make Utah Valley one of the most scenic spots in all the world. Utah Lake, which takes up much of the valley between the Wasatch Mountains on the east and the Lake Mountains along the western shore, is a feature found only in one other Utah valley: Bear Lake Valley, far to the north. There are occasions, especially when traveling along the west shore of the lake, when it seems like a part of Switzerland immigrated to Utah, along with the numerous Swiss converts to Mormonism who left during the last half of the 19th century. The third feature to dominate the area is Brigham Young University. Students from all over the world attend this Mormon institution known for its strict moral and dress codes. Yet the institution is very much a part of the world, with its athletic teams, dance companies, law school, and academic programs. The university is the intellectual center for the LDS Church. It is this institution which brings most visitors to the Provo and Orem area.

HISTORY

When Fathers Francisco Atanasio Dominguez and Silvestre Velez de Escalante reached Utah Lake on September 23, 1776, on their journey from New Mexico, they found villages of Yuta (Ute) Indians who called themselves the Timpanogotzis, which means "Fish Eaters." Utah Lake was known as Lake Timpanogos, and while the mountain that looms above the lake went unnamed by the Franciscan friars, it is the only natural landmark that still bears the name Timpanogos. The Spanish padres spent only a few days at Utah Lake, anxious to hurry on toward

California before winter set in, but they were very impressed with the land and its people. Escalante recorded that "… as many Indian pueblos can fit inside the valley as there are those in New Mexico …. All over it there are good and very abundant pasturages …. And the climate here is a good one …." The men promised to return the next year and establish a mission among the Timpanogotzis, but were unable to do so.

After Dominguez and Escalante, traders from Santa Fe made infrequent journeys north into Utah and visited the Indians of Utah Valley. By the 1820s the far western fur trade was underway and in 1824, Etienne Provost, a French Canadian fur trapper, trapped as far north as Utah Lake and the Jordan River. Provost was attacked by Snake Indians along the Jordan River in October 1824 and escaped injury, although eight of his men were killed. Provost did not spend much time in Utah, but it is for him that the city of Provo and other landmarks are named.

Provost preceded the first permanent settlers by a quarter of a century, but when Mormon pioneers moved south from the Salt Lake Valley into Utah Valley in 1849, they became the nucleus of more than a dozen communities established between Alpine on the north and Santaquin on the south.

The valley was not settled without conflict. Isolated Indian battles took place, and in 1853, one of two major Indian wars in Utah, the Walker War, named for the Ute Chief Walkara, began near Springville. The immediate event that touched off the conflict was a fight that arose during a misunderstanding over the trade of three trout for a portion of flour. The war was a series of clashes throughout central Utah between Mormons and Utes, led by Chief Walkara, that lasted more than a year and left 20 Mormons dead. A peace treaty was signed by Chief Walkara in May 1854, eight months before his death.

The lake, good land, moderate climate, and close proximity to Salt Lake City ensured that Utah Valley would be one of the most prosperous areas in the region. Later, with the establishment in Provo of Brigham Young Academy, which became Brigham Young University, the community grew in importance and, for much of its history, has been the third largest city, next to Salt Lake City and Ogden, in the state.

While originally noted for its agricultural land and especially its orchards, Utah Valley has gone through an industrial revolution with the establishment of steel mills during the 1920s and World War II. In the 1980s, a "high-tech" revolution brought growth to the area, through such computer software companies as Wordperfect and Novell.

GETTING THERE
Provo is located 45 miles south of Salt Lake City on Interstate 15.

MAJOR ATTRACTIONS

Brigham Young University

In Utah, you can't escape the institution known as the Y or as BYU. Established in 1875 two years before the death of its namesake, BYU has become the largest church-related higher education institution in the country. BYU plays an important role in the educational, cultural, and recreational life of the community: A third of Provo's population is made up of students, and many residents are employed by the university. A perennial football power and "quarterback factory," with such pro stars as Gifford Nielson, Steve Young, Jim McMahon, and 1991 Heisman Trophy winner Ty Detmer, BYU football is one of the "tenants" of the Mormon religion for many Utahns. And basketball is not far behind. The Marriott Center, which seats 23,000, is the largest basketball arena in the state and is usually filled. But BYU is much more than football and basketball. The university provides training for students from all over the world who later return home with professional qualifications and—more often than not—a dedication to serving in the many church positions that make up the Mormon way of life. The university also includes four museums: the **Museum of Art; Monte L. Bean Life Science Museum, (801) 378-5051;** the **Earth Science Museum, (801) 378-3680;** and the **Museum of Peoples and Cultures, (801) 378-6112.** For first-time visitors and those who have not been on the campus for a while, the free tour offered by the university is recommended. Call **(801) 378-4678** for information.

Timpanogos Cave National Monument

Utah's most famous and most often visited cave, Timpanogos Cave is actually three connected limestone caves that were set aside by presidential proclamation in 1922. Located on the steep, northern slope of the 11,750-foot Mt. Timpanogos in American Fork Canyon, the first of the three caves was discovered by Martin Hansen in 1887 and is named **Hansen Cave.** Hansen was cutting timber on the south wall of the canyon when he noticed the tracks of a mountain lion and followed them into an opening. Later that winter he returned with three friends to explore the cave. He placed a wooden door over the natural entrance, and then for several years afterward he led groups through the cave on request. **Timpanogos Cave** was discovered in 1914 by two adventuresome teenage boys who began exploring the area while they were waiting outside for a group of relatives who were inside the Hansen Cave. The third cave, known as **Middle Cave,** was discovered in 1921 by George Heber Hansen, the son of Martin Hansen, and Wayne E. Hansen, the elder Hansen's grandson. The interior of the cave is decorated with a colorful variety of stalactites, stalagmites, dripstone, flowstone, and rimstone formed by calcium carbonate and other minerals in the groundwater that enters the caves. Manmade tunnels connect all three caves. During the 1890s, Hansen Cave was stripped of most of the onyx and other mineral deposits that lined its walls by crews working for a Chicago onyx company. After the other two caves were discovered, local groups and the forest service were determined to preserve the caves. On Oct. 14, 1922, President Warren G. Harding created Timpanogos Cave National Monument in response to recommendations by the US Forest Service and the Timpanogos Outdoor Committee, an organization of local citizens concerned about the preservation and proper maintenance of the caves. The committee had obtained a special use permit from the forest service in Apr. 1922 to collect entrance fees, conduct tours, and maintain the cave. This agreement continued for 24 years until 1946 when the National Park Service took over all activities in the monument. Electric lights were installed inside the cave in 1922. They have now been upgraded so that for the half mile or so that you walk inside the cave you have light. Still, the park ranger does turn off the lights for a few moments so that you can experience the total darkness of the cave. The temperature inside the cave is a cool 43 degrees Fahrenheit, so take a jacket or a sweater with you. The cave is located 1.5 miles up the mountain from the visitor center, requiring a strenuous zig-zag climb from 5,665 feet to 6,730 feet. Timpanogos Cave is popular with Utahns, and on weekend and holiday afternoons you can expect a long wait before entering the cave. Tick-ets for specific times can be purchased in advance, and special historic tours and candlelight and flashlight tours can be arranged. The visitor center contains exhibits, a 12-minute slide presentation, and a bookstore. It's located 2 miles up American Fork Canyon on state Hwy. 92. The cave is open from mid-May–mid-Sept. and tickets can be purchased from 9:00 am–3:30 pm in the visitor center. It's a good idea to call in advance to make reservations. For information write **Superintendent, Timpanogos Cave National Monument, Route 3, Box 200, American Fork, UT 84003; (801) 756-0351.**

OTHER ATTRACTIONS

Utah Lake

The principal access to the 150-square-mile Utah Lake is through the **Utah Lake State Park**, 4 miles east of the Provo city center. Utah Lake is a remnant of Lake Bonneville. Shorelines of old Lake Bonneville can be seen on the Traverse Mountains on the west side of the lake and the Wasatch Range on the east side. It is estimated that 13,000 feet of lake sediments lie beneath the central part of Utah Valley. Fed by streams coming down from the mountains, and with an outlet (the Jordan River) at the north end, Utah Lake has remained a freshwater lake since it was an arm of Lake Bonneville. As you might expect, the primary activity here is boating. There are 144 boat spaces at the 30-acre marina, four concrete boat launching ramps, and boat and trailer storage. Although the average depth of the lake is only 10 feet, Utah Lake is still good for boating, waterskiing, windsurfing, and fishing. Carp, catfish, and yellow perch are plentiful, while trophy-size bass and walleye have been taken. In winter there is ice fishing and ice-skating on an Olympic-size artificial skating rink. The lake has a **visitor center/museum** and **120 camping spaces** with picnic tables, modern restrooms, and showers available year-round on a first-come, first-served basis.

FESTIVALS AND EVENTS

Lehi Round-Up Rodeo
last full week of June

The Lehi Round-Up began in 1938 and is one of Utah's oldest continuous rodeos. The rodeo runs three nights (Thurs., Fri., and Sat.) during the last full week of June and attracts cowboys from all over the country. In addition to the rodeo, other activities include a cowboy poetry gathering, fine arts display, parade, carnival, free museum tours, and plenty of food. For information and rodeo ticket reservations call **(801) 768-9581.**

Freedom Festival
July 4th

Provo goes all out to celebrate the 4th of July. A month-long celebration, which draws politicians from around the state, culminates with the state's largest Independence Day parade down Freedom Blvd. The hot-air balloon display includes as many as 40 balloons and is one is the largest in the state. Other activities continue throughout the day, with the climax being a huge fireworks extravaganza held in the 65,000-seat Cougar Stadium.

Spanish Fork Fiesta Days
end of July

Spanish Fork takes its name from its location along the 1776 Dominguez-Escalante Trail and the route used by subsequent fur trappers out of Taos, New Mexico, into the Utah Valley area. The community celebrates its namesake, along with Pioneer Day the week of July 24 with a series of activities ranging from parades, dances, sporting activities, arts and crafts shows, children's activities, to a professional rodeo. Call **(801) 798-5000** for more information.

———— OUTDOOR ACTIVITIES ————

BIKING
Utah Lake Loop—

This 100-mile-long bike ride takes you around Utah Lake over fairly level terrain. A modified route skirts the west side of the lake along state Hwy. 68, a distance of 34 miles one way between the junction of Hwy. 68 and Hwy. 73 (a couple of miles west of Lehi) and the fruit-growing town of Elberta on US Hwy. 6. The west side of the lake is my favorite as it offers a unique view of the Wasatch Mountains, with Utah Lake in the foreground. It is a much less traveled road than those on the east side of the lake. If you want to circumnavigate the lake on a bike, pick up a copy of the Utah County map at the Utah County Travel Council office and ask the helpful staff to show you the alternate routes on the east side of the lake.

BOATING

See Utah Lake in the Other Attractions section, and Deer Creek Reservoir in the **Heber Valley** chapter.

FISHING
American Fork Creek—

Although this stream tends to yield smaller-sized German browns and stocked rainbow trout, its clear, pristine water cascading over rocks between the towering Wasatch Peaks makes fishing this stream an aesthetic delight.

Deer Creek Reservoir—

See the **Heber Valley** chapter.

Provo River—

The Provo River offers one of Utah's most popular fly-fishing streams that has been designated by *Field and Stream* magazine as one of the 10 "blue ribbon" trout streams in the West. You will find rainbow, cutthroat, and brown trout, and Rocky Mountain whitefish.

GOLF
Cascade Fairways—

Located in Orem near the mouth of Provo Canyon, this course draws golfers from Provo and Orem and is one of the busiest public course in Utah Valley. The course is both compact and difficult, demanding accuracy both on the fairways and on the greens. The course was built in the mid-1960s in the middle of a peach orchard, and peach trees continue to line both the east and west boundaries of the course. **1313 East 800 North** in Orem; **(801) 225-6677.**

East Bay—

If you like the challenge of water, then Provo's East Bay Golf Course is for you. Located near Utah Lake, water is a factor on 13 of the 18 holes, making this the wettest golf course in the state. A number of the holes have water on both sides of the course. The water provides a natural habitat for a variety of waterfowl, including Canadian geese, pelicans, blue herons, snowy egrets, ducks, and other birds that frequent the marshlands surrounding the golf course. Their soaring and gliding is a pure delight. The course is very flat, in contrast with the towering mountains behind it. One of the unique features of the course is the yardage to the green is given on the sprinkler heads. You can also easily get confused here as some of the holes are located some distance from each other, while others require crossing or going around one tee box to get to the other. This course is located near the south end of University Ave., just off Interstate 15. Take exit 266 and turn right at the first light off the interstate, then follow East Bay Blvd. until you see the course. **1860 South East Bay Blvd.; (801) 379-6612.**

Gladstan Golf Course—

In case you are wondering how this course was named, the answer is simple. When Stan and Gladys Wilson donated the original Payson Golf Course to the city, they did so with the stipulation that the course name be a combination of their two first names. The original 9-hole course was later sold and the present course established, but the old name stuck. This course has a lot going for it. Tucked against the Wasatch Mountains, with Loafer Mountain and Dry Mountain looming to the east and south and the beautiful Utah Valley and Utah Lake spreading out to the north and west, nearly every hole has its own wonderful view. The autumn leaves make this an especially beautiful course in the fall. The third, fourth, and fifth holes surround an RV campground with 21 units, providing good accommodations almost right on the golf course. There is a good variety of holes. The front 9 are on flat or rolling hill terrain, but the back 9 wind up the canyons and hills below Loafer Mountain, making an electric golf cart almost a necessity. Gladstan is located northeast of Payson. To get there, follow the signs from exit 254 off Interstate 15; **(801) 465-2549.**

Hobble Creek Golf Course—

You will not find any debate that this is one of the most picturesque golf courses in Utah; in spring 1994 readers of the *Deseret News* voted it their favorite golf course to

play in Utah. Located in Hobble Creek Canyon, east of Springville, the course is laid out in the narrow bottom of the canyon along the course of Hobble Creek. The brightly colored leaves on the trees on both sides of the course make this a breathtaking course in the fall, while the towering mountains, well-maintained fairways and greens, and bridges across Hobble Creek give this course a charm that is unforgettable. To reach the course, take the 263 exit off Interstate 15 and head east for 7 miles along 400 South as it winds into Hobble Creek Canyon; **(801) 489-6297.**

Spanish Oaks Course—

Located at the mouth of Spanish Fork Canyon, just off Hwy. 6, the course spreads out beneath the large white cross on top of Dominguez Hill, which marks the spot where Dominguez and Escalante entered Utah Valley in 1776. The Franciscan fathers followed the Spanish Fork River north toward Utah Lake. The same river cuts through the front 9 of the course,. The river also cuts across the 6th hole, but it is not a factor unless you really duff the shot. The front 9 are characterized by wide fairways and level terrain. The back 9 are played on the slope under Dominguez Hill and are more challenging as the scrub oak brush seems to attract balls and the uphill-downhill layout adds difficulty to most of the holes. The course is located about 4 miles off Interstate 15 at exit 261. For reservations, call **(801) 798-9816.**

Tri-City Golf Course

Three towns—American Fork, Pleasant Grove, and Lehi—pooled their resources in 1973 to build this challenging golf course. The challenge can be found in two words: distance and trees. The middle tees play a total of 6,710 yards; if you go to the back tees, it's 7,077 yards. This course probably has more cottonwood trees than the rest of Utah's golf courses put together, even though some 300 trees have been removed over the years. Golfers rate this as one of the five most difficult courses in the state. But the trees and the spectacular view of Mt. Timpanogos and isolation from traffic and noise combine create a beautiful course. **1400 North 200 East** in American Fork; **(801) 756-3594.**

HIKING

Provo River Parkway Trail—

This 8-mile-long trail runs along the Provo River, from Utah Lake through Provo and up Provo Canyon past Bridal Veil Falls, Nunns Power Plant and Park, to Vivian Park. The route is also popular with joggers and bicyclists. For information, call the **Provo Parks and Recreation Office; (801) 379-6600.**

Santaquin Peak and Loafer Mountain—

Named for a Ute Indian Chief, Santaquin Peak rises to 10,685 feet. The 10-mile up and back hike climbs about 3,000 feet from the trailhead to the peak. The trailhead is located on the north side of the road, near the Payson Lakes Campground on the Mount Nebo Scenic Loop Rd.

Stewart Falls Trail—

From the main lodge at Sundance Resort, you can take the 1.5-mile-long trail to Stewart Falls for a fairly easy walk to a series of stepped waterfalls called Stewart Cascades.

Timpanogos Peak—

Many Utahns consider this the best hike in the entire state; historically it is one of the most popular. The history books do not record who was the first to climb to the top of the peak, but many family histories record the treks of their ancestors. Starting in 1912, Brigham Young University sponsored an annual Timp Hike, but when the number of hikers grew to more than 7,000 by the late 1960s, the hike was canceled because of the large crowds and their impact on the fragile mountain environment. Some Utah Valley residents who vied with each other to see who could establish the longest string of annual hikes were disappointed with the decision. What was once a collective rite of passage for BYU students has become an outing for smaller groups. Today, some summer weekends see in excess of 500 hikers on the trail at one time. The distance from the trailhead at Aspen Grove to the summit is 9.4 miles. The trail starts at an elevation of 6,900 feet and climbs to 11,750 feet. Most people require five to six hours to make the ascent and three to four hours for the descent. Strong hikers can make it to the top in three hours: the record—90 minutes up and 45 back down—was set in 1967 by Michael R. Kelsey, who has become a prolific author of Utah hiking books including one on Mt. Timpanogos. The major landmark en route to the top is Emerald Lake, 6.9 miles from the trailhead. On the way to the lake, you pass a dozen or so waterfalls. Some hikers are satisfied to make Emerald Lake their goal and avoid the more dangerous rock and snowfields and the acrophobia-inducing perch on the peak. But if you go all the way to the top, keep an eye out for mountain goats, which were reintroduced into the area in 1981. Although it is a tradition to slide down the "glacier" above Emerald Lake, forest service rangers strongly discourage it because of the jagged rocks, holes, and varying hardness of snow. If you are worried about accidents, you might want to hike the trail on weekends, when an emergency response team is on duty with a mission to respond to all injuries within 30 minutes. The Aspen Grove trailhead is located in Provo Canyon, past the Sundance Ski Resort, in the west end of Aspen Grove. While the Aspen Grove route is the most popular, there are several other possible routes.

HORSEBACK RIDING

Big Springs Riding Stable—

Located on the South Fork of the Provo River, hourly rides around the ranch are available on a drop-in basis, while longer trips of six hours to Windy Pass or the Provo Overlook and overnight pack trips need to be scheduled in advance. The ranch is located 3.5 miles northeast of the confluence of the South Fork with the Provo River at Vivian Park; **(801) 225-8589.**

Boyer's Riding Stables—

Horseback rides can be scheduled Mon.–Sat. **2449 North 600 West, Pleasant Grove; (801) 785-2857.**

MOUNTAIN CLIMBING

Hansen Mountaineering—

If you want to progress from hiking to rock climbing, ice climbing, or spelunking, you can arrange for professional guides through Hansen Mountaineering. **757 North State St., Orem, UT 84057; (801) 226-7498.**

SKIING
CROSS-COUNTRY
Alpine Loop—

What better use for a scenic road closed by snow in the winter than to turn it into a cross-country ski trail? The Alpine Loop, famous for its autumn leaves, offers a good outing for about any level of cross-country skier. The ascent is gradual, starting at 6,850 feet at Aspen Grove (the trailhead for the Mount Timpanogos climb—see the Hiking section) and rising to 8,060 feet at the summit of Utah Hwy. 92. As with the scenic drive, you can start either in Provo Canyon, at Aspen Grove, or in American Fork Canyon, just above Mutual Dell. The distance from Aspen Grove to Mutual Dell is 8 miles. You can either do part of the trail or complete the entire distance and arrange to be shuttled back. Alternatively, if you want a longer jaunt, cross from American Fork Canyon to Aspen Grove, then to Sundance in the morning. Enjoy lunch at the Sundance Resort, then return to your car in the afternoon.

See also Sundance, below.

DOWNHILL
Sundance—

Sundance may be the only ski resort named for a western outlaw. When actor Robert Redford acquired what was a small local ski area called Timphaven in 1969, he named it Sundance in honor of the nickname for the bad man Harry Longabaugh Redford played in the now classic film *Butch Cassidy and the Sundance Kid.* Yes, in anticipation of your question, you do, on occasion, see Redford at the resort. Despite its big-time name, Sundance still maintains the feel of a small-time resort. Lift tickets are less than the Park City and Little Cottonwood Canyon resorts, and the lift lines … well, what lift lines? The resort has the feel of a community with no massive lodges or hotels. Accommodations are in privately owned homes and cottages, which are put into a lodging pool. If you can afford them, these are the places to stay for a quiet, relaxing ski trip. If you can't, the 15-mile drive from Provo takes less than a half hour. The view of the towering snow-covered peaks of Mount Timpanogos from the slopes and lifts rivals that of any other ski resort in the world. There are four lifts, two triple-chair lifts and two double-chair lifts that provide access to 400 acres of skiing along 41 trails. The elevations ranges from 6,100 feet at the base to 8,250 feet at the top of the highest lift. A ski school offers full-day programs for children, a learn-to-ski program for beginners that includes lesson, equipment rental, and lift ticket, and specialized instruction for skiers at any level. Senior citizens over 65 ski free. There are 10 kilometers of marked trails for cross-country skiers. The ski season usually runs from late Nov.–mid-Apr. The resort is located in Provo Canyon, 15 miles north of Provo. To get to Sundance, take Hwy. 189 up Provo Canyon and watch for the turnoff on to Hwy. 92 to reach the resort. For lodging and general information, call **(801) 225-4107.** For skiing information, call **(801) 225-4100.**

SWIMMING
Provo Recreation Center and Swimming Pool—

This pool offers lessons, aerobics, lap swimming, and open swimming. The complex also has racquetball courts and a weight room. Open during summer 1 pm–8 pm Mon.–Fri. The rest of the year from 5:30 pm–8:00 pm, and until 6 pm on Sat. year-round). Admission fee charged. **1155 North University Ave.** in Provo; **(801) 379-6610.**

SEEING AND DOING

AMUSEMENTS

Seven Peaks Resort—

During the few years that the Seven Peaks Resort has been open, it has become one of Utah's most popular water parks. Located a few blocks from Brigham Young University, at the foot of Y Mountain, the park is convenient for students and youngsters from the Provo area. The resort also seeks to draw in overnight visitors with special accommodation/golf/water park packages. The water park boasts more than 45 heated water attractions, including Utah's largest wave pool, with 5-foot swells and numerous different wave patterns. The park claims among its 12 slides one of the world's longest water slides, 550 feet of which is through darkness punctuated with lights, foggers, misters, and sound effects. It also boasts the Tallest Slides in the World. One, the Lazer's Edge, is a 10-story water rollercoaster that delights youngsters and may seem to last an eternity for oldsters who dare try it. Another, the Sky Breaker, flushes you down a dark tunnel from which you emerge into a 95-foot waterfall. If you want to enjoy the water without the heart-seizing slides, "The Lazy River" allows you to lie back in a tube and enjoy an 800-foot-long float ride on the shallow artificial river. There are plenty of picnic tables available on the expansive lawns. The water park is open, weather permitting, from mid-May–Labor Day. To get there, follow Provo's Center St. east toward the mountain until you come to the park. For information and price information, call **(801) 377-4700;** or in Utah, call **1-800-824-4193.** The nationwide toll-free number is **1-800-824-3676.**

Trafalga Family Fun Center—

This recreational center has a giant water slide, game room, miniature golf, and batting cages. Trafalga is located in Orem and can be seen from Interstate 15. Take the Orem Center St. exit from Interstate 15 and turn south. Open Mon.–Sat. 10 am–midnight. **165 South 580 West; (801) 225-0195.**

HISTORIC SITES

Camp Floyd-Stagecoach Inn State Park—

In 1857, President James Buchanan sent 2,500 soldiers—approximately a third of the entire US Army—from Fort Leavenworth, Kansas, to Utah, to put down an alleged Mormon Rebellion. After spending the winter near Fort Bridger, blocked by Mormon militiamen who had set up fortifications east of Salt Lake City, the army, under the command of Albert Sidney Johnston, finally negotiated a truce and was allowed to pass through a deserted Salt Lake City on June 26, 1858. They continued without stopping for another 40 miles southwest of the city, where they established Camp Floyd. Until the outbreak of the Civil War, in 1861, Camp Floyd was the nation's largest military encampment and Utah's second largest community. Approximately 400 structures were built, and a large civilian population moved into the adjacent village of Fairfield. In 1858, the Overland Stage route was established through Fairfield and John Carson built an inn and stagecoach stop that has been preserved as a museum and historic site in this state park. The inn was also a Pony Express station from the time the Pony Express was first established, in April 1860, until its demise in Oct. 1861, after the completion of the transcontinental telegraph line. Camp Floyd closed in July 1861, when the last troops were ordered east as soldiers of the North and South moved to their first bloody encounter at Bull Run. Today, you can visit the restored Stagecoach Inn, an old army commissary building, and the Camp Floyd military cemetery, where 84 soldiers are buried. The cemetery is open year-round and the Stagecoach Inn and commissary from Mar.–Oct. Open daily, 11 am–5 pm. To reach Camp Floyd, take exit 262 off Interstate 15 at Lehi and drive west on Hwy. 73 for 14 miles until you get to the town of Cedar Fort. Continue on the road as it turns south for 5 miles to Fairfield. **18035 West 1540 North** in Fairfield; **(801) 768-8932.**

John Moyle's Indian Tower—

The Black Hawk War raged throughout Utah during the mid-1860s, when John R. Moyle, an 1856 immigrant from England, moved out of the protection of the Mountainville fort at present-day Alpine to build his home. But in case he came under attack by Utes, Moyle built a circular tower, approximately 10 feet in diameter and 15 feet tall, in which he and his family could take refuge and protect themselves. A tunnel was to connect the Moyle home with the rock tower, but the Ute Indians were sent east to the Uintah Reservation before the tunnel could be completed. The Moyle family has donated the tower and home to the city of Alpine. The city has constructed a park at the site, preserved the historic tower and remodeled Moyle home, and moved in an old timbered house and barn along with more than two dozen pieces of farm machinery and equipment. To reach the park, take Grove Dr. to 770 North, turn right and then left on the first street, Moyle Dr.

Mercur and Ophir—

These two 19th-century mining areas are hard to classify because they aren't exactly ghost towns. In the case of Ophir, people still live there, while Mercur was destroyed in a fire but mining operations continue. These old mining communities are located on the west slope and at the south end of the Oquirrh Mountains. Mercury was discovered here by a Bavarian prospector in the late 1860s (the name Mercur comes from the German word for "mercury"). Ophir, which is a name from the Bible, has a particularly interesting city hall. The false-fronted frame structure, built in 1890, has a bell tower and is an historic remnant from the days of early western mining. To get there, take Hwy. 73 west from Lehi and follow it past Fairfield, across Five Mile Pass, where the road turns in a northwesterly direction for approximately

8 miles. Watch for the road to Mercur as it heads back eastward. The road to Ophir, located in the canyon just north of Mercur, is another mile or so farther north, off Hwy. 73. The 3.5-mile drive up Ophir Canyon from Hwy. 73 is particularly beautiful in the fall when the trees are decked out in their autumn leaves.

Provo Historic Buildings—

Pick up a free copy of the **Provo Historic Buildings Tour booklet** from the Utah County Travel Council, which is located in the center of the tour, inside the old **Utah County Courthouse** at **51 South University St.**, just south of Center St. The 1920s Classical Revival–style courthouse has been restored, so take time to view each of the three floors where the combinations of marble and polished stone are simply stunning. Most of the 22 buildings can be visited on foot, but you might want to drive to some of the outlying locations. The tour features turn-of-the-century homes including those of Karl Maeser, founder of Brigham Young University; James E. Talmage, a prominent Mormon apostle; Jesse Knight, a millionaire miner, businessman, and philanthropist; and Reed Smoot, a Mormon apostle and US senator from 1903 to 1933. The historic Provo Tabernacle, constructed between 1883 and 1896 to seat 2,000 people, is located across University St. from the courthouse. Also included are the downtown commercial buildings, most of which date from the turn of the century. The large red Knight Block with its clock tower constructed in 1900 is of interest. It is located on the northeast corner of Center St. and University St.

Utah County Historic Sites—

This is a handsome nine-page booklet that describes 19 historic buildings and sites throughout Utah County, of which Provo is the county seat. Some of the sites include the **Lehi Roller Millers, American Fork Presbyterian Church,** the **Provo Town Square,** the **Provo Tabernacle,** and the **Peteetneet Academy.** The booklet is illustrated with beautiful full-page watercolor paintings by John Johnson of six of the sites and is an excellent source of information and a wonderful souvenir of your visit to Utah Valley. Published by the **Utah County Travel Council,** the booklet is free to the public.

MUSEUMS

Brigham Young University Museum of Art—

The 100,000-square-foot Brigham Young University Art Museum opened in Oct. 1993 and is the largest art museum between Denver and San Francisco. The university has more than 14,000 art objects in its collection, and the new museum, with its numerous galleries, offers curators plenty of opportunities to exhibit the collection. An orientation theater introduces the museum and the collection to visitors. The museum opened with a crowd-pleasing exhibit, "The Etruscans: Legacy of a Lost Civilization," from the Gregorian Etruscan Museum of the Vatican Museums. Subsequent exhibits have included "150 Years of American Painting," with paintings by such outstanding artists as Benjamin West, Albert Bierstadt, J. Alden Weir, and Maynard Dixon, all taken from the BYU art collection. Changing exhibits are a feature of this museum. Admission is free, unless there is a special exhibit. Open Mon.–Sat. 9 am–10 pm. For information, call **(801) 378-2787.**

Earth Science Museum—

Brigham Young University's third and smallest museum, this one has some of the largest exhibits with an allosaurus and camptosaurus dinosaurs. There is also a monstrous fish and crocodile heads, and the skull of a diceratops—a close relative of the triceratops and other items from the university's dinosaur collection. There is a petrified tree trunk, dinosaur footprints, an exhibit explaining a dozen ways in which fossils are formed, a mural depicting the relative size of dinosaurs including the unbelievably huge ultrasaurus. There is also a view area to watch scientists working with the fossil collection. Open Mon. 9

am–9 pm, Tues.–Fri. 9 am–5 pm, and Sat. noon–4 pm. Located just across the street from the south end of the football stadium next to the 1912 Page Elementary School at **1683 Canyon Rd.; (801) 378-3680.**

John Hutchings Museum of Natural History—

One of Utah's oldest museums, the John Hutchings Museum of Natural History began in 1913 as a family project to collect artifacts. With no particular theme, the collection includes items representing the area's Native Americans to the present-day computer industry. The museum is located in a Spanish Revival–style building constructed in 1920 as a Carnegie Library and Memorial to World War I veterans. John has passed on, but two of his sons, H. C. and John, are on hand most days to show visitors through the museum. A modest admission fee is charged. The museum is open daily 9:00 am–5:30 pm, except Sun. and holidays. **685 North Center** in Lehi; **(801) 768-8710.**

McCurdy Historical Doll Museum—

This is my wife's favorite Utah museum. In 1910, Laura McCurdy Clark began collecting dolls from all over the world. Eventually, in 1979, this museum opened as a showcase for the McCurdy dolls, which now number in excess of 4,000 dolls. The museum includes both a permanent exhibit and a monthly display. Lectures, films, and craft classes are offerd. There are storytelling sessions for the children, with the "McCurdy Story Princess," who uses dolls in her presentations. The museum is open Tues.–Sat. noon–6 pm; winter hours are 1 pm–5:00 pm. A modest admission fee is charged. **246 North 100 East** in Provo; **(801) 377-9935.**

Monte L. Bean Life Science Museum—

About 300 yards to the north of the Museum of Art, across the road on the hill, the Monte L. Bean Life Science Museum is a favorite with children and those who like to watch the wonderment of children as they encounter mounted or preserved animals from all over the world. The two floors of this eclectic collection include such animals as caribou, elk, moose, deer, pronghorned antelope, mountain goats, bobcats, timber wolf, mountain lion, bison, five different kinds of bear (Kodiak, polar, grizzly, black, and brown), a leopard, tiger, emperor penguin, and a European boar. In the Monte L. Bean memorial room, which displays the mounted heads of large game animals from Africa, push-button-activated screens show pictures of the animals in their natural habitat. There are displays of shells and snakes. A children's discovery room offers a hands-on experience for everyone. A gift shop offers plenty of opportunities to buy a special gift for all types and ages of animal lovers. A research library is also open to the public. Open Mon. 10 am–9 pm, Tues.–Sat 10 am–5 pm. No admission fee; **(801) 378-5053.**

Provo Daughters of Utah Pioneers Museum—

The museum is open Mon.–Sat. from June–Labor Day, and Thurs. during the rest of the year. Hours are 1 pm–5 pm. Located north of the museum are a collection of original pioneer cabins. **500 North and 500 West.**

Springville Daughters of Utah Pioneer Museum—

Housed in one of a dozen or so Carnegie libraries in Utah, the Springville Library was constructed in 1920 with a $10,000 Carnegie Foundation grant and $13,000 in local funds. The library was moved in 1965, but the building was renovated in 1991 to house artifacts collected by the Daughters of Utah Pioneers. **175 South Main; (801) 489-4681.**

Springville Museum of Art—

As Utah's first and oldest museum of art, a visit to Springville, nicknamed "The Art City," is a must for art lovers. Springville was home to two famous Utah artists: John Hafen and Cyrus Dallin. In 1903, the two

artists donated some of their works to the Springville High School. Other Utah artists donated works in 1907. In 1925, the Smart Collection was given to the high school. The white stucco, Spanish Mission–style museum building was constructed with funds from the New Deal Works Progress Administration and completed in 1937. It is now listed in the National Register of Historic Places. The museum's collection includes more than a thousand works by artists from Utah and throughout the US, which are exhibited in nine galleries on the second floor. Other educational programs, including lectures, guided tours, and films, are offered. The museum is open Tues.–Sat. 10 am–5 pm, Sun. 2 pm–5 pm, with extended hours on Wed. eve. until 9 pm. No charge for admission. **126 East 400 South, PO Box 509, Springville, UT 84663; (801) 489-2727.**

SCENIC DRIVES

Alpine Loop—

When you drive the 24-mile-long Alpine Loop (Utah Hwy. 92) you have the impression that this road was constructed with only one purpose in mind: to give thousands of motorists an intimate view of spectacular Mount Timpanogos. The narrow road connects American Fork Canyon with Provo Canyon. It twists and turns as it climbs to just over 8,000 feet at the summit, making it a slow drive requiring an hour or more. Be sure to allow plenty of time, especially during the autumn, and take lots of film for your camera. You will want to stop frequently to capture the beauty of the slopes with their magnificent tapestry of autumn leaves. Stops at Timpanogos Cave, Sundance, and Cascade Springs, along with a picnic lunch, enable you to make this a full day's outing. Because of the narrow curves and steep grade, trailers are prohibited. The road is closed during the winter. To reach the loop from Interstate 15, take exit 287 and head east on Utah Hwy. 92 to American Fork Canyon, where the loop begins. Follow it to the summit, and continue past Sundance to the junction with Hwy. 189 in Provo Canyon.

Nebo Loop—

See Nephi–Tintic section.

Pony Express Trail—

For 19 months in 1860 and 1861, some 80 Pony Express riders pounded along the 1,900-mile-long trail between St. Joseph, Missouri, and Sacramento, California, to deliver letters in 10 days' time—a journey that had previously taken many weeks by wagon or stagecoach. Riding at an average speed of 7 miles an hour, riders, weighing no more than 120 pounds and dressed in bright red shirts and blue pants, covered between 60 and 120 miles, before passing the mail pouches on to the next rider. Horses were exchanged at swing stations, approximately 12 miles apart. You can drive the best-preserved portion of the old Pony Express Trail and overland stage coach route as it heads west for 133 miles from the Stage Coach Inn State Park, one of the original Pony Express stations, to Ibapah, near the Utah-Nevada border. The federal Bureau of Land Management preserves and interprets the trail. Watch for visitor information signs at the Faust Station and plan a stop at the restored Simpson Springs Station where there is a developed BLM campground with 14 sites just east of the station. Most people take time to visit the isolated Fish Springs National Wildlife Refuge (75 miles west of Hwy. 36 at Faust). Other stops include the Boyd Station ruins and the Canyon Station ruins, where, in July 1863, Indians killed a stagecoach agent and four soldiers before burning the station. Monuments, mostly erected by the Utah Pioneer Trails and Landmarks Association and men working with the Civilian Conservation Corps during the 1930s, mark most of the sites of the 16 stations from Camp Floyd to Ibapah, site of the Deep Creek station. The road passes through Callao, site of another station and several ranches that form a small community. You can also take a short detour to the old mining town of Gold Hill. The road is sand and gravel, and vehicles usually don't have much trouble; wet roads, however, can cause sections of the road to become an impassable quagmire. The route passes just south of the Great Salt Desert, offering an unforgettable view of the desert and mountains. From Ibapah, most travelers head north about 60 miles to Wendover to refuel, eat, and visit the casinos, before driving back across the Salt Desert the 120 miles to Salt Lake City on Interstate 80. There is no gas available for the more than 200 miles between Lehi and Wendover, so start out with a full tank, let people know where you are going, and take plenty of water. (Sometimes gas is available at Ibapah, but don't count on it.) You can pick up a BLM brochure at the Utah County Travel Council Office or other locations in the state, which offers a good overview of the trail. For road conditions, call the **BLM's Salt Lake District Office, 2370 South 2300 West, Salt Lake City, UT 84119; (801) 524-5348.**

Provo Canyon Scenic Byway—

Connecting Utah Valley with Heber Valley and providing access to the Sundance Resort, U.S. Hwy. 189 winds around the south side of Mt. Timpanogus and follows up the Provo River, a popular fly-fishing stream. At the top of Provo Canyon, the highway skirts around the east side of Deer Creek Reservoir, at the southern end of Heber Valley. Located at the mouth of Provo Canyon is the Olmstead hydroelectric plant. The Olmstead Power Plant was constructed in 1904 by L. L. Nunn and his brother P. N. Nunn for the Telluride Power Company. L. L. Nunn was a pioneer in the development of alternating current high-voltage transmission. They operated an institute for up to 40 students at Olmstead and it was the first corporation-sponsored electrical school in the US. Ten miles up the canyon from Provo is Bridal Veil Falls (see the Tram Rides section).

THEATER

Sundance Summer Theatre—

You won't find many places with a dramatic setting equal to that offered at the Sundance Resort. Utahns appreciate both the magnificent mountain scenery as well as the two or more excellent theater productions that are staged here from mid-June–Aug. Both bench seating and lawn seating are available. **Performances** are held Mon.–Sat. beginning at 8:30 pm. A Children's Theatre offers two plays in repertory from July–Aug., with matinees at 1 pm Thurs., Fri., Sat., and Sun., and evening performances at 6 pm on Mon., Thur., Fri., and Sat. If you attend an evening performance, be sure to bring sweaters, jackets, and even blankets. The night temperature in the mountains, even during the summer, can be uncomfortable without adequate clothing. For reservations, call **(801) 225-4100.**

TOURS

Geneva Steel Tour—
Geneva Steel is the only integrated steel mill west of the Mississippi. For directions and information about tours, call **(801) 227-9420.** Located at **10 South Geneva Rd.** in Orem.

Historic Lehi Bus Tour—
Carl Mellor is a local history enthusiast who offers an informative bus tour of the Lehi area. During the 6-hour tour, you visit the Hutchings Museum, Camp Floyd, and Fairfield Stage Coach Inn, and listen to entertaining stories about characters who are a part of Utah Valley's history. The tour, which includes lunch, begins at 9 am on Sat. throughout the summer from May 15–Labor Day. **Charter bus tours** can also be arranged for groups. For individual and group reservations call Carl Mellor at **(801) 768-8665** or **768-4578.**

Nu-Skin International Tour—
If you want to learn about the history of skin care and tour a modern office building in downtown Provo, Nu-Skin operates a visitor center and weekday tours at 10 am, 11 am, 2 pm, and 3 pm. **76 West Center St.; (801) 345-TOUR.**

Peppermint Place—
This tour of a candy factory is popular with young and old alike. Kencraft, established in the home of Ken and Marlene Matheson in 1969, as a means of providing supplementary income for their family, has grown from the home kitchen to a modern factory. The new factory produces over 500 different products, most of which are available in the factory outlet store. Kencraft is now owned by Bob Murray, and he has built on the ideas of the Mathesons in exciting and innovative ways. When you enter the store, check out the rich assortment of goodies available, then go upstairs where a series of observation windows allows you to watch the candy-making process and the hand-decorating of the candy canes and lollipops. There is also an excellent eight-minute video upstairs that takes you through the candy cane–making process from beginning to end. You won't believe the imaginative ways of dressing up candy—bubble gum buddies that look like toys, candy climbers wrapped on a stick, and traditional candy canes, lollipops, and candy sticks. If sugar is not for you, there is a wide selection of sugar-free candies and chocolates that makes this one of Utah's most popular places to buy sugar-free candy. The outlet store is open Mon.–Sat. 10 am–6 pm, but the best time to see the candy-making process is weekdays from 10 am–2pm. **155 East 200 North, Alpine, UT 84004; (801) 756-7400.**

TRAM RIDES

Bridal Veil Falls—
One of the most scenic locations in the Wasatch Mountains, Bridal Veil Falls is a short 6-mile drive up Provo Canyon. The falls were originally named the Cascade Falls in 1859 by US Army Surveyor James H. Simpson but were later changed to the more picturesque Bridal Veil. The tram that climbs 1,228 vertical feet from the Provo River to a precipice above the 600-foot double-cataract falls is said to be the steepest in the world and is the oldest recreational tram in Utah. You might want to take your binoculars along and keep an eye out for Rocky Mountain goats, which were reintroduced into the area in 1967. Tram rides are reasonably priced

WILDLIFE

Fish Springs National Wildlife Refuge—

The only way to reach the refuge is across the **Pony Express Trail** (see the Scenic Drives section). But the 10,000-acre spring-fed marsh is an almost unbelievable contrast to the desert and barren hills through which most of the trail follows. The refuge is located on the east side of the Fish Springs Range and is formed by the springs that rise from a fault zone along the edge of the mountains. Fish Springs was the site of a Pony Express station. It was acquired by the US Fish and Wildlife Service in 1959, and work on the nine impoundment pools was completed in 1964. The best time to visit the refuge is during the late fall and early spring, when migrating waterfowl, such as swans, Canadian geese, blue herons, snowy egrets, and many other species can be seen. For information write **Refuge Manager, Fish Springs National Wildlife Refuge, Dugway, UT 84022.**

Provo Bay—

The marshlands along the south shore of Provo Bay, on the east side of Utah Lake provide easy viewing of numerous wetland bird species from Apr.–Nov. Look out for white pelican, egrets, blue herons, and a variety of geese and ducks. To get there, take exit 263 off Interstate 15 and head west on Utah Hwy. 77 to the Spanish Fork River bridge. There, turn north onto a dirt road and drive to Provo Bay, where there are numerous trails you can follow along the dikes to get a close-up view of the birds.

Steele Ranch—

For an easy-to-reach winter location to view mule deer and elk, the 1,000-acre sagebrush and oak-covered range managed by the Utah Division of Wildlife Resources at Steele Ranch is a good bet. To get there, take exit 245 off Interstate 15, about 2 miles south of Santaquin, and drive south on the frontage road on the west side of the interstate for about 3 miles. Cross under the interstate and drive east into the graveled parking area. Watch the animals from your vehicle so that you don't disturb them. Don't forget your binoculars!

———— WHERE TO STAY ————

ACCOMMODATIONS

Cottontree Inn—$$ to $$$

This Best Western motel has 80 rooms, heated pool, and whirlpool, and is located three blocks from Brigham Young University in a parklike setting along the Provo River. **2230 North University Pkwy.** in Provo; **(801) 373-7044** or **1-800-528-1234.**

Escalante Bed and Breakfast— $$ to $$$

This small two-bedroom bed and breakfast operated by Blake and Melanie Barney is housed in a restored 1890s home. Each room has a queen-sized bed, antiques, and a private bath. A full country breakfast is served in the dining room. Located in Spanish Fork, 7 miles south of Provo, off Interstate 15; **733 North Main; (801) 798-6652.**

Fairfield Inn—$$ to $$$

This modern 72-room motel, part of the Marriott system, is located a just off the Interstate 15 University exit (exit 266) in Provo. Heated indoor pool and hot tub; complimentary continental breakfast. **East Bay Business Park, 1504 South 40 East; (801) 377-9500** or **1-800-228-2800.**

Kearns Hotel—$$ to $$$

This early Springville Hotel was originally constructed as a residence in 1892 and converted into a hotel in 1909. After being closed for many years, the hotel was reopened after an extensive restoration, which won the Utah Heritage Foundation's 1991 Award for Historic Preservation. The hotel, listed in the National Register of Historic Places, has three full-size suites, two mini-suites, all with kitchenettes, and four additional sleeping rooms. A free continental breakfast is served. **94 West 200 South, Springville, UT 84663; (801) 489-0737.**

Provo Park Hotel—$$ to $$$

The Provo Park Hotel is part of the Seven Peaks Resort, and many locals consider this Provo's best lodging. With 235 guest rooms and suites, the hotel is certainly the area's largest. Smoking and non-smoking floors are provided. Swimming pool and fitness center. An excellent restaurant, **Mingles**, and a private club, **Seasons**, are located within the hotel. **101 West 100 North** in Provo; **(801) 377-4700** or **1-800-777-7144.**

Sundance Cottages—$$$ to $$$$

The accommodations at Sundance Resort range from a standard room to studios, three-bedroom cottages, and five-bedroom residences. For information, rates, and reservations, write or call **RR 3, Box A-1, Sundance, UT 84604; (801) 225-4107.**

CAMPING

With the Wasatch Mountains rimming Utah Valley on the east, there are five canyons in which public camping is available from mid-May–mid- and late Oct. on forest service land. Beginning from the north and moving south, camping locations are noted for each of the five canyons.

American Fork Canyon (American Fork and Pleasant Grove)—

All campgrounds are located on state Hwy. 92.

Echo, Roadhouse, Martin, Warnick, and Mile Rock—This series of five small campgrounds is located about 12 miles from Pleasant Grove. Each has 6 sites, except for Echo, which has only 4.

Granite Flat and Timpooneke—14.1 miles northeast of Pleasant Grove. Each campground has 32 sites.

Little Mill—10 miles northeast of Pleasant Grove; 79 RV sites and 35 tent sites.

Hobble Creek Canyon (Springville, Mapleton, and Spanish Fork)—

Diamond—18.5 miles east of Spanish Fork off Hwy. 147. Thirty-six RV and tent sites.

Whiting—6.8 miles east of Springville, off Hwy. 89. Sixteen RV and tent sites.

Payson Canyon (Nebo Loop Road)—

Blackhawk—16 miles southeast of Payson; 23 RV and tent sites.

Maple Bench—7.6 miles southeast of Payson; 14 RV and tent sites.

Payson Lakes—12 miles southeast of Payson; 99 RV and tent sites.

Provo Canyon—

Hope—10 miles northeast of Provo, off Hwy. 189; 24 RV and tent sites.

Mt. Timpanogos—14 miles northeast of Provo, off Hwy. 80; 26 RV and tent sites.

Rock Canyon—4.9 miles east of Provo, off Hwy. 189; 7 RV and tent sites.

Santaquin Canyon—

Tinney Flat—8 miles southeast of Santaquin; 2 RV and 10 tent sites.

Private Campgrounds—

Most private campgrounds are located in Provo or in Provo Canyon. All are open year-round unless otherwise noted.

American Campground—All 53 RV trailer sites have complete hookups. **418 East 620 South, American Fork; (801) 756-5502.**

Deer Creek Park—A third of the 100 RV trailer sites have complete hookups. Open May–Oct. **620 Provo Canyon; (801) 225-5346.**

Frazier Trailer Park—Eight of the 26 RV trailer sites have complete hookups. Open late Mar.–Nov. Three miles east of Orem in Provo Canyon; **(801) 225-5346.**

Lakeside Campground—This is the largest private campground with 135 RV sites, all with complete hookups. Drinking water, flush toilets, showers, and laundry are available. Located adjacent to Utah Lake. **4000 West Center, Provo; (801) 373-5267**

Riverbend Trailer Park—Riverbend has 64 RV sites, 50 of which have complete hookups. Open mid-Apr.–mid-Oct. Seven miles east of Orem in Provo Canyon; **(801) 225-1863**.

Silver Fox Campground—Nearly all of the 87 sites have full hookups. **101 West 1500 South; 1-800-833-1379.**

WHERE TO EAT

Bombay House—$$ to $$$

Featuring East Indian food prepared by master chef Amber Singh, the Bombay House offers a fine luncheon buffet and dinners cooked in a Tandoori oven—an oven made of clay shaped like a big jar and insulated with a thick layer of plaster and ceramic tile that is heated by a charcoal fire producing temperatures of 850 degrees Fahrenhet inside the oven. The full-course dinners include curries, rice, Indian breads (naan), chutney, and a variety of chicken and lamb dishes. In keeping with Indian tradition, fennel seeds are offered at the end of the meal to cleanse the breath and help with digestion. But don't end your meal without trying one of their unusual desserts such as Rasamiaai—cheese patties in a sweet thickened milk sauce with nuts; kheer—mildly flavored basmati rice, raisins, cashews cooked in milk; or Kulfi—homemade Indian ice cream. Open for lunch 11:30 am–2:30 pm weekdays; noon–3 pm Sat.; and for dinner weekdays 5 pm–9:30 pm; 5 pm–10:30 pm Fri. and Sat. Closed Sun **463 North University Ave., Provo; (801) 373-6677.**

Brick Oven Pizza—$ to $$

BYU students have been coming here for the excellent pizza for decades. The menu also includes other Italian food such as spaghetti and lasagna. Open 11 am–11 pm; 11:00 am–12:30 am Fri. and Sat. Closed Sun. **150 East 800 North, Provo; (801) 374-8800.**

Brigham Young University's Skyroom—$ to $$

Located on the sixth floor of the Wilkinson Center, the Skyroom offers panoramic views of the campus and Utah Valley. If you are visiting BYU and want a special eating experience, the Skyroom is your best bet. This is where professors, administrators, and their guests meet for lunch from 11:30 am–2 pm. A soup and salad buffet is the most popular lunch item. Sandwiches are also available. It is also open for dinner on Fri. evenings 6:00 pm–7:30 pm. Reservations are recommended. The public is welcome, as long as they adhere to university dress and conduct standards; **(801) 378-5001.**

Gandolfo's New York Delicatessen—$

A New York deli seems about as out of place in downtown Provo as white-shirted Mormon missionaries in the Bronx, but since its establishment in 1990, Gandolfo's certainly has brought a unique character to the eating possibilities in Provo. Owned by native New Yorker Craig Gandolph, the delicatessen traces its lineage back to the establishment of the original Gandolfo's in New York City in 1878 by Craig's great-great-grandfather, Thomas Anthony Gandolfo. (The name was changed in the 1920s because of anti-Italian prejudice.) When I stopped for a sandwich, I stood in line behind a BYU student from New York who said he had come to see if it was "a genuine New York deli." Before I left I asked him if it was, and he replied, 'Yes, indeed!' The decor, from the outside road sign indicating "New York" to the street signs, pennants, New York Met posters, and even the nearly abrasive workers would make any New Yorker feel at home. The basement location also adds to the character. There is a good variety of sandwiches. All carry New York names, including the

Brooklyn Bridge, the Little Italy, the Central Park, the Ebbets Field, the Shea Stadium, and the Yankee Dog. **18 North University St., Provo; (801) 375-DELI.**

Govinda's Buffet—$ to $$

The most popular items in this vegetarian and natural food restaurant are the buffet lunches and dinners, which include an entrée, two homemade soups, two types of rice, vegetable dish, salad bar, and fresh rolls and bread. Other menu items include a veggie burger made from lentils seasoned with fresh spices, a grilled slice of marinated tofu, and the avocado delight made with avocados, Monterey Jack cheese, tomatoes, sprouts, and lettuce. Open for lunch 11 am–2 pm, and dinner from 5:00 pm–8:30 pm; 5:00 pm–9:00 pm on weekends; closed Sun. **260 North University Ave., Provo; (801) 375-0404.**

Joon's Cafe—$ to $$

You might be inclined to see this as just another hole-in-the wall restaurant, but Joon's offers some of the best Korean food to be found anywhere. Im Joon Park married an American Air Force officer and came to the US in 1955. During the last 40 years, she has operated restaurants in New York City, Atlantic City, Los Angeles, and Hawaii. When her two daughters married Mormons and moved to Provo, they decided to open Joon's Cafe in what was formerly Clair's Cafe. They preserved the 1950s-style serpentine counter, one of the last left in Utah, and now offer excellent Korean food at very moderate prices. For lunch you can get chicken curry and vegetable curry, a vegetarian bowl, or my favorite, the lunch bowl combo which includes a sampling of Korean dishes such as pulkogi (barbecued beef or chicken); yagi mandoo (beef filled dumplings) bae choo kimchee (pickled spicy cabbage) chap chae (clear noodles stir fried with vegetables; and vegetable tempura and steamed rice. The dinner menu offers soups and specialties and an expanded version of the lunch bowl combo that includes soup and several additional kimchee dishes. Open for

lunch weekdays 11 am–3 pm and for dinner 6 pm–9 pm; open Sat. noon–9 pm. Closed on Sun. **154 North University Ave., Provo; (801) 377-3630.**

La Casita Mexican Restaurant— $ to $$

Established in 1978 by Luis and Luz Muzquiz, the La Casita is one of the most popular places for Mexican food in Utah Valley. The menu includes five different salsas, traditional combination plates, plus specials like a crab enchilada and machaca—shredded beef cooked with onions, tomatoes, and peppers. Open 11:30 am–10 pm. Mon.–Thurs.; 11 am–11 pm on Fri. and Sat. Closed Sun. **333 North Main St., Springville; (801) 489-9543.**

La Dolce Vita—$ to $$

Giovanni Della Corte and his family immigrated from Naples to Coalville, Utah, in 1980 and worked in a restaurant there until they opened their family-style Italian restaurant in Provo on July 4, 1984. The restaurant is a three-generation operation as Giovanni, his wife Susi, their son Jerry and daughter-in-law Anna Rosa, and son Jimmy all work to make this the most authentic Italian restaurant in the Provo area. The pizza and calzones are popular, but my favorites are the pasta combo which includes two pastas, one under a white sauce and the other under a red sauce and the chef's combo, which is a specially prepared breaded beef cutlet, topped with a house sauce and melted cheese served with three different kinds of pasta. On Thurs. the traditional gnocchi (potato and flour dumplings baked with cheeses under a red sauce) is available. Open 11 am–4 pm for lunch and 5 pm–10 pm for dinner. Closed Sun. **61 North 100 East; (801) 373-8482.**

Oak Crest Inn—$$ to $$$

The Oak Creek Inn is situated on a ridge lined with scrub oak and has a nice panoramic view of the mountains and Spanish Oaks Golf Course. This is a local favorite place for lunch and special occasions. Lunch menu items include traditional dishes such as chicken-fried steak, grilled ham, pork chops, halibut, grilled ham, and sirloin steak. Dinner items include steak, prime rib, seafood, and fish. Open Tues.–Fri. noon–2 pm and 5 pm–10 pm; Sat. 5 pm–10 pm, and Sun. noon–6 pm. Closed Mon. Located just off US Hwy. 6, southeast of Spanish Fork. **2600 Canyon Rd.; (801) 798-7045.**

Osaka Japanese Restaurant—$ to $$

Located in a long narrow building, the interior is simple, exquisitely clean, and very Japanese. From the Japanese calligraphy on the walls to the lanterns over each table, the atmosphere is worth the visit, to say nothing of the excellent Japanese cuisine at very reasonable prices. Nancy Lin, who grew up in Taiwan, named her restaurant for the home city of her mother from whom she learned to cook. She opened Osaka in 1985. Her gyoza (chinese dumplings) and homemade salad dressing win raves from visitors from all over the US. The menu includes sushi and sashimi along with traditional teriyaki, sukiyaki, katsu, and tempura dishes. The chicken teriyaki donburi is the most popular menu item. For dinner try one of the combination dinners. If you want to eat in the traditional Japanese style, there are three tatami rooms, where you can take off your shoes and sit at a low table inside an enclosed dining area. Open 11:00 am–9:30 pm, until 10:00 pm on Fri. and Sat. (10 pm on the weekend) Closed Sun. **46 West Center St., Provo; (801) 373-1060.**

The Torch—$ to $$

This is one of Utah's most unique eating establishments, not only because it is the only place in the state where you can get authentic Cuban cuisine, but also because of the gourmet shake menu which includes over 100 different combinations. Most of the shakes are made from fresh fruit, such as watermelon, mango, papaya, tamarindo, guava, coconut, guanabana, and strawberries. Owner Robert Perez left Havana in 1960 and spent time in Florida and Chicago, where he met and married his wife Annabella, who had immigrated from northern Cuba. They offer a great all-you-can-eat buffet with fresh fruits for lunch and dinner. If you just want a sandwich for lunch, try the Cuban sandwich, made of ham, swiss cheese, mustard, and mayonnaise (because that's what Americans like) served on Cuban bread that is pressed and cooked. A popular favorite dinner is the picadillo (seasoned ground beef with rice and corn fritters). If you want a special dinner, call in advance for the paella valenciana, a special dish made of shrimp, lobster, fish, clams, oyster, pork, and chicken, cooked in yellow rice and served with fried plantains. Black beans are served with most dishes, and the salsa is made from a traditional recipe. Open daily for lunch from noon–2:30 pm and dinner 5 pm–11 pm. Closed Sun. **43 North University Ave., Provo; (801) 374-0202.**

Tree Room and the Grill Room— $$ to $$$$

Two excellent restaurants make dining an added plus to the special experience of visiting Sundance Resort. The Tree Room features good food and Native American art and western memorabilia collected by Robert Redford. The Grill Room, is a more informal bistro-style restaurant, with soups, sandwiches, pizza, pasta, and house specialties. The Tree Room features steaks and fish. My favorite is the pepper tree steak, served with chutney and mango sauce. Both restaurants offer outdoors eating in the summer. The Grill Room is open daily from 7 am–10 pm, and the Tree Room for dining only 5 pm–10 pm. Located at **Sundance Resort; (801) 225-4107.**

SERVICES

Mountainland Travel Region—
2545 North Canyon Rd., Provo, UT 84604-5906; (801) 377-2262.

Uinta National Forest—
88 West 100 North, Provo, UT 84601; (801) 377-5780.

Utah County Travel Council—
Located in room 111 of the historic Utah County Courthouse. **51 University Ave., Provo, UT 84606; (801) 370-8393** or **1-800-222-UTAH.**

The Kearns Hotel of Springville was originally built as a private residence for Thomas Kearns. Constructed in 1892, the hotel is listed in the National Register of Historic Places. Photo courtesy of the Utah State Historical Society.

Park City

Park City is the ideal winter destination. Promoters who hope to land the 2002 Winter Olympics for Utah use the community and its facilities as one of the key arguments in favor of Utah. It has excellent ski slopes, fine restaurants, delightful accommodations, and the ambiance of a 19th-century mining town that planners have carefully maintained—and all within a few miles drive from Salt Lake City International Airport. It is true that you can leave Salt Lake City, purchase your ski ticket, ride the ski lift, and be skiing down the slopes in less time than it takes to watch *60 Minutes* on television. Park City is actually six areas, if you count the new subdivisions and condominiums to the north of town: the ski jumping and bobsled and luge facilities in Bear Hollow; Wolf Mountain Ski Resort; Park City Ski Resort; the historic mining town of Park City; and the Deer Valley Resort. Park City has a highly developed cultural life, with an arts festival that attracts thousands, the Sundance Film Festival (which draws celebrities from all over the world, and which, under the direction of Robert Redford, is considered one of the top film festivals anywhere), and a number of art galleries and shops. Park City is much more than a winter resort town; it is also a popular summer resort, with excellent golf courses, summer activities, and hiking opportunities.

HISTORY

Three particular interests have developed Park City: pioneering, mining, and skiing. The original Mormon Pioneer Trail winds just to the north of the Park City area and enters the Salt Lake Valley through Emigration Canyon. Parley P. Pratt, a Mormon apostle and member of the first pioneer group to come west with Mormon president Brigham Young, was an explorer by nature. He examined the mountainous area near the trail and found excellent mountain meadows for his livestock in what was soon being called Parley's Park. Pratt also built a toll road into Salt Lake City, down the canyon just south of Emigration Canyon. Constructed in 1850, California gold seekers were willing to pay $1,500 in tolls that year to bypass the Emigration Canyon route into Salt Lake City. But Pratt did not stay long before being "called" to other church assignments that took him away from the canyon that continues to bear his name. In 1853, he sold his interest in what would become the Park City area to Samuel Snyder, who opened a saw mill there. A small settlement, known as Snyderville, developed around the saw mill. It remains a place name in the area, just a few miles north of Park City.

179

With Mormons content to cut timber, to graze livestock, and to abide by the admonitions of their leader Brigham Young to stay away from gold and silver mining, it was left to prospectors among the California regiment sent to Utah during the Civil War to stake some of the first claims in the Park City area. Their commander, the Irish-born Colonel Patrick Connor, encouraged his men, many of whom had plenty of mining experience in California and Nevada, to search the surrounding mountains for precious metals. He maintained that with the development of a strong mining economy, the theocracy of the Mormon Church in Utah would dissolve.

The first mining claim was recorded on December 23, 1868, and the first silver ore shipped from the Flagstaff Mine by wagons to the new railroad line in Echo City in 1871. During the July 4th celebration in 1872, George Gideon Snyder announced that the shacks and cabins that had been thrown up near the mine now constituted the new community of Park City. The city grew steadily during the 1870s and by 1880, contained 350 buildings. A newspaper, *The Park Record*, which is still published, was established in 1880. The Utah Eastern Railroad was completed that year between Park City and Salt Lake City. The 1880s were prosperous as rags-to-riches stories like those of Thomas Kearns, David Keith, John Judge, Albion Emery, and others spurred hopefuls to strike it rich themselves.

But the 1890s brought two major disasters. The first was a severe economic depression caused by the demonetization of silver and the Panic of 1893. The second occurred on June 18, 1898, when more than 200 wooden buildings and houses, including all of those on Main St., were destroyed by fire. Park City was rebuilt, prosperity returned, and the mines continued to operate. Most mines closed during the Great Depression and, although mining was revived to meet the wartime demands of the 1940s, mining was all but dead by the 1950s.

History does not record the name of the individual to first tie wooden slats to his feet and slide down the snow-covered slopes around Park City, but among the early miners there were plenty of immigrant miners from Sweden, Norway, and Finland. In all likelihood it was they who introduced skiing to Park City. By 1916, recreational skiing was beginning to develop as members of the Wasatch Mountain Club began to traverse the mountains above Park City. In 1923, the first ski-jumping exhibition was staged and, in 1928, construction of the Ecker Hill ski jump commenced. By the 1930s, representatives of Franklin D. Roosevelt's New Deal programs proposed rescuing the economy of Park City by transforming it into "the best winter sports center in America." A combination of factors delayed this reality for 30 years: to the north, in Idaho, the Union Pacific Railroad constructed its famous Sun Valley

Resort and, just across the mountains from Park City, the ski areas of Alta and Brighton lured the skiers that Park City had hoped to attract.

In 1962, with mining in rapid decline, real estate prices at rock bottom, and few jobs to keep its young people, Park City officials and businesspeople revived the dream of making Park City a skier's mecca. They announced plans to construct a 12,880-foot, 144-car gondola tramway, the Treasure Mountain Center, and two chairlifts as the nucleus of the Park City ski area. A year later, the facilities were opened and, as if by magic, Park City started the transformation from a depressed mining town to a world-class resort. The initial success led to the establishment of a second resort, Wolf Mountain, which opened in 1968 and the Deer Valley area opened in 1981. Park City continues its quest to become America's top ski center. In January 1993, ski-jumping facilities in Bear Hollow, visible just off the road into Park City from Interstate 80, were dedicated.

All this development has been done with an attempt to preserve the 19th-century mining heritage. Park City Main St. was listed in the National Register of Historic Places in 1978, and Utah's strictest preservation and zoning ordinances have been adopted by the city. Grants and low-interest loans for the preservation of historic buildings are offered to owners by the city, and the city has placed historic markers on many of its historic buildings.

GETTING THERE

Park City is an easy 35-mile drive from the Salt Lake City airport. Just take Interstate 80 east toward the city. At the junction with Interstate 15, head south on Interstate 15 for about 3 miles and stay to the left to reenter Interstate 80, which heads east up through Parley's Canyon. About 5 miles beyond Parley's Summit, take exit 145 and head south along state Hwy. 224 into the Park City area.

FESTIVALS AND EVENTS

Utah Winter Games
January

Held during the month of Jan., the Utah Winter Games include ski-jumping, downhill and slalom races, and cross-country ski races. Clinics are also offered as well as a host of other winter activities. For more information, write or call **Utah Winter Games, PO Box 25204, Salt Lake City, UT 84125; (801) 975-4515.**

Sundance Institute Film Festival
end of January

If the excitement of glamorous movie stars, nervous producers, and the drama of film premiers before discerning audiences captures your imagination, or if you just like new and innovative films, then the Sundance Institute Film Festival is the place to be. During the last half of Jan. Park City hosts the Sundance Institute Film Festival, which includes 10 days of screenings, seminars, tributes, and other activities. The festival began in 1981 under the direction of Robert Redford and has become the premiere American festival for independent filmmakers. Park City is where new filmmaking talent comes to be discovered and legends remembered. The festival seeks to show films that cover as many diverse points of view as possible. With this philosophy the festival offers an eclectic mixture of dramas, comedies, documentaries, foreign films, and films that deal with important subjects or that are produced by a selected group such as the series that includes films about and made by Native Americans. Tickets go quickly, and many showings are sold out in advance of the festival as part of package deals, but part of the adventure of a film festival is the chance to see innovative and provocative films that may not be shown anywhere else. There is a chance that tickets will be available for some showings, and even if there is a sold-out sign, you can still put your name on the waiting list in hopes that you might get one of the unfilled seats. The way to work this system is to pick up a copy of the festival program and decide what you want to take your chance on seeing. Go to the theater about an hour and a half before the scheduled time and get in line to get on the waiting list. An hour before the film begins they will take your name and money for the ticket. About 15 minutes before the film starts, if there are any empty seats in the theater, those on the waiting list will be admitted. If you pay your money and don't get in, your money is refunded. The waiting line experience can be as exciting as watching the film. Until recently all screenings have been held in Park City, but in 1993 the festival expanded to Salt Lake City's Tower Theater providing more opportunities to view the selected films. For information call **(801) 328-FILM.**

Park City 4th of July Celebration
4th of July

The day begins at 6 am with early-rising enthusiasts setting off loud blasts that can be heard all over Park City. The day-long events are centered around the park and Main St. Breakfast is available at the park, followed by the traditional not-so-traditional parade down Main St. at 11 am, where participants strive for the most unique and bizarre entries. The afternoon activities include children's games at the park; the traditional rugby game, with the local team, the Park City Muckers, taking on challengers usually from the Salt Lake Valley; food; and musical performers. The day concludes with a spectacular display of fireworks at the Resort Center.

Park City Arts Festival
1st Sat. and Sun. in August

This annual gathering of local and out-of-state artists began in 1979 and now ranks as one of the nation's top fine art events according to *Sunshine Artist* magazine. The festival is held on Main St. The street is closed off, and each year the festival sets new attendance records as attendees jostle elbow to elbow up and down the street to view the works of the 200 artists selected from nearly a thousand applicants. Art works include such items as ceramics, drawing, fiber, glass, jewelry, leather, metal, painting, paper, photography, sculpture, and wood. Live music is performed on several stages. In addition to the art, the event is something of a food festival with more than a dozen Park City and Deer Valley restaurants vying with each other to offer the most upscale and trendy edibles. The festival is held the first Sat. and Sun. in Aug. from 10:00 am–6:00 pm. Admission fee for those over 12. For further information call the Kimball Art Center, **(801) 649-8882**.

Autumn Aloft
mid-September

The sight of almost 30 balloons floating above Park City is truly spectacular. The brilliantly colored balloons crowd the sky, while below people crowd the streets of Park City for this annual event. Autumn Aloft is free to everyone, unless you want to ride in a hot-air balloon. The festival begins early in the morning, so that the balloons can take advantage of the cool weather in order to rise. Plan to arrive by 7:00 am to watch the balloons being set up and to watch them rise slowly into the sky.

—————— OUTDOOR ACTIVITIES ——————

ALPINE SLIDE

During the winter, it is the famous PayDay ski run, but in the summer, it is home to a half-mile-long snake of half pipe that twists and turns down the slope provoking thrills and screams from those who climb aboard the sleds to make the descent to the center of the ski resort. To ride the alpine slide, purchase tickets at the **Park City Resort Center,** then climb aboard the double-chair ski lift at the base of the hill for an enjoyable ride up the mountain. At the top of the mountain you pick up a sled and then climb on one of the two pipes that parallel each other down the mountain. If you plan a slow descent, warn those in back of you to give you plenty of room. Youngsters like to roar down the mountain threatening to sail out of the pipe at every turn. (Yes, you can go out of the pipe, so if you are not the daredevil type, exercise caution.) Still, it is a fun activity for all ages. The slide is open daily during the summer from 10 am–9 pm.

BIKING

When the skiers finally put their skis away in the spring, it is no longer with the same regret as in former years. The two-wheeled mountain bike has become a worthy substitute for a pair of skis or a snowboard. Ski lifts that carry skiers to the tops of the mountains in winter offer an easy way to get your bike to the top of the mountain with no effort. Ski runs that challenge the best of skiers offer the same white-knuckle experience for mountain bikers. But while there are challenging routes for the Kamikaze-style rider, there are also miles of wonderful forest land for those who want a relaxing ride. The "Park City Mountain Bike Trails" brochure is available free from the **Park City Visitor Information Center** and at other locations in the city. The guide describes 10 rides in the Park City area, ranging from an easy 1.7-mile, 30-minute ride in Telemark Park to the 10.5-mile, steep climb to Shadow Lake. Utah's first rails-to-trails bike route was opened in 1992 and follows the 30-mile route of the Union Pacific Railroad from what was the location of the railroad station in Park City to near the junction with the main Union Pacific line at Echo.

Tours—

If you are looking for an organized tour, led by guides who know the area, support personnel who will look after your equipment and provide you with snacks, meals, and drinks, then **Sport Touring Ventures** might be just your ticket. They offer rentals and half-day, full-day, and overnight tours. **4719 Silver Meadows Dr., #19, Park City, UT 84060; (801) 649-1551.**

GOLF

Park City Municipal Golf Course—

Situated at the base of the Park City Ski Resort, this course was constructed in 1962 and is quite scenic—a favorite of Utah golfers. There are plenty of water and trees, as well as condominiums built along some of the fairways, adding one more layer of stress for erratic golfers. **1800 Three Kings Rd.; (801) 521-2135.**

Park Meadows—

In the spring of 1994, readers of the *Deseret News* voted this golf course the most difficult course in Utah. Designed by golf pro Jack Nicklaus, it is certainly long and difficult with sand traps sprinkled all over the 6,666-yard course (7,338 yards, if you play the blue tees). While Utah golfers consider it expensive at (fees do include a cart), it is a bargain for those accustomed to much higher greens fees. You can cut the price by $4 by playing Mon.–Thur., or by $7 if you play after 3:00 pm without a cart. The course is characterized by beautiful scenery, no trees, and no crowds. **2000 Meadows Dr.; (801) 531-7029**

HORSEBACK RIDING

Park City Stables—

Park City Stables has two locations, one at the Park City Ski Area just under the lift that takes you up to the Alpine Slide and the other at the Deer Valley Resort. You can arrange for a one- or two-hour trail ride or special breakfast and dinner rides. Open daily from late May–mid Oct. **(801) 646-7256** or **1-800-303-7256.**

SKIING
CROSS-COUNTRY
White Pine Touring Center—

Located on the Park City Golf Course, just off Main St., the White Pine has 12 kilometers of set track, plus guided tours, lessons, and a full-service ski shop. Open daily from 9 am–6 pm; **(801) 649-8710.**

DOWNHILL

Park City is home to the US Ski Team and ranks among the top ski areas in the country, if not the world. Park City, Wolf Mountain, and Deer Valley all have excellent ski schools, rental shops, and lifts that are located within walking distance of accommodations, or a short drive or bus ride from anywhere in the Park City area. All three areas participate in multi-area programs.

Deer Valley—

Catering to the more affluent skier, Deer Valley is an unbelievable experience compared to every other ski resort in Utah, or, for that matter, in the US. *Ski Magazine* consistently rates Deer Valley one of North America's top resorts. The number of skiers allowed on the mountain is restricted, lift lines are usually nonexistent, and skiers are catered to and pampered in ways that are hard to imagine. When you arrive at the resort, ski valets unload your skis from your car, and complimentary secured ski storage corrals ensure that your skis will be where you left them. Thick padded chairlifts make the ride up the mountain as comfortable as possible, and, if you need to blow your nose or clean your glasses, tissue dispensers are available at each lift. The restaurants and lodging are first class. The 66 ski runs are meticulously groomed and spread out over 900 acres. With 13 chairlifts—two high-speed quads, nine triple chairs, and two double chairlifts, the resort capacity is 19,200 skiers per hour.

The runs are spread out over three mountains: Bald Mountain (8,400 feet elevation), Flagstaff Mountain (9,100 feet elevation), and Bald Eagle Mountain (9,400 feet elevation). Opened in 1981, the ski season usually runs from the first week in Dec.–first week in Apr. Actually, for all the amenities, skiing at Deer Valley costs only a few more dollars a day than at the Park City Resort. Multiday passes offer some savings. For reservations, lift tickets, ski school, and rentals, call **(801) 649-1000** or **1-800-424-3337**.

Park City—

During its heyday as a mining town, a tram ran from the center of Park City up the mountain to the mines. Today, a triple chairlift follows the old tram route, allowing skiers to stay on historic Main St. and walk to the chairlift for a 13-minute ride. The main resort center is located at what was the northwestern edge of Park City. Here, a four-passenger gondola takes skiers for a 23-minute ride up the mountain to the heart of the 2,200 acres of skiing terrain. In addition to the gondola and triple-chair town lift, there are a high-speed detachable quad, a fixed-grip quad, five triple and five double chairlifts, which provide access for nearly 22,200 skiers an hour to 86 trails (the longest of which is 3.5 miles), plus 650 acres of wide-open skiing in five bowls at the top of the mountain. The snowfall average for Park City is more than 300 inches a year, with the largest amount usually falling in Mar. From below, the Park City mountains are not as dramatic as those in nearby Little and Big Cottonwood canyons, but once you get on top there are plenty of runs to challenge the best of skiers. The snowfall average is about 60 percent of that at Alta, for example, but the use of snowmaking equipment ensures good skiing, even during infrequent years of little snow. The lifts are located at approximately 6,900 feet elevation and reach 10,000 feet, for a vertical drop of 3,100 feet. While the ski schools serve all ages of skiers, a special It's Never Too Late program has been developed for older skiers. Some

graduates of the school automatically qualify for free lift passes, given to all those 70 and over. Children 12 and under ski for about half price. For snow conditions, call **(801) 649-9571;** for general information, call **(801) 649-8111**.

Wolf Mountain (formerly Park West)—

Wolf Mountain has a reputation for being one of the lowest-priced ski options along the Wasatch Front. The resort's name was changed from Park West to Wolf Mountain beginning with the 1994 and 1995 ski season, but it will probably be referred to by both names for some time to come. It is the only ski resort in the Park City area that allows snowboarders, offering two "half pipes" and instruction in snowboarding. It has an excellent children's ski school, and children eight and under can ski for free when accompanied by an adult ticket holder. With easy access off Interstate 80, special ski school classes, and lower lift prices, Wolf Mountain probably has a higher percentage of Utah skiers than the other two Park City area resorts. The resort offers seven double chairlifts with a capacity of 6,700 skiers per hour. The terrain covers 850 acres between 6,800 and 9,000 feet elevation with 64 runs, 24 percent beginner, 34 percent intermediate, and 42 percent advanced or expert. Powder skiers can tackle Murdock Bowl, which requires a 600-foot vertical climb above the Ironhorse lift. For more information, call **(801) 649-5400**.

SKI-JUMPING
Utah Winter Sports Park—

In preparation for Utah's bid for the 2002 Winter Olympics, a new ski-jumping facility was opened in 1993, just north of Park City in Bear Hollow. The 90-meter jump is a year-round facility. During the summer, the jumping continues using a special plastic mat in place of the snow for the landing and a ceramiclike material for the track on the ski jump. Visitors are welcome at the facility; during the summer, you can ride up the lift alongside the 90-meter jump.

During the winter you can also try your skill at going off the 18-meter jump. A moderate fee is charged for visitors and those who use the facility, except for members of the US Ski Team. You can see the ski jumps from Interstate 80 near the Park City exit. Just follow the signs that lead off state Hwy. 224, south of the Interstate and north of Snyderville and Wolf Mountain Ski Resort. For information, call **(801) 649-5447.**

TENNIS

Many of the hotels offer private tennis courts, but there are two free courts: **Prospector Square Athletic Club** has two outdoor courts and the **Park City Racquet Club** has seven outdoor and four indoor courts.

SEEING AND DOING

BALLOONING

Most of us have imagined what it would be like to step into the basket of a hot-air balloon and slowly lift off the ground and float high above the houses, fields, and mountains below. Park City is Utah's most popular ballooning area, and visitors can take advantage of this strong interest for a never-to-be-forgotten experience. Flights can be arranged throughout the year, depending on wind and weather conditions, with the following companies:

Balloon Affaire—(801) 649-1217 or **1-800-658-8489.**

Park City's Great Balloon Escape— **(801) 287-9401** or **1-800-645-9400.**

FLYING

High Country Aviation—

You can take an airplane tour of the Wasatch Mountains and ski resorts or soar above Park City and Deer Valley in a motorless glider aircraft. For information and prices, write or call **1980 Airport Rd., PO Box 550, Heber City, UT 84032; (801) 649-5858.**

HISTORIC BUILDINGS

Miners Hospital—

On Christmas Day in 1903 more than 300 members of the Western Federation of Miners Local No. 144 met to consider and adopt plans to construct a miners' hospital and to provide better medical care for the miners. The Park City Hospital is one of 25 miners' hospitals erected by local unions of the Western Federation of Miners in the West between 1897 and 1918. As well as accidents, work in the mines brought a variety of occupational diseases including lead poisoning, miners' consumption, tuberculosis, and silicosis. The hospital was a godsend for families whose fathers and husbands could be treated in Park City rather than in far away Salt Lake City. The hospital was closed in the 1950s, and the building became a dentist's office, bar, restaurant, and skiers' dormitory. When it was threatened with demolition, the citizens of Park City insisted the building be preserved, and, in 1979, it was relocated to the nearby park. The old hospital was renovated and reopened as the Park City Library in 1982. Eight hundred people formed a human chain 3,800 feet long to pass from hand to hand the 5,000 books from the old to the new library. Park City received a commendation by the National Trust for Historic Preservation for the innovative adaptive reuse of the old hospital. In 1993, a new Park City Library was opened and the building began its 4th life as a community center and historic museum.

HISTORIC MAIN STREET

Every visitor to Park City should make the walk up and down the town's historic Main St. With its shops, restaurants, museums, galleries, theater, post office, and false-front buildings, Main St. remains the heart of Park City. The City's Historic Preservation Commission has passed Utah's strictest zoning ordinances to maintain the character and historical accuracy of the 19th-century buildings. Main St. was one of the first historic districts in Utah listed in the National Register of Historic Places, At the Park City Museum you can purchase an attractive and inexpensive booklet, "Park City Main Street Historic Walking Tour," published by the Park City Historical Society. **Guided walking tours** of Main St. are offered through the Park City Museum during the summer. **528 Main St.; (801) 645-5135.**

MUSEUMS AND GALLERIES

Alf Engen Ski Museum—

A native of Norway who arrived in the US in 1929, Alf Engen won numerous national ski-jumping championships in the 1930s and 1940s as well as the national downhill and slalom events in 1941, 1942, and 1947. He established the ski school at Alta, which he directed for over 30 years, and is known as the father of the powder skiing technique. The museum was opened in 1993 and is located at Bear Hollow in temporary quarters adjacent to the Bear Hollow Day Lodge until a permanent facility can be constructed. The museum is free and open to the public year-round. The initial exhibit includes a pictorial history of Engen's career, skis, and equipment of the past, Engen's US Olympic team uniform, metals, trophies, awards, and other memorabilia from his illustrious career. To reach Bear Hollow, just follow the signs that lead off state Hwy. 224, south of the interstate and north of Snyderville and Wolf Mountain Ski Resort. The museum is operated by the **Alf Engen Ski Museum Foundation, 4534 South Fortuna Way, Salt Lake City, UT 84124; (801) 272-4334.**

Artist Galleries—

The Gallery Association of Park City includes more than a dozen members and publishes a "Gallery Guide of Park City," which lists the names of exhibiting artists and special exhibits throughout the city. Available at the Park City Museum and other locations in the city.

Kimball Art Center—

Art is an integral part of Park City. While you are there, don't miss the Kimball Art Center located at the bottom of Main St. You will find exhibited paintings and sculpture of major American artists in the main 3,000-square-foot gallery. The **Badami Gallery**, on the lower level, features local and regional artists. An extensive gift shop offers a fine selection of ceramics, paintings, prints and posters, stained glass, handmade jewelry, wood, glass, and quilts. A nonprofit enterprise, everything that is sold in the gallery, including the gift shop items, is juried and carried on consignment. The art center also sponsors a **Summer Art Institute** with more than a dozen instructors offering seminars and workshops. During the winter, a variety of weekly classes are offered. The center also sponsors the **Park City Arts Festival.** Open daily from 10 am–6 pm and Sun. noon–6 pm. **638 Park Ave.; (801) 649-8882.**

Park City Museum—

Park City Museum is housed in the 1885 City Hall, the basement of which was used as a jail (locals and children still refer to it as the "dungeon"). Complete with the original jail cells, leg irons, and an Industrial Workers of the World inscription that has been preserved in one of the cells, the basement jail depicts what incarceration was like in a 19th-century mining town. While the dungeon is perhaps the most popular part of the museum, it is by no means all there is to it. Excellent exhibits upstairs focus on mining, early skiing, fraternal and community organizations, and early community life in Park City. One popular exhibit depicts "China Bridge"— a bridge from the eastern side of Park City down to Main St. which crossed over Park City's Chinatown. A series of videotapes on the history of Park City can be viewed in the museum. The museum is open Mon.– Sat. 10 am–7 pm and Sun. noon–6 pm.

Admission is free. The **Park City Visitor Information Center** is also located in the museum and is an excellent place to pick up additional brochures, a calendar of events, and other information about Park City. **528 Main St.; (801) 649-6104.**

SHOPPING

The Factory Outlet in Park City has become a destination for shoppers from all over the state. Located just off Interstate 80 at Kimball Junction (exit 145), the famous manufacturer outlets encircle a large parking area, giving the impression that this is a modern-day version of the wagon encirclement or a community fort. There are nearly 50 stores, offering reduced prices on quality name brand items including Levis, Van Heusen, Bass, Nike, Corning Revere, Cape Isle Knitters, and many more. The stores are open Mon.–Sat. 10 am–9 pm and Sun. 10 am–7 pm. For information, call **(801) 645-7078.**

Park City's Historic Main St., described above, is also a shopper's delight. Galleries, boutiques, and specialty shops, many of which are located in historic buildings, make shopping on Park City's Main St. a special experience.

THEATER

Park City Performances is a local non-profit acting company that utilizes both amateur and professional talent to produce six shows a year. Under the direction of managing director Nikki Lowrey, the performances include dramas, comedies, musicals, and melodramas performed in the historic Egyptian Theater, which was built in 1926 as a vaudeville and silent movie theater. The theater still contains elements of the Egyptian Revival architecture including false-front columns, a lotus blossom ceiling design, and Egyptian hieroglyphic tile motifs. **328 Main St.; (801) 649-9371.**

TOURS
Park City Mine Tour—

The United Park City Mines is planning to offer an underground mine tour beginning in 1995 or 1996 which will take visitors 1,500 feet down a vertical shaft for a tour of the 4,000-foot mine tunnel. An orientation theater will explain the history of mining and offer the necessary safety instruction before visitors are permitted inside the mine. For information about the tour, check with the **Park City Visitor Center** or write or call **United Park City Mines, PO Box 1450, Park City, UT 84060; (801) 539-4227.**

———— WHERE TO STAY ————

ACCOMMODATIONS

Park City and nearby Deer Valley have a good mix of high-quality hotels, condominiums, bed and breakfasts, and historic lodges. Central reservation service is available through **Park City Travel and Lodging, 1492 Park Ave., PO Box 1854, Park City, UT 84060; (801) 645-8200 or 1-800-421-9741;** and **Deer Valley Lodging, PO Box 3000, Park City, UT 84060; (801) 649-4040 or 1-800-453-3833.** During the off season, rooms go for about half the high season rate. For something out of the ordinary, consider the following possibilities.

Blue Church Lodge—$$$ to $$$$

This building served as the Park City Mormon Church from 1900 to 1962. The original 1897 church was destroyed in the Great Fire of 1898. The church is listed in the National Register of Historic Places. The church interior was completely renovated in 1983 and converted into seven condominiums, each with one to four bedrooms. The lodge also has four two-bedroom condominiums across the street. Indoor and outdoor spas. Located on Park Ave., one street west of Main St. **424 Park Ave.; (801) 649-8009 or (800) 626-5467.**

Château Après Lodge—$$ to $$$

If you are looking for the best bargain in lodging, the Château Après Lodge, which has been around almost since the Park City ski area opened, is a good bet. There are 32 rooms with private baths, plus dormitory-style accommodations for 52 individuals. (The dorms are available only during ski season.) The lodge is only a few minutes' walk to the lifts at the Park City resort. **1299 Norfolk Ave.; (801) 649-9372.**

Goldener Hirsch Inn—$$$$

The famous Goldener Hirsch Hotel in Salzburg, Austria, is the model for this Deer Valley inn, which opened in 1990. There are 20 luxurious mini-suites with Austrian furniture and decor. A continental breakfast is provided, and the inn's restaurant is open for breakfast, lunch, and dinner (see Where to Eat) There are indoor and outdoor hot tubs, sauna, fireside lounge, and bar; **(801) 649-7770** or **1-800-252-3373.**

Imperial Hotel—$$$

Known originally as the Bogan Boarding House, the building that now houses the Imperial Hotel was constructed for miners in 1904, after the passage of the 1901 Boarding House Bill by the Utah state legislature no longer requiring single miners to stay in company-owned boarding houses. It has been known as the Imperial Hotel for many years. During an influenza epidemic of 1918 it served as an emergency hotel. It also carries a reputation as a former brothel. The building is listed in the National Register of Historic Places. It was renovated as a bed and breakfast in 1989, and each of the 13 rooms has a private bathroom with tub large enough for two. An old-fashioned breakfast is served each morning. Located at the top of Main St. **221 Main St.; (801) 649-1904** or **1-800-669-8824.**

Old Miners' Lodge—$$$

Even older than the Bogan Boarding House, the Old Miners' Lodge was constructed in 1893 to provide housing for miners working in the nearby silver mines. The

original structure was of balloon-style construction and built of inferior-quality lumber. Following several additions, the building was renovated in the 1970s,. It is Park City's oldest full-time bed and breakfast inn. Each of the 10 rooms is named for a Park City personality, and each has a private bath. Popular rooms include the Jedediah Grant, the largest room and with a magnificent view of Main St. and the Park City Town Ski Lift; the Black Jack Murphy, with a mine entrance to the room and named for the only man ever lynched in Park City; and the Mother Urban, named for Park City's infamous 200-pound-plus madame.

Innkeepers Hugh Daniels and Susan Wynne offer a hearty country breakfast and plenty of good conversation around the large living room fireplace. There is a hot tub in back and each room is provided with terrycloth robes and down feather comforters. The Town Ski Lift passes just to the north of the Lodge. Because of its location on the side of a hill and the 20 steps to climb, access for the physically disabled is difficult. **615 Woodside Ave.; (801) 645-8068** or **1-800-648-8068.**

Resort Center Lodge and Inn—$$$ to $$$$

The elegant rooms of the Resort Center Lodge and Inn are a skier's dream. Units range from hotel rooms to four bedroom units, and you can ski in and ski out of your room, as the lodge is located close to the ski lifts at the base of Park City's Treasure Mountain. Within the lodge complex are several excellent restaurants and easy access to bus transportation to Park City's historic Main St. Other amenities include an indoor/outdoor swimming pool and whirlpool spas, sauna, tanning bed, fitness center, and ski lockers; **(801) 649-0800** or **1-800-824-5331.**

Snowed Inn—$$$ to $$$$

This unforgettably named, elegant Victorian-style inn, furnished with European antiques, is located on 5 acres of land, 2 miles north of Park City and 1 mile from the Wolf Mountain ski area. There are 10 rooms, each with its own bathroom and oversized soaking tub. The rooms are spacious, with 10-foot ceilings and furnished with European antique furnishings. Other amenities include an outdoor Jacuzzi and transportation to the ski slopes. Lodging includes breakfast downstairs in the library. During the winter, you can enjoy a delicious gourmet-style dinner, served at 6:00 pm and 8:15 pm every evening, or take an evening sleigh ride into the aspens where you can dine on a specially prepared Dutch-oven dinner of warm bread, potatoes, vegetables, beef, poultry, and fresh fish. Reservations are required for both the Victorian dinner in the lodge or the sleigh ride dinner. **3770 North Hwy. 224; (801) 649-5713 or 1-800-545-SNOW.**

Star Hotel—$$

Part of the building that houses the Star Hotel was constructed before 1889, and the rest was completed in 1929, just as the Great Depression began. The Star Hotel is now a 10-room family-style lodge that is inexpensive by Park City standards. Lodging includes breakfast and dinner. **227 Main St.; (801) 649-8333.**

Stein Eriksen Lodge—$$$$

A legend in skiing, Stein Eriksen has also become a legend in lodging with his elegant 113-unit lodge at Deer Valley. The lodge brings the rustic tradition of Norway to Utah with a personal touch that combines the best of Old World tradition with the best of Utah hospitality. It is ranked, for good reason, as one of the top 10 ski lodges in the US. Skiers can ski from the lodge down the mountain and return whenever you are ready via the Viking Chairlift. The lodge has two restaurants: the Forest Room and the **Glitretind Restaurant** (see Where to Eat) year-round outdoor pool, hot tub, sauna, exercise room, and shuttle service to anywhere in the Park City/Deer Creek area; **(801) 649-3700 or 1-800-453-1302.**

Washington School Inn— $$$ to $$$$

This bed and breakfast, listed in the National Register of Historic Places, is located in the historic 1889 Washington School. Although it was one of Utah's first public schools, Washington School became outdated in the 1930s and was used for a time as a social hall. After remaining vacant for nearly 30 years, it was restored in the 1980s. Even though it contains all modern facilities—including a private bath in each suite—there is still the feel of an old-fashioned schoolhouse. It contains 15 individually decorated suites, each bearing the name of a former schoolteacher. A full complimentary breakfast is served in the formal dining room. The Washington School Inn is located one block from the Town Lift and on a free shuttle route to three ski areas. **543 Park Ave.; (801) 649-3800 or 1-800-824-1672.**

Full-service and condominium hotels—

Copperbottom Inn; (801) 649-5111 or **1-800-243-2932.**

Olympia Hotel; (801) 649-2900 or **1-800-234-9003.**

Park Station Condominium Hotel; (801) 649-7717 or **1-800-367-1056.**

Prospector Square Hotel; (801) 649-7100 or **1-800-453-3812.**

Radisson Resort; (801) 649-5000 or **1-800-333-3333.**

Shadow Ridge Resort Hotel; (801) 649-4300 or **1-800-451-3031.**

Silver King Hotel and Silver Cliff Village; (801) 649-5500 or **1-800-331-8652.**

Yarrow Resort Hotel; (801) 649-7000 or **1-800-327-2332.**

WHERE TO EAT

You can pick up a free *Park City Menu Guide* at the Visitor Information Center on Main St. It lists menus and prices for practically every eating establishment in the Park City/Deer Valley area. The guide is published in the winter and summer. Park City has the largest concentration of good restaurants. The following is a partial list of personal and local favorites.

Adolph's Restaurant—$$$$

Offering traditional continental cuisine including Châteaubriand, roast rack of lamb, saddle of venison, fillet of beef Oscar, and Swiss fondue, Adolph's has been a Park City institution since it was established in 1977. A fine place for a special occasion. Open 6 pm–10 pm daily. Located at the **Park City Golf Course; (801) 649-7177.**

Alex's—$$$$

Alex's is Park City's French restaurant. You will find a good selection of authentic French entrées here including frog's legs, duck breast, sautéed venison, and veal. Most diners opt for the prix fix dinner, which includes appetizers—such as onion soup gratinée, soup of the day, pâté maison, or fish terrine; a house salad; and an entrée, such as beef tenderloin, lamb shanks, broiled chicken breast, or fresh Utah trout. If you want to enjoy owner/chef Alex Dusser's fine food in a quieter more intimate spot away from busy Main St., he also operates the Snowed Inn restaurant near the Wolf Mountain Resort north of Park City. It has much the same menu as the Main St. location. Open nightly for dinner during the winter, Tues.–Sat. during the summer. Reservations are recommended. **442 Main St.; (801) 649-6644.**

Bangkok Thai on Main—$$ to $$$

Park City's first Thai restaurant, opened in 1993, is located in the basement of the Park Hotel near the bottom of Main St. and is a sister restaurant to one located in Salt Lake City (1400 Foothill Blvd.). The menu features a good selection of appetizers, soups, salads, entreés, and desserts. Each dish can be prepared vegetarian. If you like curry, try the gang keow wan, which is a homemade, mildly spicy green curry with coconut milk, bamboo shoots, and fresh Thai basil. The favorite wok dish is the pad him ma parn, a stir-fry with roasted chiles, roasted cashews, assorted vegetables, and a special oyster sauce. Open daily for dinner year-round 5:30 pm–10 pm, and also for lunch during the ski season. **605 Main St., (801) 649-8424.**

Baja Cantina—$$ to $$$

Locals hail the Baja Cantina as their favorite Mexican food restaurant in Park City, even though the prices run a bit higher than most places in the area. It is a small establishment located in the Park City Resort Center. Drinks are available in a tiny bar in the restaurant. Open daily from 11:00 am–11:00 pm; **(801) 649-BAJA.**

Cisero's Ristorante—$$

Cisero's caters to locals, who, in turn, recommend it to inquiring visitors. Open for breakfast, lunch, and dinner, it is also an excellent choice for Italian food. The lunch menu features salads, sandwiches, pasta, and vegetarian casserole (spinach noodles baked with marinara sauce, topped with mozzarella and ricotta cheeses, zucchini, mushrooms, spinach, green peppers, and onions). Another favorite is the cioppino, the seafood stew. The dinner menu offers seafood, veal, and a great variety of pasta dishes. Look for the magic card in the ceiling in the front dining room. Reservations are taken. Breakfast is served 8 am–11 am; lunch is served 11:30 am–3:00 pm; dinner from 5 pm–10 pm. **306 Main St.; (801) 649-6800.**

Claim Jumper—$ to $$$

This old restaurant is located in a three-story brick building constructed in 1913 as the New Park Hotel. This was Park City's finest hotel for many years, with the Who's

Who of Park City visitors staying here, where they could take three meals a day for 50 cents a meal in the patriotic red, white, and blue dining room. The dining room has been renovated, but there is still the feel of old Park City in this restaurant. The menu features steaks, ribs, prime rib, and seafood. If you are a steak lover, try the 12-ounce baseball steak. The prime rib and Alaskan king crab legs are also popular. Open daily 5:30 pm–10 pm. **573 Main St.; (801) 649-8051.**

The Eating Establishment—$ to $$

The Eating Establishment is another Park City institution, with a casual fun atmosphere, good sandwiches and burgers, and breakfast served all day. Check out the chalkboard specials if you want something a little more unusual. Or you may want to consider the pasta and seafood menu items. **317 Main St.; (801) 649-8284.**

Glitretind—$$$$

Located in the Stein Eriksen Lodge at Deer Valley and open for breakfast, lunch, and dinner, the Glitretind describes itself as "a European Mountain Bistro." Lunch entrées include sandwiches, homemade quiche, and soup. For dinner, favorites are grilled leg of lamb, Asian duck, baked salmon, and New Zealand red deer. Also at the Stein Eriksen Lodge is the Forest Room, an intimate 40-seat dinner restaurant, with entrées on the wild side—wood pigeon, partridge, grouse, pheasant, hare, and venison. The Forest Room is open daily for dinner only from 6 pm–10 pm. Reservations are recommended for both restaurants; **(801) 645-6454.**

Goldener Hirsch Inn—$$$$

In keeping with its Salzburg motif, you can find the kind of food served in an Austrian Gaststatte—sauerbraten, Wiener schnitzel, zwiebelrostbraten, Hungarian veal goulash, and Salzburg-style trout—in the Goldener Hirsch Inn at Deer Valley. Indulge yourself in fabulous old-world desserts like Salzburger nockerl, apfel strudel, Black Forest cake, sachertorte, and topfenknodel.

Open for breakfast, lunch, and dinner daily in winter; Wed.–Sat. in summer. Reservations are recommended for dinner. **7570 Royale St. East; (801) 649-7770.**

Grappa—$$$ to $$$$

Opened during summer 1994, Grappa has already earned the reputation as one of Park City's most popular upscale dinner restaurants. Owner/chef Bill White has taken the old Alpine Prospector Hotel, and with the work of local artisans and craftspeople, turned the old three-story hotel into something that resembles a Park City version of an Italian villa. The building is sent into the hill at the top of Main St., above the hustle and bustle further down the street, and is surrounded by beautifully tiered gardens with ample seating for outside dining in the summer. Hand-painted ceramic tiles are used on the floors, windows, and throughout the restaurant.

The menu offers a variety of entreés, each one an adventure in itself. All the food is cooked over a wood-fired grill or in an oven using cherry, apple, and oak wood. If you like pizza, the gourmet pizzas are the best you'll find anywhere. Other favorites include cedar-planked sea bass, which is seasoned with chopped shallots and garlic bread crumbs, then baked in the wood-fired oven on a cedar plank to give it a delicious, slightly smoked flavor. If you are a soup lover, try the sampling of all five soups, including such tasty choices as roasted chicken soup with Romano dumplings and grilled vegetable minestrone with mixed seafood. Open daily 5:30 pm–10 pm. Reservations recommended. **151 Main St.; (801) 645-0636.**

Ichiban Sushi—$$ to $$$

Peggy Ince, a gregarious Salt Lake City native, spent two years in Japan as a Mormon missionary and then worked two years at a Salt Lake City Japanese restaurant before returning to Japan to an apprenticeship as a sushi cook. It was strange for her Japanese colleagues not only to have an American apprentice, but a female as well since traditionally Japanese women are not permitted to become sushi cooks. It was long believed that women's hands were too weak and too warm to prepare sushi properly. Peggy completed the eight-month training in Japan and returned as the first American female sushi cook. She opened Ichiban Sushi in 1988. A favorite with Park City locals, Peggy rewards her regular customers with their own set of chopsticks which are displayed in racks on the north wall in front of the sushi bar. At last count there were more than 175 regulars who have been honored.

Sushi is a combination of food and art, and it's a delight to watch Peggy prepare it. Other Japanese dishes, including tempura, teriyaki, donburi, sukiyaki, and kushi yaki—Japanese shish kebabs, are available as well. Diners can sit at tables or booths, or in private traditional Japanese dining rooms. The restaurant is located in one of Park City's old two-story frame commercial buildings that was constructed just after the 1989 fire. Open daily except Sun. 11:30 am–10 pm. **424 Main St.; (801) 649-2865.**

Miletti's—$$ to $$$.

This is Park City's oldest and favorite place for Italian food. Opened in 1973, the restaurant offers pasta as well as a selection of main courses that includes Italian sausage, chicken, beef, lamb, veal, and seafood with grilled items cooked over Texas mesquite. My favorite is the fettuccini Miletti: fettuccini tossed in heavy cream and three cheeses to which is added fresh tomatoes, mushrooms, and olives and served with chicken or shrimp. Open nightly for dinner. Reservations are recommended. **412 Main St.; (801) 649-8211.**

Pizza—$

Any ski resort worth its snow has several good pizza parlors and Park City is no exception. On Main St., there are three pizza joints. All are open for lunch and dinner daily and offer takeout service.

Main Street Pizza and Noodle, 530 Main St.; (801) 645-8878.

Park City Pizza Company, 430 Main St,; (801) 649-1591.

Red Banjo Pizza Parlour (Park City's oldest, established in 1962), **322 Main St.; (801) 649-9901.**

In Deer Valley the Olive Barrel in Silver Lake Village is a favorite; **(801) 647-7777.**

Riverhorse Cafe—$$$ to $$$$

Housed in the upper floor of one of Park City's most historic buildings, the 1908 wood-framed Masonic Hall, you can dine in the historic hall, the more intimate atrium where live music is performed, or, in summer, on the porch overlooking Main St. The menu, which includes pasta, Utah lamb, chicken, steak, salmon, halibut, and the Riverhorse vegetable plate, varies during the year. Open daily 5:30 pm–10 pm. **540 Main St.; (801) 649-3536.**

Taste of Saigon—$$ to $$$

This refined, charming, and inexpensive Vietnamese restaurant is one of my favorites. Mariette Tran and her husband Richard are the proprietors. Mariette, a member of a well-to-do family and a high school French teacher in Saigon, left her home city 10 days before it fell to the Communists in 1975. She spent 18 years in France, spending part of the time helping her brother operate a Vietnamese restaurant in Paris before she moved to Utah in 1993. The French influence is evident in some of the dishes, such as the Saigon caramel and the caramel-flavored pork or tofu. Vegetarian dishes also available. Open daily except Sun. 11:30 am–2:30 pm for lunch and 5 pm–9:30 pm for dinner. **580 Main St., (801) 647-0688.**

Texas Red's—$$

This is not the place for a quiet intimate dinner, but it is a fun location for a family or group of friends. "Pit barbecue" and "chili parlor" say it all as far as the menu is concerned, with barbecue dinners of beef, pork, chicken, turkey, ribs, and sausage. You can also get chicken-fried steak, T-bone steak, or catfish. For homesick Texans, this is about as close to the stereotypical Texas as you can get in Utah. The good food and chance to rub elbows with a room full of people enjoying themselves makes this one of the liveliest spots on Main St. Open daily 11:30 am–10:00 pm. **440 Main St.; (801) 649-REDS.**

Wasatch Brew Pub—$ to $$

This pub is a delightful place to have lunch or dinner. Seating is available on the patio or indoors. If your interest is a cold mug of beer or ale, the bar is the place to try the varieties of beer made on the premises. The Wasatch Ale, a dark amber ale, was voted one of America's 10 tastiest brews at the Great American Beer Festival. The south windows offer a spectacular view of the surrounding hills, which are especially beautiful in the fall. The lunch menu includes the Milwaukee brat with sauerkraut—it's consistently good. The beer-batter shrimp is more expensive but worth trying. The dinner menu is available after 5 pm. Daily specials are chalked up on a large blackboard on the west wall. Open daily from 11 am. The restaurant is located at the top of the hill on Main St. **250 Main St.; (801) 645-9500.**

SERVICES

ABC Reservations Central—

Reservations for everything from restaurants to **hot-air balloons, sleighs, snowmobiles,** and **helicopter skiing.** Open daily from 10 am–6 pm. **514 Main St.; (801) 649-2223.**

Bus—

Park City Transit operates a free local bus system covering most areas within Park City and runs from about 8 am–1 am in the winter and 10:30 pm during the summer. Watch for the free trolley bus that runs up and down Main St. For information, call **(801) 645-5130.**

Day Care and Baby-Sitting—

Creative Beginnings—Open Mon.-Fri. 7 am–6 pm; Sat.-Sun. 8 am–5 pm. Evening care is available with reservations; **(801) 645-7315.**

K.I.D.S. Resort—Open 8:30 am–5 pm in the **Prospector Square Hotel; (801) 649-3867** or **1-800-453-3812.**

Miss Billie's KID'S KAMPUS—Open daily from 9 am–5 pm. Located near the **Wolf Mountain ski area; (801) 649-5437.**

Nightowls Babysitting Service—

In-room child care by CPR- and first-aid-trained and licensed sitters; 24-hour service available; **(801) 649-6463.**

Deer Valley Lodging—

PO Box 3000, Park City, UT 84060; (801) 649-4040 or **1-800-453-3833.**

Interconnect Adventure Tour—

Ski up to five Utah ski areas in the same day—Park City, Brighton, Solitude, Alta and Snowbird. This unique guided tour is for strong intermediate and advanced skiers. Call **(801) 534-1907** for reservations.

Park City Chamber of Commerce/ Convention and Visitors Bureau—

Open Mon.-Fri. 8 am–5 pm. **1910 Prospector Ave., PO.Box 1630, Park City, UT 84060;(801) 649-6100** or **1-800-453-1360.**

Park City Transportation Services—

Twenty-four-hour dispatch, door-to-door airport transportation, and other transportation services. **1555 Lower Iron Horse Loop Rd.; (801) 649-8568** or **1-800-637-3803.**

Park City Travel and Lodging—
1492 Park Ave., PO Box 1854, Park City, UT 84060; (801) 645-8200 or 1-800-421-9741.

Park City Visitor Information Center—
Open Mon.–Sat. 10 am–7 pm; and Sun. noon–6 pm. **528 Main St.; (801) 649-6104.**

The rugged mountains provide a majestic backdrop to a lodge at Snowbird Ski Area. Photo by Allan Kent Powell.

Heber Valley

There more western valleys than I care to count that claim to be the "Switzerland of America." But if the votes of the Swiss immigrants who settled in Heber Valley in the 1860s count for anything, Heber Valley would win hands down. Swiss families like Probst, Huber, Kohler, Zenger, and Abegglen found the towering Wasatch Mountains to the west, the rolling Uinta Mountains to the east, and the lush meadows of the valleys to be both a reminder of their homeland and a good place for their dairy and cattle herds. The Provo River flows through the valley, and the deep snows in the mountains and springs in the valley have provided abundant water for residents. Heber Valley is a popular recreation area with residents along the Wasatch Front. Wasatch Mountain State Park and the Homestead Resort in Midway are especially busy in the summer, but winter activities—primarily cross-country skiing—are drawing more and more winter visitors. The Jordanelle Reservoir, located in the north end of the valley on the Provo River and completed in 1995, will draw thousands of fishermen and boaters, as has the Deer Valley Reservoir farther downstream, in the south end of the valley, since it was completed in 1940.

HISTORY

Heber Valley was originally called Provo Valley when it was settled in 1858; however, to avoid confusion with the city of Provo on the western side of the mountains and to honor Mormon leader, Heber C. Kimball, who was instrumental in converting many of the original English settlers of the valley to the Mormon faith, the name of the town and valley was changed in 1861 to Heber City and Heber Valley. Settlement of the valley was delayed until a 28-mile road could be constructed through the mountains from Utah Valley. The first English and American-born Mormons who settled the valley during the 1860s and 1870s were followed by Mormon converts from Switzerland. These early Swiss settlers wrote back to family and friends of the virtues of Mormonism and the beauty of Heber Valley and, as the original converts or their sons returned to Switzerland as missionaries, a small but steady stream of Swiss immigrants made their way to Midway in Heber Valley. The Swiss heritage has been preserved in a number of ways, including the popular Swiss Days held in early September. Heber City was incorporated as a town in 1889, the same year that the impressive red sandstone tabernacle was completed. A decade later, in 1899, the Rio Grande Western Railroad completed a branch line to Heber City, and the town became a shipping center for agricultural products, especially sheep. A remnant of the railroad has been preserved as Utah's only operating historic railroad: the Heber Valley Historic Railroad. Today Heber Valley has a population of nearly 10,000, contained mostly in Heber City and Midway.

GETTING THERE

The Heber Valley is 50 miles southeast of Salt Lake City, 30 miles northeast of Provo, and 20 miles south of Park City. From Salt Lake City, take Interstate 80 to its junction with state Hwy. 40, about 35 miles east of Salt Lake City, then follow US Hwy. 40 south to Heber City. From Provo, US Hwy. 189 winds through Provo Canyon, with Mt. Timpanogos rising north of the highway.

—————— MAJOR ATTRACTIONS ——————

Wasatch Mountain State Park—
In 1961, the State of Utah acquired the 22,000 acres that make up Wasatch Mountain State Park. Located on the eastern slope of the Wasatch Mountains, 35 miles southeast of Salt Lake City, the park offers year-round recreation. Golfing, picnicking, camping, fishing, horseback riding, and sightseeing are the principal summer activities, while snowmobiling and cross-country skiing are popular during the winter.

—————— FESTIVALS AND EVENTS ——————

Oakley Independence Day Celebration and Rodeo
beginning of July
During the height of the Great Depression in 1935, the Oakley Independence Day celebration and rodeo began, and it is now one of the most popular local rodeos around. Other festivities include a parade, dance, patriotic program, and fireworks. The Utah Professional Rodeo Association–sanctioned event is held on three nights and culminates on the night of July 4th; **(801) 783-5526 or 783-5356.**

Mountain Valley Stampede
2nd weekend of August
This popular local rodeo is also sanctioned by the Utah Professional Rodeo Association and is held in Heber City over three days the 2nd weekend of Aug.; **(801) 654-2198.**

Swiss Days—
1st Friday and Saturday in September
The Midway Swiss Days is known throughout Utah as one of the oldest ethnic festivals in the state. Held the first Fri. and Sat. in Sept., the festival draws more than 200 craftspeople and artists from all over. The festival includes a parade, musical programs, carnival games for children, a 10-kilometer run, and plenty of food. Swiss Days is truly a community event, with Midway residents gathering in midsummer to chop cabbage for the more than 300 gallons of sauerkraut that are served during the two days. For more information, call **(801) 654-3666.**

OUTDOOR ACTIVITIES

FISHING

Deer Creek Reservoir—

Few Utah communities have an excellent fishing spot in their backyard, but residents of Heber Valley do. Deer Creek Reservoir, constructed between 1938 and 1940 as part of a federal works project, is located on the Provo River, 8 miles southwest of Heber City, on Hwy. 189. The reservoir is about 7 miles long and is a popular spot for boating, wind surfing, and year-round fishing.

Jordanelle Reservoir—

Completed in 1992, the Jordanelle Dam is located on the Provo River, about 5 miles north of Heber City. The reservoir should be close to capacity in 1995 and promises to be a popular fishing spot with rainbow, brown, and cutthroat trout attracting fishermen from the Heber, Utah, and Salt Lake valleys.

Provo River—

The Provo River, above the Jordanelle Reservoir and below Deer Creek Reservoir, is one of the most popular fly fishing streams in Utah. There's rainbow, cutthroat and brown trout, and Rocky Mountain whitefish.

Soldier Creek Reservoir—

This reservoir, east of Strawberry Reservoir, was constructed separately in 1973. The existing Strawberry Dam and Indian Creek Dike were partially removed in 1985, allowing for the two reservoirs to be connected along the river channel now known as "the Narrows." Soldier Creek Reservoir retains its own marina, and many fishermen make it their destination.

Strawberry Reservoir—

The original Strawberry Reservoir was constructed in the 1880s by farmers in Heber Valley to secure water from the Upper Strawberry Valley that otherwise would flow in the opposite direction. The reservoir has been enlarged over the years but remains a key element of the Central Utah Project, a massive undertaking by the federal, state, and local governments to reclaim and manage the scarce water resources in the state. The reservoir is one of Utah's most popular fishing spots with Bear River cutthroat trout, kokanee salmon, and sterile rainbow trout. The Strawberry Bay Marina offers a store, cafe, boat rentals, and fishing supplies. The reservoir is located off Hwy. 40, 30 miles southeast of Heber City.

GOLF

Homestead Golf Course—

Just a little more than a three-wood shot back down the road from the Wasatch Mountain Golf Course, the Homestead Golf Course, opened in 1990, has cashed in on the popularity of its older neighbor and its association with the historic Homestead Resort. The front 9 are played uphill, west of the resort, while the back 9 open out onto the flatter terrain of the course—obviously a good decision for those who choose to walk. Because this is a private course, the fees are slightly higher than Wasatch Mountain State Park. For reservations, up to seven days in advance, call **(801) 654-1102.**

Wasatch Mountain Golf Course—

If you were to ask well-traveled Utah golfers to list their half-dozen favorite golf courses, it is a safe bet that Wasatch Mountain Golf Course would be on nearly everyone's list. The 27-hole course is located on the east slope of the Wasatch Mountains, just down off the ridge from the Brighton Ski Resort. The 27 holes are divided into three 9-hole courses, the Lake and Canyon 9s, which were built in 1967, and the Mountain 9, which was completed in 1973. The course designers have made good use of lakes, the mountain, and native trees to provide a course that is a real pleasure to play. In addition, while the course is not flat and easy, the spacious greens and large tee areas do offer some advantages to the regular hacker. As the only golf course included in the state park system, Utah golfers hold that Wasatch Mountain belongs to the entire state, not just the Heber Valley residents. And the employees here treat visitors as guests, foregoing the cliquishness that is sometimes characteristic of local courses. The Wasatch Mountain course is located at an elevation of 5,775 feet, and the summer mountain air is much more pleasant than the Salt Lake and Utah Valley courses, not to mention southern Utah's courses. My favorite time, however, is early fall, just as the leaves are turning. It is simply a golfer's heaven. The course is near Midway. Take Hwy. 40 south from Interstate 15 and after you pass Jordanelle Reservoir and come down the mountain,

watch for the sign to Wasatch Mountain State Park and take the road off Hwy. 40. From Heber City drive west from the center of town to Midway and follow the road as it winds through Midway to the Park, located northwest of Midway. For reservations, call **(801) 654-0532.**

HOT SPRINGS

See **Homestead Resort and Mountain Spa Resort** in the Accommodations section.

WINDSURFING

Deer Creek Reservoir—

Regular up-canyon afternoon winds makes this one of Utah's favorite windsurfing locations. For more information, see the Fishing section in Outdoor Activities.

SEEING AND DOING

FISH HATCHERIES

Midway Fish Hatchery—

Operated by the Utah Division of Wildlife Resources, visitors are welcome at this trout fish hatchery, located a mile south of Midway just off Utah Hwy. 113. Visitor hours are 8 am–4:30 pm.

HISTORIC SITES

Midway Historic Homes—

One of the most photographed historic homes in Utah is the John Watkins' home on the northeast corner of Center and Main streets in Midway. The Gothic Revival-style house has three gables on the front and plenty of wood "gingerbread" trim. The elaborate white-painted trim with white sandstone quoins offers a striking contrast with the dark red brick walls. John Watkins, an architect and builder from England, built the house in 1868. The house is listed in the National Register of Historic Places, and has appeared in several national publications including *Life, Ford Times*, and a color photograph of the house was used on the cover of a special architecture issue of the *Utah Historical Quarterly*.

Watkins built several other houses in Midway, which, though not as elaborate as his own home, are easily identifiable. Although none of the homes are open on a regular basis, owners are used to visitors stopping in front to take pictures.

Wasatch Stake Tabernacle—

One of Utah's most beautiful churches, the Wasatch Stake Tabernacle was constructed in 1889 from red sandstone. The tabernacle served as the center of Mormon religious activity in the Heber Valley for many years, until local church authorities decided it was time to build a more up-to-date building. Along with the decision to build a new building, it was decided to demolish the old tabernacle. This led to one of Utah's first historic preservation battles in the early 1960s. Under the leadership of Ruth Witt, wife of Heber City's sheriff, a group of local women and other heritage-conscious individuals successfully challenged the local church leader and won preservation of the building, which was acquired by the local historical society. The building was used as a summer theater, and for other activities until the late 1980s, when the interior of the building was renovated and converted into Heber City's town hall. While visiting the tabernacle, take a look at the building in back. The Amusement Hall was built around the turn of the century and originally had a steel spring dance floor, which old-timers claim was a joy to dance on. The Amusement Hall has been converted into a senior citizen center. The tabernacle is one of the few remaining 19th-century Mormon tabernacles and stands as a tribute to three generations of Heber Valley residents: the one that built it, the one that preserved it from demolition, and the one with the vision to adapt a state treasure to modern needs. The tabernacle is located on Main St. on the southwest corner of 100 North.

RAILROADS
Heber Valley Historic Railroad—

This railroad is the only operating historic railroad in the state and is a popular attraction in Heber Valley. It began operation as Utah Eastern Railway in 1899 and ran from the Rio Grande Western's main line in Provo up Provo Canyon to Heber City. Because of the steep 2 percent grade up the canyon, the trains moved slowly, earning the nickname "The Heber Creeper" from early passengers. The railroad was reestablished in 1993, under the auspices of the Heber Valley Historic Railroad Authority, a nonprofit, state-created organization. The train features restored vintage coaches and a working steam locomotive, originally built in 1904. You can travel from the station in Heber City around the west side of Deer Creek Reservoir and down Provo Canyon to Vivian Park, 32 miles round trip. The ride takes 3.5 hours, including a half-hour stop at Vivian Park. The railroad runs from Mother's Day–end of Oct. and usually makes two trips a day: 10:30 am and 2 pm. For times, prices, special events, and more information, write or call: **Heber Valley Historic Railroad Authority, 450 South 600 West, PO Box 641, Heber City, UT 84032; (801) 654-5601 or 1-800-982-3257.**

SCENIC DRIVES
Cascade Springs Backway—

This 25-mile-long, well-graded dirt road begins south of Midway, where it leaves state Hwy. 113 and heads west, climbing the mountain as it makes its way to Cascade Springs—actually a series of springs that have formed limestone terraces over which seven million gallons of mountain water cascades each day. Barrier-free walkways provide easy access to the falls; interpretive information along the way describes how springs are formed and rivers are born high in the mountains. One visitor has described the springs as like a Japanese garden with a variety of trees, shrubs, flowers, ferns, vines, pools, bubbling springs, and miniature waterfalls. Rainbow trout can be seen in the pools from the boardwalks and bridges. Songbirds, frogs, toads, squirrels, and chipmunks are another highlight of a visit here.

Mirror Lake Scenic Byway—

With an elevation of 10,687 feet at Bald Mountain Pass near Mirror Lake, Utah Hwy. 150 is the highest of all the state's scenic byways. The highway begins in Kamas, at the western edge of the Uinta Mountains, and follows up the Provo River to its headwaters in the high Uintas. About 24 miles from Kamas are the Upper Provo River Falls. Walkways near the road provide easy access to view the terraced cascades. The distance from Kamas to the Utah-Wyoming border is 65 miles. Travelers can retrace their route or continue on to Evanston, Wyoming, and Interstate 80, which is 23 miles north of the state line. As one of the most popular recreation routes in Utah, the highway provides access to numerous lakes, campgrounds, and picnic areas.

Strawberry/Diamond Fork Rd.—

From Strawberry Reservoir, you can cross the ridge of the mountains to the west and follow the Diamond Fork Rd. through the mountains to its junction with US Hwy.

6/50 in Spanish Fork Canyon. This is the route that the Dominguez and Escalante followed in 1776 enroute to Utah Lake. From Hwy. 6/50, you can retrace your route back to Strawberry Reservoir, or return to Heber City via Interstate 15 and US Hwy. 189 through Provo Canyon.

WILDLIFE

Strawberry Valley—

While Strawberry Reservoir is known mostly for its fishing, the reservoir and valley in which it is located provide an excellent opportunity to view wildlife.

Western tributaries of the reservoir, such as Crooked Creek and Streeper Creek, offer a chance to view spawning cutthroat trout in May and June. Sandhill cranes are also present during the late spring. In the spring and fall, herons and egrets can be seen around the bay. White pelicans and double-crested cormorants also visit the reservoir. Deer and elk are abundant in the entire valley. The reservoir is located 23 miles east of Heber City, off US Hwy. 40. Check in at the visitor center for more information and directions to prime viewing opportunities.

WHERE TO STAY

ACCOMMODATIONS
HEBER CITY
Cottage Bed and Breakfast—
$$ to $$$

This small bed and breakfast has two rooms, one that will accommodate four with a queen and two twin beds and a smaller room with a double bed. Continental breakfast included that features homemade muffins and fresh fruit in season, served in the dining room. **830 South Main; (801) 654-2236.**

Family Choice High Country Inn—$$

Indoor spa, nonsmoking rooms available; 38 rooms. **1000 South Main; (801) 654-0201 or 1-800-345-9198.**

Hylander Motel—$$

Pool; 22 rooms. **425 South Main; (801) 654-2150.**

Viking Motor Inn—$$

Year-round pool, Jacuzzi spa and sauna, nonsmoking rooms available; 34 rooms. **989 South Main; (801) 654-2202 or 1-800-343-2675.**

MIDWAY
Homestead Resort—$$$

Perhaps Utah's finest historic resort, the Homestead was originally known as "Schneitter's Hot Pots," when it was established in 1886. Simon Schneitter immigrated from Switzerland and brought with him a European flair for what a good resort should be. His American-born wife Fanny knew that good food was basic to a fine resort, and her heaping plates of fried chicken and other American dishes became known far and wide. In 1952 the name of the resort was changed to Homestead. Ninety-two rooms, indoor and outdoor heated pools, sauna, mineral bath, hot tub, tennis, horseback riding, buggy rides, bicycles, golf and cross country skiing, snowmobiling, and horse-drawn sleigh rides in the winter. There are two restaurants and a private club. **700 North Homestead Dr.; (801) 654-1102 or 1-800-327-7220.**

Inn on the Creek—$$$ to $$$$

This charming inn, designed by local architect George Olsen, is located on a rise above the Homestead Golf course and a small meandering stream. The structure will make you wonder if you have not just driven up to a rural Swiss château. Joel and Becky Van Leeuwen's attention to detail, cleanliness, and enthusiasm make them ideal hosts. The Inn has eight oversized suites, each with its own fireplace, Jacuzzi, and patio deck with spectacular views of the Heber Valley and nearby Wasatch Mountains. There is also an outdoor swimming pool and hot tub. A full breakfast, with such items as ham and cheese croissants, quiche, and French toast, is served in the beautiful dining room. In addition to the main bed and breakfast, there a couple of one- to three-bedroom chalets with kitchen facilities available. **375 Rainbow Ln.; (801) 654-0892.**

Mountain Spa Resort—$$ to $$$

Although much smaller than the Homestead, (see above) the Mountain Spa Resort also traces its history back to the 1880s, when, in 1888, Andrew Luke and his eldest son John purchased the land and built a popular resort known as Luke's Hot Pots. The primary attraction was the Old Long Pot, a limestone rock formed by the mineral springs in the shape of a natural swimming pool. The resort also is said to have a pot of gold buried on its premises. According to legend, in 1851 a gang of outlaws stopped for a swim in the Old Long Pot. When Indians threatened them, they buried their stolen gold in an iron kettle and fled. When one of the men returned many years later, he was unable to locate the gold. Today the resort features indoor and outdoor swimming pools, private mineral baths, horseback riding, an old-time soda fountain, a cafe and dining room. The water in the swimming pool is high in calcium and zinc, contains no sulfur, chemicals, or chlorine. Accommodations are available in the 1890 house built of native limestone by Andrew Luke and in three small cabins located just south of the old house. The resort also has 25 RV sites, some with full hookups. Lynda Payne manages the property for her mother Althea who, with her husband Eugene Payne, purchased the resort in 1957. The resort still has a 1950s or earlier feel to it. The Paynes vowed never to go into debt to maintain or "fancy up" the place. Lynda admits there is much maintenance that needs to be done and that people either love or hate the place. But if you are looking for some authentic nostaligia and something quite different from what you find in most parts of Heber Valley and Park City, give the Mountain Spa a try. Open daily from Memorial Day–Mid-Sept. and on a restricted schedule from mid-Mar.–mid-Oct. Call in advance for times. **800 North 200 East; (801) 654-0721 or 654-0807.**

CAMPING
PRIVATE
Country Estates Mobile Home Park—

Thirty-five sites will full hookups including satellite TV. Laundry facilities, restrooms, showers. Weekly and monthly rates available. Open year-round. **2997 South Hwy. 40, Heber City, (801) 654-0359.**

High Country RV Park—

Thirty-six full hookups, laundry and showers, heated pool, indoor spa, and restaurant, adjacent. Open year-round. **1000 South Main, Heber City; (801) 654-0201 or 1-800-345-9198.**

Jordan Ranch RV Park—

Eighty sites, 34 with full hookups; tent sites also available. Convenience store, laundry, restrooms, and showers. Weekly and monthly rates can be arranged. Open year-round. **7000 North, Hwy. 40,** located 6 miles north of Heber City; **(801) 654-4049.**

PUBLIC
Deer Creek State Park—

The Deer Creek Campground has 31 RV trailer sites and 10 tent sites, flush toilets, showers, drinking water, and disabled access. Deer Creek is located 7 miles southwest of Heber City, on Hwy. 189. Open Apr.–Nov. Fee charged.

Lodgepole Campground—

Located in Daniel's Canyon, 16 miles southeast of Heber City, off US Hwy. 40, the Lodgepole Campground offers 51 RV trailer sites and tent sites. The campground is equipped with drinking water and toilets and has handicap facilities. Open May–Oct.

Soldier Creek—

Both the Strawberry and Soldier Creek reservoirs are fed by the Strawberry River. A narrow channel connects the two reservoirs. The Soldier Creek Campground is also large, with 108 RV sites and 57 tent sites. It is located 34 miles southeast of Heber City. Open late May–late Oct. Fee charged.

Strawberry Reservoir—

One of Utah's most popular fishing spots, Strawberry Reservoir also boasts one of its largest public campgrounds, with 200 RV trailer and tent sites. If you come to fish, you won't mind the size and open setting, but if you are looking for a getaway campground, this is probably not the best choice. Located off Hwy. 40, 26 miles southeast of Heber City. Open late May–late Oct. Fee charged.

Wasatch Mountain State Park—

Located just north of Midway, there are 130 RV sites and tent sites in this state park. Restrooms and showers are available, a children's fishing area, and easy access to some of the finest golfing in Utah. Open year-round. Fees are charged; **(801) 654-1791** or **1-800-328-2267.**

Additional Public Campgrounds—

Hwy. 150 winds from Kamas, 15 miles northeast of Heber City, through the western flank of the Uinta Mountains to the Utah-Wyoming border and on to Evanston. The distance from Kamas to the state line is 56 miles, and, beginning with the **Yellow Pine Campground,** 6.8 miles east of Kamas, and stretching for 50 miles to the **Stateline Reservoir Campground,** there are 33 campgrounds with nearly 700 trailer sites and tent sites located in the Wasatch National Forest. For a list of these campgrounds see the current issue of *Utah Travel Guide,* published annually by the Utah Travel Council and available at most tourist information centers.

——————— # WHERE TO EAT ———————

CHARLESTON
Lakeside Cottage—$ to $$

This picturesque, affordable, and very clean restaurant is located along the north shore of Deer Creek Reservoir, on Utah Hwy. 113, a half-mile west of its junction with US Hwy. 189 and about 3 miles south of Midway on Hwy. 131. Known for years as Scrappy's, Lauren and Walter Williams are now the proprietors. My family's favaorite is the Yankee pot roast that is slow-cooked for eight hours and served with real mashed potatoes and gravy. Other favorites include grandma's meat pie, salmon, halibut, and old-fashioned malts and shakes made from hard ice cream. For lunch there's a good selection of sandwiches and hamburgers. Save room for a slice of one of Lauren's excellent pies. Senior citizen discount and childrens menu available. Select a window seat for a magnificent view of Mt. Timpanogos to the southwest. Open Wed.–Sat. 11 am–8:30 pm and 10 am–3 pm for Sun. brunch. 3761 South Charleston Rd.; **(801) 654-3456.**

HEBER CITY
Blazing Saddles—$ to $$

Mexican and American food. Open for lunch and dinner, 11 am–10 pm, Mon.–Sat.; Sun. hours noon–9 pm. **605 West 100 South; (801) 654-3300**

Granny's Drive Inn—$

Voted best milk shakes in Utah. Open Mon.–Sat. 11 am–10 pm; **511 South Main, (801) 654-3097.**

MIDWAY
Das Burgermeister Haus—$ to $$

Great homemade soup, sandwiches, knockwurst, pies, and desserts. Open for lunch and dinner, Mon.–Sat. 11:30 am–9 pm. **79 East Main; (801) 654-5370.**

Grindlehaus—$ to $$

Operated by Sandy and Paul Grindle, who have turned one of Midway's turn-of-the-century houses into an international restaurant. The Grindlehaus offers breakfast, lunch, and dinner. In addition to the good food, there is an unsurpassed view of the mountains from the patio. The international menu features omelettes and traditional American plates for breakfast, hamburgers and deli sandwiches for lunch, plus bratwurst or German weiners with sauerkraut. Mexican dishes include enchiladas and chimichangas. Sandy specializes in pastas with favorites being cajun, seafood, and vegetarian pastas. Paul discovered Heber Valley on a fishing trip and, when he called his wife Sandy in southern California to persuade her to come and see the mountain paradise for herself, he said he did not know if he would even return to LA to pack! Open 8 am–9 pm, Tues.–Sun. Closed Mon. **42 West Main, Midway; (801) 654-0805.**

Homestead Resort—$$ to $$$$

You have two options at the Homestead Resort, and both are excellent. The **Grill Room** is a more casual place, open daily during the summer from 7 am–9 pm. It features contemporary American country cuisine, with barbecue ribs, barbecue chicken, and roast beef typical lunch and dinner entrées.

Simons is open for dining only daily from 5:30–9:15 pm. Each evening two fixed-price five-course dinners are offered such as rack of lamb, filet mignon, and salmon. Simons also has a Sun. brunch from 10 am–2:30 pm. 700 **North Homestead Dr.; (801) 654-1102** or **1-800-327-7220.**

SERVICES

Heber Valley Information Center—

Located in the Swiss chalet–style Heritage Building on Hwy. 40 at the north end of Heber City, the center offers free maps, brochures, and information about accommodations, restaurants, and local events. Open 8:30 am–5 pm Mon.–Sat., May–Oct., and Mon.–Fri. the rest of the year. **475 North Main; (801) 654-3666.**

Wendover

For Utahns, Wendover and gambling are synonymous. Each week, thousands make the 120-mile drive from Salt Lake City east to Wendover to try their luck at the five casinos located just across the border in Nevada. Technically, there are two towns that share a common boundary along the Utah-Nevada state line and the same Mountain Standard Time zone. In reality, however, there is only one Wendover, and the Wendover Visitor and Convention Bureau has solved the problem of promoting a single town in two states by calling the place "Wendover, USA." For those travelers familiar with Las Vegas and Reno, Wendover is small potatoes, but when you can drive to Wendover in less than two hours it is a much greater attraction than the other Nevada gambling capitals that are 8 to 10 hours away.

Gambling was a latecomer as far as Wendover's fame is concerned. The Bonneville Salt Flats, just outside Wendover, developed international fame in the 1930s as the site where world land speed records were set. In the 1940s, archaeologists discovered 10,000-year-old paleo-Indian artifacts in Danger Cave. Surrounded by desert on all four sides, Wendover is a neon oasis that you can appreciate only after traveling to it from any direction in the heat of summer or the cold of winter. Wendover lies next to the Toana Mountain Range which rises 5,000 feet above the desert. Northwest of Wendover, 10,000-foot Pilot Peak was a landmark for early travelers across the desert and the original source of water for Wendover. To the south, the 12,000-foot Deep Creek Mountains are among the highest in the state. The more than 19,000 airmen stationed at Wendover during World War II may have had second thoughts about the government's wisdom in sending them to such an isolated spot. I'm sure they appreciated what Bob Hope said when he visited them—that the place should be called "Leftover."

HISTORY

Before human beings arrived, and even before there was a Great Salt Lake Desert, a vast area of western Utah and portions of the surrounding states (approximately 9,300 square miles) was covered by the waters of Lake Bonneville. Approximately 12,000 years ago, the lake receded, leaving a hard flat surface of crystalline salt, where no vegetation grows. During the winter and spring, the flats resemble a huge lake because the rain and snow falling on the area does not evaporate quickly and the hard salt layer means that percolation beneath the surface is very slow. The area was not so desolate more than 10,000 years ago when prehistoric humans set foot on the former lake bed. If the State Line Silver Smith Complex accommodates most visitors to Wendover today, for the first 10,000 years of human presence in and around Wendover it was Danger Cave, located a mile east of town. The cave has yielded more than 2,000 artifacts, including basketry, clothing, netting, cordage, tools made from bone, horn, and stone, arrows, knives, traps, and clay effigies. Danger Cave was occupied at various times by prehistoric peoples and native Americans until after US Army Captain John C. Fremont traversed the area in 1845, stopping at the springs at Pilot Peak, about 23 miles north of Wendover. Travelers on the Hastings Cutoff in 1846 also stopped at the Pilot Peak springs, including the ill-fated Donner Party, which left several wagons and many of its goods on the salt desert, about 35 miles northeast of Wendover. Established in 1907 as a watering stop on the just-completed Western Pacific Railroad, Wendover, in comparison with most Utah towns, is relatively new. The origin of the name has been debated for years. Some folks attribute the name's origin to the fact that the town is surrounded by desert on all sides and to get there from anywhere required "wending" over the desert. More likely, though, is that it was named for Charles Wendover, a surveyor employed by the Western Pacific Railroad.

Wendover gained a measure of lasting fame in 1914 when the transcontinental telephone line was joined at the Utah-Nevada state line in Wendover. At the time the line was completed, a cross-country call took 23 minutes to place and a three-minute station-to-station call cost $20.70—a rare case of things having gotten cheaper over the years.

About that time, automobile racers were touting the virtues of the level, hard-packed salt flats east of Wendover. In the 1930s, numerous speed records were set on the Bonneville Salt Flats, with Pontiac's Bonneville automobile model taking its name from Utah's salt desert raceway. The salt flats have also been the basis for a potash industry, which began in 1917 and today produces more than 100,000 tons of fertilizer annually.

The two most important dates in Wendover's economic history were 1926, when the Victory Hwy. was completed to Wendover from Salt Lake City, and 1931, when Nevada passed its wide-open gambling law. William and Anna Smith applied for one of the first casino licenses and, at the height of the Great Depression, took their own gamble in opening the State Line Casino. Bill Smith, who, according to tradition, was kicked off the train in Wendover in the 1920s, stayed in the desert town and purchased a gas station, to which he added the casino when the gambling law was passed. The State Line served Utahns and California-bound travelers on US Hwy. 40 until the 1980s, when three other casinos were established in Wendover.

Today Wendover has a population of approximately 3,000, but during the World War II years as many as 19,000 airmen were stationed at Wendover Air Base. High-altitude bombers trained over the salt flats, dropping bombs on cities made of salt and full-size salt battleships. At one of the gunnery ranges, the Tokyo Trolley, which consisted three machine guns located on a moving railroad car, was used by trainees to shoot at moving targets in an attempt to simulate aerial combat. The isolated location was the site selected by Col. Paul W. Tibbetts for training the 509th Composite Group in preparation for dropping the atomic bombs on Japan. Many of the original World War II–era buildings remain on what was Wendover Air Base. A new monument to the 509th Composite Group at the Wendover Welcome Center commemorates the mission's objective, with an August 1945 statement by President Harry Truman: "The atomic bomb is too dangerous to be loose in a lawless world...we pray that [God] may guide us to use it in His ways and for His purposes."

GETTING THERE

Wendover is located along Interstate 80, 120 miles west of Salt Lake City. Heading east along Interstate 80, Wendover is 400 miles east of Reno, Nevada. It's about a two-hour drive along the interstate from Salt Lake City. While most Wendover visitors do drive, there are several buses that run daily between Salt Lake City, Ogden, and Wendover. There is a charge for riding the bus, but, on weekdays, by the time you get cash back, a food discount, free drinks, Keno tickets, and lucky bets from the casino, they actually pay you to ride the bus. A typical weekday schedule has the bus leaving downtown Salt Lake City about 9 am and returning from Wendover at 5 pm. Weekends **buses** depart at 6:30 pm on Fri. and return at 2:30 am that night, or leave Sat. evening at 5 pm and return at 1 am. Call the following bus lines for schedules and offers: **Casino Caravans (801) 649-3423; Donna's Tours (801) 566-1434;** or **Nevada Tours (801) 363-9300.** This free transportation has proven so successful with buses that it has also been applied to air transportation. The **State Line and Silver Smith** casinos provide free transportation to charter flights from 90 or so cities for one- or two-night trips. Once the charter flight has been organized, all you have to do is reserve a room and show up with the required amount of cash that you plan to gamble with in Wendover. For more information about **charter flights,** call **1-800-848-7300.**

—————— MAJOR ATTRACTIONS ——————

Gambling

If it is not obvious by now, let me state it clearly: 99 percent of the people who drive to Wendover come for the gambling casinos, which are the closest casinos to Utah's Wasatch Front. While not all of the more than 1 million people who live along the Wasatch Front gamble, enough do to make Wendover a popular weekend destination. There are five casinos, with more planned in the future. All five offer the same kinds of games including poker, craps, blackjack, roulette, sports book, and keno, as well as slot and other gaming machines. All have restaurants, accommodations, and live entertainment. It is easy to visit all five casinos, either by car or by shuttle bus. Walking is also a possibility, but one that few people seem to take. The following listings begin with those closest to the Utah border and move west along Wendover Blvd.

Nevada Crossing Casino—

The indoor swimming pool and spa are special attractions at the 137-room Nevada Crossing. The restaurant is open 24 hours and features homemade soups, well-loaded omelets served with biscuits and gravy, and a special prime rib dinner, offered 4:00 pm–10:00 pm daily; **1-800-537-0207.**

Peppermill Casino—

With 90 rooms and plans to expand, the Peppermill is trying to keep up with Wendover's gambling boom. The Peppermill restaurant features the only lunchtime prime rib buffet in Wendover; **(702) 664-2900** or **1-800-648-9660.**

Red Garter Casino—

In 1994, 48 rooms were built at the Red Garter making it the fifth casino to offer lodging in Wendover. The Red Garter restaurant has a popular ham-and-egg breakfast, served 24 hours a day, along with other American and Mexican dishes; **(702) 664-2111.**

State Line and Silver Smith Hotel, Casino, and Convention Center—

The State Line Casino received one of the first licenses when the Nevada gambling law was passed in 1931. Although the original building has been replaced, the State Line is reportedly the only casino in Nevada still under the ownership of the original licensees. The State Line Casino, located on the south side of Wendover Boulevard, and the Silver Smith, on the north side, are connected by a sky walkway that keeps the gambling traffic flowing between the two casinos. If you make only one stop in Wendover, this is the one you should make. It is the home of the neon sign "Wendover Will" and is the largest casino in Wendover. The two casinos have 500 rooms, with 248 rooms at the State Line and 250 at the Silver Smith. There are also 56 sites at the RV park below the State Line. Entertainment is offered nightly in the State Line lounge and the Silver Smith cabaret lounge. Well-known stars make appearances from time to time. There are outdoor pools with Jacuzzis at both facilities. The Silver Smith has two tennis courts and an exercise room. Both casinos offer a midweek golf package, which includes 18 holes of golf with a cart for a modest fee.

You won't go hungry—each casino has three restaurants. I like the all-you-can-eat buffets in the **Bonneville Room** at the State Line and at the **White Swan Restaurant** at the Silver Smith. They are open evenings after 5 pm. **The Pantry** at the Silver Smith and **Anna's Kitchen** at the State Line are open 24 hours a day and offer similar fare for breakfast, lunch, and dinner—eggs, omelets, pancakes, burgers, sandwiches, soups, salads, chicken, beef, and seafood. The Pantry also serves Mexican dishes. **Gene's Deli** at the Silver Smith makes good sandwiches, while the **Salt Cellar** at the State Line is the fanciest and highest-priced restaurant in town offering homemade pasta daily and more elaborate fare, such as lobster, veal, steaks, prime rib, and fish. The Salt Cellar is open daily 6:00

pm–10:00 pm and 6:00 pm–11:00 pm on Fri. and Sat.; closed Mon.

Weekday rooms are generally available, but weekends usually fill up in advance. For information and reservations, call **1-800-848-7300**.

Racing

Bonneville Salt Flats Raceway—

At one time, the Bonneville Salt Flats were synonymous with world land speed records; they still attract plenty of racers each year. The salt flats, which range in thickness from less than 1 inch to 6 feet, were formed about 12,000 years ago when prehistoric Lake Bonneville disappeared at the end of the Ice Age. During the summer months, when water evaporates and the salt is compacted, the flats make a natural speedway. They were first used as early as 1911, when two race car pioneers, W. D. Rishel and Ferg Johnson, began promoting the salt flats as an ideal venue. Three years later, in 1914, Terry Tetzlaff set an unofficial land speed record of 141 miles an hour there, and, soon after a 10-mile-long speedway was established, along with an oval track. Over the years, many different

kinds of speed records have been made. Some of the most famous drivers include Ab Jenkins, who established a number of 24-hour speed records during the 1930s; Sir Malcolm Campbell, who established a land speed record of 301.129 mph for 1 mile on Sept. 3, 1935; and Gary Gabelich who set a 1-mile speed record of 622.407 mph on Oct. 23, 1970. Deterioration of the salt flats has been a serious problem for the last couple of decades, and it is doubtful that another world land speed record will ever be set on the Bonneville Salt Flats. Nevertheless, several racing associations continue to sponsor races (one vehicle at a time against the clock) usually between June and Oct. Visitors are permitted in the pit area, on the starting line, and at the timing stands down the track. There are no permanent facilities at the raceway, which can be reached by taking exit 4 off Interstate 80 and following the paved road 1.4 miles north, then 3.7 miles east, to the end of the pavement. For information about events, contact the **Bureau of Land Management, Salt Lake District** at **(801) 977-4300** or the **Wendover USA Visitor and Convention Bureau** at **(702) 664-3414** or **1-800-426-6862**.

FESTIVALS AND EVENTS

Bordertown Mountain Bike Challenge

1st weekend in May

The Bordertown Bike Challenge offers a variety of activities for serious racers as well as the more laid-back bike tourers. Races include a 15-mile cross-country race; a high-speed, 1.5-mile, downhill sprint from Wendover Peak; and 50- and 75-mile road races. Bike tours for nonracers are held on Sat. and Sun., with a Beginning Bike Clinic available as part of the Sat. tour. For information, call **(801) 582-4425**, or the **Wendover Welcome Center** at **1-800-476-6862**.

Cinco de Mayo

May 5th

Nearly two-thirds of Wendover's permanent population is Hispanic, and most of them are from Juchipila, Zacatecas, Mexico. They followed family members and friends to Wendover for the employment opportunities in the casinos. In May 1990 the Hispanic community held its first Cinco de Mayo celebration. It has continued to grow since then with a parade, fiesta, and Mexican dance. For more information, call the **Wendover Welcome Center** at **1-800-426-6862**.

July 4th Celebration
July 4th

This small-town celebration includes a parade down Wendover Blvd., a carnival, a barbecue, and a fireworks display.

Speed Week
3rd week of August

This is the largest speed event on the Bonneville Salt Flats. It is usually held during the 3rd week in Aug. The event, which dates from 1948, draws up to 360 cars and motorcycles. For specific times and activities, contact the **Wendover Welcome Center** at **1-800-426-6862.**

Deer Hunter Widows Weekend
3rd weekend in October

The 3rd weekend in Oct. is Utah's traditional deer hunt. With thousands of Utah males taking to the hills in pursuit of a trophy mule deer, many of the wives decided they were entitled to an outing as well. Wendover has become the "hot spot" for women who invade by the thousands while their husbands and boyfriends are off on the deer hunt. Among the most popular activities are the exotic male dancer revues. As one lady wrote, "For the most part, the weekend is a couple of days of harmless fun that manages to capture that special feeling high school girlfriends share."

———— OUTDOOR ACTIVITIES ————

BIKING

One of the tours offered during the Wendover Bordertown Bike Challenge can be taken by bikers at any time, weather permitting. It is a 12.8-mile circular course that begins and ends at the Wendover Welcome Center. The course starts out at an elevation of 4,600 feet and has four ascents, with 5,200 feet as the highest point along the course. The climbs can be taxing, but the breakneck downhills are thrilling. The route is a combination of dirt roads, pavements, and single track. The scenery is breathtaking, as the seemingly endless desert stretches to the south and east, and 10,600-foot Pilot Peak rises above you to the north. Pick up a map and course description at the **Wendover Welcome Center.**

GOLF

Toana Vista Golf Course—

If the brown and white of the Great Salt Lake Desert gets to you, or the lights and noise of the casinos give you a case of "casino fever," you can find your "cure" at the Toana Vista Golf Course. Some insist that this is the only patch of green in the whole 500 miles between Salt Lake City and California. The 18-hole championship course was opened in 1987 and is popular with Wendover visitors. This is a challenging links-style course, with narrow fairways and plenty of chances to hit your ball into the desert surrounding the course. Perhaps the most memorable feature of the course is the tremendous view out across the desert and salt flats; you can almost see forever. The course is open from Mar.–Nov. and is located at the west end of Wendover. Dr. down Wendover Blvd. to the street just past the Pizza Hut restaurant. Turn left and follow the road to the golf course. Reservations are taken two weeks in advance and are highly recommended on weekends. **2319 Pueblo Blvd.; (702) 664-4300** or **1-800-852-4330.**

TENNIS

There are two lighted public tennis courts adjacent to the Wendover Visitor Center. The **Silver Smith Casino and Resorts** has two tennis courts available for guests.

SEEING AND DOING

ARCHAEOLOGICAL AND HISTORIC SITES

Danger Cave—

Archaeologists seem to have a knack for naming sites, and Danger Cave is no exception. Danger Cave received its moniker in 1941, when a large slab of rock fell from the ceiling during an archaeological excavation, narrowly missing one of the workers. Excavation of the 11 feet of deposits in the late 1940s and early 1950s produced a stratigraphy indicating that the cave had been occupied sequentially by a number of groups from about 10,000 years ago to the present—a much earlier regional occupation than had previously been proven. The cave, and radiocarbon dating of material found in it helped establish a chronological framework that was a landmark in archaeological studies in Utah. Nowadays, if you ask any archaeologist to name the most famous and the most significant site in Utah, it's a safe bet that the response will be Danger Cave. Danger Cave was under the waters of Lake Bonneville until about 12,000 years ago. The cave remains undeveloped, with no visitor center, exhibits, or even signs. Still, it is worth the short drive from Wendover to see the cave and ponder the human story that has been played out inside and around the cave over the millennia. To reach the cave, take exit 4 off Interstate 80, east of Wendover, and drive north for a half mile, then turn left (west) onto a paved road for 1.4 miles. Turn right (if you keep going the pavement and road end) onto a gravel road and follow it for 1.8 miles to the cave. Be sure to bear to the left or you will end up in a gravel pit. You will drive parallel to Interstate 80 back to the west until you reach the bridge across the highway that takes you back into Wendover (part of exit 2). The bridge is south of the cave about 300 yards. The cave entrance is above the road, a short distance to the north. Visitors should not attempt to enter the cave and should avoid disturbing anything at the site.

Wendover Army Air Field—

Long before Wendover became the mecca for Wasatch Front gamblers, it was a temporary home to thousands of members of the Army Air Corps who were stationed there during World War II. The army needed a large, uninhabited, isolated, and open area for bombing and gunnery ranges. The deserts around Wendover were a good choice and in 1941 nearly 2 million acres of land were set aside as a training ground for high-altitude formation flying, long-range navigation, and simulated combat missions. The first detachment of trainees arrived less than four months before the US entered World War II, following the attack on Pearl Harbor. The most famous group to train at Wendover was the 509th Composite Group under the command of Colonel Paul W. Tibbets, Jr. It was Tibbets and his crew who, aboard the "Enola Gay," dropped the atomic bomb on Hiroshima, Japan, which brought the end of World War II eight days later. In preparation for the historic event, the 509th Composite Group made 155 test drops over the Wendover range in 1944 and 1945. Although the military continues to use the Wendover Bombing and Gunnery ranges for training, Wendover Field was closed permanently in 1969. You can still see some of the World War II hangars and other buildings if you drive to the southern end of Wendover, on the Utah side. Also look at the rock ledges above Wendover, where some of the World War II airmen spent their free time with what seems to be an overabundance of paint.

ATTRACTIONS

Tree of Utah—

About 100 miles west of Salt Lake City and 26 miles east of Wendover is Karl Momen's Tree of Utah. This somewhat controversial but nevertheless interesting sculpture, completed in 1981, is an 87-foot-tall "tree" built from 255 tons of cement, 1,800 ceramic tiles, and 5 tons of welding rod. There are six spheres on the tree which are coated with natural rock and minerals found within the state of Utah. The pods below symbolize the changing seasons and natural transformation of trees, while the tree itself came about out of Momen's desire to have a thing of beauty growing out of the seemingly sterile salt.

Wendover Will—

Wendover's symbol and landmark, Wendover Will, was constructed in 1951 and has been welcoming visitors to Wendover for nearly half a century. This neon sign stands more than 50 feet tall and is a wonderful example of neon technology from an earlier era. Built for the State Line Casino, the double-sided Will greets visitors coming from both the east and west. One arm waves a hello while the other hand points down to the State Line Casino. Will sports red boots, blue jeans, green shirt, yellow bandanna, white hat, and an orange holster slung low on his hip, and he winks at you with one eye and offers an almost audible greeting with a cigarette flapping up and down in his mouth.

COMMUNITIES AND GHOST TOWNS

Callao—

The first settlers arrived at Callao, or Willow Springs, between 1859 and 1860. With the coming of the Pony Express, they found a good market for hay and wood at the string of stations that stretched across the uninhabited western half of Utah. You can still see a number of log structures that date from the 19th century, including the one-room schoolhouse, reportedly the last one in use in the state. The Willow Springs Pony Express Station at Callao is one of the best preserved along the entire trail. Willow Springs became Callao in 1895 to avoid confusion with the several other Willow Springs in Utah. An old prospector who had visited Peru suggested the name Callao because of its resemblance to Callao, Peru, and his proposal was adopted.

Gold Hill—

Gold Hill, located 23 miles north of Callao, is one of Utah's best-preserved mining ghost towns. The Clifton Mining District was designated in 1889, and in 1892 the town of Gold Hill was established. It was named for a low, gold-bearing mountain east of the town, where James P. Woodman, the discoverer in 1869 of the famous Emma Mine at Alta above Salt Lake City, had several claims, which, during a three-year gold boom, produced nearly $300,000. The initial gold boom faded by the turn of the century; however, a copper boom during World War I boosted the population of Gold Hill to 3,000. In 1917, a railroad was constructed from Wendover to Gold Hill (a total of 51 miles) to transport more than a million dollars' worth of copper ore to the Salt Lake City smelters. Tungsten and arsenic were also mined at Gold Hill until about 1924, when the second boom ended. Most of the remaining buildings date from this period. A third boom struck with the outbreak of World War II, and tungsten and arsenic mines that had been idle for two decades were reopened as part of the total war effort. Some 8,000 tons of ore were shipped between 1944 and 1945, but when the government had all the arsenic it needed, production was shut down. There are still a number of old stores, warehouses, dwellings, foundations, mines, abandoned vehicles, and equipment, in Gold Hill—enough to stir the imagination and make this ghost town a worthy stop.

MUSEUMS

Bonneville Museum—

Richard Dixon first came to the Bonneville Speedway in 1947 with his stepfather and fell in love with automobiles and the speedway lore. The Speedway Museum, built by Dixon in 1979, offers an interesting collection of photographs and memorabilia from speedway events and racing automobiles. The museum houses two Indian Bonneville motorcycles and a number of cars, including a 1909 Electric Opera Coupe, a 1928 Essex boattail roadster, a Gullwing

Mercedes SL 300, a 1959 Jaguar, and, when it is not on tour, the four-engined Golden Rod, which set a world's speed record in 1965. The museum is usually open daily June–Nov. 10:00 am–6:00 pm. Call to be sure, though, since, as Dixon admits, the hours are sometimes erratic. **1000 State Hwy.**, on the Utah side of the border; **(801) 665-7721.**

SCENIC DRIVES

Deep Creek Mountains Backway—
The 15-mile road from Callao south to Trout Creek has been designated a Scenic Backway, as it provides spectacular views and access to the east side of the southern end of the Deep Creek Mountains. The mountains seem deceptively low, but Haystack Peak, the highest point in the range, is actually 12,101 feet in elevation. The Deep Creek Mountains have no developed hiking trails, but the road passes five canyons coming out of the Deep Creeks, which you can explore with a four-wheel-drive vehicle or on foot. The mountains are among Utah's most isolated ranges and are habitat for mule deer, elk, mountain lions, and bighorn sheep. Callao is nearly 100 miles south of Wendover, with about a third of the distance being on a graveled road, much of which was the old Pony Express trail between Ibapah and Callao. You can combine the drive to Trout Creek with a stop in Callao and Ibapah, where Pony Express stations were located, and which are traditional cattle ranching centers; a visit to the Fish Springs Wildlife Refuge (see the **Provo and Orem** chapter); and a tour of the old mining district and town of Gold Hill. The backway is usually closed by snow accumulations late Nov.–April. Because of the distance involved, you should allow the better part of a day for the drive. Travel with a full tank of gas, and let people know of your planned itinerary.

Silver Island Mountain Loop—
The mountains northeast of Wendover look like islands floating in the distance as the white salt flats appear to give way to water. But it is all illusion as the water seems to recede as you move towards the mountains. The Silver Island Mountain Loop drive covers 54 miles on a graded gravel and dirt road that circles the mountains. The loop begins a mile north of Interstate 80, off exit 4, and takes a couple of hours to complete. A four-wheel-drive vehicle is recommended, especially if you plan to do any exploring in the canyons and washes. The drive offers a unique perspective on distance, with the unencumbered landscape seeming to stretch forever—although the heat, reflections, and the earth's curvature do play tricks on your perception. The loop takes you near the route taken by the ill-fated Donner Party, which, in 1846, struggled across an 80-mile, waterless stretch of the salt desert along what was suppose to be a time-saving cutoff to California. The Donner Party lost animals, had to abandon wagons, and suffered so many delays that early snows in California's Sierra Nevada mountains claimed many of the party. (Survivors were forced to cannibalize the dead to make it through the winter.) The Silver Island Mountain area gives you some perspective of the distance and difficulties that early travelers encountered trying to cross the Great Salt Lake Desert. The road is most passable when it is dry, with summer and fall the best times to make the drive.

WILDLIFE

Goshute Research Site—
Between mid-Aug. and mid-Oct., thousands of hawks fly over the Goshute Research Site, during their annual migration. An average of 100 to 200 raptors are counted each day; as many as 800 birds a day have been noted during the peak third week in Sept. In cooperation with the BLM, HawkWatch International, a volunteer group based in New Mexico, does annual counts of migratory birds at the research site. Visitors are welcome and anyone can take part in the counts.

The Goshute Research Site, located about 25 miles southwest of Wendover, is in a wilderness study area and somewhat difficult to reach. Head south out of Wendover on Alternate Hwy. 93 toward Ely, Nevada, for 25 miles, then turn right (northwest) onto a dirt road a mile beyond the Ferguson Springs Highway Maintenance Station. Follow the dirt road for 3.2 miles, then take the left fork at a junction on top of the hill and continue another 2 miles on a four-wheel-drive road to the parking area. After leaving your vehicle, it's a good hour's hike up the 2-mile-long steep trail to the ridge top and observation post. The best time to view the hawks is between 10 am–2 pm. For more information, contact **HawkWatch International** in Albuquerque, New Mexico, **(505) 255-7622;** or check at the **Wendover Welcome Center, 1-800-426-6862.**

WHERE TO STAY

ACCOMMODATIONS

Accommodations can be difficult to find on weekends, and the Wendover Visitor and Convention Bureau staff reports that some weekends hundreds of people are turned away with every casino and motel being full. If you plan to stay in Wendover, be sure to make reservations in advance. Rates are quite reasonable, with weekday prices about half the price of weekends. Casinos offer special rates and incentives, even on weekends, so inquire about their offerings when you call. (For casino accommodations see Gambling in the Major Attractions section.)

Best Western Salt Flat Inn—$$
Heated pool, sauna, whirlpool, steam room, and exercise room; 24 rooms. 295 East Wendover Blvd.; (801) 665-7811, 1-800-648-9668, or 1-800-848-7300.

Bonneville Motel—$$
Heated swimming pool; 87 rooms. 389 Wendover Blvd.; (801) 665-2500.

Heritage Motel—$$
Swimming pool; 50 rooms. 505 East Wendover Blvd.; (801) 665-7744.

Motel 6—$$
One hundred thirty rooms. 505 East Wendover Blvd.; (801) 665-2267.

State Line Inn—$$
This motel in Utah is part of the State Line and Silver Smith enterprise and is within walking distance of the parent facility on the Nevada side. There are 101 rooms and a heated pool and whirlpool. The Inn is a nice option for families traveling with children and for those who do not want to stay at one of the casinos; (801) 665-2226.

Super 8—$$
Adjacent to the Red Garter Casino; 74 rooms; (702) 664-2888.

Western Motel—$ to $$.
Swimming pool; 30 rooms. 645 East Wendover Blvd.; (801) 665-2215.

Western Ridge Motel—$$
Fifty-five units. 10 two-bedrooms units. Heated pool. 895 East Wendover Blvd.; (801) 665-2211.

CAMPGROUNDS

State Line RV Park—
Fifty-six full hookups. Showers, compete laundry facilities, tennis courts, Jacuzzi, spa, and swimming pool. Located within walking distance of the State Line Casino; (702) 664-2221 or 1-800-648-9668.

Wendover KOA Kampground—
One hundred sites, 80 pullthroughs with full hookups. Tent spaces. Outdoor heated pool, large store, laundry playground, and a casino shuttle service. Open year-round. Located off Interstate 80, exit 410, on Camper Dr.; (702) 664-3221

WHERE TO EAT

Most visitors eat in one of the five casinos described above. If you don't want to eat there, your choices are limited to Pizza Hut, Burger Time, Taco Burger, Subway, and the Salt Flats Grill. The latter is located on the Utah side and has the character of a 1950s roadside cafe. It is the unofficial headquarters for the speedway crews when they gather in Wendover, and there are photographs of race cars on the east wall.

SERVICES

Day Care—
    Ginger's Child Care; (702) 664-2630.

Wendover Welcome Center—
    Located across Wendover Blvd. from the Peppermill Casino, the Welcome Center has an ample supply of brochures and maps about the area and can provide information about events and other things to do and see. There are several interesting displays about the Bonneville Salt Flats Speedway, wildlife, and travel opportunities in Nevada. The east wall is devoted to the 509th Composite Group and displays a flight jacket and other World War II memorabilia. Outside, near the east end of the parking area, a peace memorial to the 509th was erected in 1990. The center is open 9:00 am–5:00 pm Wed.–Sun. Kelly Housley, director of the center and the Wendover Visitor and Convention Bureau, is happy to answer questions about the area and to send, upon request, literature about the facilities, activities, and events. Call **(702) 664-3414 or 1-800-426-6862.**

Wendover Casino and Community Shuttle Bus—
    This community bus service has two routes: the Casino Route runs from the Red Garter Casino on the west, down Wendover Blvd., to the State Line and Silver Smith Casino on the east. The Town Loop continues east on Wendover Blvd. to all of the motels on the Utah side and, on the Nevada side, as far west as the Toana Vista Golf Course. The Casino Loop operates every half hour from 7:30 am–midnight, Sun.–Thurs. (until 2:00 am on Fri., Sat., and Sun. nights prior to a Mon. holiday). The Town Loop operates hourly 7:20 am–8 pm daily.

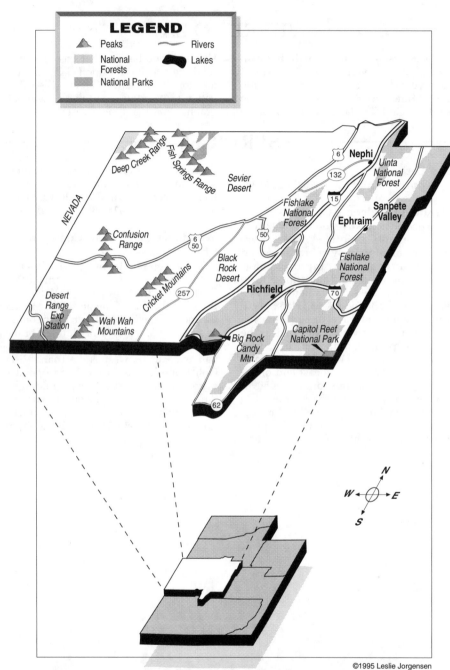

Central Region

CENTRAL REGION

Nephi and Eureka

If two communities ever reflected the diverging forces of 19th-century Utah, it is the towns of Nephi and Eureka. Nephi, established on Salt Creek in 1851, was named by early Mormon settlers for the first of several principle prophets who wrote the Book of Mormon. Nephi is typical of the hundreds of Mormon communities established in Utah by early settlers. Eureka, on the other hand, takes its name from the Greek word meaning "I have found it." What early miners found were rich deposits of silver ore that led to the establishment of a mining town in 1869. Eureka is located high in the Tintic Mountains, and its narrow, twisting streets, and mine dumps, head frames, and other signs of mining activities visible from about any place in town, are in sharp contrast to the well-ordered grid street system of Nephi, which was laid out according to a plan for communities developed by Mormon founder Joseph Smith. Nephi sits at the base of the 11,877-foot Mt. Nebo, the southernmost mountain in the Wasatch Range and a landmark that can be seen from much of central Utah. Proceeding westward to the Nevada border, like the folds of an accordion, are a series of mountain ranges that include the East Tintic Range, the West Tintic Range, the Thomas Range, the Fish Springs Range, and the Deep Creek Range. Except for the Tintic Range, the rest of region to the Nevada border and beyond is unoccupied and provides plenty of space for exploring. Nephi is the Juab County seat and, with about 4,000 people, it is the largest community. A smaller community, Mona, is located to the north; south of Nephi is another small town, Levan. The name of the latter community is the subject of some speculation. Some wags claim that it was named by a practical joker who realized the town was located in the center of the state and, reversing the spelling of "Navel," called it Levan!

HISTORY

Fremont Indians occupied the valley until about AD 1300. They left important archaeological sites, such as the Nephi Mounds, just north of Nephi along the western slope of the mountains. The Fremont were supplanted by incoming Utes in the eastern part of Juab County, while in western Juab County, Goshiute Indians became dominant. (Tintic is named for a Goshiute Indian chief whose band lived in the valleys west of Utah Lake.) Nephi sits on an historic travel corridor, which was used by Dominguez and Escalante in 1776, Jedediah S. Smith in 1826 through 1827, and John C. Fremont in 1843 through 1844. Early Mormon explorers noted the favorable location, and, in 1851, a settlement on Salt Creek came into being at the point where the valley reaches the mountains. Nephi became a farming community and, as the railroad was extended south from Salt Lake City in the 1870s, an important livestock shipping center, which acquired the nickname Little Chicago. The railroad also brought miners, and the Tintic Mining District was organized on December 13, 1869. The Tintic Mining District joined Park City and Bingham Canyon as one of the top three precious metal producers in the state. By 1976, the total production of base and precious metals from the district over a period of more than 100 years was estimated at 16,654,377 tons, with a value of $570 million. Eureka sits at the center of the district, but it is surrounded by Silver City, Diamond, Mammoth, and Knightsville, mining towns that have now become ghost towns. Hundreds of mines operated in the district, but the "big four" producers were Eureka Hill, Bullion Beck, Blue Rock, and Gemini. Much of the early mining history has been documented and preserved by the Tintic Historical Society, which has received national recognition as one of the best local historical societies in the country. Visit their museum in Eureka and inquire about the driving tour of the district, what mining activities are still going on, and purchase a copy of the excellent history *Faith, Hope and Prosperity: The Tintic Mining District*, authored by a prominent Utah Historian, Philip F. Notarianni and published by the Tintic Historical Society.

GETTING THERE

Nephi is 85 miles south of Salt Lake City on Interstate 15 at exit 228. Eureka, located northwest of Nephi, sits astride Hwy. 6 and is 21 miles west of the Santaquin exit (exit 245) off Interstate 15.

MAJOR ATTRACTIONS

Little Sahara Recreation Area

"Little" does not seem quite right for this Bureau of Land Management–administered recreation area, which consists of miles of free-blowing dune sand. The actual recreation area includes 60,000 acres of sand dunes and, in keeping with a multiuse recreation philosophy, there are specific areas for nature study, picnicking and playing in the sand, and vehicle recreation. The Dunes, as they are also called, are Utah's most popular area for off-road-vehicle recreation. Dune buggies, four-wheelers, motor bikes, and four-wheel-drive vehicles tear across the dunes, and Sand Mountain, with its steep sand slopes, challenges the most skilled drivers. But if you don't have a sand vehicle, the Dunes are still an unforgettable experience. This is a place to build sand castles, to run barefoot through the sand, to jump off sand hills. Even if you are past middle age, you can't help acting like a kid again. Easter is an especially popular time, but fall is also a nice season at Little Sahara. To get there, turn west off Hwy. 6 at Jericho Junction, 20 miles south of Eureka, and follow the paved road until you reach the recreation area. From Nephi, head west on Hwy. 132 for 13 miles, then turn right onto the paved road to Jericho Junction, about 8 miles to the northwest. Four campgrounds have been developed by the BLM. The **Sand Mountain Campground,** with room for 300 trailers, is the largest. **Oasis** has 114 sites and **White Sands 99. Jericho** offers 40 tent sites. All have drinking water and flush toilets, but none have showers.

FESTIVALS AND EVENTS

Ute Stampede

2nd weekend in July

This popular rodeo is held in Nephi, usually the 2nd weekend in July. **PO Box 404, Nephi, UT 84648; (801) 623-0643.**

Tintic Silver Festival Celebration

3rd weekend in August

Around the third weekend in Aug., Eureka hosts its Tintic Silver Festival Celebration. With an emphasis on the mining heritage and tradition, the festival includes a parade, tours of the mining museum and the old Tintic Mining District, food, displays, foot and bicycle races, a dance, and other activities. Call June and Coleen McNulty at **(801) 433-6842.**

OUTDOOR ACTIVITIES

BOATING AND FISHING

Mona Lake—

With easy access off Interstate 15 at the Mona exit (exit 236), Mona Reservoir offers good boating and fishing facilities.

Yuba Lake—

See the **Fillmore and Delta** chapter.

GOLF

Canyon Hills Golf Course—

Located at the mouth of Salt Creek Canyon, just off Interstate 15 at exit 225 in

Nephi, the 9-hole Canyon Hills Course is easily accessible. No reservations are taken, and there is no need. If there are more than a dozen players on the course at any one time, it is considered crowded. Golf junkees traveling up or down Interstate 15 can pull into the golf parking area, pay their fees, play a round in under two hours, experience a golfer's high with what should be one of their better scores, and be back on the road with time to get wherever you are going. The course offers some spectacular views of Mt. Nebo to the north, and Salt Creek Canyon to the east. Rates are about the lowest in the state. **East Canyon Rd., Nephi, UT 84548; (801) 623-9930.**

HIKING
Mt. Nebo Hike—
You can hike to the top of Mt. Nebo along a strenuous 6-mile route that begins near the Ponderosa Forest Campground, 10 miles northeast of Nephi, off Hwy. 132. The elevation gain is 5,000 feet to the top of Mt. Nebo's south summit. From the summit you have an unbelievable view of the other peaks that comprise Mt. Nebo and farther to the northeast the peaks of the Wasatch Range extend off beyond the horizon. To the east and south is the Wasatch Plateau and to the west, the basins and ranges of the Great Basin seem to stretch into infinity. It's a good idea to check with the Uinta National Forest Office about conditions before you set out. **740 South Main, Nephi, UT 84648; (801) 623-2735.**

SEEING AND DOING

HISTORIC BUILDINGS
Juab County Jail—
There are not many historic jails preserved in Utah, but one of the most interesting is the 1892 Juab County Jail, which remained in use until 1974. As with most jails that have been around for a few years, many stories are told about the old jail, including one about three of the jail's first prisoners, who made a hole in the brick wall and escaped only to be recaptured and returned to the jail. One inmate, incarcerated for drunkenness, spent the summer in jail, but was given a key to the jail by the sheriff, so that he could let himself out of the jail during the day and return at night after spending the day doing volunteer work on the city golf course. Open Mon.–Fri. 9 am–5 pm. The jail is located at 4 South Main St. adjacent to the Old Juab County Courthouse; Nephi; **(801) 633-5202.**

MUSEUMS
Tintic Mining Museum—
Located on Main St. and operated by the Tintic Historical Society, this is one of the best small-town museums in the state. There are artifacts here from throughout Eureka's history, but the focus is on its heyday as one of the largest mining towns in the Utah. One of the most interesting artifacts is a three-dimensional model of the inside of a silver mine. The museum is not open on a regular basis, but you can call the numbers listed on the door and one of the faithful members will be only too glad to come down and give you a personal tour. Or, if you want to make arrangements in advance, call June or Coleen McNulty at **(801) 433-6842.**

SCENIC DRIVES
Nebo Loop Scenic Byway—
Mt. Nebo was named by Mormon pioneers for the highest mountain east of the Jordan River in the Holy Land where Moses died. The pioneers, in recognition of their own Zion, chose to honor the highest mountain in the Wasatch Range, which runs just to the east of Utah's Jordan River, with the name Mt. Nebo. The 38-mile-long Nebo Loop Scenic Byway loops around the 11,877-foot-high Mt. Nebo. The byway can be followed south from its northern terminus at Payson in Utah County, or north from the

turnoff off Hwy. 132 about 3 miles east of Nephi, in Salt Creek Canyon. The drive leads to the Payson Lakes Recreation Area, 12 miles south of Payson, and takes in breath-taking views of Utah Valley, the Wasatch Mountains, and Mt. Nebo from various over-looks. Magnificent autumn colors makes this one of the top five drives in the state in late Sept. and early Oct. On the north side of Mt. Nebo, chances are good of seeing elk and deer as the herds number an estimated 500 and 5,000, respectively.

Tintic District Driving Tour—

The Tintic Historical Society has pre-pared a suggested driving tour booklet of the Tintic Mining District, which takes you to some of the historic mining towns and past several of the old mine head frames and buildings. Highlights of the tour in-clude the Bullion-Beck Headframe and the sites and ghost towns of Knightsville, Divi-dend, Silver City, and Mammoth.

WHERE TO STAY

ACCOMMODATIONS

Best Western Paradise Inn—$$
Heated pool; 40 units. **1025 South Main, Nephi; (801) 623-0624.**

Budget Host Motor Inn Roberta's Cove—$$
Six of the 39 rooms have private whirlpool baths. Located off Interstate 15 at exit 222. **2250 South Main, Nephi; (801) 623-2629.**

Super 8 Motel—
Forty-one rooms. **1901 South Main St., Nephi; (801) 623-0888.**

Whitmore Mansion Bed and Breakfast—$$ to $$$
Abandoned for many years and hid-den behind a used car lot, the 1898 Whitmore Mansion was acquired and re-stored by Bob and Dorothy Gliske in the 1970s and became one of central Utah's first bed and breakfast inns. The mansion retains many of the original features, in-cluding a magnificent open stairway, leaded glass windows, sliding oak doors, and original 19th-century furnishings from the time it was constructed for local busi-nessman George Whitmore. The house is listed in the National Register of Historic Places. There are six nonsmoking rooms

with a country breakfast served in the din-ing room. **110 South Main St., Nephi; (801) 623-2047.**

CAMPING

PRIVATE

High Country RV Camp—
Located in the south end of Nephi, the campground has 45 sites, most with full hookups, flush toilets, showers, laundry facilities, and disabled-access facilities. Open year-round. **899 South Main; (801) 623-2624.**

Horseshoe Bar Ranch KOA Campground—
This KOA campground provides a mountain setting that is only a few miles from Nephi. It has 90 sites, 28 of which have full hookups, and there are flush toi-lets, showers, and laundry. In Salt Creek Canyon along Utah Hwy. 132, near the Mt. Nebo Scenic Loop; **(801) 623-0811.**

PUBLIC

There are two campgrounds located on national forest lands northeast of Nephi, on the Mt. Nebo Loop Rd. The **Ponderosa Campground** is 11 miles from Nephi and has 28 sites. The **Bear Canyon Campground** is 2 miles farther up the road with 4 sites. The latter campground has flush toilets. Both campgrounds are open from late May–Oct.

WHERE TO EAT

Cedar Hollow—$ to $$

A convenient and popular place just off the Interstate 15 at exit 222. Serves burgers, sandwiches, and traditional American dishes. Breakfast, lunch, and dinner. Open daily 7 am–10 pm; **(801) 623-2633.**

Mickelson's Restaurant—$ to $$

One of only a handful of long-established restaurants in the southern half of the state, Mickelson's was established by Jay Mickelson, a traveling salesman who knew what a good meal away from home should be. After Jay's retirement, his son Jens and daughter-in-law Jacqueline took over the restaurant, keeping the same cooks and same basic menu of American food that had made the restaurant so popular among locals and travelers. Open Mon.–Sat. 6:30 am–9:45 pm. **793 North Main; (801) 623-0152.**

SERVICES

Nephi Chamber of Commerce—

PO Box 71, Nephi, UT 84648; (801) 623-2411.

Uinta National Forest—

740 South Main, Nephi, UT 84648; (801) 623-2735.

Miners Dry at the Tintic Mining District. This structure was built about 1923 as a change room for the miners at the Tintic Standard. Photo by Allan Kent Powell.

Fillmore and Delta

The Pahvant Mountains, to the east of Fillmore, and the Pahvant Valley, in which are located the towns of Fillmore, Holden, Meadow, Kanosh, Delta, Deseret, and Hinkley, are named for the Indian tribe that occupied the area when the Mormons arrived here in 1851. Beyond the string of towns along the mountains and the farms clustered around Delta on the Sevier River, the rest of the area is considered uninhabitable. The West Desert stretches toward the Nevada border and the Great Basin National Park and what is left of the Sevier River, after providing water to most of the south central Utah communities, sinks into the intermittent Sevier Lake in the Great Basin. Rock hounds will enjoy collecting some unique gems in the desert. Outdoor buffs have no shortage of miles in which to roam.

HISTORY

Judging by the number of places in Utah that bear his name, Millard Fillmore, who served as president of the US (1850–1852), when Franklin Pierce died in office, is the most honored president in Utah. No other county and county seat carry both names of an American president. Millard County is Utah's third largest county, and Fillmore, the county seat, was once the territorial capital. Fillmore became the territorial capital practically before it was settled in 1851. Pioneer settlers were sent out from Salt Lake City in October of that year; three months later, the new territorial capital was announced. A territorial statehouse was constructed, but the relocation of the capital 150 miles south of Salt Lake City proved impractical after a few years. The region gained national attention when John W. Gunnison, surveying a route for the transcontinental railroad along the 38th parallel, was killed by Indians west of Fillmore. During the 1860s two forts—Fort Deseret and Cove Fort—were constructed as protection from Indian unrest, which grew as more and more Mormon settlers competed for precious resources. But Indians were not the real challenge for settlers, it was the lack of water. The construction of the Yuba Dam and other dams along the Sevier River made possible the extensive agricultural development of West Millard County, and the town of Delta was established in 1907. During World War II, Topaz became the largest city in the area, when about 9,000 Japanese-Americans were relocated from their homes in the San Francisco area to a camp northwest of Delta. The most significant postwar development in the county was the construction of the huge coal-burning Intermountain Power Plant north of Delta in the 1970s.

GETTING THERE

Fillmore is 150 miles south of Salt Lake City on Interstate 15. Delta is about 40 miles northwest of Fillmore and 133 miles south of Salt Lake City. Take Interstate 15 south to Santaquin, exit 248, and then take Hwy. 6 west through Eureka and southwest to Delta. Another interesting route to Delta is to take Hwy. 132 west out of Nephi to its junction with Hwy. 6 at Lynndyl. The former route takes you through the historic Tintic Mining District, past the Little Sahara Sand Dunes Recreation Area; the latter passes through Leamington with its interesting beehive-shaped pioneer charcoal kilns.

———— MAJOR ATTRACTIONS ————

Great Basin National Park

Introduction—

Delta is the gateway city to the Great Basin National Park. Located about 100 miles west of Delta, off Hwy. 6, this newest of the western national parks was created in 1986 and is just across the border in Nevada. The 77,000-acre desert park preserves features common to the Great Basin, a name explorer John C. Fremont gave to the desert region between Utah's Wasatch Mountains and Plateau on the east and Nevada's Sierra Nevada Mountains on the west because it offered no outlet to the ocean. The Great Basin is characterized by a series of mountain ranges with lofty peaks, mountain meadows, alpine lakes, a wide range of plant and animal habitats, broad sweeping valleys and deserts, and rivers and streams that flow inward to soak into the earth, evaporate, or form lakes because they have no access to the sea. The main attractions in the park are the Lehman Caves, 13,063-foot Wheeler Peak, and the Lexington Arch. (Note: The national park is located in the Pacific Time Zone, which is one hour later than in the rest of Utah.)

Visitor Center—

Great Basin Visitor Center is located 10 miles south of US Hwy. 6 and 5 miles west of the town of Baker, on Utah Route 488, at the entrance to Lehman Caves. The center is open daily, except Thanksgiving, Christmas, and New Year's Day, 8 am–5 pm; **(702) 234-7331.**

Baker Creek Trailhead—

As you drive up the Wheeler Peak Scenic Drive, watch for the turnoff to Baker Creek, about 4 miles up the road. If you drive past the Baker Creek Campground to the end of the road, you reach the Baker Creek Trailhead. Here there are several possibilities for spending the day hiking to Baker Lake, Johnson Lake, along Baker Creek and its south fork. If you fish, the creek offers good opportunities to cast a line and hook one of the brown, brook, rainbow, or cutthroat trout that inhabits its waters. You follow Baker Creek for about 3 miles before the trail switchbacks up the mountain to the log cabin of Peter Dieschman, an early prospector. It's another 1.5 miles from the cabin to Baker Lake, situated in a paintinglike setting beneath the 12,300-foot Baker Peak. From Baker Lake you can either return on the trail you came for an out and back hike of 11 miles, or follow a trail south for 1.4 miles over Johnson Pass to Johnson Lake. En route you pass the remains of a mine, concentrating mill, and cabins of a tungsten mining operation established by Alfred Johnson about 1913.

Johnson Lake is another mountain jewel. From the lake, the trail starts down Snake Creek and then crosses the Snake Creek divide as you return to the Baker Creek Trailhead along the south fork of Baker Creek. The total distance for the loop hike is 11 miles with an elevation gain of 3,250 feet as you cross Johnson Pass (elevation 11,250 feet). The climb to Baker Lake is 2,600 feet from the trailhead. Along the trail keep a watch for old beaver dams along the creek, rock squirrels, mule deer, and birds like the Clark's nutcracker—distinguishable by its loud shrieks—and the yellow-bellied sapsucker, a woodpecker that you can hear drilling holes in trees for sap.

Camping—

There are four campgrounds within the park. **Baker Creek Campground,** south of the visitor center, has 32 spaces. Along the Wheeler Peak Scenic Drive, **Lower Lehman Campground** has 11 spaces; **Upper Lehman Creek Campground** has 24 spaces; and the **Wheeler Creek Campground**, at 9,950 feet, has 37 spaces.

Icefield Trail—

This trail also begins at the "horse loading" parking area and heads generally south toward Teresa Lake. At the fork in the trail, take the left (east) fork which takes you through the bristlecone pine forest, where some of the world's oldest living trees—nearly 3,000 years old, can be found.

After a jaunt to the east, the trail resumes a southerly course as you pass the Wheeler Peak Rock Glacier—quartzite boulders that have fallen off the wall of the Wheeler Cirque above. At the end of the trail, you can look ahead and see the ice field. The icefield has been called a glacier because it demonstrates many of the features of active glaciers. Because it does not move, however, the designation remains an icefield. The hike is 3 miles one way with an elevation gain of 1,400 feet. Portions of the trail are quite rocky.

Lehman Caves—

About 550 million years ago the area was covered by a shallow inland sea. Sea creatures died and their shells and bones piled up on the sea floor, eventually hardening into limestone, thousands of feet thick. Lehman Caves were formed by water. Part of it was hollowed out by an underground stream. About 20 million years ago, the Snake Range was formed and as water percolated down through the soil, combining with carbon dioxide gas to form a weak carbonic acid that eroded the limestone even more. In time the caves were emptied of groundwater, leaving smooth, well-scrubbed walls. Then a different chemical process kicked into gear. Calcite deposits, left by the slow dripping calcite-laden water, began to form on the roofs and floors of the caves as stalactites and stalagmites, which sometimes grew together to become thick columns. Other deposits were left millions of years ago that are called flowstone, cave popcorn or cave coral, helictites (which resembles dried chow mein noodles), small delicate argonite crystals, shields, and draperies.

Lehman Caves are named for Absalom Lehman, who established a ranch and orchard near the caves about 1870. He discovered the cave system in 1885, and soon hundreds of visitors arrived to explore the caves. A .6-mile, 1.5-hour, ranger-led tour leaves from the visitor center hourly during the summer between 8 am–5 pm daily (about every two hours in the winter). Highlights of the tour are the **Gothic Palace, Grand Palace,** and **Cypress Swamp.** The temperature inside the cave is a cool 50 degrees Fahrenheit, so a jacket or sweater is recommended. A candlelight tour is offered daily during the summer and on summer weekends. Spelunking tours, lasting 2.5 hours, take you to parts of the cave system not seen on the regular tour, but they involve considerable crawling and the use of cave equipment. Children under 16 years must be accompanied by an adult. The spelunking tour is limited to those 14 years or older.

Lehman Creek—

This 4-mile-long trail connects the **Wheeler Peak Campground**, located at the end of Wheeler Peak Scenic Drive, with the **Upper Lehman Creek Campground** located further down the scenic drive. The trail follows the north side of Lehman Creek. Most hikers catch a ride to the Wheeler Peak Campground or arrange for a ride back up the road to pick up their vehicle. It is an easy 2,100-foot descent through meadows, aspen groves, spruce and fir forests, mountain mahogany, single leaf piñon (the source of the delicious pine nuts used by Indians for centuries and enjoyed by westerners today as a fall and early winter snack). Around the Upper Lehman Creek Campground you begin to encounter the sagebrush and cactus vegetation of this elevation.

Lexington Arch—

Unlike all the other arches described and noted in this guide which are of sandstone, Lexington Arch is a natural limestone arch that stands 75 feet above you with a span of 120 feet. To reach the arch drive south on Nevada Hwy. 487 from the visitor center to Baker and on to Garrison, Utah. Continue south of Utah Hwy. 21 for 4.5 miles and watch for a dirt road on your right. After you turn onto the dirt road, follow the signs indicating Lexington Arch. Its a 12-mile drive across the desert valley to the road's end at the base of the Snake Creek Range. From the end of the road, its a one mile hike to the arch as you climb 1,000 feet up Arch Canyon. As you hike you will see remnants of mining activity including the remains of an old miner's cabin. The view of Lexington Arch is magnificent. On one side, the massive rampart stands like a fortress protecting the arch while the jagged top of the arch has not yet been worn flat as is characteristic of most sandstone arches. Geologists theorize that the arch may have been a passage in a cave system at one time and point to the flowstone at the arches' base in support of their position. Other counter that it is not an arch at all, but rather a natural bridge carved by an ancient stream.

Stella and Teresa Lakes—

This pleasant hike also begins at the "horse loading" parking area and is the same as the Wheeler Peak Trail for the first mile. When the trail branches, stay to the left and in a short distance you will reach Stella Lake, a beautiful alpine lake surrounded by pine and spruce. Teresa Lake is approximately a mile away. Both lakes are quite shallow, no more than 10 feet deep. The elevation gain is only about 400 feet from the trailhead to Stella Lake. After that it is relatively level and then downhill. This is one of the most beautiful hikes anywhere. Take your time and enjoy it. Plan a period of reflection and meditation at both lakes. Your soul will be refreshed, if you let the beauty sink in for a while.

Wheeler Peak—

A 12-mile scenic drive begins east of the visitor center and climbs the northern slope of Wheeler Peak to an elevation of about 10,000 feet. The peak is named for George Montague Wheeler, who conducted a reconnaissance survey in 1869 to map, collect natural history items, and determine anything of potential military value in the Great Basin for the US Army. Wheeler and his party climbed the peak in July 1869 and determined its elevation to be 13,000 feet. The peak was regarded for many years as the tallest mountain in Nevada. (Boundary Peak on the border between Nevada and California is higher at 13,145 feet.) Wheeler spent nine years with his survey of the Great Basin.

At the end of the scenic drive you can choose from several different hiking trails to get a closer look at the country. Maps, trail descriptions, and backcountry permits are available at the visitor center.

Wheeler Peak Summit—

This is the most strenuous of the several hikes near and at the end of the Wheeler Peak Scenic Drive. The trail climbs 2,900 feet from the trailhead at the "horse loading" parking area—elevation 10,161 feet to the top of Wheeler Peak at 13,063 feet. The route to the peak covers 5 miles one way and usually requires 6 to 8 hours to make the 10 mile roundtrip. The trail up Wheeler Peak is well marked. During the first mile the trail is fairly level with only a 200-foot elevation gain until you reach the fork to the left that takes you to Stella Lake. The 2nd mile is also fairly gentle as the trail winds through groves of limber pine and, in summer, hillsides covered with purple-flowering mint. As you reach the 2nd mile, the trail leaves the tree line of stunted spruce and junipers and continues across rock and boulder fields in an ever steeper climb across the 600-million-year-old quartzite rock, which was laid down during the early Cambrian period when seas covered the area. Finally, after what seems like a maximum effort, especially given the thin air at 13,000 feet, you reach the summit. The 360-degree panoramic view is well worth the effort. To the west and east desert valleys with lonely towns and ranches are visible in the distance beyond the sheer dropoff on the west and the 1,500-foot cirque wall formed over millions of years by glaciers atop Wheeler Peak. Also visible to the west are four distinct mountain ranges— the Schell Creek, Egan, Grant and White Pine mountains. The Snake Range, of which Wheeler Peak is the tallest, stretches to the south with Baker, Pyramid, and Mt. Washington peaks usually visible. Be prepared for this hike with plenty of water, warm clothing, and good hiking boots.

FESTIVALS AND EVENTS

National ATV Jamboree
last week in June
If you have to ask what ATV (all-terrain vehicle) means, this probably isn't for you. But for hundreds of people who enjoy bouncing around on the small four-wheel motorized vehicles, the National ATV Jamboree is a must. Riders come from all over North America to participate in the four-day event along the 200-mile Paiute ATV Trail, which crosses three mountain ranges, winds through rugged canyons, and spans sections of Utah's deserts. For information call **1-800-441-4ATV or (801) 743-5154.**

Days of the Old West Rodeo
2nd weekend in August
This three-night rodeo is held the 2nd weekend in Aug. in Delta; **(801) 864-3888.**

Leamarado Day
Labor Day
This annual celebration began on Aug. 15, 1945, when word was received that the Japanese had surrendered and World War II was over. The news that husbands, sons, and brothers would soon be returning was met with such joy that the people of Leamington marched through the town, beating on pans and shouting and singing. Later in the day, everyone gathered in the park for a potluck dinner. After a few years, the date of the celebration was changed to Labor Day, an amateur rodeo was added, and attendance continued to increase. Leamarado Day is an old-fashioned celebration, with a morning program, a barbecue at noon, and children's sports in the afternoon, followed by the rodeo.

———— OUTDOOR ACTIVITIES ————

ALL-TERRAIN VEHICLES

Little Sahara Recreation Area—
(See the **Nephi and Eureka** chapter.)

Piute ATV Trail—
This 200-mile-long trail over public lands loops through four Utah counties and provides ATV riders with a unique opportunity to spend days exploring central Utah. Promoted by tourism officials and ATV dealers, the Piute ATV Trail is actually a series of trails across backcountry roads, mining roads, and newly cut tracks. The trail is also the site of the National ATV Jamboree, described in the Festivals and Events section. Fillmore is located at the northern end of the trail and provides accommodations, good access, ATV repairs, information, and maps; **1-800-441-4ATV** or **(801) 743-5154.**

BOATING AND FISHING

Gunnison Bend Reservoir—
Locals brag about the excellent water-skiing on Gunnison Bend Reservoir, where a large peninsula juts into the lake and prevents large waves from forming. The lake is quite shallow, making for warmer water temperatures for which swimmers, water-skiers, and sail-boaters are thankful. The reservoir is located east of Delta, on the Sevier River. To get there, take the road to Sutherland out of Delta to 3000 West, then turn left and follow the road for 2 miles to the reservoir.

Yuba Lake—
While Yuba Lake would not merit a high rating by *Field and Stream*, it is a favorite fishing and boating spot for local residents, perhaps because it is the only body of water within a 50-mile radius on which to launch a boat. Located north of Scipio, off Interstate 15, exit 188, coming from the south, or exit 202 from the north, Yuba Lake is a reservoir on the Sevier River, which was constructed by local farmers between 1903 and 1907. Enlarged in 1916, the lake stores irrigation water for farms and ranches along the river and when full has a surface area of more than 10,000 acres along 20 miles of the Sevier River. The lake has a year-round campground, with 28 camping spaces, and a marina near the dam at the north end of the reservoir.

GOLF

Sunset View Golf Course—
In 1983, floods covered the original Delta Golf Course, so county officials decided to build a new course above the Sevier River on the sage and rabbit brush plain 2 miles north of Delta on Hwy. 6. The course is flat and easy, with fairly wide fairways . A few trees have been planted along the edges of the course, but what is impressive is that you can see for miles and miles in every direction. The course is an island in a sea of sagebrush, and the horizon is broken only by Pahvant Butte and mountain ranges in the distance. Although serious golfers need not go out of their way to play this course, it offers enough challenge to make it fun for most. No reservations are necessary. It is also the least expensive public golf course in Utah; **(801) 864-2508.**

HIKING

Great Stone Face—
Locals claim that a formation in the ancient lava flow south of Delta is the spitting image of Joseph Smith, founder of the Mormon church. A short hike leads to the rock formation. To get to the trail, drive south out of Deseret on Hwy. 257 for 3 miles and then turn west, just south of Fort Deseret, onto a dirt road. After a 4-mile drive, you reach the end of the road, where you can park your vehicle and hike up to the Great Stone Face. Also along the dirt road, you pass the Gunnison Massacre Site Monu-

ment. Near this spot, Captain John W. Gunnison and seven members of his 12-man group were killed by Indians while the men were carrying out a survey for a trans-continental railroad along the 40th parallel.

Pavant Butte—

Rising 1,000 feet above the valley floor, this extinct volcano is one of the area's most interesting geologic features. The ancient waters of Lake Bonneville covered about half of the butte before vanishing at the end of the last Ice Age, about 10,000 years ago. Remnants of the ancient shoreline can be seen on the butte. Other remnants are man-made. In 1923, the construction of a wind-powered electric power plant began but was never completed. Two concrete pylons and a large underground structure remain, stimulating a thousand questions about why it was attempted, why it failed, and how it was to operate. To reach the butte drive south on Hwy. 257, which begins 6 miles west of Delta off Hwy. 6-50. Follow 257 for 16 miles to Clear Lake, then turn east and drive through the Clear Lake State Water-fowl Management Area for 11 miles. Take the lefthand fork where the roads branch and follow it in a northeasterly direction for about 4 miles to Pahvant Butte. Coming from the east, head west out of Fillmore toward Flowell on Hwy. 100. After about 4 miles, before you reach Flowell, Hwy. 100 turns north. Continue north for about 10 miles until you reach a dirt road that turns west. Follow the dirt road for about 7 miles to Pahvant Butte. Park your vehicle and hike up the old road on the south side of the butte. After an elevation gain of about 400 feet in .7 mile, you reach the old wind-power plant ruins. Here, the road ends, and it is another .5 mile to the summit.

Tabernacle Hill—

Like Pahvant Butte, Tabernacle Hill was formed by volcanic eruptions between 12,000 and 24,000 years ago, while Lake Bonneville was still in existence. Cinder and ash built a circular ring of tuff more than 200 feet high above the waters of Lake Bonneville. The lava hill is said to resemble the Salt Lake Tabernacle, hence its name. From the end of the road, it is a 2.5-mile hike to Tabernacle Hill. The easiest way to reach the hill is to take Interstate 15 to Meadow, exit 158, then follow the gravel road west then northwest for 8 miles. Look for a domed-shaped hill south of the road.

HORSEBACK RIDING
Utah Blue Phantom Trail Guides—

Headquartered in Fillmore, Blue Phantom Trail Guides offer a choice of one-to five-day trail rides, from the third week of June to the third week of Sept. John Cooper, a life-long resident of Fillmore, except for two years he spent living on the Navajo Reservation, offers a variety of tours from a base camp on the Pavant Range of the Fishlake National Forest below Mt. Katherine. Among the options are participating in an authentic cattle drive on a working cattle ranch or fishing the difficult-to-reach, left-hand fork of Chalk Creek, home to native trout. Groups are limited to 14, with a usual minimum of 5—although smaller groups can be arranged. The trips are fully catered, with horses and gear provided; **175 South 100 West, PO Box 192, Fillmore, UT 84631; (801) 743-6884.**

SWIMMING
West Millard County Swimming Pool—

Located at the northern end of Delta, just west of the Middle School are pool, racquetball courts, and a weight room. Admission fee charged. Open Mon.–Fri. 5:30 am–9 am, 1:30 pm–5 pm, and 6 pm–10 pm., Sat. 10 am–10 pm. **200 East and 300 North; (801) 864-3133.**

—————————— SEEING AND DOING ——————————

HISTORIC SITES

Cove Fort—

Modern interstate travelers can appreciate the strategic importance of Cove Fort when they realize that the 1867 fort was constructed at what would become, more than 100 years later, the intersection of Interstate 15 and Interstate 70. The 100-foot-square, 18-foot-high, dark basalt fort, situated about halfway between Fillmore and Beaver, was constructed during the Black Hawk Indian War to provide safety for Anglo travelers from Indian attacks. The 50 miles between the two settlements, across steep hills, was often too far for slow-moving wagons to cover in a day. Other forts were built by early Utah settlers, but none have been preserved or restored. In the late 1980s, the fort was donated to the LDS Church. After a thorough renovation, the fort was reopened to visitors in 1992. Tour guides conduct you through the fort, and each of the 12 rooms—six on the north and six on the south side walls—have been outfitted with pioneer-era furnishings. The second phase will include construction of a blacksmith shop, a barn, icehouse, chicken coops, and pig pens in an attempt to recreate the environment of a small Mormon settlement in 19th-century Utah. To reach the fort from the north, take exit 135 off Interstate 15; if you are coming from the south, take exit 132. If you are headed west on Interstate 70, watch for the road that heads north to Cove Fort, about a mile before the intersection with Interstate 15. Open daily 10 am–dusk. No admission charge.

Fort Deseret—

Constructed in response to the Black Hawk War in 1866, and located about 60 miles to the north of Cove Fort, Fort Deseret was built under orders from Brigham Young to "fort up" for protection against the Indians. Unlike the rock-solid Cove Fort, which took seven months to construct, the 10-foot-high 550-foot-square adobe walls of Fort Deseret were completed in nine and a half days by 98 men divided into two teams competing against each other to see which one could finish its two sides first. After it was completed, the fort was never used for protection against the Indians, in fact, the Indians used the fort themselves. The adobe walls of the abandoned fort are slowly dissolving, but visitors can still see the ruins, which are located 2 miles south of Deseret on Utah Hwy. 257.

Territorial Capitol Building—

It is hard to believe that the founder of Salt Lake City, Brigham Young, decided that the capital of Utah should be moved south 150 miles. Yet, four years after Salt Lake City was established, Young appointed a commission to select a new, more centrally located, site for the capital, and, in Jan. 1852, he concurred with their selection of Fillmore. Truman O. Angell, architect for the Salt Lake City Temple, designed an elaborate capitol building, with four wings and an imposing dome. Construction on the south wing began during the summer of 1852. Despite the use of federal appropriations, work progressed slowly, and it was not until three years later that the south wing was dedicated and used as the location for legislative sessions from 1856 to 1858. In 1858, Young was replaced as territorial governor by Alfred Cumming and Salt Lake City became the territorial capital once more. The Fillmore capitol was used for public meetings, social events, offices, a school, a jail, and a theater, but by the turn of the century had fallen into disuse. In the 1920s, the Daughters of Utah Pioneers spearheaded its preservation as one of that organization's first projects. Today it is maintained and operated as one of the historic sites in the Utah State Parks system. The original rooms, including the upstairs assembly room, have been preserved. An excellent collection of pioneer artifacts is on display. The Territorial Capitol Building is open daily (except Thanksgiving, Christmas, and New Year's Day) 9 am–6 pm Memorial Day–Labor Day and 9 am–5 pm the rest of the year. The building is located in the center of the block behind the Millard County Courthouse between Main St. and 100 West and Center St. and 100 North. Southwest of the building, on the same block, is the 1867 rock schoolhouse.

Topaz Japanese-American War Relocation Camp—

During World War II, 9,000 Japanese-Americans from the San Francisco area were relocated to the Central Utah War Relocation Center, as part of a wartime policy that saw the removal of about 100,000 West Coast residents of Japanese ancestry. The Utah camp, named Topaz for the nearby Topaz Mountain, was one of 10 camps located in the western states. Constructed at an estimated cost of $5 million by 800 men, Topaz required another $5 million annually for operation. The camp covered 19,800 acres, but most of the 623 buildings were located within a 42-block, 1 mile-square area. The camp opened on Sept. 11, 1942, and closed in Oct. 1945. Critics of the relocation camps argue that they were a waste of money and manpower since Japanese-Americans proved their loyalty time and time again to the US. Defenders point out that relocation was a justifiable precaution in the aftermath of the sneak attack on Pearl Harbor and that the Japanese-Americans could be protected from violence fostered by anti-Japanese sentiment. At Topaz, 3,000 students attended school, a newspaper was published, and young men volunteered for service in the US Army. After the war, the camp was dismantled; today, only a few foundations and traces of streets can be seen. The Japanese-American Civic League erected a monument at the camp site in 1976. Many of the Japanese-Americans sent to Topaz chose to remain in Utah after the war, and they and their families return to the site from time to time to remember the dark days of World War II. For all Americans, the camp raises the oft-debated question whether a nation dedicated to the pursuit of life and liberty can or should arbitrarily restrict the freedoms of its citizens without due process. Located 15 miles northwest of Delta, the easiest way to reach the site is to head west out of Delta on Hwy. 6 and, after crossing the viaduct, continue west toward Sutherland and Abraham. As you drive north and west, you will see green signs with white lettering pointing toward Topaz Relocation Site. The paved road continues for 10 miles to 7000 West and 3000 North, where you continue north on a gravel road for 1.5 miles to 4500 North. Turn left (west) onto 4500 North and follow it for 3.8 miles to the site. There is no visitor center, no telephones or facilities at the site, and no admission charge.

MUSEUMS

Great Basin Museum—

This museum is operated by the local historical society and housed in a building previously used as a maintenance shop for the local telephone company. Exhibits and artifacts focus on the agricultural history of the area, its geology, and the World War II–era Japanese Relocation Camp at Topaz. Work is under way to restore one of the original recreation buildings from the Topaz Camp and to reconstruct an original barracks adjacent to the Great Basin Museum. Some of the other interesting items include a huge steam engine used to operate a sawmill, a telephone switchboard that was used until 1984 for local calls, and a trunk full of hats from past decades that children can try on and model in front of the mirror. Admission is free. Open Mon.–Fri. 9 am-5 pm., and Sat. and Sun. 1 pm–5 pm. **328 West 100 North in Delta; (801) 864-5013.**

ROCK HOUNDING

Rock hounds and fossil hunters will think they've arrived in heaven when they reach the Delta area. A wide variety of rocks and fossils can be taken from land administered by the Bureau of Land Management, including, obsidian, topaz, red beryl, bixbyite, sunstones, garnet, muscovite, pyrite, quartz, geodes, agate, trilobite fossils, and petrified wood. Visit the **West Desert Collections** at **298 West Main in Delta** to see what can be found and to ask about directions to a dozen or more locations around Delta. The local BLM office in Fillmore is also a good source of information; **Warm Springs Resource Area, PO Box 778, Fillmore, UT 84631; (801) 743-6811.** The two most popular areas are Topaz Mountain and Antelope Springs.

Antelope Springs—

Here you can find trilobite fossils. These Cambrian Age anthropods were compressed between stratified layers of shale millions of years ago and have become the unofficial symbol for the area. (You can pick up a trilobite souvenir pin at the Delta Area Chamber of Commerce.) Antelope Springs is located west of Delta. Take Hwy. 6 and 50 west from Delta for 12 miles, then turn north onto a gravel road and follow it northwest for about 8.5 miles.

Topaz Mountain—

As you might guess, Topaz Mountain is a source of topaz crystals. The mountain is mined commercially, but a section has been reserved for amateur collectors. Topaz Mountain, with an elevation of 7,113 feet, is located at the southern end of the Thomas Range about 40 miles northwest of Delta. To reach the mountain, drive northwest on Hwy. 174, past the Intermountain Power Plant and continue to the end of the paved highway.

SCENIC DRIVES
Notch Peak Loop Backway—

Notch Peak in the House Range Mountains is a 9,700-foot peak of exposed sedimentary rock layers said to be the largest limestone formation in Utah. It dominates the surrounding desert, and the Notch Peak Loop road provides access to a little-traveled part of Utah. The 50-mile loop circles the House Range Mountains on a maintained gravel road that passenger cars can use, except when blocked by snow or heavy rains. The loop begins 43 miles west of Delta on Hwy. 50 and heads north.

TOURS
Intermountain Power Plant—

Opened in 1987, IPP is one of the world's largest coal-fired power plants. The plant employs more than 600 people and is located a few miles north of Delta. Just look for the two 300-foot-tall buildings and a 710-foot chimney. Guided tours of the plant can be arranged by calling the public relations department; **(801) 864-4414.**

WILDLIFE
Clear Lake State Waterfowl Management Area—

This marsh area of the West Desert with its water, cattails and bulrushes, provides a good habitat for a variety of wetland species, including ducks, egrets, coots, curlews, and other birds. To reach the management area, drive west from Delta on Hwy. 6 for 5 miles, then turn south onto Hwy. 257. Continue for just under 16 miles, then turn east onto a gravel road and continue for 6 miles to the viewing area.

—————— WHERE TO STAY ——————

ACCOMMODATIONS
Best Western Motor Inn—$$

Eighty-three rooms. Coin laundry and swimming pool. Located at the junction of Hwys. 6 and 50. **527 East Topaz Blvd., Delta; (801) 862-3882.**

Best Western Paradise Inn—$$

Dining room, coffee shop, heated indoor swimming pool, and whirlpool, 80 rooms. Near exit 167 off Interstate 15; **800 North Main, Fillmore; (801) 743-6895.**

Budget Motel—$ to $$
Twenty-nine rooms. 75 South 350 East, Delta; (801) 864-4533.

Fillmore Motel—$ to $$
Twenty rooms. 61 North Main, Fillmore; (801) 743-5454.

Killpack Motor Lodge—$ to $$
Seventeen rooms. 201 West Main St., Delta; (801) 864-2734.

Spinning Wheel Motel—$ to $$
Sixteen rooms. 65 South Main, Fillmore; (801) 743-6260.

CAMPING
PRIVATE
Antelope Valley RV Park—
Ninety-six full hookups, laundry facilities, restrooms, showers, a children's play area, volleyball court, and horseshoe pits. 766 West Main, just west of the overpass; (801) 864-1813.

B Kitten Klean Trailer Park—
Open year-round; 30 sites, all with complete hookups. 200 East Main in Delta; (801) 864-2614.

Fillmore KOA Campground—
Opened in 1993, the campground has 50 hookups, 7 large tent sites, and 5 camping cabins, a game room, playground, Laundromat, showers, and convenience store. Located at the south end of Fillmore off Interstate 15 at exit 163; (801) 743-4420.

Wagons West Campground—
The largest private campground in the area: 50 trailer sites, 42 of which have complete hookups. Showers, laundry facilities, convenience store. Open year-round. 501 North Main in Fillmore; (801) 743-6188.

PUBLIC
Oak Creek—
Located 4.5 miles east of Oak City, off Hwy. 135, in the Fishlake National Forest; 23 trailer and tent sites. Open late May–Sept.

Also see Public Camping at Little Sahara Sand Dunes and Yuba Lake in the **WHAT?** chapter.

WHERE TO EAT

DELTA
Bennett's Drive In—$
Burgers and ice cream. Open Mon.–Sat. 11 am–10 pm. 303 East Main; (801) 864-2511.

Chef's Palace, Too—$$ to $$$
Steak dinners, open from 5:30 pm–10 pm. Mon–Sat. 225 East Main; (801) 864-2421.

Delta Valley Farms Restaurant—$
This cheese factory has a restaurant that serves homemade soups, burgers, sandwiche,s and daily specials. The cheese store is open 8 am–6 pm where you can purchase fresh curd or any of the 15 varieties of cheese they make. The restaurant is open Mon.–Sat. 10 am–4 pm. Located 2 miles north of Delta on Hwy. 6; (801) 864-3566.

Jade Garden—$ to $$
American and Chinese food. Open daily for breakfast, lunch, and dinner. Located across from the Best Western Motor Inn at 640 Topaz Blvd.; (801) 864-2947.

Mariza's Cosina—$
Mexican fast food. Open 10:30 am–10:00 pm; 340 East Main; (801) 864-2928.

Pizza House—$ to $$
Pizza, soup and salad bar, sandwiches, and pasta dinners. Open Mon.–Sat. 11 am–10 pm. 69 South 300 East; (801) 864-2207.

FILLMORE
Cowboy Cafe—$ to $$
Open daily 6 am–10 pm. 30 North Main; (801) 743-4302.

Deano's Pizza—$ to $$

Homemade pizza, chicken, sandwiches, salad bar. Open Mon.–Sat. 10 am–10 pm. **90 South Main; (801) 743-6385.**

Garden of Eat'n—$ to $$.

Located at the Paradise Inn. Open for breakfast, lunch, and dinner; **(801) 743-5414.**

SERVICES

Bureau of Land Management—

Warm Springs Resource Area, PO Box 778, Fillmore, UT 84631; (801) 743-6811.

East Millard Travel Council—

PO Box 848, Fillmore, UT 84631; (801) 743-5154.

Delta Area Chamber of Commerce—

80 North 200 West, Delta, UT 84624; (801) 864-4316.

Saltair, the largest and most famous bathing resort near the Great Salt Lake, was built in 1893 and known for its roller coaster, dance floor, and buoyant waters. Photo courtesy of Utah State Historical Society.

Sanpete Valley

While many communities claim that they have been saved by being astride the interstate highway system, the fact that the interstate bypasses Sanpete Valley has actually saved what has been described as the best concentration of houses, structures, and cultural elements reflecting 19th-century Mormon Utah in the state. Another factor that has helped preserve the character of the valley is the lack of one major city, as is more typical in the rest of rural Utah. The towns of Moroni, Mt. Pleasant, Ephraim, Manti, and Gunnison, with about 1,500 to 3,000 residents each, all have institutions vital to the valley. Moroni, named for the last prophet in the Book of Mormon, has a turkey-processing plant that employs 200 permanent and 500 seasonal employees. The birds sent to the plant are raised by over a hundred turkey farmers in Sanpete Valley. Mt. Pleasant was the sheep capital of Utah around the turn of the century. Those prosperous times are still evident in the well-preserved main street, the magnificent houses, and Wasatch Academy, a 125-year-old private institution that draws students from all over the country. Ephraim has Snow College, which, with its 2,000 students, is a major cultural and economic institution in the valley. Seven miles south of Ephraim is Manti, the county seat of Sanpete County and the location of one of four pioneer Mormon temples constructed in Utah. Named for a city in the Book of Mormon, Manti, which dates from 1849, was the first Mormon settlement in the Sanpete Valley. To the south lies Gunnison, a small town named for Captain. John W. Gunnison, who was killed by Indians along the Sevier River in 1853. It was established in 1859 and, since the mid-1980s, has been the home of a regional state prison facility. Other communities within the valley include Fairview, Fountain Green, Spring City, Wales, Sterling, and Mayfield.

Sanpete Valley is part of the Great Basin geographical province and lies between the mountains of the Wasatch Plateau on the east and a western range known by four different names—the Sanpete Plateau, Gunnison Plateau, the West Mountains, and the Sanpitch Mountains—with lower hills to the north and south. The valley is more than a mile high, with most communities located at around 5,800 feet. The dominant physical feature is Horseshoe Mountain, which rises to more than 11,000 feet east of the valley. The horseshoe shape of the mountain, an ice-cut scallop, is easy to recognize from most locations in the valley. Water flowing down from the mountains to the east forms the Sanpitch River, which flows south through the valley to its junction with the Sevier River near Gunnison. Most of the river is appropriated for culinary and irrigation use within the valley. Although

Interstate 15 bypasses Sanpete Valley to the west, about 30 miles on the other side of the Sanpitch Mountains, Hwy. 89 does pass through the valley, providing good access for travelers.

There are about 15,000 residents in Sanpete Valley and ties to the valley run deep. Many are descendants of 19th-century Mormon converts from Denmark and Sweden. As one 10-year resident of the valley observes, "They really are a tough breed of people, to stay and not be enticed to better areas to farm or to the city for jobs. Most were born and raised here and really like it. Professionals would like to come back after college if they could make a living. Some return for retirement, and if they leave they're invariably buried back here."

In 1987, Gary B. Peterson and Lowell C. Bennion published *Sanpete Scenes: A Guide to Utah's Heart.* The book won national recognition by the American Association for State and Local History. The beautifully illustrated history and guide includes a discussion of the Mormon landscape, architecture in Sanpete Valley, the geography, and the economy. It provides a close and personal look at Sanpete Valley and is highly recommended. The book is available at the Ephraim United Order Cooperative Store, in most local bookstores, or by writing Basin Plateau Press, PO Box 155, Eureka, UT 84628.

HISTORY

On November 19, 1849, Isaac Morley and 50 families of Mormon settlers completed the 125-mile journey from Salt Lake City into the Sanpete Valley. The group was sent by Brigham Young after Ute Chief Walker invited the Mormon leader to establish a colony alongside Chief Sanpeetch and his people in the Sanpete Valley. The names Sanpitch, for the river, and Sanpete, for the valley and county, come from the undefined Ute word "Sanpeetch." The original 220 settlers were later supplemented by others, and during the first decade, communities were established from Gunnison to the south and Fairview to the north. Sanpete Valley had a special attraction for Scandinavian converts to the Mormon Church. Most were from Denmark, but Sweden and Norway were also well represented. Sanpete Valley became known throughout Utah as Little Scandinavia, and with good reason: Of the total population, first-and second-generation Scandinavians comprised 80 percent in 1870 and 70 percent in 1880. In 1870, Ephraim counted 94 percent of its population as Scandinavian. The Jutland region of Denmark was an especially fruitful field for Mormon missionaries in the 1850s. Converts there came mostly from peasants who did not own the land they farmed and felt oppressed by their landlords as well as clergy of the Lutheran Church, who exacted tithes from everyone and charged substantial fees for important sacraments such as marriages and burials. Mormon missionaries, promising free land in America, a new religion in which the people could participate as leaders, and the means to reach Utah through the Perpetual Emigration Fund, converted hundreds of Danes and sent them off to America on board ships from Copenhagen and Hamburg.

But, even in Sanpete Valley, the streets were not paved with gold. The Scandinavians worked hard as farmers and helped Sanpete Valley win renown as the "granary of Utah." But limited land and water resources demanded alternatives. Many Sanpeters moved south to settle the Sevier Valley and east into Castle Valley. Those who stayed turned to sheep, sugar beets, and later turkeys for a livelihood. But the Mormons were not the only ones who saw the promise of a new life in Sanpete County. In 1911, 12 Jewish farmers representing 200 immigrant families arrived in Utah and created an agricultural colony 3 miles west of Gunnison, which they named Clarion. Clarion was one of 40 such Jewish settlements in America, established as part of an international back-to-the-soil movement among Jewish people seeking to leave the crowded urban slums and inhuman sweatshops of the East for the countryside.

Human conflict and natural obstacles brought an early end to Clarion, but some Mormons of Sanpete County saw the attempt as part of a grand unfolding strategy that would usher in Christ's Second Coming. Even more important in this strategy was the completion of the Manti Temple on May 21, 1888. Eleven years in construction, the Manti Temple was the third temple in Utah. Situated roughly halfway between the temples of St. George and Logan, which were 400 miles apart, the Manti Temple was the most centrally located temple for most Utahns until the completion of the Salt Lake Temple in 1893. The temple united and strengthened Sanpete Mormons more than anything, save perhaps, the Atlantic crossing and wagon or handcart trek to Utah. The temple remains the focus of community life in Sanpete Valley. The Mormon Miracle Pageant held at the Manti Temple in July involves hundreds of valley residents and draws hundreds of thousands of spectators.

GETTING THERE

Fairview and Mt. Pleasant, in the north end of Sanpete Valley, are approximately 100 miles south of Salt Lake City. Manti, the county seat of Sanpete County, is 123 miles south of the state capital. Hwy. 89 passes through the valley and is reached from Salt Lake City by taking Interstate 15 south to Spanish Fork (exit 256), then heading southeast on Hwy. 6 for 13 miles to its junction with Hwy. 89. Another option is to continue on Interstate 15 south to Nephi and take Hwy. 132 east, then southeast into Sanpete Valley, through Fountain Green and Moroni to its junction with Hwy. 89. If you are traveling on Interstate 70, exit in Salina and head north on Hwy. 89 for about 15 miles to Gunnison or 30 miles to Manti.

FESTIVALS AND EVENTS

Scandinavian Festival
Friday and Saturday
before Memorial Day

The Scandinavian Festival, held in Ephraim, is an eclectic kind of event that borrows from Sanpete Valley's Scandinavian tradition but includes a healthy dose of American activities. Scandinavian activities include a Little Denmark supper, a Scandinavian breakfast, old-world crafts, and an ugly trolls contest. Other activities include historical tours, an art show, craft booths, food booths, a tennis tournament, a fun run, a rodeo, a parade, and a selection of festival royalty.

Spring City
Heritage Days
Saturday before Memorial Day

Also held the Saturday before Memorial Day, you might consider Spring City Heritage Days a part of the Scandinavian Festival since many visitors to Sanpete County take in both events. Spring City is only 10 miles north of Ephraim. This is one day a year when owners of most of the historic homes in Spring City open them as part of the home tour. The home tour runs from noon–5 pm, and you can spend most of the time visiting the houses, especially if you park your car and walk—an activity that gives you glimpses and insights into the community that are missed just driving around the town. It also helps you work up a good appetite for the turkey barbecue that follows the tour.

Independence Day
July 4th

Mt. Pleasant, Moroni, Manti, and Gunnison all hold July 4th celebrations, with parades, races, games, art shows, dances, and, at Mt. Pleasant, a rodeo.

Mormon Miracle Pageant
July 10th through July 20th

Every year, thousands travel to Manti to witness the Mormon Miracle Pageant held on Temple Hill. The pageant opens with the notes of a trumpet from atop the spires of the Manti Temple, and then, during the next two hours, the early history of the Mormon Church is presented. While most of the audience are members of the Mormon faith and familiar with the scenes that are portrayed, those not of the Mormon faith are offered a warm welcome and will find the pageantry, if not the story, an unforgettable experience. Foreign language interpretation of the dialogue is provided at no cost to those who request it. The first pageant in 1967 attracted 2,000 people for the single performance. Now, the audience tops 30,000 each night of the pageant. A third of the audience uses the 10,000 chairs provided, while the rest of the audience views the pageant from blankets and lawn chairs they bring themselves.

The gates for seating open at 6 pm, and the performance begins around 9:30 pm. I recommend arriving at 6 pm and taking a blanket with you and spreading it across the seats or the spot of ground that you want to claim for the evening, then heading downtown for dinner and a tour of the historic sites in the town. Since seats are available on a first-come, first-served basis, this system of saving or reserving seats is a long-standing tradition at the pageant. Be sure to bring jackets and sweaters since the evenings can be cool. The event seems to involve the entire community as performers or in assisting with seating, parking, and food. Visitors arrive early in Manti to walk around the historic community and to partake of the famous barbecued turkey dinner prepared by local residents. The dinner is available from 5 pm–8 pm at the Manti Tabernacle at 1st South and Main St. and at the Manti

Stake Center located at 300 South and Main St. A pancake, ham, and eggs breakfast is also served from 7 am–10 a.m. There is no cost for the pageant, although there is a modest charge for breakfast and dinner.

Lamb Day Festival
end of July

There is no better place than the small town of Fountain Green for a lamb day festival. Usually held the 3rd Sat. in July or the Sat. just before Utah's State Holiday, the 24th of July, this festival recalls the days when Sheep County was another word for Sanpete County. Thousands of head of sheep brought the elusive prosperity to the county, and although you will see more turkeys in Fountain Green than sheep these days, the wooly animals are still an important part of the local economy. The festival features a lamb show, a lamb auction, a lamb barbecue, a parade, children's activities, and a dance.

Sanpete County Fair
3rd week in August

The fair, held in Manti, includes livestock judging, exhibits, a horse show, a car show, a demolition derby, a parade, a western concert, and a two-night rodeo.

———— OUTDOOR ACTIVITIES ————

ALL-TERRAIN VEHICLES

Pinchot ATV Trail—

The 4-mile Pinchot ATV Trail was developed in 1993. The trailhead is located in Twelve Mile Canyon, east of Mayfield, and consists of two major loops, the easternmost of which extends to the summit ridge. The Twelve Mile Canyon road was closed in 1984 by landslides, and part of the trail follows the old road.

BIKING

Ephraim Canyon—

This is a steep climb that demands caution because of the vehicle traffic up the canyon. But if you want a leg-burning ride into one of Utah's most beautiful canyons, give this route a try (see Scenic Drives in the Seeing and Doing section).

Sanpete Valley—

There are a series of back roads that connect most of the Sanpete Valley communities. It is fun to get on your bike and explore these roads and see where they take you. Take time to ride through the communities to see the historic homes and buildings and perhaps spot as many of the Mormon Landscape elements as you can (see Historic Sites in the Seeing and Doing section). For example, you can start at the north end of the valley and follow the southernmost street in town as it heads east. After it leaves Fairview, it turns south and you can follow the road on to Mt. Pleasant (7 miles). From Mt. Pleasant, follow Hwy. 89 south about 2 miles to the turnoff to Spring City (4 miles). Follow the road into Spring City, take time to ride the streets of this historic town (see Historic Sites in the Seeing and Doing section), then continue south out of town. You return to Hwy. 89 just north of Ephraim. From Ephraim you can continue south along Hwy. 89 to Manti (7 miles) and Sterling (6 miles) and even Mayfield (4 miles) and Gunnison (8 miles) in the south end of Sanpete County and return the way you came, or arrange for a shuttle to pick you up. Another option is to backtrack from Ephraim a few miles on Hwy. 89 to the Pigeon Hollow Junction. Take Hwy. 132 north to Moroni, (8 miles from the junction) then back to Mountain Pleasant (9 miles) and Fairview (5 miles). From Moroni you can also continue north to Fountain Green (12 miles), where you can turn east to follow a road that connects with Hwy. 89 just north of Fairview (about 12 miles). Another alternative to this latter route that adds a little distance and takes you to the town of Wales (the home of some 19th-century coal miners from Wales who were sent to Sanpete Valley by Brigham Young) is to ride north from the Pigeon Hollow Junction to Chester (4 miles), leave Hwy. 132, and turn west on Hwy. 116 and ride to Wales (4 miles). From Wales there's a road that heads straight north to Fountain Green (10 miles).

Skyline Drive—
This is a popular mountain bike ride in the summer (see Scenic Drives in the Seing and Doing section).

For rentals and equipment, as well as directions and advice for other area rides, check at **Skyline Cycle** at **71 South Main in Ephraim; (801) 283-5007.**

FISHING
Palisade Lake—
Open for year-round fishing, Palisade Lake is the most accessible fishing spot in the Sanpete Valley. Only human-powered boats are allowed on the lake. The northern end of the lake is a popular swimming area, but there is plenty of room for anglers looking for the trout that inhabit the lake. The lake is part of Palisade State Park and is located 2 miles east of the small community of Sterling off Hwy. 89.

GOLF
Palisade Golf Course—
This is an ideal course for those traveling with motor homes and trailers. You can camp at Palisade State Park and walk to the golf course. The course is fairly easy, with wide fairways, very little water, and few sand traps. It has some of the best maintained greens to be found anywhere. To reach the course, drive south out of Manti along Hwy. 89 for 5 miles to the town of Sterling and watch for the turnoff to Palisade State Park. The golf course is located about 2 miles off the highway. Generally, the course is not too busy, but reservations can be made by calling **(801) 835-GOLF.**

HIKING
You can pick up a list of hiking trails on the Manti-La Sal National Forest at the US Forest Service Headquarters on Main St. in Ephraim. Here are some favorite trails.

Canal Canyon Trail—
This is a scenic and good hiking trail with the possibility of seeing plenty of wildlife, including deer, elk, and just possibly a black bear. The trail is steep but only a couple of miles long. The trailhead is located southeast of Spring City. If you are driving, you will need to park your car a mile or so west of the trailhead and hike up the road.

Maple Canyon—
Two trails: the 1.5-mile Maple Canyon Loop Trail and the 2-mile Left Fork Trail can be hiked in a few hours. The Maple Canyon Trail is easier, offers a nice viewpoint, and passes a natural arch. The Left Fork Trail is steep and strenuous, as it climbs to the top of the plateau for a nice scenic view. Indian Petroglyphs are located near the trail. They have been fenced for protection, so keep a careful eye out for them. The trailhead is located in Maple Canyon Campground, which is reached by following the road west out of Moroni for about 8 miles.

Oak Creek Trail—
This 8-mile long trail requires a shuttle from the trailhead on top of the Skyline Dr. above Fairview. Oak Creek enters the Sanpete Valley about 3 miles north of Fairview.

TENNIS
There are six lighted tennis courts behind Manti High School, which is located west of the temple across Hwy. 89. In Ephraim, there are six lighted courts open to the public in the center of the Snow College campus.

SEEING AND DOING

CULTURAL ACTIVITIES

Snow College—

Named for Lorenzo Snow, president of the Mormon Church when the institution was founded as a church academy in 1888, and for Erastus Snow, an important southern Utah church leader, Snow College became a state institution in 1932. Students come from all over the state because of the college's reputation and to enjoy the small-town life in Ephraim. The school has excellent theater and music departments. Theater productions staged by the college are an important part of the cultural life of Sanpete Valley. The football and basketball teams have a long tradition of success.

HISTORIC SITES

MORMON LANDSCAPE

Visitors to Utah have long recognized that the human-made landscape that resulted from the Mormon encounter with the western environment has distinctive characteristics; it has produced a recognizable geographical region that writers such as the late Wallace Stegner and geographer Donald Meinig have called Mormon Country. Another student of the Mormon region, Richard V. Francaviglia, published a book in 1978 entitled, *The Mormon Landscape* that summarized the characteristics that make up this unique cultural geographical region. Since the publication of Francaviglia's study, others have added to his list. While some of these elements, notably the irrigation ditches, have disappeared since Francaviglia completed his study, Sanpete County remains one of the best locations to view this distinctive landscape heritage. To view these elements, simply drive the highways, streets, and back roads of the county and see how many of them you can identify: rectangular or square fields intensively irrigated, used for hay pasture and separated by unpainted cedar posts and barbed wire fences; erect, spirelike lombardy poplar

trees; cattle and sheep grazing in the same pasture; hay derricks (often called Mormon stackers; the main feature of the hay derrick is the long pole used to stack hay); biblical and Book of Mormon names for communities; the town's initial on a hill; north—south—east—west orientation of streets; ragged, overgrown streets and a rural feeling to the community because open pastures, barns, granaries, and haystacks are found right in town; roadside irrigation ditches; unpainted barns; inside-outside granaries—grain storage sheds where the studs are on the outside walls rather than on the inside as in most structures to allow easier emptying of the granaries and better support of the weight of the grain pushing against the walls; shed rooftops made of loose or baled hay; an LDS ward chapel; cemeteries with Mormon themes on the tombstones, and footstones on the older graves made out of the same materials as headstones with the deceased's initials on them; a parallel canal system consisting of the first ditches, which were diverted low in the creeks to irrigate river bottom land, and the later highline canals constructed to carry water to the bench lands.

Historic Houses of Sanpete—

One of the most obvious and prolific elements of the Mormon Landscape are the stone, adobe, and brick houses built to house the early settlers of Sanpete Valley and their children. Sanpete County has the highest concentration of these houses, which were constructed in the second half of the 19th century. The houses demonstrate much about the lifestyle and priorities of the early residents. The early homes were symmetrical structures that characteristically used the Federalist and Greek Revival styles with which pioneers were familiar. As Scandinavian immigrants arrived, they built in a style similar to that of their homeland. These "pair houses," usually one story, were marked by a central entrance and two rooms of equal size on each side. Beginning about 1890, a second generation of homes, different from the earlier straight-lined homes of the pioneer, was constructed. The asymmetrical Victorian houses were now distinguished by their gingerbread ornamentation, eye-brow windows, porches that broke up the square facade, and a look that suggested the pioneer era was over. A third generation of houses was built between 1910 and 1930; these reflected the influence of the bungalow style of architecture. These houses can be found in all Sanpete communities, but Spring City, Manti, and Ephraim seem to have the greatest number.

Canute Peterson House—There was no individual more important in the early history of Sanpete County than Canute Peterson. Born in Norway in 1824, he immigrated to the US as a teenager with his parents and joined the Mormon faith at the age of 18. He returned to Scandinavia three times to do missionary work, and many of those he converted followed him to Sanpete County. He was selected president of the Sanpete Stake, an ecclesiastical position that carried responsibility for all of the Mormon churches in the Sanpete Valley. As husband to three wives, Peterson constructed the surviving rock home in 1869 for his first wife and had two places of concealment built into the house. Known as "polygamy pits" because they were used to hide from federal marshalls seeking to arrest polygamists, one pit was built under the dining room floor as a diversion for a larger one located in a small sitting room next to the kitchen. The home is now owned by Nadine Nibley who has a craft shop on the first floor. **10 North Main.**

Ephraim Co-op Building—As you visit this building, look for the inscription "Ephraim U.O. Mercantile Institution," and a beehive encircled by the words, "Holiness to the Lord." If it seems strange to apply a religious connotation to mercantile activities, just remember that for 19th-century Mormons, the building of the Kingdom of God included both. In an effort to promote self-sufficiency, Brigham Young directed Mormons to avoid buying all imported goods, especially those sold by non-Mormon merchants. He argued that the wealth that such merchants would acquire could better be used to build up the Mormon Church and the Kingdom of the Saints in Utah. A solution to the problem was seen in cooperative merchandising, a plan where Mormons would establish a wholesale house or parent institution that would purchase all goods imported to Utah. In turn, each Mormon settlement would establish a cooperative retailing store that would deal only with goods delivered by the parent institution from Salt Lake City. The Ephraim United Order Cooperative Store, constructed of native oolite limestone in 1872, is Utah's best remaining example of one of these stores and one of Utah's best examples of the Greek Revival style. The cooperative was located on the main floor, and the second story was used for dances, theatrical productions, meetings, and for the first classes of what is now Snow College. After standing vacant for years, the building was restored and opened in 1990 by the Sanpete Trade Association for handicrafts and other locally produced items under the name Sanpete Sampler. Open Mon.–Sat. 10 am–6 pm. **96 North Main.**

Next door to the Co-op Building, the old mill has been restored as an art gallery, with work by local artists on display and available for purchase. Open noon–5 pm. **100 North Main, Ephraim; (801) 283-6654.**

Great Basin Experimental Range Station—Now known as the Great Basin Environmental Education Center and operated by Snow College, this historic experimental station was constructed by the US Forest Service between 1912 and 1914 at at the base of Haystack Mountain, 10 miles up Ephraim Canyon. The station was the first of its kind in the US and perhaps the world. For three-quarters of a century, the dozen or so buildings served as a field headquarters for scientists interested in studying ecology and the management of range and forest lands. The founder and first director of the station, Dr. Arthur W. Sampson, pioneered the science of range management. By arrangement with the forest service, Snow College took over maintenance and operation of the station in 1992. Under the leadership of director David Lanier, the college has preserved the buildings, established a museum, maintained the historic laboratory, and uses the facilities for summer school classes and special conferences. The station is one of the stops on the Ephraim Canyon Scenic Drive described later in this chapter.

John Patten House—Perhaps the oldest remaining residence in the Sanpete Valley, the Patten House was built in the mid-1850s for John Patten, an early convert to Mormonism and one of the first settlers of Manti in 1850. Built of native limestone using sticky adobe to hold the stone together, the house has an almost medieval style to it. The building has been renovated and houses a museum maintained by the Manti Daughters of Utah Pioneers. You can visit the full basement, main floor, and upstairs. The hours vary, and it may be necessary to call the telephone number posted on the door. **95 West 400 North, Manti.**

Manti—

A few years ago, the honor students at Manti High School prepared a walking map of Manti that lists 27 historic buildings and sites in the community. The free map is available at the Manti city offices at the John Patten House.

Manti Temple—When Brigham Young visited the infant settlement of Manti in 1850, he pointed to the hill where many of the settlers had spent the first winter and prophesied that a temple would one day be built on the hill. Twenty-five years later, in 1875, Brigham Young dedicated the temple site and construction work began. The temple was completed in 1888 and is one of Utah's most remarkable buildings. Constructed of native oolite limestone quarried at the site, the temple presented its

architect, William Folsom, with a special problem. The temple was located on the hill overlooking Manti to the west, yet Mormon temples are oriented with their front to the east in anticipation of the resurrected Christ coming from that direction. The solution was the construction of two different towers. The larger slightly higher one on the east faces the mountains, while the western tower appears to be level with the eastern tower and gives the appearance that the building faces west. As you travel along Hwy. 89, the temple looms over the valley like an ancient, strangely designed cathedral or castle. A blending of the Gothic Revival, French Renaissance Revival, and the French Second Empire styles, according to Mormon architectural historian Paul Anderson, the temple is "perhaps the crowning achievement of 19th-century Mormon architecture." In the 1980s, the interior of the temple was renovated, however, unlike the Logan Temple, which was completely gutted and modernized in the 1970s, great pains were taken to ensure that the interior work of the pioneer artisans was preserved. Only faithful members of the LDS faith are permitted inside the temple, but a visitor center just outside the temple provides information.

Mt. Pleasant Main St.—The two blocks that make up the northern side of Mt. Pleasant's Main St. are the best-preserved, turn-of-the-century, commercial district left in Utah. The prosperous sheep industry stimulated the construction of the two- and three-story buildings, which, in recent years, city fathers have seen as a real asset and have encouraged their preservation. Located on the south side of the street is the district's oldest building, the 1875 Liberal Hall. The hall was built by disaffected Mormons and was the first home for the Wasatch Academy, established by Presbyterians in 1875 to educate and "christianize" Mormon youth. If you are traveling on Hwy. 89, it is easy to miss Main St., since it intersects the north-south highway at its western end. Watch for the junction of Hwy. 89 and Hwy. 116.

Spring City—The large number of 19th-century buildings in the well-preserved Mormon agrarian village of Spring City led to it being has been listed in the National Register of Historic Places on Oct. 20, 1980. If you want to see the inside of some of these remarkable buildings, mark the Sat. before Memorial Day on your calendar and come for Spring City Heritage Days and Home Tour. If that date doesn't fit your schedule, you can call **(801) 462-2211,** or write **Kaye Watson, 187 North Main, Spring City, UT 84662** to arrange a tour for small groups. In any case, a visit to Spring City still should not be missed. Since Spring City was "discovered" by architectural historians in the 1970s, the 850 residents have grown accustomed to visitors driving around town shooting pictures of their homes and buildings. The town of Spring City has prepared a pamphlet that highlights 60 of the buildings' and town's histories. Available from Kaye Watson or at the Ephraim Cooperative Building. The community has attracted several artists including Bennion's Horseshoe Pottery.

Wasatch Academy—Established in 1875 by Reverend Duncan McMillian, a Presbyterian minister who came west to regain his health and who had been assigned missionary work among the Mormons of Sanpete Valley, Wasatch Academy continues as one of the state's most prestigious private academies. The academy operated in Liberal Hall on Main St. until it outgrew the building and relocated two blocks to the south in 1888. The entire school, with its 20 buildings, has been listed in the National Register of Historic Places. The oldest buildings are the 1893 Lincoln Hall, 1895 President's House, and the 1900 Indiana Hall.

MUSEUMS

Fairview Museum—
The old Fairview schoolhouse has been home to the Fairview Museum since 1966. The museum is an eclectic collection of more than 2,000 objects on exhibit that relate to the history of Sanpete Valley and its citizens. A recent addition is the replica of an ancient Columbian mammoth, which was uncovered in the mountains west of Fairview in 1988. The museum is free, although donations are accepted. Open Memorial Day weekend–Oct., Mon.–Sat. 10 am–5pm and Sun. 1 pm–8 pm. You can make special arrangements to see the museum during the rest of the year by contacting the Fairview City Hall.

SCENIC DRIVES

Eccles Canyon Scenic Byway—
If you are traveling in a passenger vehicle that you don't want to subject to the rigors of Skyline Drive, you can see some of the same beautiful scenery by taking Hwy. 264 from Hwy. 31, above Fairview east to Clearcreek and its junction with Hwy. 96. The road is 16 miles long and worth driving in both directions. The high mountain valleys with their pine-forested, steep-sloped mountains could be mistaken for Germany's Black Forest.

Ephraim Canyon—
The forest service has prepared an excellent 16-mile automobile tour booklet for Ephraim Canyon to the 10,500-foot summit near the junction with the Skyline Drive Rd. The road climbs nearly a mile in elevation from downtown Ephraim to the summit and passes through five life zones: Upper Sonoran, characterized by piñon and juniper; Transition with ponderosa pine; Canadian, where aspen and fir are found; Hudsonian, with spruce and fir; and Alpine tundra, near the summit beyond treeline. Pick up the free Auto Tour Guide at the forest service office in Ephraim, or if you are starting the tour from the top of the canyon, a box with guides is located at the summit. Along the drive, there are nine signs and pullout areas where you can learn much about the human and natural history of the Wasatch Plateau. Highlights include the Sanpete overlook, where you can look down on the Sanpete Valley from an elevation of 8,400 feet; the Great Basin Experimental Range Headquarters

(see Historic Sites in the Seeing and Doing section); the stream gauge, at an elevation of 8,900 feet, where the stream flow is measured by forest rangers; and the alpine meadows and millions of wildflowers that bloom in summer between 9,000 and 10,500 feet. The road is graveled and easily passable for automobiles, except when wet or blocked by snow. The road begins at 400 South and Main St. (Hwy. 89) in Ephraim. Turn right at the first stop sign as you head east on 400 South, then follow the road eastward up the canyon.

Skyline Drive—

One of Utah's most remarkable drives, Skyline Drive follows the 10,900-foot summit of the Wasatch Plateau, which divides the Great Basin from the Colorado Plateau. Most travelers cover the 30-mile section from Hwy. 31 to the Ephraim-Orangeville Rd., which offers an eagle's view of the Sanpete Valley below and Mt. Nebo and other mountains in the distance. Extensions from the heart of the drive take you farther south to the Mayfield-Ferron Rd., and even as far as Interstate 70. An 87-mile northern extension from Hwy. 31 intersects with Hwy. 6 at Tucker, but is only passable with a four-wheel-drive vehicle. The drive is impassable in winter. There is an abundance of wildlife along the drive. In summer, you can watch eagles soar overhead and deer bound through the trees on either side. In the winter, the road is used by snowmobilers and cross-country skiers.

WHERE TO STAY

ACCOMMODATIONS
BED AND BREAKFASTS
Brigham House Inn Bed and Breakfast—$$$

Owned by Helen and Lee Thurston and located in one of Manti's pioneer rock homes, the four nonsmoking rooms all have private baths and antique furnishings. There are two communal living rooms. The Indian room upstairs has Indian rugs, blankets, and other antiques, while the downstairs room has a player piano. **123 East Union, Manti, UT 84642; (801) 835-8381.**

Cedar Crest Inn—$$$

Looking to the top of the hill east of Sterling you can see the Cedar Crest Inn. If you were in Europe, this would have been an ideal location for a castle, and that is probably what inspired a German immigrant named Mussig to select the spot for his home, instead of building below on the more level bench land in Sterling. The feeling at Cedar Crest is certainly one of a rural German inn. An old German linden tree, which grew from a seed brought by Mussig from his homeland adds charm, and each of the nine rooms at Cedar Crest Inn has a balcony with beautiful views of the orchards and flower gardens. The rooms are all non-smoking and have private baths. Breakfast is served in the dining room and includes apple crepes and eggs Benedict as specialties. Other special features are the "cookie jar," where guests can help themselves any time, and a library with about 200 videos where guests can select up to four movies to watch in their rooms. The inn is operated by Ron and Dori Kelsch and is located 5 miles south of Manti at **Palisade Lake and State Park Rd.; (801) 835-6352.**

Ephraim Homestead Bed and Breakfast—$$$

This unique homestead consists of two buildings; the House, and the Granary. The former is an 1880s cottage with two bedrooms, one full and one half bath, a parlor, a dining room, and a kitchen; the latter is an 1860s Scandinavian cabin with a bedroom, full bath, and kitchen. Be sure to look at the photograph album of the house before it was rescued from certain demise in 1978 by Sherron and McKay Andreasen, who opened the bed and breakfast in 1986. The house and cabin are full of antiques that recall another era, including a Danish bed and operational wood-and coal-burning stoves; you feel you have actually gone back in time. A typical hearty breakfast consists of pancakes with warm apricot syrup made from home-grown apricots. A nighttime treat is also served such as apple crisp or pie. All rooms are nonsmoking. **135 West 100 North, Ephraim, UT 84627; (801) 283-6367.**

Grist Mill Inn—$$ to $$$

The historic grist mill at the mouth of Manti Canyon dates from the 1850s and has 3-foot-thick stone walls. It has been converted into a delightful bed and breakfast with eight guest rooms, each with a private bath. The creek flows just south of the house. If you like the sound of the water, Joanie Ferrin has a couple of south-facing rooms where you can let the water sing you to sleep. You can also sit on the stream banks or gaze at the star-filled sky through a telescope on the balcony. From the front porch, you have a magnificent view of the Manti Temple in the distance. Located east of Manti. **780 East Canyon Rd.; (801) 835-MILL.**

Mansion House Bed and Breakfast—$$ to $$$

By Utah standards, this Victorian-style home, built in the 1890s for James Larsen, a prominent Utah sheepman, is a mansion. The hand-painted ceilings, scrolled oak staircase, and stained glass windows have been preserved, and the home converted into a bed and breakfast with four bedrooms, each with a private bath. All rooms are nonsmoking. Owners Denis and Terri Andelin are congenial hosts. **298 South State St., Mt. Pleasant, UT 84647; (801) 467-3031.**

Manti House Inn—$$$

Built in 1880 to house skilled workers who came throughout central and southern Utah to help construct the Manti Temple, the Manti House Inn is constructed from the same oolite limestone as the temple and other buildings in Manti and Sanpete County. After the construction workers left, it changed hands several times until it fell into disrepair. In 1983, the building was renovated by Jim and Sonya Burnidge and opened as one of the area's first bed and breakfasts. In 1992, the Burnidges sold the

inn to Beverly and Charles Futrell, who fell in love with it when they spent their honeymoon in Manti in 1989. The inn's bridal suite has a balcony and hot tub. The other five rooms all have private baths. All rooms are nonsmoking, and guests can enjoy an in-house spa, ice cream parlor, and a hearty country breakfast. **401 North Main St., Manti, UT 84642;, (801) 835-0161.**

W. Pherson House Bed and Breakfast—$$ to $$$

This turn-of-the-century electic Victorian-style house built for Willard Pherson has been an Ephraim landmark for more than 100 years. Now owned by Karen Graser and used as a bed and breakfast, the Pherson House offers three nonsmoking bedrooms with a shared bath. (The bathtub invites long leisurely soaks.) **244 South Main St., Ephraim, UT 84627; (801) 283-4197.**

Yardley Inn—$$ to $$$

Located in a remodeled, turn-of-the-century Victorian home, guests are faced with a hard choice: whether to take breakfast in the formal dining room or have it served in bed. Gill and Marlene Yardley are the owners of the inn which has five bedrooms and with a private bath and cable TV in all the rooms. The suite has wood-burning fireplace, private balcony, and white marbled Jacuzzi with room for two. In addition to the full breakfast included, you can arrange for a candlelight dinner. There is an outside deck and hot tub room. Inside, guests can enjoy the library, the music room, and a large living room, and are welcome in the old-fashioned kitchen. Also ask about the mystery weekends. **190 South 200 West, Manti, UT 84642; (801) 835-1861 or 1-800-858-6634.**

MOTELS

Manti Country Village—$$

Thirty units. **145 North Main in Manti; (801) 835-9300.**

Travel Inn Motel—$$

Fourteen units. **330 North Main in Ephraim; (801) 283-4071.**

SCANDINAVIAN HUMOR

If you spend any time in Sanpete County, you will soon begin to hear about the humor of early Scandinavian pioneers from Denmark, Sweden, and Norway. The humor ranges from the nicknames they gave each other, to humorous incidents involving their use of the English language and their unmistakable accents, to elaborate stories involving social relationships and situations that brought out their individual human characters. As you travel around Sanpete County looking at the buildings they built, the homes in which they lived, the churches where they worshipped, and the fields they worked, you might want to reflect on a people that could laugh at themselves and who were not inclined to take the actions of their neighbors too seriously. The following is just a taste of the Scandinavian humor as it relates to nicknames and one of my favorite Sanpete characters, Old Okerman.

NICKNAMES

In an area where practically everyone shared his Scandinavian name with several other people, the Jens Jensens, Neils Andersons, Hans Hansens, Lars Larsen, Olof Ottosons, Peter Petersons, and others with commonly shared names were given nicknames by their peers that stayed with them all their lives, and for some became more real than their given name. For example, a man arrived in Ephraim and informed a group of Danes gathered around the post office that he was looking for a man named Jacob Jensen. No one could help him, but the stranger persisted, indicating he had his address. "He lives in the South Ward, four blocks east of Main Street. Are you sure you don't know Jacob Jensen?" Finally a light came on as Jake Butcher, one of the old-timers, scratched his head and said, "Hell, that's me." Others were given names like Painter Hansen, Dan Wheelmaker Jensen, Chris Cellar, Chris Tallerass Christensen, Big Mart, Dirty Mart, Soren Chickenheart, Faithful Andrew, Long Peter Peterson, Olof Coffee Pot, False Bottom Larsen, Chris Golddigger, Stinkbug Anderson, Fat Lars, Peephole Soren, Alphabet Hansen, Absolutely Anderson, Bert Fiddlesticks, Otto By-Yingo Anderson, Pete Woodenhead, Little Peter, and Salt Peter.

OLD OKERMAN

One LDS bishop had to contend with Old Okerman, a habitual drunk. After berating him for his drinking problem in front of a group of other church members the church leader asked if Okerman had anything to say for himself. He responded sadly, "Vel, Biscop and Brodders, you haf all de time asked me how much visky I haf drunk, and scolded me for drinking it; but you nefer did ask me how tirsty I vas."

Old Okerman had run up against the Mormon church teaching known as the "Word of Wisdom," which strongly discouraged the consumption of alcohol, tobacco, tea, and coffee. This proved to be a real trial for the coffee-loving Danes. At the funeral of one Dane, the speaker reported that his friend had gone to that "happy hunting ground where there is no pain nor tears—nor Word of Wisdom." On another occasion when members of the congregation could stand and express their thoughts in the church meeting, one member boasted that he did not use coffee, tea, liquor, or tobacco and claimed that these things were only for the "Yentiles" (Gentiles—or non-Mormons). When he sat down, another brother jumped up and asked, "Brodders and sisters, vy iss it dat all the good tings shall be for the Yentiles?"

CAMPING
PRIVATE
Yogi Bear's Jellystone Park—

The only private campground in the Sanpete Valley, don't let the name discourage or encourage you. Located off Hwy. 89, .25 mile northeast of the Manti Temple, the campground serves many visitors to the temple. There are 54 sites, 20 of which have complete hookups, and 15 tent sites. Flush toilets, showers, and a laundry. Open from mid-May–end of Sept.; **(801) 835-2267.**

PUBLIC

Most of the public campgrounds are located east of the Sanpete communities in the mountains of the Wasatch Plateau. Access to these campgrounds is by way of the canyons that open into the Sanpete Valley.

Ephraim Canyon—

Off Hwy. 29, 8.5 miles east of Ephraim, Lake Hill Campground has 9 sites. Open mid-June–mid-Sept.

Fairview Canyon—

Located on forest service land 10 and 12 miles east of Fairview, off Hwy. 31, are two small campgrounds: Gooseberry, with 6 trailer sites and Flat Canyon with 13 sites. Open mid-June–mid-Sept.

Manti Canyon—

Nine camping sites located in the Manti Community Campground, 7 miles east of Manti on the Manti Canyon Rd. Open mid-June–early Sept.

Mayfield Canyon—

Twelve Mile Flat Campground has 16 sites. Located 19 miles east of Mayfield at an elevation of 9,800 feet, the campground is open July–early Sept.

Palisade State Park—

Located 2 miles east of Sterling, the state park offers 53 camping units with modern wheelchair-accessible restrooms and showers. The camping units are located along Palisade Lake, within easy reach of fishing and swimming facilities at the lake, the adjacent 9-hole golf course, and nearby hiking trails.

WHERE TO EAT

Sanpete Valley needs a good restaurant to go with its historic buildings, beautiful mountains, popular community college, and fine bed and breakfast inns. The local sources of lamb and turkey, the wonderful recipes that circulate around the valley, and the Scandinavian tradition offer the basics for a unique dining experience. But, until that happens, the following restaurants are the best that Sanpete has to offer.

Backroads Restaurant—$ to $$

Open daily for breakfast, lunch, and dinner. 7:30 am–10:30 pm. **70 North Main, Mt. Pleasant; (801) 462-3111.**

Chad's City Cafe—$ to $4

Open daily for breakfast, lunch, and dinner. Mon.–Sat. 6 am–10 pm, Sun. 7 am–9 pm. **350 North Main, Ephraim; (801) 283-6364.**

China Gate Cafe—$ to $$

Open daily for lunch and dinner. 11:30 am–9 pm weekdays, until 10 pm weekends. **290 North Main, Ephraim; (801) 283-4614.**

Fat Jack's Pizza—$ to $$

81 South Main, Ephraim. Open daily 11 am–10:30 pm. **(801) 283-4222.**

Manti Country Village Restaurant—$ to $$

Open Mon.–Sat. 6 am–10:30 pm; Sun. 7 am–8 pm. **145 North Main St., Manti; (801) 835-9550.**

Stu's Home Plate—$ to $$

Open daily 6:30 am–9 pm weekdays; 6:30 am–10 pm on weekends. **215 North State, Fairview; (801) 427-9300.**

Richfield

Richfield is the major commercial center in central Utah. The city, which lies at an elevation of 5,280 feet and has a population of 5,600, is the county seat for Sevier County and the gateway to Fish Lake. Richfield sits in a valley bordered by the Pahvant Range on the west and the Wasatch and Fishlake plateaus on the south. The valley's most dominant feature is 11,227-foot Monroe Mountain, southeast of town. Historically the most important feature of the valley has been the Sevier River, which flows north out of Marysvale Canyon to provide irrigation water to the farms along its banks. While Richfield is the center, Salina, located at the mouth of Salina Canyon, is also an important community because it sits on the historic route out of the Great Basin and into Colorado Plateau country to the east. Other settlements in the valley include Redmond, Aurora, Sigurd, Venice, Glenwood, Annabella, Central, Monroe, Elsinore, Joseph, and Sevier. To the south, also along the Sevier River, are Marysvale, Junction, and Circleville in Piute County. Piute County, with a population of 1,500 and only 754 square miles in size, is one of Utah's smallest counties. Two important reservoirs, Otter Creek and Piute Reservoirs, are found there. Piute County was the boyhood home of the famous western outlaw Butch Cassidy.

HISTORY

The Richfield area was heavily used by prehistoric peoples. Excavations at Sudden Shelter, east of Salina on Ivie Creek, indicate that this site was occupied for more than 7,000 years. Most of the communities in the area, including Richfield, were established in former Fremont villages. Like their neighbors, the Anasazi, the Fremont people were farmers but tended to live in pithouses and to rely heavily on hunting and gathering. They made pottery, but are best known for their spectacular rock art. They occupied the Richfield area from about the time of Christ and reached the height of their civilization about AD 1000. Around AD 1250 traces of their culture began to disappear, perhaps absorbed into another tribe's. By AD 1500 they were completely gone. The culture of this people is documented at the Fremont State Park just off Interstate 70 in Clear Creek Canyon and in Capitol Reef National Park. During the late 1820s, fur trappers, including Jedediah Smith and others, crossed the area. What is now Sevier County lay squarely along the Old Spanish Trail, which ran from Santa Fe to California and was used by travelers between 1830 and 1850. Those using the trail left the Colorado Plateau and entered the Great Basin by way of Salina Canyon. At the mouth of Salina Canyon, they encountered the Sevier River and followed it the length of the valley. Mormons settled near Richfield and other locations beginning in 1864, but these early settlements were abandoned in April 1867 during the conflict with the Ute Indians known as the Black Hawk War. Resettled in 1871, Richfield grew rapidly to become a regional center.

By 1891, the Denver and Rio Grande Railroad reached Salina and a decade later was extended through the entire valley to Marysvale. The railroad proved a boon to the agricultural economy of the area and made mining possible at places like Kimberly in the Tushar Mountains. But Kimberly was not like earlier hell-raising, rip-roaring mining camps. As one former resident recalled, "Kimberly was too small and not rich enough to get the drifters...and the 'boys' were too close to home to 'cut up' much." Although Kimberly was not another Virginia City or even a Park City, the area still has an exciting history.

GETTING THERE

Richfield is located on Hwy. 89 and Interstate 70. The 160 miles to Richfield from Salt Lake City may be driven via Interstate 15. From the interstate four routes lead to Hwy. 89, which you can follow all the way to Richfield: (1) Take exit 261 at Spanish Fork and follow Hwy. 6 for 13 miles to its junction with Hwy. 89, then turn south; (2) take exit 224 at Nephi and follow Hwy. 132 to its junction with Hwy. 89 just north of Ephraim; (3) take exit 222 at Nephi and follow Hwy. 28 south to Levan and on to its junction with Hwy. 89 at Gunnison; or (4) take exit 188 at Scipio and follow Hwy. 50 to its junction with Hwy. 89 and Interstate 70 at Salina. Coming from southwestern Utah on Interstate 15, take exit 132 at Cove Fort onto Interstate 70 and follow the Interstate east to Richfield.

———— FESTIVALS AND EVENTS ————

Independence Day Celebration

July 4th

The 4th of July in Richfield features a parade down Main St., food, races, and activities at the park, a dance in the evening, and a fireworks display. The celebration also features performances of an historical pageant, A Field of Stars, which depicts events from the American Revolution including the Boston Tea Party, Paul Revere's Ride, and the Battle of Bunker Hill. For information call **(801) 896-4513.**

OUTDOOR ACTIVITIES

ALL-TERRAIN VEHICLES

Utah ATV trails are unique, not only because of the varied and beautiful terrain through which they pass but because of the hundreds of miles of public land open to ATVs. You can leave the trail and obtain gas, lodging, and supplies at nearby communities, such as Salina, Richfield, Marysvale, and Junction. You can learn to drive an ATV in less than an hour; after that you will be able to reach areas that would otherwise be inaccessible to many people. ATVs are proving more and more popular with senior citizens and others who like access to remote areas of Utah's mountains and deserts, without the physical strain of long, multiday hikes.

If you have your own ATV, maps of the **Piute Trail** can be acquired at the US Forest Service Office in Richfield. For guided ATV tours (ATVs provided) or ATV rentals contact:

Big Rock Candy Mountain River and ATV Trips—
PO Box 161, Richfield, UT 84701; (801) 326-4321 (May 15–Sept. 30) or **(619) 379-4616** (Oct.–May 14).

Bushwackers—
At the general store along Hwy. 89 in Marysvale, UT 84750; (801) 326-4549.

Iron Hoss ATV Trail Rides—
Marysvale, UT 84750; (801) 326-4553.

Piute ATV Trail Tours—
Operating out of the Grass Valley Inn in Koosharem, half-day and one- to three-day rides over the Paiute ATV Trail are offered. Box 440014, Koosharem, UT 84744; (801) 638-7563.

Piute Trail OHV Service—
Box 155, Aurora, UT 84620; (801) 529-7825.

BIKING

Clear Creek Canyon Narrows—
This loop begins 2 miles west of Fremont Indian State Park and follows the old highway through the Clear Creek Canyon Narrows for 13 miles to Service Rd. 114. Here you can either return the way you came or follow the service road as it passes beneath Interstate 70, across Shingle Creek, and continues for another mile to an old grass airstrip and a fine view of the 12,000-foot Tushar Mountains to the south. The trail heads east across Fish Creek, which you cross twice, and then runs parallel to Interstate 70 until you come to an underpass; after that it's a 3-mile ride back to the starting point. The ride has a combination of asphalt, gravel, and dirt trails with an elevation gain of about 1,200 feet.

Fishlake—
The Fishlake area offers some beautiful summer and fall rides. The 25-mile Mytoge Mountain Loop, climbs the mountain east of Fishlake from an elevation of 8,845 feet to nearly 10,000 feet. You can begin the ride from the northwest side of Fishlake on Hwy. 25 and ride southwest to Forest Rd. 046 which loops over Mytoge Mountain to the east of Fishlake and then past Crater Lakes onto Forest Rd. 045 which rejoins Hwy. 25 about midway between Fishlake and the Johnson Valley Reservoir. This is an especially beautiful ride through aspen trees in the fall.

Larry Theivagt, a former recreation officer at the Fishlake National Forest, has written a 24-page booklet describing 21 mountain bicycle routes on the Fishlake National Forest. The booklet, "Mountain Bicycle Trails on the Fishlake National Forest," is available from the US Forest Service, Richfield Office, 115 East 900 North, Richfield, UT 84701; (801) 896-9233. Mountain bikes are available for rent at Bushwackers at the General Store in Marysvale; (801) 326-4549.

Richfield to Fremont Indian State Park—

This 46-mile out-and-back ride provides a chance to tour the villages south of Richfield and the Fremont Indian State Park. The route follows along paved roads through the towns of Annabella, Elsinore, Joseph, and Sevier (old Hwy. 89) before heading up Clear Creek Canyon to Fremont Indian State Park (see Museums in the Seeing and Doing section). You can add a little distance and see the community of Monroe if you take Hwy. 118 east from Joseph on your return trip then head north from Monroe to reconnect with Hwy. 89. The ride is generally level, with a gradual climb as you pedal up the canyon to Fremont Indian State Park. Keep an eye out for the rock art along the canyon walls.

Soldier Canyon—

Soldier Canyon takes its name from the time known as the Black Hawk War, during which the local militia fought Ute Indians from 1865 to 1869. During the war at least 25 towns were temporarily abandoned, including Salina and Richfield, and 70 whites were killed. A company of 84 men on horseback pursued the Utes up Salina Canyon after two men were killed in the canyon and their cattle taken. A battle between the militia and Utes left two more whites dead and two wounded before the Utes made their escape to the east. This 18-mile loop follows part of the route taken by the militia as it leaves the city park a mile southeast of Salina on Hwy 89. You ride east on the frontage road for 2 miles to the Soldier Canyon Rd. at the Interstate 70 overpass. Follow the gravel road as it climbs 1,200 feet in about 10 miles before it drops into Gooseberry Valley. Turn onto the Gooseberry Rd. (Service Rd. 640) and follow it as it makes a gradual descent to the Salina Creek Frontage Rd. Follow the frontage road back into Salina.

BOATING AND FISHING

The US Forest Service and Sevier Travel Council have pooled their resources to produce a handy guide, "Fishing Opportunities on the Fishlake National Forest," which lists more than 40 fishing spots. It is available at forest service's **Richfield Ranger District, 115 East 900 North, Richfield, UT 84701; (801) 896-9233.** The following are some of the most popular fishing locations in the region.

Fish Lake—

One of central and southern Utah's largest natural lakes, Fish Lake covers 2,500 acres, with an average depth of 85 feet. The lake is stocked with lake trout, rainbow trout, and splake, while native brown trout are able to sustain their population without planting. Most fishing is done from boats, which can be rented at the Fish Lake Lodge. The lake is extremely popular during the summer. Located at an elevation of 8,000 feet, the lake freezes over during the winter and is an excellent location for ice fishing from Dec–spring. To reach Fish Lake, take Hwy. 24 to the junction with Hwy. 25, then go 7 miles on Hwy. 25 to Fish Lake.

Gooseberry Area—

A number of small reservoirs and ponds in the Gooseberry area are well stocked with trout. To reach the area, take exit 61 off Interstate 70 east of Salina and follow the Gooseberry-Sevenmile Rd. (Forest Rd. 640) to the Gooseberry Campground. Near the campground, Gooseberry Creek is stocked monthly with small rainbow trout and is one of a few opportunities to try stream fishing.

Johnson Valley Reservoir—

Located 3 miles northeast of Fish Lake, this human-made reservoir covers just over 700 acres. Like Fish Lake, it is well stocked with trout and is a popular ice fishing spot.

Otter Creek Reservoir and State Park—

Constructed on a tributary of the Sevier River in the southern end of Piute County, Otter Creek Reservoir was built by local farmers in the 1890s. It is one of the oldest reservoirs in the south-central part of the state. Otter Creek State Park is located at the southern end of the reservoir. Large rainbow and cutthroat trout, have been taken from the reservoir which is a popular fishing location in the summer, with ice fishing in the winter. Fly fishermen can try a large pool below the dam. To reach the reservoir, turn east on Hwy. 62 2 miles south of Junction and drive 10 miles to the reservoir.

Piute Reservoir and State Park—

Located downstream from the Otter Creek Dam, between the towns of Junction and Marysvale, the Piute Reservoir was created in 1908 to impound water for irrigation purposes. The 2,250-acre-foot reservoir is a popular fishing location for cutthroat and rainbow trout. Piute State Park is located at the north end of the lake about 5 miles north of Junction.

GOLF

Cove View Golf Course—

This is one of the older public courses in the southern half of the state, and it is not as well maintained as others. For example, it is still watered by above-ground sprinklers, which stretch in single file down some of the fairways, resembling the lighting apparatus on the end of an airport runway. The clubhouse is nice and clean, but the fairways and greens could use more attention. Still, Cove View is the only public course along Hwy. 89 in the nearly 200 miles between Manti and Kanab. (For travelers along Interstate 70, the next closest course is more than 200 miles away in Grand Junction, Colorado.) Inexpensive, uncrowded, flat, with wide fairways, you can get on just about anytime. The course is located just east of exit 37 off Interstate 70,

just west of the Richfield Airport; **(801) 896-9987.**

HORSEBACK RIDING

Color Country Outfitters—

Hourly rentals and trail rides, as well as hunting and fishing pack trips in the Fish Lake and Dixie national forests can be arranged. **PO Box 49, Sigurd, UT 84657; (801) 425-3598.**

RIVER RUNNING

A 4-mile stretch of the Sevier River through Marysvale Canyon is a great place for a fun-filled 1.5-hour ride on inflated rafts. You can usually make arrangements at the Big Rock Candy Mountain along Hwy. 89, where the trip begins, or contact **Big Rock Candy Mountain River and ATV Trips, PO Box 161, Richfield, UT 84701; (801) 326-4321** (May 15–Sept.) or **(619) 379-4616 (Oct.–May 14).**

SWIMMING

Richfield Community Pool—

Open year-round with lap swimming from 5 am–9 am Mon.–Fri., and open swimming 1 pm–9 pm Mon.–Sat. Admission fee charged. **600 West and 500 North; (801) 896-8572.**

Sunrise Fitness Center—

Has a swimming pool, along with racquetball courts and a weight room. Open Mon–Fri. 6 am–9 pm, closed Sat. and Sun. **80 East 1100 North; (801) 896-6708**

TENNIS

Tennis courts (four courts) are located at **Richfield High School** at approximately **560 West and 100 North.**

SEEING AND DOING

HISTORIC BUILDINGS AND SITES

Big Rock Candy Mountain—

Driving south on Hwy. 89 through Marysvale Canyon, you will see a wonderfully colored mountain of yellow, pink, brown, tan, green, gray, and orange with a lemonade spring—colored yellow by calcium and iron rather than lemons. In 1897, "Haywire Mac" McClintock a brakeman on the railroad that ran through the canyon, wrote a song called "In the Big Rock Candy Mountain." The song was recorded by Burl Ives and Tex Ritter, and its lyrics about chocolate bars, gumdrops, and peppermint sticks has reached the stature of a genuine American folk song. A motel and resort operated on the 200-acre site for decades but closed recently. Efforts are now underway to revive the old resort.

Maximillian Parker Cabin—

Even before Paul Newman and Robert Redford made the hit movie, *Butch Cassidy and the Sundance Kid* in 1969, the Utah-born outlaw was a western folk hero. Stories have circulated throughout southern and eastern Utah for nearly a hundred years of how Cassidy, in true Robin Hood fashion, robbed from the rich to give to the poor. Though many of the stories are apocryphal, it is a fact that Cassidy, born Robert LeRoy Parker in 1866, spent his teenage years on the Parker Ranch, about 2 miles south of Circleville. In 1879, Maximillian Parker purchased the ranch and a two-room cabin from the James family and moved his wife and six children into the homestead. At 13, Robert was the eldest child. Like many rural Utah ranchers, the elder Parker spent much of his time away from the family, earning a livelihood in the mining towns or on the freight roads. He left his eldest son in charge of the ranching operation. Shortly after his 18th birthday, Robert Parker left the ranch for Telluride, Colorado, where he worked at various jobs for five years. On June 24, 1889, Parker, now known as Butch Cassidy, along with Matt Warner and Tom McCarty robbed the Telluride Bank of $31,000. The three men hit the outlaw trail in a big way. Between 1889 and 1900, Cassidy committed robberies in Colorado, Utah, Wyoming, and Idaho. When an attempt to negotiate an amnesty agreement with Utah officials failed, Cassidy headed east via Texas to New York City where he, Etta Place, and the Sundance Kid sailed for South America in 1901. The two outlaws were reportedly killed in a gun battle in 1909, but many people did not believe the story. Lula Parker Betenson, who was born on April 5, 1884, a few days before Cassidy left home for Colorado, claims that her older brother returned to the family ranch and visited with the family at their Circleville home in 1925. In her book, *Butch Cassidy, My Brother*, Mrs. Betenson recounts the escapades both here and in South America that her brother related to the family with the promise that they not talk about them. (A promise she kept until after her brother's death.) Mrs. Betenson concludes her account noting that her brother lived in the Northwest under the alias Bob Parks, until his death in 1937, at the age of 71. The old Parker Cabin is located on private land, but it is visible from the highway. Set off by the towering Lombardy poplars that, according to Lula Betenson, were planted by her mother with the help of her now famous brother, the ranch is a favorite picture stop for travelers in the area—especially those who know its association with Butch Cassidy.

Piute County Courthouse—

A jewel of a public building, the Piute County Courthouse was constructed of red burnt brick made on-site and placed on top of granite slabs hauled by wagon from nearby Kingston. The courthouse has been in continual use since 1903 and, with its parklike setting, is a popular stop for photographers driving through Junction.

Ralph Ramsay Home—

Operated by Richfield City as a pioneer museum, there are important reasons to visit this historic home beyond the fact that it was built between 1873 and 1874 by my great grandfather. In 1856, at the age of 32, Ralph Ramsay immigrated to Utah from England as a convert to the Mormon Church. That summer, he and his wife Elizabeth spent 15 weeks pulling a handcart 1,400 miles from Iowa City to Salt Lake City. During the journey, two of their children died and were buried along the trail. A master woodcarver, Ralph Ramsay carved the famous eagle atop the Eagle Gate in Salt Lake City and left many pieces of fine furniture in the city, before moving to Richfield in 1872, at the request of Brigham Young. The upstairs of his home was used as a workshop, and his wife operated a pill and herb remedy dispensary out of a small room on the main floor. The house contains some of the wood carvings done by Ramsay. The house remained in the Ramsay family until the death of its long-time occupant, Ettene Ramsay, a granddaughter of the builder. It was donated to Richfield City. It is open Tues.–Fri. from 11 am–4 pm; **57 East 200 North.**

Richfield Walking Tour—

Available at the Richfield Visitor Center and at a number of locations in Richfield at no cost, the pamphlet, "One Mile Walking Tour of Richfield, Utah" identifies 18 sites and buildings along a 1-mile route. This walking tour is an excellent way to get acquainted with the town's history.

MUSEUMS

Fremont Indian State Park—

One of Utah's newest state parks and museums, Fremont Indian State Park was established by the state legislature in 1985 to preserve the archaeological sites and rock art left by the Fremont Indians during their occupation of the area more than a thousand years ago. The museum was completed in 1987 and now houses the material excavated from a large Fremont Village site that was uncovered, in November 1983, during construction of Interstate 70 through Clear Creek Canyon. Working under extreme time pressure, archeologists collected artifacts from what has been identified as the largest Fremont village in Utah. The village includes 80 residential structures and pithouses and numerous storage granaries. Although the freeway construction led to the destruction of the village, Fremont State Park provides an excellent opportunity to learn more about Fremont culture. The visitor center includes exhibits, a replica of a Fremont pithouse, a statue of a Fremont woman (which was constructed using a plaster cast from a well-preserved skull uncovered while digging a natural gas pipeline), and orientation videos. A paved, handicapped-accessible, interpretive trail begins at the visitor center. More than 500 panels of rock art, both pictographs (painted) and petroglyphs (carved), are located along the north and south sides of Clear Creek Canyon and can be reached by the access road and hiking trails. During the summer, keep an eye out for snakes. In winter, deer and bald eagles can be seen here. The park is open daily, except Thanksgiving, Christmas, and New Year's Day, 9 am–6 pm Memorial Day–Labor Day; 9 am–5 pm the rest of the year). Admission fee charged per person or per vehicle. The park is located about 20 miles southwest of Richfield, off Interstate 70. Take exit 23 if you are traveling from Richfield, or exit 17 if you are coming east from Interstate 15 (17 miles to the west). **11550 West Clear Creek Canyon Rd., Sevier, UT 84766; (801) 527-4631.**

SCENIC DRIVES

Cove Mountain Road Scenic Backway—

Another scenic autumn drive is the 25-mile-long graded dirt road across Cove Mountain from Koosharem to Glenwood, just east of Richfield. The road is closed during winter, but during summer and early fall, offers breathtaking views of the Sevier and Koosharem valleys. The backway passes the 1910 Koosharem Guard Station, which was one of Utah's first forest service buildings. It is an interesting reminder of the time when forest rangers traveled into the mountains on horseback and spent weeks alone carrying out their duties. The Koosharem Guard Station is open free of charge to visitors during the summer on a limited schedule.

Fishlake Scenic Byway—

Designated as one of Utah's official Scenic Byways, Utah Hwy. 25 to Fish Lake, is a beautiful, high-country drive that winds through aspen forests, providing good opportunities to view autumn leaves, deer, prairie dogs, and other small forest animals. If you are lucky, you might spot elk or some of the moose that were introduced into the area a few years ago. The drive begins at the junction of Hwy. 25 with Hwy. 24, the road between Richfield and Capitol Reef National Park. It runs for 13 miles around the eastern and northern ends of Fish Lake as far as Johnson Reservoir, where the paved road ends. At that point, you can either retrace your route to Hwy. 25 or continue on the unpaved road southeast from Johnson Reservoir for about 12 miles to its junction with Hwy. 72. This section of the road is part of the Gooseberry/Fremont Road Scenic Backway. From Hwy. 72, continue south about 3 miles to Loa and its junction with Hwy. 24.

Gooseberry/Fremont Road—

Forty miles in length and recently paved, this road runs through the Fishlake National Forest and part of the Wasatch Plateau from Interstate 70 to its junction with Hwy. 72, 2 miles north of Fremont. The road is closed during winter and has steep grades, but it offers one of the best opportunities in central Utah to view autumn leaves. It connects with the Fishlake Scenic Byway at Johnson Reservoir. From Salina, take Interstate 70 east 7 miles to exit 61, then follow the road south.

Kimberly/Big John Road Scenic Backway—

From Fremont State Park, you can take the Kimberly/Big John Scenic Backway, south into the Tushar Mountains. After 7.5 miles, you reach the old mining town of Kimberly. Now a ghost town, Kimberly dates from the late 1890s, when the Annie Laurie Consolidated Gold Mining Company established a cyanide leaching mill to extract gold from ore taken from the mountains. At its height, 500 people lived in the two sections—upper and lower—Kimberly. A daily stagecoach service provided contact with Richfield, and heavily loaded wagons made their way up from the Sevier Valley and back down again. In 1908 the company went bankrupt, and most of the residents moved away. Mining was revived between 1932 and 1938, but today the ruins of the Annie Laurie Mill and other structures are a silent monument to another abandoned mining town.

The road to Kimberly is steep, narrow in sections, and can be rough in some areas; high-clearance vehicles are recommended. From Kimberly, the road continues south through the Tushar Mountains, reaches an elevation of 11,000 feet, then turns east to drop off the mountain and intersect Hwy. 89 at Junction. The drive is approximately 40 miles long and takes about three hours, with a stop in Kimberly. From Junction, you can drive back north about 30 miles, through Marysvale, along the Sevier River through scenic Marysvale Canyon, past the multi-colored Big Rock Candy Mountain, to the junction of Hwy. 89 with Interstate 70.

WHERE TO STAY

ACCOMMODATIONS
BED AND BREAKFASTS

Fish Lake Lodge—$$ to $$$

The present Fish Lake Lodge was constructed between 1928 and 1932. At 360 feet long and 80 feet wide, with a 160-foot-long ballroom, it was considered the largest wooden structure west of the Mississippi at the time of its completion. This is actually the third lodge built at Fish Lake. The first, built in 1911, burned down; the second collapsed into the lake. The rustic lodge includes 25 wooden cabins, some dating from the 1930s and others of recent vintage. Nearby, the Lakeside Resort has 24 units and 24 RV spaces. During the 1960s and 1970s, the lodge went through difficult times, but since 1983, under the guidance of Gary and Stephanie Moulton, it has been rehabilitated. It is now an attractive location for a peaceful stay at one of Utah's best and most beautiful fishing spots. The dining room is open for weekend dinners early in the season and regular hours during the summer; **(801) 638-1000.**

Peterson Bed and Breakfast—$$ to $$$

This bed and breakfast, under the management of Mary Ann Peterson and located in one of Monroe's old homes, has three nonsmoking rooms; generous country breakfast included. **95 North 300 West, PO Box 142, Monroe, UT 84754-0142; (801) 527-4830.**

Rockin' R Ranch—$$$

Would you like to stay at a real working ranch, where they still brand cattle, grow and harvest hay, and preserve old western traditions while still having fun? The Rockin' R Ranch near Antimony, with a 1,000-acre ranch site and 40,000 acres of grazing land in the mountains, is such a place. Guests are provided three meals a day and can participate in a variety of activities, from cattle drives and roundups to hikes, Dutch-oven cookouts, fishing, horseback riding, riding a bucking bull barrel, western dances, songfests, and storytelling. Rockin' R Ranch and Lodge Office, **9160 South 300 West #20, Sandy, UT 84070; (801) 565-8588** or **1-800-767-4386.**

Victorian Inn—$$$

Owned and operated by Ron, Debbie, Sarah, and Rebecca Van Horn, who leave their southern Florida home to spend the summers in Utah. The two-story Victorian house, listed in the National Register of Historic Places, was built in 1896 and restored in 1987. The three rooms are all air-conditioned and have king-size beds and private baths. Children are welcome. Breakfasts are huge family-style all-you-can-eat affairs with fresh fruits, fresh breads. Travel tips available on special places to see in the area and the most scenic routes to get to your next destination. Open mid-June – mid-Aug. **190 West Main St., Salina, UT 84654; (801) 529-7342** or **1-800-972-7183.**

MOTELS

Best Western Apple Tree Inn—$$

Heated pool. Sixty-three rooms, five available with two bedrooms. **145 South Main; (801) 896-5481,** or **1-800-528-1234.**

Days Inn—$$

Heated pool, whirlpool, sauna, and exercise room with a coffee shop and restaurant inside the inn; 51 rooms, some nonsmoking. Located at **333 North Main; (801) 896-6476** or **1-800-325-2525.**

HoJo Inn—$$

Heated pool, whirlpool, and restaurant; 40 rooms. **60 North State in Salina; (801) 529-7467.**

Quality Inn—$$

Swimming pool, laundry room, and some rooms with kitchen facilities; 58 rooms. **540 South Main; (801) 896-5465.**

Romanico Inn—$$

Twenty-eight rooms, some nonsmoking. Located on the outskirts of Richfield, near exit 37 off Interstate 70. **1170 South Main; (801) 896-8471.**

Shaheens Best Western—$$

Heated pool, restaurant; 40 rooms. **1225 South State in Salina,** just off exit 54. **(801) 529-7455.**

Weston Inn—$$

Indoor pool and spa; 40 rooms. **647 South Main; (801) 896-9271.**

CAMPING

PRIVATE

Butch Cassidy Campground—

Located in the south end of Salina, just off exit 54 from Interstate 70. Forty camp sites, but none with hookups. Flush toilets, showers, and laundry facilities; **(801) 529-7400.**

At Fish Lake—

Bowery Haven has 67 sites; **(801) 638-1040.** Lakeside Resort has 24 sites; **(801) 638-1000.** All sites have complete hookups. Flush toilets, showers, and laundry facilities available at both caompgrounds. There is a dump site at Bowery Haven. A maximum 14-day stay at both campgrounds. Open late May–end of Oct.

KOA Campground—

This KOA has 90 sites, most of which have full hookups. Also 50 tent sites. Flush toilets, showers, laundry facilities, and swimming pool. Open year-round. **600 South 600 West, Richfield; (801) 896-6674.**

Salina Creek RV and Campground—

All 22 sites have full hookups. Flush toilets, showers, and laundry facilities. Open year-round. **1385 South Main, Salina; (801) 529-3711**

PUBLIC

At Fish Lake and Johnson Reservoir—

The best and most used public campgrounds are at **Fish Lake** and **Johnson Reservoir** about 50 miles southeast of Richfield, via Hwy. 24 and Hwy. 25. The **Doctor Creek Campground** is located on the southwestern shore of Fish Lake, 7 miles from the junction of Hwy. 24 and Hwy. 25. Twenty-nine RV and 29 tent sites are available from late May–end of Oct. Two miles north on the eastern side of the lake, **Mackinaw Campground,** the largest campground, has 68 RV and 68 tent sites. Situated in an aspen grove overlooking the lake, the campground has drinking water and flush toilets. Five miles up the road near the Johnson Valley Reservoir, the **Frying Pan Campground** has 12 RV and 12 tent sites, drinking water, and flush toilets. Less than a half mile away, the **Piute Parking Campground** has 16 RV sites. If you are driving a large outfit, this is the public campground for you since it accommodates RVs up to 48 feet in length, while the other three campgrounds can handle vehicles no longer than 22 feet. For more information, call **1-800-280-2267.**

At Otter Creek Reservoir—

Camping facilities include 34 RV sites and 6 tent sites. Modern restrooms with wheelchair accessibility, showers, picnic tables, drinking water, a sewage disposal station, a fish cleaning sink, paved boat ramp, and a floating dock adjacent to the campground are available. **(801) 624-3268.**

Near Richfield—

Although Richfield is surrounded on three sides by Fishlake National Forest, there are relatively few public campgrounds in the immediate vicinity. The closest to Richfield is the Castlerock Campground at Fremont State Park. Open year-round, 21 miles southeast from Richfield in Clear Creek Canyon. Fifteen RV sites and camp sites. Drinking water, flush toilets, and handicap facilities.

North of Richfield and 14 miles west of Salina on Highway 50, the Maple Grove Campground offers 11 RV and 11 tent sites on forest service land. The campground has picnic tables and drinking water. It is not far from Scipio Reservoir.

WHERE TO EAT

Fats County Cafe—$ to $$

As the only eating establishment in the county seat of Junction, the Fats offers good home-cooked food at reasonable prices. Specialties include homemade soup (I enjoyed a wonderfully creamy bowl of potato soup with large chunks of potato and parsley), homemade pie, and a nightly special. Breakfasts are hearty—fit for ranchers and others whose main meal comes early in the morning. Lunch includes a basic selection of sandwiches; the dinner menu offers steak, shrimp, and vegetables. The cafe is a rural Utah version of a German Gasthouse, with booths along the walls, a pool table dominating the center of the room, color televisions in opposite corners, an interesting collection of antiques and knickknacks on the walls, and raffle items at a dollar a ticket sponsored by local groups. When I stopped by, the Horseman's Association was raffling off a two-burner campstove and the Jeep Posse proffered a handcrafted doll. Even if this is the only choice in town, it is still a good one. One block west of the courthouse in **Junction. 135 West Center; (801)577-2672.**

Hoover's—$

Established in 1936 by Kenneth and Ada Hoover near the mouth of Marysvale Canyon, this campground, gas station, convenience store, and small cafe has been a landmark on Hwy. 89 for nearly 60 years. Located just south of the Big Rock Candy Mountain. Though the exterior might discourage some, the food—basic sandwiches and burgers—is good and reasonably priced.

Topsfield Lodge—$$ to $$$

Serving steak and seafood dinners after 5 pm, Steve and Madeline Christensen have built up a long tradition of good food. This is where locals go for a special evening. **1200 South Main, Richfield; (801) 896-5437.**

Hamburgers seem to be a favorite food in the Richfield area. The following locations were given high marks by both locals and visitors to the area

Burger Mill—$

Open daily except Sun., May–Sept. 11 AM–10 PM and 11 AM–11 PM Fri. and Sat.; the rest of the year hours are 11 AM–9 PM weekdays and 11 AM–10 PM Fri. and Sat. **499 South Main, Richfield; (801) 896-6666**

Kay's Kafe—$

Although Kay has been the cook there for years and is responsible for the fantastic burgers, the sign still says Larry's Cafe. Open daily during the summer from 7:30 am–7:00 pm. Located at **30 West Main, Circleville; (801) 577-2839.**

Robertson's Roost—$

35 North Center, Elsinore; (801) 527-4129.

SERVICES

Sevier Travel Council—

Open Mon.–Fri. 9 am–5 pm. **220 North 600 West, Richfield, UT 84701; (801) 896-8898** or **1-800-662-8898.**

US Forest Service, Richfield Ranger District, Fishlake National Forest—

Open Mon.–Fri. 9 am–5 pm. **115 East 900 North, Richfield, UT 84701; (801) 896-9233.**

Visitors Information Center—

Open daily during the summer months and located in the Richfield City Park at **390 North Main.**

⹀ Capitol Reef National Park ⹀

For many Utah natives, Capitol Reef is their favorite national park in Utah. Ward Roylance, who devoted much of his life to writing about Capitol Reef, wrote that the park "...features splendid erosive forms-grand cliffs, goblin rocks, carved pinnacles, stone arches, great butte-forms and deep gorges. It combines the fantasy of Bryce and the grandeur of Zion national parks, with more variety of color than either, and is larger than both combined (378 square miles). It also contains archeological and historic resources." The park was set aside to protect the bizarre Waterpocket Fold, named by Almon Thompson in the 1870s for the numerous waterpockets created by erosion in the sandstone formation, of which Capitol Reef is part. The "reef" is an upthrust ridge with a cliff face that rises above its surroundings and stands as a forbidding barrier to travel, hence the name "reef." On top of Capitol Reef itself are white domes of Navajo sandstone that early pioneers thought resembled the dome of the US Capitol in Washington, DC. The Capitol Reef is just one of many smooth-domed formations atop the Waterpocket Fold, a long bulge on the earth's surface. This great hump stretches nearly 100 miles from Thousand Lake Mountain on the north to the southern boundary of the national park where the Escalante Canyon Wilderness meets the Glen Canyon National Recreation Area and Lake Powell. The southern reaches of the park along the Waterpocket Fold are relatively narrow—10 or so miles wide. It is accessible by car along the 47-mile long dirt road that runs down the east side of the fold from Notom to Bullfrog Basin on Lake Powell. Coming from the west, the Burr Trail bisects the Waterpocket Fold and the national park as it connects the Bryce Canyon/Escalante/Boulder area with Lake Powell. The northern section of the park, Cathedral Valley, is remote and can be reached only by four-wheel-drive or high-clearance vehicles. The prehistoric Fremont Indians take their name from the river that flows through Capitol Reef Monument. There are many sites left by this ancient people within the park and rangers have given special attention to their preservation and interpretation. The richness and variety of colors, the towering cliffs, the close confinement of the tight and deep gorges, the historic buildings and orchards of Fruita, the prehistoric Indian rock art, the opportunity to hike through canyons cut through the Waterpocket Fold, and the lack of crowds—at least during the spring and fall—make a visit to Capitol Reef an inspiring, stimulating, and relaxing experience.

HISTORY

Human ties to Capitol Reef have been tenuous, even though they stretch back more than 1,000 years to the prehistoric Fremont Indians who made the area their home. Archaeologists believe the Fremont occupied the area between AD 700 and AD 1300. Because of its continual source of water, the Indians made their home along the Fremont River. In the late 1920s, archaeologist Noel Morss identified the prehistoric residents along the Fremont River as a separate and distinct culture from the more widespread and populated Anasazi group to the south and east. Morss named this newly identified people the Fremont culture because he had done most of his research along the Fremont River. While the scientific origins of the Fremont culture begin within Capitol Reef National Park, the culture area covers a large part of Utah, extending north to the Uinta Mountains and west to the deserts of southwestern Utah. The Fremont people left a wealth of petroglyphs and pictographs. Although similar in many ways, the Fremont are distinguishable from their neighbors—the Anasazi—by their use of leather moccasins fashioned with heels made from the dewclaw of a deer instead of woven fiber sandals; their continued use of pithouse dwellings instead of the large masonry buildings the Anasazi went on to build; the crafting of small unfired clay figurines; and the absence of domesticated dogs and turkeys as could be found among the Anasazi.

Archaeologists speculate that a severe, long-lasting drought and competition for scarce land and resources, or both, account for the demise of these two important prehistoric cultures. By AD 1300, both cultures had abandoned the region. While archaeologists trace the movement of the Anasazi to the Rio Grande and Little Colorado River drainages to the south, it is unclear what happened to the Fremont people. They may have been absorbed by other tribes, no one knows. When government explorers, gold prospectors, and Mormon settlers penetrated the area in the 1870s, they found abundant evidence of the presence of earlier prehistoric peoples. Beginning with Nels Johnson in 1878, several families homesteaded along the Fremont River within the present park boundaries. One of the settlers was Eph Hanks, a polygamist, who perhaps sought refuge from arrest in the remote region of the Fremont River. It was Hanks who realized that the heat-absorbing cliffs and the fertile river bottom land would be ideal for fruit growing and planted the first 200 fruit trees at Floral Ranch, 10 miles south of the visitor center. Nels Johnson followed Hanks' example and planted fruit trees at what was called Junction. Around the turn of the century, when the residents sought to establish a post office, they were not allowed to use the original name as there were already too many Junctions. Instead, they chose the name Fruita, to honor their excellent orchards and vineyards.

Although the population of Fruita was never large (the largest population, 46, was recorded in the 1900, 1910, and 1940 census), a sense of community was established in part with the construction of the one-room schoolhouse in 1896, which still stands. As early as 1910, a few local movers and shakers began to promote the area's potential and were successful in getting the Utah state legislature to set aside 160 acres as a state park. Boosters promoted Wayne Wonderland. Local legislators twisted arms and both kept their crusade for national recognition before the public. Success came in 1937 when Capitol Reef was set aside as a National Monument. Access to the area was enhanced with the construction of a paved road through the area in 1962. After 1937 the monument was enlarged several times until 1971 when Capitol Reef became a national park. The National Park Service bought out the last residents of Fruita and now the old town is park headquarters. It is the best base for exploring the park by several hiking trails and as the beginning point for the scenic drive. The Fruita Campground offers the only accommodations in the park. Fruit continues to grow and can be picked. As it was undoubtedly in earlier centuries, the Fruita area remains a welcome oasis to visitors.

GEOLOGY

For millions of years shallow seas, rivers, and tidal flats laid down many layers of deposits that eventually hardened into rock formations. In time they were covered by massive sand dunes which also hardened. About 65 million years ago, the earth began to move beneath the California coast resulting in a period of intense mountain building, known as the Laramide Orogeny. The sedimentary rock that had been laid down by water and sand dunes was pushed upward in a series of monoclines or folds, of which the Waterpocket Fold is one of the most spectacular. Later, volcanic activity began. The deep molten rock pushed up the sedimentary rock and the landscape was reshaped once again. The Henry Mountains were created through this process. To the north of Capitol Reef, lava came to the surface along faults and helped create Thousand Lake Mountain. A third movement of the earth's surface caused the Colorado Plateau to be lifted between 1 and 2 miles above sea level. The forces of erosion began to work the new canvas of the earth's surface and the result is a masterpiece of cliffs, towers, spires, natural bridges, canyons, and valleys that now constitute Capitol Reef National Monument.

GETTING THERE

Even though Capitol Reef is the most isolated of Utah's national parks, you can get to it from all four directions. From Salt Lake City and northern locations, take Interstate 15 south to Nephi, then pick up Hwy.

28 and continue south to Salina. Get on Interstate 70 for a few miles then take the Sigurd exit to Hwy. 24 which takes you to Capitol Reef (about 80 miles). Total distance from Salt Lake City is 225 miles, so plan a four-hour drive. If you enter Utah from the east, via Interstate 70, take exit 147 onto Hwy. 24, about 12 miles west of Green River. At Hanksville (44 miles south) the road turns west and continues for another 40 miles to Capitol Reef. From the south, take Hwy. 12 from Bryce Canyon to Escalante and Boulder, then cross the eastern flank of Boulder Mountain to Torrey and the intersection with state Hwy. 24, a few miles west of Capitol Reef. Roads can be snowpacked in the winter, so you might want to take Hwy. 89 north to Hwy. 62, just south of Junction, then continue past Otter Creek Reservoir as it heads north to Koosharem and the junction with Hwy. 24, 5 miles north of Koosharem. From Monument Valley or Natural Bridges National Monument, follow Hwy. 95, the bicentennial highway, northwest to Hanksville, then turn west on Hwy. 24 which continues through Capitol Reef.

VISITOR INFORMATION

Located on Hwy. 24, at Fruita, 11 miles east of Torrey, you will want to make the visitor center your first stop to check on guided hikes, evening programs, obtain backcountry permits, purchase maps and other publications, and to view the exhibits and large relief map of the park. The visitor center is open 8 am–7 pm mid-Apr.–Oct., and 8 am–4:30 pm during the winter. The Scenic Drive begins at the visitor center. Visitors register and pay for camping at the campground. The entrance fee for the park is paid beyond the campground at a self-pay station on the scenic drive. There is no food or lodging available in the park.

———— FESTIVALS AND EVENTS ————

Harvest Homecoming Days
September

Held to coincide with the apple harvest in September, the Harvest Homecoming Days Festival offers a glimpse of the traditions and customs of the former occupants of Fruita, including quiltmaking, making jerky, and other activities. Most of these demonstrations are held near the amphitheater in Campground C.

OUTDOOR ACTIVITIES

BIKING

Bikes are not allowed to travel off-road or on any of the park trails or backcountry routes. Nevertheless, bikers can find plenty of challenges in the following four routes recommended by park rangers.

Cathedral Valley Loop—

This ride takes you through the beautiful Cathedral Valley section in the northern end of the park, a place that most visitors do not see. It is a strenuous 60 miles plus ride up steep hills, switchbacks, through stretches of deep sand and requires a river ford. The ride is best made in the spring and fall to avoid the extreme summer temperatures. Bring your own water, as none is available. (See Scenic Drives in the Seeing and Doing section.)

Notom Road-Burr Trail-Boulder Mountain Loop—

Recommended for only the fittest bikers, this ride of 80 to 130 miles depending on shuttles, allows you to loop up across Boulder Mountain along Hwy. 12 (the highest point is about 9,200 feet), then pickup the Burr Trail Road at the village of Boulder and follow it eastward to its junction with the Notom Rd. You follow Notom Rd. north, along the east side of the Waterpocket Fold to its junction with Hwy. 24 just outside the east entrance to the park.

Scenic Drive—

You can follow the Scenic Drive on your bike for its entire length if you choose, although the the narrow road is full of curves and extra care must be given to watch for automobiles. The road leaves from the visitor center and passes the campground and is the best place to spend an hour or two on your bike. The road is 25 miles long, but you can return whenever you are ready (see Scenic Drives in the Seeing and Doing section).

South Draw—

This is a good summer ride since it begins on Boulder Mountain at an elevation of 8,500 feet and descends to 5,500 feet where it joins the Scenic Drive at Pleasant Creek. You make the 3,000-foot descent in a distance of about 12 miles, so brakes in good working order are a must. The ride begins at the junction of the Bowns Reservoir Rd. and Hwy. 12 on Boulder Mountain. You follow Bowns Reservoir Rd. to Jorgeson and Tantalus Flats where you pick up South Draw Rd. and follow it east into its junction with the Scenic Drive. With this ride there are three options: Leave a shuttle vehicle at Pleasant Creek, a 12-mile ride; continue on from Pleasant Creek to the visitor center, a 22-mile ride; or ride the entire distance from the visitor center following Hwy. 24 then Hwy. 12 for 30 miles to the Bowns Reservoir Rd. for a total distance of 52 miles. Park rangers recommend taking a map of the area with you to avoid the confusing side roads along the ride.

HIKING TRAILS

Capitol Reef is for hikers, but hiking here is not like most other places. Experts warn that "rough terrain, scarce water, and extreme weather make good physical condition a must. It is unwise to judge your abilities or water needs here based on experience elsewhere." Temperatures rise to almost unbearable levels, and the difficult terrain becomes even harder going in excessive heat. Spring and fall are the best times to enjoy the many hiking opportunities in the park. The hiking map and guide available for sale at the visitor center lists 25 hiking routes from less than a mile to nearly 25 miles in length. Twelve of the trails are maintained and begin close to the visitor center at Fruita. Most visitors hike at least one of the trails, usually several of the shorter routes such as the Grand Wash or the Fremont River trails. What makes hiking in Capitol Reef so appealing is the variety of trails and the easy access. Narrow canyons rising 800 feet above you, natural bridges, panoramic overlooks, ancient Indian rock art, and strolls along the Fremont River and through the orchards all make for long-lasting memories.

For those traveling the Notom-Bull-frog Rd. there are several excellent hikes ranging in length from 2.5 miles to the 27-mile round-trip hike from Halls Creek Overlook to Halls Creek Narrows. In the Cathedral Valley area, there are several hikes that are well worth the time to get to and to take. Backcountry hiking may be done throughout the park on rugged, unmarked terrain. Permits are required for backcountry camping. The following are some of the more popular hikes within the park.

TRAILS OFF HIGHWAY 24
Chimney Rock and Spring Canyon to the Fremont River Ford—

For a more extended hike that requires most of the day and a shuttle, you can continue east from the loop trail and drop into Spring Canyon, following it for approximately 10 miles to the Fremont River, which must be forded. This is usually no problem, especially in the summer when the stream is only a few inches deep; however, during the spring runoff it can be up to waist deep. Get an early start and carry plenty of water if you take this trail. You can also make this an extended hike by turning left into Upper Spring Canyon, then retracing your route either to your vehicle at Chimney Rock trailhead or continue down the canyon to the Fremont River. This is a good trail for overnight hikers because of the easy access from Hwy. 24 and the many good places to pitch your tent. Pick up a copy of the Spring Canyon trail guide at the visitor center.

Chimney Rock Loop Trail—

If you enter Capitol Reef from the west, the Chimney Rock trailhead is the first you will encounter; coming from the visitor center, it is 3 miles west. You can see the 400-foot-high, multilayered Chimney Rock from the highway. The 3.5-mile-long loop takes you round the rock and to the mesa above for a panoramic view of Capitol Reef and the 12,000-foot Henry Mountains to the east.

Gooseneck Point Trail—

Only .1 mile long, this does not qualify as a hiking trail for most people, but still it is one not to be missed. The view down from the cliff into the 800-foot-deep gorge is spectacular. You can see why it is called Gooseneck Point as Sulphur Creek makes a dramatic loop, resembling a gooseneck, through the gorge. Take the road off Hwy. 24 about 2.5 miles west of the visitor center and head south for about a mile. Stop first for a view from Panorama Point, but make sure you continue along the dirt road to its end, where you will see signs for the Gooseneck Point Trail and Sunset Point Trail.

Grand Wash—

You can enter Grand Wash from either the parking area off Hwy. 24, about 4 miles east of the visitor center, or off the Scenic Drive. If you don't want to retrace the 2.2-mile-long hike and have access to two vehicles, you can arrange for a shuttle vehicle at either end. However you do it, this is one hike that you will want to make. An easy hike without any climbing, it takes you through the depths of the Waterpocket Fold into narrows where the cliffs rise hundreds of feet above you in a passage only a few yards wide. Here, you feel the power and majesty of the land, as you are enveloped by the rocks and become part of them rather than just an onlooker. Along the walls, watch for debris and other signs of the flash floods that have roared down the canyon. Do not hike when summer rainstorms are expected: Rainwater is quickly funnelled down these narrow canyons and destroys everything in its path.

Hickman Bridge Trail—

There are few national parks in Utah without a natural bridge or arch. Capitol Reef's Hickman Bridge ranks with any in the state and the hiking trail to the bridge offers breathtaking views of the Capitol

Dome, Fruita, and the Fremont River Gorge. The trail is 2 miles round-trip and climbs in a steady, but gradual ascent from the trailhead located where the Fremont River crosses to the north side of the highway on the north side of Hwy. 24, about 2 miles east of the visitor center. Along the trail, you pass the foundation of a Fremont Indian pithouse, a Fremont granary in a ledge just above the trail, and a series of potholes (waterpockets) and low-lying natural bridges carved by water. Named for Joseph S. Hickman, a local educator who worked to see Capitol Reef established as a national park, the natural bridge is 133 feet wide and 125 feet high. Pick up a copy of the trail guide, either at the visitor center or at the trailhead, and use it at each of the 18 numbered posts. Be sure to continue on the trail, around the back side of the bridge, rather than returning along the trail in front of the bridge. Then you can view the Fruita area and the junction of the Fremont River and Sulphur Creek from a high vantage point. One of the most popular trails in Capitol Reef, this is not to be missed.

Rim Overlook Trail—

About .3 mile up the Hickman Bridge Trail, you can head to the right (north) and take the Rim Overlook Trail. From the junction, the trail is 2 miles long as it climbs to the top of the cliffs on the north side of the Fremont River Gorge. Part of the trail is across smooth slickrock, where your route is marked by rock cairns. The trail circles above Hickman Bridge as it heads west to the overlook point. From the overlook you have an unobstructed view of Fruita below and the Scenic Drive road, as it follows the west side of Waterpocket Fold. Total length of the trail from the Hickman Bridge Trailhead to the rim and back is 4.6 miles.

Sunset Point Trail—

After viewing the goosenecks, take the .6-mile trail to Sunset Point for a panoramic view of Capitol Reef, the Waterpocket Fold, and the Henry Mountains in the distance. Looking from the west toward the east, with the sun behind you, this is an especially fine

location to watch the fading sunlight play across the rocks and formations. No wonder it's called Sunset Point.

TRAILS NEAR THE CAMPGROUND

Capitol Gorge—

This hike is 1.6 miles round-trip, unless the 1.5-mile road into the gorge to the trailhead is closed to automobile traffic as we found during one Easter weekend trip. Like the Grand Wash hike, the Capitol Gorge route requires no climbing. It winds along narrow canyon bottoms beneath sheer-walled cliffs offering some shade early in the morning and late in the afternoon. There is nothing quite like the confining walls of a narrow canyon to turn your thoughts inward and to find peace within yourself. Within the gorge is an inscription rock, known as the Pioneer Register and the waterpockets, or "tanks," which hold water in depressions in the rock. The earliest inscriptions are those of "Wal. Batemen" and "J. A. Call" in 1871. They were probably prospectors passing through looking for gold.

Cassidy Arch Trail—

From the Grand Wash parking area, you can head downstream about .2 mile and watch for the Cassidy Arch Trail as it branches to the left. The 3.5-mile round-trip hike takes you onto the high cliffs above Grand Wash for an excellent view of Cassidy Arch. The arch is named for the outlaw Butch Cassidy, who, according to legend, had one of his hideouts in Grand Wash. The elevation gain to the arch is nearly 1,000 feet in less than 2 miles, so be prepared. Unlike the Hickman Bridge, which was formed over a stream, the Cassidy Arch is the result of wind erosion.

Cohab Canyon Trail and the Frying Pan Trail—

From the Fruita Campground, two strenuous trails—Cohab Canyon and Frying Pan—take you to the top of Capitol Reef for a breathtaking overview of the center of Capitol Reef National Park. The Cohab Canyon Trail begins across the road from the campground and heads east along steep switchbacks for .25 mile, after which the remaining 1.5 miles are a more moderate climb to a hidden canyon. According to tradition, the canyon was a secret hiding place for local polygamists hiding from federal marshalls. The Frying Pan Trail heads south off the Cohab Canyon Trail 1.1 miles from the trailhead to connect with the Cassidy Arch Trail and Grand Wash. The trail follows the top of Capitol Reef and is a strenuous hike because of the many ups and downs; however, it is one that offers unique views of the park, away from the more populated and easier trails.

Fremont River Trail—

Near the Fruita Campground, this 2.5-mile round-trip hike is really two trails in one. The first .5 mile is a level, pleasant walk along the river, past orchards and pastures. It is the only trail within the park that offers disabled access. The last mile is a strenuous hike up the north face of the cliff for a panoramic view of Fruita below and Capitol Reef to the east. This is a nice morning or evening hike. If you are not staying in the campground, you can park your car in the ampitheater parking in Campground C.

Golden Throne Trail—

This is a 4-mile round-trip hike from the Capitol Gorge parking area to the base of the Golden Throne, one of the domes atop the Navajo sandstone formation, nearly 1,000 feet above the gorge.

Grand Wash—

See under Trails off Highway 24.

Pleasant Creek—

A third trail into the Waterpocket Fold lies at the end of the Scenic Drive, along Pleasant Creek. Although the cliff walls are not as dramatic as in Grand Wash or Capitol Gorge, this is a longer hike (7 miles round-trip) and much less traveled. There are a number of side canyons to be explored, and you can easily spend the entire day on this route. The trail follows east along the perennial Pleasant Creek and ends after the stream exits the Waterpocket Fold and turns north to join the Fremont River.

HORSEBACK RIDING

Hondoo Rivers and Trails—

Trail rides into Capitol Reef National Park and pack trips into surrounding areas. **PO Box 98, Torrey, UT 84775; (801) 425-3519.**

Scenic Rim Trail Rides—

Horseback rides from one hour up to all-day rides into the park. Clint Mecham, whose family has been in the outfitting business for years, takes care of even the greenest tenderfoot. Located just east of the Best Western Capitol Reef Inn along Hwy. 24 east of Torrey. For information, call **(801) 425-3761.**

———— SEEING AND DOING ————

HISTORIC SITES

Elijah Cutler Behunin Cabin—

Constructed in 1882 of red sandstone, this small cabin housed a family of 10 while Behunin attempted to homestead along the Fremont River. All 10 could not sleep in the cabin, so the girls slept in a wagon box and the boys in a dugout. Watch for the cabin along Hwy. 24 near the eastern boundary of the park. There is a parking area and interpretive sign at the cabin.

Historic Fruita—

The Capitol Reef Visitors Center sits at the edge of the old Fruita town site. Park service officials have done a good job of preserving and interpreting the historic Mormon settlement. Within the radius of less than a mile, you can visit several interesting buildings and sites. The historic Pendleton-Gifford Barn was constructed in 1895 by Calvin Pendleton to store hay. The 2,000-square-foot barn is typical of hay barns constructed throughout Utah and the Intermountain West. The Merin Smith Shed and Blacksmith Shop, built in 1925, housed the first tractor in Fruita, which was known as a power horse." The Johnson Orchard has been replanted with varieties of trees from the World War I era, as part of a living history exhibit and demonstration. The Blue Dugway, which served as the road between Fruita and Hanksville until 1961, can still be seen along the western exposure of the Waterpocket Fold. The one-room Fruita schoolhouse, built in 1896, was used until 1941, when students were transported by bus over dirt roads to schools in Bicknell and Torrey. Built of squared logs and chinked with lime mortar produced from a nearby lime kiln, the school was built on a foundation of sandstone blocks. The original flat, bentonite clay roof was replaced with a peaked shingled roof just before World War I. Tape-recorded recollections by Merin Smith talking about the blacksmith shop, and Mrs. Torgerson, one of the teachers in the one-roomed school, relating her experiences as a teacher, are a particularly nice feature of the interpretation provided here. Historic preservationists employed by the National Park Service have been at work to document the historic orchards (apple, cherry, pear, peach, and apricots) and nominate the historic Fruita landscape to the National Register of Historic Places. You can pick up a brochure at the visitor center, which describes the historic Fruita area and other sites to visit.

Oyler Uranium Mine—

At the junction of the Scenic Drive and Grand Wash there are two mine tunnels and two small stone foundations that date from about 1904. Little is known about the mine or its original owner, and apparently very little ore was ever taken from the mine. However, it is representative of a number of one- or two-man dug mines throughout south central and southeast Utah that were shoveled out in response to the discovery in 1902 by Marie Curie that radium could be produced from uranium.

The Park—

One of the most striking features of Capitol Reef is the beautiful park in the Fruita area through which the Fremont River and Sulphur Creek run. It is a refreshing oasis in the otherwise harsh desert and mountains of stone. Take time to walk through the park, across the bridge and, if you want a nice place to relax, read a book, stretch out for a nap, or enjoy a nice picnic lunch or evening barbeque. The tall cottonwood and walnut trees offer ample shade even on the hottest of days.

Wolverton Mill—

The mill was constructed by Edwin Thatcher Wolverton at a remote site on Mt. Pennell in the Henry Mountains in 1921. The BLM moved it to Hanksville in 1974 because it was being vandalized. Located behind the BLM office in the southwestern part of Hanksville, a self-guided tour explains the mill's use and technology. Wolverton believed that he had found lost Spanish gold mines in the Henry Mountains and constructed his mill to process the gold from the mines. Reports of lost Spanish mines echo throughout Utah, and the Henry Mountain mines seem to have proven as intangible as the others that enthusiasts claim still exist.

ROCK ART

Fremont Culture Walk—

About a mile east of the visitor center off Hwy. 24, you can view some of the finest and most accessible Fremont Indian rock art in the park and anywhere in Utah. The petroglyphs are pecked into the south-facing sandstone ledges and include mountain goats, trapeizoidal anthropomorphs, and other figures. The largest panel is just in front of you, as you take the main trail from the parking area. But don't be content with these easy-to-spot figures. Continue east along the trail as it runs parallel to the cliffs and to Highway 24. If you look carefully, you will spot other petroglyphs on the sandstone walls. When you come to a small alcove, go inside to see the intials and date, 1882, left by early travelers through the area.

SCENIC DRIVES
Cathedral Valley—
It is a shame that only a few visitors to Capitol Reef National Park see The Cathedral Valley section of the park. The red entrada sandstone monoliths are reminiscent of European cathedrals. The tallest rocks reach more than 500 feet skyward from their base—the same height as Germany's world-famous Cologne Cathedral. Cathedral Valley is located in the extreme northern end of the park and laps the flanks of Thousand Lake Mountain. It is accessible only over dirt roads by high-clearance vehicles. Ward J. Roylance prepared an excellent, inexpensive guide to Cathedral Valley, which is published in newspaper format, by the Capitol Reef Natural History Association. The tour describes the roads into Cathedral Valley and outlines a 59-mile loop that begins at the Fremont River Ford off Hwy. 24, 11.5 miles east of the visitor center, and returns to Hwy. 24 at Cainsville, outside the park, 19 miles east of the visitor center. Travelers can purchase a copy of the guide and obtain current information on road conditions into the area at the visitor center. The Fremont River Ford is just that: There is no bridge, and you must drive your vehicle through the river—usually not much more than a foot deep. But it is advisable to get the river crossing out of the way at the beginning of the trip in case the river level rises. From the Fremont River Ford, the dirt road heads northwestward through the South Desert to the Lower Cathedral Valley Overlook, 17.5 miles from the ford. A 1 mile hike to the overlook provides a spectacular view of the Temple of the Sun, the Temple of the Moon, and other formations. Ten miles up the road is the Upper Cathedral Valley Overlook, which marks the halfway point of the loop and contains the tallest of the area's formations. It is impossible to describe all of the

terrain you will cover in this loop, but it is a drive that you will not soon forget.

Loa to Hanksville Scenic Byway—
Utah Hwy. 24 through Wayne County and Capitol Reef National Park has been officially designated one of Utah's 27 Scenic Byways. The 70-mile stretch passes through spectacular scenery with the Waterpocket Fold at its center. In Loa, there are two interesting Mormon buildings you can visit: the Loa Stake Tabernacle, at 100 West and 100 North, constructed between 1906 and 1909, and the earlier Loa Tithing Office, at 100 West and Center St., which dates from 1897. Continuing eastward, the highway passes through high valley farmlands and by the Bicknell Gristmill, located in a beautiful meadow near a poplar-lined stream, about 3 miles east of Bicknell on the north side of the road. The two-story frame gristmill was constructed in 1890 for Hans Peter Nielsen. Nielsen immigrated from Denmark to Utah in 1863. He was a miller in his native country and operated the Bicknell mill until his death in 1909. Wayne County was fortunate in obtaining the services of an experienced miller for nearly two decades, and the Bicknell Gristmill was an important part of the local economy for nearly 50 years. The mill was operated by various individuals until 1935, when the long arm of the Great Depression ended operations at the mill. Much of the original machinery and equipment remain inside the mill, but it is unfortunately not open to the public. Past Bicknell, the road continues through Torrey and into Capitol Reef National Park, where it follows the Fremont River past the red rock formations then the blue-colored Mancos shale hills on to Hanksville.

Notom Road Backway—
This road is recommended for high-clearance vehicles only, as it connects state Hwy. 24 at the eastern boundary of Capitol Reef with the Burr Trail at the southern end of the park. The road parallels the eastern exposure of the Waterpocket Fold for the entire 29-mile length of the Fold south of Hwy. 24. As you continue southward, the

"breakers" of the Fold get deeper and deeper. The road offers fantastic views of the Fold and the Henry Mountains in the distance.

Scenic Drive—

Every visitor to Capitol Reef must take the 25-mile Scenic Drive that follows the old Blue Dugway wagon road and provides access to Grand Wash, Capitol Gorge, Golden Throne, and Pleasant Creek. Pick up the free brochure "A Guide to the Scenic Drive," along with the pamphlet "The Ancient Rock: A Guide to the Scenic Drive," edited by retired park historian George Davidson, which sells for $1 at the visitor center. Use these for information on the 11 designated stops along the drive. The Scenic Drive leaves the visitor center and winds through part of historic Fruita, then heads south along the western side of the Waterpocket Fold. The road is paved for the 12 or so miles to Sleeping Rainbow Ranch (Sleeping Rainbow was the Paiute name for the Waterpocket Fold because of its many soft colors), but the narrow, twisty, road (and National Park Service policy) does not permit speeds of more than 30 miles an hour. Plan to spend at least a half day. This should allow time to stop at each of the designated stops, to hike Capitol Wash, and, if you want, to make the strenuous trek up the Golden Throne Trail.

WILDLIFE

The park offers plenty of opportunity to view wildlife. In the morning mule deer can be seen in the orchards and pastures in Fruita. Drivers must exercise great caution along the roads to watch for deer and to watch for visitors who stop suddenly to photograph the deer that come down to feed and drink. Other "quiet desert" residents of the park include: gray foxes, cougars, mountain lions, bobcats, coyotes, many varieties of lizards, water snakes, gopher snakes, and two varieties of poisonious rattlesnakes, the prairie rattlesnake, and the small faded midget rattlesnake. You have the best chance of seeing the shy wildlife at twilight along the river and in the canyon bottoms. Golden eagles, hawks, warblers, grosbeaks, and many species of swallows also reside in the park.

———— WHERE TO STAY ————

ACCOMMODATIONS

There are no accommodations, other than a campground, within Capitol Reef National Park; however in the nearby communities of Torrey, Teasdale, Bicknell, Loa, and Hanksville, you can find the following.

BICKNELL

Aquarius Motel—$$ to $$$

Twenty-seven rooms. 240 West Main, PO Box 304, Bicknell, UT 84715; (801) 425-3835 or 1-800-833-5379.

Sun Glow Motel—$$

Nineteen rooms. 63 East Main, PO Box 158, Bicknell, UT 84715; (801) 425-3821.

HANKSVILLE

Desert Inn—$$

Twenty rooms. 197 East Hwy. 24, PO Box 111, Hanksville, UT 84734; (801) 542-3241.

Fern's Place—$$

Eight rooms with kitchenettes. 99 East 100 North, PO Box 181, Hanksville, UT 84734; (801) 542-3252.

Whispering Sands Motel—$$

Ten rooms. 44 South Hwy. 95, PO Box 68, Hanksville, UT 84734; (801) 542-3238.

LOA

Road Creek Inn Bed and Breakfast—$$$

If you are looking for the most luxurious and most intimate lodging experience within 200 miles of Capitol Reef National Park, the Road Creek Inn is without peer. The 1912 Loa General Store was renovated into a 14-room inn in the late 1980s and has drawn acclaim from near and far. The spacious, quiet rooms are a welcome oasis after a long day of travel or sightseeing. Breakfast is included—fresh fruit, juice, coffee, pancakes, bacon, and eggs. In the basement of the two-story building there is an exercise room, whirlpool, sauna, and showers. Three full-sized billiard tables and video theater with a good selection of movie videos, plus a popcorn machine and soda fountain are provided. Eighteen nonsmoking rooms. **90 South Main, PO Box 310, Loa, UT 84747; (801) 836-2485 or 1-800-388-7688.**

Wayne Wonderland Motel—$$ to $$$

Twelve rooms. **42 North Main, PO Box 98, Loa, UT 84747; (801) 836-9692.**

TEASDALE
Cockscomb Inn—$$–$$$

Teasdale is a small town not far from Capitol Reef where Elissa Stevens has established a pleasant three-room bed and breakfast in a 1905 house originally owned by the Coleman family who raised seventeen children here. Elissa named her bed and breakfast for the rock formation outside her front door—a ridge that resembles a cockscomb. Elissa came to Teasdale to enjoy the outdoors, and she can offer plenty of tips on hiking, biking and cross-country skiing. All rooms are nonsmoking with private baths. Breakfasts include fresh fruit and juice, granola, waffles, pancakes, and eggs. **97 South State, PO Box B, Teasdale, UT 84773; (801) 425-3511.**

TORREY
Best Western Capitol Reef Resort—$$ to $$$

Swimming pool; 30 rooms. **2600 East Hwy. 24, PO Box 750160, Torrey, UT 84775; (801) 425-3761 or 1-800-528-1234.**

Capitol Reef Inn—$$

Ten rooms. **360 West Main, PO Box 100, Torrey, UT 84775; (801) 425-3271.**

Chuck Wagon Motel—$$

Ten rooms. **12 West Main, PO Box 80, Torrey, UT 84775; (801) 425-3288.**

Rim Rock Ranch Resort Ranch—$$ to $$$

Thirty-one rooms; swimming pool. **2523 East Hwy. 24, Torrey, UT 84775; (801) 425-3843.**

Skyridge Bed and Breakfast—$$$

Karen Kesler served as executive director of the Mendocino Art Center for 10 years and decided when she left Mendocino it would have to be for a place at least as nice. It is no wonder that she chose Torrey. Karen has applied her artistic skills to everything from designing the building itself to painting, furniture-making and creating unique items such as the fire place mantel in which she used over 30 pounds of roofing nails to form a most engaging design. Skyridge, which opened in 1994, has a western touch but is not cliché western. It has a steep pitched roof, dormers and a wide front porch. Karen has dyed the concrete floor to give it a slatelike appearance and the unusual sand–painted interior walls blend in with perfect harmony with the red sandy soil of the 75 acres on which Skyridge is located. The three-story inn sits on top of a ridge so that each of the five nonsmoking rooms has a unique view of either the Capitol Reef area, Boulder Mountain or the Torrey Valley. All rooms have private baths and TVs with VCRs. Some have a private deck, and the patio, hot tub and living room/library are available. Sally Elliot, the co-owner and chef, gives special care in offering a full breakfast with homemade granola, fresh fruit and juice, and a hot entrée such as southwest quiche, croissant French toast, or frittata. Located on Hwy. 24, just east of the intersection of Hwys 12 and 24. **PO Box 750220, Torrey, UT 84775; (801) 425-3222.**

Wonderland Inn—$$ to $$$

Fifty rooms. Junction of Hwy. 12 and Hwy. 24. **PO Box 67, Torrey, UT 84775; (801) 425-3775 or 1-800-458-0216.**

CAMPING
PRIVATE

Aquarius Mobile and RV Campground—

Twenty-four sites, with complete hookups. Open year-round. **220 South 100 East in Bicknell; (801) 425-3835.**

Chuckwagon Campground—

Twenty-five RV sites, 10 with complete hookups. Toilets, showers, laundry facilities, and drinking water. Open Apr.–Nov. **12 West Main in Torrey, (801) 425-3288.**

Red Rock Campground—

Forty-five RV trailer sites, 38 of which have complete hookups, and 15 tent sites. Toilets, showers, and a laundry. Open Apr.–Oct. At the junction of Hwy. 95 and Hwy. 24 in Hanksville; **(801) 542-3235.**

Rim Rock Ranch Motel and RV Park—

Located between Torrey and the park, it is the closest private campground to Capitol Reef. Fifty-two units with complete hookups and 20 tent sites. The campground is open year-around and has drinking water, toilets, showers, and laundry facilities; **(801) 425-3843.**

Thousand Lakes RV Park—

Located a mile west of Torrey on Hwy. 24. Forty-four RV sites, 38 with complete hookups and 50 tent sites. Drinking water, toilets, showers, and laundry facilities. Open Apr.–Oct.; **(801) 425-3288.**

PUBLIC

There are three campgrounds within the national park; however, two are small, primitive, and difficult to reach. Most campers in the park stay at the **Fruita Campground,** a mile from the visitor center and located along the Scenic Drive. Within the Fruita Campground, there are 63 RV trailer sites and a large open tent area. The campground has drinking water, toilets, and handicap facilities. The two primitive campgrounds are the **Cathedral Campground,** in Cathedral Valley, with 5 tent sites, and in the southern section, **Cedar Mesa Campground,** also with 5 tent sites. No fees are charged at Cathedral and Cedar Mesa, but campers must bring their own water. Fees are charged at Fruita. All three campgrounds are open year-round.

Other public campgrounds are located on forest service land outside the park. A mile east of Bicknell off Hwy. 24, the **Sunglow Campground** is open mid-May–end Oct., with 7 RV trailer and tent sites. South of Torrey, about 15 miles down Hwy. 12, there are three campgrounds in a 7-mile stretch that are open late May–late Oct. **Single Tree** has 31 RV and tent sites, **Pleasant Creek** has 9 RV and 11 tent sites, and **Oak Creek** has 8 RV and tent sites. All have drinking water and toilets and are located at elevations between 8,600 and 8,800 feet.

———— WHERE TO EAT ————

Aquarius Restaurant—$

Located in part of the Aquarius Motel in Bicknell, the restaurant has western decor, including a collection of Indian paintings and artifacts and 60 authentic cattle brands used by ranches surrounding Capitol Reef National Park. Ted Stallman prides himself on creating a unique experience for all his guests. From playing his harmonica for an evening singalong in the restaurant, or telling stories about the famous and not-so-famous guests, Ted makes your visit to the Aquarius something you will not soon forget. Specialties include locally grown trout, rib-eye steak, and omelets for breakfast, and an old-fashioned soda fountain. This is a favorite of locals, especially since it is about the only place that is open year-round. Open daily 6 am–10 pm. **240 West Main, Bicknell; (801) 425-3835.**

Capitol Reef Cafe—$ to $$

Part of the Capitol Reef Inn, the Capitol Reef Cafe is part of a private shangri-la that

Southey Swede has established for himself in the isolated reaches of south-central Utah. Southey gave up a successful psychology career in California and moved to Torrey about a decade ago. His cafe offers a strong vegetarian menu with such dishes as stir-fry vegetables served with brown and wild rice, mushroom lasagna, fettuccine primavera, and a vegetarian omelet for breakfast. The Capitol Reef dinner salad is a delicious mixture of ten fresh vegetables. Other entrées include trout, steak, and chicken. Freshly squeezed juices and espresso drinks are a delight. The Cafe also features a well-stocked bookstore that features local and regional history and natural history books. on the Capitol Reef area. Open daily 7 am–11 am and 5 pm–9 pm. **360 West Main St., Torrey; (801) 425-3271.**

Chappell Cheese Company—$

You can purchase several varieties of local cheese, produced by brothers Matthew and William B. Chappell who opened the plant in 1977. They inherited their cheese-making skills from their father Blaine Chappell, who was a perennial winner of the Utah Dairyman's Association Best Cheese Award. You can watch the cheese-making process from the upstairs viewing room and may purchase cheese in the factory store. Open Mon.–Sat. 8 am–6 pm. Located 1.5 miles west of Loa, on Hwy. 24. **PO Box 307, Loa; (801) 836-2821.**

John and Jan's—$ to $$

Located in the Best Western Capitol Reef Resort, between Torrey and the national park, John and Jan Peterson have established a friendly and clean restaurant with a reputation for good food. In the evenings, you can have Dutch-oven-cooked beef and chicken with real mashed potatoes and homemade rolls. For breakfast, the breakfast bar offers all-you-can-eat bacon, sausage, scrambled eggs, pancakes, biscuits and gravy, hash browns, and fresh fruit at a reasonable price for adults, and a special price for children under 10. Without any drapes on the windows, you can enjoy a 270-degree panoramic view of the landscape.

La Buena Vida Mexican Food—$

Located in a little white house with red trim on the west edge of Torrey. Beth Humphries took over the restaurant from her parents Peggy Lopez Garver, who, with Beth's Father operated the restaurant for nine years, first in Cainville and then in Torrey. Enchiladas and burritos are among the specialties. Open daily for lunch and dinner, noon –10 pm (closed on Tues.), Apr.–Nov. **599 West Hwy. 24; (801) 425-3759.**

Red Rock Restaurant—$

Breakfast lunch and dinner. Closed during the winter. Located at the junction of Hwy. 24 and Hwy. 95; Hanksville; **(801) 542-3235.**

Road Creek Inn Restaurant—$$

Road Creek, which originates in the mountains above Loa, is the source for the excellent trout that have become the trademark of the Road Creek Inn. You can get trout cooked eight different ways, with charbroiled, smoked, and sautéed my favorites. For hardy eaters the New York steak and charbroiled trout is the ultimate. If you want something unique, try a trout served on a hoagie bun. Burgers, soup, and salads round out the menu. The restaurant is located on the main floor of the Road Creek Inn. Open for dinner 5 pm–8 pm. **90 South Main, Loa; (801)-836-2485.**

Wonderland Inn Restaurant—$ to $$

A part of the Wonderland Inn Motel located at the junction of Hwys 12 and 24 just a few miles west of Capitol Reef National Park, this restaurant serves steaks and trout for dinner, sandwiches for lunch (with sack lunches to go) and hearty breakfasts. A breakfast favorite is the Wonderlands Haystack with melted cheese, diced ham, bell peppers, onions and two eggs (any style) piled high on hash browns. Open daily 7 am–9 pm, Mar.–Oct. and closes at 7 pm the rest of the year. Located off Hwy 24 a mile east of Torrey. **(801) 425-3775.**

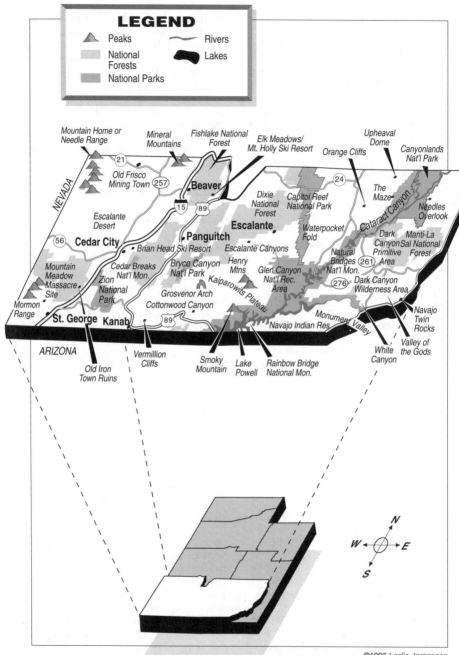

Southern Region

SOUTHERN REGION

Beaver

Situated halfway between Salt Lake City and Las Vegas, Nevada, Beaver is one of southern Utah's undiscovered treasures. Relatively few skiers have discovered the uncrowded slopes at Elk Meadows. Puffer Lake remains a spot primarily for local fishermen. Hiking trails in the Tushar Mountains see little use. The treasure of historic rock and brick pioneer homes in Beaver are seldom noticed, and the ghost towns of Frisco and Newhouse largely unexplored. Rock hounds have only begun to scratch the surface (so to speak) of the treasure house of minerals and gems found throughout the area. One of the attractions of Beaver is that it does not appear that these resources will soon be overdeveloped. If you're seeking a chance to catch your breath and unwind from the hectic pace of today's world in a place full of activities that does not draw the crowds that other southern Utah locations do, Beaver might just be for you.

HISTORY

A number of prehistoric sites, dating back to the Archaic and Sevier Fremont periods, have been identified in Beaver County, including obsidian quarry sites in the Mineral Mountains that apparently supplied stone tools for many of central and southern Utah's prehistoric inhabitants. Southern Paiutes met members of the 1776 Dominguez-Escalante expedition as the Spaniards journeyed from north to south through present-day Milford. Described by Escalante as "the Bearded Utes," 80 years later the Southern Paiutes encountered Mormon settlers moving into Beaver Valley from Parowan 35 miles to the south. Beaver was initially settled because of its potential for livestock grazing. Raising cattle and sheep has also been an important part of the area's economy. Beaver's economy was enhanced by four factors during the 1870s: an aggressive move to establish a woolen mill, tannery, and dairy industry; the establishment of Ft. Cameron by the US Army in 1873; a mining boom launched in the 1870s; and the arrival the Utah Southern Railroad at Milford in 1880. A local newspaper editor boasted that Beaver would soon be the largest city in the territory with 20-story skyscrapers pushing upward to rival the mighty Tushar Mountains looming over the city. But by World War I, mining was on the wane, Ft. Cameron had long been abandoned by the army, and, while there are no 20-story skyscrapers in Beaver, an impressive number of brick and stone homes and buildings leave a legacy of historic buildings unrivaled by few towns in the West.

GETTING THERE

Beaver is 200 miles south of Salt Lake City and 100 miles north of St. George on Interstate 15.

FESTIVALS AND EVENTS

Pioneer Days
July 24th
Horse races at the racetrack, more than 100 floats in the parade, a full day of events, tricycle race, and a 5-kilometer race.

OUTDOOR ACTIVITIES

BIKING

The Tushar Mountains east of Beaver offer a number of good bike routes that allow you to experience the beauty and isolation of the seldom-traveled routes in the area. Maps are available at the **US Forest Service** office in Beaver.

Beaver Canyon—

This 36-mile roundtrip route travels Hwy. 153 to Elk Meadows Ski and Summer Resort. The route starts in the center of Beaver, just north of the high school building on Main St. The first 2 miles take you past the Canyon Breeze Golf Course, rodeo grounds and racetrack, and the site of Ft. Cameron, before entering Beaver Canyon. The route follows Beaver Creek to Ponderosa Picnic Ground, near Mile Nine, and Mahogany Cove Picnic Ground at Mile Eleven. The first 10 miles of the route climb gradually from 6,000 feet, just east of Beaver, to 7,000 feet. At Mahogany Cove Picnic Ground the road becomes noticeably steeper as it switches back and forth up the side of the mountain. Merchant Valley Dam is located near the 15-mile mark, and the end of the ride at Elk Meadows Ski Resort is at 9,200 feet, 3 miles beyond the dam. If you don't mind a steep climb and sharing a narrow road with a few automobiles and trucks, this route promises a good workout to the top and exhilarating descent down the mountain on the return leg.

Big John Flat Kimberly Trail—

This one-way alpine ride offers the solitude of pine forests and alpine meadows, breathtaking vistas of the surrounding mountains, wildlife, relief from the summer heat, and the historic Kimberly Mine. The first 6 miles of the 23-mile trail climbs steadily from about 8,800 feet at the beginning point in Big John Flat to 11,000 feet near Mud Lake. The remaining 17 miles drops nearly a mile in elevation to 5,900 feet at the junction of Forest Rd. 113 and Interstate 70 in Clear Creek Canyon. Designated a Scenic Backway, the trail is reached from Beaver by driving on Hwy. 153 about 16 miles up Beaver Canyon toward Elk Meadows Ski Resort. Watch for Forest Rd. 123, which heads north from the highway 1.5 miles beyond the Merchant Valley Dam and 2 miles below Elk Mountain Resort. Follow Forest Rd. 123 3 miles north to Big John Flat, where the trail begins. After 13 miles, the road intersects Forest Rd. 113 coming up from Marysvale to the east. The last 10 miles are along Forest Rd. 113, with the Kimberly Mine located 2 miles northwest of the junction. The route requires arrangements for a shuttle pick-up on Interstate 70, 30 miles by automobile from Beaver. For riders who do not want to hassle with shuttle arrangements, an alternate out-and-back ride is the 6-mile climb up to Mud Lake and back.

Puffer Lake Loop—

For riders looking for a scenic high-country loop road, the 8-mile Puffer Lake Loop is one of Utah's best. The ride begins just beyond the Big Flat Ranger Station, 24 miles east of Beaver. To reach the ranger station, follow Hwy. 153 east from Beaver for 18 miles to where the paved road ends and the gravel road begins near Elk Meadows (see the Beaver Canyon route). Continue along the gravel road past Puffer Lake to Big Flat, then continue for 6 miles to Forest Rd. 581, which begins just south of the Big Flat Ranger Station and heads east. This is the beginning point of the loop. Follow the road east, then keep to the left as the trail turns north to climb past City Creek Peak 2 miles into the ride. Continuing north another 2 miles, the trail follows the ridge overlooking Piute Reservoir to the east and continues along the Skyline Trail toward Lake Peak and Mt. Holly. At the intersection with Forest Rd. 129, turn left and head west around the north shore of Puffer Lake to the intersection of Hwy.

153 at the northwestern end of the lake. Turn back south and follow Hwy. 153 about 3 miles back to the starting point.

South Creek Trail—

For novice to intermediate bike riders, the South Creek Trail offers a traffic-free descent along a dirt road for 18 miles from the 10,000-foot elevation Anderson Meadow through four plant communities—pine, aspen, juniper and piñon, and sagebrush—into Beaver. The route requires transportation to its beginning point at Anderson Meadow. Take Hwy. 153 east from Beaver for about 10 miles to the point where Forest Rd. 137 to Kent's Lake heads south. Follow the road past Kent's Lake and Anderson Meadow Reservoir to Forest Rd. 575, an old logging and four-wheel-drive road southeast of the reservoir. The trail from Anderson Meadow climbs uphill for the first 1.5 miles along Forest Rd. 575, before it becomes Forest Rd. 68 at the summit. Designated for four-wheelers, the trail is wide and well marked. The first 4 miles from the summit are a fairly steep descent along some switchbacks to the 8,000-foot level. After that, the descent is much more gradual, as the route meets the north fork of South Creek and follows the stream for several miles. The road for the last 10 miles of the ride is Forest Rd. 008, a dirt road that heads northwest passing through sagebrush into Beaver.

FISHING

Kent's Lake—

Named for Kent Farnsworth, who acquired the land through squatter's rights and built a dam on the upper Beaver River, the lake is stocked with rainbow, German brown, brook, and cutthroat trout. Farnsworth developed a small resort at the lake, which has since been closed, only unimproved camping facilities are available. Kent's Lake is located 15 miles east of Beaver, on Hwy. 153.

LaBaron Reservoir—

Situated 3 miles beyond Kent's Lake, LaBaron Lake is located near the head of

LaBaron Peak and is surrounded by a large meadow. The lake offers trout fishing and unimproved camping facilities.

Little Reservoir—

This small lake is the first body of water after the turnoff onto Kent's Lake Rd. The lake has disabled access.

Minersville Lake State Recreation Area—

The most accessible and most popular boating and fishing spot in the area, Minersville Reservoir is located on the Beaver River, about 10 miles west of the town of Beaver along Hwy. 21. Although Mormon pioneers had constructed dams on the river as early as 1860, a permanent dam on the river was not built until 1914. Named the Rocky Ford Dam, after the boulder-strewn wagon road crossing of the river just below the dam, the original structure continues to impound the waters of the 1,130 surface acre Minersville Reservoir. Open for year-round fishing, the reservoir has been treated several times to kill off the carp and chub, most recently in 1991 when the reservoir was closed to fishing for two years, then reopened for trophy fishing. The reservoir is maintained as a state park, and a fee is charged. Facilities include picnic sites, drinking water, modern restrooms, showers, sewage disposal, electrical hookups for 29 units, and 18 tent sites.

Puffer Lake—

Puffer Lake is a natural mountain lake that was discovered by James Puffer in 1865. Located at an elevation of 9,700 feet, 22 miles east of Beaver on Hwy. 153, the lake is fed by the snow fields of the surrounding 12,000-foot-plus peaks of Mts. Belnap, Baldy, and Delano. According to tradition, the lake was not only named in honor of its discoverer but in gratitude by an early group of fishermen who were guided to the lake by James Puffer. You can fish either from the shore or from boats. The lake is privately owned and boat rentals are available.

GOLF

Canyon Breeze Golf Course—

If it's a nice summer day and the urge for a quick game of golf hits as you are driving along Interstate 15 through southern Utah, you won't do any better than to stop in Beaver to play the Canyon Breeze Course. This 9-hole, 2,746-yard, par 34 golf course was laid out in 1965 on part of the site of old Ft. Cameron at the mouth of Beaver Canyon. It's also the only golf course I know that is closed for horse races. No reservations are needed. Simply show up and expect to be sent out to the first hole. The trees along the course are mature and add to the beauty of the course, along with a nice one-and-a-half story pink rock house and well-weathered barn and outbuildings along the right side of the 3rd hole. Weather permitting, the course is open from Mar.–Nov., **(801) 438-2601.**

HIKING

Delano Peak/Mt. Holly—

At 12,129 feet Delano Peak is the highest peak in the Tushar Mountains. It can be reached by a 6-mile hike from Elk Meadows Ski Resort. The trailhead begins at an elevation of about 9,700 feet, and the route generally follows a northeasterly course for approximately 4 miles to the saddle between Mt. Holly and Delano Peak. The elevation gain to this point is approximately 2,000 feet. Once you reach the saddle, you can turn right for a half-mile climb to the top of Mt. Holly, or turn left for the mile ascent to Delano Peak. Whichever route you choose, you will have panoramic views of the Tushar Mountains, the Great Basin ranges to the west, and Piute Reservoir and the Fishlake Mountains to the east. The round-trip hike of 12 miles is a good day-long hike for most hikers and is best taken in the middle of the summer, when the days are long and the high mountain temperatures cool but pleasant.

Wah Wah Mountains—

It's hard to believe that the Indian name for these mountains means "good, clear water." But descriptive names are relative to the local circumstances. Given the surrounding desert and the fact that Wah Wah Springs, located on the east slope of the mountains about 7 miles west of the mining town of Newhouse, was an important water source for travelers, livestock men, and the 6,000 residents of Newhouse, no doubt water from these western Utah mountains did seem "good and clear" to early visitors and residents of the area. The hike along the ridge of the mountains is generally cross-country, without a well-defined trail. From the trailhead at about 8,100 feet, the route climbs to Wah Peak at 9,383 feet, a distance of 3.5 miles. Bristle-cone pines, several thousand years old, can be seen on the ridge to the east of Wah Peak. Plan four to five hours to make the round-trip hike. There are few travelers, let alone hikers, in this area, making isolation and solitude attractive features of this hike. The hike also offers spectacular views of Pine Valley and the desert 4,000 feet below. The trailhead is reached by taking Hwy. 21 west from Milford about 24 miles, before turning left (south) off the highway onto a gravel road near Milepost 54. Follow the road in a southwesterly direction along the eastern slope for 15.5 miles to the highest point on the backbone of the mountains and begin your hike at this point. For further information, contact **Beaver River Resource Area, Bureau of Land Management, 444 South Main, Cedar City, UT 84720; (801) 586-2458.**

ROCK HOUNDING

The mountain ranges west of Beaver offer some of the best rock-hounding locations in America. The Mineral Mountains and San Francisco Mountains are dotted with old mines and mine dumps. Rock shops in Beaver and Milford make for interesting stops and are a good source for information about locations, access, and ownership. Some sites are located on private property, while others are isolated and difficult to find. The following have been recommended by the Beaver County Travel Council and represent the diversity of minerals and stones available within the area.

Antelope District of the Northern Mineral Mountains—

This is a good source for galena, barite, magnetite, malachite, and pyrite. Take Hwy. 257 north from Milford for 11 miles, then turn east onto a dirt road that leads to the western slope of the Mineral Mountains.

Indian Creek—

If panning for gold is your long-held dream, Indian Creek offers an opportunity, if you bring your own pan. Head north out of Beaver for 10 miles, through the hamlet of Manderfield to the Indian Creek Recreation Area, then follow the trace into the canyon.

Mineral Mountains—

The Mineral Mountains provide a wide range of minerals and are one of the closest and most accessible areas to Beaver. Follow Hwy. 21 west from Beaver for approximately 5 miles to Pass Rd. Turn north on Pass Rd. and follow it into the Mineral Mountains to the top of the pass. Here you will see a number of old mines and workings.

San Francisco Mountains—

Near the site of the Cactus Mine and the old town site of Newhouse, exotic minerals such as chalcopyrite, hematite, azurite, rutile, serpentine, stibite, tourmaline, galena, and even gold can be picked up from the foothills and low ridges on the west side of the San Francisco Mountains. To reach the site, take Hwy. 21 about 26 miles west of Milford, then turn north to Newhouse, where a few foundations remain. Turn east at the town site and follow the road to Copper Gulch.

South Creek—

Located 7 miles southeast of Beaver, South Creek is a source of a variety of colored agate, which may be found on the low ridges on both sides of the road. Take Hwy. 160 south from Beaver for 1 mile to the South Creek Rd., then follow it for 6 miles to the area where the mountains begin.

SKIING
DOWNHILL SKIING
Elk Meadows Ski Area—

If you are looking for an out-of-the-way, uncrowded but easily accessible ski area committed to teaching beginning skiers of all ages, Elk Meadows deserves careful consideration. Here, the emphasis is on skiing rather than on fashion, nightlife, and other amenities of the big expensive resorts. *Ski* magazine has given the ski school its highest possible ranking for teaching children. The SkiWee half-day and full-day programs for 4- to 12-year-olds offer all levels of instruction, lift passes, ski rentals, supervision, and lunch at reasonable rates. Lift tickets are usually the lowest in the state and, in a generous gesture to the agelessness of skiing, skiers who are 65 and over ski for free! Elk Meadows consists of two areas: the Upper Meadows, with two lifts for beginners and those who enjoy their skiing away from the deep powder, steep slopes, and man-eating moguls of the more advanced runs. These lifts that descend from Tushar Ridge at 10,400 feed to the West Village Base Lodge at 9,200 feet.

The 2nd area is located below Tushar Ridge, close to the Lodge, and caters to more advanced skiers. Located just four hours from Salt Lake City or Las Vegas on Interstate 15, or nine hours from Los Angeles and Phoenix. The ski season usually runs from Thanksgiving–Apr. Open daily 9 am–4 pm. Lodging is available a short walk from the ski lifts, at prices considerably lower than at other resorts, or at very modest rates 18 miles away in Beaver.

TENNIS

Two public tennis courts are located on the canyon highway across the road south of the horse-racing grandstand.

SEEING AND DOING

GHOST TOWNS

Newhouse—

This ghost town, located 7 miles northwest of Frisco, bears one of the most famous names in Utah mining history. Samuel Newhouse made successful investments in the Bingham Copper Mine near Salt Lake City and, in 1900, along with investors from England and France, opened the Cactus Mine. Five years later the town of Newhouse was established. Residences of stucco adobe, brick, rock, and wood were constructed near a business district that included several stores, a livery stable, hospital, library, opera house, dance hall, and hotel. About 1910 the Cactus Mine gave out, putting miners out of work and causing the town's sudden demise. It also saw the end of an ambitious plan by Newhouse to set up a non-Mormon business district in Salt Lake City that would rival the older Mormon business district to the north near the Temple. Partly with earnings from the Cactus Mine, Newhouse constructed several buildings that still remain Salt Lake City landmarks, including the Boston and Newhouse buildings, two of Utah's first skyscrapers. Newhouse is reached by traveling 4.7 miles west on Hwy. 21 then 2 miles north along a dirt road.

Old Frisco—

The Frisco charcoal kilns stand today more like ancient religious shrines than the most visible reminder of the once prosperous silver mining area of Frisco. The five beehive kilns were constructed in 1877 by the Frisco Mining and Smelting Company to provide fuel for the smelting of ore from the nearby Horn Silver Mine. Charcoal was produced until about 1884, at which time the smelter was closed, and ore from the mines was shipped to coke-fired smelters in Salt Lake City. Still, the Frisco charcoal kilns are a reminder of a time when mining held the promise of prosperity in an otherwise desolate land. Frisco is located 15 miles west of Milford on Hwy. 21. A dirt road leads off the highway to the right (northwest) into the former town, which was inhabited by some 6,000 people between 1880 and 1885.

HISTORIC BUILDINGS

If you are looking for a Utah town that is a veritable museum of 19th-century houses, you need search no further than Beaver. There are more than 100 historic buildings ranging from the early log cabins and one-story adobe houses of the 1860s to beautiful examples of black rock, pink rock, and brick homes built during the 1870s and 1880s. Characteristic of Beaver architecture are the black basalt rock houses and pink tuff houses, which were built during the prosperous years of the last quarter of the 19th century by two Scottish stonemasons, Thomas Fraser and Alexander Boyter. Thomas Frazer, a convert to the Mormon church while living in Scotland, had emigrated to Utah in the 1860s and was asked by church authorities to move to in Beaver in 1868 in order to improve the quality of building construction in the town. Unlike Frazer, Alexander Boyter had come to Beaver with the US Army as a non-Mormon. Boyter learned his stonemason skills while serving at Ft. Cameron, just east of Beaver, rather than in "the old country" as had Frazer. Frazer initially worked with black basalt, whereas, Boyter made principal use of the pink tuff, which was softer and easier to work than the hard basalt. While all of these houses are private residences and not open to visitors, a walking or driving tour of the following buildings will give you a good idea of some of the remarkable architectural treasures of Beaver. Each of these buildings has been listed in the National Register of Historic Places. But don't be tied to the following list. A fun exercise, especially with children, is to cover a section of the town and see how many black rock, pink rock, old brick, stuccoed adobe, and log homes you can identify.

Alexander Boyter House—

Scottish stonemason Alexander "Scotty" Boyter built his house of pink tuff in 1882. According to local folklore, Boyter quarried the stone for his house three times, but sold it all twice before constructing the one-and-a-half-story house for his family. When he finally began work on his own house, he made sure that it would be a showcase of his skill. The stone was tooled to a smooth finish and the mortar was dyed to match the pink rock. **590 North 200 West.**

Beaver Carnegie Library—

The Scottish-born American industrialist Andrew Carnegie believed that the wealthy should use their money to help their fellow human beings. One of the most worthwhile ways he accomplished this was to help construct more than 2,500 public library buildings around the world. This effort began in 1881, when Carnegie built a library for his hometown of Dunfermline, Scotland, and continued for nearly four decades until 1917. One of the last libraries financed by Carnegie was the Beaver Library, built in 1917 at **50 West Center St.** The arrangement with Carnegie was that each community furnished the building site, books, interior furnishings, and an annual maintenance budget equal to one-tenth the building cost, which was used to pay for the upkeep and operation of the building, the salary of a librarian, and the purchase of new books. The building has served the community of Beaver for three-quarters of a century and, with a recent addition to the rear, the library will continue at this location for many years.

Beaver Historical Park/Philo T. Farnsworth Memorial—

There are few individuals who have challenged Brigham Young for equal billing as Utah's most important historic figure, but, in 1987, 110 years after the death of the Mormon leader, Beaver-born Philo T. Farnsworth did. That year, following a campaign launched by a Salt Lake City 6th grade class, Farnsworth was chosen as Utah's 2nd person (Brigham Young being the first) to be honored with a statue in Statuary Hall in the US Capitol in Washington, DC. Named for his grandfather, an early Mormon pioneer to Utah and one of the original 1856 founders of Beaver, Philo T. Farnsworth was born Aug. 19, 1906, in his grandfather's log cabin on Indian Creek just north of Beaver. While Brigham Young has been praised as "the Great Colonizer," Philo T. Farnsworth's star shines even brighter as "the Father of Television." In 1927, at the age of 21, Farnsworth demonstrated the first all-electrical television system and, later, successfully defended his -Farnsworth had a natural talent for physics, and his experiments helped in the development of radar, electron microscopes, aircraft guidance systems, and incubators for newborn babies. He made millions with his inventions, but died in debt at the age of 64. Though he lived in Beaver for only the first few years of his life, Beaverites are convinced that his humble birthplace was the most important element in his brilliance. A statue of Farnsworth as a young man has been placed in the Beaver Heritage Park, located just west of the old courthouse. Plans are to develop the park even further by moving the old Farnsworth cabin to the park. About 500 miles to the north, in Rigby, Idaho, the community is trying to establish the Farnsworth Memorial Museum to "mark the birthplace of television." The Farnsworths moved to Idaho in 1918, and Rigby claims to be the birthplace of television since this was where Farnsworth, as a high school freshman, conceived the idea of all-electrical television and explained it to his chemistry teacher.

Beaver Opera House—

It is estimated that as many as 30 opera houses were built in Utah before World War I. Most of them have been demolished or severely altered, leaving the Beaver Opera House as the best-preserved opera house in the state. Constructed between 1908 and 1909, at a cost of $20,000, the theater provided seating for 1,000 people and was considered by one commentator to be the "finest playhouse south of Salt Lake...." In addition to theatrical perfor-mances, the building was used as a dance pavilion, a gymnasium, and, in later years, a movie theater. Between 1929 and 1955, the local unit of the National Guard was housed here. It served as storage for another 30 years until it was renovated in 1988. It is now the Beaver Civic Center. **55 East Center.**

Charles D. White House—

One of Thomas Frazer's best-designed houses, this large one-and-a-half story black basalt house, trimmed with gray granite, was constructed about 1882. Charles White was a prominent cattle and sheep man, the superintendent of the Beaver Co-op Store, a polygamist, and served in the highest Mormon ecclesiastical position in Beaver from 1891 until 1908. **115 East 400 North.**

David Muir House—

David Muir was another Scottish stonemason who worked often as Thomas Frazer's trusted assistant. Muir came to Beaver more than a decade before Frazer and had also learned the stonemason craft in Scotland. But he seemed content to work as an assistant to Frazer. This home is the only one in Beaver that was completely designed and built by David Muir. The stonework bears the mark of a master, and the unusual stone cross gable is unique in Beaver. **295 North 300 West**

Duckworth Grimshaw House—

The crown jewel of Thomas Frazer's work, the one-and-a-half-story black rock house was constructed at a cost of $2,000 between Mar. and Dec. 1877, so that the Duckworth Grimshaw family could move in time for Christmas. A Mormon convert from England and local farmer, Grimshaw who, incidentally, was not pleased that he had been given as a first name the family name of his grandmother, was a polygamist who was eventually convicted and sent to the territorial prison in Salt Lake City for "unlawful cohabitation." The Grimshaw House became the model for other houses constructed by Thomas Frazer in Beaver. **95 North 400 West.**

Fort Cameron—

Named for Civil War hero Colonel James Cameron, who was killed during the Battle of Bull Run, Ft. Cameron was established in 1873 to control the "Indian problem" in southern Utah. After more than two decades in the area, Mormons had effectively handled the Indians, and it was really the "Mormon problem" that federal troops were sent to southern Utah to keep in check. Despite congressional action outlawing it, Mormons continued to practice polygamy amidst a continual suspicion of disloyalty toward the federal government. About 250 soldiers were stationed at Ft. Cameron until 1882, when the fort was abandoned. The dozen or so buildings and the land were sold for a song to the Mormons the army had come to watch. Church leaders established an educational academy, known first as the Beaver Branch of Brigham Young Academy, the forerunner of Brigham Young University and later Murdock Academy, which provided high school training until the early 1920s when a public high school was established. During the 1920s, all of the buildings were demolished except one, the laundress quarters, which was last used in 1937 and 1938 to house a branch of the Civilian Conservation Corps.

George Fennemore House—

Beaver's first doctor of medicine had this house built about 1890. Built of tooled pink rock on a black rock foundation, the dormer windows and mansard roof reflect a move away from the more formal Federalist style of the 1870s and 1880s. **90 South 100 West.**

Harriet S. Shepherd House—

Townspeople considered this home to be Beaver's mansion. Constructed in 1876, it is indeed still one of the largest homes in Beaver and was built by a prominent sheepman and local church leader, Marcus L. Shepherd. Shepherd did not spend much time here, though. Following the counsel of Brigham Young, Shepherd became a polygamist when, in addition to

his first wife, Harriet, he took a second, Cedaressa Cartwright, nearly 30 years his junior. Shepherd's two wives did not get along and apparently never shared the same house. Harriet became the owner of this house, while Marcus lived the latter part of his life in another house with the younger second wife. The granary behind the house, which served on occasion as the town jail, was built by Thomas Frazer, but the builder of the Federalist-style house is unknown. One room of the house served as a school, and dances were held upstairs in the early days. **190 North 200 East.**

James Boyter House—

In 1883, a year after Alexander Boyter built his pink rock house, his younger brother and partner James Boyter constructed one of Beaver's finest brick houses. Just as Alexander Boyter's house was an advertisement for the brothers' stonework, the brick house constructed by James stands as a fitting monument to their skill with brick. **90 West 200 North.**

John Grimshaw House—

After the turn of the century, the style of house construction changed dramatically. The traditional symmetrical design of local craftsmen working with stone and brick was replaced by a new wood frame, asymmetrical form, taken from pattern book designs ordered from eastern catalogs such as the Sears Roebuck catalog. The John Grimshaw House, built in 1909, is one of the best examples of the new style and construction. Like the earlier stonemasons, however, John Grimshaw was a craftsman in his own right. As a skilled carpenter, he manufactured cornices and lathe-turned fancy woodwork trim that were used for decoration in this new style of house. **290 North 200 East.**

Old Beaver County Court House—

One of Utah's oldest courthouses (begun in 1876 and finished in 1882), the Beaver County Courthouse remains an impressive public building. Built under the direction of William Stokes, the US marshall, the building has a deep basement foundation of black basalt, two stories, and an attic. The tower houses a clock facing all four directions, which can be seen from almost anywhere in the town. Partially destroyed by fire in 1889, the building was immediately rebuilt and served as the county courthouse until the new building across the street was completed in the 1970s. Today, the building houses a museum operated by the Daughters of Utah Pioneers. The 2nd floor courtroom has been preserved and is used during the summer for theatrical performances.

Thomas Frazer House—
Built in three stages by the master stonemason, the Frazer House is both unpretentious and very interesting. The oldest section, the middle part, was constructed in 1870 of black basalt, followed by an addition to the east in 1872. Eighteen years later, the 3rd section was constructed of pink tufa rock. Attached to this addition is a bas-relief portrait in green granite of Frazer and his wife Annie. **590 North 300 West.**

SCENIC DRIVES

Beaver Canyon Scenic Byway—
Utah Hwy. 153 is the main access to most of the recreation spots in the mountains east of Beaver. The route from Beaver

to Elk Meadows has already been described for its access to the area's ski resort, as a biking route, and its plentiful hiking opportunities. The 17-mile route has also been designated as one of 28 Scenic Byways within the state. This is another example of the journey, rather than the destination, being of primary importance. Beaver Canyon is a beautiful drive during all seasons of the year, but especially in the fall when the yellow leaves of the aspens glow in contrast to the dark colors of the pine forests.

Kimberly/Big John Road Scenic Backway—
See the Biking section.

WILDLIFE
Big Flat Area—
Wildlife can be seen throughout the Tushar Mountains, but one of the most likely areas to spot mule deer is the Big Flat area, which sits on forest service land along the ridge of the mountains, approximately 23 miles east of Beaver, off Hwy. 153. Big Flat, a large meadow surrounded by a conifer forest, extends approximately 4 miles south from Hwy. 153 to Gunsight Flat. In addition to deer, the area is home to elk, hawks, golden eagles, other mountain birds, and coyotes, whose howls can sometimes be heard at night.

———— WHERE TO STAY ————

ACCOMMODATIONS
Best Western Paice Inn—$$
Heated pool, sauna, whirlpool, and restaurant; 24 rooms. **161 South Main; (801) 438-2438.**

Best Western Paradise Inn—$$
Fifty-three units. At the north end of Beaver near Interstate 15, exit 112; **(801) 438-2438.**

Comfort Inn—$$
Fifty-one rooms. **645 North Main; (801) 438-2409.**

Country Inn—$$
Thirty-seven rooms. Swimming pool. **1450 North 300 West,** near Interstate 15, exit 112; **(801) 438-2484.**

Elk Meadows—$$$ to $$$$
The ski and summer resort at Elk Meadows, high in the mountains, 18 miles east of Beaver; 39 condominiums available; **(801) 438-5433.**

Quality Inn—$$
Heated indoor pool and whirlpool; 52 rooms. **1540 South 450 West,** near Interstate 15, exit 109; **(801) 438-5426.**

Sleepy Lagoon Motel—$ to $$
Located in the southern end of Beaver, this 20-room motel, with its delightful pond and quiet setting, seems like an anachronism among the more modern motels that hug the interstate exits. **882 South Main; (801) 438-5681.**

Station Motel—$ to $$
The only motel in Milford; 25 rooms. **485 South 100 West; (801) 387-2481.**

CAMPING
PRIVATE
There are three excellent private campgrounds located to the south, east, and north of Beaver.

Beaver Canyon Campground—
With 105 RV trailer sites, this is the largest of the private campgrounds, though only a third are equipped with complete hookups. There are also 45 tent sites, flush toilets, showers, laundry, and dump sites. One of the attractions of this campground is **Maria's Cocina** Mexican restaurant. Located east of Beaver on Canyon Rd. and Hwy. 153; **(801) 438-5654.**

Beaver KOA—
This KOA has 70 RV sites, 25 of which have complete hookups. There are 20 tent sites, and the campground is equipped with all the facilities of a modern campground including a swimming pool. Located north of Beaver on Manderfield Rd.; **(801) 438-2924.**

United Beaver Campground—
With 85 RV trailer sites (80 have complete hookups), 30 tent sites, flush toilets, a swimming pool, showers, laundry, and other facilities, this is a popular campground. Its popularity is enhanced by its owners. A few years ago, five women from the Phoenix area decided it was time they became their own bosses and, looking around for an opportunity, came across the United Beaver Campground which was for sale. The women delight in making their guests' stay memorable, with activities planned throughout the entire year. Betty Miller, one of the five, is the chairperson of the Beaver County Travel Council and, as one of the movers and shakers in the community, she has made a great difference since her arrival. Located at the southern end of Beaver just off Interstate 15 at exit 109; **(801) 438-2808.**

PUBLIC
There are four public campgrounds located in the Fishlake National Forest in the Tushar Mountains east of Beaver. All are located off Hwy. 153, have picnic tables, drinking water, and charge a fee.

Little Cottonwood Campground is located 6.7 miles from Beaver. It has 9 RV trailer sites and 9 tent sites and is the only campground with flush toilets. Located at 6,500 feet, it has the longest season, mid-May–mid-Nov. Three miles farther up the canyon, **Little Reservoir Campground** has 7 RV trailer sites and 7 tent sites, as does **Mahogany Cove Campground,** a half mile beyond Little Reservoir Campground. Both campgrounds are usually open early June–end Oct. **Anderson Meadow Campground** is located just beyond Elk Meadows Resort, 18.2 miles from Beaver. With 10 RV trailer and 10 tent sites, this campground is at 9,000 feet elevation and has the shortest season, June 1–mid-Sept. For further information, contact the **Beaver Ranger District, Fishlake National Forest, 190 North 100 East, PO Box E, Beaver, UT 84713; (801) 438-2436.**

WHERE TO EAT

Arshel's Cafe—$ to $$

Arshel's has been a Beaver tradition since the 1930s, when Arshel Hollingshead established a gas station and a grill here. The grill expanded to a cafe, and the gas station and cafe were operated by the Hollingsheads until Arshel's death in 1972. At that time, their son Dale returned from military service and took over the cafe. The original name has been retained and a photograph of Dale's parents during their courting days graces the menu. Dale has preserved the original character of the cafe, with such hard-to-find items as "real" french fries and hash browns. He continues to use a number of the old family recipes but supplements the menu with some of his own experiments. Some of the local favorites are the chicken and noodles, which is usually the Wed. special, the honey pecan chicken, which appears from time to time as the Sun. special, and the chicken-fried steak with homemade gravy that is available anytime. Homemade soups include broccoli, potato, clam chowder, tomato macaroni, and chicken noodle. Informed travelers between Salt Lake City and California always stop at Arshel's on their journey. Arshel's is also a favorite of local residents, especially the older set, with whom Dale has a particularly good rapport. Save room for the homemade deserts, which include peach cobbler and a variety of pies. For lemon meringue fans, the meringue on Dale's pie seems to imitate the 12,000-foot Tushar Mountains visible to the east from the cafe windows. Open daily 7 am–9 pm. **711 North Main; (801) 438-2977.**

Cottage Inn—$ to $$

Located in a renovated 1960s split-level house, this is an attractively decorated restaurant. Open for breakfast, lunch, and dinner. The menu includes a wide assortment of burgers, sandwiches, hot sandwiches, Mexican dishes, a vegetable casserole, barbecue baby back ribs, a 1-pound T-bone steak, shrimp, and prime rib. **161 South Main** in Beaver; **(801) 438-5855.**

El Bambi Cafe—$ to $$

This truck stop is open 24 hours a day, so if you are headed up or down Interstate 15 at a time when you should be in bed, the El Bambi can provide a good hot meal. **935 North Main; (801) 438-2983.**

Hong Kong Restaurant—$ to $$

The origins of the Hong Kong Restaurant go back several decades, when a Chinese immigrant, whose name has been lost to history, established a restaurant in Milford and secured a contract from the Union Pacific Railroad to provide meals 24 hours a day for railroad workers. Johnny Yee came to Milford in the 1950s to work in the restaurant; in the 1960s he and a partner purchased it. The partner moved on to Cedar City and opened the China Garden Restaurant there. Johnny turned the restaurant over to his son, Thomas, and daughter-in-law, Selina, in 1976, and they have continued the tradition of 24-hour service for railroad workers and anyone else who needs breakfast, lunch, or dinner, anytime of day. **433 South Main; (801) 387-2251.**

Joe Yee's Station Restaurant—$ to $$

The Hong Kong and the Station Restaurant are both owned by Yee families, but they are not related. Joe Yee moved to Milford in the early 1980s to work in the Hong Kong Restaurant. When the Station Restaurant became available in 1987, Joe and his wife, Waifan, took out a lease and have operated a successful restaurant ever since. Open daily 8 am–10 pm. **485 South 100 West; (801) 387-5024.**

Kan Kun—$$

The large double-poled sign that you see on the west side of Interstate 15 at exit 109 on the south end of Beaver reads "Mexican Food." I have driven past it many times, thinking it was another fast-food taco place, but when I finally stopped I had a very pleasant surprise. Rita and Santiago Amezcua became the proprietors of Kan Kun in Jan. 1992 and have already established a reputation for good Mexican food. This charming young couple are from the town of Jiquilpan, in the state of Michoacan, two hours south of Guadalajara. They have brought several traditional dishes such as carneas asada (broiled flank steak with special spices), carnitas (deep-fried pork), authentic fajitas, home style chili verde, and salsa that should please every Mexican food lover. The restaurant is a cheery place, and it's easy to engage others in conversation. Open seven days a week 11 am–9 pm; until 10 pm Fri. and Sat.; **(801) 438-5908.**

Mama Sarty's—$ to $$
Beaver's only pizza parlor, Mama Sarty's offers pizzas from 8 to 23 inches in diameter, plus a variety of sandwiches and pasta dinners. Open Mon.–Sat. 10 am–9 pm. Of interest is the collection of police patches from all over the US. Located at the corner of Center and Main on the first floor of the old Beaver Hotel; **(801) 438-5868.**

Maria's Cocina—$$
Located at the Beaver Canyon Campground, 1.5 miles east of Main St. on the road up Beaver Canyon—state Hwy. 15—the fare is Mexican and the location is a rustic log cabin with a central fireplace. The restaurant is open daily May 1–Nov. 1; the rest of the year on Fri. and Sat. only for dinner from 4 pm–9 pm; **(801) 438-6564.**

SERVICES

Beaver County Travel Council—
    Box 272, Beaver, UT 84713; (801) 438-2975 or 438-2808.

These abandoned charcoal kilns were built by the Frisco Mining and Smelting Company in 1877 to provide fuel for the smelting of ore from the nearby Horn Silver Mine. Photo by Allan Kent Powell.

Panguitch

It is the scenery that brings hundreds of thousands of visitors to Panguitch each year. Most come to gaze upon the fairy castlelike formations of Bryce Canyon National Park. Others seek solace and rejuvenation backpacking along the Escalante River. Fishermen enjoy the beautiful Panguitch Lake or the more remote mountain lakes on Boulder Mountain. There are few inhabitants in the area. Panguitch has a population of about 1,500 people, and the next largest town, Escalante, is half that size. The other towns—Hatch, Henrieville, Tropic, Boulder, Cannonville, and Antimony—all have fewer than 200 inhabitants. There are about 4,000 people in all of Garfield County, or one person per square mile, with 1,158 square miles left over.

Most of the residents still trace their ancestors back to the 1860s and 1870s, when Panguitch, Escalante, and other hamlets were settled. They are fiercely loyal to their homeland, and many have strong opinions about how public lands should be used. A recent legal battle erupted over paving the Burr Trail—a victory for Garfield County over those who would preserve the trail as a gravel road connecting Boulder with the Notom-Bullfrog road, which runs down the eastern exposure of the Waterpocket Fold in Capitol Reef National Park to Lake Powell. It is hoped that the newly paved road will increase tourism by providing access to Lake Powell through Garfield County, and that it will give Lake Powell visitors better access to Bryce Canyon and other Garfield County attractions. Local residents, who have struggled for years to wrest a living from the wilderness, mostly by raising cattle and sheep and doing some timber harvesting, are willing to promote almost any enterprise that will allow them and their children to remain in the area, even when their income (primarily through farming or service jobs) remains half or even a third of Utah's urban residents. This is not to say that locals do not appreciate the wilderness or have no desire to see it preserved. It is the encounter with the wilderness that has shaped the people of Garfield County and for which they have their own respect and reverence, though not always in ways that are apparent to outsiders.

But if there are elements of combativeness and independence, there is also a strong thread of humor that has existed in the area since it was founded. The original settlers named their town Panguitch, the Indian word meaning "big fish." At an elevation of 6,650 feet, Panguitch is one of the highest cities in Utah and consequently one of the coldest places in the state. Local wags joke, "There are two seasons in Panguitch, Fourth of July and winter." Or, "There are nine months winter and three months darn cold weather." When the small hamlet on the east side of Bryce Canyon was settled (6,350 feet elevation), it was named Tropic because it supposedly had a milder climate than Panguitch. Local jokers proposed that Tropic's neighbor Cannonville be called Shotgun because it was not big enough to be a cannon. Early Panguitch residents named their only store "The Old Sow," suggesting its role in providing nourishment to the community. That same kind of humor is evident in the now-famous (perhaps apocryphal) statement about Bryce Canyon attributed to the settler Ebenezer Bryce, who grazed livestock there: "It's a hell of a place to lose a cow."

HISTORY

Panguitch was first settled on March 16, 1864, under the direction of Jens Nielsen, a Danish convert to Mormonism who, eight years earlier, had suffered severely in the early winter storms as he pulled a handcart across Wyoming to Salt Lake City. Nielsen led a group of pioneers from Parowan and Beaver eastward across the mountains to establish the settlement near the Sevier River.

The settlers faced difficult times as crops did not mature because of the high elevation. Unstable Indian relations threatened the fledgling community. During the first winter there, seven men left Panguitch for Parowan, 40 miles across the mountain, to try and get flour and food for their starving families. The trek became known as the "Quilt Walk," when, according to tradition, the men had to abandon their wagon and oxen and make their way on foot across the snow fields by laying one quilt down and then another. In 1867 the newcomers were forced to abandon the settlement during what was known throughout central and southern Utah as the Black Hawk War. Panguitch was officially resettled in 1871 and began to prosper. Houses were built outside the fort, and farmers constructed an irrigation ditch. Other residents built lumber mills, shingle mills, and a flour mill. The livestock industry provided a good-enough income that substantial red brick homes could be built during the 1880s and 1890s. After World War I, though, the livestock market dried up and ranchers scraped by until World War II brought better times. Livestock never has regained its earlier preeminence, and tourism has come to play a large role in the local economy.

Bryce Canyon was established as a national park in 1928. It grew in popularity during the 1930s, with the completion of the Rim Road in 1934 and the construction of lodges by the Union Pacific Railroad which bussed visitors from the railroad station in Cedar City across the high plateau country to Bryce Canyon. Tourism has placed Garfield County on the map, but there were earlier events that also helped interject outside influences into the community life and economy of the area. In

1902, under President Theodore Roosevelt, federal lands were withdrawn as forest reserves and designated national forests in 1907. That same year a US Forest Service office was established in Panguitch, which continues today to oversee grazing, timber cutting, conservation, and recreation in what is now the Dixie National Forest. The next year, 1908, millionaire philanthropist Andrew Carnegie gave money to Panguitch for the construction of the public library building which still services children and adults throughout the area.

The New Deal public works programs of the 1930s had a significant impact on the area. One of the most interesting projects is the barnlike Bryce Canyon Airport constructed in 1936 and 1937. The federal presence is still felt and, as suggested, sometimes resented. Nevertheless, with the principles of multiple use, for land not included in wilderness areas which may only be entered on foot and used in a very low-impact way, forest service and Bureau of Land Management professionals seek a balance that prevents excessive exploitation of fragile desert land, permits controlled development, and preserves as much of its pristine character as possible.

GETTING THERE

Panguitch is 236 miles south of Salt Lake City on Hwy. 89. To reach Panguitch from Salt Lake City, head south on Interstate 15; then you have several choices to reach US 89. Most locals leave the Interstate at Nephi and take Hwy. 28 south through Levan to its junction with Hwy. 89 at Gunnison. You can also leave the Interstate farther south at Scipio and take Hwy. 50 to its junction with Interstate 70 and Hwy. 89 near Richfield. If you want to visit Cove Fort and Fremont State Park before reaching Panguitch, take Interstate 70 east from Interstate 15 south of Fillmore to its junction with Hwy. 89 near Sevier. To follow the 1864 pioneer route, leave Interstate 15 at exit 94 and take Hwy. 20 across Bear Valley to its junction with Hwy. 89, 10 miles north of Panguitch. Coming from the south on Interstate 15, take Hwy. 9, 10 miles north of St. George and travel through Zion National Park and on to Hwy. 89 at Mt. Carmel Junction 50 miles south of Panguitch.

FESTIVALS AND EVENTS

Bryce Canyon Winter Festival
February

Held over the three-day President's Day weekend in Feb., this festival includes cross-country ski races, snow sculpture contests, ski archery competitions, evening entertainment, and free ski, archery, and photography clinics.

Bryce Canyon Country Fat Tire Festival
early June

Held over three days in early June, guided tours are scheduled throughout the area to introduce mountain bikers to the many biking possibilities around Bryce Canyon.

Old-Time Bear Festival
2nd weekend in July

Held in Cannonville, this festival features old-time fiddle music and bear burgers (made from real bear!). There are also regular hamburgers and Dutch-oven potatoes. The festival takes its name from a bear that came into town during the fruit season and pestered residents of Cannonville. They destroyed the bear, but the bear hide is on display in town

Harvest Festival
last Friday and Saturday in September

Tropic is the scene of this festival. Activities include a scarecrow contest, children's games, horse obstacle course, native American dancers, Dutch-oven cookoff, arts and crafts, black powder shoot, and dances on both nights. For information, call **(801) 679-8796** or **679-8546.**

For further information about these and other events during the year contact **Garfield County Travel Council, PO Box 200, Panguitch, UT 84759; 1-800-444-6689.**

OUTDOOR ACTIVITIES

BIKING

Birch Spring Knoll Lava Beds—

According to the Garfield County Travel Council, this bike route "will take you through one of the most diversified forests in the West; several varieties of fir, ponderosa pine, aspen, bristlecone pine, mahogany, juniper, and piñon are growing side by side. Awesome vistas are seen looking south across red hills and black lava rock contrasted against the green trees and brilliant blue sky." The ride begins at the Birch Spring Knoll turnoff, 2.6 miles east of the Panguitch Lake Store on Hwy. 143. It follows Forest Rd. 069 for 1.7 miles, and then turns left onto Forest Rd. 309, which continues eastward along a fairly steep descent. It's a 2-mile ride through meadows to Cameron Wash, about 7 miles from the beginning point. Turn right along the Cameron Wash Rd. and head south for 1.5 miles to Forest Rd. 071. Head back west to Birch Spring Knoll along the most scenic part of the ride. This 5-mile ride is slightly uphill to its junction with Forest Rd. 309. The last 1.7 miles take you back to Hwy. 143 west along Forest Rd. 069, the beginning section of the ride.

Casto Canyon—

If you are looking for a downhill ride through one of the most scenic areas around Panguitch, the 17-mile-long route through the red-rock country into Casto Canyon offers easy access from Hwy. 12, with shuttle service available from nearby Ruby's Inn. The route leaves from Hwy. 12 east of Red Canyon, about 4 miles west of the Bryce Canyon junction, and heads north on Forest Rd. 117 also known as the Tom Best Rd. After 3 miles the trail turns left onto the Berry Spring Creek Rd. (Forest Rd. 120), as the Tom Best Rd. heads northeast. After another 3 miles, Forest Rd. intersects with Cabin Hollow Rd. (Forest Rd. 120). Turn right and follow this road north for 3 more miles to Casto Canyon. The single-track, 5-mile stretch through Casto Canyon, with its redrock pinnacles is unforgettable. The last section of the ride—what else but 3 miles—heads south at the bottom of Casto Canyon back to Hwy. 12.

Dave's Hollow—

This easy 8-mile out-and-back ride through ponderosa forests and meadows along a double-track road begins a mile south of Ruby's Inn at the northern boundary of Bryce Canyon National Park. Take the dirt road heading west and, after .75 mile turn right onto the Dave's Hollow Trail. Follow it for approximately 3 miles to its junction with Forest Rd. 087 near Dave's Hollow Forest Service Station. You can either return the way you came or head north along Forest Rd. 087 to its junction with Hwy. 12 and then east to the junction with the Bryce Canyon Rd. and back to Ruby's Inn. The latter route adds another 4 miles, for a total distance of 12 miles.

Horse Valley/Caddy Creek—

One of the appeals of this 17-mile loop is its high-country isolation. The ride begins in Horse Valley north of Panguitch Lake. Take Forest Rd. 076, which leaves the North Shore Rd. at Panguitch Lake from the northeastern corner of the lake. The dirt road goes 6 miles to the Horse Valley / Myers Valley junction. Here, the ride begins, heading north through the grassy meadows of Horse Valley. At about 5 miles, the road crosses a small pass and descends for a mile to the Caddy Creek Jeep Rd. (Forest Rd. 396). Head east for about 4 miles to Forest Rd. 082. Then turn south on Forest Rd. 082 and follow it back to the beginning point. The route begins at 8,800 feet and reaches 9,300 feet at its highest point. But don't worry: There are lots of ups and downs. The lush alpine meadows are an ideal habitat for deer, elk, and antelope, so watch for these animals.

Indian Hollow—

If you are staying in Panguitch and want a good four- to six-hour ride, head west out of Panguitch from the main intersection on Main St. and follow Forest Rd. 085 through Five Mile Hollow. Turn left onto Forest Rd. 310 and follow it along Five Mile Ridge to its intersection with Forest Rd. 082. Follow Forest Rd. 082 for 1 to 2 miles in a northwesterly direction, then turn right into Indian Hollow along Forest Rd. 039; the road heads northeast before turning back to the east, where it rejoins Forest Rd. 085 for the return ride through Five Mile Hollow to Panguitch. The 18-mile ride takes you through wooded stretches in a relatively untraveled area close to Panguitch.

Panguitch Lake Loop—

If you would rather ride than drive along Forest Rd. 076, an alternative to the Horse Valley / Caddy Creek ride is to begin where Forest Rd. 076 leaves the North Shore Rd. at Panguitch Lake. Follow Forest Rd. 076 for about 4 miles (the route climbs nearly 1,200 feet!), then turn right (north) onto Forest Rd. 082, which ascends through heavy timber toward the route's highest point (9,200 feet), at the right fork of Haycock Creek. After that it is a pleasant downhill ride through Myers Valley, home to herds of deer and elk. This is also an especially beautiful ride during the fall. Forest Rd. 082 reaches Hwy. 143 at White Bridge Campground, where it is a mile back along the highway to the beginning point. The entire loop is about 15 miles, but you can add several miles by circling around Panguitch Lake.

Pine Lake—

Located toward Antimony from its junction near Bryce Canyon with Hwys. 12 and 63. Eleven miles from the junction is a gravel road that heads east. Look for the sign Pine Lake Table Cliff Plateau, Campground, Dixie

National Forest, Forest Rd. 132. The bike route begins at this point and climbs along Forest Rd. 132 for about 5 miles to Pine Lake. You can stop here or continue another 3.5 miles along Forest Rd. 282 to the turnaround point at Henderson Canyon Viewpoint. The ride along Forest Rd. 282 winds through pine forests and aspen groves, and the over-look into Henderson Canyon provides a breathtaking view of what has been called a "miniature Bryce Canyon."

Skunk & Badger Creeks (Sunset Cliffs)—

This is a classic up-and-down loop through meadows, wildflowers, pine for-ests, and with a magnificent view of the Sunset Cliffs from the summit. The ride climbs from 7,875 feet to 9,240 feet. The route leaves the King's Creek Campground at Tropic Reservoir on the East Fork of the Sevier River and heads south to Forest Rd. 109 and up Badger Creek, a total distance of 7 miles, to another junction. Turn left or south and continue for another 2 miles to the summit for a well-deserved rest and a view of the Sunset Cliffs that will leave you speech-less. The 9-mile return route is all downhill along Forest Rd. 233, which follows Skunk Creek to its junction with the East Fork of the Sevier River, then turns north back to Tropic Reservoir. If you prefer starting from Bryce Canyon or Ruby's Inn, you can take the Johnson Hollow Connector Rd. which leaves the Bryce Canyon Rd. at the northern bound-ary of the park and heads west for about 2.5 miles to Forest Rd. 088. Turn left onto Forest Rd. 088 and head south for a mile to Johnson Mill. Turn right onto Forest Rd. 096 for less than a mile, until you reach the junction with Forest Rd. 088. Turn right along Forest Rd. 088 in a west/northwesterly direction for 2 miles until you come to the main road (For-est Rd. 087) to Tropic Reservoir. Turn south for another 2 miles to Tropic Reservoir.

Tropic Reservoir Loop—

The Tropic Reservoir Loop covers some of the same area described in the Dave's Hollow ride, but it begins and ends at the junction of Hwy. 12 and Forest Rd.

87. The 17-mile loop is ideal for novice bikers and is also recommended as a handi-capped off-road route. The elevation gain is only 225 feet, which comes during the first half of the ride. Forest Rd. 087 begins 4 miles northwest of Bryce Canyon. Begin the ride here and, after less than a mile turn west (right) at the sign to Blue Fly Creek. Follow Forest Rd. 091 through the mead-ows for 8 miles until you reach Tropic Reservoir. If you are ready to head back, turn left on the road north of the reservoir and continue to its junction with Forest Rd. 087 and follow the road back to Hwy. 12. Most riders will opt to continue another 2 miles along the western shore of the reser-voir to its southern junction with Forest Rd. 087 to complete the 17-mile loop.

BIKE RENTALS

Ruby's Inn, near Bryce Canyon; **(801) 834-5341.**

Rustic Lodge, Panguitch Lake; (801) 676-2639.

Kolowisi Tours, Antimony; (801) 967-1161.

FISHING

Panguitch Lake—

Speak of fishing in southern Utah, and Panguitch Lake comes to mind for most long-time Utah fishermen. Located 17 miles southwest of Panguitch, the lake is fed by three streams: Blue Spring, Ipson, and Clear creeks. The natural lake once had a depth of 38 feet, but a dam constructed in the 1890s increased the depth to 61 feet. Chances are you will not snag any of the "big fish" for which Panguitch was named, but the lake's cool water is home to plenty of rainbow, brook, cutthroat, and brown trout. The high country location and cold temperatures make this an excellent ice fishing lake. Boat rentals are available, and there are two public boat launching ramps on the north and south sides of the lake. Lodging is available at four locations near the lake (see the Accommodations section).

A number of other lakes in the area are stocked with trout and offer the opportunity for peaceful, uncrowded, and usually successful fishing trips. Many of the lakes must be hiked into or reached by four-wheel-drive vehicle. Antimony Lake, Barker Reservoir, Deer Creek Lake, Garkane Power Reservoir, Lower Bowns Reservoir, Oak Creek Reservoir, Pine Lake, Posey Lake, Tropic Reservoir, and Wide Hollow Reservoir are the best-known lakes and reservoirs in the area. Fly-fishing is best done at Antimony Creek, Asay Creek, Mammoth Creek, Panguitch Creek, and the East and South forks of the Sevier River. Additional information is available at the US Forest Service offices in Panguitch and Escalante. **Powell Ranger District, 225 East Center, PO Box 80, Panguitch, UT 84759; (801) 676-8815. Escalante Ranger District, 270 West Main, PO Box 246, Escalante, UT 84726; (801) 826-4221.**

HIKING

Birdseye Trail—

From the visitor center near the western end of Red Rock Canyon, this trail climbs for 1.3 miles through the pink and red formations for a true bird's eye view of the spectacular terrain. A shorter, easier route, the **Pink Ledges Trail,** also begins at the visitor center and loops for .75 mile through the formations. It is probably the most popular trail in the canyon.

Buckhorn Trail—

This trail begins in the Red Canyon Campground and climbs past fragile red-rock formations for 2 miles to a magnificent viewpoint high above the canyon floor. Because of the elevation gain, this trail is considered moderate to strenuous.

East Fork of the Sevier River—

Near the Red Canyon Campground adjacent to Hwy. 12, on the way to Bryce Canyon National Park, there are a dozen hiking trails from a mile round-trip to 14 miles from point to point. The longest, the Cassidy Trail, named for the outlaw Butch Cassidy, who supposedly used the trail, leaves Hwy. 12 about .4 mile from the Red

Canyon Campground and heads north through the picturesque red rock formations. At about 8 miles, the route meets another trail coming up Casto Canyon from the west. At this point, you can either retrace your route back to Hwy. 12, for a round-trip hike of 16 miles, or take the Casto Canyon Trail for about 5.5 miles to the mouth of the canyon and its intersection with a gravel road that loops off of Hwy. 89, just south of Panguitch. The trail winds through the bottom of the canyon and is considered one of the most scenic hikes in the area. The entire distance can be covered in one day of vigorous hiking, or two days at a slower pace. If you choose to spend more than a day in the area, there are other trails that branch off the Cassidy Trail. The main route is also a popular horse trail. Off-road vehicles are permitted in Casto Canyon but not on the Cassidy Trail. No water is available, so carry your own.

Golden Wall Trail—

The Golden Wall Trail begins about a mile west of the Red Canyon Campground and heads south up the bottom of a canyon for just over a mile. Plans are to extend the trail east for about 1.5 miles to intersect with the Buckhorn Trail. A detour off the Golden Wall Trail is along the .7-mile-long Castle Bridge Trail, a steep switchbacked route up the east side of the canyon, which rejoins the Golden Wall Trail near its present terminus.

Tunnel Trail—

Tunnel Trail begins just west of the tunnels on the south side of Hwy. 12 in Red Canyon and is only a mile in length. A foot route only, the trail provides some of the most spectacular views of Red Canyon and is a pleasant, uncrowded, moderate walk.

All these trails are located on forest service land. For further information, contact the **US Forest Service, Powell Ranger District, 57 North Main St., Panguitch, UT 84759; (801) 676-8815.**

HORSEBACK RIDING

Scenic Safaris, Inc.—

Horseback rides from one hour to five days can be arranged. Shorter rides feature trips through Kodachrome State Park, while the longer rides head north from Cannonville into the Escalante Mountains and the Acquarius Plateau. **PO Box 278, Cannonville, UT 84718 (801) 679-8536.**

ROCK HOUNDING

The Panguitch area offers many opportunities for rock hunters. Nedra Johnson, who with her husband Howard owns the Bear Valley Trading Company, 10 miles north of Panguitch, is a local lapidarist who offers information for rock hounds. Among other rocks, blue and red agate may be found at the southern end of Panguitch Lake in an area called the Meadows and unfractured red agate is prevalent along the Hole-in-the-Rock Rd. east of Escalante.

SKIING

CROSS-COUNTRY SKIING

Duck Creek Village—

Located along Scenic Byway Hwy. 14, about 30 miles southwest of Panguitch, Duck Creek Village has groomed cross-country skiing trails, ski rentals, and instructors; **1-800-223-8264.**

Ruby's Inn Cross Country—

See the **Bryce Canyon National Park** section.

SNOWMOBILING

The Panguitch and Escalante areas offer hundreds of miles of snowmobile trails. Duck Creek Village, located on Hwy. 14 offers snowmobile rentals and daily guided tours over three groomed routes. A 45-mile loop reaches Cedar Breaks National Monument on the north and Cascade Overlook on the southern end of the

loop. Another route heads to Strawberry Point and its magnificent view south into Arizona. From the Panguitch Lake Trailhead, a trail heads south to connect with the groomed trails north of Duck Creek Village. From Ruby's Inn, just outside Bryce Canyon, or the Tropic Reservoir Trailhead south of Hwy. 12, a groomed trail encircles Tropic Reservoir, with other snowmobile trails heading west up Badger and Skunk creeks, or south along the east fork of the Sevier River. The Escalante Mountain Trailhead begins north of Bryce Canyon, at Widtsoe, and follows Escalante Canyon to the mountain summit. It then descends on the eastern side along the Main Canyon Rd. down Birch Creek to the trailhead, about 5 miles west of the town of Escalante, for a one-way distance of about 20 miles. A much longer route heads north from the Escalante Mountain summit along Forest Rd. 140, then angles to the northeast, then east to the southern end of the Aquarius Plateau. Here, the route joins Forest Rd. 154 near Green Lake and turns southeast, passing Posy Lake before it intersects with the Hell's Backbone Rd. (Forest Rd. 153) and continues to the trailhead, about a mile north of Escalante. The Dixie National Forest has published a snowmobile trail guide, which covers these and other routes. Because snow conditions vary, it is also good to check in at one of the US Forest Service district offices. For trail guides and additional information contact the **Powell Ranger District, 225 East Center, PO Box 291, Panguitch, UT 84759; (801) 676-8815;** or **Escalante Ranger District, 270 West Main, PO Box 246, Escalante, UT 84726; (801) 826-4221.**

TENNIS

At the northern end of town, just east of the visitor center is a park with two tennis courts, a playground, picnic area, and a rodeo arena and racetrack. The old grandstand dates from early in this century.

SEEING AND DOING

AMUSEMENTS

Old Bryce Town—

Located across the highway from Ruby's Inn, Old Bryce Town offers a number of "Old West" entertainments and amusements including a chuck wagon dinner ride, old-time hoedown, rodeo, gold panning, and trail rides. For further information, write **Ruby's Inn, UT 84764;** or call **(801) 834-5301.**

FISH HATCHERIES

Mammoth Creek Hatchery—

Operated by the Utah Division of Wildlife Resources, this hatchery produces more than a half million fish each year, many of which find their way into the lakes, reservoirs, and streams of southern Utah. Visitors are welcome during the day, where 16 fish runs and other facilities make for an interesting stop. The hatchery is located off Hwy. 89, a mile south of Hatch, then 2 miles west along a paved road to the hatchery.

GHOST TOWNS

Traveling the road between Bryce Canyon and Antimony, you will pass two ghost towns—definitive evidence that not all pioneering efforts in the West were successful. Widtsoe, just east of Hwy. 22 and 13 miles north of the Bryce Canyon junction with Hwy. 12, was established in 1876. By 1920, it boasted four stores, a post office, two hotels, an LDS church, a social hall, a school, and a number of homes. But the agricultural depression and drought of the 1920s saw one family after another move away as crops failed. In 1935, the last 17 families, with federal government assistance, abandoned the town, leaving for more productive locations. Fourteen miles farther north on Hwy. 22, the site of Osiris is worth a stop to photograph the remains of a rock-walled creamery, a red-stained frame, four-story grain elevator, and four concrete silos that date from the prosperous days before and during World War I.

HISTORIC BUILDINGS

Bryce Canyon Airport—

The Bryce Canyon Airport Building is one of the most unique historic buildings in Utah. The story of the building and its construction is a self-contained history lecture. Built between 1936 and 1937, this was one of the projects of Franklin D. Roosevelt's Work Progress Administration New Deal program. Men, who were the children and grandchildren of those who had settled this frontier, found themselves without work or income during the Great Depression and were appreciative of the opportunity to earn money from this joint project of Garfield County and the federal government. With an eye to attracting air service and more tourists to Bryce Canyon, the Ruby Syrett family used tractors to level the 7,586-foot runway. The barnlike airport building was constructed of native ponderosa pine logs, infested with the black beetle. Civilian Conservation Corps workers cut down the trees which were sawed at a nearby sawmill and hauled to the construction site with teams of horses. The corrugated tin used for the gabled roof was manufactured outside the area and represented perhaps the largest nonlabor expenditure on the building. The airport is still in use. It is one of the oldest remaining airports in the US.

Historic Panguitch Homes—

If you want to really see Panguitch, take time to walk or drive around the town. There are nearly two dozen houses of locally produced brick that give the town a distinctive character. Most were built in the 1890s and reflect a period of architecture when Utah builders were just beginning to break away from the symmetrical Federalist style to more asymmetrical Victorian styles.

Panguitch Business District—

The economic prosperity of Panguitch a century ago is still visible in the historic commercial buildings that remain on Main St. between Center St. and 1st North. The Garfield Exchange, located on the corner of Main and 1st North, was established in 1899 as a general mercantile business. Next to it, the bank building saw several locally organized banks attempt to establish an economic foothold in the community, but they succeeded only as long as the national economy was strong, in the first two decades of the 20th century. The Southern Utah Equitable, known throughout southern Utah as SUE, finally closed its doors in the 1980s. This stately building was, according to local tradition, the source of difficulty for one young man who spent the summer in Panguitch. When he returned home to his parents in the northern part of the state, they asked, "Who is this SUE to whom you've been writing all those checks?"

Panguitch Historic Public Buildings—

From the number of public buildings constructed then, it seems that the years 1907 and 1908 were the most active construction periods in Panguitch's history. Within two blocks, you can see four buildings that served as the political, social, educational, and religious hubs of the community. In 1907, the **Garfield County Courthouse** was constructed at **55 South Main.** This handsome building of native brick has served as the center of political activity in the county for more than 90 years, and with the sympathetic addition on its north side in 1984, the building should still be in service when it celebrates its 100th birthday. The **Social Hall**, located on **Center St.**, was built in 1908, then immediately rebuilt after a fire destroyed the first building. As the social center of the community, it was used mostly for public dances, but it continues to be used for basketball, dancing, gymnastics, and summer musicals. Just south of the Social Hall, the **library** was also built in 1908. Panguitch was one of more than 20 Utah communities that took advantage of start-up money for public libraries offered by Andrew

Carnegie. Across the street from the library, the **Panguitch Bishop's Storehouse** was built in 1907 and is now used as the Pioneer Museum (see below).

Panguitch Tithing Office/Bishop's Storehouse/Daughters of Utah Pioneers Museum—

If Escalante and Panguitch are representative Mormon villages, it seems that the early settlers of these towns built their tithing offices so that they could be later used by the Daughters of Utah Pioneers as museums. In truth, if it were not for these committed women, the buildings would probably have been demolished long before now. The Panguitch Tithing Office offers an interesting contrast to the Escalante office and reflects the obvious transition from pioneer times to more modern ones. Built in 1907 of red brick, the Panguitch Tithing Office was designed from one of at least three standard plans that Salt Lake City authorities created for tithing offices around 1905. You can see almost identical buildings in Sandy, Richmond, Manti, Spring City, and Fountain Green. The building was leased by the local Daughters of Utah Pioneers organization in 1964. They use the building for meetings and as a museum to house artifacts from the pioneer days of Panguitch. The museum is open during summer Mon.– Sat. 1 pm–5 pm and by appointment during the rest of the year. If you come when the museum is not open, look for a phone number posted on the building; someone will come and open the museum for you. **100 East Center.**

SCENIC DRIVES

Brian Head/Panguitch Lake Scenic Byway—

See the **Cedar City** Chapter 6.

Highway 12 Scenic Byway—

As you travel throughout the Panguitch/Escalante region, you will put in a good number of miles on Hwy. 12. The entire route—122 miles from Panguitch past Bryce Canyon, through Tropic,

Cannonville, Henrieville, Escalante, and Boulder to Torrey in Wayne County—has been designated a Scenic Byway. If you are staying at Panguitch or Bryce Canyon and want a full day's outing, you can take Hwy. 12, making stops at Anasazi State Park in Boulder and at Capitol Reef National Park, just east of Torrey. Return via Hwy. 24 through Wayne County, then follow Hwy. 62 south through Koosharem, past Otter Creek Reservoir, Antimony, and Widtsoe Junction back to Bryce Canyon, or west from Otter Creek Reservoir to Hwy. 89 and back to Panguitch. Plan an early start if you want to spend a few hours in Capitol Reef National Park.

WHERE TO STAY

ACCOMMODATIONS
PANGUITCH

The high tourist season is late spring, summer, and early fall. The rest of the year, it can be very quiet in Panguitch, although more and more people are discovering its cross-country skiing potential and that it is easier to reach Brian Head Ski Resort from the Panguitch side than the Parowan side. Travelers will find the accommodations in Panguitch meet the basic needs without the frills, and cost, of overdeveloped resort towns.

Best Western New Western Motel—$$

Thirty-seven rooms. Heated pool and coin laundry. Open year-around. **200 East and Center; (801) 676-8876.**

Color Country—$$

Twenty-six rooms. Heated pool. Open Apr.–mid-Nov. **600 N. Main; (801) 676-2386.**

Horizon Motel—$$

Five of the 12 rooms are two-bedroom units. Open mid-Feb.–mid-Nov. **730 North Main; (801) 676-2651.**

Hiett Lamp Lighter Inn—$$

Twelve nonsmoking rooms, most with refrigerators. Open Apr.–Oct. **581 North Main; (801) 676-8362.**

MaeMae's Bed and Breakfast—$$

NidaMae Jensen was called MaeMae by her children, and the name seemed appropriate for the bed and breakfast she established with her husband Douglas in 1993. NidaMae was director of the Panguitch Job Service office for 31 years, and after her retirement she decided to turn their 1890s red brick home into a bed and breakfast. The house was originally owned by the Henrie family, one of the founding families of Panguitch. There are three rooms with shared bath, but Douglas is working on an addition to provide private baths for all three rooms. A continental breakfast of homemade cinnamon rolls, cereal, fruit, and juice is included. **501 East Center St., PO Box 387, Panguitch, UT 84759; (801) 675-1388.**

Marianna Inn—$$

Twenty-four rooms. **699 North Main; (801) 676-8340.**

PANGUITCH LAKE
Beaver Dam Lodge and Restaurant—$$

Located along the north shore, is open year-round to accommodate open water and ice fishermen. **PO Box 278, Panguitch, UT 84759; (801) 676-8339.**

Deer Trail Lodge—$$

Located northwest of the lake on the Clear Creek tributary. Offers housekeeping cabins with and without kitchens. **PO Box 647, Panguitch, UT 84759; (801) 676-2211.**

Lake View Resort—$$$

Open from Memorial Day–Labor Day. Offers housekeeping cabins. **PO Box 397, Panguitch, UT 84759; (801) 676-2639.**

Rustic Lodge—$$ to $$$

Located along the West Shore Rd.

Offers cabins with fireplaces, a restaurant, lounge, grocery store, boat and mountain bike rentals, and hunting and fishing licenses and supplies. **PO Box 373, Panguitch, UT 84759; (801) 676-2639.**

TROPIC
Bryce Point Bed and Breakfast—$$$
LaMar and Ethyl LeFevre went through high school together and married in 1944 while LaMar was a US Navy copsman in World War II. They returned to Tropic after retirement and opened the town's first bed and breakfast in 1990. There are six nonsmoking rooms, each with a private bath, television, and VCR. There is an extensive video library. Each of the rooms is named for one of the LeFevre's five children; the 6th room is the Grandkids' Room. A seventh unit, separate from the house, is the honeymoon cabin; it is one of the early cabins from Bryce Canyon that has been relocated to Tropic and renovated. The LeFevres know the area intimately and can help you plan your activities in and around Tropic. Open year-round. Reservations are highly recommended. **61 North 400 West, PO Box 96, Tropic, UT; (801) 679-8629.**

Francisco's Bed and Breakfast—$$$
Evadean Francisco took in her first guests in 1991 when Ethyl LeFevre (see the Bryce Point Bed and Breakfast, above) called in desperation asking if she wouldn't take in some visitors who had arrived with no place to stay. Evadean agreed and says that plea for help was a turning point in her life. The log home is surrounded by a beautiful flower garden that Evadean maintains. Her husband, Charlie, is a lifelong resident of the area. He was a guide for horseback trips at Bryce Canyon and still keeps horses on their 10-acre working ranch. He will even let you ride "Jack" up and down the lane. If you want, you can do chores with Charlie—gather eggs, milk the goats, and feed the horses.

There are three nonsmoking rooms, each with a private bath. Breakfast includes homemade bread and marmalade, fresh eggs, and pancakes and waffles. The house is located a half mile south of Tropic off Hwy. 12 at **51 Francisco Ln. PO Box 3, Tropic, UT 84776; (801) 679-8721**

Half House Bed and Breakfast—$$$
The Half House is indeed half a house that was built just after the turn of the century and is Tropic's oldest remaining home. The front of the house slopes to the road in perfect symmetry, but the back is a straight wall that begs the question, Why wasn't it finished? The house is being renovated as a museum for the Daughters of Utah Pioneers by Bill and Carol Nieman. The Niemans built a modern and spacious log house next door to the half house, and they've operated a bed and breakfast in the house since 1993. There are three nonsmoking rooms, each with a private bath. Carol's caramel French toast is a breakfast favorite. Open Apr.–Sept. **320 Hwy. 12, Tropic, UT 84776; (801) 679-8643.**

CAMPING
PRIVATE
Hitch-N-Post Campground—
Facilities include flush toilets, showers, laundry, a dump site, some tent sites, and disabled facilities; 34 RV trailer sites, 28 of which have full hookups. Open year-round. **420 North Main, Panguitch; (801) 676-2436.**

Mountain Ridge RV Park—
Eighteen sites with full hookups and 8 tent sites. Open May–Nov.; **(801) 735-4258.**

Panguitch Big Fish KOA—
Offers the usual facilities and a swimming pool; 70 RV sites (20 with full hookups) and 20 tent sites. Open Apr.–Oct. **555 South Main, Panguitch; (801) 676-2225.**

Panguitch Lake Resort—
Restrooms, showers, laundry, picnic tables, drinking water, and easy access to Panguitch Lake make this a popular campground during the summer. Seventy-two RV trailer sites with complete hookups. Open early May–Labor Day. **791 South Resort Rd.; (801) 676-2657.**

Riverside Campground—

Flush toilets, showers, laundry, swimming, and fishing are available; 124 RV trailer sites, 45 with full hookups. The **Cactus Cowboy Restaurant** is located nearby. Open May–Nov.; **(801) 735-4223.**

Sportsman Paradise RV Park—

Restrooms, hot showers, laundry, game room, pavilion picnic area, and snackbar within the park; 32 pullthrough sites with full hookups (15 with power and water) and 8 tent sites. Open year-round. Located 2 miles north of Panguitch on Hwy. 89; **(801) 676-8348.**

PUBLIC

Ten miles southeast of Panguitch on Hwy. 12 not far from Bryce Canyon, two national forest campgrounds provide space for visitors to Bryce Canyon and hikers in Red Canyon.

King's Creek Campground—

Located near Tropic Reservoir, the campground can be reached by turning off Hwy. 12 onto Forest Rd. 87 about 4 miles west of the road to Bryce Canyon, and following it for about 5 miles south. With 36 tent sites and only 8 RV sites, this is a good campground for tenters. Open June–mid-Sept.

Panguitch Lake North and Panguitch Lake South Campgrounds—

The North Campground serves RVs with 31 spots, while tenters can find 20 sites at the North Campground and 18 at the South Campground. Flush toilets are available at both campgrounds and showers at the South Campground. Open June–mid-Sept.

Pine Lake Campground—

It is located northeast of Bryce Canyon and is reached by taking Hwy. 22 toward Antimony for 11 miles, then turning east on Forest Rd. 132 for 6 miles to the lake. Has 32 RV and tent sites. Open June–mid-Sept.

Red Canyon Campground—

Open mid-Apr.–mid-Nov.; 15 RV spaces and 22 tent sites with flush toilets.

White Bridge Campground—

Open June–mid-Sept.; 22 RV spaces and 2 tent sites.

WHERE TO EAT

Bishop's Cafe—$ to $$

Open daily for breakfast, lunch, and dinner with homestyle cooking. Closed during winter. **429 North Main; (801) 676-8006.**

Country Corner Cafe—$ to $$

This long-time cafe is a favorite of local residents. **80 North Main; (801) 676-8851.**

Cowboy's Smokehouse—$ to $$

This is one place you will want to write home about. The warm hospitality, excellent food, western music, artifacts, and collection of local moose, elk, and deer heads on the wall all make this an unforgettable experience. Bill and Edie Collier are transplanted Texans who came to Utah because of the Mormon Church. Intending to move to Salt Lake City, they stopped in Panguitch and fell in love with the people, the scenery, and the area's ranching tradition. They opened their smokehouse in 1993, in one of the beautiful turn-of-the-century brick commercial buildings on Main St. It has become a favorite with both locals and tourists. Bill smokes the beef, pork, turkey, and chicken in his own smokehouse using mesquite charcoal. He makes his own barbecue sauce from 15 secret ingredients and serves a bowl of tasty home-cooked pinto beans with each meal. The history of these items is described on the back of the menu in paragraphs that would have earned Bill an A in any college writing class. Edie's homemade cobbler with ice cream is a must.

Peach is her favorite (mine too) but the apricot and cherry are also delicious. Chris Gilbert, who grew up on a southern Colorado ranch, helps out in the evenings and sings delightful old cowboy songs on the weekends and on other occasions. Open for lunch Mon.–Sat. 11:30 am–3 pm and for dinner 5:30 pm–10:00 pm. **95 North Main; (801) 676-8030.**

Flying M Restaurant—$ to $$

Known for its homemade pancakes and huge sweet rolls. **614 North Main; (801) 676-8008.**

Lazy J Steak House—$$ to $$$

Features steak, shrimp, and lobster. Open daily 5 pm–11 pm. Closed during winter. **523 North Main; (801) 676-8118.**

SERVICES

Dixie National Forest Powell Ranger District—

225 East Center, PO Box 80, Panguitch, UT 84759; (801) 676-8815.

Garfield County Travel Council—

PO Box 200, Panguitch, UT 84759; 1-800-444-6689.

An example of the fairy castlelike formations of Bryce Canyon. Photo by Allan Kent Powell.

Escalante

The small towns of Escalante and Boulder lie in the heart of some of the most beautiful desert scenery in the Southwest. For most of this century, they have been isolated and host to only a few hearty visitors. With the discovery of the excellent hiking opportunities, the paving of Hwy. 12 from Boulder to Grover which provides an excellent connection between Bryce Canyon and Capitol Reef national parks, and better access to Lake Powell via the recently paved Burr Trail, however, Escalante has come to occupy an important place on the travel map of Utah. Escalante and Boulder lie within Garfield County, which is also home to Panguitch and to Bryce Canyon National Park. Hwy. 12 connects the three locations as well as the smaller towns of Tropic, Cannonville, and Henrieville.

As you stand atop the Aquarius Plateau on the east rim of the Escalante County the country has changed little since Clarence Dutton penned this description in the 1870s: "It is a sublime panorama. The heart of the inner Plateau Country is spread out before us in a bird's eye view. It is a maze of cliffs and terraces lined off with stratification, of crumbling buttes, red and white domes, rock platforms gashed with profound canyons, burning plains barren even of sage—all glowing with bright color and flooded with blazing sunlight. Everything visible tells of ruin and decay. It is the extreme of desolation, the blankest of solitude, a superlative desert." As Dutton and other members of the Powell Survey looked over the land they could see four major landforms all running in something of a southeasterly direction and all quite different in nature. To the south they could see the Kaiparowits Plateau, some times called "Fifty Mile Mountain," for the distance it stretches from south of Escalante to the Colorado River. The historic Hole-in-the-Rock Trail parallels the Plateau on the north. The middle feature is Escalante Canyon, through which flows the Escalante River carrying water from the Escalante Mountains and the Aquarius Plateau historically to the Colorado River and now to the waters of Lake Powell. North of Escalante Canyon are the Circle Cliffs and the Waterpocket Fold, both upthrusts of rock which occurred about 85 million years ago. The Waterpocket Fold is included within Capitol Reef National Park. Flanking the Aquarius Plateau to the north is Boulder Mountain, over which passes Hwy. 10 as it heads north to connect with Hwy. 24 near the entrance to Capitol Reef National Park.

The Aquarius Plateau is an elevated tableland rising to over 10,000 feet in elevation on whose surface can be seen deposits from relatively recent volcanic and glacial deposits. Throughout the Escalante Canyon you will find different layers of sandstone, mudstone, siltstone, gypsum, and reddish shales. These are the remains of deposits from ancient seas, rivers, and sand dunes which have hardened into sedimentary rocks that are thousands of feet thick and include such formations as the Kayenta, Wingate, and Navajo sandstones. Water and wind have worked on these layers to produce an elaborate collection of fins, domes, buttes, cliffs, arches, bridges, and deep-cut canyons.

HISTORY

During the Black Hawk Indian War of the mid-1860s, the southern Utah militiamen, under the leadership of Captain James Andrus, passed through the Escalante area on a journey from St. George to Green River. During the journey they found wild potatoes growing here, which they cooked and ate, leaving the name Potato Valley to describe the area just east of the Escalante Mountains. In 1872 a group of Panguitch citizens investigated the valley for potential settlement and met Frederick S. Dellenbaugh and Almon Harris Thompson, members of Major John Wesley Powell's expedition. They recommended that any new settlement in the area be called Escalante, in honor of the 1776 Franciscan father, who, ironically, was never within 100 miles of his namesake.

Escalante was settled in 1875 and has been one of the most isolated towns in Utah ever since. But even more remote is the town of Boulder, 30 miles north of Escalante. Established as a ranching community in 1889, it has been dubbed the "last frontier in America." Its location is ideal for cattle raising, with the lush summer pastures on Boulder Mountain and the more moderate winter range on the deserts and in the canyons to the east. Boulder was connected to the outside world, if you can call Escalante the outside world, by a treacherous mule and horse trail, known as the Boulder Mail Trail, across which mail and small packaged goods were transported three times a week by horse and mule from 1902 until 1940, making Boulder probably the last town in America to receive its mail service in this ancient manner. Within Boulder, Anasazi State Park has been established to preserve and exhibit the ruins left by the ancient inhabitants of the area.

GETTING THERE

Escalante is located about 300 miles south of Salt Lake City, 40 miles east of Bryce Canyon National Park, and 70 miles southwest of Capitol Reef National Park. Escalante is located along Hwy. 12 which runs from its junction with Hwy. 89 just south of Panguitch to Hwy. 24 at Torrey at the west entrance to Capitol Reef.

MAJOR ATTRACTIONS

Anasazi Indian Village State Park

Like a number of other Utah towns, Boulder is located on the site of an earlier prehistoric village but, unlike all other Utah towns, only the ancient pueblos in Boulder and Blanding in San Juan County have become museums. (The museum in Blanding is called **Edge of the Cedars.**) Anasazi State Park was established in 1960, after a two-year excavation by archaeologists from the University of Utah uncovered 87 rooms in the pueblo which were variously used for storage, living quarters, religious ceremonies, and burial chambers. Later excavations were undertaken, beginning in 1978 and continuing to the present. A museum building was constructed in 1970; later a full-scale, six-room replica of a representative Indian dwelling from the period of AD 1075 to 1275 was built. Trails wind their way through the stabilized ruins. A self-guided brochure is available in the museum.

The village was situated on a branch of the Escalante River and, with an estimated population of 200 people, was one of the largest Anasazi settlements in the region. The Indians cultivated beans, corn, and squash in fields adjacent to the village. Apparently the village suffered a major fire, either because of war or through natural causes, and was abandoned by about AD 1150, less than 100 years after it was established.

The museum is open year-round, except for major holidays, 8 am–6 pm, mid-May–mid-Sept.; 9 am–5 pm the rest of the year. A modest admission fee is charged. For further information, call **(801) 335-7308.**

Escalante Petrified Forest State Reserve

There are a number of locations in Utah where you can find petrified wood, but nowhere is there a greater abundance

or easier access than at Escalante Petrified Forest State Park, 2 miles west of the town of Escalante. The 1,784-acre reserve was established as a state park in 1963. You can view a good collection in the petrified wood cove, a short distance from the parking lot. The hiking trails withing the park cover about 1.75 miles. There is a trail guide to the 1-mile petrified forest trail that climbs up the hill from the parking lot for a fine view of the ridge of Wide Hollow Reservoir to the west and the town of Escalante to the east just before you enter the petrified wood preserve. You can see plenty of petrified wood along this trail, but for an even greater concentration of petrified logs, the .77-mile-long Trail of Sleeping Rainbows, which loops off the main trail, is well worth the effort. The latter trail requires a steep descent then ascent. Even though tons of petrified wood were hauled away from the park before collecting was prohibited, there is still a vast amount of it to be seen. Tree trunks and stumps have been preserved by volcanic silica that entered the wood through groundwater. One explanation holds that the trees fell during a time of intense volcanic activity. They became buried in mud, which cut off oxygen, thereby preserving them. Silica mixed with groundwater was deposited in the wood from the fine volcanic ash. It is these silicates that led to the mineralization of the interior of the trees and the colorful gems preserved inside them. Within the state park is Wide Hollow Reservoir, which was constructed in 1954 for irrigation purposes. A popular local recreation area, there are boating facilities, swimming, open-water fishing, and ice fishing at the reservoir. There are picnic facilities, modern restrooms, showers, and 22 camping units within the park; **(801) 826-4466.**

Kodachrome State Park

You may wonder how Kodak could get a 2,500-acre park named for its most popular brand of film. Known locally as

Thorley's Basin, this colorful valley was visited by members of a National Geographic Society expedition in 1948. They named the area Kodachrome Flat, after the color film that first appeared on the market in 1935 and was first used in *National Geographic* in 1939. The valley was established as a state park in 1963.

The most distinctive feature within the park are the 67 slender, gray limestone stratified, stone columns called "chimney rocks." These columns are found nowhere else in the world in such a large group. While the chimney rocks look like they might be toppled by a good push or a strong wind, they have stood for thousands of years. Located a few miles east of Bryce Canyon National Park, the limestone chimneys offer an interesting contrast to the sandstone formations at Bryce. Some geologists postulate that the chimney rocks were ancient geyser plugs, vents, or tubes that filled with a harder limestone material than the sandstone that encased them. As the sandstone weathered away, the limestone chimney rocks were left. Cowboys had another theory, suggesting to gullible visitors that they were really petrified postholes!

Getting There—

To reach Kodachrome State Park, turn south out of Cannonville off Hwy. 12 and follow the scenic Cottonwood Cutoff Rd. for 7 miles to the park.

Camping—

There are 24 camping sites at the park, and a modest fee is charged.

Hiking—

Seven short hiking trails provide access to much of the area.

Angel's Palace Trail—Beginning just east of the campground, this trail makes a scenic loop in less than a mile through a narrow canyon onto a plateau where you can look down over the park.

Big Bear Geyser Trail—Named for a spire that looks like a big bear, this 2-mile loop trail off the Panorama Trail is the newest trail in the park. The trail also takes you to Cool Cave, a spectacular box-canyon cave well worth the hike.

Eagles View Trail—This old cattle trail north to Henrieville is a steep climb to the top of the cliffs 1,000 feet above the campground.

Grand Parade Trail—This 1 mile long trail takes you to the base of several fins and spires that look like they are lined up in parade formation.

Panorama Trail—An easy 3-mile round trip that circles among the chimneys and colorful rocks.

Shakespeare Arch Trail—This .25-mile-long trail takes you to an arch discovered several years ago by park ranger Tom Shakespeare. A brochure is available to explain the flora and fauna of the park.

Horseback Rides—

Guided horseback rides can be arranged through **Scenic Safaris Box 278, Cannonville, UT 84718; (801) 679-8536 or 679-8787.** Within the park is a natural sandstone arch named in 1979 for its discoverer, park ranger Tom Shakespeare. The arch may be reached via a short hike along Arch Trail. Outside the park boundaries 10 miles to the southeast is a larger double arch named for Gilbert M. Grosvenor, president of the National Geographic Society, by the 1948 National Geographic expedition.

OUTDOOR ACTIVITIES

BIKING

Hell's Backbone Route—

Until completion of Hwy. 12, this was the only route from Escalante to Boulder, and books could be written about the stories of travel over the dangerous route. Hell's Backbone is a thin ridge with precipitous walls on both sides that drops hundreds of feet alongside the Box/Death Hollow Wilderness Area to the west and Sand Creek Canyon to the east. On top of the ridge is a deep narrow crevice first spanned by a bridge constructed by the Civilian Conservation Corps in the late 1930s. While the route was first used by horses and mules, today mountain bikes are common. The designated bike route is rated from moderate to difficult because of the steep climbs and descents. The ride ends in Escalante, and a shuttle is required to take riders to its beginning point. The Hell's Backbone Rd. begins about 3 miles west of Boulder off Hwy. 12. Follow Forest Rd. 153 for about 7 miles from Hwy. 12 to the junction with Forest Rd. 109. Here is the beginning of the 30-mile ride over Hell's Backbone to Escalante. If you want to camp overnight, you can do so at the **Blue Spruce Campground.**

Hole-in-the-Rock Trail—

See the Scenic Drives section.

FISHING

Boulder Mountain Area—

Located north of the town of Boulder off Hwy. 12 Boulder Mountain is a fisherman's delight, with many small lakes, reservoirs, and streams that attract anglers from all over the state. Usually you will find brook and cutthroat in abundance. Pleasant, Raft, Green, Fish Creek, Cook's, Round, Left Hand, Donkey, Blind, and Pear are just some of the lakes on Boulder Mountain. Access to most of the lakes is with a four-wheel-drive vehicle over rugged roads. Roads connect off Hwy. 12, but check with the Escalante Ranger District

Dixie Forest Service Office in Escalante **(270 West Main St.)** for a forest service map that shows access to the various lakes and where you can get information on road conditions. One lake that you can reach with a passenger vehicle is Bown's Reservoir. Head north out of Boulder on Hwy. 12 for 19 miles and take the road to the right (east) for about 4 miles to the reservoir. The reservoir is usually well stocked with rainbow trout.

Posey Lake—

This lake has good brook and rainbow trout.

Wide Hollow Reservoir—

A part of Escalante State Park and located 2 miles west of Escalante, this is a popular and easy-to-get-to fishing spot for trout and bluegill.

HIKING

Calf Creek Falls—

Located 17 miles east of Escalante and 12 miles south of Boulder, the Calf Creek Recreation Area and Campground offers access to the 126-foot Lower Calf Creek Falls. The falls are reached along a 2.75-mile (5.5 miles round-trip) trail that is quite sandy, and, although the trail is not too steep, it can be quite strenuous, especially in the heat of the day. Yet the hike is well worth the effort, as the falls have created a miniature Shangri-la in this desert region. The refreshing falls; pool; "hanging gardens" of ferns, mosses and colorful wildflowers; and shade are a welcome relief before you make the return trip. The sight of water plunging over the red sandstone cliff is one that you won't soon forget. Along the hike there are two locations where you can see Fremont-style pictographs on the cliffs. One panel includes three anthropomorphs 6 to 8 feet high, which are apparently painted on top of older paintings. They are adorned with horns and seem to carry shields, a trademark of Fremont rock art. There is a trail guide that corresponds with 24 markers along the trail. You can pick up the guide at the trailhead.

Hiking the Escalante Wilderness—

The Escalante River, a tributary of the Colorado, provides access to some of the most pristine and glorious backpacking country anywhere in the world. A designated wilderness area, the region is open only to foot travelers. Spring and fall, when temperatures are cooler and the weather more settled, are the best times to hike the desert. Because of the numerous side canyons, hundreds of miles of hiking possibilities, and the wilderness designation, you generally encounter few people. Even though the waters of Lake Powell back up into Escalante Canyon, the area still remains as difficult to reach as before the lake. Only one road, Hwy. 12, crosses the river along the 85-mile-long course of the river between the town of Escalante and Lake Powell. You can reach the canyon from trailheads off two historic trails: the Hole-in-the-Rock Road, which parallels the canyon to the south, and the Burr Trail, which parallels the canyon to the north. Outdoor recreationists see Escalante Canyon as a great hiking preserve. Backcountry permits are required for more than day hikes. These can be obtained at the Escalante Resource Area Office of the Bureau of Land Management in Escalante. They also have a map for sale that outlines the trails, locates the trailheads and indicates mileage.

Also available for purchase is Rudi Lambrechtse's *Hiking the Escalante,* an indispensable reference if you are unfamiliar with Escalante Canyon. It offers 43 different routes that can be taken and gives a good introduction to the geology, history, wildlife, plant life, and backpacking dos and don'ts.

While most visitors who take the time to reach Escalante usually spend several days backpacking, camping, and exploring in the canyon, a nice day hike can be made along the 15-mile stretch of river from Escalante to the Hwy. 12 bridge. The river cuts through the great cliffs of the Escalante Monocline offering magnificent scenery and a wilderness experience just outside of town. Begin the hike by entering the Escalante River at the bridge next to the sawmill in Escalante. There is no established trail for the entire length, and much of the time you will be hiking in the ankle-deep river. (If the river is running higher than ankle deep, you probably won't want to make the hike.) Either leave a shuttle vehicle at the Hwy. 12 bridge or arrange for someone to pick you up.

The best place to get supplies, equipment, information, and maps about hiking in the area is at **Escalante Outfitters, 310 West Main St.; (801) 826-4266.** Barry and Celeste Bernards can offer good suggestions for all levels of experience and interest. They have on hand USGS maps and most items hikers would need.

——— SEEING AND DOING ———

MUSEUMS

Escalante Tithing Office/Daughters of Utah Pioneers Museum—Constructed in 1894, this rock building has been a museum for more than 50 years. According to principles of the Mormon faith, each member is to pay 10 percent of his or her income. Until after World War I, most LDS Church members paid their 10 percent tithe in kind, i.e., 1 out of every 10 eggs, 1 out of every 10 bushels of wheat, 1 out of every 10

calves that were born. To receive and disburse these tithes, tithing offices were constructed and tithing lots maintained in every Mormon village. The Escalante Tithing Office is one of the oldest and best-preserved tithing offices and has been used as a museum by the Escalante Daughters of Utah Pioneers since 1938. If the building is not open, look for the telephone number posted there. One of the faithful DUP ladies will be happy to come and give you a personal tour. **40 South Center St.**

SCENIC DRIVES

Burr Trail—

Shortly after the Burr Trail was opened, in October 1892, Josephine Catherine Chatterly Wood, a traveler on the trail, wrote, "All well in health but we had the life frightened right out of us all. I don't know what they call this place, but I'll call it the Devil's Twist and that's a Sunday name for it. For all of the roads on earth, I don't think there are any worse than there are here. It is the most God-forsaken and wild looking country that was ever traveled." The paving of the Burr Trail from Boulder to Lake Powell was one of the most controversial environmental issues of the 1980s in Utah. Local residents fought long and hard—and finally succeeded—in getting the road paved, arguing that the trail forms an essential link for travelers between Lake Powell and Bryce and Zion national parks. Seventeen miles of this 70-mile-long is still unpaved: 13 miles through South Capitol Reef National Park and 4 miles through Glen Canyon National Recreation Area. The road begins at Boulder, passes across the Waterpocket Fold at the southern end of Capitol Reef National Park, joins the Scenic Backway Notom-Bullfrog Rd., and intersects Hwy. 276 a few miles north of the Bullfrog Marina on Lake Powell. There are eight designated overlooks along the trail, which offer spectacular views of Long Canyon, the Circle Cliffs, Muley Twist Canyon, the Waterpocket Fold, the Henry Mountains, the southern parts of Capitol Reef National Park, Bullfrog Creek, Clay Canyon, and Lake Powell. Plan about four hours for your drive. This unforgettable drive cuts through the heart of southern Utah.

Cottonwood Canyon Road—

Another backway that connects Hwy. 12 with Hwy. 89 is the Cottonwood Canyon Road, which heads south from Cannonville, past Kodachrome State Park, and Grosvenor Arch. As the road follows Cottonwood Creek through Cottonwood Canyon, the prominent monocline (also called a hogback) known locally as the Cockscomb (because of the crest), looms above to the east. At the end of Cottonwood Canyon, the creek joins the Paria River, and the road follows the river some distance before heading southeast to its intersection with Hwy. 89 near the Paria Ranger Station. The road is 46 miles long and requires a couple of hours to travel—in good weather. During wet weather, the road south of Kodachrome State Park is impassable to most vehicles. During dry weather, the road can be dusty and washboarded, but it is heavily used during the summer as a scenic drive and a connecting route between Bryce Canyon National Park and the southern end of Lake Powell.

Griffin Top Road Backway—

If you want a shorter loop road, one alternative to continuing on to Bicknell over the Posey Lake Rd. is to turn west at Posey Lake and follow the Griffin Top Rd. for 32 miles, as it curves back to the southwest along the top of the Escalante Mountains. The road is a narrow, single-lane dirt and gravel road, with turnouts. It offers excellent possibilities for viewing wildlife, and once you reach the Escalante Canyon Rd., you can either return to Escalante or head west past the ghost town of Widtsoe, then south to Bryce Canyon and Panguitch, or north to Antimony and Piute County.

Hell's Backbone Road—

This 38-mile-long drive heads north from Escalante along Forest Rd. 153 following the Posey Lake Rd. for 14 miles to the lake, where the road branches. Keep to the right and follow the road to its junction with Hwy. 12. Passenger cars can usually travel the road in dry weather. The road reaches an elevation of 9,200 feet and is closed by snow in winter. (It reopens by late May.) For a more detailed description see the description in the Biking section.

Hole-in-the-Rock Trail Scenic Backway—

The 180-mile-long Hole-in-the-Rock Trail between Escalante and Bluff on the San Juan River was the most difficult of any of America's western pioneer trails. Today it is the best preserved of any of

America's western pioneer trails. The route was opened during the winter of 1879–1880 by a group of 250 men, women, and children who left their homes in Cedar City, Parowan, Paragonah, and other southern Utah communities to establish a new settlement on the San Juan River. The route passes Dance Hall Rock, a famous landmark on the trail. It was near Dance Hall Rock that the various groups converged to unite for their journey on to the San Juan River. Dances were held in the amphitheaterlike Dance Hall Rock. In some places, evidence of the pioneer trail can still be seen. Just above the Colorado River, at the end of this drive, the pioneers chipped and blasted an unbelievable slit in the sandstone cliffs down which they drove their loaded wagons. The nearly 60-mile-long section west of the Colorado River begins 5 miles east of Escalante off Hwy. 12. The road is a good gravel road, suitable for passenger cars, for all but the last 5 miles of the road. As the road approaches the Hole-in-the-Rock down to the Colorado River, it goes over hills of slickrock that may not be suitable for passenger cars and which require caution even in higher clearance vans and four-wheel-drive vehicles. In addition, there are sandy spots that you need to watch for. If you can locate a copy of David E. Miller's book, *Hole-in-the-Rock*, take it along as a guide to the trail and as an excellent history of the expedition, which took six months to cover the 180 miles. This backway is seldom traveled during parts of the year, so let someone know where you are going and when to expect you back. A few years ago, some retired friends from Kanab drove out to the Hole-in-the-Rock; their vehicle broke down and they

spent a couple of days and nights waiting for someone to come along to rescue them. Be prepared with food, water, and blankets.

Posey Lake Road—

While most travelers north from Escalante to Wayne County will take the all paved Boulder-Grover Rd. (Hwy. 12), there is another route north out of Escalante along Forest Rd. 153 across the Aquarius Plateau, to the town of Bicknell. The 40-mile, single-lane dirt road offers access to Posey Lake and large, open meadows on top of the plateau, punctuated with dense stands of spruce and fir. Plan an hour and a half for this drive, plus stops.

Smoky Mountain Road Scenic Backway—

If you want a Scenic Backway taken by very few people through one of the most isolated parts of the state, the Smoky Mountain Rd. offers such an opportunity. The 78-mile-long road runs south from Escalante to Big Water City on Hwy. 89, near the Utah-Arizona border, just east of Glen Canyon Dam and the city of Page, Arizona. The road is graded dirt and gravel. The steep climb up the Kelly Grade (5 miles of switchbacks up the 1,200-foot face of Smoky Mountain) is impassable when wet, as are other portions of the road, and should not be attempted. If it is dry you are likely to find plenty of dust and rutted roads, and high-clearance vehicles are strongly recommended. The route offers spectacular views of the Kaiparowits Plateau, Lake Powell, Navajo Mountain, and other landmarks. Plan several hours for this route, and take extra food and water, just in case.

--------------------------- **WHERE TO STAY** ---------------------------

ACCOMMODATIONS

Escalante is a small town and while it is well known to many Utah travelers, camping tends to be more popular than staying in motels. So if you are looking for fancy, modern accommodations in Escalante, you won't find them. But if you need a place to sleep and take a refreshing shower after a day of hiking, biking, or sightseeing, the following Escalante motels provide the necessities.

Boulder Mountain Ranch—$$$

Operated by Bob and Sioux Cochran and located 7 miles from Boulder on Hells Backbone Rd. adjacent to the Box Death Hollow Wilderness Area, this working cattle ranch has lodge rooms and cabins for its guests. Horseback riding, cattle drives, and pack trips are available. **PO Box 1373, Boulder, UT 84716; (801) 335-7480.**

Circle D Motel—$ to $$

Twenty-seven rooms, some with kitchenettes. **475 West Main; (801) 826-4297.**

Escalante Outfitters—$

Seven log cabin bunkhouses—three with double beds and four with bunk beds. These small cabins have heaters and a fan, but no air conditioning. Toilets and showers are located in a common bath house. The cabins are located around a common lawn with barbecues. **310 West Main St., (801) 826-4266.**

Moqui Motel—$ to $$

Ten rooms. **480 West Main; (801) 826-4210.**

Padre Motel—$ to $$

Twelve rooms. **20 East Main; (801) 826-4276.**

Prospector Inn—$$

Opened during the summer of 1994, this 52-room motel is the largest in Escalante. **400 West Main; (801) 826-4653.**

Quiet Falls Motel—$ to $$

Twelve rooms. **75 South 100 West; (801) 826-4250.**

CAMPING

PRIVATE

In Escalante, the **Triple S RV Park** offers 29 spaces with hookups and 19 tent spaces. Restrooms and hot showers are available. **495 West Main; (801) 826-4959.** Across the street, the **Moqui Motel Campground** has 10 RV spaces all with complete hookups. **480 West Main; (801) 826-4210.**

PUBLIC

About 20 miles north of Escalante, on the Hell's Backbone Rd. (Forest Rd. 153), there are two forest service campgrounds. Open June–mid-Sept., **Posey Lake** has 19 RV sites and 23 camping sites, while the smaller **Blue Spruce** campground has 6 tent sites. Swimming, boating, and fishing are available at Posey Lake; however, neither campground has flush toilets or showers.

Calf Creek Campground—

Fifteen miles east of Escalante, on Hwy. 12, the BLM maintains the **Calf Creek Campground**. Open mid-Apr.–late Nov., the campground has 5 RV sites and 14 tent sites. Flush toilets. Six miles southeast of Boulder, on the Burr Trail, the **Deer Creek Campground**, another BLM facility, has 2 RV sites and 5 tent sites.

Escalante Petrified Forest State Park—

Twenty-one RV and tent sites. Restrooms and showers. Located 2 miles west of Escalante.

EVERETT RUESS

In 1934, a 21-year-old-adventurer, artist, and writer mysteriously vanished from his camp in the rugged canyons east of Escalante. A native of California, Ruess had forsaken the comforts of Los Angeles for the wilderness of southeastern Utah and northern Arizona. Traveling by foot with his faithful pack mule, Ruess made the road his home and beauty and nature were his passion. Unlike the jobless folks wandering the southwest, Ruess came from a family of means and rejected convention. His letters and descriptions inspired later regional writers, such as Wallace Stegner and Edward Abbey. He has become a folk hero for many Utahns and visitors to the state because of his appreciation for and devotion to the canyons and wilderness he loved so much. While few visitors have the means or nature to forsake all worldly goods in pursuit of the secrets of canyon country as Ruess did, most visitors can still appreciate the area's impact on a young man like Ruess. In the last letter he wrote before he disappeared, written on November 11, 1934, from the Escalante Rim to his older brother Waldo, Ruess reveals a contentment with life and an appreciation for beauty that the Escalante canyons had helped him discover.

As to when I shall visit civilization, it will not be soon, I think. I have not tired of the wilderness; rather I enjoy its beauty and the vagrant life I lead, more keenly all the time. I prefer the saddle to the streetcar and star-sprinkled sky to a roof, the obscure and difficult trail leading into the unknown, to any paved highway, and the deep peace of the wild to the discontent bred by cities. Do you blame me then for staying here, where I feel that I belong and am one with the world around me? It is true that I miss intelligent companionship, but there are so few with whom I can share the things that mean so much to me that I have learned to contain myself. It is enough that I am surrounded with beauty and carry it with me in things that are a constant delight, like my gorgeous Navajo saddle blankets, and the silver bracelet on my wrist, whose three turquoises gleam in the firelight. ...

A few days ago I rode into the red rocks and sandy desert again, and it was like coming home again. I even met a couple of wandering Navajos, and we stayed up most of the night talking, eating roast mutton with black coffee, and singing songs. ...

I have not seen a human being or any wildlife but squirrels or birds for two or three days. Yesterday was a loss as far as travel was concerned for I got into an impasse in the head of a canyon system, and had to return almost to where I had started. Last night I camped under tall pines by a stream that flowed under a towering orange yellow cliff, and the tall straight ones that grew part way up the face of it. It was glorious at sunrise. Today I have ridden over miles of rough country, forcing my way through tall sage and stubborn oak brush, and driving the burros down canyon slopes so steep that they could hardly keep from falling.

At last I found a trail and have just left it to make dry camp on what seems like the rim of the world. My camp is on the very point of the divide, with the country falling away to the blue horizon on east and west. The last rays of the sun at evening and the first at dawn reach me. Below are steep cliffs where the canyon has cut its way up to the rim of the divide. Northward is the sheer face of Mount Kaiparowits, pale vermilion capped with white, a forested summit. West and south are desert and distant mountains. Tonight the pale crescent of the new moon appeared for a little while, low on the skyline, at sunset. Often as I wander, there are dream-like tinges when life seems impossibly strange and unreal. I think it is, too, only most people have so dulled their sense that they do not realize it.

W.L. Rusho, *Everett Ruess: A Vagabond for Beauty*, Salt Lake City, Peregrine Smith Books, 1983, pp. 178–180.

WHERE TO EAT

Circle D Restaurant—$ to $$

Located adjacent to the Circle D Motel. Offers both American and Mexican food. Breakfast served until 11 am. Open daily 6 am–9:30 pm.; winter hours 7 am–2 pm and 5 pm–8 pm. **475 West Main; (801) 826-4282.**

Cowboy Blues Diner—$ to $$

Traditional breakfasts, sandwiches, Navajo tacos, burritos, enchiladas, and traditional steaks, roast beef, chicken and trout for lunch or dinner. Try AJ's chili verde, made with a recipe from Mexican sheepherders. Open daily 7 am–9pm. **530 West Main; (801) 826-4251.**

Golden Loop Cafe—$ to $$

Big breakfasts, sandwiches for lunch, and American-style food for dinner. Open daily 6:30 am–9 pm; winter hours 7 am–8 pm. **39 West Main; (801) 826-4433.**

SERVICES

An interagency visitor center, operated by the BLM, the US Forest Service, and the National Park Service, is located just off Hwy. 12 at the western end of Escalante.

Dixie National Forest Escalante Ranger District—
270 West Main, PO Box 246, Escalante, UT 84726; (801) 826-4221.

Dance Hall Rock, a famous landmark on the Hole-in-the-Rock Trail. Dances were held by pioneers in the amphitheater like structure. Photo by Allan Kent Powell.

Cedar City

When Cedar City was settled in 1851, the band of settlers who made their way 250 miles south from Salt Lake City envisioned that the "Iron Mission" would become the industrial center of the Mormon empire. Iron ore had been discovered in the mountains to the west and coal in the mountains to the east. While church president Brigham Young had no use for gold and silver mines because they seemed to demand more in resources and labor than they ever produced, the iron and coal mines were another matter. They could be used to build self-sufficiency and independence from eastern manufacturers. With Mormon converts being recruited to Cedar City from the mines and industrial centers of England, the vital labor force was available.

Brigham Young and others did not foresee that Cedar City would become a grimy soot-choked city as England's Leeds or Manchester once were; instead it was understood that Cedar City's new inhabitants would be hard-working, sober followers of the Mormon faith.

In light of the city's origins, Cedar City's founders may today be taken aback by the city's promotional slogan, "the festival city," and would wonder why the iron and coal mines and other manifestations of industry are now absent from the city. But recreation, tourism, and festivals have come to characterize Cedar City. One of Utah's oldest and best-known festivals is Southern Utah University's Shakespearean Festival held the last week of June through the first week of September. The Shakespearean Festival and the Olympic-caliber Utah Summer Games attract participants from all over the state.

These and other nearby attractions, such as Cedar Breaks National Monument and Zion National Park, make Cedar City a tourist destination in the summer. Less well known, but growing in popularity, Brian Head Ski Resort, a few miles east of the city, atop the 11,000-foot Markagunt Plateau, serves all of southern Utah and has become a popular destination for Las Vegas and California skiers. Cedar City is also the home of Southern Utah University.

HISTORY

Human presence in the Cedar City area stretches back into prehistoric times. Rock art in Parowan Gap, just north of Cedar City, covers a long period of time from the Desert Archaic period of several thousand years ago to the Fremont and Anasazi cultures which matured about 700 years ago. Evidence of prehistoric occupation is found throughout the county and at least two of the area's pioneer settlements, Paragonah and

313

Summit, were built on extensive Fremont sites that were occupied between AD 1000 and 1300.

When the first Europeans, the Dominguez-Escalante Expedition, reached the area in 1776, they met ancestors of the present-day Southern Paiute Indians and learned that they were part of an Indian trading network that extended into southern Arizona and beyond. It was at a site about 30 miles west of present-day Cedar City that the two Franciscan friars decided to end their quest for an overland route from Santa Fe, New Mexico, to Monterey, California, and to return to Santa Fe. The "casting of the lots" was a dramatic moment in the history of this celebrated expedition, as the two clergymen had concluded they must return to Santa Fe, while others were still set on Monterey. Fifty years later, another man of deep religious faith, the Bible-packing, Methodist fur trapper Jedediah Smith, succeeded in making the journey from present-day Utah to California, passing through the Cedar City area in 1826. Both the 1776 Dominguez-Escalante Expedition and the 1826 Jedediah Smith trek contributed to the successful opening of the Old Spanish Trail in 1830, which connected Los Angeles with Santa Fe. The Old Spanish Trail passed near present-day Parowan, Summit, and Cedar City. Spanish coins and crosses and signs carved in rocks have been reported in the foothills east of these locations.

The Spanish Trail was still in use in 1849 when the first Mormon explorers, under the command of Parley P. Pratt, came south from Salt Lake City, with orders from Brigham Young to explore the southern region for colonization. It was this group that named the area the Little Salt Lake Valley, dedicated and marked the future site of the City of the Little Salt Lake with a flagpole and an American flag, and discovered the iron deposits on Iron Mountain 9 miles west of Cedar City that were such welcome news to Brigham Young.

Young lost no time in organizing a two-prong colonization of what was called the "Iron Mission." The vanguard group, which was made up of those with the right skills was called by Brigham Young to undertake the assignment. The first group would provide a good agricultural base for the mission, and consisted of 120 men, 30 women, and 18 children. They arrived on January 13, 1851, a year and five days after Parley P. Pratt, and raised the liberty pole and dedicated the location for settlement.

With the agricultural needs provided, the second phase, or the industrial phase, of the mission began. Beginning in November 1851, Cedar City was settled. By April 1852, English workers were being recruited from the mines as part of the Deseret Iron Company. The Iron Mission was both a colossal failure and a brilliant success. Little iron was produced and, after disappointment after disappointment, the dream of a self-sufficient iron industry was abandoned, even though the hills still yield abundant iron. Parowan and Cedar City prospered as Mormon settlements, however, and supplied colonists for a host of other later settlements throughout southern Utah, Arizona, Nevada, and Colorado. It is with great pride that Parowan still calls itself the Mother Colony.

While Cedar City and Parowan have built their 20th-century success on agriculture, mining, and tourism, the pioneer past remains a strong element in the mentality and heritage of these communities.

GETTING THERE

Cedar City is located 250 miles south of Salt Lake City on Interstate 15. Most travelers get there by automobile, but you can also fly into Cedar City from Salt Lake City. **Greyhound** bus service from Salt Lake City and Las Vegas is also available.

MAJOR ATTRACTIONS

Cedar Breaks National Monument

The Paiutes are said to have called it "circle-of-painted cliffs," and the name is most appropriate, as Cedar Breaks National Monument is a 3-mile-wide, 2,000-feet-deep amphitheater of eroded and beautifully colored ledges ranging in color from white or orange at the top to deep rose and coral further down. The colors and shades are constantly changing as sunlight, clouds, and shadows play on the cliffs. Visitors often compare Cedar Breaks with Bryce Canyon National Park, and for good reason. Both are cut from the same geological formation and are located close to one another in southern Utah. However, Cedar Breaks, at 10,350 feet, sits 2,000 feet higher than Bryce Canyon National Park and is completely in the subalpine zone.

Both are part of the Claron Formation, which consists of soft pink and white siltstone, sandstone, dolomite, and limestone layers. These strata were deposited in a Paleocene lake that filled a series of near-sea-level basins surrounded by lowlands about 50 million years ago. Fresh-water creatures lived in the lakes and when they died, their shells formed deposits that filled the lake bottoms. The lake ebbed and flowed over a long period. Eventually the limey skeletons of the marine creatures and other sediments compressed into rock. Violent seismic activity caused the region to lift up and split, about 15 million years ago, leaving the former lake bed on top of what are now known as the Markagunt Plateau (Cedar Breaks) and the Paunsaugunt Plateau (Bryce Canyon). Exposed to rain, snow, wind, and 200 to 300 freeze-thaw cycles a year, the poorly cemented sedimentary rocks began to erode at an uneven rate, leaving a deep amphitheater that remains pristine compared with Bryce Canyon. The 9.5-square-mile Cedar Breaks National Monument was set aside by Franklin D. Roosevelt in 1933.

Getting There—
Because of heavy snowfall, this park is closed from Oct.–late May. There are two routes to Cedar Breaks National Monument. From Cedar City, take Hwy. 14 (a Scenic Byway) for 20.4 miles to its intersection with Hwy. 143. Then drive north for 3

miles to the park entrance. From the north, follow Hwy. 143 19 miles south from Parowan, past Brian Head Ski Resort to the national monument. If you want to continue on to Bryce Canyon National Park, follow Hwy. 143 east to Panguitch for 33 miles, then continue another 20 miles to Bryce. Or follow Hwy. 14 east for 25 miles to its junction with Hwy. 89, then continue north 34 miles to the national park.

Camping—

There is one small campground within Cedar Breaks, Point Supreme, 2 miles north of the south entrance, next to the visitor center. It has 30 RV and tent sites. Like the park, the campground is open only from mid-June to mid-Sept. It is equipped with drinking water and toilets. A fee is charged. There are no other accommodations or restaurants in the park, so bring a picnic.

Hiking—

Unlike Bryce Canyon, which offers several trails from the top of the plateau down through the eroded formations to the bottom of the canyon, there is only one rough US Forest Service trail to the bottom of the amphitheater. Descent into the steep amphitheater is discouraged by the National Park Service, which tries to keep the Breaks as pristine as possible. However, two rim-level trails provide space to stretch your legs and give you an opportunity to view the exposed rim and forest environments that make up the Breaks.

Alpine Pond Trail—This short loop through the forest is 2 miles long and begins at the Chessmen Ridge Overlook. It passes through aspen, fir, and spruce forest close to the rim and circles an alpine pond. You will see bluebells, columbines, and other glorious woodland flowers in the shady glades and may bump into marmots lazily enjoying the summer bounty.

Rattlesnake Creek and Ashdown Gorge—See Hiking in the Outdoor Activities section.

Spectra Point Trail—Beginning at the visitor center, the Spectra Point and Wasatch Ramparts Trail follow the southern rim of the Cedar Breaks amphitheater for 2 miles around the exposed rim, past Elkweed and Indian paintbrush, to a stand of ancient bristlecone pines (one specimen is 1,600 years old) on Spectra Point. Beyond Spectra Point, a rugged promontory that sticks out into the Breaks continues into the forest alongside a bubbling stream, past woodland flowers, until you reach the end of the Wasatch Ramparts. The trail is mostly level, with a few ups and downs, and makes an excellent introduction to this unusual park. Allow about two hours round-trip.

Historic Sites—

Cedar Breaks was designated a national monument in 1933. Four years later, the Civilian Conservation Corps constructed two buildings that because of their age, architecture, and association with Franklin Roosevelt's New Deal program have been listed in the National Register of Historic Places. The visitor center and the caretaker's cabin are both of log and masonry construction. Their rustic architecture is characteristic of many of the buildings constructed in America's national parks from the turn of the century and into the 1930s. Nearly 60 years after their construction, the two buildings fit the character of Cedar Breaks to a T, and their rustic style enhances the visit to the National Monument for many people. There was a Cedar Breaks Lodge built by the Utah Parks Company but it was pulled down in the 1970s because of its deteriorated state. The small visitor center has a beautiful "picture window." It has interpretive displays and a small bookstore.

Scenic Drives—

Cedar Breaks may be viewed from your car along the 5-mile Rim Drive, which winds through stands of subalpine fir, Englemann spruce, quaking aspen, and flower-dressed alpine meadows. Along the Rim Drive are four view areas, starting with Point Supreme at the visitor center near the southern boundary of the monument. The other turnouts are Sunset View, Chessmen Ridge Overlook, and North View.

Cedar Breaks Scenic Byway—The 6-mile road between Hwy. 14 and Hwy. 143 that provides access to Cedar Breaks National Monument has been designated a Scenic Byway and is especially beautiful during the summer when many thousands of colorful wildflowers cover the mountain meadows.

Southern Utah University

In 1990, this nearly century-old institution attained state university status. The journey to university status was a long one. The institution was established as a branch normal school in 1897, then became a branch agricultural college in 1913. It was recognized as part of the state junior college system in 1953, when the name was changed to College of Southern Utah. In 1965, the school changed from a two-year junior college to a four-year college and was renamed Southern Utah State College in 1971. Its new status and name should outlast all the others. Southern Utah University is the center of much of the social, cultural, and recreational life of the area, with the famous Shakespeare festival, its popular athletic programs, and other activities. The two original buildings, the ivy-covered Old Main and the Braithwaite Liberal Arts Center-date from 1898 and 1899, respectively, and remain at the heart of the campus.

FESTIVALS AND EVENTS

Parowan's Birthday Celebration
January 13th

Parowan was settled on Jan. 13, 1851, and each year the community commemorates its birthday with pioneer dancing by elementary and high school students, a town meeting, a luncheon, and a birthday ball. For more information, call **(801) 477-3331.**

Iron County Cowboy Days and Poetry Gathering
3rd weekend in April

The 3rd weekend in Apr. draws cowboy poets, horse owners, and others interested in the lore of the old West to Parowan. In addition to cowboy poetry readings, activities include horse and mule races, sheep-shearing demonstrations, and a western heritage exposition. For information, call **(801) 477-3331.**

Parowan Memorial Weekend Horse Races
Memorial Day weekend

Each Memorial Day weekend, the Parowan Lions Club sponsors sanctioned horse races at the Parowan Equestrian Park. Post time is 2 pm on Sat. and Mon.

Utah Summer Games
June

Who said you have to travel halfway around the world to attend or even participate in the Olympic Games? While Utah's Summer Olympic Games do not attract international or even national media coverage, it is still a big event in Utah. The brainchild of university president Gerald R. Sherratt, after he witnessed the highly successful 1984 Summer Olympic Games in Los Angeles, the idea was enthusiastically adopted by Cedar City civic leaders, and the first Utah games were held in 1986. Now, each year, nearly 7,000 participants from all over the state compete in regional qualifying meets for the privilege of traveling to Cedar City in June for the finals of the Utah Summer Games. Olympic-style opening and closing ceremonies, dinners, intense coverage by Utah television stations, and more than 3,000 volunteers make this a never-to-be-forgotten experience for the athletes and their families. The competition covers 28 sports: archery, basketball, bowling, cycling, diving, equestrian, fencing, golf, gymnastics, horseshoes, judo, karate, mountain biking, power tumbling, shooting, soccer, softball fast pitch, softball slow pitch, swimming, table tennis, tennis, 10K race, track and field, trap shooting, triathlon, volleyball, weight lifting, and wrestling. For more information, call **(801) 586-4484.**

Paiute Restoration Gathering
2nd weekend in June

Held in Cedar City, this Paiute tribal celebration includes a pow-wow, a parade, a queen and princess contest, a dinner, a talent night, and a softball tournament. The Paiutes lost their status as a tribe in the 1950s and were reinstated in June 1980. Cedar City is the tribal headquarters for what is now known as Paiute Indian Tribe of Utah. For more information contact the **Paiute Indian Tribe Administrative Office, 600 North 100 East, Cedar City, UT 84720; (801) 586-1112.**

Utah Shakespearean Festival
end of June through September

In 1962, Fred C. Adams and his small group of students and volunteers launched the first Utah Shakespearean Festival. Today, the festival has grown to be one of Utah's most renowned cultural events. While the focus remains on the presentation of three or four Shakespeare plays (both well- nown and obscure), works by other famous playwrights, such as Ben Jonson, George Bernard Shaw, and Arthur Miller are also performed. During the 10-week festival, which runs from the end of June until the 1st of Sept., visitors can spend an entire week and see a different play every day. A good number of Utahns schedule a week's vacation in Cedar City for the festival. For serious students of the theater, a series of seminars, preperformance lectures, and backstage tours, provide insights and knowledge that enrich the audience's experience of the plays. The festival spirit is enhanced by jugglers, dancers, musicians, Punch and Judy shows, and Renaissance games, as well as entertainment that affords a new appreciation for the people of Shakespeare's England. Tarts, horehound and humbug candies, and oranges are sold by strolling maidens who banter with the audience using the authentic language and dialect of the 16th century. For those who want to treat their taste buds to more than tidbits of the period, there is "The Renaissance Feaste," which consists of a seven-course meal served by "winsome wenches" and accompanied by "roguish entertainment and lively humor," under the jocular eye of Henry VIII. The permanent festival site is located on the campus of Southern Utah University and consists of three theaters, including the 825-seat Adams Memorial Shakespearean Theater, constructed as a perfect replica of Shakespeare's Globe Theatre in London. It is best to order tickets well in advance by calling **(801) 586-7878,** or by writing **Box Office, Utah Shakespearean Festival, Cedar City, UT 84720.** A few tickets are made available the morning of each performance and a courtesy booth offers last-minute tickets for resale, if any are available.

Independence Day
July 4th

Celebrations are held in both Cedar City and Parowan.

Midsummer Renaissance Faire
2nd weekend in July

Held the 2nd weekend in July on Thurs., Fri., and Sat. in Cedar City during the height of the Shakespeare Festival. Offers games, entertainment, displays, crafts, and food.

American Folk Ballet Festival
mid-July
A week-long ballet festival with matinee and evening performances by the American Folk Ballet, a dance group now in its fourth decade.

Pioneer Day
July 24th
Celebrated in Cedar City and Parowan to remember the arrival of the first Mormon pioneers in Utah in 1847.

Jedediah Smith High Mountain Rendezvous
1st Saturday in August
This is a mountain man's delight and, for that matter, anyone interested in the costumes and activities of the mountain

men who roamed the West during the 1820s and 1830s. Activities include black powder competition, games, displays, and stories. Held in the mountains above Cedar City. Call **(801) 586-5124.**

Cedar City Birthday Ball
November 11th
Cedar City began to be settled on Nov. 11, 1851, 67 years before the rest of the nation would recognize the date as Armistice Day. Every year, Cedar City celebrates its founding with activities and events that culminate in a grand birthday ball.

Christmas in the Country
last Saturday in November
Held in Parowan, this unique candlelight parade followed by a Christmas lighting ceremony is a memorable way to start the Christmas season. Santa Claus pays a visit, home tours are scheduled, melodramas performed and a country dance caps off the celebration. For information, call **(801) 477-8190** or **(801) 477-3331.**

OUTDOOR ACTIVITIES

BIKING
The Bike Route—
Mark Gunderson, owner of The Bike Route, has done much to promote biking in the Cedar City area. The shop offers maps, half-day and full-day guided tours of trails in the area, bike rentals, spare parts, and repairs and good advice on trails and rides for beginning to advanced riders. **70 West Center, Cedar City; (801) 586-4242.**

The "C"—
This 16.5 mile loop begins on Center St. in Cedar City and follows Hwy. 14 for 5 miles up Cedar Canyon. At Milt's Stage Stop turn south, into Right-Hand Canyon. After a mile, the paved road becomes a double-track jeep road, as it continues into the canyon. Follow the jeep road for 4.7 miles to where the road splits, keep to the right as the route follows to the southwest,

then turns northwest and heads back into Cedar City. The last third of the ride is downhill and passes through groves of pinons and junipers, then sagebrush and wildflowers, as the elevation drops. It offers a grand view of Cedar City and Cedar Valley.

New Harmony Trail—
This ride follows an ancient Indian trail west from the early pioneer settlement of New Harmony, for 10 miles along Forest Rd. 011 to Big Water Lake. The route is along a single track that has rocky sections as it follows Comanche Creek. The first 4 miles are quite level and give you a spectacular view of the vermilion-colored Finger and Kolob section of Zion National Park. But the next 4 miles climb from 5,600 feet to 6,800 feet making this a ride for advanced bikers. To reach the trail, drive

south on Interstate 15 and take the New Harmony exit. Travel past the few houses that now constitute New Harmony to the end of the paved road. Take the left road, Forest Rd. 011, and watch for the New Harmony Trail sign that marks the beginning of the bicycle trail.

Red Mountain Ride—

If you want a short scenic ride from Cedar City that offers some challenge to intermediate riders, the 3.2-mile Red Mountain loop can be made in about an hour, including stops at a couple of viewpoints for overviews of Cedar City and the surrounding mountains. The loop begins a mile up Hwy. 14 from Cedar City and heads north. The ride is a single track marked with orange ribbon tape.

Sidney Peak and 2nd Left Hand Canyon—

Although this ride requires a shuttle to the beginning point and a pick-up at the end of the 17-mile-long ride, the hassle is still well worth it. The ride begins along a trail northeast of 11,307-foot at Brian Head Peak and descends to 6,400 feet. The trail winds around Sidney Peak as it passes through ponderosa pines and junipers. The ride takes you down Second Left-Hand Canyon, along Forest Rd. 048, until it intersects with Hwy. 143, about 4 miles up the canyon from Parowan. The lower portion of the trail weaves through sculpted red rock, sandstone, and limestone formations, similar to those found in nearby Bryce Canyon and Cedar Breaks, offering the rider a unique close-up look at the pinnacles and buttes of Vermillion Castle and other rock features. The upper portion of the route begins along a trail northeast of Brian Head Peak, located south of Brian Head Ski resort and off of Highway 143. Although the ride is all downhill, along a double-track and single-track dirt road, still plan four to five hours to make the ride.

Twisted Forest—

Perhaps the most popular ride from Brian Head Ski Resort starts at Upper Bear Flat, at the south end of Brian Head. The 9-mile round-trip route leaves Hwy. 143 and follows Forest Rd. 304, a jeep road that climbs across the downhill ski run before it intersects with Forest Rd. 265. After turning left on 265, the route heads southwest for 1.5 miles before reaching Forest Rd. 051 to High Mountain. Turn left (south) onto Forest Rd. 051, which passes through Twisted Forest, named for its gnarled forest of ancient bristlecone pines before reaching a spectacular overlook of Cedar Breaks and the Ashdown Gorge Wilderness Area at the end of the trail. The ride is good for intermediate bikers.

FISHING

If you like to fish, then don't forget your fishing gear when traveling to the Cedar City area. Several excellent reservoirs and streams provide a variety of opportunities.

Enterprise Reservoir—

One of the most isolated reservoirs in the area, Enterprise Reservoir is situated 10 miles southwest of Enterprise, and nearly 50 miles west of Cedar City. Stocked with rainbow, German brown, and brook trout, the reservoir has a boat launch and excellent camping facilities.

Navajo Lake—

All four types of trout—rainbow, German brown, brook, and cutthroat—can be found in this natural lake, located off scenic Hwy. 14, about 25 miles east of Cedar City. Boating is permitted, and both improved and unimproved camping sites are available. Although Navajo Indians do not and did not inhabit the area, bands of Navajos who had evaded the Long March to New Mexico made their way across the Colorado River and entered Utah from the southeast in the late 1860s. Hungry and angry with whites, the Navajos retaliated by stealing the cattle belonging to the settlers in southern Utah. One Navajo raiding party fought a skirmish with Cedar City cattlemen near Navajo Lake, which was named to commemorate the encounter. The Paiute Indians, who inhabited the area, called the lake Pah-cu-ay, which means Cloud Lake. Located atop the 10,000–11,000-foot Markagunt Plateau, there is good reason for it to be called Cloud Lake. The road to Navajo Lake is closed by snow in the winter.

Newcastle Reservoir—

Thirty miles west of Cedar City, the farming area of Newcastle receives water from a reservoir located just southeast of the town that is fed by waters of Pinto Creek. Stocked with rainbow trout, the reservoir can offer good fishing, though its setting appears to be more of a desert than a mountain location.

Panguitch Lake—

See the **Panguitch** chapter.

Paragonah Reservoir or Red Creek Reservoir—

If you are looking exclusively for rainbow trout, take the Red Creek Rd. out of Paragonah, approximately 7 miles east to this quiet reservoir.

Parowan Creek—

If you want to test your fly-fishing skills in a rapid, narrow stream, Parowan Creek might be just the ticket. The fishing area begins 5 miles south of Parowan, at the road to Yankee Meadows, and continues most of the way up to Brian Head Resort. The stream is stocked with brook, rainbow, and German brown and cutthroat trout.

Yankee Meadow Reservoir—

This reservoir is located 13 miles from Parowan. It stores irrigation water for the Parowan area and is stocked with rainbow and cutthroat trout. Small boats are permitted on the lake. Take the 7-mile dirt road off Hwy. 143, 5 miles south of Parowan.

GOLF

Cedar Ridge Golf Course—

Expanded to an 18-hole golf course in 1993, Cedar Ridge offers a good variety of holes, easy access from Cedar City's Main St., and no reservations needed. Pro John Evans all but guarantees to have you on the course within a half hour of your arrival. Located in the northeast sector of Cedar City, the course winds around the foothills and uses the natural terrain to good advantage. **900 North 200 East; (801) 586-2970.**

HIKING

Dominguez-Escalante National Historic Trail—

Although California was their objective when they set out from Santa Fe on July 29, 1776, by early Oct. Father Francisco Atanasio Dominguez and Father Silvestre Velez Escalante and their party faced blizzards, a shortage of food, and an unknown distance and terrain to complete their journey to California. Today, part of the route they followed, as their course swung from westward to southward near Cedar City, has been designated a hiking trail by the Bureau of Land Management. To reach the marked portion of the trail, 30 miles northwest of Cedar City, head out of Cedar City on Hwy. 56 for 1 mile, then turn right onto Hwy. 19 and drive to Lund. At Lund, turn right at the railroad tracks and follow them to the sign indicating Thermo Hot Springs. Follow the 25-mile hiking trail back to where the trail intersects Hwy. 56, 2 miles west of Cedar City. After leaving Thermo Hot Springs, you hike for about 1 mile, and then reach the site of the Casting of the Lots. The expedition's journey through this area (including "the casting of the lots") to Ash Creek, south of Cedar City, took four days, from Oct. 10 to Oct. 13, 1776. If you are serious about making this hike, it will be enhanced a thousandfold by taking a copy of the Dominguez-Escalante journal for these days with you. The most complete edition is the translation by Fray Angelico Chavez, edited by Ted J. Warner, and published in 1976 by Brigham Young University Press. Perhaps more accessible is the earlier translation by Herbert E. Bolton, published by the Utah State Historical Society in 1972, under the title *Pageant in the Wilderness: The Story of the Escalante Expedition to the Interior Basin: 1776.*

Rattlesnake Creek and Ashdown Gorge—

This steep 10-mile hike along a forest service trail descends 3,400 feet via Rattlesnake Creek through the Ashdown Gorge Wilderness Area. In places the footing is very poor and the trail is exposed and dangerous in the summer when thunderstorms and flash floods occur. Always check with a National Park Service or US Forest Service ranger before setting out. The trailhead is located off Hwy. 143, past the Brian Head Ski Resort and just before you reach the northern entrance to Cedar Breaks National Monument.

Spring Creek Canyon Trail—

If you want a spectacular hiking trail close to Interstate 15, the Spring Creek Canyon Trail offers easy access and an unforgettable experience in the narrow redrock canyon just outside the northern boundary of Zion National Park. The area is under study by the Bureau of Land Management for possible wilderness designation. From Cedar City, take Interstate 15 south to exit 51, then follow the road on the east side of the Interstate for 5 miles to Kanarraville, and another .5 mile south to Spring Creek Canyon. Coming from the north, take exit 42 and follow the frontage road north toward Kanarraville.

HORSEBACK RIDING

Cougar Country Outfitters—

One of the best-equipped outfitters in southern Utah, Cougar Country Outfitters offers horse and mule pack trips and day rides along with specialized fishing trips, cattle drives, family trips, ladies pack trips, and multilingual guides. **PO Box 550, New Harmony, UT 84757; (801) 586-3823.**

Eagle Basin Outfitting—

Located in Parowan, Eagle Basin Outfitting offers horseback rides of 3 to 10 days in length through the mountains and deserts of southern Utah. Groups are limited to no more than eight guests. **PO Box 947, Parowan, UT 84761; (801) 477-8837.**

ROCK HOUNDING

Wah Wah Mountains—

The southeast section of the Wah Wah Mountains is a good source of dendrites, fossils, calcite, magnetite, rhodochrosite, and other minerals. To reach the area, which is located 35 miles northwest of Cedar City, take the road from Cedar City northwest to Lund (head west on Hwy. 56 and watch for the road to Lund which is less than a mile after you cross under Interstate 15), then continue another 10 miles on the road that heads north, paralleling the eastern slope of the Wah Wah Mountains.

SKIING
DOWNHILL

Brian Head Ski Resort—

Uncrowded, well-groomed hills, distinguished ski schools, breathtaking scenery, and excellent accommodations best describe this fast-growing ski resort, which is located at the top of Parowan Canyon and nestled between Navajo Peak and 11,307-foot Brian Head Peak. This is the highest ski resort in Utah and the town of Brian Head is the highest town. While Brian Head Resort draws skiers from Cedar City and St. George, the biggest clientele seems to be from Nevada and California. Three and a half hours away, Brian Head is the closest ski resort for Las Vegans, and the quiet serenity of the resort makes it an ideal retreat from the never-ending nightlife of Utah's neighbors to the southwest. In a word, après skiing is not the emphasis here, making it all the more attractive for families and those for whom a busy nightlife is not essential. The seven lifts, two double-chair and five triple-chair, provide access to more than 4,000 acres of mountain terrain. The lifts are placed at three locations in the canyon, and this adds to the uncrowded feeling. The Riviera lift is for first-time skiers and offers a nice gentle hill to learn the basics of skiing. The adjacent Stardust Lift, 3,895 feet in length, is one of the longest lifts at the resort, but is primarily for beginning skiers or those who like a gentle slope. The Navajo Lift provides access to a good selection of intermediate runs and can be reached via the Stardust Lift. The Giant Steps area, serviced by three triple-chair lifts, offers runs for all levels. Ski rentals are available, and an attractive beginners package that includes rentals, a two-hour lesson, and an all-day lift pass is popular. Lift prices compare with most northern Utah resorts, but if you want to ski for free, just show up on your birthday with proper identification and the lifts are yours at no cost. There are several restaurants and a total of nearly a thousand rooms. Reservations can be made by calling **(801) 677-2035** or **1-800-272-7426.** Brian Head is located on Hwy. 143, 12 miles off the Parowan exit on Interstate 15.

The high-country meadows found in the Brian Head Ski / Cedar Breaks National Monument area are excellent places for cross-country skiing. For information on trails and ski rentals, check at the **Brian Head cross-country shop,** located at the **Brian Head Hotel. (801) 677-2012.**

Duck Creek Village—
Located 30 miles east of Cedar City on Hwy. 14, Duck Creek Village offers groomed cross-country skiing trails, rentals, and instruction; **(801) 682-2495.**

TENNIS
Southern Utah University—
Six lighted public courts are available at Southern Utah University, **1025 West and 200 South.** Although SU students and faculty have priority, you can call **(801) 586-7762** for times.

---------------- SEEING AND DOING ----------------

CEMETERIES
Parowan Cemetery—
The Parowan Cemetery has a number of historic headstones which make this a worthwhile visit. One of the most famous headstones is that of Ed Dalton, shot and killed by a US marshall on Dec. 16, 1886. The 34-year-old man was one of the first children born in Parowan on Aug. 25, 1852. His crime was marrying two women, in accordance with the Mormon practice of polygamy and then trying to escape from the marshall, who was trying to arrest him for violating federal laws against cohabitation. Dalton had been in hiding in Arizona, but when marshalls in Beaver, 32 miles away, learned that he had returned to his home, they made their way to Parowan under the cover of darkness. In the morning, as Dalton was taking his stock to graze on the range west of town, the fatal shooting occurred. Dalton died a Mormon martyr, and his headstone memorializes the injustice that Utah Mormons felt in being persecuted for their religious beliefs. The north side of the monument proclaims:

Here lies a victim of a Nation's blunder,
Which many to untimely graves hath brought,
It nature's holy ties hath torn asunder,
And, untold suffering, woe, and anguish wrought,
By ruthless hand this man crossed death's dark river,
His was the sacred blood of innocence,
The taker of his life will meet the giver,
Before the Tribune of Omnipotence.

On the south side, the statement is less poetic and oblique in explaining Dalton's fate: "He was shot and Killed December 16th, 1886, in cold blood by a deputy United States Marshal, while under indictment for a misdemeanor under the Edmunds Anti-polygamy law."

GHOST TOWNS
Old Irontown—
There is not much left at Old Irontown, except for a well-preserved charcoal kiln and a brick chimney; but if you are interested in kicking through the sagebrush to

discover the stone foundations of houses and other buildings and trying to imagine a town of several hundred inhabitants, the 22-mile drive west from Cedar City to Old Irontown is worth the effort. Old Irontown, or Iron City as it is sometimes called, was the second attempt to establish an iron industry in the region. The initial pioneer attempt, which began with the settlement of Cedar City in 1851 and lasted until about 1858, failed for a number of reasons—mostly problems with the blast furnace and the lack of a suitable source of coke or charcoal. When larger ore deposits were located on Iron Mountain in 1870 a second attempt was launched. More successful than the first attempt at Cedar City, which only produced 25 tons of iron, daily production of iron reached 1 ton a day in 1870 and climbed to 5 tons a day for a while after 1874.

The plant operated throughout much of the 1880s, but the lack of coke and the availability of cheaper eastern iron led to the abandonment of the project. By 1890, the plant had been dismantled, the equipment sold, and the former population of Irontown had relocated to Newcastle, Cedar City, and other places. Because of its significance in the early industrial history of Utah, the site has been listed in the National Register of Historic Places.

From Cedar City, take Hwy. 56 approximately 20 miles to the sign for Old Irontown, then follow the road southwest for 2.6 miles. Also of interest as you travel along Hwy. 56 is the open-pit iron mine on Iron Mountain, north of the highway before you reach the Irontown turnoff. The iron mine was reopened during the 1920s and greatly expanded during World War II, from a production of 300,000 tons in 1940 to 3,000,000 tons in 1950. Peak production was 4,000,000 tons in 1957, but after that production declined, until today when mining takes place on a limited scale.

HISTORIC BUILDINGS
CEDAR CITY

The Iron County Historical Society has prepared a pamphlet entitled "Historical Tour of Cedar City, Utah," which describes

14 sites, buildings, and markers in the city. It is available at the visitor center and other locations around the city. Except for the George Wood House, located at Iron Mission State Park, there is only one other significant house from the 19th century. Two important public buildings remain from the 1920s and 1930s.

Cedar City Railroad Depot—
The depot was constructed in 1923, when the Union Pacific Railroad line reached Cedar City. The railroad was a great boon to the agriculture and mining activities of the area and helped to make Cedar City a gateway city to the national parks. Tour buses provided transportation to the parks from Cedar City, and the railroad got into the park concession business, building lodges in Bryce, Cedar Breaks, and Zion in the 1920s and 1930s. One of the first passengers on the railroad was US President Warren G. Harding, who visited Cedar City and Zion National Park in late June 1923, shortly before his death. The railroad to Cedar City was actually a 30-mile-long spur from Lund and the main line between Salt Lake City and Los Angeles. For the best part of 36 years the "Doddlebug," a one-coach train, carried passengers from Lund to Cedar City. By the 1950s, the automobile had greatly overshadowed the railroad for passenger transportation, and the depot was closed in 1959. Still conspicuous as you drive through town, the depot has since been renovated as a restaurant, convenience store, and, in the summer, an antique and craft shop. Located on the northwest corner of **200 North and Main St.**

Cedar City Rock Church—
The Cedar City Rock Church is a monument to latter-day Mormons who, without money for materials and wages during the Great Depression, constructed this church with native materials and donated labor. Red cedar (juniper) from the mountains around Cedar City is used inside, while colorful stones from nearby creek beds were gathered and carefully

placed on the exterior walls. Especially stunning is the rock baptismal font in the basement of the church. The church is a very popular landmark. Don't miss it. Open for tours from mid-Jun.–Labor Day, Mon.–Sat., 11 am–5 pm. Center St. between Main and 100 East.

Joseph S. Hunter House—

Across the street from the rock church on the south side of Center St., the Joseph S. Hunter House was constructed in three stages between 1866 and 1924. Joseph Hunter and his family immigrated to America from Scotland as Mormon converts in 1849. While en route to Utah, Hunter's wife and two of his five children died. In 1852 Hunter was part of the colonizing group sent to Cedar City from Salt Lake City. In 1865 he married an English convert to Mormonism, Elizabeth Catherine Pinnock. Shortly after his marriage, he began construction of this house, where 10 children were born to the couple. Successful as a farmer and livestockman and active in church and civic affairs, Hunter was one of Cedar City's most prominent citizens. The house is now the office for the Century 21 real estate company. **86 East Center St.**

PARAGONAH

If you want to catch a glimpse of a fading Mormon village that has more pioneer homes and barns than any other remaining town in this area, drive the 4 miles northeast from Parowan. The name Paragonah comes from the Piede Indians, a group of Paiute Indians living in the area, who used the term as the name for the salty springs and marshlands nearby, which Mormons called the Little Salt Lake. Paragonah has a number of early adobe and fired-brick houses as well as log-and-wood barns, which are becoming an increasingly rare site in rural Utah. One unique style of construction was to build the log barns with spaces between the logs, supposedly to provide better air circulation to the stored hay. Another unique construction technique was mud concrete

or poured adobe houses, made possible because of the high lime content of the native clay. A lime mortar mixture was made from lime, sand, and animal hair then poured into forms that were 12 inches high and ran the length of the house. After one level hardened, the forms were removed and placed above for the next 12 inch layer. It doesn't take long to drive up and down the streets of this hamlet of 300 people and, while all of the buildings that are not vacant are private residences and not open to visitors, there is a museumlike quality to the town. The following buildings are of special interest.

Edward Morgan Edwards House—

Constructed in the 1880s, this is probably the best remaining example of the poured-adobe construction technique. After the walls were poured, they were covered with plaster. **19 South 200 East.**

Helen Bell Robb House—

The most elaborate of Paragonah's pioneer houses, this large brick home was built in 1861 for Helen Bell, the first of William Robb's two wives. She emigrated to Utah from Australia with her husband and used money she had earned in a successful Australian business to finance the construction of the house in Paragonah. William Robb arrived in Paragonah in 1858, but in 1861 moved about 50 miles farther south, to Harrisburg, with his second wife, Susannah Drummond. When Susannah died, after giving birth to her seventh child, Helen agreed that William could return to Paragonah with Susannah's children who were raised by Helen. **128 North Main.**

Marius Ensign/Silas S. Smith House—

Constructed about 1862 of locally produced red-clay adobe by Marius Ensign, one of the original settlers of Paragonah, the house was sold to Silas S. Smith in 1872. The older brother of Jesse N. Smith (see below), Silas S. Smith, like his younger brother, was one of the stalwarts of western Mormon colonization. He was appointed leader of the San Juan Mission, which blazed a 180-mile-long pioneer trail from Escalante across the Colorado River at the Hole-in-the-Rock Crossing and on to Bluff on the San Juan River in 1879 to 1880. The adobe remains in remarkably good condition more than 130 years since its construction. **96 North Main.**

PAROWAN

Travelers to Parowan will want to take time to visit a few of the historic sites still standing in this historic town.

Jesse N. Smith House—

Built of stuccoed adobe, between 1856 and 1858, this early pioneer home stands on the north side of the block just south of the two churches. Jesse N. Smith was the youngest cousin of LDS Church founder Joseph Smith. Born in 1834, he lived in all of the eastern gathering places—Kirtland, Ohio; Missouri; and Nauvoo, Illinois—before coming west at the age of 13, during the Mormon exodus. Smith was in his early twenties when he constructed his Parowan house. At the age of 26, he left his two wives and children in Parowan to travel to Denmark as a missionary for the Mormon faith. He was gone for five years! Call one of the numbers posted at the house to set up a tour.

Parowan Rock Church—

Parowan's landmark church, located in the center of the block in the town center, is one of the oldest remaining churches in Utah. The rock church was constructed between 1862 and 1866 and, with its separate entries for men and women, reflects the New England origins of many early Parowan residents. According to local tradition, men used the west side and women the east side and sat separated from each other until Brother Watson rebelled, marched up the east steps, and sat by his wife. Within a few weeks others followed and soon the congregation was sitting together as families. The church is built of an orange-brown sandstone laid in coursed rubble and has two levels: the lower level

of six classrooms and the upper level assembly hall with seating for up to 800 people. Since much of the Mormon settlement of southern Utah, northern Arizona, and the San Juan River area was under the direction of LDS Church authorities in Parowan, this church has special significance, for it was here that many Mormons were "called" to leave and help establish new settlements. The building currently houses a museum operated by the Daughters of Utah Pioneers, who will give you a tour of the building on request. A list of phone numbers to call is posted on the church.

Parowan Third Ward—

Standing on the same block as the rock church but facing east on the west side of Main St., the Parowan Third Ward Chapel makes an interesting contrast to the old pioneer church. Designed in 1916, and dedicated in 1918, the building is one of the most impressive examples of the "Prairie School" style of architecture, which was adopted by the Mormon church for several buildings. Salt Lake City architect Miles Miller was familiar with the work of Frank Lloyd Wright, and the new style of architecture served as a physical symbol that the Mormon faith was progressive and forward-looking— a statement that had particular importance shortly after the turn of the century and the long fight over polygamy. An addition was made to the church in 1958, and it is still used for worship services.

MUSEUMS

Iron Mission State Park—

Iron Mission State Park is one of a half dozen history museums operated by the Utah Division of Parks and Recreation. The museum is based on a unique collection of horse-drawn vehicles collected from throughout Utah by Cedar City native Gronway Parry beginning in 1911. Parry ran the first buses to Cedar Breaks. The unique collection includes buggies, surreys, sleighs, a milk wagon, a white hearse— used for children—a replica of a Wells Fargo stagecoach, and an authentic bullet-marked stagecoach that operated between Price and San Juan County around the turn of the century. There are hundreds of pieces of horse-drawn farm machinery, freight wagons, and other vehicles that were essential to Utah's early economic development. The museum, as you might expect, also tells the story of the development of the iron industry in the area. It has on display items made from the iron manufactured in Cedar City. These include a bell that was cast in 1854 and an iron cage jail that was last used at Lund. Two early log cabins are exhibited, outside in the grounds, one of which is the George Wood Cabin, constructed in 1851 and recognized as the oldest remaining residence in southern Utah. The house was actually built in Parowan, then moved to Cedar City later that year shortly after the new settlement was established. Open daily, except major holidays 9 am–7 pm in summer; 9 am–5 pm in winter. A modest admission fee is charged. **595 North Main in Cedar City, (801) 586-9290.**

ROCK ART

Parowan Gap—

Parowan Gap is known to rock art scholars throughout the world. Listed in the National Register of Historic Places, it has some of the finest Indian petroglyphs in the state. Unlike much of Utah's rock art, which is painted, the hundreds of Parowan Gap designs have been pecked and cut into the stone; however, like the painted anthropomorphs of eastern and southern Utah, those at the Parowan site have broad shoulders, tapered trunks, and headdresses which are considered characteristic of the Fremont. Other forms and designs are clearly from the older Archaic period.

Parowan Gap separates Cedar Valley to the west and Parowan Valley to the east. The Gap is 2 miles long. The petroglyph panels can be found on the northern side of the Gap, with the primary panel being near the western end and the other near the eastern end. There is plenty of parking at the

western end. The major petroglyphs have been fenced, but spend some time looking along the cliffs on the north and south side of the road, inside the Gap, for petroglyphs that have not been fenced. Parowan Gap is located about 15 miles northwest of Cedar City. Take Main St. to Hwy. 130, where it passes under Interstate 15, and continue north for 13.5 miles. Turn east (right) onto a good gravel road, which takes you the 2.5 miles to the rock art. From Parowan, head west at 400 North under Interstate 15 and continue for 10.5 miles to the Parowan Gap.

SCENIC DRIVES
Brian Head/Panguitch Lake Scenic Byway—

If you want to make a day of touring, you can take the two roads mentioned above and continue north from Long Valley Junction along Hwy. 89. Make a detour to Bryce Canyon then continue into Panguitch, later returning to Cedar City via Hwy. 143, a 55-mile-long Scenic Byway, which cuts through the Vermillion Cliffs, past Panguitch Lake, and on to Brian Head before descending Parowan Canyon to intersect with Interstate 15.

Take time to drive up to Vista Point. Located 1.5 miles east of Brian Head and .5 miles before the north entrance to Cedar Breaks, this gravel road is just under 3 miles long and is passable by passenger cars. The steep climb takes you to the top of Brian Head to an elevation of 11,307 feet, one of the highest points in Utah that you can reach by car. At the end of the road is a parking area with a 100-yard walk to a stone shelter, from which you can look down upon the highway, meadows, Brian Head Ski Resort, Cedar Breaks, the Parowan Valley, and, in the distance, Bryce Canyon National Park. Four states can also be seen here—Arizona, Colorado, New Mexico, and Utah. If you stop at the Rattlesnake Trailhead, at the north entrance to Cedar Breaks, you can look to the northwest and see the shelter on top of Brian Head Peak. Hwy. 148, which intersects with Hwy. 143 at Cedar Breaks, is closed by snow in winter.

Dry Lakes/Summit Canyon Scenic Backway—

If you want to enjoy a bird's-eye view of the Parowan Valley, the 19-mile-long Dry Lakes/Summit Canyon Rd. provides the opportunity. An improved dirt road, with gravel in essential places, the route is usually passable by passenger car, though not in wet weather or during the winter. It is also steep and narrow in places, especially during the first part of the road, as it climbs to the top of Sugarloaf Mountain (9,000 feet elevation). The road can be driven in either direction, but most people leave Interstate 15 at Summit and, beginning just north of the town on old Hwy. 91, follow the road as it heads south and east. The route passes through the Hurricane Cliffs, then up Sugarloaf Mountain, whose summit is about 10 miles from the beginning of the route. From Sugarloaf Mountain, the road turns in a northeasterly direction, as it follows below Navajo Ridge across several small streams and through mountain meadows to its intersection with Hwy. 143, 8 miles from Parowan.

Kolob Reservoir Scenic Backway—

For a unique view of the western part of Zion National Park, and a memorable drive that begins in the piñon forests east of Cedar City, passes by the picturesque Kolob Reservoir and Blue Springs Reservoir and descends through the red and white sandstone ledges of Zion National Park to the old Mormon pioneer town of Virgin, the Kolob Reservoir Scenic Backway is a drive that you will not soon forget. The Scenic Backway leaves Hwy. 14 6 miles east of Cedar City and heads south over a gravel and dirt road for approximately 25 miles to the northern boundary of Zion National Park. From here, the paved road takes you past ranches, in and out of the park, to the junction with Hwy. 9 at Virgin, approximately 20 miles to the south.

Markagunt Scenic Byway—

Chances are if you spend any time in the Cedar City area at all, you will travel over this Scenic Byway, which is also known as Hwy. 14 either to Cedar Breaks or to Hwy. 89 for access to Bryce Canyon. The Markagunt Scenic Byway climbs through Cedar Canyon, east of Cedar City, to the top of the lofty Markagunt Plateau, then descends to intersect Hwy. 89 at Long Valley Junction. The 40-mile drive can be made in an hour, but travelers will want to plan more time for stops since the twisting road does not offer time to view scenes like Ashdown Gorge Wilderness where sheer cliffs rise above both sides of the canyon, or the Zion Overlook at the top of the canyon which provides a panoramic view of the Kolob Terrace in the northern part of Zion National Park and the monoliths and canyons in the main park. Navajo Lake, a 3.5-mile-long lake, is visible from the highway, or you can take a dirt road that heads south, providing access to the lake and Cascade Falls, a picturesque waterfall that can be reached by a short hike. Navajo Lake is drained by sinkholes, which carry the water into the north fork of the Virgin River. Like many Utah canyons, this is an especially beautiful drive in the fall, but places like Navajo Lake, Cedar Breaks, and Cascade Falls are usually closed by heavy winter snows.

Strawberry Point Overview—

If you want to add distance to the Markagunt Scenic Byway and don't mind a 9-mile drive across an unpaved road, the route to Strawberry Point on top of the Pink Cliffs is well worth your time. From Strawberry Point, you can see the Arizona Strip to the south, and to the west, the silhouettes of Zion National Park are visible. Just below the point, there is an enchanting natural bridge. The road turns to the south off Hwy. 14, 5 miles east of Duck Creek pond.

SCENIC FLIGHTS

The Cedar City Air Service offers scenic flights over southern Utah's national parks, including the Grand Canyon and Lake Powell. For further information, rates, and reservations, call or write: **Cedar City Air Service, PO Box 458 Cedar City, UT 84720; (801) 586-3881.**

WILDLIFE

As you drive from Cedar City or Parowan to Cedar Breaks, you will pass through four distinct life zones which are identified because of their elevation and the flora and fauna which inhabit them. The Upper Sonoran Zone (4,000 to 6,800 feet) is characterized by sagebrush, rabbit-brush, piñon pine, and juniper trees and wildflowers such as the creamy trumpet-flowered sacred datura, known locally as the Zion lily. Animals include the Western rattlesnake, short-horned toad lizard, the desert jackrabbit, cottontail rabbit, grey rock squirrel, sage sparrow, sage grouse, and lark sparrow. The Transition Zone (6,800 to 8,000 feet) is distinguished by the gambel oak and ponderosa pine and at, the upper levels Douglas fir and white fir. Wildflowers include bluebells, geraniums, and globemallows. Mule deer and elk inhabit this zone. The Canadian Zone (8,000 to 9,500 feet), is distinguished by groves of aspen, blue spruce, and Douglas fir. Mule deer and elk extend into this zone along with smaller animals such as chipmunks, ground squirrels, prairie dogs, marmots, the hairy woodpecker and the hermit thrush. In the tops of the Utah mountains, the Hudsonian Zone (9,500 to 11,000 feet) the Engelmann spruce, subalpine fir, and bristlecone pine (considered the oldest living trees in the world) mark this zone. A canopy of wildflowers including bluebells, delphinium, Indian paintbrush, penstemon, white-and blue-spurred columbines, to mention a few, covers the high mountain meadows in summer.

Parowan Front Area—

One of the best places to see mule deer in winter is located between Cedar City and Summit, 8 miles to the north. You can view the deer by driving the gravel front-age road, which runs adjacent to and just east of Interstate 15. In order to preserve the habitat, motorized vehicles are limited to existing roads from Jan. 1–Apr. 30—which is also the best time for viewing the deer herds.

Wild Horses—

There is nothing more symbolic of the Old West and thrilling than seeing a herd of wild horses running free across the open range. Wild horse herds can still be seen west of Cedar City, including horses that display the characteristics of the extinct wild tarpan, which were brought to America in the blood lines of the "Spanish barbs"—the mounts of the early Spanish explorers. According to BLM professionals in charge of managing the horses, "While most wild horses come in a variety of colors (black, bay, sorrel, or grey) the descendants of the tarpan are shades of dun and grulla. They have a dorsal stripe running from the mane into the tail, and stripes appear on the legs near the hocks, knees, and sometimes on the withers. Their manes and tails are multicolored, and they have dark fringed ears." If you are lucky, you might see these horses in the Sulphur Wild Horse Management Area early in the morning or late in the evening. For further information and directions, contact the **Cedar City District Office of the Bureau of Land Management, 176 East D.L. Sargent Drive, Cedar City, UT 84720; (801) 586-2401.**

There are numerous prairie Dog areas, sage grouse strutting grounds, golden eagle nest and perch sites, and deer, elk, and moose ranges around Cedar City under the management of the Bureau of Land Management and the US Forest Service. For further information about opportunities to view the area's wildlife, call or write: **Cedar City District Office of the Bureau of Land Management, 176 East D.L. Sargent Dr., Cedar City, UT 84720; (801) 586-2401,** or the **Cedar City Ranger District, Dixie National Forest, 82 North 100 East, Cedar City, UT 84720; (801) 865-3200.**

WHERE TO STAY

ACCOMMODATIONS
BED AND BREAKFASTS (CEDAR CITY)

Bard's Inn—$$

At the Bard's Inn you can enjoy the ambiance of old country living with the comforts of today. The inn offers a suite, studio apartment, cottage, and three bedrooms, beautifully furnished with and all with private baths. **150 South 100 West; (801) 586-6612.**

Paxman's Summer House—$$$

The three bedrooms with private baths and furnished with antiques are located on the second story of a turn-of-the-century Victorian house only two blocks from where the Shakespearean Festival is held. The main floor master bedroom with private porch and bath is available during the summer. Breakfast features fruit, cheese, homemade breads and rolls, and beverages. **170 North 400 West; (801) 586-3755.**

Willow Glen Inn—$$

Located on a 10-acre farm, 5 miles from downtown Cedar City, the house has three bedrooms and a nearby two-bedroom cottage. The farm has landscaped lawns, gardens, orchards, and picnic areas. Sheep, peacocks, turkeys, pheasants, and ducks add to the rural character of the inn. **3308 North Bulldog Rd. (801) 586-3275.**

MOTELS (CEDAR CITY)

Abbey Inn—$$

Opened in 1993, with 81 rooms and plans to double in size in the future, the inn has an indoor swimming pool, whirlpool, and is located next door to **Shoney's Restaurant** at **940 West 200 North; (801) 586-9966 or 1-800-325-5411.**

Best Western El Rey Inn—$$ to $$$

One of Cedar City's oldest motels, owner Ray Knell was one of two charter members of the Best Western system. New units have been constructed over the years.

Today, the El Rey has 75 rooms, including family suites that sleep up to six and two suites featuring a hot tub and Jacuzzi. There is a heated pool, Jacuzzi, sauna, and game room. Poolside rooms are available, and an elevator provides easy access to the second floor rooms. Centrally located on Cedar City's Main St., the El Rey is within a couple blocks of SUU campus and is popular with visitors to the Shakespearean Festival. **80 South Main; (801) 581-6518 or 1-800-528-1234.**

Best Western Town and Country Inns—$$ to $$$

The two inns are located on the south and north sides of Main St. With 161 modern rooms, two heated pools, and located in the center of Cedar City, this is one of the city's most popular lodging facilities. **200 North on the west side of Main St., (801) 586-9911 or 1-800-528-1234.**

Holiday Inn—$$ to $$$

One hundred units. Heated pool, whirlpool, and sauna. Located west of Interstate 15 at **1575 West 200 North; (801) 586-8888.**

Village Inn—$$

Used as a dormitory during the school year, the inn has two- and three-bedroom units with kitchenettes. Ideal for families. **840 South Main; (801) 586-9926.**

BED AND BREAKFASTS (PAROWAN)

Adam's Historic Home—$$$

Charles Adams built this home in 1870, and one of his descendants, Fred Adams, is the founder of the Shakespearean Festival. The bed and breakfast has three rooms, each with a private bath. The family suite can sleep up to six people. Furnished with antiques and located on a quiet street in Parowan, this is a popular establishment with festival attenders and Brian Head skiers. **94 North 100 East; (801) 477-3384.**

Grandma Bess' Cottage—$$

The three upstairs bedrooms have queen-sized beds and a shared bath. Guests share the family front room for TV watching and piano playing. 291 West 200 South; (801) 477-8224.

MOTELS (PAROWAN)
Best West Swiss Village—$$ to $$$

Twenty-eight units. Pool and restaurant adjacent. 580 North Main; (801) 477-3391.

Jedediah's Inn—$$

Forty units. Restaurant adjacent. 200 South 600 West; (801) 477-3326.

BRIAN HEAD SKI RESORT
Accommodation Station—$$$

The 110 units come equipped with kitchens and fireplaces. There is an indoor pool, sauna, whirlpool, exercise room, game room, and covered parking. 259 South Hwy. 143, Brian Head, UT 84719; (801) 677-3333 or 1-800-572-9705.

Aspen Condominiums—$$$

These two- and three-bedroom units in a rustic wooded setting are equipped with kitchens and fireplaces and are available at daily or weekly rates. 312 South Hwy 143, PO Box 190176, Brian Head, UT 84719; (801) 677-2018.

Brian Head Hotel—$$$

The largest facility at Brian Head, with 183 rooms—some equipped with refrigerators. Pool, whirlpools, sauna, exercise room, garage, dining room, and coffee shop. Summer rates are about half the winter rates. Bicycles can be rented and guided mountain tours can be arranged. 228 Hunter Ridge Dr.; (801) 677-3000.

Bristlecone Hostel—$$ to $$$

Sixteen dorm spaces and cabins. 1037 South Nordic Circle, Brian Head, UT 84719; (801) 677-2059.

Chalet Village—$$$

Thirty-five units, some with two-story loft bedrooms; all have kitchens and fireplaces. Sauna and whirlpool. 226 South Hwy. 143, PO Box 180188, Brian Head, UT 84719; (801) 677-2025 or 1-800-942-8908.

Lodge at Brian Head—$$$

Ninety-three rooms, some with kitchenettes. Sauna and whirlpool. 314 Hunter Ridge Dr., Brian Head, UT 84719; (801) 677-3222.

Timberbrook Village Condominiums—$$$

Sixty-five units with kitchens. Indoor pool, exercise room, and covered parking. 424 North Hwy. 143, PO Box 190186, Brian Head, UT 84719; (801) 677-2806.

CAMPING
PRIVATE

There are five excellent private campgrounds in the Cedar City area: two in Cedar City, two in Parowan, and one in Kanarraville.

Cedar City KOA Kampground—

One hundred sites, with 55 pull-throughs and 68 with complete hookups. Restrooms and showers, laundry, heated pool, game room, playground, and barbecue. 1121 North Main; (801) 586-9872.

Country Aire RV Park—

This Good Sam park is also located in the northern end of Cedar City; 48 RV sites, all of which have complete hookups and 28 of which are pullthroughs, and 15 tent sites. Restrooms and showers, laundry facilities, convenience store, playground, and pool. 1700 North Main; (801) 586-2550.

Foothills RV Park—

Situated at exit 75 off Interstate 15 this Parowan RV park has 79 sites, all of which have complete hookups. Laundry facilities, showers, and restrooms with handicap facilities. 1435 West 200 South; (801) 477-3535.

Pit Stop Campground—

This small campground has 20 RV sites with complete hookups and 8 tent sites. Restrooms and showers. **492 North Main, Parowan; (801) 477-9990.**

Red Ledge Campground—
Another small campground with 24 complete hookups and 8 tent sites. Restrooms, showers, and laundry facilities. **15 North Main, Kanarraville; (801) 586-9150.**

PUBLIC
Most of the public campgrounds in the Cedar City area are located east of town on national forest land just off Hwy. 14. There are seven campgrounds, beginning 13 miles east of Cedar City along a 17-mile stretch of the highway.

Cedar Canyon—
This is the closest campground to Cedar City at an elevation of 8,100 feet; 10 RV trailer sites and 9 tent sites. Open mid-May–end of Oct.

Deer Haven—
Twenty RV and tent sites. Elevation 8,900 feet. Open Jun.-Sept. Located 19 miles from Cedar City. Reservations are required for the group site. **(801) 865-3200.**

Duck Creek—
Eighty-three RV and tent sites. Drinking water, toilets, and picnic tables. Open mid-June–mid-Sept. Thirty miles from Cedar City.

Navajo Lake and the Spruces Campgrounds—
Twenty-eight RV and tent sites at each campground. Drinking water, toilets, and picnic tables. Open mid-June–mid-Sept. Twenty-five miles from Cedar City.

Te-Ah Campground—
Forty-two RV and tent sites. Drinking water, toilets, and picnic tables. Open mid-June–mid-Sept. Twenty-seven miles from Cedar City.

Vermillion Campground—
The only public campground between Parowan and Cedar Breaks National Monument; 14 RV and tent sites, with drinking water and toilets. Located on forest service land. Open June–Sept. Located southeast of Parowan, 5.5 miles on Hwy. 143.

——————— WHERE TO EAT ———————

Adriana's—$$ to $$$
"Good sister, let us dine and never fret." So spoke Adriana in Shakespeare's "Comedy of Errors," and that has become the watchword for this fine eating establishment. In keeping with Cedar City's Shakespearean theme, this is a charming bungalow-style house that has been redecorated to resemble a quaint English inn. Heavy dark woods, a stunning antique fireplace imported from England, an impressive staircase, beautiful buffets in each end of the house, quaint booths, pewter dishes, and lace tablecloths all add to the character. The menu features salads, sandwiches, and fish and chips for lunch; steaks, fish, chicken, and pasta for dinner. Open daily year-round for lunch 11 am–3 pm and dinner 3:30 pm–10 pm; 5 pm–9 pm during winter. Reservations are strongly recommended during the Shakespearean Festival. Located at **164 South 100 West; (801) 865-1234.**

China Garden—$ to $$
The gigantic sign of a smiling Chinese lady in traditional costume captures your attention as you drive down Cedar City's Main St. The sign has been there as long as I can remember and graces the entrance to the China Garden Restaurant. The restaurant offers both American and Chinese food—chow mein, chop suey, fried rice, beef, pork, and chicken dishes. Open 10 am–10 pm, Sun.–Thurs.; 10 am–11 pm Fri. and Sat. **64 North Main; (801) 586-6042.**

Escobar's—$ to $$

Martin Escobar came to southern Utah from a small village in the Mexican state of Guerrero approximately equi-distant between Mexico City and Acapulco. He opened his first restaurant in Utah in 1984 in the small town of Hatch, across the mountain from Cedar City. His unpretentious Cedar City restaurant was opened in 1991 and has become popular with local residents. Operated by Martin's son, Leo, and daughter-in-law, Rosa, Escobar's specializes in combination plates. Open 11 am–9:30 am, Sun.–Fri. Closed Sat. **155 North Main; (801) 865-0155.**

LaTajada Steak and Seafood House—$$ to $$$

Offers Italian cuisine, in addition to steaks and seafood. Located upstairs above Sullivan's, LaTajada is much more quiet and intimate. It is one of the few places in town that serves wine and mixed drinks. Open daily for dinner. **86 South Main; (801) 586-6761.**

Market Grill—$ to $$

Located near the livestock auction yards, this is a local favorite. It is used to feeding hungry farmers and livestock men with tasty, plentiful home cooking. Well known for its chicken fried steak. **2290 West 400 North; (801) 586-9325.**

Milt's Stage Stop—$$$

Milt's has been around for a long long time and is a legend in southern Utah. It features steaks and prime rib. With a beautiful canyon location, this is the place local residents go for special occasions. Reservations are recommended. Open daily 6 pm–10 pm. **5 miles east of Cedar City on Hwy. 14; (801) 586-9344.**

Pancho and Lefty's—$$ to $$$

When Russ Dains established his restaurant, he held a contest to pick the name of the establishment. A Willie Nelson fan nominated the title of Nelson's country and western song. Russ liked it and ever since, it has been known as Pancho and Lefty's. The building and interior looks like a re-created Spanish villa, and it is the only place in Utah where you can sit on the front veranda and drink margaritas, daiquiris, or wine—as long as you purchase food to go with your drinks. As one of only three eating places in Cedar City where liquor is available and open seven days a week from 4 pm–10 pm, this is one of Cedar City's most popular eating places. You can get anything from a taco or burrito to the house special—Pancho's steak and enchilada. If you are a steak fan, try the carne asada, a New York steak sautéed with salsa and spices. **2107 North Main; (801) 586-7501.**

Pizza Factory—$ to $$

If pizza is part of your regular diet, you won't find a lot of choices in southern Utah. But the Pizza Factory, patronized by Southern Utah University students and local families, carries the reputation for the best pizza in this part of the state. **124 South Main; (801) 586-3900.**

Sugar Loaf—$ to $$

With a complete menu of traditional American breakfasts served all day long, the Sugar Loaf has a large local following. Specialties include rolls, pies, and its famous homemade cinnamon rolls, which stand more than 3 inches tall and fill the entire plate. The menu warns you'll never eat all of it, and it's true. Open daily 6 am–10 pm. **281 South Main; (801) 586-6593.**

Sullivan's Cafe—$ to $$

Opened in 1946, Sullivan's is operated by Dayton Sullivan, grandson of the founder. Sullivan's offers homemade food, a 32-item salad bar and breakfast served anytime. With its unusual shaped counter, traditional booths and tables, and reasonable prices, it is a local favorite. Open daily 6 am–10 pm. **86 South Main; (801) 586-6761.**

Yogurt Junction—$

This little place features soup in a bread bowl. It has a wonderful decor and is a good place for lunch. The low-fat, sugar-free yogurt is delicious. Open Mon.–Sat. 11 am–9 pm. **911 South Main; (801) 586-2345.**

BRIAN HEAD
Brianhead Station Cafeteria— $ to $$

If you are watching your budget and looking for a quick in-and-out place while you are skiing, the cafeteria will fit the bill. Open during the winter only for breakfast and lunch; **(801) 677-2035.**

Columbine Cafe and Summit Dining Room, Brian Head Hotel— $$ to $$$

This is the special-occasion place at Brian Head. The Columbine Cafe is open for breakfast and lunch and the Summit Dining Room for dinner. The chefs at the Columbine are health-conscious and try to offer items that are low in fat and cholesterol. The breakfast buffet is especially appealing with fresh fruits and whole grain products. For lunch there are a number of sandwiches and pasta dishes with salmon pasta and smoked chicken pasta being the two favorites. The Columbine Cafe is open daily from 7 am–2 pm. The Summit Dining Room keeps the focus on healthy dishes with such entrées as citrus scalloped pasta, and Ahi tuna—cooked oriental style in a dark oyster sauce. If you want to splurge, try the ribeye steak smothered with onions, mushrooms, and garlic. The downstairs seating area has a beautiful view of the surrounding mountains including Brian Head Peak; **(801) 677-3000.**

The Edge—$$ to $$$

Located at the south end of Brian Head, the Edge dining room offers a spectacular view of the ski mountain and the Brian Head Valley. Luncheon items include specialty burgers and sandwiches. Dinner items feature steaks, chicken, and pasta. The filet mignon is a favorite. Open daily during the summer 11:30 am–4 pm for lunch and 5 pm–10 pm for dinner with a Sun. brunch served from 10 am–3 pm. During the ski season the Edge is open only for dinner, daily from 5 pm–10 pm and for Sun. brunch from 8 am–3 pm; **(801) 677-3343.**

SERVICES

Bureau of Land Management—

Cedar City District, 176 East D. L. Sargent Drive, Cedar City, UT 84720; (801) 586-2401.

Dixie National Forest—

82 North 100 East, PO Box 0580, Cedar City, UT 84721-0580; (801) 865-3700.

Iron County Tourism and Convention Bureau and the Cedar City Chamber of Commerce—

Open 8 am–5 pm Mon.–Fri. **PO Box 1007, 286 North Main, Cedar City, UT 84720; (801) 586-5124 or 1-800-354-4849.**

St. George

"Utah's all season resort city" is the slogan adopted by the St. George Area Chamber of Commerce to lure visitors to what early Mormon pioneers labeled "Utah's Dixie," for the cotton that grew there. Driving in early morning rush hour traffic on the 14th day of a January inversion that has blocked the sun and turned the Salt Lake Valley into a western version of London fog, these alluring radio spots offering an escape from the depression of winter 300 miles to the south are almost irresistible. Even if the commitment to duty does triumph and the winter-weary worker continues on to the office, there remains the dream of retirement to St. George, a dream that during the last 20 years has become a reality for thousands.

Utah's "snowbirds" begin their migration southward in October and November, returning north in April and May. Some purchase houses or condominiums and, after a few years of maintaining two households, give up their northern home to stay in St. George year-round. Others rent homes or condominiums, often succumbing to the lure of purchase once bitten by the "Dixie" bug. A good number travel in motor homes and trailers to spend the winter months in one of several well-equipped RV parks in the area.

But St. George is not just a retirement center. During spring break in late March, St. George becomes Utah's answer to Daytona Beach, as thousands of high school and college students head south to get a jump on summer. Dixie College, a two-year community college in St. George, is one of the state's most popular destinations for beginning college students. Other visitors come to attend the Vic Braden Tennis College or shed some unwanted pounds at the National Institute of Fitness in Snow Canyon. Although summer high temperatures in this desert location seldom drop below 100 degrees Fahrenheit, St. George is still an excellent summer vacation destination. You can play an early morning round of golf on one of the many golf courses that have sprung up here, or walk in Snow Canyon before the heat gets you, then retire to the patio to read or visit one of the four historic sites maintained by the LDS Church in the area. There are plenty of places to go for a leisurely lunch. This might be followed by an afternoon swim or a hike up the Virgin Narrows in nearby Zion National Park, or perhaps a drive west to Pine Valley and Mountain Meadows. In the evening, head just 36 miles down Interstate 15 from St. George and visit the casino at Mesquite, Nevada. Those with a more intellectual bent might consider one of the history lectures or musical programs offered in St. George.

With its close proximity to Zion National Park, Cedar City, and Las Vegas, an historical consciousness that still permeates the community despite its rapid development, and plenty of activities for residents and visitors of all ages, there is no question why St. George is one of Utah's most popular areas.

HISTORY

After Dominguez and Escalante made the decision to abandon their effort to journey to California and to return to Santa Fe, they reached present-day Washington County on October 13, 1776. They traveled along Ash Creek just east of the present route of Interstate 15, before heading southeast back to New Mexico.

In 1830, another group of travelers from Santa Fe accomplished what the Franciscan friars had been unable to do in opening a route between Santa Fe and Los Angeles. The 1830 group entered Washington County from the north on the western side of the Pine Valley Mountains, where they rested in the Mountain Meadows, before continuing on the arduous journey across the Nevada desert. (Mountain Meadows is infamous as the site of the massacre of 120 California-bound immigrants in 1857.) Mormon explorers led by Parley P. Pratt entered the area on a reconnaissance mission from Salt Lake City in 1849 and spent New Year's Day 1850 at the junction of the Santa Clara and Virgin rivers. The first settlement in Washington County was made at Fort Harmony in 1852, one year after Parowan was established, 35 miles to the north. Communities were later established at Santa Clara (1854), Washington (1857), and St. George (1861).

St. George was named in honor of Mormon Apostle George A. Smith who, although he did not participate in his namesake's settlement, did select most of the 309 original families called to settle near the Virgin River. Saints, like Mormons, was an abbreviated name that members of the Church of Jesus Christ of Latter-day Saints often applied to themselves. The combination of Saint with George made perfectly good theological sense to 19th-century Mormons.

The settlement of St. George coincided with the outbreak of the Civil War. Settlers already had been experimenting with cotton-growing in Santa Clara and Washington and Brigham Young wanted to take advantage of this opportunity to further the Mormon self-sufficiency by having a locally grown and controlled source of cotton, especially as the war threatened to cut off shipments of the essential material to Utah. Young also saw in St. George the opportunity to establish a larger community for a number of converts to the faith from the southern states. This, and St. George's location in the southern part of the state, quickly led to its designation as "Utah's Dixie." A cotton factory was constructed in

Washington and cotton was grown along Santa Clara Creek and the Rio Virgin until the 1890s, when a depression and competition from other parts of the country led to its demise.

If cotton was not the salvation for St. George, the construction of the Mormon Temple in the community was. Completed in 1877, it was the first Mormon Temple in Utah and the only one completed before Brigham Young's death. St. George was, and remains, a religious center for Mormons. In 1911, 50 years after St. George was settled, the residents commemorated the event with the establishment of the St. George Academy, a normal school, which became Dixie College in 1933.

The population of St. George remained fairly constant until after World War II, when postwar travel to the West boomed. Beginning in the 1960s, St. George has grown faster than any other part of the state, because of its prominence as a retirement community. Between 1960 and 1990 the population grew from just over 5,000 to nearly 30,000.

Since the cotton days, St. George's economy has diversified and, while agriculture is still an important element, recreation, tourism, and the town's popularity as a retirement center have led to its unprecedented growth.

GETTING THERE

St. George is located 300 miles south of Salt Lake City and 120 miles northeast of Las Vegas, Nevada, on Interstate 15. Air transportation is available from Salt Lake City and Las Vegas on **Sky West/Delta Connection; 1-800-453-9417. Greyhound** provides bus service to the city; call **(801) 673-2933.**

MAJOR ATTRACTIONS

St. George Tabernacle

This is arguably the finest Mormon church building constructed in Utah and is one of the best-preserved pioneer buildings in the entire state. Work began on June 1, 1863, a few months after the settlement of St. George. The tabernacle was dedicated by Brigham Young 13 years later. Designed by pioneer architect Miles Romney, the graceful clock tower rises to a height of 140 feet. Sandstone was quarried nearby, and a close examination of the exterior of the building reveals the chisel marks of the early craftsmen. The glass in the tabernacle is also special. It was transported by ship from the East to the West Coast, and then shipped by wagon to St. George. The interior has a horseshoe balcony, which is also found in the Salt Lake Tabernacle and other larger early Mormon church buildings. It is still used for special meetings and programs. Open daily 9 am–6 pm. Corner of **Main St. and Tabernacle Ave.**

St. George Temple

As the first Mormon temple completed after the exodus to Utah, and the oldest temple still in use, the St. George Temple has attracted Mormons from all over the world since its completion in 1877. Historian Nels Anderson explains the significance of the St. George temple in his book *Desert Saints* noting, "No event in Mormon church history exceeded in spiritual importance the dedication of the St. George Temple. Here was the first sign that God's people had permanently established themselves in the valleys of the mountains. Other temples had been planned or begun, but here was one dedicated eternally. It was a kind of victory monument for thirty years of effort."

The stunningly white building is actually constructed of native red sandstone covered in white stucco. Only worthy Mormons are allowed inside the temple, where sacred ordinances such as marriages and baptisms are performed. A visitor center is located on the beautiful temple grounds, where guides explain the purpose of Mormon temples and relate interesting information about the construction of the temple. The temple, which occupies an entire block, is located between **200 and 300 East and 400 and 500 South**. The **visitor center** is open daily 9 am–9 pm.

OTHER ATTRACTIONS

Dixie College

A two-year community college of approximately 3,000 students, Dixie College is at the center of much of the cultural and educational activity in the St. George area. Exhibits, a concert series, lectures, sporting events, and other activities are all part of a concerted effort by the administration to integrate the college into the mainstream of community life and to expand the academic experience for its students. Located in the southeastern section of St. George, chances are if you spend any time at all in the area you will find yourself on the Dixie College campus. It is worth a special trip to view the 15-foot by-127-foot mosaic mural on the south wall of the Fine Arts Building, which depicts events from Dixie's history. An interpretive marker is provided explaining the mural. The college mascot is the "Rebel" and "Dixie Rebel" clothing and souvenirs, available at the bookstore, are popular items for both young and old. For information about the college, its programs, and activities, call **(801) 673-4811.**

Gunlock State Park

Built in 1969 to 1970 to impound waters of the Santa Clara River for irrigation and flood control purposes, Gunlock Reservoir is 2 miles long and .5 mile wide with a maximum depth of 115 feet. Recreation activities include swimming, boating (power boats and sailing craft), and fishing. The Utah Division of Wildlife Resources stocks the lake with largemouth bass, black crappie, threadfin shad, and channel catfish. The reservoir is located 1 mile south of the hamlet of Gunlock, which was settled by Will Hamblin in 1857. Hamblin was known as "Gunlock" because he reportedly kept in such good condition the locks of guns belonging to those in his pioneer company as they journeyed to Utah. Will Hamblin was the brother of Jacob Hamblin, president of southern Utah's Indian Mission and a friend to the Paiutes. Jacob Hamblin's home is located about 20 miles below the reservoir in Santa Clara. It is now an historic site operated by the LDS Church. Gunlock State Park is open year-round. Camping is available, though amenities are scarce. The reservoir and state park may be reached by driving west from St. George to Santa Clara, then continuing another 8 miles to Shivwits, where you turn north for approximately 7 miles until you reach the lake. The reservoir sits on the Old Spanish Trail. The little community of Gunlock is nearby, but it is not the original site of the Hamblin/Leavitt settlement.

Quail Creek State Park

Quail Creek Reservoir, though one of the state's newest reservoirs, already has a colorful past. The reservoir, visible from Interstate 15, 14 miles north of St. George, inundates part of the old Harrisburg town site. Harrisburg was located along Quail Creek, on the eastern slope of the Pine Valley Mountains, in 1859 by Moses Harris and his sons. The original site was abandoned in 1862, when spring floods forced the Harrises to relocate farther upstream. Two of the stone ruins of old Harrisburg have been preserved as part of the Harrisburg Lakeside RV Park. The Interstate actually cuts through the Harrisburg town site, and other house ruins may be found west of the Interstate.

Work on the **Quail Creek Reservoir Dam** was completed in 1985. The 40,000-acre-foot lake impounded water from Quail Creek, but its principal source was water from the Virgin River, which was supplied through an 8-mile-long diversion tunnel fed by a pipeline from a concrete dam near the town of Virgin to the east. In the early hours of New Year's Day 1989 the dam gave way, sending a wall of water rushing down the Virgin River, which inundated homes downriver in Bloomington causing millions of dollars of damage. The reconstructed dam was completed in 1991.

Quail Creek State Park is open year-round for camping at group camp sites or in one of the 23 individual units. The facility is well equipped with modern restrooms that are wheelchair-accessible, drinking water, group pavilions, and picnicking facilities. Recreation activities include swimming, boating, and fishing. Rainbow trout, bluegill, channel catfish, crayfish, and a well-deserved reputation as the best largemouth bass hatchery in Utah make this one of the most popular fishing spots in the area.

Snow Canyon State Park

Despite the fantasies of some Utah ski enthusiasts, Snow Canyon State Park is not the St. George area ski resort. In fact, this redrock and volcanic desert canyon is a stark contrast to locations like Snowbird and Snow Basin to the north. Named for Erastus Snow, who directed the settlement of St. George as the highest-ranking Mor-

mon leader in southern Utah, Snow Canyon is a 3-mile-long, 1,000-foot-deep gorge cut by water and wind erosion.

There are two ways to enter the canyon. To enter from the north, take Hwy. 18 north out of St. George for 8 miles and watch for the Snow Canyon road on your left. To enter from the south, take the old Hwy. 91 road west out of St. George through the town of Santa Clara, then watch for the sign indicating a right turn to reach Snow Canyon. You drive north, passing through the town of Ivins, then turn back to the east and follow the road as it curves north to enter the State Park.

Within Snow Park three different kinds of rocks are visible. The oldest rocks are of the Kayenta Formation which originated about 180 million years ago. Large, slow-moving, silt-, mud-, and sand-bearing rivers left deposits which in time hardened into siltstone, mudstone, and fine grained sandstone. After the streams dried up the area became a vast sand desert. The wind-blown sands eventually hardened about 183 million to 173 million years ago and the 1,000 foot layer is known today as Navajo sandstone. About 3 million years ago a period of volcanic activity began which spued hot, molten rocks down the canyons, over the streams, and across the valleys. As the rocks cooled, they formed thick sheets of basalt. A second period of volcanic activity began sometime between 1,000 and 10,000 years ago and the hot lava rocks once again spread over the landscape from the cinder cones located in the north end of the park. Geologically speaking these lava flows are very recent, and you have a feeling that the once molten rock cooled just hours ago. The contrast of the black basalt with the red, pink, orange, and white sandstone of the Kayenta and Navajo formations offers a panorama that is a photographer's delight. The swirling Navajo sandstone rock formations, towering cliffs, and subtle colors insure that no two pictures will be just the same.

Getting There—

The best way to drive through the park is to head north from St. George on

Hwy. 18 to the Snow Canyon turnoff. Start at the top of the canyon and drive down, returning by way of Ivins and Santa Clara, if you don't want to make the drive back up to Hwy. 18. Spring and fall are the most popular times to visit the canyon, although an early-summer morning excursion when temperatures are still cool makes for a delightful outing. Camping facilities are available in the park.

Hiking—

Cinder Cone Trail—I'm still not sure that there is a trail up the cinder cone. I climbed about two-thirds of the way up the cone and decided that one slip on the ashlike lava rock could be painful and dangerous. The Cinder Cone is located north on Hwy. 18 about a mile past the north entrance into Snow Canyon. The cone looks like a volcano, and if you can negotiate a route to the top, you can see on the south side where the lava flow has covered the older sandstone. Even though the cone has not been active for over a thousand years, you have both the feeling that this is something very ancient dating back when the world was very young as well as quite recent with millions of tons of black basalt rock covering the area.

Johnson's Arch Trail—For years this 1.5-mile round-trip hike was the most popular in Snow Canyon. The sandstone arch is named for Maude Johnson, a St. George pioneer, and has been a well-known local landmark for over a century. Unfortunately, the trail to the arch crosses private land and recently the land owner decided to prevent access to the arch by constructing a barbed wire fence with ominous no trespassing signs. The state parks consider access to the arch a top priority and is working to reopen the trail. Watch for a sign indicating the trailhead at the south entrance to the park. If you don't see it, inquire at the ranger's hut at the entrance to the campground about the status of the trail.

Lava Caves and West Canyon Overlook Trail—Located in the northern portion of the park, the Lava Caves Trail is a 1.5-mile out-and-back hike that takes you to caves that have been formed in the lava rock. The caves can be hard to find. As you walk down the trail and leave sight of your vehicle at the trailhead, look for a ridge of lava rock almost straight ahead of you. The most prominent area of the black rock is where the cave is located. Keep your eyes open as you come down the lava ridge and watch for a depression to the right of the trail. The cave looks like an old mining shaft. It is unfenced, open, and can be dangerous if you get too close. As you continue down the trail you will come to another cave located in a ridge of basalt rock perhaps 20 feet thick. Continue down the trail to the West Canyon Overlook. Here you can look down into West Canyon from the south side of a side canyon of pink and white checkerboarded sandstone from which time has scoured all the lava rock that once covered it.

Three Ponds Trail—This is my personal favorite in Snow Canyon. At 6 miles out and back, it is long enough for a couple of hours' hike, and the terrain through which the trail passes is varied and interesting. The trail begins across the road from the entrance to the campground. During the first mile you cross three low-lying ridges, one of basalt and two of sandstone, before you descend a .25 mile to the gravel road up West Canyon. The first half of the trail to the gravel road is well marked and easy to follow. After you cross the road in a westerly direction, the trail becomes less defined as you walk through heavy sand toward a gigantic U-shaped opening between the sandstone walls formed by the intermittent stream that flows down out of the cliffs. After you pass between the sandstone walls hiking along the bottom of the wash, you enter a broad, circular area. Keep the white dome on top of the sandstone walls ahead of you in sight and follow the wash and trail toward the dome. Don't be tempted to head to the left but follow the wash as it curves to the right until you come up against the sandstone walls where you will find the three ponds. They are really three potholes, usually with some water in them, but hardly enough to qualify as ponds. The ponds were used by Indians as a water source and later by local pioneers. The ponds are located almost on top of each other—one at the base of the sandstone cliff and the two above in the sandstone rock inside a V-shaped notch cut by the water into the sandstone. As you return out of the canyon and head back toward the West Canyon Rd., keep your eyes on the ridge straight ahead. This is the ridge over which you just hiked. You will see three windows or small arches along the ridge line.

In addition to these designated trails, there are other unnamed and undeveloped trails, some marked by the sign of a hiker, throughout the park. These trails follow wash bottoms and are often animal and old cattle trails. If you are in doubt about hiking in a particular area, check with the state park ranger.

Plant and Animal Life—
You can pick up a trail guide to the 1.5-mile **Hidden Pinyon Trail** which offers an excellent introduction to the plant life of the area. Plants described include Mormon tea, cliffrose, lichens, desert almond, englemann prickly pear, hackberry, squawbrush, sand or old-man sagebruch, Utah juniper, datil or banana yucca, narrow-leaf yucca, purple torch cactus, shrub live oak, blackbrush, brittle bush, and creosote bush. In addition to these plants, you will also find piñon pine, chaparral, chola cactus, prickly pear cactus, sego lilies, and other perennial and annual flowers.
The sandy washes and sand dunes offer an excellent opportunity to see the tracks of the area's wildlife including lizards, kangaroo rats, piñon mice, lizards, diamondback and sidewinder rattlesnakes, gila monsters, chipmunks, ground squirrels, rabbits, skunks, porcupines, kit foxes, coyotes, desert mule deer, bobcats, badgers, coyotes, owls, blue jays, robins, crows, and hawks.

Sand Dunes—
Children and adults love the sand dunes located in the lower (southern) end of the canyon. You can run barefoot through the sand, write messages in the sand, and pretend that you are in the middle of the Sahara.

———— FESTIVALS AND EVENTS ————

Dixie College Invitational Art Show
Presidents' Day weekend–late March
Presidents' Day weekend opens the Dixie College Invitational Art Show, which is held in the Graff Fine Arts Center at Dixie College and runs through late Mar. Call **(801) 673-4811** for more information.

St. George Art Festival
Easter weekend
Held on Fri. and Sat., Easter weekend, the St. George Art Festival began in 1978. It has become southern Utah's largest art celebration, with more than 100 booths, live entertainment, food, and activities for all ages. The festival is held along Main St. in front of the tabernacle, library, and St. George Arts Center. Sponsored by the St. George City Leisure Services Department. For more information, call **(801) 634-5850.**

Dixie International Folkfest
week of July 24th
We sat in the Dixie College Stadium on a July evening when the temperature was still over 100 degrees watching with amazement as wool-clothed senior-aged dancers from Europe performed traditional folk dances with smiles on their faces and no apparent discomfort from the scorching heat. The festival, which began in 1991, now includes nearly a dozen folk groups from such places as Europe, the Far East, the former

Soviet Union, and the US, who spend the week of July 24 performing traditional dances and music to the delight of hundreds of local residents and tourists from across the nation and all corners of the world. All of the performers are housed with local hosts and the good will that the performances and activities generate is heart-warming. The festival has adopted as its theme a statement by one of the Utah native American groups: "Our world is like a giant mosaic made up of many different pieces. Each piece with its own beauty and importance, is dependent on all the others to make up a beautiful interesting design. Every part plays its role, and if even one is missing, it leaves a flaw that distracts from the beauty of the whole. For the mosaic of mankind, harmony comes only through the tolerance that comes with mutual understanding." Performances are held at Dixie College, the O. C. Tanner Amphitheater in Springdale outside Zion National Park, and at other locations around the St. George area. For information call **(801) 634-5747** or **1-800-869-6635.**

Washington County Fair
August
Held in Hurricane, it features prize-winning fruit crops, exhibits, and a carnival.

Lions Dixie Roundup
September
A three-day Professional Rodeo Cowboy's Association–approved rodeo held each Sept. in the Sun Bowl in St. George; **(801) 628-2898.**

Santa Clara Swiss Days
last Friday and Saturday in September
The last Fri. and Sat. in Sept. finds the small town of Santa Clara celebrating its Swiss heritage. Swiss converts to the Mormon church were among the communities early settlers in the 1860s, and people have wondered ever since how the natives of the forested mountains and lush valleys of Switzerland coped with the red rock, sand, scarce water, and heat of their new desert

home. Presented by the Santa Clara Historical Society, activities include displays, a pageant, a fun run, crafts, food, game booths, entertainment, a parade, and tour of historic homes. For more information call **(801) 673-6712.**

St. George Marathon
1st Saturday in October
This is one of Utah's most popular marathon runs. The course starts in the Pine Valley Mountains north of St. George and follows Hwy. 18 down to St. George. The long, descending course offers runners the chance to post personal bests in a race that attracts more than 2,000 participants annually. For more information, call **(801) 634-5850.**

World Senior Games
mid-October
Held throughout the St. George area, this two-week event attracts hundreds of senior athletes (age 50 and over) from all over the world. They participate in a wide range of sporting activities, such as tennis, golf, basketball, cycling, racquetball, softball, swimming, running, horseshoes, bowling, race walking, and table tennis. Sponsored by the Huntsman Chemical Corporation, headquartered in Salt Lake City. For information contact **Sylvia Wunderli, Executive Director—Huntsman World Senior Games, 1355 South Foothill Dr., Salt Lake City, UT 84108; (801) 583-6231** or **1-800-562-1268.**

Jubilee of Trees
week before Thanksgiving
This five-day event, usually held the week before Thanksgiving, launches the Christmas season in St. George. Trees sporting original decorations are displayed. There is something for everyone, including booths, fashion shows, gift ideas, live entertainment, and food including a gala dinner, a parade, auction, and activities for the children. Call **(801) 673-5235** or **673-7942** for more information.

Dixie Rotary Bowl Football Game

1st Saturday in December

The Dixie Rotary Bowl started in 1986 and has turned into one of the most successful junior college football bowl games in the nation. Bowl festivities include a parade, a marching band competition, a banquet, and a tailgate party.

———— OUTDOOR ACTIVITIES ————

BIKING

Pine Valley Loop—

Unless you enjoy riding in dry 100-degree-plus desert temperatures, much of the Dixie area does not lend itself to long bike rides in the summer. One exception is the 35-mile-long Pine Valley Loop. In addition to the spectacular views of the west side of the Pine Valley Mountains, the route offers three interesting historic sites to visit during the ride: the Pine Valley chapel, the remains of the Jacob Hamblin homestead, and the Mountain Meadows Massacre Site. Take Hwy. 18 north from St. George for 25 miles to Central, then turn east and follow the road (Forest Rd. 035) for 6 miles into Pine Valley. The loop begins in Pine Valley and winds north on Forest Rd. 011 through Grass Valley for 12 miles to Pinto. Turn left (west) at Pinto and follow Forest Rd. 009 for about 5 miles to its junction with Hwy. 18. Before you reach the paved road, you pass the Hamblin homestead. From Hwy. 18, turn left and head south, making a stop at Mountain Meadows about a mile from the junction. From there it's another 10 miles back to the beginning point—unless you forget to turn left (east) at Central.

Snow Canyon Loop—

This is an excellent early morning ride that offers the spectacular scenery of Snow Canyon, the chance to leave directly from your lodging in St. George for a strenuous uphill workout, and a thrilling downhill schuss at the end of the ride. You can begin the 24-mile loop by following old Hwy. 91 (Sunset Blvd.) west to Santa Clara from the junction at Bluff St. Continue west through Santa Clara and, about a mile past the historic Jacob Hamblin house, turn north toward the town of Ivins. At the crossroads in Ivins, turn right (east) and follow the road as it turns northward, to begin the long climb up Snow Canyon. When Snow Canyon Rd. intersects Hwy. 18, turn right (south) for the well-earned coast back to St. George.

For more information about other biking routes in the St. George area, repairs, and rentals, visit **Bicycles Unlimited, Inc.** Open Mon–Sat. 8 am–7 pm. **90 South 100 East in St. George; (801) 673-4492.**

FISHING

Few Utahns go to St. George to fish. But there are several nice reservoirs in the area that are usually well stocked with rainbow, German brown, brook, and cutthroat trout. In addition to the state parks—Gunlock and Quail Creek—mentioned above, Baker Reservoir, located on Hwy. 18, 16 miles north of St. George; and Enterprise Reservoir located about 50 miles from St. George—40 miles north on Hwy. 18 to Enterprise and another 11 miles west—are all local favorites.

FITNESS RESORTS

National Institute of Fitness—

If you drive through Snow Canyon early in the morning, chances are you will see guests staying at the National Institute of Fitness—called "Niffers"—toiling up the steep road. Rated as one of the 10 best fitness resorts in the world, the National Institute of Fitness was established by Drs. Marc and Vicki Sorenson to help people lose weight using a variety of aerobic activities and a modified diet. Most participants spend a week, with the option of on- or off-campus accommodations. National Institute of Fitness, **202 North Snow Canyon Rd., PO Box 938-T, Ivins, UT 84738; (801) 673-4905.**

GOLF

What makes golf special in St. George is that you can golf year-round at reasonable rates and there are enough courses to play a different one every day of the week and still have one left over for the next week. The St. George area boasts six public courses. Just down Interstate 15, two more courses—the **Beaver Dam Golf Course,** 28 miles away in Arizona, and the **Peppermill Golf Course,** 36 miles away in Mesquite, Nevada—are considered home courses by St. Georgites. Winter daytime temperatures average in the 50s and 60s, and any "serious" Utah golfer makes at least one pilgrimage during the winter to play St. George. Unfortunately, between Oct. and May, there is plenty of competition for tee times from local residents and the hundreds of "snowbirds."

During the summer, when the temperatures push past 100 degrees Fahrenheit, there are fewer golfers, but if you are properly prepared—that is, with plenty of cold drinks, light clothing, suitable hat, and, if necessary, a golf cart—two or four hours perspiring on the golf course can be an enjoyable form of sauna—if your golf game is on—and makes the post-game plunge into the swimming pool all the more wonderful.

Dixie Red Hills—

Opened in 1965, this is St. George's first golf course and still a favorite of many golfers. On a couple of holes, the red cliffs can be either a hazard or a help when errant drives ricochet off the walls and bounce back onto the fairway. **1000 North 700 West, St. George; (801) 634-5852.**

Green Spring Golf Course—

Owned by the city of Washington, this course is located north of Interstate 15 and is reached from St. George by taking the Washington exit and turning left back under the interstate. The course is rated as one of the most difficult in the state, and most golfers can plan to lose at least one ball trying to play the treacherous 6th hole. If you are not a very good golfer and are prone to frustration on challenging courses, you might want to save the green fees and opt for a course that is a little more forgiving of those who don't shoot straight. **588 Green Spring, Washington; (801) 673-7888.**

Peppermill Golf Course—

This 18-hole course is part of the Peppermill Resort located in Mesquite, Nevada. The desert course has lakes and more than 200 palm trees—a novelty for Utah golfers. **Exit 120 on Interstate 15; 1-800-621-0187.**

St. George Golf Club—

This city-owned course snakes along Fort Pierce Wash as it drains toward the Virgin River. **2190 South 1400 East; (801) 634-5854.**

Southgate Golf Course—

Local golfers consider this course one of the easiest in the area. **1975 South Tonaquint; (801) 628-0000.**

Sunbrook Golf Course—

As St. George's newest municipal golf course, Sunbrook is a must for real golf enthusiasts. Keep in mind that green fees are about double the price of other public courses within the state. **2240 West Sunbrook Dr.; (801) 634-5866.**

Twin Lakes—

As you approach St. George on Interstate 15 from the north, look off to the right and you will see the Twin Lakes course. Even from the Interstate, you realize that it is a tricky course that requires precision shots to keep out of trouble. Plenty of hills, valleys, and water obstacles, it is especially good for people who want to work on their short game. **660 North Twin Lakes; (801) 673-4441.**

HIKING

There are three popular areas for hiking in the St. George area: **Zion National Park, Pine Valley,** and **Snow Canyon.** For additional hikes pick up a copy of Bart Anderson and Max Bertola's *Top Hikes of the St. George Area,* which provides a brief description of 25 short hikes ranging from .5 to 6 miles in length.

Forsyth Trail—

This 5-mile trail begins in the town of Pine Valley and follows Forsyth Creek to its terminus near Burger Peak. The elevation gain is 3,000 feet. The trail is noted for its beautiful mountain scenery, and the wildlife—including mule deer, elk, squirrels, chipmunks—that can be observed. Allow six to seven hours to make the hike.

Snow Canyon—

See the Major Attractions section.

Temple Quarry Trail—

You will find an interesting historic trail on Black Hill, west of St. George. The Temple Quarry Trail is part of the old wagon road that was used to haul black rock from the quarry on the west side of Black Hill for use in the foundation of the St. George Temple. The trail is level as it heads south around the hill. At the quarry site, chisel marks, partly worked stones, and other evidence remain from pioneer times. To reach the trail, drive up the hill of Bluff St. to Black Hill View Park, then head southwest until you intersect the trail.

Whipple Valley Trail—

The 15-mile trail begins east of the Blue Springs Campground at the road terminus in Pine Valley and climbs 2,000 feet in 3.5 miles to Whipple Valley, where it intersects with the Summit Trail. For hardy hikers who don't mind the up and down of following the ridge line, you can continue on the Summit Trail for 7 miles and then return to Pine Valley along the Brown's Point Trail, which terminates near Lion's Lodge on the road a mile west of the Blue Springs Campground. It is a strenuous hike with portions of the trail not well marked. The area borders the Pine Valley Wilderness (50,000 acres), administered by the US Forest Service. The Whipple Valley Trail is a good workout and is recommended for those who want to experience the beauty and solitude of the Pine Valley Mountains. For more information about trails in the Pine Valley Mountains, contact the **USFS, Pine Valley Ranger District, Dixie National Forest, Box 584 St. George, UT 84770; (801) 673-3431.**

Zion National Park—

See the **Zion National Park** section.

HORSEBACK RIDING
Snow Canyon Riding Stables—

Located in Snow Canyon, 8 miles north of St. George, these stables offer a variety of trail rides, from one-hour guided rides in the Snow Canyon area to several-day pack trips in the Pine Valley Mountains and other southwestern Utah locations. Riding lessons are available, and special attention is given to beginning riders. Hay-wagon rides and western cookouts are available for larger groups. For information and reservations write **PO Box 658, Ivins, UT 84738; (801) 628-6677.**

SWIMMING

Public swimming facilities are available at the **St. George City Pool, 250 East 700 South,** an outdoor pool open late May–Sept.; **(801) 634-5867;** and the **Dixie Center Natatorium, 425 South 700 East; (801) 673-8368.** The **Veyo Pool,** located 18 miles north of St. George on Hwy. 18 is a unique pool, fed by hot springs; **287 East Veyo Resort Rd.; (801) 574-2744.** The Resort at Green Valley has three pools, including an indoor pool and an outside diving pool.

TENNIS
Vic Braden Tennis College—

Green Valley, just west across or around the ridge from St. George, is home to the Vic Braden Tennis College, one of the most popular tennis programs in the world. The college includes courts, hitting lanes, and practice areas. Group and private lessons are available for players at all levels. Tennis vacation packages attract people from all over the world. For more information, write or call, **Vic Braden Tennis College, 1515 West Canyon View Dr., St. George, UT 84770; (801) 628-8060.**

Six public tennis courts are located on the **Dixie College Campus.**

SEEING AND DOING

CULTURAL ACTIVITIES

Elderhostel—
This highly successful program operated by Dixie College is for seniors 60 years of age and older. Between 30 and 50 participants come together for a week and undertake a variety of classes, field trips, and group activities that focus on learning and interaction without any homework or onerous assignments. The week usually begins Sun. evening and concludes the next Sat. morning. The instigators of the program—former Dixie College president Douglas Alder and former St. George mayor Karl Brooks—usually begin the week with a highly informative historical overview of the St. George area. For more information, contact **Dixie College, 225 South 700 East, St. George, UT 84770; (801) 673-4811.**

GAMBLING

Located 36 miles southwest of St. George on Interstate 15, Mesquite, Nevada, is considered part of the St. George area since it draws 90 percent of its visitors from Utah. Most come to participate in an activity that is forbidden in their home state—gambling. Resorts are located at both ends of this town that was started and abandoned by Mormons twice before succeeding in 1894.

Peppermill Resort, Hotel, and Casino—
Nearly 1,000 people are employed at this complex. The casino offers more than 700 slot and poker machines, 2 crap tables, 1 roulette wheel, 15 blackjack tables, 4 poker tables, and other betting games. The casino is open 24 hours a day. The well-landscaped resort includes in excess of 700 rooms, a 500-seat convention center, 6 swimming pools, 4 restaurants, a health club, a gun club, lighted tennis courts, an 18-hole golf course, miniature golf, horseback riding, an animal park, and a children's petting zoo. Check about the special packages and discounted rooms. Located off **exit 120 on Interstate 15; 1-800-621-0187.**

Virgin River Hotel and Casino—
Closer to St. George by 2 miles, the Virgin River Hotel and Casino also offers plenty of gambling plus 375 rooms. Located off **exit 122 on Interstate 15; 1-800-346-7721.**

GHOST TOWNS

Grafton—
Initially settled in 1859, "the Great Flood" of 1861 destroyed the settlement, causing the town to be relocated to a higher location. Succeeding floods continued to batter the little community until unrest during the Blackhawk War caused it to be abandoned until 1868. Today, the remains of the church and some pioneer homes and the use of the town for the 1969 movie *Butch Cassidy and the Sundance Kid* make this one of Utah's most popular ghost towns. The little pioneer cemetery includes a headstone commemorating the massacre of the Berry family by Indians at Short Creek in 1866. To reach Grafton, turn south on Bridge Ln. in Rockville and follow it across the Virgin River. After crossing the

river, turn right (west) and follow the dirt road as it parallels the river for about 2.5 miles until you reach Grafton.

Harrisburg—

After you visit Silver Reef, return to Leeds and follow the road south past the interstate for about 2 miles to the Harrisburg RV resort. Take a few minutes to look at the ruins of the 19th-century houses, then drive west under the freeway to see the other ruins of this one-time Mormon settlement.

Silver Reef—

In the 1870s and 1880s, Silver Reef was a rip-roaring mining town with a reputation unsurpassed by few western mining towns. There is enough left of the old town, especially with the restored Wells Fargo Building (originally constructed in 1877 and restored in 1986 to house the Silver Reef Museum), and the bank building across the street to give a good indication of what was going on there. Within the museum there is an art gallery with bronze works by sculptor Jerry Anderson. In back of the Wells Fargo is the old powder house which contains a scale model of Silver Reef during its heyday of the 1880s. Old mine tailings, early mining equipment, and Catholic and Protestant cemeteries remain from the glory days.

Silver Reef is unique among western mining towns because it is the only place where silver has been discovered in sandstone. The silver may have originated in volcanic tuffs in the Chinle Formation. Ancient streambeds deposited sand and fragments of petrified trees, bushes, and reeds over the silver. Water dissolved the silver and carried it upward. As the silver-bearing water solution reached the decaying vegetation, chemical changes caused the water to precipitate out and become deposited in both the sand and petrified material. Miners kept a close watch for petrified wood with some petrified logs, saturated with silver, worth hundreds and even thousands of dollars. There were 37 mines within the Silver Reef district. At its peak, five mills processed the ore from the mines.

During the late 1870s the mining town grew rapidly. Homes, schools, churches, a newspaper, bakeries, blacksmith and butcher shops, grocery, hardware, furniture, clothing, and drug stores sprang up. Saloons, a dance hall, a gambling house, brothel, and a Chinatown made Silver Reef unique among all southern Utah communities. When it was proposed to relocate the county seat from St. George to Silver Reef, politicians, acting with the support of the Mormon-controlled territorial legislature, had the boundary of Washington County moved north 20 miles to include enough voters to defeat such a proposal. But while Silver Reef proved a challenge to the moral and political life of the area, it also greatly aided the local Mormon economy in providing a much-needed market for local agricultural products and handmade items, including hay that sold for as much as $40 a ton and Dixie wine that had an inexhaustible market.

Silver Reef's glory years did not last long, especially with the Panic of 1893 severely affecting all western silver mining. Around the turn of the century, many of the town's buildings were offered for sale. A rush to purchase the buildings occurred after Peter Anderson purchased the old dance hall and found $2,000 in gold coins apparently left hidden in the building by the original owner who had been shot in the hall and died of his wounds before he told anyone about the money. Other buildings were demolished but no other hidden treasures were found. Mining activity resumed and halted abruptly until the 1960s, never, however, with the intensity of the early years.

To reach Silver Reef, take Leeds exit 2 off Interstate 15, 17 miles north of St. George, and follow the road through pretty little Leeds until, at the north end of town, you see a sign indicating Silver Reef to the west. Follow the road under the freeway then about 2 miles to the Wells Fargo Building.

HISTORIC BUILDINGS AND SITES

The St. George area is rich in pioneer historic buildings. Historic homes, public buildings, churches, business buildings, trails, and ruins provide the casual visitor and the avid history buff with plenty of opportunities to immerse themselves in the history of this unique region. *The Washington County Visitor Guide* (which you can pick up free of charge in the Old Washington Court House) provides a walking guide to 22 St. George buildings within a few blocks. The guide also contains information about historic sites in the area. More detailed information is available in a guide to historic sites published by the Washington County Historical Society. The LDS Church maintains five historic buildings within the area: the **St. George Tabernacle**, the **St. George Temple**, the **Brigham Young Winter Home**, the **Jacob Hamblin House** in Santa Clara, and the **Pine Valley Chapel**—staffing them with volunteer guides at each location. Because pioneer history still permeates the area so strongly, we like to visit one or two buildings and sites each day we are in the area. The following are not to be missed.

Brigham Young Winter Home—

Mormon leader Brigham Young is credited with setting the trend followed by thousands of Utahns—"going to Dixie for the winter." While the warmer weather of the south was indeed good medicine for the aging rheumatic pioneer, the 300-mile annual journey also allowed Young to visit the string of settlements between the two spiritual centers of Salt Lake City and St. George, to supervise work on the St. George Temple, and to give support and encouragement to those seeking to establish a foothold on the southern Mormon frontier. Brigham Young, a carpenter and builder himself, was partial to the use of adobe and chose this material over the native red sandstone or black basalt, although both are used in the foundation. The house was started in 1869 and finished

in 1873. It is one of the best restored homes in the state and houses many personal things such as Youngs corn cob mattress. Free guided tours begin in the one-room office, adjacent to the home, and are offered daily from 9 am–dusk. Located on the corner of **200 North and 100 West.**

Fort Pearce—

During the mid-1860s, Navajo unrest and the threat of raids into southwestern Utah led to the construction of Fort Pearce for defensive purposes. Although it never came under attack, the small rock-walled fort is an interesting reminder of frontier conditions and has been preserved by the Bureau of Land Management. It is located 12 miles southeast of Washington and can be reached by turning south off Main St. in Washington onto 400 South St. and following it south across the Virgin River toward Warner Valley.

Hurricane Heritage Park—

Located in the Center of Hurricane, Heritage Park is a fine memorial to the heroic struggle that brought the town into existence. In the center of the park is a monumental statue of a family. The father stands, hat at his side, touching his wife's hand who holds a baby in the other arm. A young boy kneels apparently in a prayer of thanksgiving as a basket with corn, grapes, and other vegetables lies at their feet. The monument gives a brief history of the construction of the Hurricane Canal and the founding of the town.

The construction of the Hurricane Canal to bring water up from the Virgin River onto the Hurricane Bench is a story of determination and endurance that spanned two centuries. The possibility of constructing a canal was first investigated by Erastus Snow and several companions in 1863. As they descended the steep hill above the town, a whirlwind blew off the top of their buggy. Snow remarked, "Well, that was a hurricane! We'll call this the Hurricane Hill." Thirty years after the initial visit by Erastus Snow, a stock company was organized and a survey made which determined that it would take a 7-mile long canal constructed along the precipitous limestone walls of the Virgin River Canyon to bring water to the Hurricane Bench. With picks, shovels, handmade drills, crowbars, wheelbarrows, and blasting powder, workers commenced construction. Several tunnels had to be blasted and numerous sections of rock walls erected as the canal was constructed under the most difficult of circumstances. To look at the canal today, it appears that the water had to flow up hill from the diversion dam in the canyon bottom to the bench high above the river. Most of the construction work was done in the winters so that the men and boys could take care of their farm work the rest of the year. During the first couple of years, there were as many as 300 men in the canyon at work on the canal. The farmers were assisted by unemployed miners who worked for their board during the winter and the promise of a horse and saddle in the spring. The miners expertise with blasting powder was a great help in building the tunnels through the chert-impregnated limestone.

The success of the canal would allow the establishment of a new community and in 1896 the builders surveyed the future town and drew lots for homesites. It was not until 10 years later in 1906 that the first families moved onto their lots and another 2 years before the first permanent home was built. After working on the canal for nearly a decade, the builders were at the end of their rope financially. Help came when the LDS Church bought $5,000 worth of stock in the canal and work pressed forward to completion in 1904. Nevertheless maintenance of the canal required extraordinary effort as the tunnels filled in, the rock walls broke, and wood fumes had to be replaced. The canal was used until 1985 when a piping system was installed. Listed in the National Register of Historic Places, you can still follow the canal out of the river gorge and onto the Hurricane Bench.

The nicely landscaped park has a nice collection of historic artifacts including wagons, a handcart, buggy, plow, and other farm machinery. Also on the grounds is the community **museum**, located in the Library–City Hall building that was constructed of local red sandstone between 1938 and 1940 as a New Deal WPA project. The museum includes pioneer and Indian artifacts. It is open Mon.–Sat. 10 am–7 pm; **(801) 635-3245.** At the museum you can pick up a pamphlet entitled, "Hurricane Historic Tour," which describes thirteen historic sites and buildings including the Ira Elsey Bradshaw and Marion Hinton House which was built as the first permanent home in Hurricane in 1908 and is being restored by the Hurricane Historical Preservation Commission. The house is known as the Bradshaw Hotel and is located across the street from the park on the northeast corner of **Main and 100 South.**

Jacob Hamblin House—

A contemporary of Brigham Young, Jacob Hamblin holds a special place in Mormon history as first president of the Southern Indian Mission. He came to the area in 1854 as one of the first Mormons to undertake missionary work with the Indians. During the next 20 years, Hamblin worked among the Paiute, Navajo, and Zuni Indians, explaining Mormon beliefs to them, interceding during disputes, and acting as a fair-minded colleague. His travels among the Indians meant exploring much of the Southwest, and Hamblin became the first white man to circumnavigate the Grand Canyon—a barrier to western travelers since the first Spanish travelers in the region. He also assisted Major John Wesley Powell with his surveys of the Colorado River area and during negotiations for a peace treaty with the Navajos in 1870. Hamblin's Santa Clara home was constructed in 1863 of sandrock quarried nearby. He and his two wives, Rachel Judd and Pricilla Leavitt, occupied the home until 1871, when Hamblin was sent by church leaders to the newly established settlement of Kanab. Although polygamy was a complex and multifaceted experience, which sometimes produced antagonisms between wives, Rachel and Pricilla seemed to get along very well, and the Santa Clara house is an interesting example of the arrangement for two wives living in the same house. The two rooms on the main floor are nearly identical with stairs ascending to the second floor from the back of each room. The second floor could also be reached directly from the outside and was something of a community center for religious, civic, and social events. Otherwise the second floor was the work area for the Hamblin household. Like other LDS Church–owned historic sites, free guided tours are offered 9:00 am–dusk. To reach the Jacob Hamblin House, head north on Bluff Rd., then turn left onto Sunset Blvd. and drive west until the road becomes Santa Clara Dr. Watch for the Hamblin House on the right (north) side of the road.

Mountain Meadows Massacre Site—

A dozen books and hundreds of articles have been written in an attempt to explain the tragic event that occurred at Mountain Meadows, just west of St. George, in early September 1857. In 1990, in an act of reconciliation, descendants of both victims and perpetrators came together to erect a simple, granite monument engraved with the names of 120 California-bound emigrants who were killed in the grassy valley by southern Utah militiamen and their Indian allies. Despite a promise of safe conduct through this area of Utah, the victims were executed and their bodies strewn across the rolling hills of this popular rest stop. Eighteen small children were spared and adopted by local Mormon families, with whom they lived for two years before federal officials collected them and returned them to relatives in Arkansas and Missouri.

The Mountain Meadows Massacre is a complex tragedy, that grew out of a legacy of persecution of Mormons in Missouri and Illinois before their exodus to Utah. In the summer of 1857, a large force of federal troops was en route to Utah to put down an alleged "Mormon Rebellion," a situation that provoked anxiety among Mormons who felt all too keenly the pressure of their non-conformist lifestyle. Added to this was the perceived need for Mormons to maintain their Native American neighbors as allies against the invading "Mericats," as non-Mormon Americans were called, and the alleged misconduct on the part of the immigrants as they proceeded south from Salt Lake City in the midst of Mormon preparations for war. Last, but not least, there were communication difficulties, which left local leaders unsure of what action Brigham Young would have them take. This confusion had tragic consequences. Men who participated in the atrocity vowed never to talk about it, and, until recent years, the massacre was discussed in hushed and secret tones. Only one man, the respected Mormon pioneer John D. Lee, was convicted for participating in the massacre. He was taken to Mountain Meadows in 1877, where he was executed by federal authorities. He is generally acknowledged to have given himself up, knowing he would be tried, found guilty, and executed to atone for the sins of his fellow Mormons. In 1950 a courageous St. George teacher and housewife, the late Juanita Brooks, published what is still regarded as the definitive study of the tragedy: *The Mountain Meadows Massacre*. Despite the storm of protest from those who would rather have ignored and forgotten the event—and a certain amount of criticism from the LDS Church—her book began the important process of healing and understanding. For her courage, her scholarship, and her commitment to truth, Juanita Brooks has become a Utah heroine. Her other writings include a biography of John D. Lee, several other southern Utah pioneers, and her autobiographical *Quicksand and Cactus*.

To reach Mountain Meadows, head north on Hwy. 18 from St. George for approximately 25 miles and watch for the signs to the left (west) of the road. You can go right up to the monument, which, perched high above this vast, lonely valley, has much of the same impact as the Vietnam Memorial in Washington, DC.

Old Washington County Courthouse—

As the headquarters for the St. George Area Chamber of Commerce, the impressive old courthouse, located in the center of town ,is recommended as a first stop. The helpful volunteers provide plenty of information about the area, including special events and activities. Construction of the courthouse began in 1866, three years after the settlement of St. George, and was completed 10 years later. The brick and mortar were manufactured locally. The second-story courtroom has been restored and is used for a weekly history lecture program given by local historian Bart Anderson. Open Mon.–Sat. 9 am–5 pm. **100 East St. George Blvd.**

Pine Valley Chapel—

Perhaps the most photogenic church in all of Utah is the Pine Valley Chapel. The symmetrical, two-story, white-frame building in the picturesque Pine Valley was constructed in 1868 and is the oldest Mormon chapel still in continuous use. According to tradition, the chapel was designed and built by Ebenezer Bryce, for whom Bryce Canyon National Park is named. Before coming to Utah, Bryce was a ship builder in Australia. Using shipbuilding techniques, the wood frame walls were assembled on the ground, raised into position, and joined with wooden pegs and rawhide, which can still be seen in the attic. Just east of the chapel is a small, red brick tithing office constructed in the 1880s. The chapel is open for free tours during the summer from 9:00 am–dusk. To reach Pine Valley, head north out of St. George on Bluff Blvd. onto Hwy. 18 for 25 miles, along the western side of the Pine Valley Mountains, then turn right (east) at Central and follow the road for 7 miles.

Washington Cotton Mill—

In 1986, Norma Cannizzaro, a lady of vision, restored one of Utah's most important industrial buildings. St. George was established in 1861, as what was to be the center of a Mormon cotton industry, and the cotton mill is virtually all that is left of that effort. The mill was constructed of red sandstone in 1866 and expanded in 1870. It is privately owned and not open to the public. To reach the building head north on Interstate 15, take the Washington exit, turn left onto Telegraph and follow the road toward Washington. Look for the building on the right (south) side of the road just before you enter the town.

HOT SPRINGS

Pah Tempe Hot Springs—

Located on the Virgin River below the bridge on the northwestern end of Hurricane, the hot springs were recorded by Dominguez and Escalante in 1776, when they named the river Rio Sulfureo. Today, the springs fill seven pools and a swimming pool with 100-degree-Fahrenheit water. The private resort includes a **bed and breakfast, a campground, and a health food cafe**. It is open daily. For times and prices, call **(801) 635-2879.**

NIGHTLIFE

Tuacahn Amphitheater—

The 1,800-seat Tuacahn Amphitheater is scheduled to open in the summer of 1995 with 64 performances of a spectacular drama entitled *Utah!* The performance will depict historic events and characters such as Father Escalante, Kit Carson, Brigham Young, and the settlement of southern Utah through singing, dancing, and special effects such as controlled lightning and controlled floods. The finale will be a dramatic fireworks display. Before the evening performance, a Dutch-oven and barbecue dinner will be offered along with Native American and pioneer dances and songs. The complex will also include replicas of Anasazi, Navajo, and Paiute dwellings. Tuacahn, meaning "Canyon of the Gods" is located 10 miles northwest of St. George off state Hwy. 300 just south of the entrance to Snow Canyon. For information and reservations write or call:**Tuacahn, 1030 South Valley View Dr., St. George, UT 84770; (801) 674-0012.**

SCENIC DRIVES
Mojave Desert/Joshua Tree Road—

One of the most unusual scenic drives in Utah is a gravel-and-dirt road suitable for passenger cars that goes through the Joshua Tree National Landmark west of St. George. This area—in Washington County's extreme southern section—marks the northernmost region in which Joshua trees grow and, here, you are in a classic Mojave Desert landscape rather than among the red hills, blue mountains, and black volcanic ridges characteristic of the rest of Washington County. Wildflowers blooming in the spring make this a particularly good time to travel this 16- mile loop. The road begins on old Hwy. 91, 2 miles west of the Gunlock turnoff. The road heads toward the south, past the Helca Mining Operation. The first 3 miles pass through the Shivwits Paiute Indian Reservation and climb up Wittwer Canyon (Widow Canyon), its phonetic name probably given for or by one of the 1856 Swiss settlers sent to Santa Clara. The road then skirts the base of Jarvis Peak, paralleling the boundary of the Beaver Dam Mountains Wilderness located to the south. About 8 miles from Hwy. 91, the well-maintained mining road ends, and you must keep to the left, following a narrow dirt road that climbs to a ridge before reaching the Joshua trees. It then traverses Bulldog Canyon and intersects Hwy. 91 about 4 miles from the Utah-Nevada border. The road can be taken in either direction.

Smithsonian Butte Scenic Backway—

This 9-mile long drive between Hwy. 9 and the Arizona Strip offers one of the most spectacular panoramic views of Zion National Park, as well as to other landmarks, including Canaan Mountain, Smithsonian Butte, the Virgin River Valley, the Eagle Crags, and the 2,000-foot headwall at the Pines. To appreciate the varied landscape, plan to drive the route in both directions. Begin in Rockville at the bridge across the Virgin River, then head south (past the turnoff for the ghost town of Grafton) and continue to the junction with Hwy. 59, 8 miles northwest of Hildale and 15 miles southeast of Hurricane.

Virgin River Gorge—

Interstate 15 cuts north-south through Utah for 400 miles. The most spectacular stretch begins just south of St. George through the Virgin River Gorge. Flying through the twisting canyon at 65 miles an hour is no way to enjoy a scenic drive, but the 20-mile stretch from St. George to Littlefield, Arizona, following the Virgin River as it cuts through the Beaver Dam Mountains, is one that few drivers will soon forget.

SHOPPING
Artist Co-op Gallery—

If you want to check out the work of 30 of the top artists in the St. George area, visit their Artist Co-op Gallery located in downtown St. George. Artists manage and run the store, so you can be assured of a great opportunity to discuss the local art scene. **4 West St. George Blvd.** in Ancestor Square; **(801) 628-9293.**

Chums—

In the early 1980s Mike Taggett began manufacturing Chums, the world's best eyeglass retainer. Mike spent his summers working as a river guide on the Colorado River and learned quickly that eyeglasses and sunglasses did not stand a chance of survival in some of the heavy rapids unless they were properly secured. After brainstorming with his friends about what the perfect retainer should be, he invented Chums. The attractive and practical eyeglass retainers survived the rigors of the Colorado River with flying colors and now some 60 employees provide Chums to more than 30 countries around the world. Building on the success of Chums, Mike expanded into comfortable clothes under the HelloWear line. The Chums factory and a retail store—where you can purchase Chums and HelloWear, including seconds at inexpensive prices—

is located in Hurricane at **120 South Main St.** The store is open Mon.–Sat. 9 am–6 pm.; **1-800-323-3707.**

Factory Outlet Stores—

At the east end of St. George Blvd., across Interstate 15 are the St. George Factory Outlet Stores. There are over 30 stores ranging from clothing and shoe stores to sports and bookstores. The stores are open from 10 am–8 pm Mon.–Sat.

WILDLIFE

Two of the best locations for viewing wildlife in the St. George have already been noted: **Pine Valley** and **Snow Canyon State Park,** both off Hwy. 18 as it heads north from St. George. Pine Valley offers a high probability for seeing mule deer, along with smaller animals and birds common to Utah's forests. Snow Canyon State Park is more desert than forest and features reptiles like the endangered desert tortoises, gila monsters, lizards, and rattlesnakes. Spring through fall is the best viewing season.

Another good area to see desert wildlife is the **Lytle Ranch Preserve.** Operated by Brigham Young University, Lytle Ranch

is open year-round, although the best time to view wildlife is in the spring and late fall. The Lytle Preserve is located along the Beaver Dam Wash drainage where the Mojave Desert of the Basin and Range Province overlaps with the Colorado Plateau. Plant life of the uplands is characterized by Joshua trees, datil yucca, creosote bushes, black brush, and cholla cactus. The lowlands along the wash support cottonwoods, black and desert willows. Animals include coyotes, cottontail and jackrabbits, mule deer, beaver—along the wash, lizards, Gila monsters, rattlesnakes, roadrunners, and the desert tortoise, an endangered species. There is a full-time manager at the preserve and limited camping facilities are available. To reach the ranch, follow Hwy. 56 through Santa Clara on to Shivwits. Approximately .5 mile west of the junction of the Gunlock Rd., watch for a sign pointing to the Lytle Ranch. Follow the gravel road in a northwesterly direction approximately 11 miles to the ranch headquarters. For information write or call the **Lytle Preserve, 290 MLBM, Brigham Young University, Provo, UT 84602; (801) 378-5052.**

WHERE TO STAY

ACCOMMODATIONS

There are nearly 60 lodging facilities in the St. George area. Although this is a prime travel area, motel rates are generally reasonable, especially during the summer. Unlike other high-travel destinations, such as Moab, Blanding, or Monticello, there are usually plenty of vacancy signs out. However, certain events and weekends such as Presidents' Day and Easter can make finding a room difficult. St. George was a national leader in providing nonsmoking rooms. Almost all motels offer nonsmoking rooms; one motel—the Clairidge Inn— is completely smoke-free.

For information on accommodations in the St. George/Washington County area call pick up copies of the *Utah Travel Guide,* which lists current rates, and the *Washing-*

ton County Travel Guide, which provides a brief description of available accommodations. Both publications are available at the Old Washington County Courthouse Visitor Center on St. George Blvd. or at the Utah State Visitor Center located just off Interstate 15, after you cross the Utah state line headed north. The following are some of my favorites:

BED AND BREAKFASTS
(ST. GEORGE)
Greene Gate Village Historic Bed and Breakfast Inn—$$ to $$$

St. Georgites who have watched the evolution of Greene Gate Village are lavish in their praise for Dr. Mark and Barbara Greene who have transformed several pioneer homes slated for demolition into a unique bed and breakfast. Their efforts have earned praise from historic preservationists everywhere. Located across the street north of the tabernacle, Greene Gate is a complex of eight historic buildings, some of which have been moved to their present location. Thirteen rooms with private baths are included in the complex. Breakfast is served in the Orson Pratt house, which is also the location for the Bentley Supper House, where dinner is offered by reservation to guests and the public Thurs., Fri., and Sat. evenings. **76 West Tabernacle; (801) 628-6999 or 1-800-350-6999.**

Seven Wives Inn—$$ to $$$

There are no bed-and-breakfast operations anywhere that are better than the Seven Wives Inn, which is run by Jay and Donna Curtis and their daughter and son-in-law Jon and Alison Bowcutt. Opened in 1981, the inn is located in two historic homes: the Edwin Woolley House (c.1875) and the adjacent George Whitehead House (1883). Each of the 13 rooms is decorated with period furnishings. Each room has its own private bath, although the plumbing has improved considerably since George Whitehead ran a pipe from the irrigation ditch outside to a bathroom upstairs to provide running water, albeit cold, for baths. As to the name Seven Wives Inn— ask Donna about her great-grandfather Benjamin Franklin Johnson, a polygamist who found sanctuary from the law in a secret hideout in the Wooley House. **217 North 100 West; (801) 628-3737.**

CONDOMINIUMS AND RESORTS (ST. GEORGE)
Bloomington Condominiums—$$$

Forty units. Located on the Bloomington Golf Course (private). **141 Brigham Rd.; (801) 673-6172.**

Green Valley Resort Condominium Rental—$$$ to $$$$

Seventy units. Plenty of recreation opportunities, including swimming pools, outdoor and indoor tennis courts, racquetball courts, basketball courts, putting

area, and children's playground. **1515 W. Canyon View Dr.; (801) 628-8060 or 1-800-237-1068.**

HOTELS AND MOTELS (ST. GEORGE)
Best Western Coral Hills—$$ to $$$

Ninety-eight units. An excellent downtown location, (just across the street from the Old Court House and a block from Ancestor Square and the St. George Tabernacle. Indoor and outdoor pools, children's pool, spas, exercise room, game room. A nice, clean, well-run motel. **125 East St. George Blvd.; (801) 673-4844 or 1-800-542-7733.**

Claridge Inn—$$ to $$$

All rooms are nonsmoking. Heated pool and Jacuzzi; 50 units. **1187 South Bluff; (801) 673-7222.**

Comfort Suites—$$$

Outdoor heated pool and Jacuzzi; 123 units. **1239 South Main** just off Interstate 15 at exit 6; **1-800-228-2150.**

Hilton Inn of St. George—$$$

One hundred units. The only lodging in St. George which carries AAA's 4-star rating. **1450 South Bluff; (801) 628-4481 or 1-800-231-4488.**

Holiday Inn Resort Hotel and Convention Center—$$$

One hundred sixty-four units. **850 South Bluff; (801) 628-4235 or 1-800-457-9800.**

Ramada—$$$

Heated pool, Jacuzzi, hot tub, free continental breakfast; 90 units. **1440 East St. George Blvd.; (801) 628-2828 or 1-800-228-2828.**

Sun Time Inn—$$ to $$$

All 46 rooms are nonsmoking. Complimentary continental breakfast. Some kitchenettes and one room with disabled access. **420 East St. George Blvd.; (801) 673-6181 or 1-800-237-6253.**

Weston's Lamplighter—$$

I've stayed at this 49-unit motel a number of times and have found it clean, quiet, with competitive rates. **460 East St. George Blvd.; (801) 673-4861.**

BED AND BREAKFASTS (TOQUERVILLE, HURRICANE, AND LAVERKIN)

Pah Tempe Hot Springs Spa Resort Bed and Breakfast—$$$

This is one of Utah's most unusual bed and breakfasts with its location in the bottom of the Virgin River canyon. The hot springs are located along the banks of the river in a secluded grove of trees. The hot springs were noted by early explorers and are an ancient Paiute healing ground that was rededicated a few years ago by a Paiute medicine man to be used for its original healing purposes. A small gourmet restaurant serves vegetarian food and nonalcoholic beverages. All rooms are nonsmoking. The rooms are very small and open off the kitchen, affording little privacy. **825 North 800 East, Hurricane; (801) 635-2879 or 635-2353.**

Your Inn—$$$

Four spacious rooms with king-size beds and private baths located on a 10-acre site, with orchards and a stream running through the property. A full country breakfast is included. **650 Springs Drive, Toquerville; (801) 635-9964.**

MOTELS (TOQUERVILLE, HURRICANE, AND LAVERKIN)

Best Western Weston's Lamplighter Motel—$$

Pool and Jacuzzi and adjacent gift shop and restaurant; 32 rooms. **280 West State St., Hurricane; (801) 635-2879 or 1-800-528-1234.**

Motel Park Villa—$$

Twenty-three units, 17 of which have kitchens. A clean, charming, motel considered the best deal in Hurricane and very popular with European travelers. **650 West State, Hurricane; (801) 635-4010.**

CAMPGROUNDS

PRIVATE

Because the St. George area is a nesting ground for thousands of snowbirds from Oct.–May, and many spend the winter in trailers or fifth-wheels, **RV parks** are of special importance in the area. The RV parks can fill to capacity during the winter, but are practically abandoned during the summer. Most of the parks have elaborate facilities—stores, laundries, clubhouses, swimming pools, hot tubs, saunas, game areas, cable hookups, and, in the winter, organized activities. Rates also vary, so if you are planning to spend any length of time in the area in your recreation vehicle or trailer, you will want to get the particulars on prices and amenities. The following list of major RV resorts and parks should provide what you need, otherwise contact the **St. George Area Travel Office.**

Brentwood RV Resort—

One hundred eighty-seven full hookups. Water slide, indoor swimming pool, bowling and amusement center. This is a popular RV park with children. Located 5 miles east of Interstate 15 (exit 16) along Hwy. 9; **(801) 635-2320.**

Harrisburg Lakeside RV Resort—

Two hundred plus hookups. Located off Interstate 15. Northbound take exit 22; southbound exit 23, then follow the frontage road 2 miles south from Leeds to the resort. Within the resort and just across the interstate are ruins of the 19th-century pioneer stone houses built by the pioneers of Harrisburg. **(801) 879-2312.**

McArthur's Temple View RV Resort—

Two hundred fifty full hookups. **975 South Main, St. George; (801) 673-6400.**

Quail Lake RV Park—

One hundred fifty full hookups. Located **3 miles east of Interstate 15 (exit 16) along Hwy. 9; (801) 635-9960.**

"ONCE I LIVED IN COTTONWOOD"

It's not the catchy tune that my friends at the St. George Area Chamber of Commerce hum as they cheerfully go about promoting "Utah's Dixie," nor was it without irritation to most Mormon authorities, including one who wrote to its composer, George A. Hicks, that he "...would make a good-looking tassel on the end of a rope." But "Once I Lived in Cottonwood," composed about 1865 and sung to the tune of "The Georgia Volunteer," is a statement of pioneer Dixie that captures the difficulties, the Spartan way of life, and the small undercurrents of "near heresy" that added flavor and life to most Mormon villages. Sung with a strong dose of self-effacing humor, it helped make the arduous pioneer life a bit more tolerable. Even though Hicks was rebuked by the leader of the Mormons in Utah's Dixie and told never to sing the song again, it is beloved by most Utah Mormons and continued to be sung long after Hicks death in 1924.

> Oh, once I lived in Cottonwood and owned a little farm.
> But I was called to Dixie, which gave me much alarm.
> To raise the cane and cotton I right away must go,
> But the reason why they sent me, I'm sure I do not know.
>
> I yoked old Jim and Bally up, all for to make a start,
> To leave my house and garden, it almost broke my heart,
> We moved along quite slowly and often looked behind,
> For the sands and rocks of Dixie kept running through my mind.
>
> At length we reached the Black Ridge where I broke my wagon down,
> I could not find a carpenter, we were twenty miles from town,
> So with a clumsy cedar pole I fixed an awkward slide,
> My wagon pulled so heavy then that Betsy couldn't ride.
>
> While Betsy was a-walking, I told her to take care,
> When all upon a sudden she struck a prickly pear,
> Then she began to blubber out as loud as she could bawl,
> If I was back in Cottonwood, I wouldn't come at all.
>
> And when we reached the Sandy, we could not move at all,
> For poor old Jim and Bally began to puff and bawl,
> I whipped and swore a little but could not make the route,
> For myself, the team and Betsy were all of us give out.
>
> And next we got to Washington where we stayed a little while,
> To see if April showers would make the verdure smile,
> But oh I was mistaken, and so I went away
> For the red hills of November looked just the same in May.
>
> I feel so sad and lonely now, there's nothing here to cheer,
> Except prophetic sermons which we very often hear.
> They will hand them out by the dozen and prove them by the Book,
> I'd rather have some roasting ears to stay at home and cook.

I feel so weak and hungry now I think I'm nearly dead,
'tis seven weeks next Sunday since I have tasted bread,
Of carrot tops and lucerne greens we have enough to eat,
But I'd like to change my diet off for buckwheat cakes and meat.

I brought this old coat with me about two years ago,
And how I'll get another one I'm sure I do not know.
May Providence protect me against the wind and wet,
I think myself and Betsy, these times we'll ne'er forget.

My shirt is died with wild dockroot with greasewood for to set,
I fear the colors all will fade when once it does get wet.
They said we could raise madder and indigo so blue,
But that turned out a humbug, the story was not true.

The hot winds whirl around me and take away my breath,
I've had the chills and fever till I'm nearly shook to death.
"All earthly tribulations are but a moment here,"
And oh, if I prove faithful a righteous crown shall wear.

My wagon's sold for sorghum seed to make a little bread,
And poor old Jim and Bally long, long ago are dead.
There's only me and Betsy left to hoe the cotton tree,
May Heaven help the Dixie-ite wherever he may be.

Redlands RV Park—

Two hundred full hookups. Take the Washington exit (exit 10) off Interstate 15. **650 West Telegraph, Washington; (801) 673-9700.**

St. George Campground and RV Park—

One hundred full hookups. **2100 East Middleton Dr., St. George; (801) 673-2970.**

Settlers RV Park—

One hundred fifty-five full hookups. **1333 East 100 South, St. George; (801) 628-1624.**

Valley View Trailer Park—

Ninety-three RV sites with 60 complete hookups. **2300 East Middleton Dr.; (801) 673-3367.**

PUBLIC

In Pine Valley—

Three miles east of the town at the end of the road there are three small US Forest Service campgrounds, **Blue Springs** has 18 RV and 3 tent sites; **Juniper Park** has 10 RV and 12 tent sites; and **Pines** has 2 RV and 6 tent sites. All three have picnic tables, drinking water, and flush toilets and charge a fee. Open from mid-May–end of Oct.

At Quail Creek Reservoir—

Fourteen miles northeast of St. George, off Interstate 15, there are 23 RV and 23 tent sites maintained by the State Parks Division. There are flush toilets, drinking water, and plenty of boating, fishing, and swimming in the adjacent reservoir. Open all year. A fee is charged.

At Red Cliffs Recreation Area —

Operated by the Bureau of Land Management; 10 RV and 10 tent sites. Equipped with drinking water and flush toilets. Open year-round. A fee is charged. From Interstate 15, take exit 22, turn back to Harrisburg, then follow the road west under the interstate, past Harrisburg for a couple of miles. The recreation area is nestled under the east slope of the Pine Valley Mountains.

In Snow Canyon State Park—

Closer to St. George, in Snow Canyon State Park, there are 14 RV and 34 tent sites. The campground includes showers, flush toilets, drinking water, and a dump site. Open year-round.

WHERE TO EAT

Andelin's Gable House—$ to $$$

Located in a quaint cottage-style building, Andelin's is two restaurants in one. On the main floor, diners can enjoy modestly priced breakfasts, lunches, and dinners. Downstairs, the special five-course dinner is more expensive and a worthy St. George tradition. Open for breakfast 7 am–11:30 am, lunch 11:30 am–5 pm, and dinner 5 pm–10 pm. Reservations are recommended for the five-course dinner. **290 East St. George Blvd.; (801) 673-6796.**

Basila's—$$ to $$$

This is arguably the best Greek restaurant in Utah—something of a surprise, since although there are significant enclaves of Greeks in other parts of the state, very few have found their way to southern Utah.

John and Basila Melonas moved to St. George in 1982, and their restaurant has become renowned for its excellent food and friendly service. John's grandparents immigrated to Utah from Argos, Greece, in the 1920s. Basila traces her roots back to Chaldea, and her Arabic heritage is evident in the food they serve. Spices from Beruit, Greece, Lebanon, Italy, and even Iraq are imported to give the food a unique flavor. Both John and Basila's parents and grandparents were involved in the food preparation business, and they learned the food business from the bottom up and through professional training. Their three children, John, Anthony, and Demetrius and daughter-in-law Noel work as cooks and waiters. They pride themselves on their friendliness and excellent food.

Two recommendations for dinner are the Greek combination platter, which includes dolmathes (marinated vine leaves stuffed with finely ground sirloin), spinakopala (phyllo pastry stuffed with spinach and feta cheese at least 4 inches thick!), shish kebab, carrots, and an Arabic-style rice with raisins and almonds. The Greek dressing is exceptional. They also offer Italian cuisine and the cheese ravioli is highly recommended. The restaurant is very intimate with instrumental Greek music playing in the background at just the right level to be heard and add atmosphere to the wonderful food, but not too loud to drown out conversations. Open for lunch, Tues.–Sat 11 am–2:30 pm, and for dinner 5 pm–9 pm. Located in Ancestor Square, **2 West St. George Boulevard; (801) 673-7671.**

J. J. Hunan-$ to $$

St. George's other Chinese restaurant is located in Ancestor Square on the 2nd floor of the Tower Building. The luncheon menu offers 50 different choices. There's even more choices for dinner with Canton, Szechuan, Mandarin, Hunan, and Shanghai-dinners plus vegetarian entrées. Open 11:30 am–9:45 pm, Mon.–Fri.; noon–9:45 pm Sat. and noon–8:45 pm Sun.; **(801) 628-7219.**

Los Hermanos—$ to $$

The history of the 1871 house in which this Mexican restaurant is located makes it a worthwhile stop, and if you are a Butch Cassidy fan, it will be doubly rewarding. Built in 1871 by Poore Hardy, the sheriff of St. George, you still get a feel for the pioneer era with two first story and one second story dining areas, despite some remodeling. The St. George jail was located adjacent to the house. One prisoner, Tom Forrest, killed a Silver Reef resident. After he was incarcerated by Sheriff Hardy, a group of 50 men overwhelmed Hardy removed the prisoner and hanged him first on a telegraph pole in front of the building and when the pole proved not strong enough, they took Forrest to a cottonwood tree a block away and finished the vigilante-style execution. Los Hermanos owner, Steve McQueen, is a western his-

tory and Butch Cassidy buff. Pictures of Butch Cassidy and his cohorts line the walls of the restaurant. The Mexican food is made fresh without preservatives and carries such names as Butch Cassidy's Vegetarian Vitals, Robert Parker's Beef or Chicken Burrito Dinner (Robert Parker was Butch's given name). There are three sizes of combination dinners and all food is cooked using canola oil. Open Mon.–Sat 11:30 am–9:30 pm. Ancestor Square, **46 West St. George Blvd.; (801) 628-5989.**

McGuire's—$$ to $$$

Located on busy Bluff Blvd., the restaurant resembles a small stuccoed Irish cottage, but it is best known by locals for its Italian cuisine. The interior scheme is based on green—green wainscoting with a touch of blue and brown, making it a rich and pleasant interior with room for about 30 people. The menu includes pasta, veal, chicken, shrimp, and steaks, all prepared with original recipes. Open daily 5:30 pm–10:00 pm. **531 North Bluff; (801) 628-4066.**

New Garden Cafe—$ to $$

Formerly known as Chumleys and run as part of the Chums operation in Hurricane, the New Garden Cafe is now under the management of Howard Ostler and maintains its emphasis on healthful vegetarian food. The most popular menu item is the veggie lasagna, but you can get a burger made from wheat meat, veggie and bean burritos, salads, and soups. The cafe is something of a center for the environmentally conscious and is a good place for locals, transplants, and visitors to rub shoulders. Open 7:30 am–9:00 pm Mon.–Sat and 9 am–6 pm Sun. **138 South Main, Hurricane; (801) 635-9825.**

Panda Garden Chinese Restaurant—$ to $$

Ivan Szu and Dena Chen are the owners of this popular Chinese restaurant. The menu is extensive with something for everyone, Cantonese-style dishes, spicy selections, family-style dinners, and a dozen entrées for vegetarians. Open daily 11 am–10 pm. **212 North 900 East; (801) 674-1538.**

Paula's Cazuela—$$

Paula Dominguez brought Mexican food to St. George in the early 1960s when she, her husband, Coronado, and children arrived in town from south Texas via Nevada. Looking for work, she was hired by Sue Cannon to cook at the Desert Kitchen Truck Stop and began offering Mexican food to Sue's customers. Now Sue, who is semiretired, works four days a week for Paula as her cashier and hostess. Paula's Cazuela (or Paula's Clay Cooking Pot) opened nearly 20 years ago and has been at the present location since 1985. After more than 30 years Paula's Mexican food is still the favorite of St. George locals.

A la carte entrées are available and, while the bestseller is Paula's special deep-fried burrito, my favorite is the enchilada grande, which comes with two beef or cheese enchiladas topped with sour cream, guacamole, tomatoes, lettuce, and olives. Although the food is the main attraction, a close second is the fabulous view of St. George. The restaurant is located on the hill at the west end of St. George and offers a panoramic view of St. George below. Ask for a window seat, even if you have to wait. Open Mon.–Sat. 11 am–10 pm. Located off Bluff Blvd. at **745 West Ridgecrest Dr.; (801) 673-6568.**

Pizza Factory—$ to $$

Serving pizza made from scratch, locals claim this is the best pizza in town. We ate there on a Fri. evening in May and found the restaurant busy and full of teenagers and families with children. The waitresses were cheery, and the customers enthused about the weekend and dinner out. We left full of good food and good feelings. In addition to pizza, the menu includes a full range of sandwiches, an excellent salad bar, spaghetti, delicious soups, and homemade cheesecake and chocolate chip cookies. Open Mon–Thurs. 11 am–10 pm; Fri. and Sat. 11 am–11 pm. Located in **Ancestor Square on St. George Blvd. and Main St.; (801) 634-1234.**

Tom's Delicatessen—$

Tom and Carol Verhaeren have been making sandwiches in St. George since 1978, and their sandwiches—35 different kinds and combinations—are considered by locals to be the best around. Also recommended is Carol's homemade potato salad. Located at **175 West 900 South Bluff**, just south of the Holiday Inn. Open 11 am–6:00 pm with takeout orders available; call **(801) 628-1822.**

——— SERVICES ———

Visitors to the St. George area will want to pick up copies of two local publications, *The Daily Spectrum,* a newspaper that carries local, national, and international news items, and *St. George Magazine.* Edited by a long-time journalist and excellent writer, Lyman Hafen, whose lifelong assignment has been to come to know the St. George area and its people with an impressive breadth and focus, the bimonthly St. George Magazine focuses on both individuals and topics such as the local national parks, history, golf, art, upcoming events, and other recreational pursuits. St. George Magazine, **165 North 100 East, Suite 2, St. George, UT 84770; (801) 673-6333.**

St. George Area Chamber of Commerce—

Open Mon–Sat. 9 am–5 pm. **Old Washington County Courthouse, 97 East St. George Blvd., (801) 628-1658.**

Utah Visitor Center—

Off Interstate 15, just across the Arizona-Utah border. Open daily 8 am–9 pm in summer; 8 am–5 pm in winter.

Washington County Travel and Convention Bureau—

Open Mon.–Fri. 9 am–5 pm. **The Dixie Center, 425 South 70 East, St. George, UT 84770; (801) 634-5747** or **1-800-869-6635.**

Kanab

The tourist gods must have inspired the selection of the town site of Kanab in 1870, since it is located in the center of the world's most magnificent landscape. Like spokes connecting with the hub of a wheel, the roads branch out from Kanab in all four directions to three national parks, three national monuments, one national recreation area, a nationally significant historic ferry crossing on the Colorado River, two nearby Indian reservations, two national forests, two state parks, and numerous opportunities to experience the American West as it has existed for thousands of years.

The image of the American West held by millions of movie buffs all over the world is the reality of Kanab. Kanab's sheer vermilion sandstone cliffs, nearby coral sand dunes, and unending vistas have brought the movie industry to southern Utah for three-quarters of a century. Beginning in 1922, with the filming of *Deadwood Coach,* starring Tom Mix, and more recent films such as *How the West Was Won,* dozens of westerns have been filmed around Kanab. Movie sets—now historic sites themselves—remain in the canyons around Kanab, waiting for appreciative visitors. Kanab still prides itself on its nickname, Little Hollywood.

But even before Hollywood discovered Kanab, it had a long tradition as a western frontier outpost and headquarters for cattle outfits whose herds ranged across the thousands of acres along the Utah-Arizona border. If state makers had followed natural boundaries instead of artificial political boundaries in drawing the line between Arizona and Utah, the extreme northwestern corner of Arizona would have been included in Utah. Known as the Arizona Strip, the area west and north of the Colorado River and the Grand Canyon is isolated from the rest of Arizona, but is a natural extension of southern Utah. The two small settlements in the Arizona Strip, Fredonia and Short Creek (now known as Colorado City), straddle the Utah-Arizona border, with historic, social, economic, and religious contacts extending north into Utah.

Travelers from the north approach Kanab along Hwy. 89 through Long Valley, which begins in the subalpine meadows at the extreme southeastern edge of the Markagunt Plateau at an elevation of 7,500 feet on the rim of the Great Basin. The Markagunt drops off on the west to form the Great Basin Province. The road along the western edge of the Colorado Plateau, through Long Valley, follows the east fork of the Virgin River in its southerly course until, at Mt. Carmel Junction, it flows west through the southern boundary of Zion National Park. The Long Valley drive is one of the most scenic in all of Utah. The historic Mormon villages of Glendale, Orderville, and Mt. Carmel suggest a sympathetic, almost reverent, accommodation to the land.

The descent along US 89 also takes you down a geological grand staircase of rock formations—the Pink Cliffs, White Cliffs, and Vermillion Cliffs—with each formation a step back into the geological past, ending at the Grand Canyon. Kanab Creek, a tributary of the Colorado, originates in the high plateau meadows east of Hwy. 89 and follows a southerly course through the series of cliffs and into Kanab. From Kanab, it continues on across the state line and through the eastern corner of the Kaibab Paiute Indian Reservation, through the Kanab Creek Wilderness Area, and into Grand Canyon National Park, where it flows into the Colorado River. Stretching from just south of Zion National Park on the west to the Paria River on the east, the fiery walls of the Vermillion Cliffs form something of a northern boundary to the Arizona Strip and leave an unforgettable impression, especially where communities like Colorado City and Kanab nestle at their feet.

HISTORY

The combination of precipitous cliffs, ancient Indian ruins, vast expanses, and isolation of this area have generated a rich tradition of stories and myths that rival the magnificent scenery in color and perhaps unbelievability. The tallest of tales center on reports that the Aztec leader Montezuma dispatched 2,000 warriors to carry much of his treasure to a hiding place in the canyons north of Tenochtitan, just before the Aztec capital fell to Spaniard Hernan Cortes in 1521. In 1914, a treasure seeker named Freddie Crystal arrived in Kanab with a map in hand that identified the Johnson Canyon area as the location for Montezuma's buried treasure. Eight years after his initial arrival, the treasure seeker discovered a series of tunnels, some of which were sealed with rock-hard mortar. Crystal and most of Kanab took the discovery as evidence that the Aztec warriors had indeed hauled Montezuma's treasure more than 1,600 miles north, across the Colorado River to the remote cliffs of Johnson Canyon. In 1922, gold fever struck Kanab, as residents took up the search and were issued shares in the treasure based on the amount of work they did. No gold was found, and after two years the search ended—though not necessarily a belief that the gold did exist. A few years ago a Kanab resident, who grew up hearing the stories of Montezuma's treasure, concluded that the tunnels in Johnson Canyon were only a diversion and that the gold had been ingeniously hidden in a water trap at the bottom of nearby Three Lakes.

Located a few miles north of Kanab on the west side of Hwy. 89, Three Lakes is a popular local fishing hole. According to the treasure theory, the Aztecs drained the lake, buried the treasure in a chamber carved into the sandstone cliff, and allowed the lake to refill. Recently, divers have attempted to carry out underwater explorations of the lake, only to experience choking sensations, attempts to suck them into an underwater chamber, and visions of mysterious figures and forms. It is proposed to drain the lakes to continue the search for the treasure, but it seems that the visionary Aztecs selected as their hiding place the home of a rare amber-colored snail, which is protected by the Endangered Species Act. With underwater spirits, on-land environmentalists, and government bureaucrats having joined forces to see that the lake is not disturbed, the treasure, if it is indeed there, may remain undiscovered for another five centuries.

The Kanab area was first visited by Mormon missionaries under the leadership of Jacob Hamblin, president of the Southern Utah Indian Mission. They made their way from Santa Clara, 90 miles west of Kanab, to the Hopi Indian villages in northern Arizona, where they hoped to convert the Indians to their faith. After Hamblin's visit, Mormon cattle-men moved into the area from Washington and Iron counties to the west. The cattlemen built dugouts along Kanab Creek (Kanab is a Paiute Indian name for the willows growing along the creek). Concern about gathering Indian unrest led them to construct a primitive fort during the winter of 1865 to 1866. Kanab was the first point of contact with Mormons along the route from the Navajo homeland to the southwest to the older southern Utah settlements. Bands of Navajos, who had evaded capture by Kit Carson and his troops, undertook raids to capture livestock from the Mormons, which sometimes resulted in deadly confrontations between the two peoples.

Late spring of 1870 marked a new milestone in Kanab's history, as a group of settlers arrived from the Salt Lake Valley to homestead. They were joined the following year by Mormon settlers from the Muddy River settlements in Nevada, who left their homes unable to pay back taxes in the hard currency demanded by Nevada state officials. The Mormon settlers wrested a living from the land, growing crops along the east fork of the Virgin River and Kanab Creek and grazing cattle on the mountains, plateaus, and deserts surrounding Kanab. A rich cowboy tradition developed, as Kanab became a regional ranching center. Cattle dominated the local economy until after World War II, when tourism and service industries took over.

The vanishing cowboy tradition, so much a part of Kanab and the Arizona Strip, has been preserved through the collections of cowboy stories and the restoration and interpretation of Pipe Spring National Monument, just to the west, in the Arizona Strip. At the same time as the solid cowboy tradition was developing in the Kanab area during the 19th century, two more extreme Mormon practices, polygamy and the United

Order movement, were taking hold. At Orderville, established in 1874, 23 miles north of Kanab in Long Valley, a group of Mormon exiles from the Muddy Mission practiced the purest form of the United Order. Members of the order owned everything in common, took their meals together, and undertook a variety of joint economic endeavors that were designed to produce a harmonious communal society in the best tradition of America's pre–Civil War religious utopian settlements.

In some ways, the Orderville community resembled the prosperous Shaker communal villages of the East. But at the other end of the spectrum from the celibate Shakers, 19th-century Mormons practiced their belief in polygamy. That practice continued openly in Kanab, Orderville, and other Mormon villages until 1890, when LDS Church president Wilford Woodruff, under pressure from the US government, issued the "Manifesto," ending more than a half century's practice of what the 1856 Republican election platform labeled, along with slavery, as one of the "twin relics of barbarism." But some committed polygamists were more willing to deny that God had finally spoken through the Church prophet on the polygamy issue than to give up the practice.

By the second decade of the 20th century, fundamentalist Mormons, i.e., those who still believed in and practiced polygamy, founded the settlement of Short Creek on the Utah-Arizona border, about 30 miles west of Kanab. The Short Creek Raid of 1953 received national attention as more than 100 Arizona law enforcement officers, accompanied by 25 carloads of newspaper reporters, attempted to carry out a surprise raid on the town. But it was the officers and reporters who were surprised. When they roared into Short Creek, they found the entire town congregated around the flagpole in the town square singing "America." Still, 107 Short Creek adult males were arrested, then brought to trial in Kingman, Arizona, in a futile attempt to eradicate polygamy. The town name was changed to Colorado City in 1961. But more than a century after polygamy was officially ended by Mormon church authorities, it continues to flourish in remote places such as Colorado City, primarily because of public tolerance for alternative lifestyles. Such communities go about their business quietly and discourage outsiders.

Perhaps local tolerance of polygamists comes from three sources: the area's recent frontier heritage with its emphasis on freedom of individual action; a tradition of openness that saw Kanab become the first incorporated town in the US to elect a female mayor and an all-woman council in 1912; and the willingness to accept and encourage visitors from a diversity of backgrounds to come and experience the wonders that make Kanab a regional tourism center.

In 1871 through 1872, within a year or two of Kanab's establishment, members of John Wesley Powell's US Geological Survey party made the

Kanab area its headquarters for surveying much of the Colorado Plateau region. It hired local men and enriched the town with all-too-scarce federal dollars. It was Powell who first noted that the area just south and west of Kanab was in Arizona, not in Utah, hence the name Arizona Strip.

Efforts to promote Kanab as a tourist destination began in the 1880s, when Edwin Wooley and Daniel Seegmiller tried to persuade a group of English aristocrats to visit Kanab and establish a private recreation area there. But the long trip by horseback and wagon only impressed on the aristocrats that Kanab was too inaccessible. The expanded availability of the automobile; the construction of passable roads; the designation of Zion and Bryce as national parks in 1919 and 1920, respectively; the beginning of the movie industry in 1922; and later, the construction of Glen Canyon Dam and gradual filling of Lake Powell in the 1950s and 1960s all contributed immeasurably to Kanab's rise as a tourist center.

GETTING THERE

Kanab is located on the Utah-Arizona border 300 miles south of Salt Lake City on Hwy. 89. Traveling south from Salt Lake City, locals claim the quickest route is along Interstate 15 to Nephi, then along Hwy. 28 to its intersection with Hwy. 89 at Gunnison. If you have an extra hour and want to travel through historic Sanpete Valley along Hwy. 89, exit Interstate 15 at Spanish Fork and take Hwy. 6 southeast for 13 miles to the Thistle Junction, then turn south on Hwy. 89. Coming north into Utah from Nevada, along Interstate 15, Kanab is 75 miles east of St. George and is reached by taking exit 16, 10 miles north of St. George, and following Hwy. 9 to Hurricane. At Hurricane you have two choices: the southern route (the fastest) along Hwy. 59 across the Arizona Strip, or a route that takes you through the Virgin River Valley and cuts across Zion National Park to Mt. Carmel Junction and Hwy. 89. Those folks coming from northern Arizona continue on Hwy. 89 past the turnoff for the Grand Canyon across the Kaibab Plateau and then down into Kanab, Utah. This drive is dramatic toward the end as you descend from the plateau with all of southern Utah's canyon country in front of you.

MAJOR ATTRACTIONS

National Parks

Three of the nation's best-known national parks are within a 1.5-hour drive of Kanab. Closest is **Zion National Park**, 40 miles to the northwest (see the **Zion National Park** chapter). **Bryce Canyon National Park** (see the Bryce Canyon National Park chapter) is 77 miles up Hwy. 89 to the north, while the Grand Canyon is 78 miles to the south in Arizona.

OTHER ATTRACTIONS

Coral Pink Sand Dunes State Park

If a visit to the West requires hiking and frolicking on Sahara-size sand dunes, then visitors to Kanab are in luck. Three thousand seven hundred acres of sand dunes are located west of Kanab in the Coral Pink Sand Dunes State Park. The sand dunes have formed in a sheltered depression along the Sevier Fault—a 200-mile-long fault that runs from western Arizona to the mountains north of Panguitch. The depression has filled with dunes of very fine coral-colored sand that has eroded from the surrounding cliffs and hills. The sand dunes rise as high as 20 feet or more.

In an effort to meet different needs, certain areas of the park are designated for off-road vehicles, while others are restricted to foot traffic only. Dune buggies, motorcycles, and other motorized vehicles are prohibited from 10 pm–9 am. Camping at 22 sites (no hookups) is available from Apr.–Nov., with modern wheelchair-accessible restrooms and hot showers. Picnic tables are also available. Dawn and sunset are especially attractive to photographers as the coral sand seems to change color and accentuated shadows make the landscape even more unbelievable. The easiest way to the state park is to go north on Hwy. 89 from Kanab for 17.5 miles, then west along a paved road for 11 miles. Entrance and camping fees are charged. You can also get to the park via Cane Beds from Hwy. 59, along a 16-mile dirt road. (See also Biking in the Outdoor Activities section.)

Pipe Spring National Monument

Although it is located in Arizona, Pipe Spring, used by Indians as a rest stop and watering hole for thousands of years, was discovered and named by the 1856 Jacob Hamblin expedition to the Hopi Mesas for the purpose of launching missionary work there. Pipe Spring was settled seven years later by St. George resident James Montgomery Whitmore. At that time the Utah-Arizona boundary had not yet been surveyed by Major John Wesley Powell, and Whitmore and the Washington County official who issued the land certificate granting ownership to Whitmore assumed that the spring was in Utah, not 10 miles south of the Utah line. Whitmore had run cattle in Texas before his conversion to Mormonism, and when he and his wife and two small children came west to the Salt Lake Valley in the mid-1850s, he reportedly drove a herd of 500 cattle with them. Whitmore helped found St. George in 1861 and noted then the vast rangelands of what would later be called the Arizona Strip. He recognized its grazing potential for cattle and, after 1863, divided his time between the ranch and his home and family in St. George.

He constructed a dugout at the ranch site and continued ranching activities in partnership with his brother-in-law Robert McIntire and young son, even though Indian tensions threatened all the fledgling southern Utah Mormon settlements. The concern was justified. In Jan. 1866, a group of Indians stole livestock from the ranch. Whitmore and McIntire were killed 4 miles south of their dugout at Pipe Spring as they pursued the lost livestock through heavy snows. Current opinion is that the perpetrators were Navajos working alongside disgruntled Paiutes. The unrest continued for the next four years, leading Utah militiamen to erect a small rock fort at Pipe Spring in 1868. A year later, Brigham Young purchased Pipe Spring for the LDS Church and organized the Canaan Cooperative Stock Company, a quasi-church corporation, which took over operations at Pipe Spring. Brigham "called" the bishop of Grafton, Anson Perry Winsor, to run the ranch for a salary of $1,200 a year. It was Winsor who supervised construction of the impressive rock fort/ranch headquarters at Pipe Spring, leading it to be called Winsor's Castle—a play on the good bishop's British heritage. The fort was stocked with beef cattle that were "tithed" to the LDS Church by Mormon stockmen. Eventually, more than 100 dairy cattle were brought to Pipe Spring to produce beef, butter, and cheese for the workers on the new St. George Temple in the 1870s. As ranching declined in the late 1870s, Pipe Spring became an important stopping point on the Honeymoon Trail that connected St. George and the Mormon temple there (where faithful Mormons are married) with the Mormon settlements on the Little Colorado River in northeastern Arizona. During the early 1880s, Pipe Spring was managed as part of the Orderville United Order Cooperative, but the Mormon church lost ownership of Pipe Spring through the Edmunds-Tucker Act of 1887, which allowed the federal government to confiscate church property because of the polygamy issue.

The ranch was sold at auction to a rancher with Mormon connections, but eventually it passed to private non-Mormon interests. Although heavy grazing had irreparably damaged what were once lush grasslands, Pipe Spring continued as a working ranch for a few more years and as a quasi-public facility providing lodging and free meals to all wayfarers, except sheepmen, tramps, and salesmen.

Eventually the Heaton family, unable to make a go of the ranch, negotiated with Stephen Mather, first director of the National Park Service, to purchase Pipe Spring for the nation. It was set aside as Pipe Spring National Monument in 1923 "as a memorial of western pioneer life." Today, the monument interprets Pipe Spring's significance to the native people of the area, the early Mormon ranching efforts on the Arizona Strip, the cabin Maj. Powell stayed in while staying at Pipe Spring in 1871, domestic ranch life, and the everyday life and equipment of late 19th-century and early 20th-century western cowboys. Historic exhibits, longhorn cattle, animals, and living history demonstrations of quilting, weaving, spinning, baking, gardening, and cattle branding, in addition to the restored ranchhouse and grounds, make Pipe Spring a popular stop for travelers of all ages. Pipe Spring is located about 20 miles southwest of Kanab on Hwy. 389, inside the small Kaibab Paiute Indian Reservation. The Paiute tribe runs a small adjoining campground. A cafeteria in the monument serves western fare. An admission fee is charged. The visitor center, exhibits, and gift shop are open daily 7:30 am–5:30 pm during the summer; 8 am–4 pm the rest of the year. **(602) 643-7105.**

OUTDOOR ACTIVITIES

BIKING

Coral Pink Sand Dunes State Park—

The 11-mile paved access road from Hwy. 89 to Coral Pink Sand Dunes State Park is an excellent bike route. It's 22 miles round-trip from the Hwy. 89 turnoff, but bikers can add another 6 miles by riding from Mt. Carmel Junction to the turnoff. The 3 miles from Mt. Carmel Junction are all uphill, and riders need to be attentive to the traffic; however, once you are on the access road there is usually little traffic. The paved road skirts the northwest side of the sand dunes and is perhaps the only place in Utah where sand dunes dominate the vista.

Hancock Road/Coral Pink Sand Dunes State Park—

An intermediate ride to Coral Pink Sand Dunes can be made from Kanab over the Hancock Rd. and back. Hancock Rd. is a paved road that leaves Hwy. 89 to the southeast about 6 miles north of Kanab. A sign points to the Hancock Rd., which you follow eastward for about 9 miles to its intersection with the paved access road to the state park described above. The paved road continues another 7 miles along the edge of the park, making a 25-mile out-and-back ride from Kanab.

Johnson Canyon—

In the 1920s, Kanab residents searched for Montezuma's treasure in this canyon, but today it offers an excellent opportunity for an undisturbed ride past the vermilion cliffs, ancient Indian pictographs, a ranch-house with a windmill, pastures, Eagle Arch, and an old movie set where segments of *Gunsmoke* and *Have Gun Will Travel* were filmed. Johnson Canyon is located east of Kanab, about 9 miles off Hwy. 89. The Johnson Canyon Rd., marked by a road sign, heads north and is paved for about 10 miles. This makes an excellent 20-mile ride for novice bikers and also offers disabled access. If you want a longer ride, don't want to transport your bicycles, and don't mind highway traffic, you can leave from Kanab and ride the 9 miles east on Hwy. 89 to the Johnson Canyon turnoff. You can also make a 65-mile loop from Kanab by continuing north after the pavement ends and following the road as it heads back east to intersect with Hwy. 89 at Glendale. From Glendale, it's a 25-mile ride into Kanab along Hwy. 89, or 40 miles back the way you came.

FISHING

While the Kanab area has a lot going for it, fishing does not top the list. Few fishermen would look to the area to indulge their

hobby. However, if you are in the area and want to try your hand at fishing, the east fork of the Virgin River near Glendale and Orderville is home to rainbow, German brown, brook, and cutthroat trout.

GOLF

Coral Cliffs Golf Course—

Although this 9-hole golf course has been in existence for only a few years, the excellent design and use of native junipers make it seem mature. This is a fun course—challenging enough for most golfers yet not to the point of frustration. The course is generally flat and the soaring ledges to the west, north, and south make this one of Utah's most picturesque courses. Located about 1 mile east of Kanab. **700 East and Hwy. 89; (801) 644-5005.**

HIKING

Paria Canyon—

Pronounced "Pah-ree-ah," a Paiute Indian word meaning "muddy water," this hike follows the Paria River, a tributary of the Colorado River, through the Paria Canyon Wilderness Area to Lee's Ferry on the Colorado River. It covers a distance of 35 miles and takes at least three—preferably six—days to complete. You will need to be prepared with backcountry camping gear. During the hike you will experience the spectacular red-rock country at its best with a feeling of total seclusion. You will pass Indian ruins, old ranch sites, a 200-foot-high natural arch, rock slides, springs, seeps, and canyons 1,500 feet high and only 12 feet wide where you pass. There is no great abundance of animals, but deer, bobcats, bighorn sheep, and mountain lions have been spotted along the trail. The canyon was one of the first BLM-designated primitive areas (1969) in the country. Access to the trailhead, located about 45 miles east of Kanab along Hwy. 89, is easy; but a shuttle is necessary if you want to get back from Lee's Ferry. The wilderness area, which is only accessible on foot, is administered by the BLM, and hiking permits are required. The permits are free and are used to help monitor foot traffic through the narrow canyon when summer flash floods threaten. Inquire about permits at the Kanab office of the BLM or ask the ranger stationed at the Paria Canyon Trailhead. A brochure on the Paria Canyon Wilderness Area is also available. A more difficult alternate route for part of the hike is through Buckskin Canyon, where the canyon width at the bottom averages only 15 feet for 12 miles. Check with the BLM office about the condition of this trail.

Squaw Trail—

If you are staying in Kanab and want a nice early-morning summer hike, the 3-mile round-trip Squaw Trail is ideal. The trail is well graded, and a **trail guide** is usually available at the trailhead. You can also pick one up at the **Kane County Information Center** or **Kanab Bureau of Land Management Office.** A somewhat strenuous hike, the trail, which begins near the city park at the north end of 100 East, climbs 800 feet in elevation as it penetrates the Vermillion Cliffs north of Kanab. From the top of the mesa the view south is spectacular, taking in Kanab and the Kaibab Plateau beyond it. Looking north, you get a great view of the rest of the top "steps" of the geological Grand Staircase—the White, Gray, and Pink cliffs—as they climb into the distance.

SEEING AND DOING

ANIMALS

Best Friends Animal Sanctuary—

Located on a 100-acre site in Angel Canyon, Best Friends Animal Sanctuary is a home for unwanted animals. At any given time the sanctuary houses over 1,500 dogs, cats, and other abused, abandoned, or neglected animals. You can tour the facility, which has dog kennels, catteries with separate areas for cats who prefer the outdoors and those that are indoor cats, and pastures for horses, burros, and goats. To reach the sanctuary, take Hwy. 89 north out of Kanab for about 5 miles to the Kanab Canyon Rd. on your right. Turn onto the road and follow it for about 2 miles to the sanctuary. You can also make arrangements for hiking tours of Angel Canyon that take you to prehistoric and historic sites. **(801) 644-2001.**

Kanab Critter Corral—

This is a special place for children and anyone who loves animals. There are llamas, a zebra, potbellied pigs, miniature horses, donkeys, goats, wallabies, bunnies, ducks, and geese to be petted and loved. A modest admission fee is charged. Located at **830 East 1000 South; (801) 644-2850** or **(801) 644-2862.**

GHOST TOWNS

The Paria River Valley is the location for the ruins of the historic Mormon farming community of Pahreah, which was settled in the early 1870s and abandoned by the mid-1880s. All that remains of the historic community are a small cemetery and some ruins. Nearby is the movie set of a pioneer town built in 1963 for the film *Sergeants Three*. To reach the Paria River Valley, head east from Kanab on Hwy. 89 for 40 miles, then follow the 5-mile-long graded dirt road as it heads north. The road is regularly maintained and usually suitable for passenger cars unless there have been recent rainstorms (usually in summer).

HISTORIC BUILDINGS

Heritage House Museum—

The Heritage House was a Kanab City Bicentennial Project in 1976. Constructed between 1892 and 1894 for Henry E. Bowman, a prosperous Kanab merchant, the house is an ambitious (for southern Utah at least) example of Victorian Queen Anne architecture. The orange-red brick walls, combination hip-and-gable/wood-shingled roof, sculpted brick chimneys, "gingerbread" porch, and tower mark a radical departure from the symmetrical adobe homes of the two previous decades. By 1892, changes in architectural fashion had reached Kanab. The house now serves as a museum and contains furniture and other items from turn-of-the-century Kanab. Located on the **southeast corner of 100 South Main St.**, the museum is usually open in the summer during the day, or can be visited by calling the number posted at the house.

Mt. Carmel School and Church—

Located on the west side of Hwy. 89 in Mt. Carmel, this stone building with its four-sided roof and bell tower recalls an era when religious, educational, civic, and recreational needs were met in one public building in some small American towns. The building was used for church services, school classes, public meetings, dances, and other social activities. The original building was constructed in the 1890s and rebuilt in 1923 to 1924, after a 1919 fire. After the fire, school was held for two years in the nearby tithing office after which students were transported to nearby Orderville. The building was used as a church until 1961 and for other church programs until 1983.

SCENIC DRIVES

Johnson Canyon/Alton Amphitheater Backway—

Part of this route is described in the Biking section. The Johnson Canyon Rd. begins 9 miles east of Kanab, off Hwy. 89, and heads north. The first 15 miles are paved, and the rest of the road is a well-maintained gravel road suitable for passenger cars. Instead of turning west off the road to Glendale, the 9-mile drive continues north

to the tiny ranching community of Alton is especially scenic, as it provides a closer view of the Claron Formation, or Pink Cliffs, in what is called the Alton Amphitheater (on the other side of the plateau from Bryce Canyon) and of volcanic cinder cones. At Alton, turn west to Hwy. 89, taking the road past several lovely small lakes.

Kanab to Junction Scenic Byway—

Hwy. 89 has already been described as the major highway to Kanab from Salt Lake City and as the principal road from Kanab north to Zion and Bryce Canyon national parks. The 60-mile section of Hwy. 89 through Long Valley, from Kanab to its junction with Hwy. 12, the road to Bryce Canyon, has been given official designation as a Scenic Byway. The drive north from Kanab is truly spectacular, as the highway ascends part of what Major John Wesley Powell dubbed the Grand Staircase—a succession of progressively younger rock formations known as the Vermillion, White, and Pink cliffs, the base rock of southern Utah's canyon country. The road climbs from Kanab's desert setting through Long Valley to the subalpine meadows and headwaters of the Sevier River, passing through the lovely little historic communities of Mt. Carmel, Orderville, and Glendale. If you do any traveling north of Kanab, you will certainly follow Hwy. 89. This stretch of highway is one of the most beautiful in all of Utah, so, if you are not driving, sit back and enjoy it.

Ponderosa/Coral Pink Sand Dunes Backway—

This Scenic Backway is described as a bicycle route in the Outdoor Activities section.

WHERE TO STAY

ACCOMMODATIONS

GLENDALE

Home Place—$$

Home Place is owned by retired teachers Bob and Ruth Palmer who enjoy conversing with guests and sharing their knowledge of the area. There are three nonsmoking guest rooms with queen beds, TV, and private baths. The kitchen/dining room, where a full country breakfast is served, is equipped with a wood-burning cookstove. Located in Glendale, 26 miles north of Kanab. **200 South Main; (801) 648-2194.**

Smith Hotel—$$

One of the few historic hotels still in operation, the Smith Hotel was built in Glendale in 1927. Its seven nonsmoking rooms are newly decorated, and each has a private bath. A continental breakfast is served in the dining room. Off Hwy. 89 at the **north end of Glendale; (801) 648-2156.**

KANAB

Best Western Red Hills—$$ to $$$

Heated pool and whirlpool; 72 rooms. **125 West Center; (801) 644-2675 or 1-800-528-1234.**

Four Seasons Motor Inn—$$ to $$$

Forty-one rooms. **36 North 300 West; (801) 644-2635.**

Miss Sophie's Bed and Breakfast—$$

Built in the 1890s by Frederick A. Lundquist and furnished with turn-of-the-century antiques, Miss Sophie's has four rooms with queen-size beds and private baths. Open May–Oct. Reservations can be made during the winter by calling **(801) 628-3987.** Located at **30 North 200 West.**

Nine Gables Inn Bed and Breakfast—$$$

This bed and breakfast is steeped in local history. Started in 1872 by Levi Stewart, the first LDS bishop in Kanab, it was sold to Edwin Dilworth Woolley. It was the childhood home of Mary Wooley Chamberlain, the first woman mayor in Kanab—perhaps in all of the US. Because there were no hotels in Kanab, the house was used to accommodate visitors to Kanab while it was still a private home. Some of those who roomed here were Mormon church president Heber J. Grant, novelist Zane Grey, and the famous showman Buffalo Bill Cody. Today, the house is furnished with many family antiques. There are four nonsmoking rooms, each with a private bath. Proprietors Frank and Jeanne Bantlin offer an excellent breakfast. **106 West 100 North; (801) 644-5079.**

Parry Lodge—$$ to $$$

Kanab's oldest motel, the Parry Lodge was established in 1929 and has been the home away from home for many Hollywood stars while they were making movies in Kanab. During the 1980s, the marquee at the motel boldly boasted that "Ronald Reagan Slept Here." In fact, he stayed in room 125. The most popular star, at least based on requests for his room, is John Wayne, who had an oversize bathtub installed in his room—192. Other stars whose names appear above individual rooms include James Garner, Frank Sinatra, Telly Savalas, Dean Martin, Arlene Dahl, Tyrone Power, Robert Preston, Sammy Davis Jr., Julie Newman, Anne Blythe, and Robert Taylor. The lodge has expanded from the original 15 rooms to 89 units with a nice heated outdoor swimming pool and adjoining restaurant. **89 East Center; (801) 644-2601 or 1-800-748-4104.**

Shilo Inn—$$ to $$$

One hundred nineteen rooms, some with refrigerators. Heated pool, whirlpool, coin laundry, and restaurant adjacent. **169 West 100 North; (801) 644-2562.**

MT. CARMEL

Thunderbird Motel—$$

Sixty-six rooms. Heated pool, adjacent restaurant, and 9-hole golf course.

Located in Mt. Carmel at the **junction of Hwy. 89 and Hwy. 9**, 17 miles north of Kanab and 24 miles from the east entrance to Zion National Park. **(801) 648-2203.**

CAMPING
PUBLIC
Coral Pink Sand Dunes State Park Campground—
Twenty-two RV sites and 22 tent sites. Flush toilets and showers available. Open Apr. or May–late Nov.

Ponderosa Grove Campground—
Seven RV sites, picnic tables, flush toilets, and a few tent sites. Near the northern section of Coral Pink Sand Dunes State Park. Open Apr. or May–late Nov.

PRIVATE
Crazy Horse Campground—
Seventy-four RV sites with full hookups and pullthrough locations plus sites for tenters. Clean restrooms, showers, a swimming pool, game room, arcade, playground, picnic tables, and the adjacent Coral Hills Golf Course provide plenty of recreational opportunities. The campground is open year-round. Just east of Kanab, off Hwy. 89. **625 East 300 South, PO Box 699, Kanab, UT 84741; (801) 644-2782** or **1-800-382-4908.**

East Zion Trailer Park—
Twenty RV hookups and 11 tent sites. **Junction of Hwy. 9 and Hwy. 89 in Mt. Carmel; (801) 648-2326.**

Hitch n Post Campground—
Twenty RV sites and 4 tent sites. **196 East 300 South on Hwy. 89 in Kanab; (801) 644-2681.**

Kamping Kabins KOA Campground—
Sixty spaces with hookups and 25 tent sites. Toilets, showers, a heated pool, game room, playground, and close to the trout fishing in the East Fork of the Virgin River. Open May–mid-Oct. Five miles north of Glendale on Hwy. 89. **(801) 648-2490.**

Mt. Carmel Campground—
Ten RV hookup sites and 6 tent sites. One mile north of junction of **Hwy. 9 and Hwy. 89 in Mt. Carmel; (801) 648-2323.**

The Tortoise & The Hare Campground—
Fifteen RV hookups. Toilets, showers, pool. A mile north of Orderville **on Hwy. 89; (801) 648-2012.**

———— WHERE TO EAT ————

Chef's Palace Restaurant—$$ to $$$
The Dude Room is open for dinner in the evenings and serves steaks, prime rib, and fish. Open daily 6 am–11 pm; 6 am–10 pm Nov.–May. **151 West Center; (801) 644-5052.**

Four Seasons 50s Style Restaurant—$ to $$
Capturing the flavor of a 1950s malt shop with its black-and-white-checked tile floor, light green vinyl booths, and a 1952 Seeburg jukebox playing hits from the 1950s and 1960s for a dime a song, this is a fun place to eat and socialize. Drinks are served in old-fashioned pointed paper cups in plastic holders (parents need to be prepared to explain to children the logic of this antiquated drinking system!). The food is touted as '50s style with sandwiches and burgers (hand-formed, with onions cooked into the patty) for lunch. Dinners feature steaks, fried chicken, stewed chicken and dumplings, pork chops, fried shrimp, spaghetti, homemade soups, and a 1980s-style salad bar. Malts and shakes are made with an old-fashioned mixer; you get the mixer cup half filled with the amount that will not fit in the traditional soda glass. Open daily, summer hours May–Oct. 6:30

am–10 pm; hours the rest of the year generally 7 am–7 pm. **36 North 300 West; (801) 644-2635.**

Houston's Trail's End Restaurant— $ to $$

A family restaurant with a western atmosphere. Waitresses are dressed in cowboy shirts, denim skirts, and holstered six shooters. Fare includes typical western breakfasts, burgers, hot sandwiches, steaks, halibut, and trout. Open daily 6 am–11 pm (until 10 pm Sept.–June.) **32 East Center; (801) 644-2488.**

Parry's Lodge Restaurant—$$ to $$$

This charming houselike restaurant is part of the Parry's Lodge Motel (see the Where to Stay section). It carries the lodge's association with movie stars—with dozens of photographs, many of them inscribed— hung on the restaurant walls. You will see pictures of stars that only experienced travelers will remember—Gabby Hayes, Ava Gardner, Walter Brennan, Jane Russell, Robert Taylor, Rhonda Fleming, Frederic Marsh, Anne Bancroft, Roy Rogers, and Dale Evans. Breakfast items include omeletes, ham steak, country-fried steak, corned beef and eggs, pancakes. For lunch there are sandwiches, soup, and salads or the hungry man lunches—chicken and dumplings, chicken-fried steak, grilled beef liver, or breaded veal. The dinner menu offers prime rib, steaks, fried shrimp, salmon, halibut, trout, veal, and pork chops. You can also order a box lunch to take with you. Open daily 7 am–10 am for breakfast, 11 am–2 pm for lunch, and 5 pm–10 pm for dinner in summer; open only for breakfast and dinner in winter. **89 East Center; (801) 644-2601.**

SERVICES

Kanab Resource Area Bureau of Land Management—

318 North 100 East, Kanab, UT 84741; (801) 644-2672.

Kane County Travel Council—

41 South 100 East, Kanab, UT 84741; (801) 644-5033.

Bryce Canyon National Park

In 1936, Indian Dick, an elderly Paiute, explained the Paiute tradition of how Bryce Canyon was formed to a National Park Service naturalist. He described that the Legend People lived in the place long before there were any Indians. The Legend People were numerous and many of them had the power to make themselves look like birds, animals, and lizards. "For some reason the Legend People in that place were bad; they did something that was not good, perhaps a fight, perhaps some stole something. … Because they were bad, Coyote turned them all into rocks. You can see them in that place now, all turned into rocks; some standing in rows, some sitting down, some holding onto others. You can see their faces, with paint on them just as they were before they became rocks."

A more scientific interpretation of the origin of Bryce Canyon attributes the odd-shaped pinnacles and rocks (called "Hoodoos") to the forces of erosion. Part of the Bryce Canyon experience is interpreting the spires, temples, turrets, and crenelated ridges for yourself. This fairyland has been seen as a natural manifestation of western Europe's baroque architecture, compared with the music of Rossini "all whimsy and delight," and explained "as the graphic representation of a magnificently insane mind."

Technically Bryce Canyon National Park is not one canyon in the traditional western sense, but rather a series of 14 amphitheaters cut into the eastern edge of the Paunsaugunt Plateau and extending approximately 20 miles from north to south. Like Cedar Breaks, atop the Markagunt Plateau to the west, it is cut into the Claron Formation, which consists of soft pink and white siltstone, sandstone, dolomite, and limestone layers that were deposited in a Paleocene lake system. Geologists think that these deposits were laid down about 60 million years ago, when lime-rich sand and mud carried along by streams and rivers for many miles were deposited into shallow lakes. The heavy sand particles were deposited close to the shores of these lakes, while the lighter silt and clay particles settled to the bottom of the lakes farther from shore. Through millions of years, wet and dry cycles changed the size of the lakes and created limestone rock layers of different hardness that are known today as the Claron Formation.

Earth forces began pushing the land upward in this area about 10 million years ago, creating what is now called the Colorado Plateau. The tremendous pressure caused the large plateau to fracture and separate into smaller plateaus, including the Paunsaugunt Plateau, on whose east slope Bryce Canyon is located, and the Aquarius Plateau, which can be seen in the distance east of Bryce Canyon.

After this uplift occurred, the Paria River began to cut through the rock layers as it flowed down off the eastern side of the Paunsaugunt Plateau, acting as a natural shovel to scoop out great bowl-shaped areas which are called "amphitheaters." The Paria removed the weak rock layers and left the more durable layers in the fantastic formations that make Bryce Canyon so unique.

The erosion of Bryce Canyon continues year-round. In the summer, thundershowers drop heavy rainfall onto the formations, carrying away dirt and gravel and carving gullies in the steep slopes. The rainwater also seeps into cracks in the rock and dissolves the calcium carbonate cement which holds the rock particles together. In the winter, water enters the cracks from melting snow during the day, then freezes and expands during the night, exerting tremendous force and causing large boulders to break off. As the tall ridges, fins, and pinnacles emerge, the iron and manganese in the rocks oxidize into colorful hues of red, pink, orange, yellow, and purple.

HISTORY

The canyon takes its name from the first white settler to graze cattle in it: Ebenezer Bryce, a Scottish Mormon who established a homestead in what is now the town of Tropic in the fall of 1875. Like the other pioneers, Bryce was not given to eloquence. He used the amphitheaters to graze his livestock and is said to have remarked that it was a hell of a place to lose a cow. In time, the canyon became known as Bryce's Canyon. Other cattlemen and people traveling through the area may have seen the wonders of Bryce Canyon before Bryce took up his homestead, but the earliest written description comes from T. C. Bailey, a US deputy surveyor, who wrote with unrestrained enthusiasm in 1876: "There are thousands of red, white, purple and vermilion rocks, of all sizes, resembling sentinels on the Walls of Castles; monks and priests with their robes, attendants, cathedrals and congregations. There are deep caverns and rooms resembling ruins of prisons, Castles, Churches, with their guarded walls, battlements, spires and steeples, niches and recesses, presenting the wildest and most wonderful scene that the eye of man ever beheld, in fact it is one of the wonders of the world." Glowing descriptions such as these led President Theodore Roosevelt to set aside Bryce Canyon and the surrounding forest as a national forest in 1905. And it began to receive more visitors, as word spread and a rough road was built to it.

The real pioneer of Bryce Canyon as a scenic resource was Ruben C. Syrett, who took up a homestead at the entrance to the future national park in 1916. Four years later, in 1920, he built a small lodge and cabins, the Tourist Rest, near Sunset Point. Visitation grew, and, in 1923, Bryce Canyon was designated a national monument. That same year, the newly formed Utah Parks Company (a division of the Union Pacific Railroad) acquired the Tourist Rest from Syrett and began to construct Bryce Lodge. Syrett returned to his old homestead and built Ruby's Inn, which today is a large hotel complex. The construction of these facilities coincided with the completion of a passable automobile road to the canyon. Bryce Canyon had come to the attention of Horace M. Albright, director of the National Park Service, during a visit to Zion Canyon in 1917; however, it was not until 1928 that Bryce Canyon National Park was established. It was enlarged to its present size in 1931. Today, Bryce Canyon National Park is one of Utah's top five tourist attractions, drawing nearly 1.5 million visitors in 1992. Visitors drive the scenic park road and stop to gaze at the fantastic formations which make Bryce Canyon and the surrounding area included in the national park such a unique place. More adventuresome visitors will take one of the many hiking trails to mingle with the formations.

FLORA AND FAUNA

Bryce Canyon is located between an elevation of 6,600 feet and 9,100 feet, which includes three separate life zones. In the Upper Sonoran Zone (6,600 to 7,000 feet), in the lower reaches of the canyon, you will find pygmy piñon, juniper trees, Gambel oak, and sagebrush. In the 7,000- to 8,500-foot Transition Zone the stately ponderosa pine dominates, and above 8,500 feet, in the Canadian Zone, the ponderosa pine are replaced by stands of white fir, blue spruce, aspen, and bristlecone pine. The high elevation and abundant water produce a wonderful variety of wildflowers including Indian paintbrush, penstemon, wild iris, yellow evening primrose, dwarf blue columbine, and goldenweed that spread across meadows and along the trails. Mule deer and ground squirrels are plentiful along the roads and hiking trails, and red-tailed hawks ride the air currents overhead. Piñon jays and sparrows are found in the forests; meadowlarks, sage grouse, and mountain bluebirds are at home in the meadows. Yellow-bellied marmots, prairie dogs, pocket gophers, chipmunks, and skunks are among the animals that live in the meadows, while in the lower reaches of the park, coyotes, bobcats, whipsnakes, and lizards can be found.

GETTING THERE

Bryce Canyon National Park is located in south-central Utah, just off Hwy. 12 about 24 miles east of Panguitch, 260 miles south of Salt Lake City, and 125 miles northeast of St. George. To reach the park from Salt Lake City, take Interstate 15 south to Nephi. Exit onto Hwy. 28 and follow it south to Gunnison where you join Hwy 89. Follow Hwy. 89 south (for a 30-mile stretch between Salina and Joseph, you will be on Interstate 70) to Hwy. 12, 7 miles south of Panguitch. From the junction of Hwy. 89 and Hwy. 12, it is about 17 miles to the park.

VISITOR CENTER

The Bryce Canyon National Park Visitor Center is located just inside the entrance to the park and is open year-round with hours that vary seasonally. Inside the visitor center are interpretive programs, a bookstore, and information. For more information write **Superintendent, Bryce Canyon National Park, Bryce Canyon, UT 84717;** or call **(801) 834-5322.**

OUTDOOR ACTIVITIES

BIKING

Biking is not recommended in the park because roadways are narrow and congested in the summer months. In keeping with policies in all national parks, no off-pavement biking is permitted.

DISABLED-ACCESS RECREATION

The National Park Service has made efforts to accommodate travelers with special needs. Many park buildings, restrooms, and viewpoints in Bryce Canyon meet current accessibility standards in providing disabled access, and the level, paved trail between Sunrise and Sunset points is well adapted for wheelchairs. A few campsites are reserved for mobility-impaired campers at the North Campground, and some of the ranger-led interpretive activities are available to all visitors. For further information, obtain a copy of the "Bryce Canyon Access Guide," available at the visitor center or by writing **Bryce Canyon National Park, Bryce Canyon, UT 84717;** or by calling **(801) 834-5322.**

For more outdoor activities and seeing and doing possibilities outside of the national park, see the **Panguitch** chapter.

HIKING

Walking is, without a doubt, the best way to see Bryce Canyon. There are 60 miles of trails that wind their way among Bryce's pinnacles and hoodoos and along the rim of the canyon, offering an ever-changing perspective on the intricacies of nature's handiwork. Inexperienced or infrequent hikers should note that the elevations of the park range between 6,500 and just over 9,000 feet. At this elevation, there is less oxygen and you will be exerting yourself more than usual. Take it easy, particularly on the return hike out of the canyon, rest often, and drink plenty of water. The trails begin at the rim and descend along well-maintained paths to the bottom of the amphitheaters. The descent seems easy, but most falls and injuries come on downhill treks, and what seemed an easy stroll on the way down can seem like climbing a 1000-foot cliff on the way back! Remember, too, that as you descend the temperature will get warmer, especially as the sun warms the ridges and rocks of this high desert country. In summer, watch out for sudden thunderstorms, which can produce lightning strikes and water runoff very rapidly. For extended hikes, bring along rain gear and a warm jacket or sweater. Check at the visitor center for backcountry camping information and backcountry hiking directions and permits. For most visitors, the following trails provide plenty of options to see the canyons in all their glory.

Bristlecone Loop—

Located at the southern end of the park, this short, easy, 1-mile loop at Rainbow Point takes you past some of the ancient bristlecone pine trees within the park, which have withstood lightning storms, deep snow and cold, and extreme changes in temperature for more than 1,700 years.

Fairyland Loop—

This strenuous 8-mile-long loop, which takes you through the amphitheater that has a fairylandlike quality, begins at Sunrise Point and descends 900 feet into the northern part of the park. During the hike you will see the amphitheaters of Fairyland and Campbell canyons as you pass by such formations as Boat Mesa, Chinese Wall, Tower Bridge, and Seal Castle. Because this is such a long climb back out, you will find the trail much less crowded than other trails in the park.

Mossy Cave Trail—

This .5-mile round-trip trail follows the Tropic Ditch most of its length. After you cross the second wooden bridge across the ditch, the trail forks. The left-hand route takes you up to Mossy Cave, a cool alcove with green moss and dripping water that forms a perennial natural stream. In the winter, the frozen spring with its icicles and sheets of ice takes on a completely

different, but just as beautiful, appearance, and the ice often lasts until early June. The trail to the right takes you to a small waterfall. Locals call this Water Canyon. It is the only place where water is taken out of the Great Basin into the Colorado Plateau. The water comes from the East Fork of the Sevier River. It is stored in the Tropic Reservoir and then reaches the town of Tropic by a system of human-made ditches and natural waterways between mid-Apr. and mid-Oct. Along this hike, the water follows a natural course. At the waterfall, see if you can count the seven windows in the rock formation atop the ridge above the stream. The Mossy Cave/Water Canyon Trail is located off Hwy. 12, west of Tropic, 3.7 miles east of the Bryce Canyon Rd. and Hwy. 12. There is a parking area at the trailhead just east of the highway bridge.

Navajo Trail—

Much steeper than the Queen's Garden Trail, the Navajo Trail begins at Sunset Point and drops 520 feet in elevation during the .75-mile hike through a narrow canyon to the bottom. Some of the colorful names for the formations along this trail include The Pope, Thor's Hammer, Temple of Osiris, and Wall Street—a deep, narrow, .5-mile-long canyon entered by a side trail at the bottom of Navajo Trail. Park rangers conduct guided hikes along this trail a couple of times a day. Check at the visitor center for times. At the bottom of the Navajo Trail, there are several options. You can retrace your route back to Sunset Point, make the ascent along the more gradual Queen's Garden Trail to Sunrise Point, and follow the Peekaboo Loop (a strenuous 3.5-mile hike that goes up and down and has connecting trails to both the Navajo and Queen's Garden trails); or you can head east for 1.5 miles to the town of Tropic, where you will need a shuttle to return to your vehicle inside the park.

Queen's Garden Trail—

The easiest trail into the canyon (if that's possible), the 1.5-mile round-trip Queen's Garden Trail begins at Sunrise

Point and descends 320 feet into the Bryce Canyon amphitheater. The amphitheater is full of strange-shaped hoodoos, castles, pillars, and balanced rocks, some with fanciful names like Gullivers Castle and Queen Victoria, which does resemble the British monarch who reigned from 1837 to 1901 and was the inspiration for this area's designation as the Queen's Garden. Plan an hour or two to make this hike. And remember that the return trip is all uphill.

Riggs Spring Loop—

The most strenuous of all the day hikes within the park, the Riggs Spring Loop begins at Rainbow Point and descends 1,657 feet in 4.4 miles into the southern canyons of the park. Plan the entire day for this hike, or check with park rangers about the possibility of an overnight backcountry camp.

Rim Trail—

The best overview of Bryce Canyon is along the Rim Trail, which follows the rim of the plateau for 5.5 miles in the northern part of the park. The most heavily traveled segment of the trail is the .5-mile paved portion between Sunrise and Sunset points. Since it is nearly level and located close to parking facilities, the trail offers the best disabled access to the park. There are a number of benches provided for those who need frequent rest stops or who want to sit and contemplate the beauties of the canyon.

Trail to the Hat Shop—

Like the Fairyland Loop, this trail also descends 900 feet into the canyon, but it does so in less than 2 miles, making this out-and-back hike from Bryce Point the steepest of the day trails within the park. If you give license to your imagination, you will find the fanciful forms and shapes to be just like those you would find in an outlandish hat shop.

Under the Rim Trail—

The ultimate hiking experience within the park is the Under the Rim Trail, which begins at various points along the rim between Bryce Point and Rainbow Point. The trail is up to 22 miles in length and follows the bottom of the canyon with many ups and downs. Plan at least two days of strenuous hiking to complete the hike, or, if you are going to be in the park for several days, you can cover the entire trail in four segments that descend from the scenic drive. If, after 22 miles of hiking, you still want more, you can add more distance by continuing along the Riggs Spring Loop from Rainbow Point.

HORSEBACK RIDES

Two-hour and half-day guided horseback rides along Bryce Canyon trails are offered Apr.–Oct. Sign up at the lodge first. The rides begin at the corral near Bryce Canyon Lodge. Advance reservations are recommended. Write **Bryce-Zion Grand Trail Rides, PO Box 58, Tropic, UT 84776;** or call **(801) 679-8665.**

SKIING
CROSS-COUNTRY SKIING

Cross-country skiing is encouraged within Bryce Canyon National Park and offers visitors a unique way to see the park in winter. The winter beauty of the snow-dusted pinnacles and hoodoos and lack of crowds make this an attractive time to visit the park. Several ski trails are marked out within the park. The Fairyland and Paria roads are unplowed during the winter so they can be used as cross-country routes. Park rangers strongly discourage skiers from skiing down the trails into the canyon. The steep grades, narrow trails, and lack of snow generally make this entirely unsafe. Inquire at the visitors center for further information about which trails are open and about snow conditions.

At Ruby's Inn, just outside the park, the **Ruby's Inn Nordic Center** maintains more than 18 miles of groomed and set track. There are many miles of backcountry trails, some along the biking trails described in the **Parguitch** chapter. Cross-country ski rentals are available.

SNOWSHOEING

If you have always wanted to try snowshoeing, Bryce Canyon provides an excellent opportunity. Snowshoes are available at the visitor center (for adults and children) free of charge, with the deposit of a driver's license, on a first-come, first-served basis.

WHERE TO STAY

ACCOMMODATIONS

Bryce Canyon Lodge—$$

Bryce Canyon Lodge offers the only accommodations within the park, but you will have to book up to a year in advance to stay at this historic lodge on the canyon rim. The rustic lodge has 114 units, including 70 rooms, 40 historic cabins—some duplex and some quadaplex—with fireplaces now warmed by gas logs, and 4 suites in the lodge upstairs. The lodge was built between 1923 and 1925 by the Utah Parks Company, and the cabins were built during the 1920s and 1930s. The lodge and cabins have been listed in the National Register of Historic Places. Open Apr.–Oct. **TW Services, Box 400, Cedar City, Utah 84720; (801) 586-7686.**

Bryce Canyon Pines—$$

The 50 units at Bryce Canyon Pines are located just off Hwy. 12 about 6 miles from the entrance to the park. Open year-round. The heated pool is enclosed during the winter. The restaurant and coffee shop are open 6:30 am–9:30 pm. **Bryce Canyon Pines, Bryce, UT 84764; (801) 834-5335.**

Bryce Valley Inn—$$ to $$$

Seven miles southeast of Bryce Canyon, in the small town of Tropic, the Bryce Valley Inn offers 61 rooms. Open Mar.–Oct. The restaurant is open 6 am–11 pm. **Bryce Valley Inn, Tropic, UT 84776; (801) 679-8811.**

Ruby's Inn—$$ to $$$

Located just outside the park entrance, Ruby's Inn is a landmark in the Bryce Canyon area. The historic lodge was, unfortunately, destroyed by fire, but the new motel has been expanded to 216 units, making it one of the largest motels in Utah. Some rooms have two bedrooms and ktichenettes. The inn has an indoor swimming pool, restaurant, general store, and laundromat. Trail rides, van tours, helicopter flights, and mountain bike rentals are available. Open year-round. **Ruby's Inn, Bryce, Utah 84764; (801) 834-5341 or 1-800-468-8660.**

CAMPING

PRIVATE

These campgrounds are located outside the park.

Bryce Canyon Pines Country Store & Campground—

Bryce Canyon Pines offers 45 campsites, of which 17 are pullthroughs and 25 have full hookups. Other facilities include restrooms, showers, laundry, limited groceries and snacks, RV supplies, playground, game room, and indoor pool. Five miles from the entrance to Bryce Canyon on Hwy. 12. **Bryce Canyon Pines Campground, Bryce, UT 84764; (801) 834-5218.**

Ruby's Inn RV Campground—

This RV campground offers 80 pullthrough sites. In addition to restrooms, showers, and laundry facilities, it offers plenty of recreation opportunities with an indoor heated swimming pool, recreation hall, arcade, and planned activities. Open Apr.–Dec. Located outside the north entrance to Bryce Canyon on Hwy. 63. **Ruby's Inn RV Campground, Bryce, UT 84764; (801) 834-5301.**

PUBLIC

There are two campgrounds within the park. The **North Campground** and

Sunset Campground are located within a few miles of each not far from the visitors center. With a total of 206 campsites, the first-come, first-served campgrounds are often unable to accommodate all visitors to the park during the summer months. Your best bet is to stake out a campsite during the mid-morning hours. The North Campground has 55 RV and 55 tent sites; Sunset Campground has 50 RV and 50 tent sites. Fees are charged and there is a seven-day limit. There are no hookup facilities, but a fee sewage dump station, located near the North Campground, is available until cold weather sets in. Laundry and showers are located at the general store at Sunrise Point and are usually in service early May–mid-Oct. The campgrounds are officially closed during the winter months. If you want to enjoy a campfire, bring your own firewood since no wood gathering is allowed within the national park.

WHERE TO EAT

Bryce Canyon Lodge—$ to $$

Located in the historic 1924 lodge, the dining room is a long hall that constitutes the middle wing of three parallel sections that form the lodge. There are large stone fireplaces on both sides of the hall and seven trusses span the hall. It is the only facility within the park. Reservations are advised during the peak season and expect slow service. Menu items include sandwiches for lunch with mountain red trout and barbecued pork riblets featured for lunch. The dinner menu include the trout and prok riblets plus prime rib, ribeye steak, halibut, shrimp, roast loin of pork. Vegetarian dishes include wagon wheel pasta with marinara, eggplant parmesan, chef's salad, and chili. Open daily, 7 am–9 pm, Apr.–Oct. **TW Services, Box 400, Cedar City, UT 84720; (801) 586-7686.**

Ruby's Inn—$$ to $$$

The dining room at Ruby's Inn serves more Bryce Canyon establishment than any other facility. Most patrons opt for the buffet, which is offered all day long. The breakfast buffet includes hot cakes, French toast, eggs, hash browns, biscuits and gravy, cereal, and fruit. The lunch and dinner buffet offers beef, pork, chicken, pasta, vegetables, fresh fruit, garden salad, and a variety of prepared salads. If the buffet does not attract your attention, there are sandwiches for lunch and rainbow trout, red snapper, shrimp, prime rib, and steaks you can order. If you want to get something quick, there is the Canyon Room, a self-service deli inside the lodge where you can cook your own hamburgers, or pick up tacos, chili, pizza, baked potatoes, and sandwiches. Open daily 6:30 am–9:30 pm. Year-round. Located on Hwy. 63 near the entrance to Bryce Canyon; **(801) 834-5341 or 1-800-468-8660.**

See also the Accommodations section in the **Panguitch** chapter.

═══ Zion National Park ═══

There is good reason why this Utah park is so popular. Sheer cliffs of creamy Navajo sandstone rise 2,000 feet above a verdant valley floor; the Virgin River has cut narrow canyons into the rock barely 40 feet wide in places; hand-carved hiking trails, 75 years old, switchback along cliffs with vertical drops of hundreds of feet; scenic drives wind along the canyon floor or take you up the face of the mountain and through a mile-long tunnel carved through a solid sandstone cliff; and mountains of sunset-hued stone, with names like The Sentinel, The Watchman, West Temple, Mountain of the Sun, Angel's Landing, The Three Patriarchs, and The Great White Throne, watch over this sanctuary of living things. Zion is many things to many people.

Within the 229-square-mile park, every spot is a photo opportunity—a place to marvel at the incredible beauty of this location. Zion is a gigantic unroofed cathedral where the sheer size and glory of the mountains demand a reverence and awe that cleanse and restore the spirit. Its beauty and inspiration are nature's gift. Long after your visit to Zion, visions of great stone temples appear as reassuring reminders that the world we inhabit is magnificent.

With nearly 3 million visitors each year, Zion is the eighth most-visited park in the US. Zion's popularity is also its greatest liability. It is being "loved to death." The area is fragile and, especially during the summer, overcrowded. You can enjoy the park much more in the off-seasons, especially in the early spring and late fall when most of the crowds have disappeared. Denny Davies, a longtime National Park Service and chief of interpretation at Zion, offers five suggestions to make the most of your visit to Zion National Park:

1. Have information on the park before you arrive.

2. Take sufficient time and don't rush through just so that you can add one more park to your list of places visited.

3. On arrival, get updated information.

4. Have maps and necessary equipment.

5. Remember that visitors share in the stewardship of the national park. There simply are not enough staff and funds for the National Park Service, or any agency, to pick up after and restore the thoughtless and/or malicious damage caused by visitors.

HISTORY

The Anasazi lived in Zion Canyon and the environs from about AD 500 to 1200. Throughout the park, abandoned cliff houses, rock art, and chipping sites remain as evidence of their ephemeral presence. When the Anasazi moved on, the hunter-gatherers moved into the area surrounding the canyon but were reluctant to enter Zion Canyon for fear of retribution from evil spirits living there. Nephi Johnson, a young missionary sent by Brigham Young to the Indians along the Virgin River, may have been the first white to see the Zion Canyon area in Sept. 1858. Johnson told family members that his Paiute guide refused to go all the way up the canyon with him, leaving him to make the journey into the depths alone. He reported that he had found places in the canyon where the sun never reached because the canyon walls were so high and narrow. (Johnson helped found the settlement of Virgin in Dec. of 1858.)

During the fall and winter of 1862 to 1863, Springdale, just west of Zion, was settled. One of the settlers, Isaac Behunin, built the first one-room log cabin in Zion Canyon, at a site near the present location of Zion Lodge. It was Behunin who gave the name Zion to the canyon he called home. Behunin had joined the Mormon church shortly after its founding in 1830 and had lived through persecutions in Missouri and Illinois before making the trek to Utah. In Mormon theology, Zion means a resting place, where the pure in heart dwell. When Behunin unhitched his wagon and made his home, he believed that his lifelong journey had brought him to a place of safety and peace.

A few other settlers built cabins within the canyon, but there was little room for farming along the narrow valley floor. In 1872, Major John Wesley Powell surveyed the area and gave the canyon its Indian name, Mukuntuweap, without recording which of several possible meanings or origins was correct. (It could mean "Straight Canyon," "Big Canyon," "Red Dirt," "the Place of the Gods," or "God's Land." It also may have been named for Chief Mokun of the Virgin River Indians, with Mukuntuweap meaning "Land of Mokun." It could also be a derivative of a desert plant called muk-unk.) Beginning in 1900 young David Flanigan began experimenting with a cable system which would lower timber from the high mountain forests to the valley floor via what is now Cable Mountain. So successful was his device that, by 1906, he had lowered 200,000 board feet of sawed lumber down the cliff. Four years later, people with nerves of steel started to "ride the cable"—first on a dare, then to avoid the strenuous hike up and down the 1,800-foot-high mountain.

On July 31, 1909, the canyon was designated as the Mukuntuweap National Monument, and eight years later, the first automobile road was constructed into the canyon. Renamed Zion National Monument in 1918, it became a national park in 1919. The original Zion Lodge was built in 1925 by the Utah Parks Company as part of their tourist facilities in Utah.

The first entrance fees to the park—50 cents—were levied in 1926. In 1927 construction began on the Zion–Mt. Carmel Tunnel. The 1.1-mile-long tunnel was designed to shorten the distance to Grand Canyon and Bryce Canyon by providing an east entrance to the park from Long Valley (present-day Hwy. 89). The tunnel, an engineering marvel, took three years to complete and cost $2,000,000. In 1937, the scenic Kolob Canyons region (in the northwest corner of the park) was first designated a new Zion National Monument. It was incorporated into the rest of Zion National Park in 1956.

For most of the 1930s, the Civilian Conservation Corps carried out a number of projects, including construction of the entrance stations, the South Campground and the Canyon Overlook and Watchman trails, among others. As visitation continues to increase at about 10 percent each year, park officials foresee the day when a limited number of hiking permits will be issued for the trails and a mass transit system will be necessary to ensure a quality experience for park visitors. The scenic drive is the primary Zion experience for most visitors, but take time to enjoy the excellent hiking trails which compound the memories of your Zion visit.

GETTING THERE

There are three entrances to Zion National Park. Most visitors enter through the south entrance near the town of Springdale. This entrance is reached by turning off Interstate 15 onto Hwy. 9 at exit 16. If you are heading north from St. George, drive to La Verkin. From there, it is a scenic drive through the Virgin River Valley to Springdale. From Cedar City take exit 27 onto Hwy. 17 and join Hwy. 9 in La Verkin. The park entrance is 43 miles northeast of St. George and 59 miles south of Cedar City. To reach Zion's east entrance turn off Hwy. 89 at Mt. Carmel Junction. The east entrance is 24 miles from Mt. Carmel Junction, 41 miles northwest of Kanab, and 74 miles southwest of Panguitch. The distance from Salt Lake City, following Interstate 15 south, is 309 miles. The park's third entrance takes you along a 5.5-mile scenic road to the Kolob section in the extreme northwestern portion of the park. The Kolob Unit is separated from the main park, but it is the easiest section to visit for travelers along Interstate 15, as it is located just to the east off exit 40. There are visitor centers in the main park and at the entrance to the Kolob Canyons. The National Park Service is moving forward with plans to replace the current main visitor center with a new center in the Watchman Campground. The plan also calls for the closure of the Zion Canyon Rd. to all private vehicles. Access to the park will be provided by a series of shuttle buses.

—— FESTIVALS AND EVENTS ——

Southern Utah Folklife Festival
weekend after Labor Day

Held the weekend after Labor Day, its mission is to preserve and foster an understanding of southern Utah's cultural heritage through the cultivation and celebration of traditional arts and folkways. Crafts, music, dance, storytelling, food preparation, quilting, and other activities attract over 10,000 attendees every year over a three-day period. During the early years of the festival, it was held in Zion National Park; however, changes in park policy, coupled with the tremendous success of the festival, have meant that the festival has now been moved to Springdale. For more information, write **Washington County Travel and Convention Bureau, Dixie Center, 425 South 700 East, St. George, UT 84770; (801) 673-6290.**

—— OUTDOOR ACTIVITIES ——

FISHING

Kolob Reservoir—

Located off the Kolob Terrace Rd., 23 miles north of Virgin outside the park boundary, this reservoir is stocked with rainbow, German brown, brook, and cutthroat trout. A Utah fishing license is required. The road is a designated Scenic Backway (see Scenic Drives in the Seeing and Doing section).

HIKES

Hiking is the best and, in many cases, the only way to see Zion National Park. There are a variety of trails: some that are an easy stroll down a level paved walkway and others that demand stamina and even courage to traverse the exposed cliffs and scale the dizzying heights. The Zion Natural History Association has prepared a handy hiking guide, *Hiking in Zion National Park: The Trails,* which describes 18 trails. Rod Adkison's *Utah's National Parks* guide describes 25 hikes within the park. Other guides and maps are available at the visitor centers in the Kolob Unit and the main visitor center at the park's south entrance near Springdale. Backcountry permits are required for overnight camping within the park and for the Zion Narrows. Some hikes require a shuttle. Shuttle service can be arranged through **Zion Lodge** by calling **(801) 772-3213** or inquiring at the lodge. Most of the hiking trails are located in the Zion Canyon section of the park, near the south entrance, but other trails begin at the east entrance, start from the Kolob Reservoir Rd., or are located in the Kolob section. For the longer hikes, I strongly recommend that you obtain a topographic map and consult a park ranger to obtain up-to-date trail information. The following are some of my favorite trails in the four locations.

Canyon Overlook—

The trail to the spectacular overlook is only .5 mile long and gets plenty of use. But from the overlook you can see into Pine Creek Canyon 1,000 feet below, and into one of the five portals of the Zion–Mt. Carmel tunnel. There are views of West and East temples, the Towers of the Virgin, and the streaked wall in lower Zion Canyon. Caution is needed on the uneven steps cut into the sandstone at the start of the trail and near the vertical dropoffs. (Handrails are provided in places.) An interpretive leaflet available at the Zion Canyon Visitor Center and usually at the trailhead introduces the natural history of the higher canyon area. Ranger-guided tours are conducted on this trail. Check at the visitor center for schedules. The trailhead is located just beyond the east entrance to the Zion–Mt. Carmel Tunnel, 5 miles east of the Zion Canyon Visitor Center and about 6 miles west of the east entrance.

Chinle Trail—

Located in the southern end of the park, this hike is the most popular winter hike because of its lower elevation, level terrain, and absence of snow and ice. The trail begins at a large dirt turnout on the right side of the road between Springdale and Rockville—3.5 miles from the South Entrance Station. You can begin the hike here, or drive your vehicle, if the road is passable, 1.3 miles to the park boundary. Part of the trail passes the Old Scoggins Stock Trail, built by pioneer cattlemen through a break in the cliff to move their animals. There is also an historic oil well site that dates from 1908 during the pioneer days of oil exploration in Utah. You will see petrified wood scattered throughout the area, and at one time this trail was known as the Petrified Forest Trail. Avoid any temptation to collect petrified wood as it is against park regulations and diminishes the enjoyment for future visitors. The one-way length of the trail inside the park is 6.8 miles.

East Entrance Trails—

Access to the two trails in the eastern section of the park is off Hwy. 9. Cable and Deertrap mountains trailheads are located at the east entrance of the park. Both trails offer views that are favorites for many hikers in Zion National Park. Follow the east entrance trail for 5.6 miles to the Stave Spring Junction. If you stay on the left branch, you will reach the Deertrap Mountain Overlook after 3.2 miles, with its breathtaking view of the Court of the Patriarchs, Twin Brothers, and the East Temple in the lower end of Zion Canyon. The 1.8-mile Cable Mountain Trail branches from the Deertrap Mountain Trail, 1.1 miles from the junction at Stave Spring. It offers unforgettable views of the top of the Great White Throne, Angels Landing, Observation Point, the West Rim, and David Flanigan's historic cableworks. Back at Stave Spring Junction, you can either return to the east entrance trailhead or continue for another 5 miles around the head of Echo Canyon, descending along the north side to the Zion Canyon Rd. at Weeping Rock. Most

hikers spend a couple of days hiking this area of the park; however, it is possible to make the 10.6-mile hike from the east entrance to Weeping Rock in a day and even cover the 20 miles of trails to take in Deertrap Mountain and Cable Mountain, if you are in excellent shape, have good weather, and get an early start.

Emerald Pools Trail System—

If you are staying at Zion Lodge, this will likely be the first hike you take. The trail begins across the river bridge, west of Zion Lodge. The .6-mile concrete trail to Lower Emerald Pool can be negotiated by wheelchairs, with some assistance, and by baby strollers. This is a cool, shady hike, out of sizzling summer sun. The "hanging gardens" of monkeyflower, mosses, and ferns give an almost tropiclike sensation. The .5-mile-long trail to the Upper Pool is unpaved and not maintained. The two small waterfalls and emerald pools, formed by a small perennial spring coming out of Heaps Canyon, and the views of Lady Mountain, Red Arch Mountain, the Great White Throne, and other Zion landmarks make this one of the most popular hikes in the park. Total round-trip distance to the Lower Pool is 1.2 miles (2.2 miles if you go on to the Upper Pool). Because of their small size, these pools are closed to swimming and wading.

Hidden Canyon—

Hidden Canyon was carved by water cascading between two giants—Cable Mountain and the Great White Throne. The 1.1-mile paved trail into the canyon was carved out of solid rock in some places by park service employees and Civilian Conservation Corps members during the 1920s and 1930s. It climbs 1,000 feet from the trailhead at the Weeping Rock Parking Area to its end. This trail features some steep dropoffs and is moderately strenuous.

Hop Valley—

Most hikers on the Hop Valley Trail usually make this an overnight hike, although strong hikers may be able to cover the 13.8-mile round-trip hike in a day. The trailhead is located about 13 miles north of the junction with Hwy. 9 on the left-hand side of the road. The trail drops from the trailhead almost 1,000 feet to La Verkin Creek, then winds through the beautiful Hop Valley with its green meadows and 600-foot-high Navajo sandstone cliffs. The trail intersects the La Verkin Creek Trail, and Kolob Arch is less than a mile farther north. To reach Kolob Arch, turn left at the junction and head in a westerly direction for about .3 mile then watch for the Kolob Arch. You can either return to the Hop Valley Trailhead or continue west, then north, along the La Verkin Creek Trail for 7 miles to its trailhead at Lee Pass. The latter route will require a shuttle.

Kolob Terrace Road—

Also known as the Kolob Reservoir Rd., this scenic backway provides access to the least-visited part of Zion National Park (the Kolob Unit) and offers an opportunity to be free of the crowds in other parts of the park during the summer season. The road runs north from Hwy. 9 at the eastern end of the town of Virgin, 14 miles west of the south entrance to Zion. Trails from here link the main part of the park with the remote Finger Canyons of the Kolob. Because the road is steep, some larger vehicles tend to overheat during the summertime, so take your time and watch your heat gauge.

Kolob Unit—

This section of Zion National Park is often overlooked by visitors because it seems so far from the South Entrance Visitor Center and Zion Lodge; but the easy access off Interstate 15 makes this a favorite area for informed highway travelers. There are few places in the US where you can be inside a national park less than a mile from the Interstate. The scenery in the Kolob Unit is just as magnificent as anywhere in the park, or any national park for that matter, and two good hiking trails take you into the heart of the vermilion cliffs and deep-cut canyons.

La Verkin Creek and Kolob Arch Trails—

Lee Pass, located 3.5 miles east of the Kolob Canyons Visitor Center, is the trailhead for the La Verkin Creek Trail. This trail is a popular backpacking trail because of the access to Kolob Arch which, with a span measuring 310 feet, is one of the largest free-standing arches in the world. To see the arch, you need to hike 6.6 miles to Kolob Arch Trail Junction and another .6 mile to the Kolob Arch Viewpoint, which is .25 mile from the arch. If you push it, you can make the 14.4-mile round-trip hike in a day, but keep in mind the return leg is an 800-foot climb back up to Lee Pass, and the 1.2-mile round-trip hike on the Kolob Arch Viewpoint Trail is rocky and more primitive than the main trail. One option that does not require a return hike but allows you to continue down the Hop Valley Trail is described in the Kolob Terrace Rd. section. Overnight hikes require a backcountry permit which can be obtained from the Kolob Canyons Visitor Center.

Middle Fork of Taylor Creek—

Two miles east of the Kolob Canyons Visitors Center, the Taylor Creek Trail parallels the creek for 2.5 miles to Double Arch Alcove. Along the trail, you pass two historic cabins: the Larsen Cabin—a 1929 homestead cabin built by Gustave C. Larsen of white-fir logs—located just west of the confluence of the middle fork and north fork of Taylor Creek, and farther up the trail, not far from the Double Arch Alcove, the Arthur Fife Cabin built in 1930. The elevation gain is just over 400 feet. One of the best times to make this hike is in the fall, when the autumn leaves against the blue sky and red rock are spectacular.

Observation Point—

This trail also begins at the Weeping Rock Parking Area and rises 2,200 feet in 3.7 miles. The trail was used by Indians and Mormon pioneers and winds around the base of Cable Mountain, before climbing onto the ponderosa pine–covered plateau.

From Observation Point, you have an unbelievable view of the Great White Throne, Cable Mountain, the West Rim, Angels Landing, and Zion Canyon. Plan at least a half day to make the 7.5-mile round-trip. The National Park Service rates this hike as strenuous.

Riverside Walk—

This hike is undertaken by 700,000 visitors a year, making it the most popular trail in the park. It is one hike where the higher the air temperature, the better. The trailhead is at the end of the Zion Canyon scenic road just beyond the Temple of Sinawava Parking Area. From Apr. through Oct., this parking area is so crowded that finding a parking space can be difficult, but park only in designated parking areas. The trail follows the east side of the Virgin River for a mile upstream along a paved, mostly level path, making it accessible for wheelchairs and other physically hindered visitors. The high walls keep the trail in the shade much of the time and ensure a pleasant stroll. At the end of the paved trail, though, it is decision time. You can either return at this point, or join the hundreds who plunge into the ankle-to knee-deep water for some river hiking. Note the "Danger Level" sign that is posted, as you begin the hike from the parking area. If it is low, you can wade up the river as far as you want, though few go beyond Orderville Canyon, 1.8 miles from the end of the paved trail. As you proceed upcanyon, the walls become narrower and narrower. The high cliff walls are decorated with "hanging gardens," waterfalls plunge off sheer faces, and the ever-beckoning sound of the river keeps you going to see what new wonder is just around the next corner. It is a time to forget about everything else and return to nature's womb.

Don't be afraid to get a little wet. Wear a pair of hiking boots or sneakers that you don't mind getting soaked. For late 20th-century humans, barefoot is no way to go, even with the threat of ruining a pair of shoes; you will remember the hike long after you have forgotten about the shoes. Watch out for submerged rocks that can twist your ankle, and go at your own pace. Many people carry a walking stick to keep their footing. This is especially useful when the water is quite deep. But bring your walking stick with you since park rules prohibit cutting or breaking limbs from living or dead trees for walking sticks. If you are in a group, appoint a designated photographer, or take turns carrying a camera (with a waterproof case or wrapped in a plastic bag) to take pictures that those back home simply will not believe.

Scout Lookout and Angels Landing—

This popular trail begins at the Grotto Picnic Area, about .6 mile up the canyon from Zion Lodge. The trail is paved, steep, and is no place for those prone to acrophobia. The 1.9-mile hike to Scout Lookout climbs 1,000 feet and it's another .5 mile and 500 feet of elevation gain to Angels Landing. The trail was cut into the rock in 1926. The most famous part of the trail is the 21 short switchbacks known as "Walters Wiggles"—named for Walter Ruesch, a resident of Springdale and the first custodian and acting superintendent of the park. The .5-mile trail to Angels Landing crosses a steep narrow ridge with support chains anchored into the rock (offering the illusion of security). If heights bother you, skip this trail. Young children should not be taken on the trail, and anyone who makes the hike should exercise great caution. Avoid the trail when it is wet or icy, or when thunderstorms make such exposure dangerous. Be sure to complete your hike before dark. Despite all these cautions, this amazing trail is thrilling to hike, and the views from Scout Lookout and Angels Landing into Zion Canyon are unforgettable.

Virgin River and Narrows—

While the Riverside Walk is adventure enough for the 9,999 folks, for the one in 10,000 who need more, there is the 17.5-mile stretch of the Virgin River that descends north to south from Chamberlain's Ranch and ends up at the Riverside Walk and the Temple of Sinawava. Backcountry permits are required for overnight hikes and day hikes through the length of the canyon. Because of the danger from flashf loods in the Narrows—where the canyon walls are no more than 40 feet apart—park service rangers exercise great caution and prohibit entrance into the canyon if weather forecasts are unfavorable. While most of the hike is in knee-deep water, there can be deep pools that will require swimming. The trek is a strenuous day hike, or, with proper equipment and preparation, you can make it an overnight hike. Because of the vagaries of weather and water levels, and the need for a backcountry permit, check in at the visitor center to finalize your plans. The hike requires a shuttle to the Chamberlain Ranch, reached via a gravel road from Hwy. 9. If you want to make this hike, be prepared physically, have good equipment and supplies—especially rubber-soled hiking boots with good ankle support and a walking stick—go with reliable companions, arrange the necessary logistics, and offer an adequate sacrifice, so that the weather gods will smile kindly on your venture.

Watchman Trail—

The Watchman guards the south entrance to Zion Canyon and offers a breathtaking view of West Temple, the Towers of the Virgin, the town of Springdale, and the Virgin River. The trailhead begins just east of Watchman Campground Information Station and is a 3-mile round-trip hike to the viewpoint on a plateau near the base of the Watchman.

West Rim Trail—

If you start from the West Rim Trailhead, which is east of the Lava Point Campground off the Kolob Terrace Rd., the 14.3-mile-long hike will take you to the Grotto Picnic Area, just north of the Zion Lodge in Zion Canyon. Most hikers make this a two-day hike—it is the most popular overnight hike in the park—but it is possible for well-conditioned hikers to complete it in a day. From the high country to the depths of Zion Canyon, you lose 3,100 feet in eleva-

tion. The scenic vistas from the West Rim Trail of Red Arch Mountain, Angels Landing, The Great White Throne, and East Temple are considered by many to be the finest in the park. The last 5 miles are very steep, as the trail descends into Zion Canyon along a rock, pavement, and concrete path and past the trail to Angels Landing. You will need to arrange for a shuttle to pick you up at The Grotto Picnic Area. To reach the trailhead, take the Kolob Terrace Rd. for 20 miles from Hwy. 9, then turn right at the sign for Lava Point and the West Rim Trail. Follow it for a mile, then keep to the left to reach the West Rim Trailhead 1.3 miles farther on.

Wildcat Canyon and Northgate Peaks—

Hikers and backpackers have several options from the trailhead located on the south side of the Kolob Terrace Rd., about 16 miles north of the junction with Hwy. 9. Most hikers follow the Wildcat Canyon Trail for 5.8 miles in an easterly / northeasterly direction to its junction with the West Rim Trail and include a 1.2-mile-long side trip to the Northgate Peaks Overlook for a view of the Northgate Peaks, North Guardian Angel, and the canyons of the left fork of North Creek. At the junction with the West Rim Trail, it is only .1 mile to the West Rim Trailhead, where you can meet a shuttle vehicle. The total distance for this hike is 8.4 miles, including the 2.4-mile round-trip to Northgate Peaks Overlook. The round-trip back to the Wildcat Canyon Trailhead, including the 2.4-mile Northgate Trail, is 14.4 miles. The elevation gain between the Wildcat Canyon and West Rim trailheads is 450 feet, but in between there is a 500-foot descent into Wildcat Canyon and a 500-foot ascent back out. The trails pass through ponderosa pine, aspen groves, lush meadows, and oak thickets and offer spectacular views of the mountains and red sandstone cliffs.

Zion Canyon—

The most popular hiking trails within the national park are located within Zion

Canyon. Easy access, magnificent scenery, and well-developed trails attract thousands of hikers of all levels each year. Unless you hike these trails in the off-season or at daybreak, expect to share the experience with others. But there is something about the majesty of the carved sandstone and domed peaks that seems to bring out the best in people, and everyone seems ready to share a smile, offer a word of greeting, and recount experiences along the trails. So don't avoid these hikes because they are popular; just go out and enjoy the scenery and your fellow visitors.

RANGER-CONDUCTED WALKS AND PROGRAMS

A variety of guided walks, evening programs, and talks is offered at various locations in the park late Mar.–Nov. Check at the visitor centers for a schedule of activities. At the Zion Nature Center, during the months of June, July and Aug., daily programs are offered for children ages 6–12.

Grand Circle—A National Park Odyssey

This multimedia presentation highlights the scenery, natural attractions, and history of southern Utah. The production is shown nightly at dusk from late May–early Sept.r at the Obert C. Tanner Amphitheater, located just outside the park boundaries in Springdale. For information call **(801) 673-4811 ext. 276.**

Zion Canyon Theater—

After a long and bitter debate that divided the community of Springdale on the appropriateness of constructing a six-story theater at the entrance to Zion National Park, the 482-seat theater opened in June 1994. A 37-minute film, "Treasure of the Gods," directed by Academy Award winner Keith Merrill, is shown daily on a continuous schedule from morning until evening (8:30 am–8:30 pm Apr.–Oct. and 10:30 am–6:30 pm Nov.–Mar.). The film depicts a mythical experience about the Anasazi, Paiutes, Spanish conquistadors and padres, early Mormon settlers, and a photographer. Park rangers point out the story should not be taken too literally. There are no lost Indian or Spanish gold mines, no Indian ruins as featured in the film, no hang gliders are allowed in the park, and rock climbing is carefully regulated. The film is worth viewing for the adventure, (the flash flood and the rock-climbing feats performed by a hand-picked crew from the Yosemite Search and Rescue Team will leave you breathless). The film is also an interesting interpretation of Zion Canyon and the lore of the American Southwest. There is a gift shop and snackbar at the complex. Be sure and note the display in the theater foyer of costumes and props used in the production of the film. Admission fee charged. **Zion Canyon Theater, 145 Zion Park Blvd., Springdale, UT 84767; (801) 772-2400.**

HORSEBACK TRIPS

Guided horseback rides are available at **Zion Lodge** Mar.–Oct. Reservations and information are available at the lodge, or by calling **(801) 772-3967.**

———— SEEING AND DOING ————

SCENIC DRIVES

Kolob Canyons Road—

Access to this 5.5-mile scenic drive is from exit 40, off Interstate 15 between St. George and Cedar City. This is a scenic drive that millions of people bypass each year as they zoom up and down the interstate. What a pity! The Finger Canyons of the Kolob, which, according to Mormon theology, were named for the star (Kolob) at the center of the universe and closest to the throne of God, are a spectacular set of unique sandstone formations and canyons that were added to Zion National Park in 1956. Even if you only have a half hour to drive to the end of the road and take in the vista of Kolob Canyons from the viewpoint and return to the interstate, your soul will be refreshed. A short hike at the turn around offers glorious views to the south. The Kolob Canyons Visitor Center at the entrance to the Kolob Unit is open daily, except for winter holidays. Friendly rangers here provide information, books, maps, and backcountry permits. The road also provides access to the Taylor Creek Trail and La Verkin Creek Trail (see the Hiking section). A road guide, with numbered stops along the drive describes the geology, ecology, and history of Kolob and can be obtained at the visitor center.

Kolob Reservoir Scenic Backway—

Also called the Kolob Terrace Rd., this scenic drive runs north from the town of Virgin, through part of Zion National Park. The pavement ends just beyond the northern boundary of the park (18 miles) and the road continues along graded dirt to Hwy. 14, 6 miles east of Cedar City. The road provides access to the Hop Valley, West Rim, Wildcat Canyon, and Northgate Peaks trails (see the Hiking section). The road reaches a high elevation and is closed by heavy winter snows, usually until May. However, you can drive part of the way. Additional information can be obtained in the **Cedar City** chapter and Kolob Reservoir in the Fishing section.

Zion Canyon Scenic Drive—

This paved road takes you through the heart of Zion Canyon, as it winds along the east side of the North Fork of the Virgin River from its junction with Hwy. 9 (known as the Zion–Mt. Carmel Hwy. inside the park) less than 1 mile north of the Zion Canyon Visitor Center. The drive is 6.2 miles long and dead-ends at the Temple of Sinawava Parking Area at the Gateway to the Narrows Trail. Unless you make the drive in the off-season, you will find the

traffic quite heavy and slow-moving. But the winding road and numerous viewpoints demand a leisurely drive up the canyon. It is impossible to see the tops of the high canyon walls and the magnificent formations from inside the car, so plan to stop at least at the following viewpoints.

Court of the Patriarchs (1.6 miles up the canyon)—

From the parking area, take the 50-yard-long concrete trail up to the viewpoint, where you can look across the canyon to the massive stone formations that are appropriately named the Three Patriarchs, for the Old Testament prophets—Abraham, Isaac, and Jacob. You can also see the Streaked Wall, the Sentinel, Mt. Moroni, the Spearhead, and Angels Landing. Behind you loom the Mountain of the Sun and the Twin Brothers.

Zion Lodge (2.5 miles up the canyon)—

The historic Zion Lodge harkens back to the days before World War II, when visitors to Zion Canyon often arrived by train and bus and needed a convenient and unobtrusive place to stay. Even if you do not stay at the Zion Lodge (it is usually booked well in advance), it is still fun to walk through and pretend that you are a guest, perhaps even have lunch or dinner at the lodge, and reflect on what it must have been like in the 1920s when the first guests arrived. A fire destroyed the original 1925 stone-and-timber building in 1966. Necessity dictated that a new lodge be constructed in three months with the sacrifice of Gilbert Stanley Underwood's classic "Rustic Architectural" design for the lodge. Fortunately, the present lodge facade was successfully renovated during the winter of 1989 to 1990 to reflect Underwood's original design.

Weeping Rock (4.5 miles up the canyon)—

It's a short, .2-mile hike to the Weeping Rock, where water seeps out of the canyon wall to form a light mist. On a hot summer day, this is a most refreshing stop. Information about the Cable Mountain Draw Works is provided along the trail. And you stand in amazement at how, in pioneer days, the timber could be lowered hundreds of feet over the canyon wall. An Anasazi pueblo was found in the vicinity. Weeping Rock is also the trailhead for hikes to Hidden Canyon and Observation Point. This is a popular location in the canyon, and, as with other places in the canyon, parking can be difficult to find, especially in the summer.

Great White Throne View Area (5.1 miles up the canyon)—

This famous Zion landmark is more than 2,000 feet above the canyon floor, and you do feel that if the Almighty had an earthly throne, this would be it. The size, majesty, and beauty of the Great White Throne are beyond description—most people photograph it instead. The view area is far enough from the Throne for you to enjoy the mountain in all its splendor.

Temple of Sinawava (6.2 miles up the canyon)—

The Temple of Sinawava is named for a Paiute spirit who is said to live in this great natural amphitheater by the Gateway to the Narrows Trail. Take time for a walk up the paved trail. Also notice Pulpit Rock just beyond the parking area. If you are lucky enough to visit this area just after a rainstorm, or in late winter and early spring after a good snow year, you will see beautiful waterfalls coming off the tops of the mountains.

Zion–Mt. Carmel Highway—

This drive is a must for park visitors. It follows across the park, as it switchbacks up the canyon from the junction with the Zion Canyon scenic road by the bridge. Just beyond the turnoff to the Zion Canyon and at the bottom of the switchbacks, you cross a beautifully arched stone bridge that, when viewed from one of the turnouts along the switchbacks, blends so well with the natural stone of the canyon that it is almost unnoticeable. After looping back and forth 800 feet up the side of the mountain, past the huge "blind" alcove–known as the Great Zion Arch, you reach the 1.1-mile-long Zion Mt. Carmel Tunnel, which was blasted through the Navajo sandstone in the 1920s and dedicated in July 1930. When the tunnel was completed, five portals opened through the canyon wall for visitors to stop and admire the unbelievable view. The portals are still there, but because of heavy traffic stopping is no longer allowed inside the tunnel.

On the other side of the tunnel, the landscape looks quite different. Here, the dune-formed nature of the Navajo sandstone is quite obvious. This is particularly true at Checkerboard Mesa, where wind and water have etched dramatic cracks and grooves into the cream-colored rock, creating a "checkerboard" effect. The total distance of this drive, from the visitors center to the Hwy. 89 at Mt. Carmel Junction, is 24 miles. Note that there are restrictions on vehicles using the tunnel. Call the National Park Service for information if you are driving an RV.

TRAM TOURS

An excellent way to see the park is on board the motorized tram, which, during warmer months, operates several times daily from the **Zion Canyon Lodge**. For information and reservations, call **(801) 586-7686.**

WHERE TO STAY

ACCOMMODATIONS
BED AND BREAKFASTS
Blue House Bed and Breakfast—$$$

A four-room bed and breakfast located in Rockville. **PO Box 176, Springdale, UT 84767; (801) 772-3912.**

Flanigan's Inn—$$$

This Springdale lodge opened in 1947, under the name "Zion's Rest," when John Drater purchased and moved some barracks from the Japanese War Relocation Camp at Topaz near Delta, Utah, and renovated them for use as tourist cabins. Nine of these original units are still in use, although they have been modernized since the 1940s. Two of the units have been converted into a conference room. The other 25 units are modern rooms located in several beautiful natural wood buildings, set among lawns and a pond, and with a private walkway to a hilltop vista of Zion Canyon. When Larry McKown purchased the establishment from the Draters several years ago, he changed the name to Flanigan's Inn, in honor of David Flanigan, the local inventor who designed the Cable Mountain Draw Works in Zion Canyon. An excellent restaurant is located at the inn (see Where to Eat section). **PO Box 100, 428 Zion Park Blvd., Springdale, UT 84767; (801) 772-3244 or 1-800-765-RSVP.**

Handcart House—$$$

Antique brass beds covered with homemade quilts, in a two-story stucco house shaded by a 100-year-old apricot tree, in the historic Mormon settlement of Rockville, only 5 miles from Zion National Park, make this a popular southern Utah bed and breakfast. Each of the three nonsmoking rooms has a private bath. **244 West Main St., Rockville, UT 84763; (801) 772-3867.**

Harvest House Bed and Breakfast—$$$

Fate brought Barbara and Steven Cooper together, and then intervened a 2nd time to send them to Springdale as owners of the Harvest House. Growing up as childhood friends in Massachusetts, their paths separated after high school only to cross again at their 10-year reunion. Three months later they were engaged. A few years later, they made a trip out West and stayed in Springdale, where, according to their account, "This place chose us." When the opportunity came to acquire a new bed and breakfast that was under construction, Steve gave up his advertising business and Barbara sold her share of a Boston-based catering house, and they opened the Harvest House in 1991. Their enthusiasm for Springdale and Zion National Park is captivating. There are four nonsmoking rooms, each with a private bath and air conditioning. Two rooms have private decks, with a magnificent view of the Watchman and Bridge Mountain. Barbara offers elegant breakfasts with homemade muffins and pastries. **29 Canyon View Dr., PO Box 125, Springdale, UT 84767; (801) 772-3880.**

Under the Eaves Guest House—$$$

The original house was constructed in 1929 from red sandstone blocks cut from nearby canyon walls. Two bedrooms are located on the 1st floor and, while there is a shared bath, each room has its own sink. Upstairs ("under the eaves") is a large honeymoon suite, with a large claw-foot tub in the private bath. Near the main house is the guesthouse which has two rooms, each with a private bath. All rooms are nonsmoking. Proprietors are Kathleen Brown Wilkerson, Dale Wilkerson, and John O'Shea. **980 Zion Park Blvd., PO Box 29, Springdale, UT 84767; (801) 772-3457.**

Zion House Bed and Breakfast—$$$

Lillie Baiardi is the owner of this four-room bed and breakfast. All rooms are nonsmoking and guests have access to the living room and dining room, where a full breakfast is served. **801 Zion Park Blvd., PO Box 323, Springdale, UT 84767; (801) 772-3281.**

Zion Lodge—$$$

Zion Lodge provides the only accommodations within the park and is, understandably, very popular. It has 80 motel units and 40 renovated historic cabins. There are also a restaurant, snack bar, and gift shop. For information and reservations, write **Utah Parks Division, TW Recreational Services, Inc., 451 North Main St., Cedar City, UT 84720**; or call **(801) 586-7686**. Note: You will probably have to book six months to a year in advance.

Zion's Blue Star Bed and Breakfast—$$$

Located in the town of Virgin at the entrance to the Kolob Reservoir Rd., 12 miles from the south entrance to Zion National Park, this is a spacious western ranch-style house with an eye-catching red-tiled roof. Rooms have queen-size beds and shared baths. A separate cottage sleeps seven and has a private bath and kitchen. Rates include a hearty country breakfast. **28 West Hwy., State Rd. 9, Virgin, UT 84779; (801) 635-3828.**

MOTELS

Nice motel accommodations with heated swimming pools are available at the following Springdale lodges and motels.

Best Western Driftwood Lodge—$$

Forty-eight units. **1515 Zion Park Blvd.; (801) 772-3262 or 1-800-528-1234.**

Bumbleberry Inn—$$

Twenty-four units. **897 Zion Park Blvd.; (801) 772-3224 or 1-800-828-1534.**

Canyon Ranch Motel—$$

Twenty-one units in new and remodeled cottages. **668 Zion Park Blvd.; (801) 772-3234.**

Cliffrose Lodge and Gardens—$$

Thirty-six units set in 5 acres of lawns, trees, and flower gardens. **281 Zion Park Blvd.; (801) 772-3234 or 1-800-243-UTAH.**

Pioneer Lodge—$$

Forty-one units. **838 Zion Park Blvd.; (801) 772-3233.**

Terrace Brook Lodge—$$

Twenty-four units. **990 Zion Park Blvd.; (801) 772-3932 or 1-800-342-6779.**

Zion Park Motel—$$

Twenty-one units. **855 Zion Park Blvd.; (801) 772-3251.**

CAMPGROUNDS

There are two large campgrounds located at the south entrance to the park. **South Campground** has 140 RV and tent spaces and is open from mid-Apr.–mid-Oct. **Watchman Campground** has 185 RV trailer sites and 229 tent sites and is open year-round. Both campgrounds have drinking water, toilets, and disabled facilities. No RV hookups.

Just outside the park in Springdale, the **Zion Canyon Campground** has 100 RV and tent sites, 70 with complete hookups. Open year-round, facilities include toilets, showers, and a laundry. **479 Zion Park Blvd.; (801) 772-3237.**

——— WHERE TO EAT ———

Bit and Spur Saloon and Mexican Restaurant—$$ to $$$

Before its demise, *Utah Holiday* magazine gave this restaurant its Best Mexican Restaurant in Utah award. While there are plenty of other contenders for the award, the Bit and Spur does offer great Mexican food. House favorites include chili verde, chili rellenos, pasta Sonora, and a Mexican combination plate that is the most popular menu item. There are also special dishes. For a Native American dish, try the Zuni stew made with lamb, corn, sweet potatoes, and juniper berries. The pork and shrimp Yucatan is a favorite combination of a grilled pork tenderloin and shrimp marinated with pineapple, lime, and chilies. For vegetarians, there's a curried vegetable burrito made with potatoes, egg plant, squash, and peppers wrapped in a whole wheat tortilla. Open daily for dinner 5 pm–10 pm. **1212 Zion Park Blvd., Springdale; (801) 772-3498.**

Bumbleberry Inn—$ to $$

Everyone who drives through Springdale sees the sign for the Bumbleberry Inn and asks what is a bumbleberry. No one is willing to give out the real secret, but the menu and a leaflet explains that among other things, "Bumbleberries are purple and binkel berries that grow on giggle bushes, so named because when the berries ripen the bush begins to quake, and at the precise moment that they ripen, they giggle. The size of the bumbleberry is determined by the heart of the picker." The curious will want to try a slice of bumbleberry pie to see if they can figure out what it really is. If you want something before the pie, there are hamburgers and sandwiches for lunch or turkey, chicken beef, steak, shrimp, liver and onions, or pasta for dinner. Open Mon.–Sat. 7 am–9:30 pm; 8 am–8 pm in the winter. **897 Zion Park Blvd., Springdale; (801) 772-3224.**

Flanigan's Inn Restaurant—$$ to $$$

Part of Flanigan's Inn just outside the south entrance to Zion National Park, the restaurant is open daily for breakfast, lunch, and dinner during the summer (dinner only during the winter). Specialties include their Southwest game plate, fresh trout, mixed grill, mesquite-roasted chicken, and pasta dishes made from original recipes. The dining area offers a delightful view of the cliffs at the entrance to Zion National Park. This is one of those places where southern Utahns, from as far away as St. George and Cedar City, go for special occasions. **428 Zion Park Blvd.; (801) 772-3244.**

Zion Lodge—$ to $$

The only restaurant inside the park, the Zion Lodge Restaurant is usually busy, and reservations are a must for dinner during the busy season. The restaurant is open for breakfast, lunch, and dinner, and offers sack lunches for hikers. A breakfast buffet is offered. Lunch items include burgers, sandwiches, chicken-fried steak, and Utah trout. The lodge also features a snack bar with patio seating.;**(801) 772-3213.**

SERVICES

Zion Canyon Visitor Center—

The largest and perhaps most attractive of any of the Utah national parks. It is open year-round, except Christmas Day, 8 am–8 pm late Mar.–Nov.; 8 am–5 pm the rest of the year. The visitor center is also park headquarters. It contains a **museum** with exhibits on Zion, a well-stocked **bookstore**, and offers information and free ranger talks throughout the day. Plan to make this your 1st stop if you are entering the canyon at the south entrance. **Kolob Canyons Visitor Center** is also open year-round but has a more limited range of services due to its size and location.

Zion National Park—

For information, write **Superintendent, Zion National Park, Springdale, UT 84767-1099;** or call **(801) 772-3256**, Mon.–Fri. 8 am–4:30 pm.

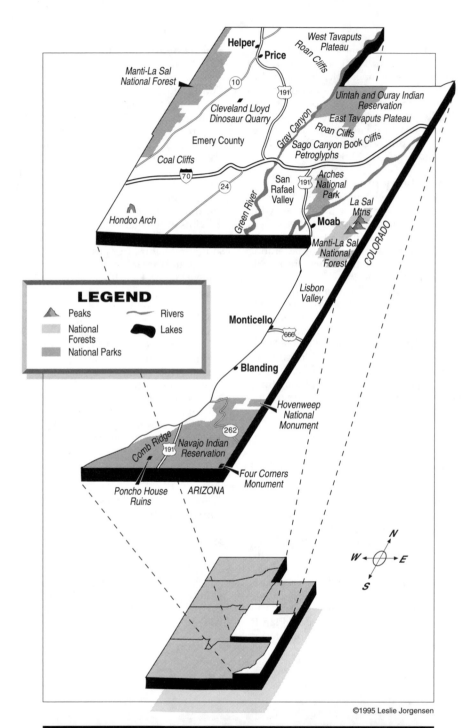

Southeast Region

SOUTHEASTERN REGION

Price

Historian Philip Notarianni has described Carbon County as "Eastern Utah's Industrialized Island." It was in fact industrialization that led to the creation of the new county of Carbon from part of what was Emery County in 1894. The coalfields stretch from the alpine settings of Scofield and Clear Creek in the northwestern corner of the county to more desert conditions in the southeast section around Sunnyside. Price is the county seat of Carbon County, which is often described as the most cosmopolitan county within the state. The reputation is well deserved. Between 1890 and the end of World War II, immigrants from around the world came to Carbon County—primarily because of the coal mining that gives the county its name. Concentrated in the coal camps and in the towns of Price and Helper, the Greeks, Italians, Finns, Slovenians, Croats, Serbs, Austrians, Chinese, Japanese, Mexican-Americans, Armenians, and others have given Carbon County a character much different from Mormon areas, such as Emery County to the south.

Catholic churches in Price and Helper and the historic Greek Orthodox church in Price symbolize the difference, though Mormon ward houses are also found in the communities. Carbonites boast that the interaction among the diverse groups has produced a much higher degree of tolerance and acceptance than in any other part of the state. While this is true today, it was not always so. The conflicts among different nationalities, Mormons, coal operators, and miners, and the rivalries between Price and Helper and Carbon County and Emery County, have left a rich, but sometimes violent history.

HISTORY

It has been nearly 120 years since the first coal was mined in the area, but the "black gold" still dominates the county. The ever-present coal trains and coal trucks along Hwy. 6 are constant reminders of this heritage, even though modern mining techniques do not require the large number of coal miners of earlier days. Coal camps and company towns have disappeared as miners and coal haulers commute to the mines from homes around and outside the county.

Old-timers recall life in the coal camps with fondness. The narrow canyons offered little living space and threw residents together in an industrial village set down in a wilderness. The closeness of the houses, the common fear of death or injury in the mines, the recreation opportunities provided at the company-owned amusement hall, the seemingly schizophrenic coal company—which both offered much-needed jobs but also demanded trade at the company store where prices were often exorbitant—all of it was a new experience, whether residents were from the Mormon farms in the valleys or the isolated villages of Italy or Greece. While community life in the coal camps led to individual friendships among the diverse groups, two events in the 1930s brought the people of the county together in ways that saw the conflict and controversy of the first 50 years give way to harmony, good feelings, and pride in the diversity. The two events were the establishment of the United Mine Workers of America to represent the area's coal miners in 1933 and, in 1937, the founding of Carbon College as the first institution for higher education in all of eastern Utah.

The union brought miners together in ways that promoted fairness and mutual respect for all miners, regardless of religion or nationality; the college provided the much-needed, inexpensive opportunity for sons and daughters of both foreign and native-born residents to complete the first two years of education, before moving on to complete four-year and advanced degrees at upstate universities or institutions around the country. Education is both the great equalizer and preserver of heritage. Carbon College, known since the mid-1960s as the College of Eastern Utah, has provided rich opportunities to its students and the entire community through such institutions as its Prehistoric Museum.

GETTING THERE

Located 120 miles south-southeast of Salt Lake City, Price is about a two-hour drive from Utah's capital. The first half of the trip is along Interstate 15 to Spanish Fork, then along Hwy. 6 for the last half. The highway crosses from the Great Basin onto the Colorado Plateau at Soldier Summit, elevation 7,477 feet. This route can be treacherous during winter snowstorms. Hwy. 6 enters Carbon County at the head of Price Canyon and follows the canyon to its mouth near the town of Helper and thence to Price. Travelers entering Utah from Colorado along Interstate 70 exit just west of Green River onto Hwy. 6 and head northwest for about 60 miles to Price.

FESTIVALS AND EVENTS

Black Diamond Stampede Rodeo

3rd weekend in June

This three-day rodeo is held in Price; **(801) 637-2788.**

Greek Festival

2nd weekend in July

The Greek-American community holds its festival the 2nd weekend in July. Homemade Greek food, music, dancing, and tours of the historic Hellenic Orthodox Church of the Assumption are all a part of the festivities; **(801) 637-0704.**

OUTDOOR ACTIVITIES

BIKING

Nine-Mile Canyon—

Nine-Mile Canyon is famous for its prehistoric Indian rock art and ruins. It, too, can be a fine ride through the canyon or along some of the routes leading off it. Two recommended rides are the Sheep Canyon route, a novice-level ride that begins 24 miles up Nine-Mile Canyon, and the Harmon Canyon/Prickly Pear loop, a ride for advanced bikers, which is located across the county line in Duchesne County. It offers a magnificent view of the Badland Cliffs.

Scofield Area—

From the Scofield Reservoir, bikers follow Hwy. 96 south past the reservoir to the old town of Scofield and on to the former company town of Clear Creek, where the houses have been acquired by private individuals for use as summer cabins. This 20-mile round-trip ride takes you through one of the most historic as well as scenic parts of the county. For those looking for a longer trip, leave the town of Scofield and head south along Hwy. 96 a couple of miles to the Eccles Canyon Scenic Byway (Hwy. 264) and turn west. This road intersects with the Skyline Drive and offers several possibilities: either return to Scofield, following the northern section of the Skyline Drive to Tucker on Hwy. 6; continue south along the middle section of the Skyline Drive; or follow Hwy. 31, down Huntington Canyon, a distance of just over

30 miles from the top of the mountain. The Tucker and Huntington routes are one-way rides requiring shuttle vehicles.

FISHING

Scofield Reservoir—

Located high in the mountains of the Wasatch Plateau at an elevation of 7,600 feet, Scofield Reservoir was constructed in the 1940s to impound waters on the upper Price River for irrigation. The reservoir is in Pleasant Valley, a most appropriate name for these lush meadowlands, where 19th-century cattlemen ranged their herds in the summer. The cool waters are ideal for trout, and the Utah Division of Wildlife Resources keeps the reservoir well stocked with rainbow trout. Native cutthroat trout also inhabit the reservoir and streams that flow into it. The reservoir is a popular place for fishermen during the summer and for ice fishing in the winter.

GOLF

Carbon Country Club Golf Course—

Built just after World War II, this course is the oldest golf course in the eastern half of the state. Located on Hwy. 6 about halfway between Price and Helper, the course is owned by the Carbon Country Club and Carbon County. In 1994 the course expanded to 18 holes and the new 9 holes, all but 8 of which are located to the south of the old course, offer an interesting contrast between the tree-lined, tight, mature front

9 and spacious open fairways on the back. The course can be busy during parts of the day as many local residents are avid golfers. An easy, pleasant course, it makes a wonderful stop on the road between Salt Lake City and southeastern Utah; **(801) 637-2388.**

SWIMMING

Price has an excellent swimming facility, located in the **Price Park.** An artificial wave pool called **Desert Wave** is open year-round; an inflated bubble is used during the winter to cover the outdoor facility. The complex also includes an indoor swimming pool, used primarily for lap swimming, water aerobics, and swimming team practices. Since few of the motels in the area have swimming pools, travelers with children whose first consideration is a swimming pool might want to make plans for a couple of hours at the Desert Wave. Operated by Price City, rates are quite reasonable for this type of facility. **500 North between 200 and 300 East; (801) 637-7946.**

TENNIS

There are six lighted tennis courts in the Price public park. The courts are just west of the College of Eastern Utah and are used by both college and high school students. There is usually one free. **400 North and 300 East.** For further information about schedules and reservations call **(801) 637-5762.**

———— SEEING AND DOING ————

CEMETERIES

Scofield Cemetery—
Located on a small rise in the eastern part of Scofield, the Scofield Cemetery contains the graves of 149 of the 200 victims of the Winter Quarters Mine Disaster, which occurred on May 1, 1900. The coal dust explosion and carbon monoxide poisoning left few survivors, and the coal camp of Winter Quarters and the town of Scofield were devastated by what, for that time, was the worst coal mining disaster in the history of the US. The youngest victim was 13 years old, 105 women were left without husbands, and 270 children lost their fathers. Condolences were sent by President William McKinley and foreign heads of state. The dead included 62 immigrant Finnish miners, among whom were seven sons and three grandsons of Abe Louma, the 70-year old patriarch of the family who, with his wife, had recently arrived from Finland to spend their last days with their family. Trenches for graves were dug, and wooden markers were produced at a local sawmill. Some of the wooden markers remain while more permanent stone markers were erected later by families for other victims. Other monuments to the disaster victims have also been erected.

CULTURAL ACTIVITIES

The College of Eastern Utah has a widespread reputation for its theatrical department and excellent productions are offered throughout the year. The college attracts special programs throughout the year, its basketball team provides exciting wintertime entertainment, and its wonderful museum is described below. For information about activities, call **(801) 637-2120.**

HISTORIC SITES

Castle Gate—
It takes little imagination to understand why Castle Gate is such an appropriate name for the massive rock formation on the east side of Hwy. 6, about 4 miles north of Helper. The top of the formation looks like a castle tower and, before the accompanying tower on the west side of the canyon was blasted away to make room for the present highway, the formation indeed looked like a gigantic castle gate being closed.

Hellenic Orthodox Church of the Assumption—

One of the buildings depicted in the mural inside the Price Municipal Building is the Hellenic Orthodox Church of the Assumption, located across the street, a block south of the Municipal Building. Constructed in 1916, the church is the oldest Greek Orthodox church in the state, preceding Salt Lake City's 1925 Holy Trinity Greek Orthodox Church by nearly a decade. The Price church was symbolic of the decision by Greek immigrants to remain in the US, and in Utah, rather than to return to their native Greece after they earned enough money to become economically self-sufficient.

Before the church was constructed, few Greek women came to Carbon County. But when the church was built, the few who were married sent for their wives and families; the majority who were single requested that Greek girls be sent over for them to marry. The church has been renovated three times—in 1940 to 1941, after a fire in 1945, and in 1961—but the basic Byzantine architectural style has been maintained. The original stained glass windows and icons had to be replaced after the 1945 fire, but the more recent ones are no less impressive. Paintings include those of the Old Testament prophets, the 12 apostles, the Virgin and Child, and inside the top of the dome, a symbolic representation of God the Father, surrounded by an angelic host, holding the world in his left hand. **61 South 200 East; (801) 637-0704.**

Millerich Hall—

When this building was first presented to the Utah Historic Sites Review Committee for nomination to the National Register of Historic Places, one of the committee members exclaimed, "That's the ugliest building I have ever seen!" Although it lacks architectural distinction, the building has served as a gathering place for Carbon County's Slovenian population since its construction in 1922. Indeed, while Millerich Hall is the historic name for the building, most people know it today as the Slovenian National Home. The present building replaced an older frame structure and was constructed mostly by striking Slovenian coal miners in 1922. In 1933, Millerich Hall became the National Miners Union headquarters for striking miners. Charged with being a communist-dominated union, the union leaders gave some credence to the charge by reportedly displaying a red flag with hammer, sickle, and a sheaf of wheat inside Millerich Hall. In the end the National Miners Union lost its strike, and its members joined the newly recognized United Mine Workers of America. In 1963 the hall was purchased from the Millerich family by members of the local Slovenian community and continues to serve social and recreational activities. Located on **Main St.** in the small town of **Spring Glen**, south of Helper about 2 miles.

Moynier House—

Just up the street from the Catholic church, the Moynier House, a private residence, has been occupied by the Moynier family since 1910. Although it is a typical frame box-style house of the time, the Moynier House has been listed in the National Register of Historic Places because of its association with the Moynier brothers, Honore (Henry) and Pierre, who left southern France in 1897. Working for five years at $30 a month as sheepherders, the two brothers saved their money until they could purchase sheep of their own in 1903. They became two of the most prominent sheepmen in eastern Utah. In 1910, the two brothers went to Bakersfield, California, a destination for many Basques, and there they married the Blanchard sisters whom they had known in southern France. Upon their return to Price, the four moved into the newly purchased house. **284 North Carbon Ave.**

Notre Dame de Lourdes Catholic Church—

Another immigrant church depicted in the Fausett Mural is the Notre Dame de Lourdes Catholic Church located two blocks west and two blocks north of the Price Municipal Building. Constructed of brick between 1919 and 1923, the architecture is bungalow style. Although Italian immigrants and their children made up the largest part of the Catholic population in Carbon County, the Price church reflects an attempt to recognize other Catholic groups—specifically French Basques who, by 1920, had become successful in the eastern Utah sheep industry and were major contributors for the construction of the church. Thus, while the Italians were represented in Helper with the naming of St. Anthony's Catholic Church for an Italian patron saint, in Price Notre Dame de Lourdes recalled the world-famous pilgrim city of Lourdes at the foot of the Pyrenees in southern France in the center of the French Basque homeland. **200 North Carbon Ave.**

Price Municipal Building—

After visiting the Prehistoric Museum (see the Seeing and Doing section) take a few minutes to go inside the foyer of the Price Municipal Building, constructed in 1938 through 1939 with local money and funds provided under the Works Progress Administration program of Franklin D. Roosevelt's New Deal. In addition to this good example of WPA architecture, the foyer contains a fascinating mural painted by Price-born artist, Lynn Fausett, as part of the Federal Arts Project of the WPA. Fausett includes 82 figures in 14 scenes on the 4-foot by 200-foot surface. The tableaux trace the early history of Carbon County, from the arrival of the first residents Abram Powell (yes, a relative of mine) and Caleb Rhodes, who entered the area as trappers in 1877 through the tremendous expansion of the local coal industry during World War I. On the east wall near the south end, there is a self-portrait of Lynn Fausett as a young boy, leading his blind Swiss immigrant grandfather, Hans Ulrich Bryner. Other scenes depict the construction of the Denver and Rio Grande Western Railroad through the area in 1882–83 by Chinese and European workers; wagon freighters

camped near the rail yards; early commercial establishments; early education efforts; a Fourth of July parade in 1911; and the diverse religious history of the county, with paintings of Catholic Bishop Lawrence Scanlan, the Greek Orthodox Priest Reverend Mark Petrakis, Methodist Reverend R. P. Nichols, and Mormon Bishop George Frandsen. A pamphlet available from the travel office explains the history depicted in the mural. Located on the corner of **200 East and Main St.**

MUSEUMS

College of Eastern Utah Prehistoric Museum—

The College of Eastern Utah Prehistoric Museum was established in 1961 by the college's geology professor, Don Burge, and a group of local rock hounds and rock art enthusiasts who were members of the Carbon County Jeep Posse. They took a geology night class that Burge offered, and in informal discussions after class, the idea of a museum to house local collections emerged. Originally located in an upstairs section of the Price Municipal Building, a newly constructed museum addition dwarfs its former home and provides an excellent facility for one of Utah's best museums.

The museum is divided into two general areas, the western wing, which is the dinosaur section and includes four skeletons from the Cleveland-Lloyd Dinosaur Quarry, 30 miles away. The replicas include an allosaurus, camptosaurus, camarasaurus, and stegosaurus. An extensive collection of dinosaur tracks found in the area's coal mines can be seen. Outside the building, an impressive 1979 bronze statue by Gary Prazen vividly depicts the life-and-death struggle between an allosaurus and a camptosaurus. Another skeleton, that of an 11,000-year-old mammoth found in Huntington Canyon in 1988, provides an excellent transition from the prehistoric animal life to the story of prehistoric man as ancient spear points and atlatl darts were found near the mammoth.

Located in the upstairs center section, and the east wing of the museum, the exhibits include a magnificent group of large photographs of rock art in the area and a full-size copy of a reproduction of the Barrier Canyon Rock Art Panel, located in Canyonlands National Park. A Ute teepee and a Fremont pithouse give examples of the lives of early Indians in the area.

The most unusual item on display is a collection of 10 unbaked clay figurines, approximately 4 to 5 inches long, which are presumed to date from the Fremont era 800–900 years ago. The figurines were discovered by Price resident Clarence Pilling in 1950, on a ranch he owned in the Range Creek area east of Price. Known as the "Pilling Figurines," the pieces are decorated with applied clay ornaments and body parts so that both sexes can be distinguished by their anatomy and dress. Open in summer 10 am–5 pm, Mon.–Sat., and Sun. noon–5 pm; in winter, Tues.–Sat. 10 am–4 pm **155 East Main St.; (801) 637-5060.**

Western Mining and Railroad Museum—

Housed in the 1913 YMCA building in the Helper Historic District, this local museum includes artifacts and exhibits on the history of coal mining and railroading in the region. The interior configuration of the YMCA has not been altered since it was constructed, and you can imagine what the three-story building with basement was like during the heyday of railroad operations in the town.

Railroading and mining history are portrayed with model trains, coal mine diagrams and models, material on the coal camps, including company stores, the miners union, and the major mine disasters of 1900, 1924, and 1984. Outside the building are large pieces of mining equipment and a caboose formerly used on the Utah Railway. Community life is also commemorated in exhibits of an old dentist and doctor's office, a pre-World War II beauty shop, a bootlegger's still from Prohibition days, wine-making equipment used by the area's Italians, an old iron jail cage, and the

first two steps from the 1890 Pleasant Valley Coal Company in Castle Gate, which was the site of the 1897 Butch Cassidy Payroll Robbery. The artifacts are of special interest to railroad and mining buffs, but one of the most enjoyable aspects of the museum is the volunteers. Retired miners, railroad men, and women answer questions about the museum and offer spontaneous stories about life in the area. Open from mid-May–Sept., Mon.–Sat. 9 am–5 pm. During the rest of the year, visits can be arranged by calling the telephone number posted on the door or by inquiring at City Hall, farther up Main St. **294 South Main; (801) 472-3009.**

SCENIC DRIVES

Eccles Canyon Scenic Byway—
See the **Sanpete Valley** chapter.

Indian Canyon Scenic Byway—

This mountain drive along Hwy. 191 leaves Hwy. 6 about 2 miles north of Helper and heads up Willow Creek past the Castle Gate Power Plant and the old Castle Gate Cemetery where town residents and victims of the 1924 coal mine explosion are buried. About 7 miles up-canyon, the road is intersected by another road coming in from the west. At this junction is the Bamberger Monument, a sandstone monument that was placed at this location by convicts from the state penitentiary who were sent to Carbon County to work on the road. The monument, according to tradition, was erected in gratitude to Governor Simon Bamberger for allowing the prisoners to work on the project. A German Jew born in Eberstadt, Germany, Simon Bamberger was Utah's first non-Mormon governor from 1917 until 1921. Just north of the monument, the road crosses into Duchesne County and reaches the summit of Indian Creek Pass at 9,100 feet. Passing through the Ashley National Forest, the vegetation ranges from pinon and juniper to aspen and Douglas fir. The road is especially beautiful during the autumn foliage. Elk and deer are often visible. From the summit, the road descends the left fork of Indian Canyon until it intersects with the right fork. The 50-mile road intersects with Hwy. 40 at Duchesne.

Nine-Mile Canyon—

One of the scenic drives not to be missed in eastern Utah is the road through Nine-Mile Canyon, which contains some of the best rock art to be found in Utah. The Fremont pictograph panels include human figures, birds, snakes, other animals, and designs. The canyon was named during Major John Wesley Powell's first expedition to explore the Green and Colorado rivers in 1869, when Frank M. Bishop did a 9-mile triangulation along what was named Nine Mile Creek. In the mid-1880s, a route was opened through the canyon to transport supplies from the Denver and Rio Grande Railroad at Price to the US Army post at Fort Duchesne. By 1889, the canyon had become became a two-way transportation route, with returning supply wagons hauling gilsonite, mined in the vicinity of the fort, back to the railroad at Price. Because of the distances involved, stage stops were established, and a telegraph line was erected to improve communications. The canyon was also used by ranchers beginning in the 1880s. The most famous of the canyon's ranches, the Nutter Ranch, was established by Preston Nutter in 1902.

The old homesteads, ranches, and stage stops are interesting, but most people visit the canyon to see the Fremont Indian rock art panels scattered throughout the canyon. Both pictographs and petroglyphs can be found along the walls, while higher up on the cliffs storage granaries and other structures dating back at least 700 years can be spotted. Binoculars are a must in order to located many of these structures. Travelers should plan the better part of a day for a good introduction to the canyon.

A Guide to Rock Art in Nine Mile Canyon, written by Mary and Jim Liddiard, can be purchased at the College of Eastern Utah Museum in Price, or pick up a free brochure from the Castle Country Travel Region, which also lists mileage and what to see. Both are highly recommended—otherwise many of the sites will go unnoticed. The Nine-Mile Canyon Rd. is located 7.5 miles east of Price off Hwy. 6. It heads north just beyond the town of Wellington. The paved road becomes gravel after 12 miles, but the road is usually in good condition and easily passable in a passenger car. The first major panels of petroglyphs are located about 26 miles after turning off Hwy. 6. Panels and other ruins are located throughout the canyon for the next 25 miles.

TOURS

Spring Canyon—

The 11 mines located in Spring Canyon beginning in 1912 can be reached by turning west at the corner of the Mining Museum and driving across Hwy. 6, then turning right (north) to follow the road as it cuts up the hill. At the top of the hill, the road heads west again, passing through the Castle Gate Subdivision (a mid-1970s development to house Castle Gate residents displaced when their town was demolished to expand coal operations). Beyond the Castle Gate Subdivision, the road enters Spring Canyon. Near the mouth of the canyon was the site of another gun battle between Greek strikers and company guards in 1922. When the coal company tried to bring in Mexican strike-breakers to take the place of strikers, young Greeks hidden in the rocks above the railroad opened fire upon armed guards accompanying the train. Arthur V. Webb was killed and four other men, including one Greek, were wounded. Spring Canyon was a heavily populated area, with 11 mines in less than 5 miles. Some of the mining towns included Peerless, Storrs, Standardville, Latuda, and Rains.

Clear Creek—

Located 6 miles south of Scofield, at an elevation of 8,300 feet, this is the highest and most picturesque of all the Carbon County coal camps. The **Clear Creek Mine** was opened around the turn of the century and the company town established shortly afterward. Signs of the coal operations remain, and coal-producing mines continue to operate in nearby Eccles Canyon. The former company houses have been sold to private individuals, mostly for summer residences.

Gordon Creek—

The Gordon Creek area is reached by heading west from the Helper Mining Museum to Hwy. 6 and turning left (south) for 2.3 miles to the Consumers Rd. Development of the area began in 1923, when the mining towns of National, Sweets, and Consumers were located approximately 15 miles up the canyon. In the 1930s, Eldon Dorman was employed by the Medical Association, comprised of both company and union men, that represented the three mining towns. His humorous and insightful experiences as a coal camp doctor are recounted in a publication edited by Philip F. Notarianni, entitled *Carbon County: Eastern Utah's Industrialized Island* (published by the Utah State Historical Society and available for purchase at the Helper Mining Museum). Lower down the canyon is the site of Coal City, formerly Dempseyville, after the world-famous boxer, Jack Dempsey, who spent time training there and considered investing part of his earnings in the nearby coal mines. When he decided not to invest, his indiscretion was rewarded by restoring the original name of Coal City. The canyon is still an active coal mining area so watch out for the large coal trucks that roll up and down the canyon.

Historic Coal Mining Areas—

The abandoned coal camps are unique attractions in this area. Pick up a copy of local historian Frances Cunningham's booklet, "Driving Tour Guide: Selected Abandoned Coal Mine Sites—Castle Coal Country Carbon and Emery Counties," from the Helper Mining Museum. The guide includes nine tours to mining districts throughout the two counties. Three major areas can be visited within a 15-mile radius of Helper.

Kenilworth—

Follow Helper's Main St. south from the Mining Museum for 1.3 miles, then turn left (east) into the community of Spring Glen and follow the Kenilworth Rd. east, then northeast, for 4.7 miles to the town of Kenilworth. This is one of the few company towns left in Utah and offers a spectacular view of the mountains and the valley below. The town was built by the Independent Coal and Coke Company which, as reflected in its name, was the first coal company in Carbon County to successfully challenge the monopoly of the Denver and Rio Grande-controlled Utah Fuel Company and Pleasant Valley Coal Company. Although the mining operations have ceased and the buildings have been sold to private individuals, the company store, the tramway, miners' homes, and other buildings remain. Kenilworth was the site of a confrontation between Greek miners and the coal company in 1911. The Greeks maintained that the company had cheated them out of pay they were due. When the Greek miners were fired for voicing their complaint, they took up positions in the rocks to the north, above the town. In the ensuing gun battle that sent bullets flying into company buildings and miners' houses, the American-born Thomas Jackson and the Greek-born Steve Kolasakis were killed.

Reflections on the Ancients—

Guided tours in four-wheel-drive vehicles by Jeanette Evans, a certified avocational archaeologist, can be arranged for the Nine-Mile Canyon area or the San Rafael Swell in nearby Emery County. This is an excellent way to see the ancient Indian writings of southeastern Utah. **PO Box 444, Wellington, UT 84542; (801) 637-5801** or **1-800-468-4060.**

WHERE TO STAY

ACCOMMODATIONS
PRICE
Carriage House Inn—$$

Restaurant, swimming pool, hot tub; 41 rooms. **590 East Main; (801) 637-5660** or **1-800-228-5732.**

Days Inn—$$$

Indoor swimming pool, hot tub, sauna, and restaurant; 148 rooms. Just off Hwy. 6 at the West Price exit. **838 Westwood Blvd.; (801) 637-8880** or **1-800-325-2525.**

Green Well Inn—$$

Restaurant; 125 rooms. **655 East Main; (801) 637-3520, 637-3520,** or **1-800-666-3520.**

Price River Inn National 9—$$

Ninety-four rooms. **641 Price River Dr.; (801) 637-7000.**

WELLINGTON
National 9 Inn—$$ to $$$

Restaurant, indoor swimming pool; 53 rooms. **720 East Main, Hwy. 6; (801) 637-7980** or **1-800-524-9999.**

CAMPGROUNDS
PRIVATE
El Rancho Motel and RV Park (Budget Host Inn of Price)—

This is a full-service RV park, open year-round, with 34 complete hookups, showers, a Laundromat, and heated pool during the summer. **145 North Carbonville Rd.; (801) 637-2424.**

Mountain View RV Park—

Twenty spaces with full hookups. Showers and adjacent restaurant. Located next to the National 9 Motel, guests have use of the motel's indoor swimming pool. Open year-round. **50 South 700 East, Wellington, UT 84542; (801) 637-7980.**

PUBLIC
Price Canyon Recreation Area—

Maintained by the BLM, there are 18 RV trailer and tent sites. Picnic tables, drinking water, and flush toilets. Open June–mid-Oct. Located off Hwy. 6 in Price Canyon, 18 miles northwest of Price.

Scofield State Park—

Two campgrounds at Scofield State Park provide camping opportunities Apr.–Nov. at this popular recreation area. Madsen Bay has 100 units; Mountain View offers 34 units. Modern restrooms, showers, handicap accessible area, and two boat launching ramps; **(801) 448-9449.**

WHERE TO EAT

China City—$ to $$

For Chinese and American dishes, at inexpensive prices, China City is a long-time favorite. Open daily 11 am–10 pm. **350 East Main; (801) 637-8211.**

Fairlaino's—$$ to $$$

The historic Mahlares and Sampinos Building, constructed in the 1910s for two Price Greek businessmen, has been recently renovated. Listed in the National Register of Historic Places, the building has included a restaurant on its main floor since its

construction. The present restaurant, Fairlaino's, has been in the building since 1987. Sam Fairlaino's grandparents came from San Giovanni in Fiore, Italy, and many of the recipes Sam prepares, including the homemade sausage, can be traced back to his grandparents' village in Calabria. Sam's menu proclaims, "To the Italians, every meal is an occasion for joy and togetherness to be enjoyed in a congenial atmosphere. It is a special time for family or friends to forget the cares of the day and enjoy the true meaning of life. It should be

CASTLE GATE PAYROLL ROBBERY

When you stop at the overlook to Castle Gate along Hwy. 6, about 4 miles north of Helper, you will find information about Utah's early coal industry, a monument to the 172 men who died in the Castle Gate Mine Explosion on March 8, 1924, and, if you put your imagination in gear, you can visualize an earlier event that took place on April 21, 1897. That day a 5-foot-5-inch-tall sunburned red head, and a 5-foot-10-inch, blue-eyed, light-complexioned companion robbed the Pleasant Valley Coal Company of $8,800 in gold and silver. The money was to meet the monthly payroll for several hundred men working at the Castle Gate mine and coke ovens. The gold was in two bags and the silver in another. After holding up the paymaster just outside the office building, the two men jumped on their horses. The bag of silver proved too cumbersome and when it fell to the ground, the robbers simply left it. As they made their getaway, coal company employees fired at them with rifles and the bandits returned the fire with their revolvers; however, no one was hit by the flying bullets. A railroad engine was pressed into service and several armed men rode it south to the city of Helper in an unsuccessful attempt to catch the thieves. Word of the robbery was delayed when the outlaws cut the telegraph wires. When the surrounding communities were finally notified, posses were sent out from Castle Gate, Helper, Price, Huntington, Castle Dale, and Green River. By nightfall the men, Butch Cassidy and Elza Lay, made their way to the San Rafael River and the next day rode on to Robbers Roost. The coal company offered a $4,000 reward for the capture of the robbers and the return of the money. But Cassidy and Lay made good their escape, repaying friends and accomplices with gold pieces during the next several months.

casual and unhurried with each course savored to its fullest." Italian dishes are offered Wed.–Sat. 5:30 pm–10 pm. The rest of the day Sam serves American-style breakfasts 7 am–11 am, then sandwiches, salads, soups, and daily lunch specials 11 am–2 pm. The evening meal is a special occasion, but Fairlaino's is also a place to pick up on the local gossip. Fairlaino family artifacts such as his grandfather's wine barrel and wine press, photographs, including one of Harry S. Truman during his campaign stop at the Price railroad station in 1948, and authentic copies at each table of the local weekly newspaper, the *Eastern Utah Advocate,* from the 1890s, are used to decorate the restaurant. Be sure to ask Sam about the Italian marble that was originally used in the restaurant and the use of the bell hidden behind the counter. **87 West Main; (801) 637-9217.**

Greek Streak—$ to $$

As the only Greek restaurant in a community with a strong Greek ethnic heritage, the restaurant is patronized by a wide spectrum of Carbon County residents. Owner George Gianoulias came to Price from Crete in 1956, after his uncle, a 1910 immigrant who had never married and had no family, returned to his village to persuade a family member to return with him to America. Twenty-three-year-old George took up the offer, left the village of Kare and its 500 residents, and came to Price, where he worked in one of the old Greek coffeehouses owned by his uncle on Carbon Ave. south of Main St. George returned to Crete and married his present wife Katherine. The couple returned to Price and opened the Greek Streak to raise money to put their two children through college. Their son Tony, an athletic scholar in high school, was nicknamed "The Greek Streak," hence the name of the restaurant. The proud parents have even hung their son's letterman's jacket as part of the restaurant decor.

Using traditional recipes from Crete, Katherine and George offer gyros, lamb roast, lamb stew, dolmades, lentil soup, lemon rice soup, Greek village salads, and other items. But save room for Katherine's Greek pastries, which are considered the best in the state. Baklava, kataifi, koulourakia, honey-nut cookies, and rolls, are the regular choices. Open from 8 am–9 pm Mon.–Sat.

84 South Carbon Ave. in one of the old Greek coffeehouses; **(801) 637-1930.**

SERVICES

Castle Country Travel Council—
Located in the College of Eastern Utah Prehistoric Museum at **155 East Main, PO**
Box 1037, Price, UT 84501; (801) 637-3009 or **1-800-842-0789.**

Mural of Sunnyside factory, circa 1917, in the Price city hall building. Photo by Allan Kent Powell.

Emery County

I suppose there is some basic psychological explanation as to why, even though I have lived in the Salt Lake Valley for a quarter of a century, when I am asked "Where are you from?" I still respond with unbridled loyalty, "Emery County!" My response is not unique, at least among my child-hood friends, with whom I still get together on a regular basis. Like me, they still subscribe to the *Emery County Progress,* the weekly paper that has been published continuously since 1900. They still make annual pilgrimages from homes along Utah's urban Wasatch Front, California, and other islands of exile, to participate in such Emery County rituals as the fall deer hunt, amateur rodeos, family reunions at Ferron Reservoir or Old Folks Flat, and to celebrate the end of winter and the promise of summer by going "eastering" on the desert.

One old-timer concluded that this seemingly excessive tie to the land was due to a secret addictive quality of alkali. The area developed an unwanted reputation for being alkaline when excessive irrigation water leeched minerals from the hay fields and pastures and left them as a white, sometimes yellow-looking crust. This is particularly true along the roads bisecting the thin edge of settlement between the hills and mountains of the Wasatch Plateau to the west and the beautiful but uninhabitable canyons and formations of the torrid San Rafael Desert to the east. Whether it is alkali in the blood, as my old-time friend claims, recollections of a childhood and youth grounded in a community in which everyone was a unique and essential part of the whole, or a new recognition of the land's inherent beauty, Emery County remains the center of this man's world.

There are three major physiographical areas within Emery County— the Wasatch Plateau, Castle Valley, and the San Rafael Swell. The highest area is the Wasatch Plateau which reaches over 11,000 feet in some places, stretching from north to south for 70 miles and east to west from about 15 to 25 miles. Four major creeks, fed by numerous springs and smaller streams, flow out of the Wasatch Plateau. The southernmost is the Muddy, which joins with the Fremont River at Hanksville to become the Dirty Devil River which flows into the Colorado River—now Lake Powell at Hite Crossing. The Huntington, Cottonwood, and Ferron creeks join east of Castle Dale to form the San Rafael River which flows into the Green River above its confluence with the Colorado River.

The oldest rocks in the county are from the Coconino Sandstone Formation and date back 250 million years ago. Cycles of dry and wet periods led to the variety of geological layers that are found within the county. Seas periodically covered the area leaving deposits of siltstone, limestone, and sandstone. Massive sand dunes produced the Wingate and Navajo sandstone formations. The Morrison Formation, the source of dinosaur bones found at the Cleveland-Lloyd Quarry, developed about 110 million years ago at a time when large forests of giant trees and shallow lakes covered the land. Seas returned to cover the area for 60 million years about 100 million years ago. The deposits left during this last great period of oceans and seas make up the Mancos Shell Formation which can be found throughout Castle Valley and the San Rafael Swell area.

The San Rafael Swell is a massive 75-mile-long, 30-mile-wide anticlinal uplift created about 65 million years ago during the mountain-building period known as the Laramide Orogeny. The San Rafael Swell was created at the same time as the Waterpocket Fold to the south in Capitol Reef National Park. The most dramatic view of the Swell is on the south and east sides which is known as the San Rafael Reef and looks like the teeth of a gigantic saw thrust upward through the valley floor. A northern extension of the uplift is Cedar Mountain. The forces of erosion have shaped narrow canyons, buttes, pinnacles, and cliffs in the San Rafael Swell. The entire area is usually referred to by locals as "the desert," but that term does not do justice to the region. The highest point of the San Rafael Swell is nearly 8,000 feet in elevation. The eroded "castles" of the Swell give the region its name. On the Swell you will find landmarks such as the Little Grand Canyon, Sids Mountain, Buckhorn Draw, Windowblind Butte, the Black Dragon, Sinbad Valley, the Chute, and hundreds of other names used to identify the nooks and crannies of this remarkable land. The San Rafael Swell remains unoccupied. Recreation, livestock grazing, and limited mining are the principal activities on the Swell.

Some 25 million or so years after the San Rafael Swell developed, the Wasatch Plateau was also created by an uplift. Later, within the plateau, faults created grabens or valleys as the land surface sunk, leaving mountains on either side from 1,500 to 3,000 feet different in elevation on either side.

Castle Valley, located between the San Rafael Swell on the east and the Wasatch Plateau on the west, is a relatively flat lowland plain interrupted here and there by small hills and benchlands of Mancos shell. It is here that the string of towns and farms along and not far from Hwy. 10 can be found.

HISTORY

The beginning of man's occupation of Emery County is as mysterious as the painted, tapered human forms and insect people found on the rock walls of canyons in the San Rafael region. What adds to the mystery about these early people is that the rock art they have left, some painted over earlier works, indicates that pictographs and petroglyphs that attract so much interest today were inscribed over a period of hundreds, if not thousands, of years. Known as the Barrier Canyon style, for the 8-foot-tall anthropomorphs in Barrier Canyon, just across the county line in present-day Wayne County, this rock art style found throughout southeastern Utah, Arizona, and Colorado, finds its northwesternmost expression in Emery County.

In 1984 archeologists discovered more than a thousand Folsom artifacts in a location south of Green River. The find indicates that the site was used over a long period of time by members of the Folsom culture and is probably the earliest village site within the state of Utah. Prior to the Green River discovery, only a few isolated Folsom points had been found within the state boundaries. In 1975, excavations by University of Utah archaeologists at Cowboy Cave, in the southeastern corner of Emery County not far from Barrier Canyon, indicate that prehistoric occupation of the region may not have been continuous. Within the cave they discovered three distinct periods of occupation: approximately 5625 BC to 4400 BC; 1685 BC to 1380 BC; and 60 AD to 455 AD. The 1988 discovery of the Huntington Reservoir Mammoth with manmade spear points nearby, indicates that early man ranged from the deserts and canyons of the San Rafael to the alpine meadows of the Wasatch Plateau.

As cattlemen and herders in the 1870s pushed into the Castle Valley area from Sanpete Valley and other locations to the west and north, they came across the remnants of these prehistoric cultures and undoubtedly wondered about a people whose rock paintings depicted unearthly forms and whose lifeways seemed so alien to their own. Those who eventually settled Emery County did so because of the lack of water and land in the older Mormon settlements which their parents had settled; the opportunities which Castle Valley held for them; and strong encouragement from Mormon Church leaders, including Brigham Young who, one week before he died, wrote to Canute Peterson, leader of the Mormon settlements in Sanpete Valley, on August 22, 1877, "There are number of the brethren in different portions of Sanpete County, who have not an abundant supply of water for their land, who would, no doubt, be happy to remove to a valley where the water is abundant and the soil good. We should like to have at least fifty families locate in Castle Valley this fall. ... In making your selection choose good, energetic God fearing young men, whether single or with families, and others who can be spared without interfering with the interests of the settlements in which they now reside."

For a people who see God's hand in almost everything, this last act by Brigham Young has been interpreted two ways. Emery County boosters interpret Brigham's death seven days later, following the August

22 letter, as "The Great Colonizer's" crowning achievement. After three decades of organizing and promoting the establishment of hundreds of settlements throughout the intermountain West, the climax of his career was to launch the settlement of Castle Valley. As reward for this accomplishment, Brigham Young was taken directly into heaven. Detractors conclude, however, that with the "call" to settle Castle Valley, it was obvious that Brigham Young was no longer an inspired leader, and in a fit of revenge and out of concern for his Mormon kingdom, God had no other choice but to remove the errant leader permanently.

Between 1880 and 1900, Emery County made a gradual transition from frontier homesteads, where 90 percent of the 453 residents were farmers or ranchers, to a string of communities whose 4,657 residents, while still mostly farmers, also included saloon keepers, musicians, ministers, teachers, a watch maker, and a life insurance salesman. The permanence of the new settlements of Emery, Ferron, Castle Dale, Orangeville, and Huntington was reflected in the construction of numerous brick homes at the turn of the century (several of which can still be seen in Castle Dale today) and civic and religious buildings in the communities, of which the Emery Church and the Castle Dale School are the best remaining examples. By 1910, the population of the entire county approached 7,000 and remained fairly consistent at that figure until after World War II. By 1970, it had dropped to around 5,000, only to rise dramatically in the energy boom during the 1970s. Today, coal mining and energy production are the key industries within the county. Third- and fourth-generation residents still farm and ranch, but perhaps more as a hobby than as the primary source of income. Though relatively undeveloped, recreation and tourism become more important each year, and civic leaders are pursuing plans that will preserve, promote, and make more accessible the unique history and resources of this area.

GETTING THERE

Emery County is located in southeastern Utah, approximately 140 miles south-southeast of Salt Lake City. Travelers from the north enter the county via Hwy. 10, after leaving Hwy. 6 at Price. Travelers on Interstate 70 exit at Fremont Junction, exit 89, and take Hwy. 10 north through the communities of Emery, Ferron, Castle Dale, and Huntington.

MAJOR ATTRACTIONS

Cleveland Lloyd Dinosaur Quarry

The Cleveland-Lloyd Dinosaur Quarry has been a source of fossil bones since 1928, when University of Utah scientists conducted the first dig at the site. Thousands of bones have been removed from the quarry for use in dinosaur reconstructions in museums located throughout the United States, Europe, and the Far East. Reconstructions of the quarry's most famous dinosaur, the allosaurus, an earlier version of the fearsome Tyrannosaurus Rex, can be seen in the Prehistoric Museum in Price and the Museum of the San Rafael in Castle Dale. The BLM runs a visitor center, with information and an exhibit, usually open weekends 10 AM–5 PM Easter weekend–Memorial Day. (Open weekends and some week days during the summer months.) To get there, follow signs east from Hwy. 10 to Cleveland then drive east on a gravel road for 12 miles. From the quarry visitor center you can take two driving tours. The shorter tour goes 7 miles southeast from the quarry to the rim of Humbug Canyon, where you can follow a .5-mile hiking trail to the bottom of the canyon. The longer drive, 252 miles long, follows along the rim of Cedar Mountain for breathtaking views of the San Rafael Swell to the south. Keep an eye out for pronghorn antelope. Brochures describing the tours are available at the center.

Huntington State Park

Located 2 miles north of Huntington, Huntington State Park includes the 129-acre Huntington North Reservoir, which was constructed in 1965–1966 by the US Bureau of Reclamation for the Emery County Conservancy District. With a maximum storage capacity of 5,600 acre-feet of water for irrigation use in the northern section of the county, and located just outside of Huntington, the reservoir is an ideal place for waterskiing and fishing for local residents and travelers. A 111-acre area around the lake was developed as a state park in 1969. Twenty-two camping units, a group pavilion area, picnic tables, modern restrooms, showers, and a sewage disposal facility are available within the park. A modest fee is charged.

Mill Site State Park

The Millsite Reservoir is a 500-acre, multipurpose reservoir constructed between 1969 and 1971 4 miles west of Ferron. The reservoir provides irrigation water for farms in the southern end of Emery County, domestic water for the city of Ferron, water for the Hunter Power Plant located between Ferron and Castle Dale, flood control, and recreation opportunities. The state park includes 20 camping units, two group shelters with 16 picnic tables, and smaller picnic areas around the reservoir. In 1989, a 9-hole golf course, the first in Emery County, was constructed adjacent to the state park (see Golfing in the Outdoors Activities section).

FESTIVALS AND EVENTS

Castle Valley Pageant

1st week in August

I can think of no more dramatic backdrop for a pageant than this one. Located on one of the side hills of East Mountain, the setting offers tremendous views of the towns of Orangeville and Castle Dale below and panoramic vistas of the San Rafael Desert with landmarks like Buckhorn Draw and Window Blind Peak visible to the east. The pageant depicts the settlement of Castle Valley in the late 1870s and portrays, in dialogue and song, historical incidents that demonstrate the hardship, commitment, community spirit, and humor of pioneer life. Before each performance writer/producer Montell Seely discusses

Castle Valley history and points out some of the landmarks visible to the audience, while covered wagons pulled by teams of horses make a half-hour journey northward from the bench below up the ridge to the performance site. That dramatic journey will remain etched in the audience's minds forever as a reminder of the pace of life in an earlier day and how tenuous man's hold on this land has been. Since seating is limited, go on a weekday if possible, and plan to arrive an hour or so early. Attendees are welcome to wander through the pageant site and visit with the performers or view one of several demonstrations such as wagon wheel making, sheep shearing, cow milking, or mule outfitting. Before driving up to the pageant site, plan a visit to the **Castle Dale City Park** where locals serve a traditional mutton dinner, offer historical demonstrations, and provide other activities for young and old alike. For information call **(801) 381-2311** or **381-2195.**

Heritage Days
end of June through beginning of July

As a youth, next to Christmas, July in Huntington was the most exciting time of the year, with celebrations July 4th and also on July 24th, Pioneer Day. Although the two celebrations were wonderful for the children, the effort eventually proved too much for those responsible for all the activities. Today, a compromise Heritage Days has been established, with activities extending from the last few days of June–1st weekend in July. Events include a parade, programs, softball tournaments, little league baseball games, contests, and a rodeo.

Ferron Peach Days
1st weekend in September

Ferron Peach Days is probably the oldest continuous celebration in Emery County and southeastern Utah. One of several areas of the state known for its peaches, Ferron commemorates the peach harvest with a three-day celebration that includes a queen pageant, horse races, road races, a golf tournament, a parade, exhibits, a children's carnival, a dance, and fireworks.

———— OUTDOOR ACTIVITIES ————

BIKING

Emery County offers two excellent areas for mountain bikers. The San Rafael area is preferable in the spring and fall, while the high Wasatch Plateau attracts riders in the summer. The free "Mountain Bike Trail Guide," published by the Castle Country Travel Council, describes a number of routes in the area. The following are some of my favorites.

Head of Sinbad—

Drive southeast about 16 miles along the road from the San Rafael Campground until you reach Interstate 70, then continue on the Interstate west about 6 miles. Exit where a road passes under the Interstate to provide access to the area on both sides of the highway. Once off the Interstate, you can ride south to Swasey's Cabin and the cave the Swaseys called "the refrigerator," where the cool temperatures allowed them to store meat during the summer. Although it dates only from the 1920s, the cabin is one of the oldest remaining structures on the desert. Up a side canyon on the south side of the Interstate are a series of pictographs, one of which locals refer to as "The Devil in the Pasture." It is a red anthropomorph about 3 feet tall with a round shield and a head somewhat square with projecting "horns." On the north side of the Interstate are other examples, including the "Bug-eyed Man," an anthropomorph with a long body, short appendages for legs and arms, and two large circles— "eyes"— in a rectangular head. A snake figure is drawn just above the head. From the Swasey Cabin to the Head of Sinbad

Overlook and the rock art on the north side of the Interstate is a ride of about 12 miles over relatively flat dirt roads with some soft sand.

Joe's Valley—

The verdant mountains to the west offer an attractive contrast to the sandstone of the San Rafael Desert. Perhaps the best-known route is the Skyline Drive, which, on a hot July or Aug. day in Utah, can be a refreshing ride in 60–70-degree temperatures. (See the **Sanpete Valley** chapter for a description of the route.) Below the Skyline Drive, within the boundaries of Emery County, is the Huntington Reservoir–Joe's Valley Rd. The road leaves Hwy. 31 east of Huntington Reservoir and traverses about 30 miles through Scad Valley beneath Bald Mountain and Bald Ridge, to Upper Joe's Valley and Hwy. 29 near Joe's Valley Reservoir. This is a beautiful alpine ride that climbs from about 7,000 feet to more than 8,500 feet in elevation. This ride can be made as an out-and-back ride, a loop ride from Joe's Valley using the Miller Flat Rd. and Lowry Water Rd., or shuttle vehicles can pick up riders at Joe's Valley Reservoir or, in Orangeville, after a 19-mile ride down Straight Canyon along Hwy. 29.

Railroad Grade—

The old railroad grade across Buckhorn Flat, along the base of Cedar Mountain, was completed in the early 1880s, but never used because the Denver and Rio Grande Railroad decided to head north to Salt Lake City rather than to continue west. The ties and rails were never laid, so you have a relatively smooth and level ride for most of the 22-mile round trip. This is both a scenic and historic ride. Side trails branch off the main route to lead to Fremont rock art and rock inscriptions left by railroad workers. The trail begins near the large power transmission line just north of The Wedge turnoff at Buckhorn Well. Gravel roads from Cleveland, Huntington, and Castle Dale lead to the trailhead.

River Road—

The San Rafael Campground makes a good starting point for bikers. One popular route is to follow the Mexican Mountain Rd. southeastward for approximately 16 miles, along the north side of the San Rafael River, until you reach Mexican Mountain. Near the end of the road, a short side trail leads to an overlook of the Black Box. The 32-mile, out-and-back ride has some short, steep grades, and a 4-mile-long gradual grade off Indian Bench.

The Wedge—

Not far from the Railroad Grade trailhead, the desert road branches, with the righthand fork heading out to The Wedge, the middle fork continuing to Buckhorn Wash, and the left fork going east to intersect with Hwy. 6 north of Green River.

Take the right fork to The Wedge and drive south .5 mile, then take the left fork and continue about 4 miles to another fork in the road where you can start your ride. Continue along the main road through the cedar trees for about 2 miles, until you come to The Wedge Overlook and its spectacular view of the Little Grand Canyon of the San Rafael River. From the overlook you can ride along the rim of the canyon in both directions for ever-changing views of the canyon. Out-and-back distance, with rides to both ends of the overlook road, is about 10 miles. You can shorten the ride by 4 miles by driving all the way to The Wedge Overlook, parking your vehicle, and riding along the rim road. This is an easy ride, with little elevation change. Keep an eye out for vehicles along the roads, however, and stop frequently along the rim for the scenic views into the canyons.

FISHING

Whether you want small, fast-flowing streams, high mountain lakes, or human-made reservoirs, Emery County give you a wide range of fishing possibilities.

Cottonwood Creek—

As the middle of three streams that join below Castle Dale to form the San

Rafael River, Cottonwood Creek flows through the towns of Orangeville and Castle Dale. Above Orangeville, the creek follows the general route of Hwy. 29 from Joe's Valley Reservoir, attracting the attention of fly fishermen in search of the trout that live in the stream.

Ferron Creek—

Emery County's 3rd fly-fishing stream, Ferron Creek has holes with brown trout, both above and below the Millsite Reservoir.

Ferron Reservoir—

Located high on the Wasatch Plateau, above Ferron, this reservoir is well stocked with trout and is popular with both fly and lure fishermen.

Huntington Canyon Reservoirs—

High in the upper meadows of the Wasatch Plateau, in Huntington Canyon, several small reservoirs—Cleveland, Huntington, Boulger, Millers Flat, and other reservoirs—were constructed to store irrigation water for the farms in the valley below. They offer good fishing for trout and are generally uncrowded, at least on weekdays, during the summer.

Huntington River—

Located along Hwy. 31, this was my first experience with fishing. My father and older brother used to take me on regular trips "up the canyon," to try and teach me the intricacies of fly-fishing. Brown trout are the usual yield from the stream. The left hand, or south fork, of the Huntington is a beautiful stream that runs through a narrow canyon away from the highway traffic.

Joe's Valley Reservoir—

As the largest lake in Emery County and as the source for some of the largest trout taken in the area (browns up to 13 pounds and rainbows up to 5 pounds), Joe's Valley is one of the most popular fishing spots in the area. The reservoir was constructed during the mid-1960s in a valley pioneers named for Joe, an Indian who helped them during their trek across the mountain from Sanpete Valley to settle Castle Valley in the 1870s.

Millsite Reservoir—

As part of Millsite State Park, the reservoir is a popular fishing spot because of its easy access and abundance of rainbow and cutthroat trout.

FOUR-WHEEL-DRIVE TRIPS

Four-wheel-drive vehicles provide an opportunity to see much of this beautiful county, which otherwise would not be accessible, except to backpackers and day hikers. Visitors can thank Owen McClenahan for his wonderful book *Utah's Scenic San Rafael*, which includes descriptions of nearly a dozen four-wheel-drive trips on the San Rafael. Self-published in 1986, *Utah's Scenic San Rafael* is the result of Owen's 35 years of traveling the desert, studying the geology, finding rock art, and collecting stories from old-timers in the area. Owen McClenahan is one of those people that Edward Abbey, in his classic *Desert Solitare*, calls "desert rats." ("There are mountain men, there are men of the sea, and there are desert rats.") McClenahan shares his experience and knowledge of the area with the reader in such a personal way that you feel the "old desert rat" himself is not only talking to you, but steering your jeep, as you wind through the rocks and up the canyons of the San Rafael. The routes described include the Wedge Loop, Buchhorn Wash Loop, Mexican Bend Loop, Head of Sinbad Loop, Copper Globe Loop, Coal Wash Loop, East San Rafael Reef Loop, Temple Mountain Loop, Hondoo Loop, and the Dinosaur Quarry and Cedar Mountain Loop. McClenahan also gives an excellent description of the boating trip from Fuller Bottoms to the Swinging Bridge over the San Rafael River. The paperback book can be purchased at the museums in Castle Dale and the Prehistoric Museum in Price. Here is one of my favorite trips.

Copper Globe Loop—

The loop begins off Interstate 70 at exit 129. Head south of the Interstate for a mile to Justesen Flat, where deer and and on rare occasions wild horses can be seen. This was a popular place for old-time cowboys to chase wild horses, so let your imagination conjure up what it must have been like for a group of a dozen or so mounted cowboys to race across the flat, lariats twirling over their heads, in pursuit of a band of free-roaming horses. Beyond Justesen Flat, you cross Devil's Canyon, which drains into the Muddy River. Six miles from Interstate 70, you come upon a monument to Henry H. Jensen, of Mayfield—a small town located west across the Wasatch Plateau in Sanpete Valley. Jensen was a sheepherder for Will and Otto Witbeck and was found shot dead on Dec. 16, 1890. Indications in the snow and on the ground was that Jensen had walked and crawled a mile after he was shot. He was carried out on a packhorse to a buckboard wagon and then into town. The monument suggests that Jensen was killed by members of the Robber's Roost gang who had warned all sheepmen to stay out of the area. Other old-time residents, however, recall that the gang never mistreated ranchers or townspeople and conclude that the murderer was not a member of the outlaw gang. About a mile beyond the monument, you reach a long stack of wood—7 feet long, two ricks deep, and 75 feet long. This is near the site of the Copper Globe Mine and was to be used to smelt copper ore taken from a source where the Navajo and Kayenta formations intersect. The mine was operated by Jessie Fugate and his son Conn between 1900 and 1905. Other remnants of the mining operation are nearby. The road continues on to Link Flat, where you can see in the distance a butte called "the Seven Sisters," or "Family Butte." Farther along, you reach "Window Overlook," where there is a hole in the wall of solid rock through which you have a picture-window view of the buttes and pinnacles of the Moenkopi Formation. Off the road, in a side canyon, is the Lucky Strike Uranium Mine. The mine was worked in the early 1950s by Frank Blackburn and Irvin Olsen, two "dog hole" miners—a term applied to uranium miners on the Colorado Plateau, who, armed with shovel, picks, wheelbarrows, and dynamite, worked out of the back of a pickup truck into which they loaded the uranium ore and hauled it over 100 miles to the mill. The route then travels out of Cat Canyon into Kimball Draw where it is about 6 miles back to Interstate 70.

GOLF

Millsite Golf Course—

If, during my growing-up years in Emery County, someone would have predicted that within a few decades many of the area's residents would turn in their tractors for golf carts, and instead of cutting fields of lucerne they would be cutting up divots on long stretches of golf fairways, they would have been laughed out of the county. But since 1989 that is exactly what has happened. That year, the Millsite Golf Course was opened, and it has proved to be one of the state's most distinctive and challenging courses. Set among sand-colored hills, with the 10,000-foot Wasatch Plateau in the background, the 9 holes are all unique. I always plan at least a sleeve or two of extra golf balls just in case I don't clear the wide canyon on the No. 2; bounce one into the rocks of the Millsite Dam, which runs along the length of the 592-yard 3rd hole; or lose a few off the rock walls that form 3 sides of the 7th hole. While you probably won't record your best score on this course, it is one that you won't forget. In fact, if you golf like me, just do your best, enjoy the scenery and the challenge, and forget to keep score—at least on the 1st round. To reach the course, follow the signs that point west off Hwy. 10 in the middle of Ferron. The course is on the **Canyon Rd. 4 miles west of Ferron; (801) 384-2887.**

HIKING AND BACKPACKING

Emery County is a unique area to hike. The high ranges of the Wasatch Plateau offer excellent opportunities for alpine hiking, while the San Rafael region offers deserts, beautifully colored canyons, and narrow gorges in which the only route is along a channel cut by the San Rafael or Muddy rivers. Recreational hiking is a relatively new activity to the San Rafael. Until the 1970s, the area was traversed primarily by horseback (like the first cattlemen entered the area in the 1870s). After World War II, a popular mode of transportation was by jeep, when they were used primarily to locate uranium claims. Steve Allen's *Canyoneering: The San Rafael Swell*, published by the University of Utah Press in 1992, describes 63 different hikes in the San Rafael area. Michael R. Kelsey's *Hiking Utah's San Rafael Swell* describes 30 hiking trails in his volume. Either guide is highly recommended for anyone planning to spend time hiking the San Rafael. Most of the hikes in the San Rafael are long and strenuous, and hiking trails are quite scarce. Most of the trails tend to follow dry creek beds, cattle and animal trails, or traces made by motorized vehicles. But there is no better way to explore the area than on foot.

Lower Black Box—

Utah hikers consider the Lower Black Box of the San Rafael, one of the most famous yet one of the least traveled hikes in the state. Just getting to the starting point is a difficult odyssey. It can be reached from Huntington and Castle Dale. Turn east from Hwy. 10, 2 miles north of Castle Dale, and follow the road through Buckhorn Draw to the Swinging Bridge across the San Rafael River, then 13 miles farther to Sink Hole Flat. From Green River, take Interstate 70 west to the exit at Milepost 129 and then follow the road north about 5.5 miles to Sink Hole Flat. At Sink Hole Flat, a sign indicates the route. Head southeast just under 2 miles to a water tank, then turn northeast 3 miles until you

reach a road that loops for 10 miles around Jackass Bench. Turn right or east for 3.6 miles until the road turns north, then look for a faint trace headed east. Leave your vehicle here. You will cross a pass after .5 mile, then begin a drop of several hundred feet over 5 miles to the San Rafael River. After another 3-mile hike along the east side of the river, you enter the Lower Black Box, walking in the river for most of the 5 miles through the Box. In some places it is necessary to float or swim, so an inner tube is essential. Once in the canyon, you pass under Swasey's or Sid's Leap, a 14-foot narrow span over the river, across which an early cowboy in the area, Sid Swasey, bet his brother a herd of 75 cattle he could jump his saddle horse across the chasm. Sid allegedly made the jump, won the bet, and gave the area one of the most dramatic stories behind any place name in the state. Today a wagon box/bridge, used to move sheep over the chasm, looms 60 feet above the river. Be sure to contact the **San Rafael Resource Area, Bureau of Land Management** before you make this hike. Ask about weather and river conditions and any problems that might be expected. **Box AB, Price, UT 84501; (801) 637-4584.**

South Fork of the Huntington River—

One of my favorite summer mountain hikes, this trail takes you along a free-flowing, clear-water mountain stream in an isolated canyon, where the water plays over the rocks offering trout fishermen plenty of opportunities. The trail has been designated a National Recreation Trail. It follows the north side of the south fork of the Huntington River for 4.5 miles through the canyon to Scad Valley. You can continue along Scad Creek to its intersection with the Miller Flat Rd., where a shuttle can pick you up, or simply retrace your route back through the canyon to the forks for an out-and-back hike of about 9 miles. The trailhead begins at the "Forks," located 18 miles up Huntington Canyon on Hwy. 31. Immediately after you cross the stream, turn west and follow the road along the north side of the creek, until you find a good parking place.

Upper San Rafael River—

As a small child, I looked down in awe from the top of the Little Grand Canyon at the chasm cut by the San Rafael River, convinced that the bottom of this canyon was one place where no human beings had ever set foot. Though there were rumors people had floated down the river in rubber rafts, they all suffered punctured boats or other difficulties and were unable to complete the journey. Later, I learned that prehistoric Indians and later cowboys had traversed the canyon. Today the section of the San Rafael River from Fuller's Bottom to the Swinging Bridge still captures my imagination. It can be run by rubber raft during the high-water spring runoff season, or traversed on foot, preferably during the low water of the fall. You can go down into the canyon by following up the river from the San Rafael Campground at the Swinging Bridge; however, the most memorable hike takes you the other way, from Fuller's Bottom southeast along the river for about 18 miles to the Swinging Bridge. With proper logistics, this can be covered in a day, providing arrangements are made to be dropped off at Fuller's Bottom, then picked up at the Swinging Bridge. To reach Fuller's Bottom, follow the road that exits Hwy. 10, 2 miles north of Castle Dale, and drive approximately 13 miles to the tank, pumphouse, and water trough at Buckhorn Well. Turn southwest along a sandy road that heads southwest for 5.4 miles to the San Rafael River. Once you have been dropped off, your driver can return to Buckhorn Well and turn right to follow the road through Buckhorn Draw for 11 miles to the Swinging Bridge and spend a leisurely day waiting for you. Another option is to leave early, drive to the campground, and leave one vehicle. Then drive to Fuller Bottom and pick up that vehicle at the end of the day. The elevation drop is less than 200 feet between Fuller's Bottom and the Swinging Bridge, but because the river carves deeply through the Carmel, Navajo, Kayenta, Wingate, and Chinle geologic formations, there is the impression of a steady descent. Several canyons—North Salt Wash, Virgin Spring Canyon, Goodwater Canyon, and Cane Wash—enter from the south and north. These side canyons offer many possibilities for exploring and are often the location for some of the region's most superb rock art—especially at Cane Wash. The hike requires numerous crossings of the river, so be prepared for some wading. The last 4 miles to the Swinging Bridge can be made along the south side of the river on an old mining road.

HORSEBACK RIDES

San Rafael Trailrides—

Horseback is the best way to see the San Rafael area, and Ron and Elora Prettyman have put together a variety of trail rides that take you to some of the area's most spectacular scenery. You half expect to meet Butch Cassidy and members of the Robbers Roost gang or Sid Swasey during your ride. If a mountain ride is more to your liking, you can also arrange for rides in beautiful Huntington Canyon. If you want an authentic western experience, this is as good as it gets. **San Rafael Trailrides, Elmo, UT 84521; (801) 653-2372.**

———— SEEING AND DOING ————

HISTORIC BUILDINGS

Historic Emery LDS Church—

Constructed between 1898 and 1900, in the 2nd decade after the settlement of Castle Valley, the Emery Church is the oldest public and religious building in the area. The clapboard traditional New England–style building still visually dominates the community of Emery. It is used today as a senior citizen's center. **100 North Center St.**

MUSEUMS

Emery County Museum—

Located in the 1909 Castle Dale School, this museum uses period rooms to depict the early days in Emery County. Among the display rooms are a school room, store, kitchen, coal mining, farming, and other artifacts. The museum is located a half block north of the Museum of the San Rafael and is managed by Dixon Peacock in conjunction with the Museum of the San Rafael. You will want to visit both museums when you stop. While one museum deals with natural and prehistory in a brand new building, the other is dedicated to the local history of the area and is housed in the county's oldest remaining public building—one that has been listed in the National Register of Historic Sites. Located on the **corner of 100 North and 100 East.** Open weekdays 10 AM–4 PM and Sat. from noon–4 PM. No entry fee, but donations are accepted; **(801) 381-5252.**

Museum of the San Rafael—

This fine local museum emphasizes the natural and prehistory of the Emery County area. The museum is designed to give an actual orientation to the area as the plants and animals along the west wall are representative of those found in the high Wasatch Plateau country to the west, while the east side of the museum is typical of the San Rafael area that spreads eastward from the mountains. In the center, between the two walls in a circular kivalike setting, artifacts of prehistoric inhabitants of the region are exhibited. In a separate wing is an exhibit of dinosaurs that includes an Allosaurus, Albertosaurus, Chasmosaurus, and Tyranosaurus Rex skull and foot. Most of the dinosaurs are taken from the nearby Cleveland-Lloyd Dinosaur Quarry. In addition to its friendly staff under the direction of Dixon Peacock, a lifelong resident of Emery County, an eye-catching attraction is the extensive collection of mounted animals taken in the area. These include bear, elk, coyotes, red fox, kit fox, badgers, bobcats, ring-tailed cats, beaver, rabbits, and rattlesnakes among others. My favor-

ite is the lifelike display of a huge mountain lion, paused almost in midair, in pursuit of a mule deer. Most of the background scenes are painted by local artist Clifford Oviatt. Among the prehistoric artifacts on exhibit are a woven rabbitskin blanket, woven figurines, and an Indian toolmaking kit dating from between 1250 and 1450 AD. that was found by a local explorer, LaVar Sitterud, 15 miles southeast of Castle Dale in 1968. Archaeologists consider the leather bundle the first of its kind recovered in the region. It contained scrapers for preparing hides; a 1.5-inch knife believed to be used for Indian ceremonial purposes, 4 bone tools including an elk antler baton for working rocks to make knives and arrowheads, a hammer stone, a leather pad to protect the palms when flaking a knife or arrowhead, and a number of other items. Open weekdays 10 am–4 pm and Sat. noon–4 pm. No entry fee, but donations are accepted. **64 North 100 East, Castle Dale; (801) 381-5252.**

ROCK ART

Some of America's best-preserved rock art is found within Emery County, and in particular in the San Rafael Swell region. Some sites are quite accessible, while others require considerable hiking; and there are undoubtedly some that remain undiscovered even today. Those interested in more than the sampling of rock art sites provided below should inquire at the **College of Eastern Utah Prehistoric Museum in Price,** the **Bureau of Land Management Office in Price,** or the **Museum of the San Rafael in Castle Dale** for more information.

Buckhorn Draw Pictographs—

This is probably the most visited pictograph site in the county and, unfortunately, the most badly vandalized. It is located 22 miles southeast of Castle Dale, on the Buckhorn Draw Rd., which makes its way to the Swinging Bridge across the San Rafael River. The 100-foot-long pictograph panel has been fenced by the BLM, and the Emery County Centennial Commission is working to restore the pictographs as its state centennial project for 1996. The panel consists of red-painted anthropomorphic figures with elongated forms, small heads, broad shoulders, and short arms and legs. Gunshots, initials, names, and dates of visitors, mostly from the early part of the 20th century, have damaged this magnificent panel, but it is certainly worth a visit. Back up the road 3.3 miles from the Buckhorn Draw panel, there is a cattle guard. Looking to the north, you can spot a trail going up toward a sand dune under a vertical ledge. Follow the trail to a large panel about 50 feet in length. This panel has stick figures of humans in pairs and one group of five holding hands. Alongside them are deer and sheep forms, arcs, footprints, and a set of concentric circles. A smaller 15-foot panel is located about 90 feet from the larger panel. These pictographs have not been vandalized. The forms at both sites are unique, suggesting they were painted at different times and perhaps by different occupants of the area.

Dry Wash Petroglyphs—

This popular site is easily reached by driving south out of Ferron along Hwy. 10 for approximately 4 miles, and then turning left off the highway onto a paved road that leads to a couple of farmhouses known as Moore. At the first junction, turn left again, heading east along a road that intersects with Interstate 70, about 15 miles away. After traveling along this road for a couple of miles look to the left, or northward, for a number of large boulders upon which can be seen snake-figure petroglyphs, some 6 to 8 feet long, which have been carved into the rocks. Park your vehicle and search among the boulders for the well-defined outline of a lizard in the stone, a small Kokopelli (hunchbacked flute player), and other figures carved into the stone.

Head of Sinbad—

See Biking in the Outdoor Activities section.

SCENIC DRIVES

Fremont Junction to Loa (Highway 72)—

This 35-mile-long road takes you from Fremont Junction, off Interstate 70, through Fishlake National Forest, to connect with Hwy. 24 near Loa in Wayne County. The road climbs through Paradise Valley, past mountain meadows, and to the west of Thousand Lake Mountain, before dropping down to the communities of upper Wayne County. The road provides access to Capitol Reef National Park. This road usually has little traffic. The autumn foliage makes this an especially nice drive in the fall.

Huntington Canyon Scenic Byway—

The 48-mile drive from Huntington to Fairview is one of the most beautiful summer and fall drives in the state—a place of pine trees, quaking aspen, and alpine meadows. One of the most popular fly fishing streams may be found here, and there's an abundance of natural lakes and manmade reservoirs. The ascent to the summit of the Wasatch Plateau from Fairview is a very steep 12-mile climb that takes you from 6,000 to 9,000 feet. The route from Huntington is much more gradual, and I prefer making the drive from Huntington to Fairview. Nevertheless, both directions provide access to the Skyline Drive, a magnificent four-wheel-drive road and mountain bike route in the summer or cross-country ski trail in the winter. (See Skyline Drive in **Sanpete Valley** chapter.) Below Skyline Drive the Upper Joe's Valley Rd. connects Huntington Canyon with Straight Canyon. Although this is a dirt road, it is generally passable for passenger vehicles and is also a delightful bike route. Look for a free guide to this scenic drive at the **Museum of the San Rafael, CEU Prehistoric Museum** or **Manti-La Sal National Forest Office in Price.** Under a joint partnership, the Forest Service and Utah Department of Transportation are developing a series of informational kiosks and interpretive panels at major points of interest along the Scenic Byway.

Orangeville to Joe's Valley Scenic Drive—

To reach Orangeville, turn off Hwy. 10 onto Hwy. 29, 6 miles south of Huntington, and drive 4 miles, passing Emery County High School. From Orangeville, Hwy. 29 follows Straight Canyon 19 miles to Joe's Valley Reservoir. The mountain valley has been known since pioneer times as Joe's Valley in honor of an Indian who directed Mormon settlers crossing the mountain from Sanpete Valley. Joe's Valley Reservoir is a popular fishing location. Although the paved road ends at the Emery-Sanpete county line, a gravel road continues west across the Wasatch Plateau to Ephraim. In the winter, the Joe's Valley area is especially popular among snowmobilers and cross-country skiers. En route to Joe's Valley, just over 2 miles from Orangeville, watch for the monument erected by the United Mine Workers of America to commemorate the 26 victims of the tragic Wilberg Mine Disaster on Dec. 19, 1984. During the first 7 miles of the drive you pass hay fields, pastures, and pioneer-era log houses as you gradually enter the mouth of Straight Canyon. Then the aromatic hay fields give way and you enter the narrow confines of the canyon as the road snakes its way another 8 miles up the north side of the canyon. The sides of the mountain and Cottonwood Creek are strewn with giant boulders around which grow juniper, fir, and pine trees. As you read the head of the canyon, the 195-foot-high, 740-foot-wide Joes Valley Dam built between 1963 and 1966 seems to block your way. But the road swings to the north and a beautiful vista unfolds below. The light blue waters of Joe's Valley Reservoir contrast with the dark tree-covered slopes of the surrounding mountains, giving an unforgettable panorama.

The Wedge Overlook/Buckhorn Draw Scenic Backway Road—

Access to the heart of the San Rafael Desert is by way of the road that heads east off Hwy. 10, a mile north of Castle Dale. In former days this was an exciting intersection, with a large stock corral used to hold livestock being moved from summer mountain pastures to winter desert range. The intersection was also marked by one of the Old Spanish Trail Marker Association markers depicting a caravan of weary Mexican travelers making their way over this historic western trail. The northernmost apex of the trail passed near the intersection; you can still see remnants of the old trail nearby. In the 1950s, the intersection was littered with what seemed like a thousand signs, all pointing to (and sometimes giving mileage for) the uranium mines and claims that were accessed from this main transportation artery during the uranium boom. The road branches 13 miles after leaving Hwy. 10.

If you go right, the road will take you up through pinon and juniper for 6 miles, until it ends abruptly at The Wedge Overlook or, as it is often called by locals, the Little Grand Canyon. The overlook provides a spectacular view of the canyon formed by the San Rafael River which flows 1,200 feet below. If this is your first visit to Emery County, try to make time to drive both segments of this road.

Back at the intersection, the "main route" (left fork) continues in a southeasterly direction through Buckhorn Draw to the San Rafael River and the historic Swinging Bridge. The drive through Buckhorn Draw is interesting on several counts. Here, you are in the northwestern corner of the magnificent red-rock country for which southeastern Utah is world-famous. The draw contains ancient Indian pictographs (see the Rock Art section). A dinosaur footprint is also located in the draw. If you happen to be traveling with locals who know where it is, they will usually point it out to you.

Buckhorn Draw was also the scene of a Wild West gun battle, when posses from Castle Dale and Huntington in pursuit of Butch Cassidy met and mistakenly opened fire on each other. No one was killed or wounded, but Butch Cassidy managed to escape to Robbers Roost. There is a nice campground at the Swinging Bridge. Here you have the option of returning the way you came, or continuing another 25 miles through open rangelands and pinon-juniper country until you intersect with Interstate 70 at exit 129. My favorite time to take this drive is in fall, when the leaves on the cottonwood trees in Buckhorn Wash and along the San Rafael have turned and the deep blue fall sky accentuates the yellow of the leaves and the red of the rocks. Designated as one of Utah's Scenic Backways, this graded road is usually easily passable for passenger cars.

WHERE TO STAY

ACCOMMODATIONS

The big draws in Emery County are the scenery, the history, and the people—certainly not fine hotels or charming bed-and-breakfast inns. Expect only basic motel accommodations.

Castle Country Motel—$ to $$

Thirteen rooms. **43 South State, Ferron; (801) 384-2311.**

Village Inn—$$

Twenty-two rooms. **310 South Main, Huntington; (801) 687-9888.**

Village Inn—$$

Twenty-one rooms. **375 East Main, Castle Dale; (801) 381-2309.**

CAMPING

PRIVATE

There is only one private campground in the Emery County area: **Esquire Estates Park** in Castle Dale is open year-round. It has 40 RV sites, all with complete hookups, drinking water, toilets, and disabled facilities. A fee is charged. **70 West 380 North; (801) 381-2778.**

PUBLIC

Ferron Canyon—

See Mill Site State Park in the Major Attractions section.

Huntington Canyon—

Bear Canyon Campground is located approximately 7 miles up the canyon from Huntington. The **Forks Campground** is located 18 miles from Huntington where the south fork joins Huntington Creek. There are 35 RV and tent sites, available on a first-come, first-serve basis, with nonpotable water and toilets. Open June–mid-Sept. Perhaps the oldest campground in the canyon is at **Old Folks Flat**, 21 miles from Huntington, so named because it was the location for one of the annual old folks' gatherings sponsored by the LDS Church. There are 8 sites with toilets and nonpotable water. Open June–mid-Sept. (See also Huntington State Park in the Major Attractions section.)

Orangeville/Joe's Valley—

Joe's Valley Campground has 46 RV and tent sites, drinking water, and toilets. Open late May–late Oct. Joe's Valley Reservoir is about 18 miles west of Orangeville on Hwy. 29.

Two miles farther west on Hwy. 29, the **Indian Creek Campground** has 28 RV and tent sites, drinking water, and toilets. Open late June–late Sept.

San Rafael Area—

The only campground located in the San Rafael area is maintained by the Bureau of Land Management at the Swinging Bridge at the mouth of Buckhorn Draw. The amenities are few—running water, picnic tables, pit toilets, and designated camping spots. Most camping in the area is done along the hiking trails or in undeveloped locations off the road or in side canyons.

WHERE TO EAT

I can recommend plenty of good places to eat, but, unfortunately, they are all in private homes. For special occasions, most local residents travel to Price, or even to Provo and Salt Lake City. Although you won't find gourmet cooking, you don't need to starve if you are visiting Emery County. Each of the larger towns—Huntington, Orangeville, Castle Dale, and Ferron—has one or two places to eat. They are geared to the locals, especially ranchers, miners, and others who want someone else to do the cooking, and are located on the main streets in each town. **The Grub Box** in Ferron, **Big Mama's Pizza** in Castle Dale, and **B.V.D.'s** located northwest of the high school between Castle Dale and Orangeville offer fast food items. Cafes include **Matties** in Orangeville; the **K Bar K** in Castle Dale; the **Lunch Box**, and **Canyon Rim Cafe** in Huntington.

Gentry Mountain as seen as a backdrop to this lush hayfield.
Photo by Allan Kent Powell.

Green River

If there is an undiscovered recreation treasure in Utah, it might just be Green River. Located at the edge of the Green River and the scenic San Rafael Swell, the area offers opportunities for river running, hiking, and four-wheel driving in a place that most travelers simply pass through on their way south to the better-known Moab area. Here, the Green River flows out of the Grey and Desolation canyons to the north and enters an open valley before continuing on its southward course into Labyrinth Canyon in Canyonlands National Park. But if you don't have a day or two for a river trip or to explore the canyons of the San Rafael Swell, a visit to the John Wesley Powell Museum, located on the east bank of the Green River, is well worth an hour's stop. If you are lucky and happen to be passing through Green River in late July, August, or early September, pick up one of the watermelons or cantaloupes from the fruit stands along the highway running through town. Demand your money back if they are not the best melons you have ever tasted.

HISTORY

The town of Green River owes its existence to the simple fact that it is the only location within a 200-mile stretch where the Green River can be crossed. Ute Indians used it as a crossing for centuries, and it was first known as Ute Crossing. It was also on the Old Spanish Trail, opened between Santa Fe, New Mexico, and Los Angeles, California, in 1830. Countless numbers of traders made their way over the trail during the quarter of a century that it was in use. In 1853, Captain John W. Gunnison, an army explorer, mapped out a transcontinental railroad route along the 38th parallel, which crossed the Green River at what was known for a time as "Gunnison's Crossing"; the Gunnison Butte is a prominent landmark north of Green River. While the 38th parallel route was not followed for the transcontinental railroad, the Denver and Rio Grande Railroad was completed between Denver and Salt Lake City in 1883. Desert Siding, north of Green River, was the location where the rails were joined. The first bridge across the Green River was completed as part of this important railroad project which led to the founding of the town of Green River.

In addition to supporting the railroad, Green River became a supply point for ranches scattered up the river and to the west in the San Rafael Swell region. During the early 1950s, Green River took on the trappings of a boomtown as uranium prospectors used the town as a base for their explorations. The real wealth of Green River, however, is found in those delicious watermelons, which are grown along the river. It must be the combination of plenty of water, cool nights, hot days, and alkali in the soil that yields the sweetest-tasting watermelons and cantaloupes to be found on this earth.

GETTING THERE

Green River is located 182 miles southeast of Salt Lake City on Interstate 70, near its junction with Hwy. 6. (Sometimes Utah's Green River is confused with Green River, Wyoming, located 150 miles to the north along Interstate 80.)

———— MAJOR ATTRACTIONS ————

Goblin Valley State Park

This is indeed, a valley inhabited by goblins—petrified goblins—as the unusual layered formations of mudstone, sandstone, and siltstone have been carved and shaped by wind and rain to resemble goblins and anything else that the imagination can conceive. The valley is long and narrow and began as a deep deposit of mud at the bottom of a primordial sea that evaporated around 150 million years ago, leaving deep deposits of marine sediments, which solidified into rock. Today, because of the forces of erosion over millions of years, much of the sedimentary rock has been carved away, leaving thousands of odd-shaped pinnacles and formations of all sizes and shapes.

Goblin Valley was noted by cowboys searching for cattle in the area. In the late 1920s Arthur Chaffin, the owner of Hite Ferry on the Colorado River to the southeast, stumbled upon the valley while traveling between Green River and Cainsville on the Fremont River. Taken with what he saw, Chaffin returned in 1949 to the area he called Mushroom Valley and spent several days photographing and exploring the area. The ensuing publicity led to an influx of visitors and concerns about how best to preserve the unique formations. The state of Utah acquired the property and maintained it as a reserve until it was officially designated a state park in Aug. 1964.

The valley is an artist's and photographer's delight. There is no other place like it in Utah, or probably in the world. It is easy to spend a day hiking through the valley. The valley is administered as part of the state park system and encompasses 3,254 acres, or about 5 square miles. There are two maintained hiking trails in the park. The Curtis Bench Trail is about 3 miles in length, and the Henry Mountains Lookout Trail is a little more than a mile in length. Most visitors spend their time wandering around the valley following their whims to see and explore the fascinating, just larger than human-size formations. Facilities include a covered observation station, picnic area, observation overlook, and a campground with 21 units, modern restrooms that are wheelchair accessible, drinking water, and showers.

To reach Goblin Valley, take Interstate 70 out of Green River to exit 147 at its junction with Hwy. 24. Follow Hwy. 24 southwest for approximately 24 miles, and watch for the turnoff to Goblin Valley on the right. You follow the paved road for 5.3 miles, then turn south onto a gravel road for 7 miles to the park entrance. Coming north from Hanksville on Hwy. 24, it is approximately 21 miles to the turnoff. The park is open year-round. Visitor and camping fees are charged. **Goblin Valley State Park, Box 93, Green River, UT 84525; (801) 564-8110.** For camping reservations, call **1-800-322-3770.**

OTHER ATTRACTIONS

Green River State Park

Located along the Green River, this state park serves the many boaters who either leave the river here after a 95-mile journey from the Uinta Basin to the north through Desolation and Gray canyons or who put in to float the river southward for 120 miles to its confluence with the Colorado River. A 9-hole golf course is scheduled to open in 1996. In addition to the boating facilities, the park includes 42 developed campsites, piped water, and lighted and heated restrooms with showers. Interpretive programs are presented at the park during the summer in a small amphitheater. Check at the Green River visitor center or at the park entrance for a schedule of programs. The park is open all year. **150 South Green River Blvd.; (801) 564-3633.**

FESTIVALS AND EVENTS

Melon Days

3rd weekend in Sept.

As noted, one of Utah's best-kept secrets is the delicious watermelons and cantaloupes grown along the banks of the Green River. These are the sweetest, best-tasting melons this side of the Garden of Eden. In season, Green River melons can be purchased from roadside stands in Green River, or from the backs of trucks or trailers at stops along the road and stores within a 125-mile radius of Green River. The 3rd weekend in Sept., Green River celebrates Melon Days with a variety of activities including a parade, city fair, music, races, games, and free melons.

OUTDOOR ACTIVITIES

BIKING

Riders can follow the east side of the Green River south for 10 miles to Crystal Geyser. The geyser shoots water 50 feet into the air twice a day for 10 minutes.

HIKING

One of Utah's little-explored hiking areas is the San Rafael Swell. A number of interesting hikes into the canyons of the San Rafael Reef for experienced hikers are described in Michael R. Kelsey's *Hiking Utah's San Rafael Swell* and Steve Allen's *Canyoneering: The San Rafael Swell.* The following hikes are located just north and west of Goblin Valley State Park. If you camp at the park for a few days, you could take most of the hikes. Otherwise, if you are just in the area for a day, you might want to combine a visit to the park with one of the shorter hikes.

Chute and Crack Canyons—

These two narrow canyons are located on the southeast side of the San Rafael Reef, just north of Goblin Valley State Park. Most hikers go up Chute Canyon and come back down Crack Canyon. The two canyons parallel each other roughly a mile apart. As Chute Canyon widens, you come to an old mining area and shack. Follow an old trace eastward for about a mile to Crack Canyon, which you can follow back down to your vehicle. The round-trip distance is approximately 16 miles, making this a good day hike. Inquire at Goblin Valley State Park for specific directions to the canyons. Once you are inside the canyons, you can't lose the trail.

Temple Mountain Loop Hike—

Temple Mountain is located at the end of the paved road that turns off Hwy. 24, about 24 miles from exit 147 off Interstate

70. Temple Mountain, named by cowboys for the twin-towered Mormon Temple in Manti, looms above the desert floor and was once the site of considerable uranium-mining activity, as the remnants of several abandoned miners' shacks and mine portals reveal. A series of abandoned mining roads constitute the 6-mile-long hiking trail around Temple Mountain.

Wild Horse Canyon—

From Temple Mountain, you can hike up Wild Horse Creek surrounded by its sheer Navajo sandstone walls darkly painted with desert varnish. If you search for them, pictographs can be found along the canyon walls. To reach the trail, follow an old mining road that runs southwest from the Temple Mountain. After about 2 miles you come to the first wash. This is Wild Horse Creek; since there is no marked trail, you simply walk down the dry wash bed. The hike is easy, and a couple of short narrow stretches make it even more interesting. The reformed outlaw, Matt Warner, left his name on the western wall just north of the junction of Wild Horse and South Temple washes. The trail heads up South Temple Wash to the paved road, which you can follow back to your vehicle. The total round-trip distance is about 9 miles.

RIVER RUNNING

The Green River offers several opportunities for all kinds of experiences, from a leisurely calm-water canoe trip to challenging, roaring, heart-stopping rapids in a rubber raft. Depending on how much time you have, trips can be arranged from a half day to a week or more in length.

The most popular day trip is the 9-mile section of the river north of town from Nefertiti Rapid to Swaseys Rapid. Known as the **Green River Daily,** there are seven rapids in the stretch, some of which range in difficulty up to Class III.

Longer runs include **Desolation and Gray canyons**, north of Green River, with 67 rapids in 84 miles. Trips usually take about 4 days. Desolation Canyon has been designated a National Historic Landmark because it remains essentially the same as when Major John Wesley Powell first floated down the Green River in 1869.

From Green River State Park, you can float downriver for 20 miles to **Ruby Ranch,** a privately owned area with a charge for parking and launching. The next takeout is at **Mineral Bottom,** 68 miles downriver from Green River. This stretch of the river is very calm and slow-moving and popular with canoeists and kayakers.

An extended trip of several days takes you down the Green River to its confluence with the Colorado River, through the infamous **Cataract Canyon**, with its 26 rapids up to Class V in difficulty and on to Hite, at the north end of Lake Powell and Hwy. 95.

Professional river guide services are provided by the following companies in Green River:

Adventure River Expeditions—185 Broadway, PO Box 96, Green River, UT 84525; (801) 564-3648 or 1-800-331-3324.

Holiday River Expeditions—1055 East Main, Green River, UT 84525; (801) 564-3273 or 1-800-624-6323.

Moki-Mac River Expeditions—100 Silliman Ln., PO Box 116, Green River, UT 84525; (801) 564-3361.

———— SEEING AND DOING ————

GEYSERS

Crystal Geyser—

Located on the east bank of the Green River, Crystal Geyser erupts three or four times a day at irregular intervals. The cold water geyser sends a powerful and impressive spray of water skyward, and if you have the time and patience to wait for the eruption this is an unforgettable experience. While you are waiting, keep watch for a herd of wild goats that can be seen on occasion. To reach the geyser, drive 1.3 miles east from the Green River Bridge, then turn left onto the frontage road (located on the south side of Interstate 70). After 2.7 miles you leave the frontage road and turn south onto a dirt road which you follow for about 10 miles to the geyser.

MUSEUMS

John Wesley Powell Museum—

One of Utah's newest museums, the John Wesley Powell Museum is located on the east bank of the Green River. It serves as both a visitor center and an excellent interpretive museum on the history of John Wesley Powell and his 1869 and 1871 explorations of the Green and Colorado rivers. An Illinois schoolmaster and ex-Union officer, Powell lost his right arm at the battle of Shiloh early in Apr. 1862 when a half-spent mini-ball shattered his arm. Powell remained in the Union Army until 1865. In 1866 he became a professor of natural sciences at Illinois State Normal University and curator of the Illinois Natural History Museum which was located on the university campus. With his joint appointments, Powell organized scientific expeditions to Colorado in 1867 and Wyoming in 1868. On May 24, 1869, Powell and nine other men set out from Green River, Wyoming, in four boats for a three-month journey to explore the unknown Green and Colorado rivers. With more than a lifetime's worth of adventure packed into the three months and following the desertion of three of his men (who died under mysterious circumstances), Powell and his group emerged from the Grand Canyon on Aug. 29, 1869, to be greeted by four Mormons, who, under instructions from Brigham Young, were watching for any survivors of the expedition. In addition to historic boats, other artifacts, and well-prepared display panels, the 171-seat auditorium features a 20-minute media presentation, *The River Experience*, that incorporates dramatic slides of the river with narration of extracts from Powell's famous river journal. Anyone who wants to gain a better perspective of the Green River, its history,

and the man who, according to the late Pulitzer Prize-winning author Wallace Stegner, "By the end of his career ... would know the West as few men did, and understand its problems better than any," will not want to miss any opportunity to visit the John Wesley Powell Museum. Open daily 8 am–8 pm. **885 East Main St., Green River, UT 84525; (801) 564-3427.**

ROCK ART

Black Dragon Canyon Pictographs—

This rock art takes its name from one of the figures that, upon first glance, resembles a black dragon. On closer examination, though, it looks more like a bird with two legs, a long neck, and odd-shaped wings. Other figures include the "praying dog," an animal standing on its hind legs, with its forelegs extending upward and forward as though it is praying, and a group of 7- to 8-foot anthropomorphs. Another panel consists of lines, dots, and dashes arranged in geometric shapes and designs such as squares, circles, rectangles, or in the shape of shields or feathers. The canyon may be reached by leaving the interstate and heading west near Milepost 145, approximately .5 mile west of the San Rafael River Bridge, then heading north through a gate for just over a mile to the head of Black Dragon Canyon. The pictograph panels are located on BLM land on both sides of the canyon about 200 yards up the dry wash.

Sego Canyon—

Travelers along Interstate 70 can see one of Utah's most spectacular rock art sites by taking exit 185 at Thompson Springs and heading north for 3 miles into Sego Canyon where a Fremont-style painted panel includes anthropomorphs (human forms) with bug eyes, antennae, earrings, snakes in hands, and legless torsos. There are also mountain sheep, deer, and other animal forms. Another panel appears to be historic Ute art from the 19th century and depicts white bison figures, horses with riders, and large human figures with a shield painted in red and white.

Temple Mountain Pictographs—

Travelers to Temple Mountain will want to take time to view an 8-foot-high, 60-foot-long pictograph panel, located just inside the mouth of South Temple Wash. Here a large Fremont figure has been painted over an earlier Barrier Canyon-style "bug-eyed man," providing archaeologists with circumstantial evidence that other Barrier Canyon-style pictographs predate the Fremont-style paintings.

SCENIC DRIVES

Interstate 70—

Department of Transportation officials could easily justify charging a heavy toll for all vehicles crossing the 100-mile stretch of Interstate 70 from Green River to Salina. This road through one of the most rugged and difficult sections in the entire nation was extremely costly to build and it has opened to travelers some fabulous scenery well worth the price of admission. The road passes through deserts, deep canyons, sheer cliffs, around 11,000-foot-high mountains, and offers panoramic views of the Colorado Plateau that even lifelong

residents of the area stop to admire as they travel along the Interstate. The Grand County Travel Council has published a brochure, "A Guide to I-70 Through Southeastern Utah," which is available at the John Wesley Powell Museum in Green River. If you are entering Utah along Interstate 70 from Colorado, stop at the Thompson Springs Welcome Center (open Memorial Day–Labor Day, 8 am–8 pm and the rest of the year from 9 am–5 pm). The guide is keyed to the visitor centers, rest areas, and view areas along the stretch. There are no services between Green River and Salina, as the Interstate passes through what was once a remote, seldom-seen part of the state. West of Green River, the Interstate cuts through the San Rafael Reef, a saw blade-like impregnable wall, 800–2,000 feet high, that required tons of dynamite to blast the road through in the late 1960s. After negotiating the Reef, the Interstate crosses the San Rafael Swell that developed as an uplift of rock 40 to 60 million years ago. Take time to stop at the **Black Dragon, Spotted Wolf, Ghost Rock, Eagle Canyon,** and **Devils Canyon** views and rest areas.

WHERE TO STAY

ACCOMMODATIONS

Bankurz Hatt Bed and Breakfast— $$ to $$$

Knowing that Hatt was a prominent name in the Green River area and that 19th-century Utahns had given their children some pretty weird names, I asked Ben and Lana Coomer who was this guy Bankurz Hatt? What I heard was an even stranger story about late 20th-century government. In 1897 J. T. Farrer, the local banker and community promoter, had this four-square gambrel roof home built. During the mid-1930s, the house was acquired by Lana's grandfather, Frank Hatt. After her grandparents passed away, the home sat vacant for several years, much to Lana's distress. She and Ben finally acquired the home and restored it as a bed and breakfast in 1993. When they applied for a business license

under the name "Banker's Hatt Bed and Breakfast," they were told that they could not use the word "banker's" in the title. To get over the bureaucratic hurdles, they used the phonetic spelling "Bankurz" to get their desired result. Ben and Lana had never stayed in a bed and breakfast before they opened their own, but their establishment ranks with the best in Utah. The master bedroom downstairs has its own bath, while the three upstairs rooms share a bath. All the rooms are furnished with antiques and there is a distinct turn-of-the-century Victorian feel to the house. The tree-shaded grounds, beautiful flower beds, and outdoor hot tub are an oasis. A full breakfast is served with waffles and eggs Benedict the standard fare. All rooms are nonsmoking; no pets and small children. Open Apr.–Dec. **214 Farrer Street, Green River, UT 84532; (801) 564-3382.**

Bookcliff Lodge—$$
Heated pool and adjacent restaurant and coffee shop. **395 East Main; (801) 564-3406.**

Motel 6—$$
One hundred three rooms. **946 East Main; (801) 564-3436.**

River Terrace Best Western—$$
This is a favorite choice because of its location on the east bank of the Green River across the road from the John Wesley Powell Museum, its swimming pool, and the **Tamarisk Restaurant,** located adjacent to the motel. **880 East Main; (801) 564-3401.**

Rodeway Inn Westwinds—$$
Forty-two rooms. **525 East Interstate 70 Business Loop; (801) 564-3495.**

GUEST RANCHES

Tavaputs Plateau Ranch provides horseback riding, jeep tours, hiking, and guided hunting trips. Located in the high country north of Green River. For information and reservations write **PO Box 139, Green River, UT 84525,** or call **(801) 564-3463.**

CAMPING
PRIVATE
Green River KOA—
Seventy-seven RV sites, 25 with hookups, and 50 tent sites. Showers, laundry facilities, store, and swimming pool. Open from early Apr.–late Oct., fees charged. **550 South Green River Blvd.; (801) 564-3651.**

Shady Acres RV Park—
Sixty-five RV sites and 25 tent sites. Showers, laundry facilities, and store. Open all year, fees charged. **360 East Main; (801) 564-8290.**

United Campground—
Sixty-five RV sites and 15 tent sites. Showers, laundry facilities, store, and swimming pool. Open all year, fees charged. **910 East Main; (801) 564-8195.**

PUBLIC
Goblin Valley State Park—
Twenty-one sites. Restrooms and showers, fee charged; **(801) 564-8110.**

Green River State Park—
Forty-two RV and 40 tent sites. Open year-round. Restrooms and showers, fees charged. **150 South Green River Blvd.; (801) 564-3633.** For reservations call **1-800-322-3770.**

———— WHERE TO EAT ————

Book Cliff Restaurant—$ to $$$
This small and pleasant restaurant is managed by Jeff and Conae Black, natives of the area who are congenial hosts willing to spend time with customers talking about the history of Green River and what to see and do. Gregory Zuniga, a native of Chile, has been the cook for 15 years and is known as one of the best cooks in all of eastern Utah. He is known for his wonderful omelets, pies and pastries, and real mashed potatoes and gravy. If you stop by when Gregory has one of his Chilean dishes as a luncheon special, be sure to give it a try. Other lunch items include soup, salads, and sandwiches (including a veggie burger and black bean burger), while the dinner menu offers steaks, roast beef, chicken, and fish. Open daily 6 am–10 pm. **395 East Main; (801) 564-3650.**

Ray's Tavern—$ to $$$
It looks like a bar and it is a bar, but Ray's is considered to have the best hamburgers in the state. Served with real potato fries and condiments on the side so that you can build the burger the way you want it, real burger connoisseurs will want to check out Ray's. You can also get charbroiled steaks and special pork chops, but

plan a 45-minute wait for the pork chops. Operated by Bob Scott, the tavern is the unofficial headquarters for river runners in Green River. **280 North Broadway; (801) 564-3511.**

Tamarisk Restaurant—$ to $$$

Named for the willowy bush that grows wild along the riverbanks and ponds of the desert region, you can see plenty of tamarisk along the Green River from the large picture windows of the restaurant which overlook the east bank of the river. The restaurant is located just across the highway from the John Wesley Powell Museum. (The Bayles family, who own and operate the restaurant, donated the land for the museum.) Menu items include omeletes, pancakes, and local watermelon and cantaloupe in season for breakfast; sandwiches, soups, and salads for lunch; steaks, chicken, turkey, seafood, and Utah trout for dinner. There are also vegetarian dishes and a daily breakfast, lunch, and dinner buffet which is especially popular with hungry travelers along Interstate 70. You won't want to leave the Tamarisk without a few pieces of the homemade fudge sold at the entrance to the restaurant. Open daily 6 am–10 pm. **870 East Main; (801) 564-8109.**

SERVICES

Green River Information Center—

Located in the John Wesley Powell River History Museum on the east side of the Green River, the Green River Information Center has a good selection of pamphlets and books about the region. **885 East Main St.; (801) 564-3526** or **1-800-635-6622.**

Ancient pictographs adorn sandstone cliffs throughout Utah. Photo by Bob Huestis.

Moab

For the traveler who seeks to enter the heaven of Utah's canyon country, Moab is the pearly gates. Although there is no St. Peter to admit or reject aspirants to this eternity of sandstone cliffs, roaring rivers, and unbelievable scenery, everyone must pass through the gates of Moab in order to visit Arches and Canyonlands national parks to embark on a journey through Cataract Canyon of the Colorado River, or to drive to the tops of the La Sal Mountains. It is no coincidence that the first European to enter Utah, Juan Maria Antonio de Rivera, found his way to what would become Moab and noted its strategic location. Moab is situated on the southeast side of the Colorado River at the only easy crossing of the Colorado River within the state of Utah. Moab provides access to the river for thousands of adventurers who want to experience the peace and beauty of drifting between enormous red sandstone cliffs and the thrill of shooting giant rapids. During the last decade, Moab has also become a mecca for thousands of mountain bikers who come for the scenery and to ride over hundreds of miles of Navajo sandstone "slickrock," which poses the ultimate challenge to daredevil bikers.

Moab is the gateway to two outstanding national parks. Accessible Arches National Park, located on a plateau just northwest of the Colorado River, is a wonderland of arches, windows, pinnacles, towers, and other formations carved by wind, water, and ice. Canyonlands National Park lies at the heart of the scenic Colorado Plateau and is one of the most rugged, isolated, and sensational natural landscapes anywhere in the world. You can spend a lifetime exploring its four units, but you will never see it all. Looming above the Moab Valley, the 12,500-foot La Sal Mountains were named by 18th-century Spanish travelers in the region. These craggy, laccolithic giants with their dark interiors stand in sharp contrast to the fiery red sandstone rocks spread across the landscape. This remarkable place has a radiance and intensity that brings awe, peace, and a sense of belonging and oneness to the human spirit. Moab has tried to build a stable economy on farming, ranching, gold, oil, uranium, and potash, but while all of these endeavors have had their day, tourism is now taking over, as Moab heads into the 21st century.

HISTORY

In 1765, the same year the British were imposing a Stamp Act on colonists on America's East Coast, Juan Maria Antonio de Rivera and his men reached and crossed the Colorado River at present-day Moab. Their expedition north from Abiquiu, New Mexico, made them the first recorded Euro-Americans to enter Utah. Rivera was familiar with the Indians of New Mexico and Arizona (who are descendants of the Anasazi) and was probably not surprised to see the vacant dwellings and rock art left by the Anasazi when they moved south during the 13th century to become part of the Pueblo Indians of New Mexico and Arizona. Rivera encountered members of the Ute tribe, who entered the region from the north and east and may have been one of the factors leading the Anasazi to abandon their centuries-old home. Rivera's 1765 mission was fivefold: to reconnoiter the land along the Indian trail north to the Colorado River and beyond; to learn more about the Indians who occupied the area; to determine their attitude toward the Spanish; to observe if the French had made contact with the Indians; and to search for precious metals.

But the northern Spanish frontier was already overextended, even before the first California missions could be established in San Diego in 1769, and there was little action in the Moab area for the next 50 years. Decades later, it was California that helped put the Colorado River crossing at Moab on the map, when the Old Spanish Trail was opened between Santa Fe and Los Angeles in 1830. It was necessary to come as far north as Moab and Green River to get around the impassable canyons of the Colorado River. The 1,100-mile trail was used chiefly by hundreds of New Mexican traders who found a ready market for woolen goods— serapes, rugs, blankets, bedspreads, yardage—in the California settlements. The traders returned to New Mexico with herds of as many as a thousand horses and mules, which were marketed in New Mexico. The Spanish Trail was actually something of a transcontinental extension of the Santa Fe Trail, which opened in the 1820s, when the Southwest became Mexican Territory and trade with the US was tolerated, if not encouraged.

In 1855, Mormon missionaries attempted to establish the first settlement at the Colorado River crossing. Known as the Elk Mountain Mission, 41 men traveled over a portion of the Spanish Trail from Sanpete Valley and constructed a rock fort, which they abandoned three months after their arrival, when Indian attacks destroyed the crops they planted and left three men dead.

Permanent settlers returned in 1878 to establish farms and ranches. They gave their new community the biblical name of Moab and looked forward to the arrival of the Denver and Rio Grande Railroad in 1881. The railroad link between Denver and Salt Lake City gave Moab access to the railroad 35 miles to the north at Thompson Springs. A ferry across the Colorado River was in operation by 1885, and the first bridge, a three-span steel bridge, was completed in 1912.

As early as 1906, the local newspaper, the *Grand Valley Times*, began promoting tourism around Moab; the designation of Arches National

Monument in 1929 further promised to put Moab on the map. But it was uranium, not scenery, that led to the first invasion of Moab. Spurred on by government bounties, miners flooded into the area and staked claims in the uranium-rich Chinle Formation. Moab's population exploded from 1,275 in 1950 to 4,682 in 1960.

Since 1898, when Marie and Pierre Curie discovered radium in uranium ore, uranium had become one of the world's most sought-after substances. A decade later, medical researchers discovered radium as an effective treatment for cancer, and the race was truly on. For the first two decades of the 20th century, miners who had come to Utah in search of radioactive treasure in the crumbly hills could sell all of the ore they could get out of the ground. One of the first was Howard Balsley, born in Connellsville, Pennsylvania, in 1886, who arrived in Moab on his birthday, December 7, 1908, and pioneered early uranium mining around Moab. In 1922, Madame Curie was presented with a gram of radium, which had been extracted from Howard Balsley's mines. As time wore on, Balsley became the only buyer of uranium ore in southeastern Utah. But with World War II and the creation of the Manhattan Project, which ushered in the atomic era with the dropping of the atomic bombs on Hiroshima and Nagasaki, the federal government established a monopoly for the purchase of uranium ore. In the early 1950s, with the outbreak of the Cold War, the government was again anxious to have a substantial supply of uranium and set the minimum price for uranium ore for over a 10-year period, offering a $10,000 bonus to anyone opening up new uranium mines. One man, Charles A. Steen, emerged as the epitome of the rags-to-riches story on the Colorado Plateau. An unemployed geologist from Texas, living with his wife and four small boys in a small trailer attached to an 8-foot-by-16-foot shack, Steen located the largest deposit of high-grade uranium ore in the United States in July 1952. His Mi Vida Mine, located south of Moab, made him an instant multimillionaire and brought an even greater number of prospectors and speculators to Moab—each convinced he or she would duplicate, if not surpass, Steen's good fortune.

The aftermath of World War II had a significant impact on tourism in Moab. The surplus rubber rafts proved ideal for running the Colorado River, providing access to the river for thousands, and the uranium boom and oil boom left a network of trails and traces that now serve four-wheel-drive vehicles and mountain bikers. The economic opportunities also introduced many people to the remarkable scenery and convinced them that significant portions of this pristine environment should be preserved. A new environmental ethic and leadership by key individuals led to the creation of Canyonlands National Park in 1964.

While tourism has continued to expand since the 1960s with an ever-increasing number of motels, restaurants, and facilities to enhance the visitor's experience, the population of remote Moab has not grown like that of places like Kanab and St. George. The closing of the uranium-processing plant has stressed the local economy. In 1980, Moab's population reached a high of 5,333, but by 1990 it had dropped to 3,971. Still, the future looks bright for Moab. It is a community that appreciates the rich scenic resources that abound and a quality of life that deserves preservation.

GETTING THERE

Moab is located 238 miles southeast of Salt Lake City. From Salt Lake City, take Interstate 15 south to Spanish Fork, exit 256, and head southeast on Hwy. 6 for 125 miles to its junction with Interstate 70 at Green River. Drive east for 22 miles on Interstate 70, then take exit 180 at Crescent Junction and continue south on Hwy. 191 for 30 miles to Moab.

———— MAJOR ATTRACTIONS ————

See the **Arches National Park** and **Canyonlands National Park** chapters.

Dead Horse Point State Park

There are a number of places to view the scenery of southeastern Utah and the workings of the Colorado River, but perhaps not even the Grand Canyon surpasses Dead Horse Point in beauty and awe. Far below you, the Colorado River makes a deep hairpin as it cuts its way through 150 million years of geologic history. To the east, the skyscraping mountains hulk over the landscape, and the forces of time and divinity seem to come together to inspire the onlooker, reminding us that our lives are but a small part of the grand scheme of things.

Dead Horse Point is a sheer-walled narrow mesa poised above the hundreds of miles of canyon country that make up Canyonlands National Park. Access to the mesa is by way of a narrow neck only 30 yards wide. According to local legend, in the late 1800s, cowboys constructed a fence across this narrow neck of land to corral wild horses. The roped the best of these wild horses and broke them for their own use. The others were left on the mesa, and, either because the fence was left up and they could not get out or they simply could not find their way out, those left behind on the waterless mesa died of thirst and exhaustion or in a futile attempt to reach the waters of the Colorado far below. Their bleached bones gave the mesa its name. Dead Horse Point State Park was established in 1959 and today covers 5,082 acres. Hang gliders have found the sheer cliffs to be an ideal spot to perform their heart-stopping hobby. If you are lucky there will be some of these daredevils taking that one step off the solid sandstone to the bench more than a thousand feet below.

The park has a visitor center, a paved 1.5-mile-long walking trail leading to the point, as well as 7 miles of additional hiking trails. The campground has 21 fully developed sites, which can be reserved in advance. The units have electrical hookups, water, grills, tables and benches, and tent pads. These are available from early

Apr.–late Oct.; winter camping is allowed, but water and electricity are turned off so come prepared. There is a picnic area for day use. The state park is located on the way to the Island in the Sky District of Canyonlands National Park. To reach it, take Hwy. 191 north from Moab for 11 miles to its junction with Hwy. 313, then follow the state highway for 23 miles to the state park. From Crescent Junction (exit 18) off Interstate 70, it is 21 miles to the junction with state Hwy. 313. The Dead Horse Point State Park Visitor Center is open daily 8 am–6 pm mid-May–mid-Sept. (9 am–5 pm the rest of the year). For more information, write **Dead Horse Point State Park, Box 609, Moab, UT 84532; (801) 259-2614.** For reservations call **1-800-322-3770.**

FESTIVALS AND EVENTS

Moab Half-Marathon

One of the most popular running races outside the Wasatch Front, this race, usually held in Mar. draws more than a thousand runners who can choose the 5-mile run or the 13.1-mile half-marathon course, both of which are run on Hwy. 128 and follow the east bank of the Colorado River.

Easter Jeep Safari

This traditional Easter outing began in 1966 and attracts four-wheel-drive fans from throughout the West. The Red Rock 4-Wheelers, a Moab ORV club, organizes several events and rides. More than 1,500 vehicles and as many as 28 different trails, ranging from relatively easy and safe trails to those reserved for daredevil jeepers who have no fear for their own safety or concern for damage to their vehicles, are used during this week-long event.

Canyonlands Rodeo

Usually held the 2nd weekend in June, this Utah Professional Rodeo Association–sanctioned event is one of the 1st held during the rodeo season in an arena located southeast of Moab just off Hwy. 191. For information call **(801) 259-8472.**

Moab Music Festival

Chamber music under the 500-foot cliffs that rim the Colorado River is the special attraction of this music festival which began in 1993. Concertgoers are transported to a magical spot on the Colorado River by jet boats, where they enjoy the exquisite music of the Old World masters in a beautifully inspiring New World wilderness setting. Performances are also held in Star Hall, and there is a family picnic concert in the Moab City Park. The festival is held over a 10-day period in mid-Sept. **Moab Music Festival, PO Box 698, Moab, UT 84532; (801) 259-8431.**

Moab Fat Tire Festival

Usually held the last week in Oct., Moabites maintain that this is the best-known mountain bike event in the country. The week-long events include a Halloween bash, guided group rides, hill climbs, time trials, and a variety of programs and activities on desert ecology, archaeology, and climbing. Call **(801) 259-5333.**

OUTDOOR ACTIVITIES

BIKING

The 1950s brought the uranium boom to Moab, but the 1980s have brought the "biker boom." Thirty years after Charlie Steen opened his Mi Vida Mine, two brothers, ex-uranium miners, opened their Rim Cyclery bike shop and began promoting off-road bicycling in the nearby slickrock. Their "discovery" of the unusual—and in many ways ideal—biking terrain has made Moab the Mecca of the mountain biking world. Where much of the weekend traffic headed south out of the Wasatch Front included amateur prospectors armed with Geiger counters and other paraphernalia that would bring wealth, today every other vehicle headed down Hwy. 6 on a Thurs. or Fri. afternoon or evening is loaded with camping gear with two or four bicycles bolted to the roof like the antlers of a mechanical animal.

Why do they come? The scenery, the camaraderie with other bikers, the free and open spaces, but above all, the miles and miles of smooth slickrock. The huge expanse of rugged, rolling Navajo sandstone, which millions of years ago was laid down when ancient sand dunes hardened into stone, offers excellent traction despite its name. The Moab Information Center has a free brochure, published by the Grand County Travel Council, called "Moab Area Mountain Bike Trails," which describes four of the most popular bike trails within a 15-mile radius of Moab. Todd Campbell has written *Above and Beyond Slick Rock*, which describes 40 bike rides in the Moab area. F. A. Barnes and Tom Kuehne have published *Mountain Biking*, which delineates 23 trails. Because of the isolated nature of the trails and the distances involved, leave word with someone, saying where you are going and when you expect to return, and carry food and extra water. In hiking, biking, and traveling throughout the area, it is essential to be responsible for your own safety and well-being. If you are not familiar with the area, it is easy to become lost, and even if you do know your way around, equipment problems and other factors can affect your ride. The local search and rescue team has had plenty of experience rescuing lost and stranded bikers, especially tourists, and they do charge the rescuee if they are called out. Be sure and wear your helmet at all times when riding. The following is a sampling of a half dozen trails you can ride. Consult the free brochure or one of the biking guide books for complete trail descriptions.

Gemini Bridges Trail—

Although this ride requires a shuttle or at least a lift to the trailhead, it is mostly downhill as it takes you through colorful rock formations and past the Gemini Bridges—a pair of natural rock spans with spectacular views of Arches National Park across Moab Canyon. The 13.5-mile-long trail leaves from Hwy. 313, 12.6 miles west of its junction with Hwy. 191. It descends the red-rock walls into the canyon. If you leave a shuttle vehicle at this point you can load up, otherwise it's about an 8-mile ride down through Moab Canyon along Hwy. 191 and across the Colorado River back to Moab.

Hurrah Pass Trail—

This is a convenient day-long loop ride that begins from the junction of Kane Creek Blvd. and Hwy. 191 in Moab. The round-trip ride is 33 miles, most of it along a paved road and graded dirt trail. If you want to get off the slickrock for a while, or if you want to get acquainted with the terrain and scenery before you tackle the slickrock, this is a good ride. The 600-foot climb up to Hurrah Pass will test your legs and get your heartrate up. The ride offers views of the Colorado River and spectacular scenery in Kane Creek and Hunter Canyon. You won't mind retracing your route later in the day, when the changing light and different perspective offer an entirely new view.

Kane Creek Canyon Rim/Pritchett Canyon Road—

More difficult and not as convenient as the Hurrah Pass Trail, this trail is a favorite of many riders because it takes you to the magnificent Behind the Rocks Area and to several large natural arches. It begins 12.5 miles south of Moab, on Hwy. 191, and heads west before turning northwest to its terminus at Kane Creek Rd. The distance is 20.3 miles, but since the road is much rougher than the Hurrah Pass Trail, the going is slower. You should plan a day for this ride. You can add another 4.5 miles by continuing along the paved Kane Creek Rd. up the Colorado River and back to Moab. This route crosses private land and the landowners have begun to charge a small fee—usually $1—to cross their land.

Kokopelli Trail—

For a multiday ride, consider the 140-mile-long Kokopelli Trail from Moab to Grand Junction, Colorado. The trail, opened in 1989, is named for the humpbacked flute player deity common to the Native Americans of the Colorado Plateau and found depicted in the area's rock art. Perhaps the most challenging part of the trail is the 4,500-vertical-foot climb over the La Sal Mountains. Bikers must carry their own water, and the ride is recommended only for experienced, well-prepared bikers. For more information about the trail, contact the **Moab BLM Office, 82 East Dogwood, Moab, UT 84532; (801) 259-6111.**

Moab Slickrock Bike Trail—

Laid out by motorbikers in 1969, the Moab Slickrock Bike Trail has been taken over by mountain bikers, although motorcycles and motorbikes are still allowed on the trail. The 10.3-mile loop demands good biking skills to handle the ups and downs across the slickrock and the sand, and to stay out of the microbiotic soil or crust, which unfortunately has been highly impacted by bikers. Please be on the lookout for these dark, "sugary" patches of new soil. Once disturbed, they will not recover for decades. If you are not sure about your biking skills, you will want to take the 2.3-mile "practice loop," which, though not as difficult as the main loop, does offer a good introduction as to what to expect. Grand views beckon, but remember you are on top of the cliffs and it is a long fall into Negro Bill Canyon or into the main canyon of the Colorado River. Both loops are outlined on a detailed map available from the Bureau of Land Management, although the trail can be clearly followed by the white dashes painted across the slickrock. Plan five to six hours for your first trip over the loop. The trail begins on Sand Flats Rd., 2.3 miles from the BLM office. To reach the trail from Moab, head east on 300 South to 400 East. Turn south and continue to Mill Creek Dr., where you turn left and follow the road, staying to the left as you reach Sand Flats Rd. and the Grand Resource Area BLM Office. Continue on Sand Flats Rd.

beyond the pavement until you reach the trailhead.

Monitor and Merrimac Trail—

For a good introduction to mountain biking, consider this 13.2-mile-long trail. It starts with a 2.2-mile ride through open desert, then follows the bottom of a wash for .6 mile before climbing out and continuing up Tusher Canyon for another 1.2 miles. Here, the trail follows the left branch of the wash through a gap in the wall dividing the Tusher and Mill canyon drainages. You will reach a jeep road, which you take to Determination Towers. Just past the towers, cross a large, flat slickrock area, with some sections of sand, for 1.2 miles to the base of Merrimac Butte. Passing to the left of Merrimac, you head south across the slickrock toward the smaller Monitor Butte. From Monitor, the trail returns down Mill Canyon. At the lower end of the canyon you will come to a gate. About .2 mile from the gate, and less than 2 miles from your vehicle, a spur road leads to the Mill Canyon Dinosaur Trail, where many dinosaur fossils can be seen. Leave your bike at the trailhead and, after you walk the dinosaur trail, you can continue on the road north to the parking area. To reach the trailhead, drive north on Hwy. 191, 14.8 miles from the Moab Visitor Center, and turn left onto a dirt road that crosses the railroad track just before a railroad bridge. Stay on the dirt road for .6 mile to an intersection where the trail begins.

Tours—

For those interested in mountain biking guided tours, join one of the bicycle tours offered by the companies listed below. They provide all the equipment you need, support vehicles, and an experienced guide. These tours range from one to several days. Be sure to make arrangements with the tours well in advance.

Bicycle Tours and Rentals—

Adrift Adventures—378 North Main, PO Box 577, Moab, UT 84532; (801) 259-8594 or 1-800-874-4483.

Kaibab Mountain/Desert Bike Tours—391 South Main, PO Box 339, Moab, UT 84532; (801) 259-7432 or 1-800-451-1133.

Nichols Expeditions—497 North Main, Moab, UT 84532; (801) 259-7882 or 1-800-635-1792.

Rim Tours—94 West 100 North, Moab, UT 84532; (801) 259-5223 or 1-800-626-7335.

Tag-a-Long Expeditions—452 North Main, Moab, UT 84532; (801) 259-8946 or 1-800-453-3292.

Western Spirit Cycling—38 South 100 West, Box 411, Moab, UT 84532; (801) 259-8732 or 1-800-845-BIKE.

CANOEING

For an inexpensive way to enjoy the Colorado River above and below Moab, canoeing offers a great opportunity. You can rent canoes, paddles, and life jackets from **Colorado River Tours**, located on the west bank of the river just off Hwy. 191 south of the bridge. From the dock, you can float down the Colorado River for 30 miles to Gold Nugget Point, where you and the canoe will be picked up and transported back to your starting point. Daily rentals include pickup of the canoe and transportation back to your vehicle. This stretch of the Colorado is placid and easy to negotiate even for unexperienced canoeists. Do keep your life jacket on at all times because if you get into the water, the swift undercurrents can be very dangerous. During your journey, you pass the boundary of the Matheson Wildlife Preserve, so keep an eye out for such birds as blue herons and other wildlife including beaver and deer. **(801) 259-BOAT.**

FOUR-WHEEL-DRIVE TOURS

There are thousands of miles of jeep trails around Moab, most of which were established by prospectors looking for uranium, gold, and oil. Avid local jeepers have devoted years and worn out vehicle after vehicle and still cannot claim to have covered every mile of four-wheel terrain in the area. Although hikers and old-time cowboys might argue, many believe there is no better way to see the canyons, deserts, and mountains of southeastern Utah than with a four-wheel-drive outfit.

The jeep made its appearance after World War II, when thousands were sold for surplus. In the Moab area, they proved as essential to the 1950s uranium boom as the Geiger counter and penny uranium stock. Unless you have your own four-wheel-drive vehicle and have some experience driving in sand and across slickrock, your best bet is to sign up for one of the half-day or full-day tours offered by one of the companies listed below. (Longer tours can be arranged.) If you go on your own, it is always best to travel with at least one other vehicle and carry plenty of water, food, topographical maps, shovels, towrope or cable or preferably a winch, and let someone know where you are going. As one old-time jeeper said, "Expect to get stuck or broke down and prepare accordingly."

The Grand County Travel Council publishes a free brochure, "Moab Area Jeep Trails," which lists five trails that can be completed in a half day. These are good introductions to the jeeping possibilities in the area and show off some of the region's most beautiful canyons, mesas, and vistas. Don't forget to take plenty of film for your camera. Most of the five trails are on public lands and range from 15 to 54 miles in length. They include the Gemini Bridges Trail, the Monitor and Merrimac Trail, the Poison Spider Mesa Trail, the Chicken Corners Trail, and the Moab Rim Trail. Four-wheel-drive trips can be arranged through the following operators.

Adrift Adventures—378 North Main, PO Box 577, Moab, UT 84532; (801) 259-8594 or 1-800-874-4483.

Canyonlands Tours—543-T North Main, Moab, UT 84532; (801) 259-5865 or 1-800-342-5938.

Lin Ottinger Tours—600 North Main, Moab, UT 84532; (801) 259-7312.

Tag-A-Long Expeditions—452 North Main, Moab, UT 84532; (801) 259-8946 or 1-800-453-3292.

Lockhart Basin Road Scenic Backway—

This route connects Moab and Hwy. 211, near the entrance to Canyonlands National Park. It passes beneath the Anticline and Needles overlooks and takes you across Kane Creek, over Hurrah Pass, along the canyon bottom of Lockhart Canyon, and back up onto a bench that skirts the base of red-rock cliffs before its intersection with the paved Hwy. 211. While part of the road can be traveled in a passenger car, the Kane Creek crossing can only be made in a high-clearance vehicle (but should not be attempted during high water); the section from Hurrah Pass to Lockheart Basin also requires four-wheel-drive. The distance from Moab Hwy. 211 is 57 miles and slow-going. Plan to spend a full day and be prepared with extra food, clothing, and water. The road starts from the intersection of Kane Creek Blvd. and Hwy. 191 in Moab. Take Kane Creek Blvd. to 500 West and follow the paved road to the left at the "Y" intersection. The road parallels the Colorado River and the pavement ends at the entrance to Kane Creek Canyon.

GOLF

Moab Golf Course—

A few years ago this golf course was expanded from 9 to 18 holes, changing this from a good rural Utah course to one of the most beautiful and fun courses in the state for the average golfer. Expert golfers who play the gold tees will find some challenging holes, but as a rule this course is user-friendly. The new holes have been integrated with the old, but it is fairly easy to tell by the design of the holes and their different character which are new and which are old. If you are playing the course for the first time, try to identify them, then check at the pro shop after your round to see if you are correct. The fairways, with one or two exceptions, are wide and without any major obstacles. The fairways tend to be hard, giving extra yards with generous bounces. The greens are usually fast and sloping, making putting perhaps the hardest part of the game on this course. Located in **Spanish Valley at 2705 East Bench Rd.** Follow Hwy. 191 south out of Moab for about 3 miles to Spanish Trail Rd. Turn left and head east for a mile, passing through a four-way stop and down then up a gully. At the top of the hill turn right and follow the road into the golf course parking area. **(801) 259-6488.**

HIKING

The Grand County Travel Council publishes a free brochure, "Moab Area Hiking Trails," which describes eight short-to-moderate hikes within a 15-mile radius of Moab. F. A. Barnes's *Slickrock Hiking & Biking* takes in more of the surrounding countryside and even more possibilities. If you plan to spend any time in the area hiking or mountain biking, Barnes's book is highly recommended. If your visit is relatively brief but you would like to take a short hike in the Moab area, one of the following trails should fit the bill.

TRAILS FROM UTAH HIGHWAY 279

(Hwy. 279 intersects with Hwy. 191 just northwest of the Colorado River Bridge and follows the west bank of the Colorado River in a southerly direction.)

Corona Arch Trail—

Located 10 miles southwest of the junction of Hwys. 279 and 191, the Corona Arch Trail takes you to the 140-by-105-foot opening of the Corona Arch and the adjacent Bow Tie Arch. The 1.5-mile hike begins from the parking lot on the north side of the highway, crosses the railroad tracks, and follows an old road through a gap in the rim before it turns onto the slickrock. Rock cairns mark the way across the slickrock to the base of the cliff, where safety cables have been installed, steps cut into the slickrock, and a ladder placed to take you up over a short ledge. Corona Arch is visible from this point.

Portal Overlook Trail—

One and one half miles long, this manmade trail, except for the sections across slickrock, follows a series of switchbacks as it climbs above the Colorado River for a breath-taking view of the Moab Valley, the La Sal Mountains, and the South Portal. The trail begins 3.7 miles southwest of the junction of Hwy. 279 and Hwy. 191. Watch for the parking area on the east side of the road. Since much of the trail is shaded by higher cliffs in the late summer afternoons, this is a good time to make the hike.

TRAILS FROM
UTAH HIGHWAY 128

(This road follows the east side of the Colorado River and joins Hwy. 191 just before you reach the bridge driving out of Moab.)

Hunters Canyon—

Kane Creek Canyon Rd. also provides access to the Hunters Canyon Trailhead, 7.5 miles west of the intersection with Hwy. 191 in Moab. From the parking area, the trail follows the canyon bottom for 3 miles, past cottonwood trees and along the intermittent spring, and eventually becomes blocked by brush. Just .5 mile above the trailhead, on the right, is a large arch.

Moab Rim—

Hikers share this trail with four-wheel-drivers along a 3-mile trail that traverses slickrock and follows a primitive road. The trail offers good views of the Colorado River, the Moab Valley, and the massive sandstone fins of the Behind the Rocks area. If you want to extend your hike, continue on the Hidden Valley Trail, which joins this trail just below the pass to Hidden Valley. The trail begins from Kane Creek Blvd., 2.6 miles northwest of its intersection with Hwy. 191 in Moab.

Negro Bill Canyon Trail—

Named for William Granstaff, an African-American prospector, Indian trader, and cattleman who ran his cattle in the canyon in the late 1870s, Negro Bill Canyon is located 3 miles upriver from the junction of Hwys. 128 and 191. The trail climbs 1.5 miles up the canyon along an old road and the stream bottom. For the last .5 mile, the trail crosses the stream and goes along a maintained trail up a side canyon. At the end of the canyon is Morning Glory Natural Bridge, which, unlike the arches in the region, was formed by a stream. The 243-foot-long bridge is the 6th longest natural rock span in the US. The picturesque setting at the end of a canyon above a spring and small pool makes this a popular hike.

South of Moab—

Hidden Valley Trail is a constructed trail 2 miles long. It follows a series of steep switchbacks as it heads north into Hidden Valley, providing an excellent view of the Moab Valley and the large sandstone fins of the Behind the Rocks area. To reach the parking area and trailhead, follow Hwy. 191 south out of Moab for 3 miles and turn right onto Angel Rock Rd. After 2 blocks, turn right onto Rimrock Rd. and stay on it until you reach the parking area. This is another trail that is shaded by the high cliffs in the late afternoon.

HORSEBACK RIDING

Horseback rides are available at the **Pack Creek Ranch, (801) 259-5505** (see the Accommodations section); through **Sunset Trail Rides, (801) 259-6574;** and **Old West Trail Rides, (801) 259-7410.** Adrift Adventures offers an excellent horseback/river combination, using horses furnished by the Pack Creek Ranch. A half day is spent on horseback in Arches National Park and the other half floating the Fisher Towers section of the Colorado River. For more information call **(801) 259-8594** or **1-800-874-4483** or write **Adrift Adventures, 378 North Main, PO Box 577, Moab, UT 84532.**

RIVER RUNNING

No one should visit Moab without spending some time on the Colorado River. Just knowing that you are floating down one of America's most historic rivers is part of the attraction—and the unbelievable desert scenery is the other. The float on a silt-laden, chocolate-colored river, with the anticipation of something new around every bend, the omnipresent red-rock cliffs, and blue-and-white La Sals in the distance offer an experience of a lifetime. River running companies operating out of Moab offer everything from a half-day calm-waters float above the confluence of the Colorado and Green rivers to a five-day Cataract Canyon trip that begins calmly in the northern section of Canyonlands National Park, then continues beyond the junction of the rivers into the funnelled white water so aptly named by Major John Wesley Powell. Cataract Canyon, which links Canyonlands National Park with Glen Canyon National Recreation Area at Lake Powell, has 26 rapids, some of which are the most thrilling (and dangerous) of any in the US. Half-day tours are available, as well as three-, four-, and five-day trips. Reservations are advised and necessary for the longer trips. Depending on your time, money, and desire for thrills, one of the following Moab-based river running companies can provide boats, guides, and all you need for what should be the adventure of a lifetime. If you want to put together a do-it-yourself trip with rented equipment and rafts, they are available from those companies indicated with an asterisk (*). (Permits are required for many sections of the river, so check with the rental companies, Canyonlands National Park Headquarters, or the Moab Information Center about specific areas you plan to float.)

Adrift Adventures—
378 North Main, PO Box 577, Moab, UT 84532; (801) 259-8594 or 1-800-874-4483.*

Canyon Voyages—
352 North Main, PO Box 416, Moab, UT 84532; (801) 259-6007 or 1-800-488-5884.*

Colorado River Tours—
1861 North Hwy. 191, PO Box 328, Moab, UT 84532; (801) 259-5261.

The Moab Wildwater Rafting Company—
PO Box 801, Moab, UT 84532; (801) 259-RAFT.

Navtec Expeditions—
321 North Main, Moab, UT 84532; (801) 259-7983 or 1-800-833-1278.

Nichols Expeditions—
497 North Main, Moab, UT 84532; (801) 259-7882 or 1-800-635-1792.

North American River Expeditions—
543-T North Main, Moab, UT 84532; (801) 259-5865 or 1-800-342-5938.

Sheri Griffith River Expeditions—
2231 South Hwy. 191, PO Box 1324, Moab, UT; (801) 259-8229 or 1-800-332-2439.

Tag-A-Long Expeditions—
452 North Main, Moab, UT 84532; (801) 259-8946 or 1-800-453-3292.*

Tex's Riverways—
PO Box 67, Moab, UT 84532; (801) 259-5101.

Western River Expeditions—
1371 North Main, Moab, UT 84532; (801) 259-7019.*

World Wide River Expeditions—
625 Riversands, Moab, UT 84532; (801) 259-7515.

RECOMMENDED GEAR AND CLOTHING FOR THE RIVER

The combination of sun, water, and bare rock demands extra precautions. Dress comfortably in clothing that will protect you from the sun and that you can get wet. Everyone going on the river should have a broad-brimmed hat; high-SPF sunscreen;

lip balm (preferably with an SPF factor); good sunglasses that can be secured with a strap; river sandals (most rafting companies will rent them for the day) or a pair of old tennis or jogging shoes (the older, the better since you may want to throw them away after your trip); a swimsuit; a T-shirt; lightweight nylon shorts; a lightweight, long-sleeved cotton shirt; long pants; and a windbreaker. Waterproof boxes (often called Ammo Cans) are provided by commercial river runners for cameras, but if you are any kind of a camera bug, you will want your camera in hand as you make the trip, so bring plenty of film and plan to protect your camera from the water. For anything longer than a day trip, consult with the outfitter for a list of items you should bring or plan to rent.

ROCK CLIMBING

There are enough challenges in Castle Valley, the Fisher Towers, along the Colorado River Valley and Indian Creek, and within Arches and Canyonlands national parks that even the most dedicated of climbers could never master all of them in a lifetime. In contrast to the hard granite faces that most mountain climbers encounter, the soft sedimentary sandstone presents a unique set of difficulties for the climbers who come to Moab each year to test themselves on Castleton Tower, Sister

Superior, Moses, Titan, Lighthouse Tower, Monster Tower, Mystery Towers, Sharks Fin, or one of any number of unique formations that the millennia have left scattered throughout southeastern Utah. Katy Cassidy and Earl Wiggins, in their beautifully illustrated and dramatically written *Canyon Country Climbs* (Pruett, 1989), describe a number of the climbs that they and their friends have made since the 1960s. They quickly show that climbing in this part of the world is not for the inexperienced or the faint-hearted. If you are interested in climbing or knowing where people may be climbing, check with the Moab Information Center.

SWIMMING
Moab Swim Center—
This outdoor swimming pool is open daily during the summer for lap swimming 12:15 pm–1:15 pm; open swimming 1:30 pm–5:30 pm; and Mon.–Sat. for night swimming from 6:30 pm–9:00 pm. Admission fee charged. **181 West 400 North; (801) 259-8226.**

TENNIS
Public tennis courts are located at the **Grand County Middle School** at **217 East Center in Moab.**

─── SEEING AND DOING ───

HISTORIC SITES
Moab Walking Tour—
The Grand County Travel Council and Dan O'Laurie Museum have prepared a free walking-tour brochure of 23 sites and buildings in the Moab area. The oldest building in town is the **Balsley Log Cabin,** constructed in 1881 and located at **68 South 100 East.** Other buildings include the 1888 LDS Church; Star Hall, built as a recreational hall in 1898; the 1892 courthouse and jail; and several business buildings and homes constructed around the turn of

the century. The brochure is available at the Dan O'Laurie Museum and the Moab Information Center.

MUSEUMS
Dan O'Laurie Museum—
Devoted to the prehistory and history of the Moab area, the Dan O'Laurie Museum has exhibits on geology, natural history, prehistory, the historic Old Spanish Trail, ranching, farming, early transportation, and the 1950s uranium boom. One of the recent acquisitions was found

by three Moab teenagers: a cone-shaped, 2.5-foot-tall Anasazi burden basket that dates from around the time of Christ. Upstairs there is an art gallery that features exhibits by local artists. The museum is named for an early supporter who came to Moab with the uranium boom of the early 1950s. Since 1989, the museum has published *Canyon Legacy*, a quarterly journal that contains excellent articles on the history of the area. There is a museum store where you can purchase copies of *Canyon Legacy* and local books; you can also obtain a free copy of the "Moab Area Historic Walking Tour" brochure. Open Mon.–Sat. 1 pm–5 pm and 7 pm–9 pm. Admission is free, but donations are accepted. **118 East Center; (801) 259-7985.**

Hollywood Stuntmen's Hall of Fame—

When you realize the number of western movies filmed in the Moab area and learn about some of the unbelievable stunts that were performed from the nearby cliffs and ledges, you will agree that Moab is as good a location as any for the Stuntman's Hall of Fame. The Hall of Fame includes costumes, weapons, equipment, and photographs from some of the most famous stunt scenes in movie history. At least as interesting as the museum is its curator, Johnny Hagner. A genuine stuntman, Hagner's credits date back to 1960, and his latest performance was as a miner in the movie *Geronimo*, which was filmed in the Moab area during the summer of 1993. The costume that Johnny wore during the filming is now on exhibit. Johnny has written the only book for movie stuntmen, *How to Be a Hollywood Stuntman*, which you can purchase at the museum. Johnny, who has worked with some of Hollywood's biggest stars, will even perform a stunt trick for you during your visit. This nonprofit museum is open Mon.–Fri. noon–9 pm; Sat. and Sun. noon–6 pm. Admission fee charged. The museum is located in an old LDS church at **111 East 100 North; (801) 259-6100.**

NIGHTLIFE

Canyonlands by Night—

Canyon country and the Colorado River are a much different experience at night. One of the most memorable ways to spend a couple of evening hours on the Colorado Plateau is to board one of the jet boats that take you upstream about 6 or 7 miles beyond the Colorado River Bridge. During the upstream journey Dee Tranter gives an informal talk about the river, points out some of the landmarks and unusual features along the canyon cliffs, and answers questions about the river and the area. When darkness comes, the boat begins the return journey accompanied by a mobile light system onboard a truck that follows along the highway down the river. The spotlights that light up the canyon present an unforgettable view of the 500 foot rock walls, while the narration covers the Indian myths about the Colorado River, geology, and history. The narration is interspersed with music, specially selected to match the scenery. One of the most memorable segments was the tape of the Sons of the Pioneers singing "Moonlight on the Colorado," as the spotlight threw a gigantic shadow of a huge cottonwood tree across the river onto the far side canyon wall. As you drift back toward the Colorado River Bridge under a brilliant canopy of stars or under a moonlit evening sky, you see another side to Utah's beauty. Canyonlands by Night has been offered since 1966 and is a popular nighttime activity in the summer. Tours usually leave at 8:30 pm and return around 10:30 pm; offered daily from May–Sept. Reservations are recommended. Stop by the **Colorado River Tours building on the west side of the Colorado River, just south of the bridge,** or call **(801) 259-5261.**

Bar M Chuckwagon—

With an emphasis on food and entertainment rather than on authentic 19th-century ranch life, the Bar M is a fun-filled and inexpensive way to spend the evening.

There are no waiters here, but after you go through the line in chuckwagon fashion, you sit down at picnic tables to enjoy the chicken and sliced beef, baked potato, baked beans, and sourdough biscuits with butter and honey. If you have room, there is peach cobbler or spice cake for dessert. The entertainment includes music by the talented Bar M Wranglers and stories, jokes, songs, and Indian dances. Open May–Sept. with dinner served at 7:30 pm. Reservations are recommended. **541 South 400 East; (801) 259-2276.**

The Canyons Edge—

This excellent 40-minute multimedia production uses photographic slides by Tom Till and Bruce Hucko, music, and narrated extracts from Utahn Terry Tempest Williams's writings to present the Colorado Plateau through the stories of its Native American inhabitants. The wonderful photography will inspire your own picture-taking and the magical prose will confirm that the beauty of southeastern Utah's canyons can also be seen in the mind. The presentation has received a special award of merit from the Utah Humanities Council. The Canyons Edge is shown twice nightly at the **Moab Information Center,** located on the **southeast corner of Center St. and Main St. in Moab.** Admission fee charged.

SCENIC AIR FLIGHTS
Redtail Aviation—

For a unique perspective of canyon country, try an airplane flight over Canyonlands National Park and the Green and Colorado rivers. One-hour tours for three- to six-passenger high-wing Cessna planes. Groups of up to 40 people can be accommodated. **Redtail Aviation, PO Box 515, Moab, UT 84532; (801) 259-7421.**

SCENIC DRIVES
Colorado River Scenic Byway—

The Colorado River is known worldwide for its unsurpassed scenery. Hwy. 128 provides the only opportunity for motorists to drive along sections of the Colorado that have not been tamed by dams. Except for the crossing at Moab and the Dewey Bridge crossing along this Scenic Byway, there are only two other points in Utah where automobiles can cross the main channel of the Colorado River along its more than 200-mile course through Utah. These are at the Hite Crossing Bridge on Hwy. 96 and via Hall's Crossing Ferry on Hwy. 278.

Hwy. 128 begins on the eastern side of the Colorado River, where Hwy. 191 crosses the river just west of Moab. It continues up the Colorado in a northeasterly direction for about 35 miles, before it crosses next to what was the Dewey Bridge. A new bridge was constructed in 1986. The historic, one-lane suspension bridge that served for 70 years as the only bridge across the river between Moab and Grand Junction has been listed in the National Register of Historic Places and preserved as an historic site. The drive concludes at Cisco, 44 miles from Moab. Unless you need to continue east or west along Interstate 70, follow the same route back to Moab.

The view and vistas are completely different coming back down the river than they are going up. The contrast between the brown-green waters of the Colorado, the red sandstone cliffs and carved formations along the river, the snow-capped La Sal Mountains, and the deep blue sky makes this a photographer's dream. Also take a few minutes to watch the rafts coming down the river. Rapids on this stretch of the river are almost nonexistent, and there is something to be said for watching boatloads of people floating by, completely relaxed and without a care in the world, except, perhaps, a water bucket attack from friends or strangers on a nearby boat. The drive also provides opportunities to view waterfowl, herons, egrets, and during the winter, bald eagles roosting in the cottonwood trees. Bighorn sheep can occasionally be seen across the river.

La Sal Mountain Scenic Loop—

While most visitors to Moab come for the magnificent red-rock scenery, the beauty of the La Sal Mountains is not to be ignored.

The La Sal Loop climbs from the desert environment of Spanish Valley up to the alpine meadows and beneath the 12,700-foot peaks. The 60-mile-long road is paved, except for a few sections of gravel. The steep climb, much of it over narrow switchbacks, is slow-going and should not be attempted by cars towing trailers or in recreation vehicles. The high-country road is closed by snow in winter, but during the rest of the year, it offers panoramic views of the Colorado Plateau and the Blue and Henry mountains in the distance. The loop leaves Hwy. 191 6 miles south of Moab and climbs the west side of the La Sals before descending through Castle Valley, where it meets Hwy. 128, which you can follow along the Colorado River back to Moab. Be sure to stop at the monument erected on the northwestern slope of the mountains to commemorate the Battle at Pinhook Draw. At Pinhook, a band of Paiute Indians that killed two men at an isolated ranch near the Utah-Colorado border in May 1881 ambushed a posse made up of cowboys and led by a brother of one of the dead ranchers. During the battle 15 to 27 men were killed, including 9 members of the posse and 7 to 18 Indians. This was one of the deadliest battles fought between whites and Indians in Utah.

Needles/Anticline Overlook Road—

This not-to-be-missed drive takes you into the heart of the sandstone formations on the eastern banks of the Colorado River, for views of the Needles District of Canyonlands National Park and the Anticline of the Colorado River. The road to both overlooks begins 35 miles south of Moab and 12 miles south of La Sal Junction off Hwy. 191. The 21-mile-long road to the Needles Overlook is paved. At the Needles Overlook, you have an excellent view of the Needles District and the Indian Creek Wilderness Study Area to the west and southwest. Looking back to the east, the volcanic La Sal Mountains offer an imposing contrast to the colorful sandstone. Retrace your route from the Needles Overlook 6 miles and you come to the junction with the gravel road that heads north for 17

miles to the Anticline Overlook. The gravel road can be traveled by passenger vehicle and is open year-round except after severe snowstorms. The Anticline Overlook is located on a narrow promontory that offers interesting views of the Colorado River, Dead Horse Point, Hurrah Pass, and Kane Creek Canyon. The total distance from the turnoff from Hwy. 161 to both overlooks is 76 miles. You should plan three or four hours for this drive.

Potash Scenic Byway—

For a shorter trip along the western bank of the Colorado River, turn off Hwy. 191 3 miles northwest of Moab and follow Hwy. 279 for 17 miles to where the paved road ends at the Moab Salt Plant. At the plant, potash is processed for fertilizer by a process that involves flushing a large amount of water through an elaborate system of tunnels, after which the water is channeled into ponds. Evaporation leaves behind the mineral potash. Though important to the local economy, many find the plant inappropriate and perhaps detrimental to the scenic resources of the area. Still, there is plenty to be seen along the route, including petroglyph panels identified by two "Indian Writing" signs. A set of dinosaur tracks is indicated by another sign. Jug Handle Arch, 46 feet high and only 3 feet wide, is located above the highway not far from the end of the paved route. If you want to combine a 3-mile round-trip hike with your drive, park your vehicle at the Corona Arch Trailhead. The 1.5-mile-long trail takes you to the 140-foot-by-105-foot Corona Arch and nearby Bow Tie Arch.

TOURS

Canyonlands Field Institute—

Established in 1984 to promote understanding and appreciation of the natural environment and the cultural heritage of the Colorado Plateau, the nonprofit Canyonlands Field Institute offers a unique series of outstanding tours and activities to explore and experience the Colorado Plateau. The institute's philosophy is that "all life is sacred. The land and those who have gone before us have much to teach." To promote that understanding it offers programs that allow participants to experience the Colorado Plateau in a variety of ways: painting, photography, geology, rock art study, ecology, canoeing, hiking, and cross-country skiing. For a catalog containing information about programs and seminars, contact the **Canyonlands Field Institute, 1320 South Hwy. 191, PO Box 68, Moab, UT 84532; (801) 259-7750.**

Hole 'N The Rock—

Some might write off this establishment as simply a tourist trap, and the gigantic lettered signs painted on the sandstone cliff in the bottom of Kane Wash (now offensive to most travelers along Hwy. 191) indicate how far our environmental consciousness has come since they were first painted in the 1950s. Nevertheless, the Hole 'N The Rock is still an interesting example of how creative humans can be with what they have. Albert Christensen spent 12 years excavating his dwelling within this sandstone monolith. After he died in 1957, his wife Gladys worked another eight years to complete the 14-room home, which has 5,000 square feet of living space. She died in 1974 and both are buried in a small alcove underneath the rock about 100 yards east of the gift shop. More than 50,000 cubic feet of sandstone were excavated from the interior of the huge rock, which is .25 mile high and through and 1 mile in circumference. Some of the interesting features include the face of Franklin D. Roosevelt sculpted into the sandstone at the entrance, cabinets built into the rock walls, and a bathtub carved out of sandstone. The tourist stop has become so popular that many people confuse this recent Hole 'N The Rock with the historic pioneer crossing of the Colorado River farther south. Open daily for tours, 8 am–8 pm during the summer; 9 am–5 pm the rest of the year. Entrance fee charged. The attraction is located on **US Hwy. 191, 15 miles south of Moab; (801) 686-2250.**

Movie Locations Tour—

If you are a movie fan, you already know that the red-rock country around Moab has been the backdrop for numerous full-length motion pictures. While in Moab, pick up a copy of the "Moab Area Movie Locations Auto Tour." Produced by the Grand County Travel Council and the Moab Film Commission, the free brochure describes the shooting locations for 16 movies filmed in the Moab area. The movies begin with the 1949 John Ford production *Wagon Master* and include such films as *The Comancheros, Cheyenne Autumn, The Greatest Story Ever Told, Rio Conchos, Indiana Jones and the Last Crusade, Thelma and Louise, Geronimo,* and *City Slickers II.* All movie locations are accessible by passenger car, and many motels and bed and breakfasts have videos of some of the movies filmed in and around Moab. If you want a detailed history of movie making in southeastern Utah, pick up a copy of Bette L. Stanton's *Where God Put the West,* a book published in Moab and available in local bookstores.

———— WHERE TO STAY ————

ACCOMMODATIONS

Moab has a good number of motels, and new ones always seem to be under construction. They remain full much of the year, however, so reservations are highly recommended. If you are traveling in the off-season (late fall and winter) be sure to ask about off-season rates.

The following is a list of 10 conventional motels and 7 condominiums followed by more detailed accounts of the hostels and bed and breakfasts in the area. For a complete list of area accommodations, contact the Grand County Travel Council. For reservations for the Moab–Green River area, call **Central Reservations** at **1-800-748-4386.**

MOTELS

Apache Motel—$$

Some kitchenettes. Heated pool. 166 South 400 East; (801) 259-5727 or 1-800-228-6882.

Best Western Canyonlands Inn—$$ to $$$

Heated pool, whirlpool, exercise room, video game room, indoor bike storage, restaurant. 16 South Main; (801) 259-2300.

Bowen Motel—$$ to $$$

Heated pool. 169 North Main; (801) 259-7132 or 1-800-874-5439.

Comfort Suites—$$$

Seventy-five rooms. Heated indoor pool, exercise room, and bike storage; microwaves and refrigerators in all rooms. 800 South Main; (801) 259-5252 or 1-800-228-5150.

Days Inn—$$ to $$$

Thirty-three rooms. Swimming pool. 426 North Main St., (801) 259-4468.

Green Well Motel—$$

Seventy-two rooms. Heated pool. Restaurant. 105 South Main; (801) 259-6151 or 1-800-528-1234.

Landmark Motel—$$ to $$$

Thirty-five rooms. Heated pool with child's wading pool, hot tub. 168 North Main; (801) 259-6147 or 1-800-441-6147.

Moab Travel-Lodge—$$$

Fifty-six rooms. Heated pool; restaurant nearby. 550 South Main; (801) 259-6171 or 1-800-325-6171.

Moab Valley Inn—$$$

One hundred twenty-seven rooms. Restaurant. 711 South Main; (801) 259-4419 or 1-800 831-6622.

Ramada Inn—$$$

Eighty-four rooms. Heated pool and whirlpool. Arches Restaurant next door, open for breakfast, lunch, and dinner. 182 South Main; (801) 259-7141 or 1-800-228-2828.

Super 8 Motel—$

One hundred forty-six rooms. Heated pool and whirlpool. 889 North Main St.; (801) 259-8868.

CONDOMINIUMS

All condominiums have kitchen facilities and are usually rented for multiday stays. Unless otherwise noted, all have televisions, are nonsmoking, and do not allow pets.

Cedar Breaks Condos—$$$

Six condos. Just off Center St. at 400 East 10 South; (801) 259-7830.

Cottonwood Condos—$$ to $$$

Seven condos. Smoking and pets permitted. 338 East 100 South; (801) 259-8897 or 1-800-447-4106.

Ron Tez Tourist Condos—$$$

Eight condos. 450 East 200 South; (801) 259-7273.

Westwood Guesthouse—$$$ to $$$$

Seven condos. 81 East 100 South; (801) 259-7283 or 1-800-526-5690.

HOSTELS

Lazy Lizard Hostel—$

A member of Rucksackers Hostel, guests are mostly young adults 18 to 30 who come to Moab to bike, although older people are also welcome. There are a number of choices from basic, single-sex dormitory lodging and teepee accommodations at less than $10 a night, to private rooms and private cabins. The hostel is nonsmoking and has laundry and kitchen facilities, along with a hot tub and television. Located at 1213 South Hwy. 191, about 1 mile south of the center of Moab in a red-and-white house behind the A-l Storage; (801) 259-6057.

BED AND BREAKFASTS

There is no place in Utah where the bed-and-breakfast movement has taken hold as it has in Moab. The following inns are a good alternative to the motels, but they too fill up fast, and reservations are almost always a necessity. On occasion there are no-shows, so don't hesitate to at least call, even on short notice. Unless otherwise noted, all rooms are nonsmoking, and no pets are allowed.

Canyon Country
Bed and Breakfast—$$ to $$$

Located in a commodious ranch-style house in a quiet part of town, Canyon Country has five rooms with both private and shared baths. Other attractions include a buffet breakfast, large enclosed yard and patio, a well-stocked travel library, a hot tub, and mountain bikes for rent. **590 North 500 West; (801) 259-5262 or 1-800-435-0284.**

Castle Valley Inn—$$$

With an unbelievable location, about 10 miles northeast of Moab along the Colorado River and set on 11 acres of fruit orchards, fields, and lawn, Castle Valley Inn is a favorite of repeat visitors to Moab. Owners Eric and Lynn Forbes Thomson are mountain bike enthusiasts and willingly share information about mountain biking. They also provide a workspace for bike repairs. There is a hot tub for soaking any stiff biking muscles. The inn has three rooms and three cottages with kitchenettes. Breakfast is included and guest meals can also be arranged. Take **Hwy. 128 north along the east side of the Colorado River from the river bridge; (801) 259-6012.**

Pack Creek Ranch—$$$ to $$$$

Though not strictly a bed and breakfast, this resort ranch located in the foothills of the La Sal Mountains operated by Jane and Ken Sleight was originally a cattle ranch. Much of the flavor of the original ranch remains, although there are amenities, such as a swimming pool, which were not a part of the cowboy's way of life. The ranch has 11 units, consisting of one- to four-bedroom units located in individual cabins. All have refrigerators and most have fireplaces. Trail rides and pack trips are offered by the ranch. They can also arrange a variety of other activities from rafting trips to four-wheel-drive tours, scenic flights, mountain bike trips, and cross-country skiing tours. The dining room is open 6 pm–9 pm and offers fresh fruit, vegetables, and a variety of main courses and desserts. Located about 14 miles southeast of Moab, off the La Sal Mountain Loop Rd. **Pack Creek Ranch, PO Box 1270, Moab, UT 84532; (801) 259-5505.**

Kane Creek Bed and Breakfast—$$$

In true European style, Albert and Connie Marsing have converted two rooms in their family home to accommodate guests. The larger room has its own TV and a private bath, while the smaller room has a shared bath. Guests are welcome in the family's living room. A large breakfast is served in the family dining room. **490 Kane Creek Blvd.; (801) 259-7345.**

Matterhorn Heights Guest House—$$$

Set in the red rock overlooking the Moab golf course, the Spanish-style home of Ron and Joyce Robertson has four bedrooms and three baths. A large game room is equipped with a TV and pool tables, while a covered patio provides comfortable access outside. No smoking and no pets. **Matterhorn Heights, PO Box 697, Moab, UT 84532; (801) 259-8000.**

Mayors House Inn Bed and Breakfast—$$$

Tom Stocks, the owner of the Rose Tree Inn, is the mayor of Moab, and, if you can catch him between his mayoral duties, he is a wealth of information about local affairs. His wife Gay provides a full breakfast. A heated swimming pool and a hot tub are available to guests. Bicycles may be stored in a locked garage. **505 Rose Tree Ln.; (801) 259-6015.**

Sandi's Family Homestyle Bed and Breakfast—$$ to $$$

This B and B is popular with bicyclists because of its location near the beginning of the Slickrock Mountain Bike Trail. There are four bedrooms with shared baths. Continental breakfast is served on the redwood deck, weather permitting. **450 Walker; (801) 259-6359.**

Slick Rock Inn—$$$

This 1907 adobe building has been carefully remodeled by Cherie Gilmore, who serves a gourmet breakfast with "the best coffee in town," either inside or outside. There are five guest rooms with two shared baths. **268 South 400 East; (801) 259-2266.**

Sunflower Hill—$$$

The guestrooms at Sunflower Hill are in three locations: a two-bedroom upstairs suite with a private bath, three bedrooms downstairs each with a private bath, and the adjacent Garden Cottage which has two suites, each with two bedrooms, bath, and sitting room. Guests are welcome to wander about the large yard and gardens. Richard and Marjorie Stucki provide a wholesome breakfast of fresh fruit and juice, homemade granola and yogurt, and homemade muffins and bread. **185 North 300 East; (801) 259-2974.**

CAMPING
PUBLIC

In the La Sal Mountains, about 22 miles east of Moab, there are two campgrounds on US Forest Service land at an elevation of 8,800 and 9,200 feet. **Oowah Lake** has 6 tent sites and is equipped with toilets but no water. **Warner Lake** has 20 RV and tent sites and is equipped with drinking water and toilets. Both are open June–Oct. and available on a first-come, first-served basis.

PRIVATE

Camping places in the Moab area can be as scarce as motel accommodations. There are 10 private campgrounds in and near Moab, with over 500 camping sites. Because of the relatively low elevation of about 4,000 feet and the consistently warmer temperatures, camping is possible all year for those prepared for it. Unless otherwise noted, all campgrounds are open year-round and charge fees.

Canyonlands Campark—

With 108 RV sites, 70 of which have full hookups, and 60 tent sites, this campground offers all of the amenities and is open year-round. **555 South Main; (801) 259-6848.**

Holiday Haven RV Park—

All of the 62 sites have complete hookups. Toilets, showers, laundry facilities, and disabled access. Open Mar.–end of Oct. **400 North 500 West; (801) 259-8526.**

Moab KOA—

The Moab KOA has 60 sites, 38 with complete hookups, 18 tent sites, and the usual KOA amenities. Closed from mid-Nov.–Jan. Located **4 miles south of Moab on Hwy. 191; (801) 259-6682.**

Pack Creek Campground—

Thirty-six trailer sites, half of which have complete hookups. Toilets, showers, and laundry facilities. **1520 Murphy Ln.; (801) 259-2982.**

Slickrock Campground—

One of the closest campgrounds to Arches National Park; 129 sites, 85 of which have complete hookups, and 52 tent sites. Amenities include disabled access. Located **off Hwy. 191 1 mile north of Moab; (801) 259-7660.**

WHERE TO EAT

"The Moab Area Restaurant Guide" lists 22 eating establishments in Moab, and in a growing tourist area like Moab, more restaurants are opening all the time. The following is a sampling of some of the more unusual locales.

Grand Old Ranch House—$$ to $$$

One of Moab's (and Utah's) finest restaurants, the Old Ranch House serves prime rib, seafood, and steaks. While the food is reason enough to stop for dinner, the location in the old Arthur Taylor ranchhouse gives this restaurant double appeal. Chances are you will spot the restaurant on the **east side of Hwy. 191, about a mile west of Moab after you cross the Colorado River Bridge.** One of Moab's most successful ranchers, Arthur Taylor had this two-story brick house built in 1896, the year Utah became a state. Open daily 5 pm–10:30 pm. Reservations are recommended. **(801) 259-5753.**

Honest Ozzies Cafe and Desert Oasis—$ to $$

In case you are inclined to ask, there is no one named Ozzie associated with this cafe. Instead Donna Rivette, owner of this unique establishment, and her employees came up with the name when customers, not too familiar with the prehistoric Indians of the area, the Anasazi, kept adding an extra "t" to their name as they asked about the "Anastazi" people of the region. You have to admit that "Honest Ozzie" and "Anastazi" sound nearly the same. Beyond the fun name, Honest Ozzies, opened in 1987, was the first Moab restaurant to focus on natural, healthy foods. The restaurant motto, "Honestly good food made better naturally," is not only a play on its name, but a goal that Donna and her staff strive for in every dish they prepare. It is "the" place in Moab for health-conscious eaters. In addition to the oatmeal, granola, and muesli for lighter breakfast eaters, the huevos rancheros and veggie potatoes are popular breakfast items. Lunch includes made-to-order sandwiches, soups, and salads. Favorite dinner items include the High Desert Vegetable Pie, a spicy mixture of vegetables layered with cheese on a blue corn tortilla and topped with a baked custard layer that is served with sour cream, salsa, rice, Anasazi beans, cilantro slaw, and a soft whole wheat tortilla; French lasagna, made with layers of spinach, sesame noodles, mushrooms, carrots, cheeses, and herbs; and the Ozzie Oriental, which is stir-fried fresh vegetables and sprouts cooked in several different glazes and served with a large portion of steamed brown rice. For nonvegetarians, there are chicken and fish dishes. The vine-covered one-story house is surrounded by trees, lawns, and a vegetable garden, which give it an oasislike appearance. The patio is an especially popular place to eat, or if the weather does not permit, the quaint dining room inside is very cozy. Donna and her staff pride themselves on maintaining a homey atmosphere where it's just like eating over at a friend's house. They succeed in doing this except when the place is overrun with mountain bikers. Credit cards not accepted. Open daily from 7 am–10 pm. **60 North 100 West; (801) 259-8442.**

Fat City Smoke House—$$ to $$$

Roger and Lyn opened this Texas barbecue–style restaurant in 1992 after deciding the warm weather of Moab was much preferable to the cold winters of their native Rock Springs, Wyoming. They had operated a bar in Rock Springs and began featuring barbecue food after Roger went to Texas for six months to try out different recipes. Using apple and cherry wood in a Ferris wheel–style smoke pit, the ribs, beef brisket, chicken, and homemade sausage make this a heaven for meat lovers. By far, the favorite is the baby back pork ribs served with smoked sweet potatoes. But even if meat is not a part of your diet, there's a nice selection of vegetarian sandwiches including a veggie club, veggie burger, grilled eggplant, and grilled ginger tofu. Open Mon.–Sat. 11:30 am–10 pm. **36 South 100 West; (801) 259-4302.**

MiVida Restaurant—$$ to $$$

Also located in an historic home, MiVida Restaurant is named for the uranium mine that lifted Charles Steen from the depths of poverty to a multimillionaire. A modern-day legend, Charlie Steen discovered the first commercial uranium deposits in the Colorado Plateau region. He built the uranium mill on the west side of the Colorado River, where uranium from the many mines all over southeastern Utah was processed. He spent his millions lavishly, and his mansion, built in 1955 atop a hill overlooking Moab, was visited by guests from all over the world. Steen's good fortune did not last, as questionable investments left him bankrupt. His hilltop mansion is now the MiVida Restaurant, which features mesquite-broiled steaks and seafoods. Open for lunch 11 am–2 pm; dinner 5 pm–10:30 pm. **900 North Hwy. 191; (801) 259-7146.**

Dos Amigos Mexican Cantina—$$

For Mexican food, try Dos Amigos. It has been around for nearly two decades and offers a good variety of enchiladas, tacos, tamales, tostadas, fajitas, relleños, and Navajo tacos. Vegetarian specialties include tostadas, vegetarian burrito, and black bean burger. There's also pizza, hamburgers, shakes, and sandwiches. Open daily 11 am–10 pm. **56 East 300 South; (801) 259-7903.**

SunDowner Restaurant—$$ to $$$

German chef Uve Weber caters to the many German tourists who visit Moab and gives the rest of us a traditional German meal without the 5,000-mile trip. Specialties include Wiener schnitzel, veal cordon bleu, steak Dijon, and shrimp scampi. Open for dinner 5 pm–10 pm. Located **north of Moab, on the south side of Hwy. 191 a mile before the Colorado River Bridge. (801) 259-5201.**

Poplar Place Pub and Eatery— $ to $$

Named for the poplar trees that used to line the streets of Moab, specialties at this favorite of locals include gourmet pizza, deli sandwiches on fresh-baked breads, homemade soups, and fresh salads. Carryout and deliveries available. Open 11 am–1 am. **100 North Main St.; (801) 259-6018.**

Eddie McStiff's Brew Pub & Restaurant—$ to $$

One of only a couple of local breweries in Utah, Eddie McStiff's offers its freshly brewed beers to go with a wide range of food. Choices include New York– and Chicago-style pizza, sandwiches, steaks, charbroiled burgers, pastas, salads, and southwestern dishes. You will find 12 different brews, including some that are quite exotic. The most popular is the Raspberry Wheat which won the People's Choice best beer award at the Southwestern Brewmeisters Festival for 1992–1993. The Amber Ale is popular and made with imported British Carastan malt. The Spruce Beer boasts a balance of root, bark, and needle, while the Jalapeno, which has a taste of chilies and a hint of heat, should appeal to the adventuresome. Those who don't want to drink alcohol can enjoy the wonderful homemade rootbeer, which uses half the sugar of normal soda, and Quillaia, a unique derivative of South American trees, along with herbs, spices, and a blend of eight different roots. There are three parts to McStiff's—the tavern and patio where liquor is served with the purchase of food for those 21 or older, and a dining room for families with children where no alcohol is served. Brittany Sheain, the hospitable manager, will greet you at the door and help you select the location best for you. Open daily for food from 3 pm–10 pm with the tavern open from 3 pm–midnight. Located in the **Western Plaza, 57 South Main; (801) 259-2337.**

Slick Rock Cafe—$$ to $$$

No one has done more to promote mountain biking in Utah than Jan Wilking. He has put together a series of nine regional biking guidebooks that have introduced hundreds of bikers to the varied terrain from the slickrock of southern Utah to the mountains of northern Utah. In 1994, he and two partners opened the Slick Rock Cafe in the historic 1906 two-story brick business building located on the **northwest corner of Main St. and Center St., across from the Moab Visitor**

Center. The interior is a bright cheerful, happy place. Breakfast items include omelets, pancakes, French toast, and "slickrock" granola. Lunch and dinner items are a good mix of Italian, Mexican, Cajun, and vegetarian dishes. For lunch, burger lovers might try the "Uranium Burger," made with a half pound of beef with fresh garlic and chunks of blue cheese mixed throughout. There is a grilled fish of the day, New York strip steak, pasta, and Utah trout. Specialties include a shrimp and chicken jambalaya and Louisiana barbecue chicken and ribs. The grilled vegetables are also very popular with the younger set that frequents this establishment. Open Mon.–Sat. from 7 am–10 pm.; **(801) 259-8004.**

Milt's Stop & Eat—$

This place has been around since the uranium boom and is known for its good traditional pancake-and-egg breakfasts. It also has burgers, real fries, shakes, and malts. Open 6 am–8 pm. **356 Millcreek; (801) 259-7424.**

SERVICES

Bureau of Land Management—
Grand Resource Area, Sand Flats Rd., PO Box M, Moab, UT 84532; (801) 259-8193.

Canyonlands National Park Headquarters—
Open Mon.–Fri. 8 am–4:30 pm. 125 West 200 South, Moab, UT 84532; (801) 259-7164.

Moab District Office—
82 East Dogwood; PO Box 970, Moab, UT 84532; (801) 259-6111.

Moab Information Center—
Center and Main streets, PO Box 550, Moab, UT 84532; (801) 259-8825 or 1-800-635-6622.

US Forest Service—
Manti–La Sal National Forest, 125 West 200 South, Moab, UT 84532; (801) 259-7155.

Balanced Rock, Moab. Photo by Allan Kent Powell.

Blanding and Monticello

Utah archaeologists half joke that the entire southeastern corner of Utah should be declared one large archaeological area and that the number of archaeological sites in the Blanding-Monticello region should be counted by the square mile, if not the acre. Only a handful of the thousands of sites have been excavated, and even fewer have been restored; others have been preserved because of their isolation and a growing awareness of their beauty and value. Ancient Anasazi ruins are one of the big draws in this area. Hovenweep National Monument, Edge of the Cedars State Park, and Grand Gulch Primitive Area offer just three of the best-known sites to study the legacy of the Anasazi. The modern Ute and Navajo tribes are also an important part of the region. The enormous Navajo Reservation begins 21 miles south of Blanding and stretches across the Utah-Arizona border and takes in a large chunk of northeastern Arizona and part of northwestern New Mexico. More than 150,000 members of the Navajo Nation, or Diné as they call themselves, live on the reservation.

The center for Utah Navajos is Monument Valley, a remarkably beautiful valley full of eroded red sandstone monoliths, pinnacles, and towers that make up one of the most famous backdrops in the world. The Monument Valley scenery is reason enough to visit southeastern Utah, but there's so much more. The small but lovely Natural Bridges National Monument, the sinuous San Juan River which cuts through the area, the Blue Mountains, and Canyonlands National Park are a few of the attractions that lure travelers. The region described in this section is known to Utahns as San Juan County, the largest of Utah's 29 counties. With an area of 7,884 square miles, it is larger than the states of Connecticut, Rhode Island, New Jersey, Delaware, and Hawaii. Visitors will find accommodations along Hwys. 191 and 163 in five locations, approximately 20 miles from each other, starting with Monticello in the north, then Blanding, Bluff, Mexican Hat, and Gouldings Trading Post on the Utah-Arizona border.

HISTORY

Man's presence in southeastern Utah for the last 12,000 years is a dramatic story of survival in a land that most of the world would regard as desolate and unappealing. Mormon pioneers did not establish a foothold here until 1880, three years after the death of the Great Colonizer Brigham Young and 33 years after the arrival of the first Mormon pioneers into the Salt Lake Valley 330 miles to the north. No area of Utah has received greater attention by archaeologists than San Juan County. Their research indicates that the earliest inhabitants, the Paleo-Indians, hunted big game in the area during the Ice Age, leaving spear points as the only trace of their presence. By 5000 BC the Paleo-Indian cultures had left the area, their destiny tied to the large herds of big game that had moved eastward onto the Great Plains. These hunters were replaced by Desert Archaic hunter-gatherers who did not establish permanent residences but moved from place to place in search of small game and wild foods. They were extremely well adapted to this desert region and pursued their practical lifestyle for at least 5,000 years. Around AD 200 corn was introduced from Mesoamerica, and the Archaic peoples began to cultivate small crops as a supplement to their wild food. To remain close to their crops, they began to establish permanent residences and to pursue a more settled lifestyle. In time, the Archaic peoples made the transition to the people we know as the Anasazi.

Over the next millennium, the Anasazi occupied what is now called the Four Corners region of Utah, Colorado, New Mexico, and Arizona, progressing from small farming hamlets to large-scale villages, or pueblos. They made exquisite baskets but soon began developing fired pottery, which was both practical and increasingly artistic. Irrigation techniques improved, and new crops, such as beans and squash, were added. As interactions with other cultures brought new ideas, between AD 1100 and 1200 Anasazi clans began to coalesce into very large villages, of which the best known are Mesa Verde in nearby Colorado and Chaco Canyon in New Mexico. Numerous examples of these pueblos also remain in San Juan County, in such places as Westwater Creek, Montezuma Canyon, and Chinle Wash. About AD 1250 the Anasazi began to move away from the San Juan area to better farmlands along the Rio Grande and the Little Colorado River. Archaeologists speculate that the move was caused by several factors: a particularly long drought that tipped the balance in this marginal land, not enough land to support the growing number of occupants, and perhaps attacks by invading nomadic Indians from the north, such as the Utes and Navajos. Pueblo Indian traditions indicate that internal strife and the need to purify people through a religious pilgrimage to a new land were the primary reason the Anasazi abandoned their homes and moved south. Navajo traditions relate that the Navajo and Anasazi lived together in peace and cooperation, as the Anasazi introduced the Navajo to corn. Disputes arose, however, and the friction left the Navajos impoverished and often enslaved by the Anasazi. Because of their wrongdoing, their unwillingness to live in harmony, and their abuse of supernatural powers given them by the gods, the Anasazi were punished in a variety of ways. Various Navajo legends recount the Anasazi were turned to fish in the

San Juan River, or beset with lockjaw and paralysis, or had the air sucked out of their lungs by a strong wind, or were burned in a great fire, or crushed by an ice storm, or drowned in a flood that destroyed everything in its path.

While the Navajo, or Diné, are the largest group of Indians living in southeastern Utah, they are relative latecomers to the area. Anthropologists indicate that they migrated from northwestern Canada with other Athapascan peoples, such as the Apache, and reached the Southwest sometime between AD 1300 and 1500. The Navajo may have pushed up to the San Juan River about the time that the Pilgrims were founding Plymouth Colony in 1620 and were as far north as Elk Ridge by the late 1700s. Navajo oral tradition says nothing of a migration from the north but does describe their arrival in this region as a journey through three worlds beneath this one. Originally hunter-gatherers, in historic times the Navajo have depended on crops such as corn, beans, and squash, which their pueblo neighbors taught them to grow, and raising livestock, especially sheep, goats, and horses, which they later obtained from Spanish settlers. The early Navajo seemed to have alternately lived alongside their neighbors peaceably and at times raided them. This was a tactic they used against Anglo settlers in Utah, New Mexico, and Arizona, after the settlers arrived in the Southwest in the 1850s and 1860s. The US government back east sent military expeditions to protect American, Pueblo, and Mexican settlers when much of the Southwest was ceded to the US in 1848. In 1864 US Army Captain Kit Carson succeeded in rounding up approximately two-thirds of the Navajo Nation, using intimidation tactics that led many of the people to surrender. They were forced to make what has come to be called the Long Walk to Fort Sumner on the dry southeastern New Mexico plain, where they were incarcerated at Bosque Redondo and forced to submit to reservation living in an area that could not support them. They were finally allowed to return to their home in 1868, after many Navajo had died and the US government conceded that the experiment had failed miserably. A number of the 4,000 Navajo who eluded capture and refused to surrender took refuge in the isolated reaches of Navajo Mountain and Elk Ridge of Utah's San Juan County.

Today, the Navajo have successfully preserved many of their old traditions, while accommodating the economic and political realities of today. As well as being a sovereign nation within the US and in charge of their own affairs, the Navajo also hold elected county offices and work in all areas of the economy. They are no longer required to send their children to government-run boarding schools. Instead the children attend high schools at Montezuma Creek and Monument Valley, built and administered by the San Juan School

District. Nevertheless, because the Navajo have not traditionally lived in a cash economy, the poverty level is high and living conditions are substandard compared to Anglo-America. Many Native Americans still feel an undercurrent of discrimination—even racism—in their relations with white neighbors.

Two hundred and fifty Mormon settlers arrived on the San Juan River on April 6, 1880, after an arduous six-month, 180-mile journey across the canyons of southeastern Utah from older Mormon settlements in southwestern Utah. Known as the Hole-in-the-Rockers, because of the narrow slit through which they had taken their wagons and livestock to cross the Colorado River, these Mormon pioneers established the towns of Bluff in 1880, Monticello in 1887, Blanding in 1905, and other Mormon outposts in Colorado and New Mexico. The Mormons succeeded economically by first working in the silver mines in nearby Colorado, and then by developing cattle and sheep herds that competed with non-Mormon outfits from Colorado and Texas. Economic and social tensions marked relations between Mormons and non-Mormons, but around the turn of the century, the non-Mormon outfits were bought out. In the 1950s, uranium and oil booms brought in non-Mormons and gave a strong boost to a stagnating economy. Over the last four decades the boom-bust cycles of uranium and oil have been a challenge. The tourism industry, which traces its origins to the turn of the century when national articles about the region led to the designation of Natural Bridges National Monument in 1908, has grown steadily, especially with the designation of Canyonlands as a national park in 1964.

GETTING THERE

Monticello is located on Hwy. 191, 291 miles southeast of Salt Lake City; and Blanding is another 25 miles farther south. From Salt Lake City, take Interstate 15 south about 60 miles to exit 261 at Spanish Fork. Exit onto Hwy. 6, which heads southeast to Price, where it joins with US Hwy. 191. Continue about 60 miles southeast to Green River to connect with Interstate 70, then stay on Interstate 70 for 20 miles east to Crescent Junction, where Hwy. 191 heads south to Moab and on to Monticello.

If you are driving west from Colorado, follow Hwy. 160 west to Cortez, then take Hwy. 666 northwest from Cortez to Monticello, which is about 50 miles away. Coming north from Arizona, follow Hwy. 160 to Kayenta, where you can take Hwy. 163 north to Monument Valley, across the border into Utah, and on to its junction with Hwy. 191 at Bluff. There is no regularly scheduled air or bus service to the area.

MAJOR ATTRACTIONS

Natural Bridges National Monument

Natural Bridges is one of the nation's earliest National Monuments. It was established by presidential proclamation in 1908, following the publication of a *National Geographic* article describing the three large natural bridges in White and Armstrong canyons. One of the bridges—Sipapu—is 2nd in size only to Rainbow Bridge in Glen Canyon, which is the largest known natural bridge in the world. The natural bridges were formed by tributaries of the Colorado River, which eroded the soft Cedar Mesa sandstone through deep bends in the river, leaving behind the bridges. The buttresses and spans that you see today have been formed by the harder caprock that tops the softer sedimentary layers.

An 8-mile, one-way loop road connects the visitors center with trailheads to the Sipapu, Kachina, and Owachomo bridges. A booklet available at the visitors center entitled "Of Wind Water and Sand: The Natural Bridges Story," offers an excellent introduction to the monument. Sipapu is 2 miles from the visitors center. It measures 220 feet in height with a span of 268 feet. The span is 31 feet wide and 53 feet thick. Sipapu is a Hopi word to describe the hole or passageway by which the ancestors of the Hopi entered this world from another world. The trail to the bridge descends 600 feet to the bottom of White Canyon, for a total round-trip distance of about 1.2 miles.

Only slightly smaller than Sipapu, the Kachina Bridge is 210 feet high with a span of 204 feet but is the most massive of the three arches, with a width of 44 feet and thickness of 93 feet. The name Kachina was given because of the Indian pictographs on the bridge abutment, which resemble the Kachina masks of the Hopi. Kachina bridge is located 5 miles from the visitors center and is reached via a 1.5-mile round-trip hike to the bottom of the canyon and back.

The smallest, oldest, and most fragile of the three bridges, Owachomo Bridge has a height of 106 feet and a span of 180 feet, but it is only 27 feet wide and 9 feet thick. Owachomo is located 7 miles from the visitors center and 2 miles beyond Kachina. It can be reached by an easy .5-mile round-trip hike that descends 300 feet. Owachomo is also a Hopi word which means "flat-rock mound," for a protrusion on the bridge. To shorten the hike to all three bridges by 2.5 miles, use a shuttle between the Sipapu and Owachomo trailheads, or start midway at the Kachina Bridge Trailhead, hike down to Sipapu, retrace your route to Kachina and continue up to Owachomo, then return to Kachina. The hike between Sipapu and Kachina bridges takes you past the 1,000-year-old Horse Collar Ruin, abandoned by the Anasazi in the 1200s. The ruin complex includes two adjacent ruins, several dwellings, two large granaries, smaller storage bins, and two nicely preserved kivas. Inside the kivas are shelves and benches along the circular walls, a plastered fire pit with an accompanying stone windbreak, and a ventilation shaft. For nonhikers, the ruin can be viewed from an overlook located at Stop Number 7 on the driving loop, 3 miles from the visitors center.

Two hundred and sixty million years ago, this area was a white sandy beach along a receding shallow sea. The sand hardened into a 1,000-foot-thick layer known today as the Cedar Mesa Sandstone Formation of the Permian geologic period. The formation is older than the more familiar Navajo, Kayenta, Wingate, Chinle, and Moenkopi formations of the Triassic period. Over time water began to cut through the siltstone and sandstone, forming entrenched meanders or large goosenecks like those seen nearby on the San Juan River. Eventually water, rocks, sand, and silt pushed down the canyons at terrific speeds by flash floods cut through the narrow necks, leaving a natural bridge above. The bridges were originally thick and massive, like that of the middle bridge—Kachina Bridge; but through gradual erosion by precipitation, percolation, and wind, they eventually become more delicate until they collapse. Given the millions of years of geologic time, the bridges occupy a relatively short time in history, though the largest spans are believed to be over 5,000 years old.

While at Natural Bridges, keep an eye out for the animals that inhabit area. Rabbits, squirrels, gophers, black ravens, magpies, several varieties of lizards, and a host of insects inhabit the potholes along the bottom of the canyon. Coyotes are seen from time to time. There are also mountain lions, bobcats, and midget faded rattlesnakes, which you are not likely to see.

Natural Bridges is located 48 miles west of Blanding, just off Hwy. 95. There is a campground located .3 mile from the visitors center, but the closest motel accommodations are in Blanding. The visitors center has exhibits, a slide show, area books and maps, and rangers to provide information about current conditions and answer questions about the monument. Open daily 8 am–4:30 pm, except for holidays during winter. There are extended hours from May–Aug. If you want to hike to all of the bridges and explore some of the surrounding attractions, plan to spend the entire day.

Hovenweep National Monument

The Ute Indians called this remote area on the Utah-Colorado border Hovenweep, meaning "deserted valley," and the six unusual villages left behind by the Anasazi in the late 1200s still convey a here-one-day, gone-the-next feeling.

The original inhabitants may have migrated westward from nearby Mesa Verde or perhaps were outcasts from that major center. Whatever their origin, they cultivated corn, beans, and squash in the scattered villages located between the Montezuma and McElmo creeks. Archaeologists postulate that many acres that have

now returned to sagebrush were cultivated fields of corn, beans, squash, and cotton. Corn was the first domesticated crop and may have been planted as early as 2,000 years ago as the inhabitants began the transition from big game hunting to agriculture. By about 1270 AD villages like the Square Tower community were populated by several hundred individuals with houses, granaries, fields, gardens, reservoirs, and dams to regulate the flow of water all visible elements of the landscape. When a major drought struck the region about AD 1200, the outlying villages were abandoned, as inhabitants relocated to canyons with permanent springs. One of the most interesting aspects of the ruins is the variety of shapes employed for these dwellings. Oval, circular, square, and D shapes were used. The towers here may possibly have been built as defensive fortifications against attack from other Anasazi clans or perhaps Shoshone Indians coming from the north. Some towers, such as the northwest end of Hovenweep Castle, may have been used to track the summer and winter solstices and the autumn and vernal equinoxes. Certain windows within the towers are placed in such a way that sunlight strikes particular points on the interior walls at those times of year. The towers may also have been used for signal fires between this area and Mesa Verde.

The oral traditions of the Pueblo Indians of Arizona and New Mexico tell of their ancestors coming from the area known today as the Four Corners region. Here they lived for hundreds of years and developed a high level of civilization before the Great Spirit directed them to abandon their homes and move to other places with better food sources and a better environment—a place where they might attain the perfection of their society. By the last quarter of the 13th century, large communities were being established to the south, perhaps with new and more elaborate religious ceremonies which, with the push of a severe drought, drew the Hovenweep Anasazi to a new homeland. It is likely that the former residents of the Hovenweep area moved southwest to the Hopi villages, south to the Zuni villages, and southeast to the Pueblo villages at Acoma and along the Rio Grande river.

Hovenweep was designated a national monument in 1923 and is administered by the National Park Service at nearby Mesa Verde National Park. The Hovenweep ruins were probably known to the early settlers on Montezuma and McElmo creeks, including Mormon frontiersman Peter Shirts who was at the mouth of Montezuma Creek in 1879. Over the next four decades, the ruins became better known and in 1917 and 1918, J. Walter Fewkes, chief of the Bureau of American Ethnology, made an archaeological survey and recommended they be designated a national monument.

A visitors center is located near the Square Tower Ruins and is open from 8 am–5 pm year-round. A trail guide is available, which indicates a number of loop trails that will take you to the most significant ruins in the Square Tower group including the famous Square Tower, Hovenweep Castle, Hovenweep House, Twin Towers, Stronghold House and Tower (entrance to which was gained by climbing up the still visible hand and toe holds chiseled into the rock), and Eroded Boulder House (which was built inside the overhang of a large boulder which incorporated the boulder into the walls and roof).

In addition to Square Tower Ruins, the Holly, Horseshoe, and Hackberry ruins may be visited along a 9-mile round-trip hiking trail. Visitors are urged to stay on existing trails and not to disturb the ruins in any way or to pick up any artifacts. Hovenweep is a treasure house for archaeologists who hope to learn more about the culture and life of the Anasazi. Its sites and ruins are also sacred places for the Pueblo Indians.

The closest accommodations are at Blanding; however, a campground is located 1 mile from the visitors center. Open Apr.–Oct., it has water and restrooms. Gas and supplies can be purchased at Hatch Trading Post or in the nearby community of Montezuma Creek. Plan a full day to

visit Hovenweep, but you can see the major ruins at Square Tower in a few hours. An especially beautiful time to view the ruins is at sunset or sunrise. If you stay overnight in the campground you can expect to enjoy a brilliant starlit night. If you find you have a little extra time, head south from the visitors center to Aneth, on the San Juan River, then follow the river as it flows westward past Montezuma Creek to Bluff. There are other ruins along this road. To reach the monument, head south from Blanding on Hwy. 191 for 15 miles, then turn east on Hwy. 262, to Hatch Trading Post, and then continue eastward for 16 miles. All but 2 miles of the road to Hovenweep are paved and the graveled 2 miles are easily negotiated by passenger vehicles. For a well-written, beautifully illustrated introduction to Hovenweep, pick up a copy of Ian Thompson's *The Towers of Hovenweep* (Mesa Verde Museum Association, 1993), which is available at the visitors center and other centers in the area.

Monument Valley

Monument Valley's eroded sandstone buttes and pinnacles fit almost everyone's notion of what the Southwest should look like. But before it became a valley of beauty to serve the imagination of thousands of visitors, the area was a solid 1,000-foot layer of sandstone. As the early Rocky Mountains deposited sediments in a vast lowland basin, they cemented into rock. About 50 million years ago, pressure from inside the earth slowly lifted the deposits to an elevation of 1 to 2 miles above sea level. Since that time the forces of wind and water have slowly chiseled away at the layers of sandstone, shaping and reshaping the rock until the last vestiges of the immense sandstone plateau remain as the pinnacles, towers, and buttes of Monument Valley. As you look at the rocks, you will see on some of them the younger and harder Shinarump Formation which serves as a cap over the De Chelly Formation which makes up the cliffs. At the base of the cliffs, the softer Organ Rock Shale or Claystone forms a kind of pedestal for the monuments. Beneath the claystone, the Cedar Mesa sandstone serves as a broad foundation for the entire valley.

Monument Valley was home to the Anasazi Indians for nearly 1,000 years until they abandoned their homes here and elsewhere in the Four Corners region around 1270 AD.

By the 1500s the Navajo Indians had entered the Four Corners region and by the 1800s had established homes in Monument Valley. As westward expansion brought contact and conflict with the Anglos from the east, the Navajo were forced to leave their traditional lands and make the long walk to Bosque Redondo in eastern New Mexico in 1864. Some escaped the ordeal by hiding out in Monument Valley and in places north of the San Juan River. When the Navajo returned in 1868, the Navajo Reservation was established with Monument Valley being the northwest corner of the original reservation. Later, in 1884, the reservation was expanded to its approximate present boundaries with the annexation of areas north and west of Monument Valley. The expansion came after four miners were killed—James Merrick and Ernest Mitchell in 1880 and Samuel Walcott and James McNally in 1884—when they went into Monument Valley looking for silver mines.

Anglo miners were not permitted on the reservation, but Anglo traders were. In 1906 John and Louisa Wetherill from Mancos, Colorado, started a trading post at Oljato ("Moonlight Water"). The Wetherills established friendly relations with the Navajo and thus were allowed to stay. Seventeen years later, another young Colorado couple, Harry and Mike Goulding, arrived to establish their trading post under the Big Rock Door Mesa. It was Harry Goulding who brought Hollywood director John Ford to Monument Valley in 1938 where he filmed *Stagecoach*. Since then Monument Valley has served as the location for hundreds of commercials and dozens of movies including: *My Darling Clementine* (1946), *Fort Apache* (1948), *She Wore a Yellow Ribbon* (1949), *Rio Grande*

(1950), *The Searchers* (1956), *How The West Was Won* (1962), *Cheyenne Autumn* (1964), *The Legend of the Lone Ranger* (1980), and *Back to the Future III* (1988).

In 1959, Monument Valley was designated a Navajo Tribal Park and a year later, a visitors center was constructed just across the state line in Arizona, 3.5 miles off Hwy. 191. A 17-mile self-guided scenic drive over a dirt road begins at the visitors center and provides access to the heart of Monument Valley. The road is native surface and can be somewhat rough, but it is passable by regular automobiles. Overlooks along the drive provide plenty of photo opportunities. Keep in mind, however, that permission to photograph the Navajo residents and their property is required and a gratuity is expected. In order to better preserve the valley and because people live in Monument Valley, hiking and off-road travel are prohibited.

After you descend the switchbacks to begin the 17-mile driving tour, you pass an old abandoned gas station that will catch the eye of any photo bug. But save plenty of film for the natural wonders. The first viewpoint is of the Mittens, East and West, and Merrick Butte. It was near this butte that James Merrick was found scalped and covered with rocks and brush in 1880 when he and his partner, Ernest Mitchell, entered the valley looking for a secret Navajo silver mine. The Navajo blamed the murder on local Paiutes, but they maintained their innocence.

The Mittens are probably the most famous and most often photographed formations in Monument Valley, and their namesake is easily recognized in the sandstone formation. Navajo myth holds that the formations are two hands left behind by the gods as a promise that someday they would return and rule with power from Monument Valley.

As the drive continues you pass other unusual formations: Elephant Butte; Three Sisters (three holly people who were turned to stone); Thunder Bird Mesa; Rain God Mesa; and Totem Pole—an important site for Navajo rain-producing ceremonies. The drive provides ever-changing perspectives of the sandstone formations while clouds and different times of day color and shade the stone with unrestrained variety.

This is a drive not to be hurried. Take your time. Drive slowly and stop often and contemplate the beauty with a singleness of mind. If you do, the rocks and the land will begin to speak to you in ways you may never have heard before. Even for the uninitiated, Monument Valley can be a very sacred place.

You can also arrange for guided tours with Navajo tour guides. There is a group of tour operators that is located in front of the visitors center, and they offer a 1.5-hour tour over the scenic drive route or a 2.5-hour tour which takes you into the restricted area where you can see natural bridges, Anasazi ruins and rock art, and a Navajo weaver at work inside a hogan. Half-day, all-day, and other specialized tours, including horseback tours, can be arranged. When you arrive at the visitors center, you are likely to be approached by several individuals about a guided tour, so it is good to decide beforehand if that is what you want, and, if so, inquire about the details of the tours being offered. Depending on the demand, prices are sometimes negotiable. One of the first Navajos to begin offering tours of the valley was the grandfather of Betty Jackson, who has lived near the Three Sisters Formation in Monument Valley all her life and has operated Jackson's Tours since 1977. The following tour operators have been approved by the Monument Valley Navajo Tribal Park.

Bennett Tours, PO Box 360341, Monument Valley, UT 84536; (801) 727-3283.

Bigman's Horseback Trailrides, PO Box 1557, Kayenta, AZ 86033; (602) 677-3219.

Blacks Van and Hiking Tours, PO Box 310393, Mexican Hat, UT 84531; (801) 739-4226.

Ed Black's Horseback Tours, PO Box 310155, Mexican Hat, UT 84531; (801) 739-4285 or 1-800-551-4039.

Fred's Adventure Tours, PO Box 310308, Mexican Hat, UT 84531; (801) 739-4294.

Homeland Tours, PO Box 662, Kayenta, AZ 86033; (602) 697-3667.

Jackson Tours, PO Box 360375, Monument Valley, UT 84536; (801) 727-3353.

Navajo Guided Tours, PO Box 3604546, Monument Valley, UT 84536.

Navajoland Tours, PO Box 131, Kayenta, AZ 86033; (602) 697-3524.

Totem Pole Tours, PO Box 360306, Monument Valley, UT 84536; (801) 727-3313.

The visitors center is open daily 7 am–8 pm mid-Apr.–mid-Oct.; 8 am–5 pm the rest of the year. Closed Christmas and New Years and at noon on Thanksgiving. Admission fee charged. Exhibits, an Indian crafts shop, and an information desk are all part of the center.

While you are in Monument Valley a stop at Goulding's Trading Post and Lodge is worthwhile. Harry and Mike Goulding established their trading post in 1923 and constructed the two-story red sandstone building in 1928. The building now serves as a museum depicting how the trading post looked during many of the 40 years it was operated by the Gouldings. The museum is open daily from 7:30 am–9 pm. A few steps in back of the museum is the movie set reproduction of Captain Nathan Brittle's Quarters which was constructed in Oct. 1949 during the filming of *She Wore a Yellow Ribbon*. There is also the Anasazi Theater, which offers three shows nightly of a 20-minute, multimedia presentation by award-winning photographer Ric Ergenbright entitled *Earth Spirit: A Celebration of Monument Valley*. Goulding's also provides the closest motel accommodations to Monument Valley.

OTHER ATTRACTIONS

Edge of the Cedars Museum

Settled in 1905, Blanding was built, in part, on an ancient Anasazi village, part of which has been excavated and is now included in the Edge of the Cedars State Park. The state park includes six clusters of ruins of which only one group has been excavated. An underground kiva, or ceremonial room, has been partly restored so that visitors can now enter it using a ladder that descends through the roof. Museum exhibits include pottery, jewelry, stone tools, baskets, sandals, and clothing as well as artifacts from the Hispanic and Anglo settlers. A gift shop sells contemporary Navajo and Ute crafts. Open daily 9 am–6 pm during the summer; 9 am–5 pm the rest of the year, except for official holidays during the winter months. Edge of the Cedars is located on the northwestern edge of Blanding and signs from Center St. direct you to the site. **660 West 400 North; (801) 678-2238.**

Four Corners Monument

The only place in the US where you can be in four states at the same time is at the meeting point of Utah, Arizona, New Mexico, and Colorado, known as the Four Corners. An inlaid concrete slab marks the point where the four states meet, and a visit to the monument makes a good geography lesson for both young and old. Since there is not much at the monument—except the chance to spread-eagle yourself across four states and have your photo taken—people usually stay less than a half hour. You will probably want to combine a stop at the monument with a visit to Hovenweep National Monument, Monument Valley, or both. There are Indian craft booths encircling the marker that sell pottery and jewelry.

To reach the Four Corners Monument from Utah, take Hwy. 191 south across the Utah-Arizona border until you reach Hwy. 160. Head east on Hwy. 160 for approximately 35 miles until you reach the monument. If you want to return along an alternate route, continue east on Hwy. 160 for about 5 miles to state Rd. 41, which turns to the north. Follow it back into Utah, where it becomes state Rd. 262, which you can follow through Aneth and Montezuma Creek to its junction with Hwy. 191, 15 miles south of Blanding.

FESTIVALS AND EVENTS

Folk Fair Festival—

This Fourth of July celebration in Blanding offers performances, folk singers, ethnic dancers, demonstrations, exhibits, booths, and Dutch-oven meals. Local craftsmen, including members of the Ute and Navajo tribes, usually participate. For more information write or call the **Blanding City Office, 50 West 100 South, Blanding, UT 84511; (801) 678-2791.**

OUTDOOR ACTIVITIES

FOUR-WHEEL-DRIVE TRIPS

I'm not sure where recreational four-wheeling began in the US, but surely one of the earliest places was southeastern Utah. After World War II, local residents purchased surplus jeeps and personnel carriers and went bouncing across slickrock and sliding down and spinning up canyons on weekend rides. The 1950s uranium boom gave what had been pure recreation the legitimacy of work, as hundreds of men and some women scoured the Four Corners area in a frenzied search for the wealth that a rich uranium find promised. The Cold War demand for uranium and the availability of four-wheel-drive jeeps made four-wheeling a popular pastime— even a necessity in San Juan County— nearly two decades before four-wheel-drive outfits became part of both rural and urban life in the rest of the country.

The carefree days of going wherever you could get a jeep are over, as federal land management policies have now brought restrictions. Still, there are hundreds of miles of four-wheel roads and trails open for travel in San Juan County.

One popular area is the Canyon Rims Recreation Area, northwest of Monticello and south of Moab, administered by the BLM. Described as "park-quality land that was left out of Canyonlands National Park," the Canyon Rims Recreation Area includes eight areas, which are described in the excellent 1991 publication by F. A. and M. M. Barnes, *Canyon Country's Canyon Rims Recreation Area*. The book describes hundreds of four-wheel-drive and hiking trails in the recreation area.

There are no commercial four-wheel-drive rental places and no four-wheel-drive tour companies in Monticello or Blanding, but **Tours of the Big Country, PO Box 309, Bluff, UT 84512; (801) 672-2281**, offers four-wheel guided tours of Monument Valley and Cedar Mesa. Other tour companies are headquartered in Moab (see the **Moab** chapter.) For information about self-guided, four-wheel-drive trips, contact the **Bureau of Land Management Office** in Monticello. **San Juan Resource Area, 435 North Main St., PO Box 7, Monticello, UT 84535; (801) 587-2141.**

GOLF

Blue Mountain Meadows Golf Course—

Operated by the city of Monticello, Blue Mountain Meadows Golf Course is located on the southern end of Monticello, just west of Hwy. 191. The 9-hole course is generally not crowded, and green fees are very reasonable. Unlike most Utah courses, the course is located in an arroyo, or wash, which means a nice downhill shot on the 1st hole, but a steep uphill climb on the 9th hole, where the flag cannot be seen for the 2nd shot. Generally open Apr.–Oct.; **(801) 587-2468.**

HIKING AND BACKPACKING

Butler Wash Interpretive Trail—

This 1-mile-long loop was developed by the BLM to provide access to the Butler Wash Anasazi ruins and to interpret the geology and native plants of the area. There are 20 markers along the trail, which identify such plants as prickly pear, yucca, sagebrush, cliffrose, rabbitbrush, and Mormon tea. A 20-room, multistory dwelling is the main structure in the Anasazi Pueblo, which was occupied approximately 700 years ago. These are some of the most interesting and accessible stabilized ruins in the area. To reach the trail, drive south from Blanding on Hwy. 191 for 3 miles, then turn west onto Hwy. 95 and follow it for 10 miles to the parking area on the north side of the road marked with an "Indian Ruins" rest area sign. A free interpretive trail brochure about the site is available at a number of locations in the area, including Edge of the Cedars State Park, and the multiagency visitors center in Monticello.

Grand Gulch—

Superlatives do not do justice to Grand Gulch. Designated a primitive area by the BLM in 1970, there is no motorized traffic in the canyon and livestock grazing is no longer allowed. It sits just below Elk Ridge at an elevation of 6,400 feet and consists of a main canyon and numerous side canyons that drop 2,700 feet through miles of carved sandstone to meet the beautiful San Juan River far below. Grand Gulch is essentially a 50-mile-long Anasazi museum in one of the most superb outdoor settings anywhere. Secreted away in the canyons are pictographs that decorate south-facing alcoves and other warm exposures. A hiker can spend anywhere from a couple of days to a month or more exploring Grand Gulch, some of the most silent and awe-inspiring places in the Southwest. Most visitors hike in for a day or two, set up camp, explore the surrounding area, and return the way they went in. Another option is to hike the entire length of the canyon and arrange for a boat to pick you up at the junction of Grand Gulch with the San Juan River. The latter option is recommended for only the hardiest and best prepared of hikers who can secure an iron-clad commitment from friends to make the rendezvous.

The largest ruins in the canyon, Junction Ruins, are located 4.5 miles from the Kane Gulch Trailhead at the junction of the Kane and Grand gulches and can be visited in a day. There are good camping spots at Junction Ruins, and most hikers plan to stay overnight there or farther down the canyon. Because of the increased use of the canyon, the BLM limits the number of hikers in the canyon. A backcountry permit is required and can be obtained at the **Kane Gulch Ranger Station** or at the **San Juan Resource Area Office of the BLM** at **435 North Main in Monticello; (801) 587-2141.** These locations are very helpful with additional information about conditions. There is a fee for overnight stays; day use is free. All hikers must sign in at the ranger station, where trail maps—an essential purchase—are available. To reach the Kane Gulch Ranger Station, open Mar.–mid-Nov., take Hwy. 95 toward Natural Bridges Monument and turn south on Hwy. 261. Drive about 4 miles south, then turn left (east) at the sign "Kane Gulch Ranger Station."

Fish Creek and Owl Creek Loop—

An alternative to Grand Gulch is the Fish Creek and Owl Creek Loop, which is located about 6 miles from the Kane Gulch Ranger Station. To reach the trailhead, drive south on Hwy. 261, 1.5 miles past the Kane Gulch Ranger Station, then turn left (east) onto a graded road, which you follow for about 5 miles to the trailhead. From the trailhead, follow the rock cairns for .25

mile to the edge of Owl Canyon. Climb down over the creamy Cedar Mesa sandstone into the canyon and watch for rock cairns that mark the trail. During the 6.5 miles from the trailhead to the junction with Fish Creek, you drop 1,400 feet in elevation, but regain the altitude on the 9-mile hike back up Fish Creek.

As with Grand Gulch, there are many Anasazi ruins to see and plenty of side canyons to explore. One special feature is Nevills' Arch, located in Owl Creek about halfway between the trailhead and the junction with Fish Creek. Exit Fish Creek by way of the left fork, located 6 miles up from the junction with Owl Creek. Follow the left fork for .5 mile to a spring, which is also a good campsite. At the spring, the trail begins a steep climb along the south side of the canyon, with an elevation gain of 600 feet to the top. Once you are on top of the canyon, follow the well-worn trail back to the south for 1.5 miles to the trailhead.

Since this area is also administered by the BLM, you can pick up information at the **Kane Gulch Ranger Station** or at the **San Juan Resource Area Office of the BLM at 435 North Main in Monticello; (801) 587-2141.**

Dark Canyon—

The Dark Canyon area west of Elk Ridge and southeast of the Colorado River's Cataract Canyon is probably the most isolated region in the entire state. In earlier days, cowboys spent weeks, even months, alone tending their cattle. Today, Dark Canyon is also a designated primitive area administered by the BLM and a wilderness area administered by the US Forest Service. Offering the ultimate in isolation and scenery, only experienced, well-prepared hikers should venture into the labyrinth of canyons and gulches that make up this convoluted area. The canyonheads on the western slope of Elk Ridge are at an elevation of 8,200 feet, where broad alpine meadows contrast dramatically with the 1,400-foot-deep sandstone walls that drop to the Colorado River and Lake Powell. A number of trails wind through the Dark Canyon area and, while a day hike can give you a taste of the region, most hikers will not be satisfied with anything less than several days. The Kane Gulch Ranger Station or the BLM Office and US Forest Service Office in Monticello are good sources of information about Dark Canyon.

Mule Canyon—

If your idea of a hike is to spend three or four peaceful hours exploring an interesting and scenic area with your family, then Mule Canyon is a good bet. Located 20 miles southwest of Blanding, off Hwy. 95, the canyon is carved from pinkish-white sandstone and supports high-elevation trees such as Douglas fir and ponderosa pine, as well as clusters of wildflowers at seeps in the walls. There are many Anasazi ruins and petroglyphs here, including the Mule Canyon Ruins, about 1 mile from the trailhead, which have been stabilized by the BLM. Visit these ruins, which are accessible for those with disabilities, then retrace your route along Hwy. 95 back to the east for .5 mile. Watch for a dirt road that heads off the highway to the north and take it for .5 mile until it crosses the bottom of Mule Canyon. You can park your car here and begin the hike up the canyon. Another option is to hike the north fork of Mule Canyon, which can be reached by continuing on the dirt road another .75 mile.

Blue Mountain and Elk Ridge—

The excellent hiking trails in the Manti–La Sal National Forest, which encompass the Abajo Mountains and Elk Ridge, are often overlooked in favor of the lower trails. The following seven trails are highly recommended by forest rangers and the San Juan Travel Council.

Lloyd's Lake—

Developed by the City of Monticello, Lloyd's Lake provides a picnic area and a 2-mile hiking trail that is very easy. Located about 2 miles west of Monticello. From Main St. (Hwy. 191) turn west onto 200 South. Follow this through the S-turn at the high school and continue west until you cross the cattle guard. Turn left on the first road on the left and proceed to the lake.

Robertson Pasture (Twin Peaks) Trail—

This trail leaves Foy Lake and travels approximately 4.5 miles to Spring Creek Trail. The trail is steep at one point for about .5 mile. This trail connects with Spring Creek Trail to make a full day's hike.

Spring Creek Trail—

This trail travels north to the paved road that you drove to reach Foy Lake. The trail is 2 miles long and leaves you about 2.5 miles from the lake. There is one short steep section near the middle of the trail. Together with the Robertson Pasture Trail, the two trails make a full day's hike.

Red Ledges Trail—

Begin at the eastern trailhead for Robertson Pasture (Twin Peaks) and Spring Creek. Follow the Robertson Pasture Trail for approximately 1 mile to the trailhead for Red Ledges Trail. Turn southwest on Red Ledges Trail and follow it 2.5 miles to Red Ledges Access Trail and on to Forest Rd. 079. Return to your beginning point, about 1.5 miles away on Forest Rd. 079.

Camp Jackson Trail—

Drive west on the north side of Recapture Reservoir on Forest Rd. 084 approximately 14 miles to the southern trailhead of Camp Jackson Trail. The trail climbs northwest for 3.5 miles to the Marvin Tunnel and the intersection with Forest Rd. 079. Going this direction the trail climbs out of Recapture Canyon, makes its way up the ridge, and ends on the side of the mountain. It may be easier to walk it in the opposite direction. In that case, leave Blanding on 100 East and travel into the national forest where the road becomes Forest Rd. 095. Follow this road to the intersection with Forest Rd. 079 and turn northeast onto Forest Rd. 079. Follow this road to the northern trailhead for the Camp Jackson Trail. From here the trail goes 3.5 miles south and east to Forest Rd. 084.

Peavine Canyon Trail—

Begin on Hwy. 275, which takes you into Natural Bridges National Monument. Turn right onto Forest Rd. 088 and travel through the geologic formation known as the Bears Ears to the intersection with Forest Rd. 108. Turn left or west and follow Forest Rd. 108 to Peavine Canyon Trailhead or stay on Forest Rd. 088 and turn right or east at the intersection (the number remains the same). If you turn west and go to the Peavine Canyon Trailhead, the trailhead is along the road and the trail travels northeast from the roadway into Peavine Canyon. There are some steep sections as you climb down into the canyon. Follow the trail 10.5 miles to the intersection of Peavine Canyon with Kigalia Canyon and the Peavine Corridor. Then follow Peavine Corridor Rd. (Forest Rd. 089) southeast to Peavine Corridor Trailhead at Forest Rd. 088 and back to the starting point. The road portion of this trip is about 5 miles. This is a good overnight hike.

Posey Trail—

Begin on Hwy. 275 going into Natural Bridges National Monument and turn onto Forest Rd. 088. Follow this past the intersection with Forest Rd. 108 and continue past intersections on the north side of the road for Forest Rd. 180 and Kigalia Canyon Trail to the intersection with Forest Rd. 092. At this point turn left or west sharply and remain on Forest Rd. 088 to the Hammond Canyon Trailhead. Follow Hammond Canyon almost its entire length, approximately 9 miles, to the intersection with the Posey Trail. Turn northwest onto Posey Trail and follow this back to Forest Rd. 200, then to Forest Rd. 088 and the starting point. There are some steep sections, many scenic overlooks, and views of Anasazi ruins. This is an overnight hike.

HORSEBACK RIDING

Monument Valley Trail Rides—

Offers a variety of rides in the valley from 1.5 hours to all day to several days. Since the summer temperatures in Monument Valley easily reach 100 degrees Fahrenheit and higher, sunrise, sunset, and moonlight rides are popular. **Monument Valley Trail Rides, PO Box 155, Mexican Hat, UT 84531; (801) 739-4285 or 1-800-551-4039.**

RIVER RUNNING: THE SAN JUAN RIVER

If you would like a river trip that can be made in one or two days, offers some of the most spectacular scenery anywhere, and has enough gentle rapids to make the run interesting but not dangerous (unless you happen to be on the river when a flash flood comes through), a float on the San Juan River between Bluff and Mexican Hat is highly recommended. The stretch can be run in a day, but if you have the time, the two-day trip is unforgettable. The extra time allows for stops at Indian pictographs, an Anasazi Pueblo ruin, and the ruins of the Barton Trading Post where Amasa M. Barton was murdered in 1887, shortly after the trading post was established at the Rincon Crossing of the San Juan River. Near the Barton Trading Post is the last stretch of the historic Hole-in-the-Rock Trail, the route up San Juan Hill. You can camp across the river from the mouth of Chinle Wash. We did and were treated to an incredibly beautiful and powerful lightning display off to the south on the Navajo Reservation. For an extended trip, you can continue down the San Juan from Mexican Hat to the Clay Hill Crossing takeout just above Lake Powell. The extended trip (three or four days) takes you through the famous Goosenecks of the San Juan, beneath soaring cliffs, and past the mouths of Grand Gulch and other side canyons to the eastern tip of Lake Powell.

Wild Rivers Expeditions, Inc.—

This Bluff outfitter offers a variety of river-running trips on the San Juan and the Colorado rivers. This company has been in the business a long time and offers a thrilling and comfortable river trip. The river guides make a concerted effort to provide insights into the archaeology, history, geology, and natural history of the area. **PO Box 118, Bluff, UT 84512; (801) 672-2244** or **1-800-422-7654.**

Ruins—

This area, as has already been noted, is full of Anasazi ruins. Many are in excellent shape and well worth the time it takes to get to them. Check at the Edge of the Cedar Museum in Blanding for more information or contact the **BLM Office.** Here are two of my favorites.

Westwater Ruins—

These ruins, which date from the 1200s, are located on Westwater Creek, along with those known as the Edge of the Cedars Ruins. The Westwater Ruins are southwest of Blanding and can be reached by heading south out of Blanding on Hwy. 191 for about 1 mile. Take the road on the right that heads west for about 2 miles. At the end of the road, it is a short hike over to the ruins, which are on BLM land.

Mule Canyon Ruins—

See Hiking and Backpacking section.

SKIING

For a number of years, the Blue Mountain Ski Area, west of Monticello, offered the only downhill skiing in the eastern half of the state. Unfortunately, the two lifts have not operated for a few years, but hope springs eternal and perhaps downhill skiing will return someday to the Blues. The Blue Mountains do, however, offer excellent cross-country skiing. For information about trails and conditions, check with the **Multi Agency Visitors Center, 117 South Main St., Monticello; (801) 587-3235,** or with the **US Forest Service in Monticello; (801) 587-2041.**

SLEDDING AND TUBING

Monticello has one of the best hills for tubing and sledding in the state. The south-sloping hills of the Monticello Golf Course offer easy access and runs free of rocks and brush. Monticello, on the eastern edge of the Blue Mountains at an elevation of 7,066 feet, usually gets plenty of snow in the winter.

SEEING AND DOING

HISTORIC BUILDINGS AND SITES

Historic Bluff Houses—

As you travel through Bluff, take a few minutes to drive around the town (it really only does take a few minutes!) and note the fine red sandstone houses. The houses were constructed after the original Bluff settlers turned from farming to cattle. The vast rangeland and juniper-clad mesas of southeastern Utah provided excellent grazing for cattle, and lucrative markets in the Colorado mining camps and farther east brought wealth to several Bluff families. The most prominent were the Redds and the Scorups.

Al Scorup's House is located on the eastern side of Bluff and faces west. Scorup

was a relative latecomer to Bluff, arriving as a 19-year-old in 1891, 11 years after the Hole-in-the-Rock pioneers founded the town. Scorup worked as a cowboy for different cattle owners until 1897, when he contracted with several cattle owners to round up missing cattle that were roaming wild in the piñon-juniper forests near Bluff. The young cowboy and his brother collected 2,000 head for which they were paid $5 each. With their $10,000 they were able to purchase their own herd of cattle and develop one of the most successful cattle operations in southeastern Utah. In 1903, construction began on the Bluff house, which is now the Bluff Bed and Breakfast operated by Rosalie Goldman (see Where to Stay section).

The **Jens Nielson House** was one of the first red sandstone homes constructed in Bluff. It is located in the center of Bluff. Jens Nielson was the quintessential Mormon pioneer. Born in Denmark in 1820, Nielson and his wife joined the Mormon church and immigrated to Utah in 1856, pulling a handcart loaded with supplies for more than 1,100 miles from Iowa to Utah. At age 60, he was the oldest of the Hole-in-the-Rock pioneers and was the bishop of the LDS Church in Bluff for 26 years until his death in 1906. He was, in the words of historian Charles S. Peterson, "the glue that held Bluff together in its early years." The house, constructed about 1890 on the corner of 1st North and 2nd West, is now the Thai House Restaurant.

The **Lemuel H. Redd, Jr.,** House is located northwest of the Jens Nielson House on the south side of the street. At 24, Lemuel H. Redd was a much younger member of the 1880 Hole-in-the-Rock group than Jens Nielson. Redd was the most prominent livestock man, religious leader, and politician in southeastern Utah, until his death in 1923. Redd was a polygamist, and his Bluff house was occupied by his 1st wife Eliza Ann Westover and her family. His 2nd wife, Lucy Zina Lyman, lived in a log house across the street until a new house was constructed in 1909. The house is now a private residence.

The **James Bean Decker House** is the 4th surviving house from Bluff's heyday as a livestock center. Unlike the other sandstone houses, Decker's home was constructed from brick in 1898 and later stuccoed. Decker was also a Hole-in-the-Rock pioneer. He lived in this house until 1900, when a diphtheria epidemic struck the town, killing Decker and four of his seven children. The house has been renovated as a guest house, known as "Pioneer House," and is connected with Recapture Lodge.

Good luck has preserved two log cabins, which date from the original settlement of Bluff. The cabins are located across the street, west of the Jens Nielson House, and have been abandoned and neglected for years. The cabins are, for the most part, constructed of cottonwood logs, which the pioneers found along the San Juan River.

Recently, Blanding resident Gary Guymon, who has a strong sense of history, acquired the property and is attempting to preserve the cabins.

St. Christopher's Episcopal Mission—

Father Harold Lieber established St. Christopher's Mission in 1943, and the school and chapel have become an important institution for Utah Navajos. Visitors are welcome to the mission, which is located 2 miles east of Bluff on Hwy. 163. Before bus transportation became the norm for Navajo students, they crossed the San Juan River on a swinging footbridge, east of the mission. You can still cross the footbridge, which is reached by continuing east past the mission for 1.3 miles, then turning right onto a dirt road for .5 mile to the bridge. Once across the bridge, you are on the Navajo Reservation.

Horsehead Peak—

I know people who have stared for years at the eastern side of the Blue Mountains, trying to see the famous horse head. When you are in Monticello, look west to the mountain and try to spot the horse head and ears formed by the terrain, shadows, and stands of trees on the mountain. Cowboys noticed it more than a century ago, though some longtime residents of Monticello claim that it is less distinct today. Nevertheless, it is there and remains an important southeastern Utah landmark. If, after trying to spot the blaze-faced horse head, you are unsuccessful, go to Monticello's city park, where specially located view pipes can help.

MUSEUMS AND GALLERIES

Monticello Museum—

Located in the Monticello Public Library, the Monticello Museum displays Anasazi artifacts, pioneer and early community items, and mineral specimens. Open during the summer weekday afternoons 2 pm–6 pm. **80 North Main.**

Four Corners Cultural Center—

This center is a part of the College of Eastern Utah and focuses on the Ute, Navajo, Spanish, and Anglo heritage of the Four Corners area. The center offers a history walking tour, western-style dinner, one-act plays, singing and folklore, and Native American dancing three evenings a week (Tues., Thurs., and Sat.) from mid-May–Sept. Located at **707 West 500 South in Blanding; (801) 678-2323.**

ROCK ART

Newspaper Rock—

Located on Hwy. 211, on the road to the Needles District of Canyonlands National Park, 12 miles west of Hwy. 191, the southwest-facing panel of petroglyphs is one of the best displays of rock art to be found in Utah or anywhere else. Hundreds of figures and designs have been "pecked" into the dark desert varnish on the sandstone face over a period of hundreds of years. Some figures are depicted on horseback shooting arrows, an apparent portrayal by Ute Indians who obtained the horse in the 1600s. Others are more symbolic and stimulate enthusiastic speculation as to their meaning. Remarkably, the rock art has survived with a minimum of vandalism. Newspaper Rock is worth spending some time to study the more than 350 distinctive inscriptions that were left by the Anasazi 800 years ago and other Indians including the Ute in the 19th century. A small campground with eight camping sites is located across Hwy. 211 from the rock.

SCENIC DRIVES

Squaw Flats Scenic Byway—

The Squaw Flats Rd., Hwy. 211, provides access to Newspaper Rock and the Needles District of Canyonlands National Park. The 35-mile-long road passes through sheer red sandstone walls along Indian Creek. This is a favorite area for rock climbers. Newspaper Rock (see above) is located within the canyon, 12 miles from the beginning of the Scenic

Byway which begins 14 miles north of Monticello on Hwy. 191. Eight miles from Newspaper Rock is the Dugout Ranch, one of the oldest cattle ranches in the region. It was headquarters for the Indian Creek Cattle Company and is still a working ranch. In 1919, Al Scorup purchased the ranch as part of his cattle enterprise. Later the ranch was acquired by another Bluff rancher, Charles Redd; it remains in the Redd family today. The road continues another 15 miles to the northwest, past South Six Shooter Peak and North Six Shooter Peak, which rise more than 1,000 feet above their bases, to the entrance to Canyonlands National Park (see the **Canyonlands National Park** chapter).

Bicentennial Scenic Byway—

If you spend any time at all in southeastern Utah, there is a good chance that you will travel over portions, if not all, of Hwy. 95, between Hanksville and Blanding. When the last segment of this road was completed in 1976, it was named the Bicentennial Highway to commemorate the 200th anniversary of American independence. The road connects Capitol Reef and Natural Bridges National Monument and leads to Canyonlands National Park, Hovenweep National Monument, and three of Lake Powell's four major marinas: Hite, Halls Crossing, and Bullfrog. The volcanic Henry Mountains, the last mountain range to be named in the US, rise to the right of the highway. About 35 miles south of Hanksville, you reach the junction with Hwy. 276, which leads to Bullfrog Marina in Lake Powell, 35 miles away. If you have plenty of time, this is a recommended detour. You can take the John Atlantic Burr Ferry across Bullfrog Bay to Halls Crossing, which was established in 1881 by Charles Hall to ferry travelers between the Mormon settlements in southern Utah and the newly established Mormon outpost of Bluff on the San Juan River. Today the ferry is the only commercially operating ferry in the state. Be prepared for some delays, especially during the heavy travel season. From Halls

Crossing, Hwy. 276 intersects the Bicentennial Highway at Natural Bridges National Monument. If this detour is not for you, and you continue on the highway, you will pass Hog Springs Campground, which offers picnic facilities, before you reach Lake Powell and the beautiful Hite Bridge.

For many people, this is the first glimpse of Lake Powell, and it is unforgettable. Stop at the Lake Powell Overlook to take pictures and enjoy the contrast of the red sandstone with the blue waters of the lake. After crossing the bridge, you reach Hite Marina, and can then follow White Canyon to Natural Bridges National Monument. As you continue to Blanding, look to the left on the mountain to see the Bears Ears, an important and highly visible landmark to early travelers in the area. A few miles east of the entrance to Natural Bridges National Monument, the highways becomes the northern segment of the Trail of the Ancients Loop, and travelers can visit prehistoric Indian ruins at Mule Canyon and Butler Wash. The distance from Hanksville to Blanding is 133 miles. While the entire drive can take more than a day, with stops at all the possible places, it can also be made in three to four hours, with one or two brief stops.

Bluff through Monument Valley—

This drive takes you literally through the heart of the West. From the time you cross the San Juan River at Mexican Hat, you are on the Navajo Reservation. The 45-mile stretch of Hwy. 163, from Bluff to the Arizona border, is designated a Utah Scenic Byway; however, you will want to continue another 25 miles into Arizona and go as far as Kayenta, so that you can see all of Monument Valley and spend a little time in one of the major towns on the Navajo Reservation (see the Monument Valley section).

The Moki Dugway—

On your return from Monument Valley to Mexican Hat take time to visit the Goosenecks of the San Juan State Park on Hwy. 361, 5 miles north of Mexican Hat. From here, the hairpin curves of the Goosenecks of the San Juan River are most dramatic, and you can wave at the river rats far, far below you. From here, continue north on Hwy. 261 for the 37-mile drive over the Moki Dugway Scenic Backway. Early white settlers referred to the Hopi and prehistoric Indians as "Moki," and this road, like others in the region, follows an ancient Indian trail. The steep gravel switchbacks of the Dugway climb 1,000 feet to the top of Cedar Mesa for a breathtaking view of Monument Valley to the south and the Valley of the Gods to the northeast. (This can be a white-knuckle ride for some, but the view is worth it.) Hwy. 261 connects with Hwy. 95 a couple of miles east of Natural Bridges National Monument, which you will want to visit now or later. Blanding is 42 miles to the east.

The Elk Ridge Road—

Elk Ridge lies to the west of the Blue Mountains and runs in a north-south direction. Located at the south end of the ridge are the famous "Bears Ears." This Scenic Backway takes you right between them. The road then continues through piñon, juniper, ponderosa pine, and aspen forests along Elk Ridge, offering panoramic views of Monument Valley to the south, Dark Canyon Primitive Area, the Henry Mountains to the west, Hammond and Allen canyons to the east, and Canyonlands National Park and the La Sal Mountains to the north. This single-lane dirt road is about 50 miles long and climbs to an elevation of 8,700 feet. It is only for high-clearance vehicles and is impassable in the winter and after heavy rains. To reach the road, follow Hwy. 95 west to Hwy. 275, which turns off to provide access to Natural Bridges National Monument. A mile after you turn onto Hwy. 275, watch for Forest Rd. 088, which continues to the right (north) as the highway turns to the northwest.

Abajo Loop Scenic Backway—

This high-country, single-lane, dirt-and-gravel road reaches nearly 11,000 feet in elevation, as it climbs to the top of the Abajos (Blue Mountains). The road is about 22 miles long and loops between Monticello and Blanding west of Hwy. 191. High-clearance vehicles are recommended. The road is impassable in winter and after heavy rains. From Monticello, head west into the mountains and turn left (south) on Forest Rd. 079, which climbs over the mountains to Blanding. The drive offers beautiful alpine scenery and spectacular views of Sleeping Ute Mountain and the La Plata Mountains to the east in Colorado. The La Sal Mountains near Moab to the north are also visible.

SCENIC AIR TOURS

The view of the rugged canyons and mesas from the air offers a unique perspective to places like Canyonlands National Park, Lake Powell, Rainbow Bridge, The Hole-in-the-Rock Trail, Monument Valley, Natural Bridges National Monument, Blue Mountains, Navajo Mountain, and other places within San Juan County. A one- to two-hour flight from Blanding or Monticello can cover an incredible amount of territory, giving you enough time to take photographs and to collect memories that will last a lifetime.

Scenic Aviation—

This air tour company operates year-round, offering flights of one to two hours in length. Its largest plane carries 15 persons. **Scenic Aviation, Box 67, Blanding, UT 84511; (801) 678-3222.**

Needles Outpost—

This air tour operator flies out of Monticello, primarily over Canyonlands National Park. Flights are half hour long and accommodate one to five people per plane. Mid-Mar.–Oct. **Needles Outpost, PO Box 1107, Monticello, UT 84535; (801) 259-2032.**

Midway Aviation—

This company operates year-round, and offers scenic flights from .5 to 2 hours in length for $35–$140 with a two person minimum. They offer a three and a five passenger plane. **Midway Aviation, PO Box 1131, Monticello, UT 84535; (801) 587-2774.**

WHERE TO STAY

ACCOMMODATIONS

Motel and bed and breakfast accommodations can be found in Monticello, Blanding, Bluff, Mexican Hat, and at Gouldings Lodge in Monument Valley. Rooms can be difficult to find during the heavy tourist season—late spring to early fall—so it is a good idea to make reservations beforehand.

MONTICELLO
Best Western Wayside Inn—$$$

Thirty-five rooms, some nonsmoking. Heated pool and whirlpool. **195 East on Hwy. 666, PO Box 669, Monticello, UT 84535; (801) 587-2261 or 1-800-528-1234.**

Canyonlands Motor Inn—$ to $$

Thirty-two rooms. My children give this a high rating because of the enclosed pool and playground. **197 North Main, PO Box 1142, Monticello, UT 84535; (801) 587-2266.**

Days Inn—$$ to $$$

With 43 rooms, this is the largest motel in Monticello. Heated indoor pool and whirlpool. **549 North Main, PO Box 759, Monticello, UT 84535; (801) 587-2458 or 1-800-325-2525.**

Navajo Trail National 9—$$ to $$$

This is an older facility, nicely kept, with a new addition; 27 rooms, 3 suites, and 3 kitchenettes. **248 North Main, PO Box 849, Monticello, UT 84535; (801) 587-2251.**

Triangle H Motel—$$

An older, very well-kept, one-level motel with good clean rooms, some nonsmoking and some with two bedrooms. **164 East on Hwy. 666, PO Box 876, Monticello, UT 84535; (801) 587-2274 or 1-800-657-6622.**

The Grist Mill Inn Bed and Breakfast—$$ to $$$

Ten guest rooms, all nonsmoking and with private bathrooms, in the old Monticello Flour Mill. There is a Jacuzzi, outside deck, main-floor sitting room with fireplace, 2nd-floor TV room, and 3rd-floor library. Operated by Dianne and Rye Nielson. **64 South 300 East, PO Box 156, Monticello, UT 84535; (801) 587-2597 or 1-800-645-3762.**

Dalton Gang Adventures—$$$

This working cattle ranch offers year-round bookings for a minimum of three days. Stay with working cowboys at cow camps where hats and boots are a must and bedrolls can be rented. Two meals and a box lunch are included. Children 12 and older are welcome. **Dalton Gang Adventures, PO Box 8, Monticello, UT 94535; (801) 587-2416.**

BLANDING
Gateway Motel—$$

Due to its 59 rooms, most travelers to Blanding stay at the Gateway. One of the oldest motels in southeastern Utah, the motel was built in at least three stages. Older rooms are usually available at a lower price. There is an outdoor heated pool and playground. The Elk Ridge Restaurant is just east of the motel. **88 East Center** (located on the south side of Hwy. 191 as it winds through Blanding); **(801) 678-2278 or 1-800-528-1234.**

Cliff Palace Motel—$$

Constructed in the early 1960s, this 16-room motel is interesting architecturally because of its prairie-style influences. Located on Hwy. 191. **132 South Main; (801) 678-2264 or 1-800-553-8093.**

Old Hotel Bed and Breakfast— $$ to $$$

Eight rooms, all with private bathrooms. Located in one of Blanding's historic homes. Operated by Ora Bayles and Bernice Perkings; open Apr.–Oct. **118 East 300 South, PO Box 866, Blanding, UT 84511; (801) 678-2388.**

BLUFF
Recapture Lodge—$$

Jim and Luanne Hook have taken over operation of the Recapture Lodge, with its 28 rooms and heated pool. Also part of the lodge are two restored historic pioneer houses: the Decker House, with four units, and the Adams House, which, with four bedrooms and kitchen facilities, can accommodate large families or small groups. **PO Box 309, Bluff, UT 84512; (801) 672-2281.**

Kokopelli Inn—$$

Named for the legendary Indian humpbacked flute player, the Kokopelli Inn offers 26 rooms. **PO Box 309, Bluff, UT 84512; (801) 672-2322.**

Mokee Motel—$$

Seven rooms. An older motel but nicely kept. **Hwy. 191 in Bluff; (801) 672-2217.**

Bluff Bed and Breakfast—$$$

Two rooms, both nonsmoking. Located in the historic Al Scorup House, now owned by Rosalie Goldman. **PO Box 158, Bluff, UT 84512; (801) 672-2220.**

Calabre Bed and Breakfast—$$

Two rooms. Extra amenities include guided half-day trips to see ruins, the swinging bridge across the San Juan River, and a Navajo hogan. Owner Pat Cook speaks Italian and German. **PO Box 85, Bluff, UT 84512; (801) 672-2252.**

MEXICAN HAT
Valley of the Gods Bed and Breakfast—$$$

If you want to get away from it all, the Valley of the Gods Bed and Breakfast at the Lee Ranch is an ideal place. Located just off Hwy. 261 between Monument Valley, the San Juan River, Grand Gulch, and Natural Bridges National Monument, there are plenty of activities and tours that can be arranged. The rustic old stone ranch house has been renovated to function on a solar-powdered system. The broad front porch provides a panoramic view of the Valley of the Gods. Open all year; has two suites. **PO Box 310307, Mexican Hat, UT 84531; (303) 749-1164.**

San Juan Inn—$$

Thirty five units. Located along a cliff above the north side of the San Juan River. The adjacent Olde Bridge Bar and Grille is a part of the complex (see Where to Eat section). **PO Box 535, Mexican Hat, UT 84531; (801) 683-2220 or 1-800-447-2022.**

Valley of the Gods Inn—$$

Thirty rooms. Located near the banks of the San Juan River. Restaurant with live music in the evenings. **Hwy. 163; (801) 683-2221.**

Canyonlands Motel—$$

A small (10 rooms) but serviceable motel located in Mexican Hat. **(801) 683-2230.**

Mexican Hat Lodge—$$

Ten rooms. Evening steak fry. **(801) 683-2222.**

MONUMENT VALLEY
Goulding's Trading Post and Lodge—$$ to $$$

Sixty-two rooms located within Monument Valley. Some rooms offer a panoramic view of the valley. Heated indoor pool and refrigerators in most rooms. A slide show and tours of Monument Valley are available for a fee. The original trading post was established by Harry Goulding and his wife, Mike, in 1923 and remained under their ownership for 40 years. The original trading post, a flat-roofed structure of locally quarried sandstone blocks, is now a museum and has been listed in the National Register of Historic Places. This is a popular stop for international tour groups, so don't be surprised if they are booked. **PO Box 1, Monument Valley, UT 84536; (801) 727-3231 or 1-800-874-0902.**

CAMPING
PUBLIC

West of Monticello on Blue Mountain are two US Forest Service campgrounds. **Dalton Springs,** 5 miles west of Monticello, has 13 RV and tent sites, while 1.5 miles farther west, **Buck Board Campground** has 12 sites. Both are open late May–end of Oct.

Devil's Canyon, located approximately halfway between Blanding and Monticello on Hwy. 191, is the largest public campground in the area with 33 RV trailer sites and tent sites. The campground is open mid-May–Oct.

At Bluff, **Sand Island Campground,** operated by the BLM, has 6 tent sites, which are used primarily by rafters on the San Juan River.

At **Newspaper Rock,** 20 miles northwest of Monticello on Hwy. 211, there are 8 tent sites.

PRIVATE
Blanding
Kampark—

Fifty-two complete hookups with 20 tent sites. Open year-round with drinking water, toilets, showers, and a laundry. **South of Blanding on Hwy. 191; (801) 678-2770.**

Monticello
Monticello KOA—

Located 5 miles east of town on Hwy. 666, this campground offers 36 RV sites, 7 of which are complete hookups, and 11 tent sites. Toilets, showers, laundry, and dump site. Open May–Oct. **(801) 587-2884.**

Mountain View RV Park—

Located on the north end of Monticello, this campground has 36 RV sites, 12 of which are complete hookups, and 18 grassy tent sites, 8 of which are partial hookups. Toilets, showers, and laundry. It is open year-round. **632 North Main; (801) 587-2974.**

Mexican Hat/Monument Valley
Burches Trading Post—
Located in Mexican Hat. Contains 15 RV sites with full hookups and 20 tent sites. Toilets, showers, laundry, and dump site. Open year-round; **(801) 683-2221.**

Valle's Trailer Park—
Also in Mexican Hat, this campground has 31 RV sites, 25 of which have full hookups; 4 tent sites. Toilets, showers, laundry, dump site, and disabled facilities. Open year-round; **(801) 683-2226.**

Goulding's Good Sam Park—
Located near the historic Goulding's Trading Post in Monument Valley. Offers 100 RV sites, 80 of which are complete hookups, and 45 tent sites. Toilets, showers, laundry, dump sites, and handicap facilities. Open mid-Mar.–Nov.; **(801) 727-3280.**

The Navajo Tribal Park—
In Monument Valley in Arizona. Offers 99 trailer sites, but no hookups, 46 tent sites, and only toilets and showers. Open year-round; **(602) 725-3287.**

—————— WHERE TO EAT ——————

Despite the heavy tourist travel in San Juan County, there is a shortage of good restaurants in the area. With the exception of La Casita, a Mexican restaurant in Monticello, the choices are, as my children would say, "American."

BLANDING
The **Elk Ridge Restaurant** located on the **south side of Hwy. 191** offers generous breakfasts and dinners. Another option in Blanding is **Kenny's Restaurant.** If a hamburger and fries will suffice, then the **Patio Drive-In** is usually a good bet. If you hit Blanding on Sunday, chances are that in the off-season only one restaurant will be open.

MONTICELLO
Monticello offers a little more variety with **Hogies** at **261 East Central**—a good choice. I have found their omelets—stuffed with cheese, olives, mushrooms, and other goodies—a very memorable breakfast. A little more expensive, the **Juniper Tree** at **133 East Central** offers good lunches and dinners while the **La Casita** east on **Hwy. 666** should handle any cravings for Mexican food that arise. If you want pizza, the **Wagon Wheel Pizza** at **164 South Main,** while the only choice, is still a good one. For steak and fish dinners served with home-baked bread, the **Lamp Light Restaurant** is a local favorite. Open Mon.–Sat. 4 pm–11 pm; **655 East Central. (801) 587-2170.**

BLUFF
Cow Canyon Trading Post
Restaurant—$$
Located in an old trading post on the northeast edge of town, the Cow Canyon Trading Post Restaurant is an unpretentious building that is home to one of the best eating establishments in southeastern Utah. Operated by Liza Doran since 1987, she combines her understanding of what makes a good restaurant with the culinary skills of local Navajo cooks. A variety of home-cooked dishes are available—squash blossom stew, lamb kebabs, lemon ginger garlic chicken, chicken teriyaki, lasagna, Navajo-style quiche, ash bread, minted cucumber and bell pepper buttermilk soup, gazpacho, and special desserts like peach dumplings. Hours seem to vary, so you might want to call ahead; **(801) 672-2208.**

The Thai House—$$
The old Hole-in-the-Rock pioneer Jens Nielsen would find it strange that a Thai restaurant has been opened in his stately red sandstone house (see the Historic Buildings and Sites section), but Rich and Sombat Becker have preserved the house, using the upstairs as their residence and the main floor as a fine Thai restaurant. Sombat is from Bangkok, Thailand, and, as Rick maintains and Sombat readily proves, she has a natural talent as a cook. Both hot and mild selections are offered,

BLUE MOUNTAIN

The song "Blue Mountain," penned by Fred W. Keller, who arrived in Monticello as a young lawyer in 1919, has become a real Utah folksong. Its words tell of events in the early history of Monticello (settled in 1887) from the point of view of a non-Mormon Texas cowboy who has fallen in love with Blue Mountain. It mentions the profile of the "Horse's Head" that is still visible on the mountain, if you know where to look. The song has been adopted by both Mormons and non-Mormons of Monticello and was always sung at farewell parties for departing servicemen during World War II and on other occasions. A local songwriter, Stan Bronson, who has composed a number of his own songs to relate the history of the San Juan area, has recorded the song on a cassette tape along with a number of his own songs about the San Juan area. The cassette is called "Down from the Mountain" and can be obtained by writing **Proud Earth Records, Box 75-B, Blanding, UT 84511; (801) 678-2805,** or ask for it in the local stores. If you want an interesting experience, ask one of the locals to explain the history mentioned in the "Blue Mountain" lyrics. If your curiosity is not satisfied, then get a copy of Fawn McConkie Tanner's *The Far Country,* published in 1976, which explains the song on pp. 313–317.

My home it was in Texas. My past you must not know.
I seek a refuge from the law, where the sage and pinion grow.

For the brand "L.C." I ride and the "sleeper calves on the side."
I'll own the "Hip Side and Shoulder" when I grow older "Zap-i-ta-ro don't tan my hide."

Chorus :   Blue Mountain, you're Azure deep.
           Blue Mountain, with sides so steep.
           Blue Mountain with horse-head on your side.
           You have won my love to keep.

I chum with Laddie-Go Gordon. I drink at the Blue Goose Saloon.
I dance at night with the Mormon girls and ride home beneath the moon.

I trade at Mons 's store. With bullet holes in the door.
His calico treasure my horse can measure when I'm drunk and feeling sore.

Chorus

"Yarn Gallus" with gun and rope. "Doc Few Clothes" without any soap.
In the little green valley have made their sally and for "Slick's" there's still some hope.

In the summer time it's fine. In the winter the wind doth whine.
But say, dear brother, if you want a Mother, there's Ev on the old "Chuck-Line."

Chorus

with the Koong-Preow-Whan, shrimp with mushrooms, tomatoes and spring onions sautéed in a sweet and sour sauce; and the KoongKa Theam-Prik Thai, shrimp sautéed in garlic and black pepper, among the local favorites. There are also five vegetarian selections. Open nightly 4 pm–10 pm. It's a good idea to call for reservations; **(801) 672-2355.**

MEXICAN HAT
The Olde Bridge
Bar and Grille—$ to $$

Mark and Julie Sword came to Mexican Hat in 1975 as Vista volunteers and spend their first year of marriage living in a one-room tent in the nearby Valley of the Gods. They fell in love with the area and acquired the trading post established by Jim Hunt. The original red sandstone trading post functions as a store, while motel rooms and a cafe and bar have been constructed nearby along the north bank of the San Juan River. A sign on a door on the south side of the Old Bridge Bar and Grille reads "Parachute or raft required beyond this point." It was on this part of the San Juan River where Bill Weidman, driving a truck heavily loaded with uranium ore, tried to cross the old cable bridge on June 5, 1953. Bill got halfway across the bridge before it gave way, sending the truck into the San Juan River 50 feet below. Badly shaken, Weidman managed to swim away from the truck; his adventure underscored the need for a new bridge across the San Juan River. There is a wonderful collection of beer cans and bottles, old wanted posters, chaps, rifle scabbards, ammunition belts, road signs, blacksmith tools, a well-worn 48-star flag, and other artifacts. Native American cooks make Navajo tacos and Haani Gai, a lamb and hominy stew.

There is also beef stew, a vegetarian taco, sandwiches and burgers, steaks, omelets, pancakes, and eggs for breakfast. Open 6 am–9 pm May–Oct.; 7 am–8 pm Nov.–Apr.; **(801) 683-2220.**

Valley of the Gods
Restaurant—$-$$

A part of the Valley of the Gods Inn, this restaurant specializes in large western-style breakfasts, steaks, and Mexican and Navajo specialties. It operates with a liquor license. Open 7 am–10 pm daily; **(801) 683-2221.**

MONUMENT VALLEY
The Stagecoach Restaurant—$$

Located as part of the Goulding's Trading Post and Lodge in Monument Valley, the Stagecoach Restaurant offers a dramatic view of the northern end of Monument Valley through large picture windows. The restaurant was clearly constructed with the magnificent view in mind. Offerings at the Stagecoach include omelets, huevos rancheros, granola, hot oatmeal, and two favorites—Mike Goulding's croissant breakfast sandwich (ham and cheese with a fried egg on a warm, buttered croissant roll with breakfast potatoes) and The Duke (named for John Wayne), which is corned beef hash and eggs with toast or biscuits. Lunch items include burgers, hot beef and turkey sandwiches, beef stew with Navajo fry bread, and the Monument Valley specialty—a Navajo taco made with fry bread, a mild beef chili con carne, diced onions, grated cheese, shredded lettuce, and ripe tomatoes. Dinner items include steaks, a pasta of the day, fresh stir-fried vegetables, and other traditional American dishes. Open 7 am–10 pm; **(801) 727-3231.**

SERVICES

Located within the San Juan County Courthouse is the **Multi Agency Visitors Center** operated jointly by the US Forest Service, the Bureau of Land Management, the National Park Service, Canyonlands Natural History Association, and the San Juan County Travel Council. The center carries brochures, maps and publications for sale, and provides information about southern Utah. It is open 8 am–5 pm weekdays year-round, and 10 am–5 pm Sat., Sun., and holidays from Apr.–Oct. 117 South Main in Monticello; (801) 587-3235. For general information about the area, write **San Juan County Travel Council, 117 South Main, PO Box 490, Monticello, UT 84535; (801) 587-2231** or **1-800-574-4FUN.**

At the southern end of the county, the Navajo Nation operates the **Monument Valley Visitors Center,** providing information about accommodations, tours, and events on the Navajo Reservation; **(602) 727-3287.**

Rafting on the San Juan River. Photo by Allan Kent Powell.

Lake Powell

Lake Powell, named for the 19th-century explorer and scientist Major John Wesley Powell, was conceived on October 15, 1956, in Washington DC, when President Dwight D. Eisenhower pushed a button on his desk in the White House, setting off the first blast in the construction of the Glen Canyon Dam. By March 13, 1963, the new dam had begun to impound the waters that would eventually lead to the 1,960 miles of shoreline that form Lake Powell. Glen Canyon Dam is located 8 miles into Arizona. The 710-foot-high dam has created a lake of 250 square miles that extends 186 miles up the former channel of the Colorado River and 72 miles up the San Juan River, a tributary of the Colorado.

The lake provides access to hundreds of miles of previously inaccessible canyons and scenery that only Native American inhabitants, a few river runners, and cowboys had been able to enjoy. Now 3 to 4 million visitors a year enjoy the many recreational opportunities offered by the lake, with more than half a million visitors at the lake on Labor Day weekend alone. "Powell" is the most popular water recreation destination for Utahns. Annual family outings and reunions have become a recent tradition and, during the summer, each weekend sees long convoys of trucks and trailers headed toward the lake from all over the state. The magnificent scenery is the primary attraction, but for water-sports enthusiasts, Lake Powell warms up faster and reaches a higher summer water surface temperature, around 80 degrees Fahrenheit, than any other lake in the state.

Even before its construction, critics argued that the lake was a mistake because the silt-laden waters of the Colorado and San Juan rivers would be deposited into it creating a gigantic sandbox within a few decades. Scientists recognize that thousands of tons of sediment are being deposited into the lake each year, but hedge their bets as to just how long it will take for the lake to dry up. The "best" educated guess is somewhere between 400 and 700 years. The Glen Canyon Dam was built to meet five objectives: water storage, flood control, irrigation, generation of hydroelectric power, and to regulate the Colorado River.

Highway access to the lake is possible at only three locations: Hite Marina off Utah Hwy. 95; Bullfrog Marina on the west side and Hall's Crossing Marina on the east side of Hwy. 276; and Wahweap Marina off US Hwy. 89 just across the Utah-Arizona border. Lake Powell is located within the Glen Canyon National Recreation Area—a 1.2-million-acre reserve established by Congress on October 27, 1972, to properly manage the recreational, historical, cultural, and scenic resources of the area. The recreation area includes Rainbow Bridge National Monument, which was established by President William H. Taft in 1910. Both the recreation area and the national monument are administered by the National Park Service. Private boats are used by most visitors to the lake, but boat rentals, including houseboats, are available at the four marinas, and tour boats operate daily from Wahweep and Bullfrog marinas. At the southern end of the lake, visitors will not want to miss a tour of the Glen Canyon Dam, the Powell Museum, or a visit to Historic Lee's Ferry, located on the Colorado River just below the dam.

HISTORY

One of the great tradeoffs in the construction of Lake Powell is that while hundreds of miles of scenic landscape and recreation potential were opened to easy access, thousands of prehistoric and historic sites were inundated by the lake's waters. During construction of the dam, the Bureau of Reclamation contracted with University of Utah archaeology professor Jesse Jennings and history professors Gregory Crampton and David Miller to document the archaeological and historical sites that would disappear as the lake filled.

Two places sacred to the Navajo were also victims of the new lake. "The water children of the cloud" and "the rain people" were created by two Navajo deities at the confluence of the San Juan and Colorado rivers. Rainbow Bridge, the largest natural bridge in the world, is sacred as symbolic of male and female holy beings who created clouds, rainbows, and moisture. The lake has caused both sites to be desecrated and they are no longer used for worship.

But long before these sites became sacred to the Navajo, the canyons of the Colorado and San Juan rivers were occupied by prehistoric peoples dating back to about 9,000 years ago. Like the rest of southeastern Utah, the primary occupants were the Anasazi, who were here for 2,000 years but reached the apex of their culture between AD 900 and 1300. The Anasazi left numerous cliff dwellings, storage granaries, and rock art panels in the canyons of the Colorado, many of which were inundated by the lake; but some can still be seen in the side canyons off the main channel of the lake.

The Spanish padres Francisco Atanasio Dominguez and Silvestre Velez de Escalante left their mark on history and these canyon walls. In 1776 they made their way back to Santa Fe via the Crossing of the Fathers, just north of the present Utah-Arizona border, after their unsuccessful attempt to reach California. Padre Bay, Dominguez Butte, the Escalante River, and the Crossing of the Fathers all commemorate this important expedition.

The Crossing of the Fathers was used by other travelers from New Mexico, including Antonio Armijo and the 31 men of his trading party en route to California in December 1829. To the north, in Cataract Canyon, the fur trapper Denis Julian was one of the first Anglos to leave his inscription on the canyon walls in 1836.

With the arrival of the Mormons in Utah in 1847, the settlement of the southern Utah communities in the 1850s, and the beginning of missionary work among the Hopi Indians by Jacob Hamblin and others in the late 1850s and 1860s, the area around Lee's Ferry and the Crossing of the Fathers became known to early Mormon explorers. As Mormon settlers pushed into northern Arizona in the 1870s, the need for a ferry across the Colorado River led to the establishment of Lee's Ferry in December 1871. Eight years later, 80 miles upriver from Lee's Ferry, Mormon settlers bound for the San Juan River in the corner of southeastern Utah blasted and chiseled their way through a 40-foot cliff and down a treacherous descent known ever since as the Hole-in-the-Rock to establish another crossing of the Colorado River. By the time they moved on to settle Bluff, then Monticello and Blanding, these "Hole-in-the-Rockers" had grown to heroic stature in Mormon and Utah history for their exploits in building a seemingly impossible 180-mile-long wagon road from the town of Escalante to Bluff. Charles Hall, who had built the ferryboat at the Hole-in-the-Rock, located another crossing of the Colorado River in 1881, upstream from the original crossing. Hall's Crossing is now the middle crossing of Lake Powell.

John D. Lee's first ferry trip across the Colorado River was on January 18, 1872, when he took a group of Navajo across the river in a boat belonging to Major John Wesley Powell. Powell first traveled the length of what would become Lake Powell during his epic 1869 trip from Green River, Wyoming, through the Grand Canyon. He returned for his second expedition in 1871. Mutual respect and high-level cooperation marked relations between Powell and Mormon frontiersmen like John D. Lee and Jacob Hamblin. Powell's surveys and scientific study of the Colorado River brought national attention to the scenic wonders of southeastern Utah and explained the importance of water and irrigation in the arid West. As an explorer, reclamationist, and conservationist, Powell is one of Utah's heroes and the naming of Lake Powell in his honor has only added to his stature.

By the mid-1880s, cattlemen were expanding into the canyons of the Colorado River from both the east and west sides. From the west, small cattle outfits from Kanab, Escalante, and Hanksville pushed their livestock into the canyons and onto the mesas. On the east, larger cattle companies like the Bluff Pool, the Elk Mountain Cattle Company, the Scorup Brothers, and later the Scorup and Somerville Cattle Company used what rangeland was available east of the Colorado River and north of the San Juan River.

Contemporary with the livestock frontier in southeastern Utah was a gold rush that started in 1883, when prospector Cass Hite arrived on the Colorado River. Some gold was found, and Hite located Dandy's Crossing of the Colorado, now covered by the lake waters. A post office operated at Hite from 1889 to 1914, and during the three decades between 1883 and 1913, hundreds of prospectors hunted for gold along the Colorado and San Juan rivers. Gold was found, but for the most part it proved too expensive to mine and too powdery to be of great value.

As the gold rush began to subside, tourists began to come to enjoy the magnificent scenery that Powell and colleagues such as Frederick S. Dellenbaugh had written about. The first recreational river trip was in 1909, when Julius Stone and Nathaniel Galloway traveled from Green River, Wyoming, to Needles, California. But river running was slow to catch on, and it was not until after World War II and the availability of surplus army rubber rafts and a public anxious to ride the river and see the scenery that recreational rafting on the Colorado became big business.

The postwar period saw America refocus on domestic issues, and, in the West, no issue continued to be of greater importance than water. A series of agreements between states through which the Colorado River flows led to the completion of a master plan by the Bureau of Reclamation in 1952, which called for the construction of four large dams above Lee's Ferry. Congressional approval for the plan did not come until the spring of 1956; that fall preliminary work began on Glen Canyon Dam. Diversion tunnels were blasted through the sides of the canyon, and the Colorado River was diverted on February 11, 1959. The pouring of concrete for the dam took more than three years, with the first bucket poured on June 17, 1960, and the last on September 13, 1963. Lake Powell started to form on March 13, 1963, but it took until June 22, 1980, to first reach the high-water mark of 3,700 feet.

GETTING THERE

As noted, there are three major highways that reach Lake Powell; however, the three roads are a long way apart. It is about 100 miles between Hwy. 89, at the southern end of the lake, and Hwy. 276, between Bullfrog and Hall's Crossing, and nearly 50 miles between Hwy. 276 and Hwy. 95 at Hite. Hwy. 89 heads east from Kanab for 65 miles before it crosses the Colorado River via the Glen Canyon Dam, then heads south out of Page through the Navajo Reservation in Arizona.

The only way to cross the lake between Bullfrog and Hall's Crossing is on the ferryboat John Atlantic Burr, which can hold a maximum of eight cars, two buses, and 150 passengers. The crossing takes about a half hour and there is a charge. The ferry normally operates year-round, with departures beginning at 8 am from Hall's Crossing and returning from

Bullfrog at 9 am, then continuing on the hour. The last departure from Bullfrog is at 7 pm during the summer season (mid-May–mid-October) and 3 pm during the winter months. The northern route, the Bicentennial Highway / state Hwy. 95, crosses the lake on the beautiful Hite Crossing Bridge.

Most visitors traveling from Salt Lake City and the Wasatch Front take Interstate 15 to Spanish Fork, then join Hwy. 6 from exit 261 and follow that highway to its junction with Interstate 70, just west of Green River. After just 8 miles on Interstate 70, exit onto Hwy. 24 and take it south to Hanksville, then continue south out of Hanksville on Hwy. 95. About 30 miles south of Hanksville, you reach the junction with Hwy. 276, which most Lake Powell–bound travelers take to reach the larger Bullfrog Marina. If you stay on Hwy. 95, you will reach the bridge and marina at Hite, on the east side of the lake. The distance from Salt Lake City to Bullfrog is about 300 miles; to Hite about 280 miles. But the drive from Salt Lake City to the southern end of the lake, via Interstate 15 and Hwy. 89, is nearly 400 miles.

Recommended Reading—

I have two favorite guides to Lake Powell. The first is C. Gregory Crampton's *Ghosts of Glen Canyon: History Beneath Lake Powell* (Publishers Place, 1986). Written by an eminent Southwest historian and University of Utah history professor emeritus, the book is divided into two parts: an overview history of the Lake Powell area, then a guide to 66 locations and historic sites from Lee's Ferry at the southern end to the Dirty Devil River at the northern end of the lake. The book has good maps and the wonderful photographs, most of them taken by Crampton before the waters of Lake Powell inundated the lower sections of the canyons, are worth the price of the book alone.

The second book, Michael R. Kelsey's *Boater's Guide to Lake Powell* (Kelsey Publishing, 1989) is a comprehensive guide to the lake with hundreds of suggestions for hikes, boat trips, archaeological sites to see, and places to camp. There are 42 detailed maps of sections of the lake, starting at the north end and moving south. Introductory chapters cover history and geology and provide general information on boating, hiking, and camping.

——————— **MAJOR ATTRACTIONS** ———————

Lee's Ferry

If John D. Lee had not won fame as the scapegoat for the tragic 1857 Mountain Meadows Massacre, he would have become famous for establishing a ferry across the Colorado River just below Glen Canyon. Strangely enough, though the one event led to the other, if it hadn't been for the Mountain Meadows Massacre and the threat of arrest, it is doubtful that Lee would have ever left his prosperous farms and ranches in southwestern Utah to establish a ferry at what his 17th wife Emma would call "Lonely Dell."

The request for Lee to establish the ferry came from his old friend Brigham Young, as he began preparations for a series of Mormon settlements in northern Arizona. The settlements became a reality in 1873 and, until the Navajo Bridge was completed across the Colorado River 5 miles downstream in 1929, Lee's Ferry linked hundreds of Arizona Mormons with the St. George Temple and the Mormon capital of Salt Lake City. Lee's Ferry was so remote that Lee was safe, as along as he remained there; but when he returned to the Mormon settlements he was apprehended while visiting his family in Panguitch. After Lee's arrest, the Mormon church continued to operate the ferry until 1909. In 1910, it was acquired by Coconino County to ensure its continued operation.

The ferry site, two log buildings reportedly built by John D. Lee, a cemetery dating from 1874, segments of the pioneer road, and other historic sites now comprise the Lee's Ferry Historic Site, which is administered by the National Park Service as part of the Glen Canyon National Recreation Area. Historians W. L. Rusho and C. Gregory Crampton have published an excellent history and guide to Lee's Ferry entitled, *Desert River Crossing: Historic Lee's Ferry on the Colorado River*. Lee's Ferry is also the starting point for river trips through Marble Canyon and the Grand Canyon.

To reach Lee's Ferry, drive south from Page on Hwy. 89 for 23 miles to its junction with 89A, then turn right and follow Hwy. 89A north for 13 miles to Navajo Bridge. On the western side of the bridge, watch for the road that heads north to Lee's Ferry. There are a couple of motels, restaurants, and gas stations just beyond the turnoff, should you need them.

Rainbow Bridge National Monument

You have not really been to Lake Powell until you have left the main channel to wind your way through Forbidding Canyon into Rainbow Bridge Canyon and have stood in awe under the largest, most symmetrical, and most beautiful natural bridge in the world. The bridge rises 290 feet above Bridge Creek and spans 270 feet. The narrowest section of the bridge is 32 feet thick. The beautiful salmon-colored Navajo sandstone contrasts vividly with the dark bulk of 10,000-foot-high Navajo Mountain. This sacred mountain watches over the bridge like a colossal sentinel, while the 1,000-foot-high walls of the canyon envelop the bridge, like an oyster shell sheltering a precious pearl.

Rumors of a massive natural bridge that resembled a petrified rainbow and that was sacred to the Navajo and Paiutes were whispered for years, but it was not until 1909 that the first white men viewed Rainbow Bridge. Two expeditions led by Byron Cummings of the University of Utah and William B. Douglass of the US General Land Office joined forces and reached the bridge on Aug. 14, 1909, thanks to explorer John Wetherill and their two Paiute guides, Nasja Begay and Jim Mike. Less than a year later, President William H. Taft established the 160-acre Rainbow Bridge National Monument on May 30, 1910. Former president Theodore Roosevelt visited the bridge in 1913 and recorded that, during the moonlit night, he awoke several times to gaze in awe at the natural wonder. Until the 1960s, all visitors wishing to view the bridge had to make a tortuous overland pack trip around Navajo Mountain or a dangerous raft trip down the Colorado River through Cataract Canyon, and then an exhausting hike several miles up the canyon.

But the waters of Lake Powell, which extend under the bridge when the lake is at or near capacity, allow boaters to come within a few hundred yards of the bridge. You can now tie your boat to a floating dock and follow the well-worn path to the arch. If you don't have your own boat, you can still visit Rainbow Bridge on one of the tour boats that leave regularly from Wahweap Marina.

OTHER ATTRACTIONS

Glen Canyon Dam

The **Carl Hayden Visitors Center** at Glen Canyon Dam has a variety of audio-visual exhibits and films on the construction of the dam and the history of the area. A large-scale relief map of the Colorado Plateau helps orient visitors and longtime residents of the Colorado Plateau to the unusual geography of this unique region.

From the visitors center, you can take a self-guided tour of the dam or join one of the guided tours. The visitors center is administered by the National Park Service. Open daily (except Christmas and New Year's Day) 8 am–5 pm (extended hours in summer). The center is located 2 miles north of Page, Arizona, on the western side of the dam. **(602) 645-2511.**

FESTIVALS AND EVENTS

Hole-in-the-Rock Commemoration

4th Saturday in January

Tour boats travel down from Bullfrog Marina and up from Wahweap Marina to the Hole-in-the-Rock where Mormon pioneers labored for six weeks to construct a wagon road through a 40-foot cliff and then along the steep slope to take their wagons to the Colorado River. On Jan. 26, 1880, 40 wagons—with wagon wheels rough-locked and men holding onto ropes to slow them—were taken down through the Hole-in-the-Rock and 26 of them ferried across the Colorado River. The commemoration includes stories, songs, and lunch. Since there is no one else on the lake in the winter, and the rest of Utah is usually snowed in or under a shroud of fog,

this trip to the blue skies and sun of Lake Powell makes for a rejuvenating experience. For information about the event and special lodging and tour packages, call **1-800-528-6154.**

Wahweap Festival of Lights Parade

1st Saturday in December

One of the most remarkable Christmas activities anywhere is the parade of boats decorated with lights around Wahweap Bay. The parade is led by the Canyon King Paddlewheeler. Even if you don't have a boat, you can view the parade from Wahweap Lodge or purchase a ticket for one of the tour boats participating in the parade. This is a Christmas event you won't soon forget. **1-800-528-6154.**

SEEING AND DOING

BOAT TOURS

ARA Services—

This concessionaire offers a number of boat tours of Lake Powell from the Wahweap and Bullfrog marinas. They are an excellent way to see the lake and a good opportunity to rub shoulders with visitors

from all over the world. The lower, enclosed section, with its large windows, offers protection from the wind and sun, while the upper deck puts you in the center of the Lake Powell universe, surrounded by deep blue skies, blue-green water, and red rock. Most tours are a half day or a full day. For reservations and information, call

1-800-528-6154 or the marinas directly— Wahweap, (602) 645-2433, and Bullfrog, (801) 684-2233.

RIVER TRIPS

Wilderness River Adventures—

Offers multiday rafting tours through the Grand Canyon and half-day float trips on the Colorado River from just below the Glen Canyon Dam to Lee's Ferry. For information and reservations write or call **PO Box 717, Page, AZ 86040; 1-800-992-8022.**

SCENIC FLIGHTS

Lake Powell Air Service—

This air tour company operates out of the Page Municipal Airport and offers year-round scenic flights from a half hour in length to several hours. **Lake Powell Air**

Service, PO Box 1385, 901 North Sage, Page Municipal Airport, Page, AZ 86040; (602) 645-2494 or 1-800-245-8668.

MUSEUMS

John Wesley Powell Museum—

This fine regional history museum has exhibits on Native American culture in the area, geology, the Colorado River, and John Wesley Powell and his contributions as a river explorer, scientist, and reclamationist. The museum includes a gift shop, and videos on the geography, geology, and history are shown upon request. Admission free. Open May–Oct., Mon.–Sat. 8 am–6 pm (Sun. 10 am–6 pm); Nov., Mar., and Apr., Mon.–Fri. 9, am-5 pm. Located in Page, Arizona at **Lake Powell Blvd. and North Navajo Dr.; (602) 645-9496.**

——————— WHERE TO STAY ———————

ACCOMMODATIONS

Best Western at Lake Powell—$$$

Heated pool, whirlpool, and restaurants close by; 132 rooms. **208 North Lake Powell Blvd., PO Box MM, Page, AZ 86040; (602) 645-2478.**

Defiance House—$$$

Located on a bluff overlooking Lake Powell at the Bullfrog Marina at the end of Hwy. 276; 48 rooms. The Anasazi Restaurant is located at the lodge. **(801) 684-2233 or 1-800-528-6154.**

Holiday Inn/Lake Powell—$$$

Heated pool; 130 rooms. Dining room open 6 am–10 pm. **287 North Lake Powell Blvd., PO Box 1867, Page, AZ 86040; (602) 645-8851.**

Housekeeping Units—$$$

ARA Services offers housekeeping units for rent at Bullfrog, Hall's Crossing, and Hite for about the same price as accommodations at Bullfrog and Wahweap. These units are ideal for couples and families and

offer a living room, three bedrooms, two bathrooms, and fully equipped kitchen. For information and reservations call **1-800-528-6154,** or contact the unit directly:

> **Bullfrog—(801) 684-2233**
> **Hall's Crossing—(801) 684-2261**
> **Hite—(801) 684-2278**

Lake Powell Motel—$$ to $$$

Also operated by ARA Services, who run Defiance House and Wahweap Lodge under a concession from the National Park Service, rates are lower at the Lake Powell Motel, primarily because it is 3 miles from Wahweap Lodge on a bluff overlooking the lake; 24 rooms. **(602) 645-2477 or 1-800-528-6154.**

Wahweap Lodge—$$$

Three hundred fifty rooms provide excellent accommodations. A number of rooms have balconies and patios facing the lake. There are two heated pools and a fine restaurant, the Rainbow Room, which offers a breathtaking view of the lake through its panoramic semicircular windows. Located at Wahweap Marina, just across the Utah-Arizona state line a few miles west of Page, Arizona. **(602) 645-2433** or **1-800-528-6154.**

CAMPING

RV parks with lights, electricity, water, sewer hookups, restrooms, showers, and a coin-operated laundry are located at **Wahweap** (178 sites), **Bullfrog** (86 sites), and **Hall's Crossing** (65 sites). Cost for full hookups varies, depending on the season, with an additional charge for airconditioning and heater hookups. Call **1-800-528-6154.**

HOUSEBOAT RENTALS

Most overnight visitors to Lake Powell either camp along the beaches or sleep on their boats. The houseboats that can be rented from ARA Services at the four marinas are very popular with families and groups, and training films are available for those with no experience but who want to try their hand at navigating the floating houses. The boats range from 36-footers that sleep 6 to 50-footers that sleep 12. Call **1-800-528-6154.**

─── SERVICES ───

All concessions on the lake, including lodging, houseboats, and restaurants, are operated by ARA Services. For early reservations, call **1-800-528-6154,** Mon.–Fri. 7:30 am–4:30 pm. For reservations seven days or less in advance it is best to call direct.

Bullfrog Resort and Marina—(801) 684-2233
Hall's Crossing Marina—(801) 684-2261

Hite Marina—(801) 684-2278

Lake Powell Motel—(602) 645-2477

Painted Hills RV Park Bullfrog—24 sites; **(801) 684-2233**

Wahweap Lodge and Marina—(602) 645-2433

Rainbow Bridge National Monument at Lake Powell. Photo by Bob Huestis.

Arches National Park

Naturally formed stone arches are a rarity throughout the world, but there is no lack of them in the 114-square-mile Arches National Park. More than 2,000 sandstone arches have been counted within the park boundaries and more are being discovered all the time or are in the process of forming. The park is a masterpiece created by erosion. You won't see only arches here, but also a panoply of fiery-hued features such as fins of thin sculpted monoliths, balanced rocks, stone chimneys, buttresses, and alcoves not yet cut through—all of them laid out underneath a wide, clear sky, northwest of Moab. Spring and fall are the ideal times to visit Arches. Winter days are often beautiful, with surprisingly mild temperatures, and usually few people. Summer is the heavy tourist season so be prepared for crowds and scorching temperatures, especially from mid-morning until after sunset.

HISTORY

The first people to make steady use of the area in and around Arches National Park was the Desert Archaic culture found throughout the West 3,000 to 8,000 years ago. But the first cultures to leave a tangible trace of their passing were the Anasazi and the Fremont, culturally related peoples who lived on the Colorado Plateau from roughly AD 1 to 1300. These people became culturally distinguished around AD 1, with the basketmaker Anasazis, progressed to pit houses, then moved into multistory masonry dwellings. They flowered between AD 1000 and 1300. Arches National Park sits just outside the Fremont cultural area, which lies to the west, so the most common vestiges of ancient society are Anasazi. Within the park are fine examples of rock art (such as those in Lower Courthouse Wash and near the Wolfe Cabin on the trail to Delicate Arch) left in hidden canyons and out-of-the-way places by prehistoric residents. Associated artifacts are also found. In historic times, the Arches area was used by two different groups of Native Americans: the Ute and the Navajo. The Ute lived and hunted throughout the park area, jealously guarding their land, and driving out the first white settlers in the area in the 1850s. Arches is north of the Navajo Reservation, and although they passed through the area, there is no evidence that the Navajo lived within what is now the park.

The Old Spanish Trail traversed Spanish Valley, where Moab is now located, and crossed the Colorado River just outside the park boundaries. Perhaps travelers on the trail ventured into what is now the park. Juan Maria de Rivera, a New Mexican trader, passed nearby as early as 1765, when much of the Southwest was under Spanish rule. By the 1840s the trail was a well-used route from New Mexico to California, and functioned as an extension of the Santa Fe Trail between Franklin, Missouri, and Santa Fe, New Mexico. Mountain men frequented the area, but the only one known to have entered the present-day park boundaries was French-Canadian fur trapper Denis Julien, who left an inscription dated 1844 in the park. The first Mormon explorers, led by William Huntington, entered what is now the Moab area with wagons in 1854 and vowed to return to establish a settlement the next year. Huntington did not return, but Alfred Billings brought back 40 men to found the Elk Mountain Mission in 1855. The mission did not outlast Ute reprisals and quickly folded.

Mormons returned to found the town of Moab in 1882. However, it was not until 1898, when John Wesley Wolfe, a crusty Civil War veteran, and his son Fred settled on Salt Wash near famous Delicate Arch, that the Arches area had its first white inhabitants. In 1906, Wolfe's daughter, her husband Ed Stanley, and their two children arrived at the ranch and remained there until 1908, when they returned to Ohio. Wolfe continued to live at the ranch until 1910. Now a National Register Historic District, Wolfe Ranch provides a glimpse into the past for today's visitors.

Other Moab residents made note of the natural arches and made regular visits to the area. In 1922, a Hungarian-born local miner and prospector named Alexander Ringhoffer was so struck by the unique beauty of Arches that he contacted officials of the Denver and Rio Grande Railroad to try to persuade the railroad company to develop the area as a tourist attraction.

Through a roundabout series of events and coincidences, the National Park Service was informed of the potential of the area for inclusion in the National Park system, and Arches National Monument was created by President Hoover in 1929. A few years later, the new monument was studied in depth and many of its most famous features named and publicized. In 1938 Arches was greatly expanded under a proclamation by President Franklin Roosevelt, from its original 4,500 acres to over 34,000 acres. Despite increasing tourist interest in the area, the first paved road into Arches was not built until 1958. In 1971, President Richard Nixon signed the law that changed Arches to a national park and set its size at the present 73,379 acres.

GEOLOGY

The three "members" of Entrada sandstone in which this enormous array of arches and windows is located were laid down as sediments in ancient seas and as windblown sand during a time of great aridity. Earlier, about 300 million years ago, the evaporation of inland seas left a thick salt layer (the Paradox Formation), 3,000 feet in some places, on top of which the sediments and sand were deposited. Over time, pressure on the lower salt layer caused the salt to push upward in places, bending the upper sediments as well. Arches, which lies on a sloping highland called the Salt Valley Anticline that resulted from this uplift, was also impacted by the faults and joints that developed as part of the uplifting process. Salt domes also developed while the dissolution of salt along fissures caused fins that eventually weakened into eroded stone features such as arches. The broken layers of Entrada sandstone became very susceptible to erosion because the small, uniform-size quartz grains that make up the sandstone weather easily. Rain, ice, melting water, and plant and animal activity caused the sandstone to crack, flake, and wash away—a process that continues today.

Writer Edward Abbey, who first arrived in Arches National Park as a seasonal park ranger in 1956, later became one of the most ardent and articulate spokesmen for preservation of the wilderness as a place of refuge and hope. Many of Abbey's books have become basic texts in western environmental literature. In his best-known book, *Desert Solitaire: A Season in the Wilderness*, published in 1968, Abbey recounted his time at Arches. In that book, laced with humor, sarcasm, and love for Utah's canyon country, he offers one of the finest written descriptions of the Arches area that anyone has ever penned.

> We drive the dirt roads and walk out some of the trails. Everything is lovely and wild, with a virginal sweetness. The arches themselves, strange, impressive, grotesque, form but a small and inessential part of the general beauty of this country. When we think of rock we usually think of stones, broken rock, buried under soil and plant life, but here all is exposed and naked, dominated by the monolithic formations of sandstone which stand above the surface of the ground and extend for miles, sometimes level, sometimes tilted or warped by pressures from below, carved by erosion and weathering into an intricate maze of glens, grottoes, fissures, passageways, and deep narrow canyons.
>
> At first look it all seems like a geologic chaos, but there is method at work here, method of a fanatic order and perseverance: each groove in the rock leads to a natural channel of some kind, every channel to a ditch and gulch and ravine, each larger waterway to a canyon bottom or broad wash leading in turn to the Colorado River and the sea.

ARCHES AND BRIDGES

Southeastern Utah has the world's largest collection of natural arches and bridges, and although both terms are sometimes used interchangeably, a bridge is actually formed by the work of a stream upon rock, leaving a "bridge" that spans the streambed. Arches, sometimes called "windows," occur where there is no stream course but a variety of other erosional factors, including frost, rain, and composition of the stone, have sculpted them. To be considered an arch, the opening must be at least 3 feet in any one direction. While most of the 2,000 arches here are of the smaller variety, there are a good number of larger arches; Landscape Arch, with its unbelievable 306-foot span which is over 100 feet above the ground, is one of the largest arches in the world. A couple of years ago, a large segment fell out of the arch—a reminder that the never-ending process of erosion will destroy this arch even as it creates others.

GETTING THERE

One of the most conveniently located national parks, Arches is just 5 miles north of Moab with a visitors center located adjacent to US Hwy. 191 at the entrance to the park. For travelers on Interstate 70, it is a 26-mile drive south on Hwy. 191 from exit 180 at Crescent Junction.

VISITOR INFORMATION

After paying your nominal entrance fee (which is good for seven days), be sure to stop in at the visitors center to view the slide show and exhibits, equip yourself with books and maps, pick up backcountry permits for backpacking, and obtain information about weather conditions, guided hikes, and special programs. Open 8 am–4:30 pm with extended hours during the high season. For information write **Superintendent, Arches National Park, PO Box 907, Moab, UT 84532;** or call **(801) 259-8161.**

———— OUTDOOR ACTIVITIES ————

BIKING

Mountain biking is permitted within Arches National Park only on paved and jeep roads, but most of the potential routes in the park are sandy, washboarded, or not as interesting and challenging as other routes outside the boundaries. One ride that can be taken by mountain bikers is into the Klondike Bluffs area along the Willow Flat Rd. and the Salt Valley four-wheel-drive road. The ride covers approximately 25 miles and offers the option of a .4-mile hike to Tower Arch. You can also ride the paved road from the visitors center out to Devils Garden and back, but the usually heavy automobile traffic demands more attention to riding than enjoying the scenery.

HIKING

Balanced Rock Trail—

It looks like, at any minute, the 73-foot-high pedestal holding this huge 55-foot-tall boulder will give way and the rock will come crashing down, but this gravity-defying natural formation has stood like this for hundreds of years. Located 6.3 miles from the Park Avenue Trailhead or 8.5 miles from the visitors center, Balanced Rock is near the turnoff to the Windows section of the park. You can examine the rock more closely on a short, .2 mile-long trail that also offers views of the distant La Sal Mountains and the red rock and cliffs within the park.

Delicate Arch Trail—

Ask most frequent visitors to Arches what is the one arch everyone should see, and more than 90 percent will probably respond, "Delicate Arch." The arch is famous throughout the world, which led to its being selected as the major design element in Utah's centennial license plate. The best way to view the arch is to make the 3-mile round-trip hike from Wolfe Ranch for a close-up look at the arch, then drive to the viewpoint for a look at the arch in the perspective of the terrain, seen from the south looking north. As you leave Wolfe Ranch, you cross Salt Wash on a suspension bridge—which if you have children with you automatically becomes something of a playground attraction. On the east side of Salt Wash, the trail crosses a greasewood flat, then climbs onto the sandstone. As you leave the bridge, keep a lookout for a short trail that branches to the left. Take time to hike this trail to see the Ute pictographs that depict riders on horseback, bighorn sheep, and what look like two dogs. Returning to the main trail, you continue to climb toward the arch, making an elevation gain of 580 feet from the trailhead. The trail crosses the slickrock, and as it winds around the north side the trail narrows as it crosses the steep north face and passes beneath the small Frame Arch.

As you crest the slickrock fin, even if you are forewarned, the view of Delicate Arch is an unforgettable experience. Like the forgotten toy of some ancient giant, the arch stands alone on the lip of slickrock above a canyon with the dark La Sal Mountains in the background. Anyone with a camera will automatically reach for it to try and capture one of the most picturesque sites in all of America's national parks. Compared with other arches in the park, Delicate Arch is not large, as it rises to 46 feet in height with a span of 32 feet between the abutments. But, symbolic of man in this land, its small, tenuous yet persistent presence in a landscape so vast and rugged speaks sermons of the value of the individual.

Delicate Arch Viewpoint—

Even after the 3-mile hike to and from Delicate Arch, you won't want to leave the beautiful site. For another perspective of the arch, follow the road east to the Delicate Arch Viewpoint. The viewpoint also provides access for those who do not have the time or physical ability to hike to the arch. From the parking area, the viewpoint is located 0.4 mile to the north. The trail gains 200 feet in elevation and is mostly across slickrock, with a 200-foot drop into Winter Camp Wash beyond the end of the trail. If you have binoculars, carry them with you. Delicate Arch is about .5 mile away.

Devils Garden Trail—

Located at the north end of the paved road, 18 miles from the visitors center, the Devils Garden Trail is the most popular trail in the park. Most hikers only make the 1.6-mile round-trip to the record-breaking span of Landscape Arch—the largest arch in the park, with a height of over 100 feet and width of 306 feet. But you can see many other arches in the Devils Garden area, including Pine Tree (46 feet high and 48 feet wide), Tunnel (22 feet high by 27 feet wide), Wall (68 feet high by 41 feet wide), Navajo (13 feet high and 41 feet wide), Partition Arches (26 feet high and 28 feet wide), and Double-O Arch (with two openings, one 45 feet high and 71 feet wide and the other 9 feet high and 21 feet wide). Double-O Arch requires a 4-mile round-trip hike; to push on to the Dark Angel at the end of the trail is a 5.2-mile round-trip jaunt. With a 7-mile round-trip hike, you can visit all the arches and see a good part of the Devils Garden area. Plan most of the day if you undertake this hike and take plenty of water, some food, and protection against the sun.

Fiery Furnace—

If you have ever had a nightmare about being trapped in a labyrinth with no way out, the Fiery Furnace is one way to make such a nightmare seem real. This section of the park is full of narrow passageways, blood-red sandstone fins, and dead ends. Aptly named, it is easy to imagine that you are among gigantic coals of an enormous furnace. Even if you are an experienced hiker, it is best to join one of the ranger-guided hikes conducted twice daily during the summer. Reservations for these popular walks must be made at the visitors center no more than 48 hours in advance of the walk. Groups larger than nine people may request a special walk, but at least two weeks' lead time is required. Since the spring of 1994, anyone entering the Fiery Furnace must have a permit or be on a ranger-led hike. These new procedures have been instituted to help preserve the vegetation and cryptobiotic crust and to enhance the quality of experience for all visitors. Remember to stay on the trail. Violators are subject to fines. The trailhead is located 3 miles north of the turnoff to Delicate Arch, or 14 miles from the visitors center. In places, steps have been cut into the slickrock, just as the Anasazi did to provide access over steep sections. During the hike, you will visit Surprise Arch and Skull Arch, with its empty "eye sockets." Check at the visitors center to confirm schedules and for additional information on the guided hikes.

Park Avenue—

After you drive the switchbacks from the park entrance in Moab Canyon, you reach the Park Avenue area, about 2 miles from the visitors center, and the Park Avenue Trailhead. Aptly named for New York City's skyscraper-lined Park Avenue, the rows of sandstone slabs reaching 150 to 300 feet offer a southeastern Utah counterpart to manmade towers of steel and concrete. You can view Park Avenue from the viewpoint, about 100 yards from the parking area, or hike along the avenue—an easy downhill stroll just under 1 mile in length. You will see the evocatively named Egyptian Queen, Sausage Rock, the Organ, the Three Gossips, and the Tower of Babel. If you don't want to hike back, you can have someone drive your vehicle down to the end of the trail at the highway. Don't walk back along the road. The zooming traffic and no shoulder make for potential accidents. Return via the trail.

Sand Dune and Broken Arches—

As you continue north 2.4 miles past the Fiery Furnace turnoff, you reach the trailhead for Sand Dune and Broken arches. The trail to both arches is 1.2 miles round-trip and is a nice stroll, compared with the slickrock climbing in the Fiery Furnace. The small, 30-foot-long, 8-foot-high Sand Dune Arch is located 200 yards off the trail to Broken Arch. Taking its name from a deep notch in the harder caprock on top of the arch, the 43-foot-high, 59-foot-wide Broken Arch is not really broken.

Skyline Arch—

You can see Skyline Arch from Interstate 70, 10 miles to the north if you know where to look. It is the only arch within the park visible from the highway. Inside the park, though, the arch is visible from the main road as well as the Devils Garden Campground. It is only a .2-mile walk to the base of the sandstone fin, in which the arch is located. The arch is 45 feet high and 69 feet wide. It expanded to its present size in 1940, when a large slab of stone fell from the top of the arch.

Windows Section—

From the turnoff at Balanced Rock, the 3-mile-long paved road leads to the Windows section. This section of the park offers five magnificent arches—Double Arch, Turret Arch, and North and South Windows—grouped together and connected by a network of trails that make a loop a little more than 1.5 miles long. With such easy access, this is one of the most popular sections of the park. Double Arch is located in the Windows, and the two arches extend outward from each side, like jughandles, a nickname sometimes applied to the two arches. The larger of the two arches spans 144 feet and is 112 feet high, while the smaller one is 61 feet wide and 86 feet high. Turret Arch is unique as one of the few arches that is taller, 65 feet high, than it is wide, 35 feet across. North Window is 48 feet high and 90 feet wide and offers breathtaking vistas that capture the attention of photographers who try to frame the magnificent scenery within the window of the arch. Nearby South Window is 56 feet high and 115 feet wide. Plan a couple of hours to visit and examine these arches, and, on hot days, carry drinking water with you and protect yourself from the sun.

Wolfe Ranch National Historic District—

Listed in the National Register of Historic Places, the historic district includes the restored 1906 cabin that was the home of John Wesley Wolfe for four years. The cabin, nearby cellar, and corrals offer an excellent example of what life was like on the Utah frontier well into the 20th century. The ranch is located 2.5 miles north of the Windows section and another 1.8 miles off the main road to the right. The ranch also lies at the trailhead to Delicate Arch.

OFF-TRAIL HIKING AND BACKPACKING

While there are plenty of hiking opportunities along the established trails outlined above, if you want to get off the beaten paths for a day's cross-country hike or to backpack and camp in the remote sections of the park, the following are four good possibilities. Remember, backcountry permits, which can be obtained at the visitors center, are required for overnight stays. The National Park Service is considering different management strategies for the backcountry camping. It is always a good idea to check in at the visitors center for information on trail conditions and weather forecasts. In summer, violent thunderstorms often cause flash floods that are extremely dangerous. These trails and other possibilities are described in detail in the excellent publication by Ron Adkison, *Utah's National Parks: Hiking, Camping and Vacationing in Utah's Canyon Country*.

Clover Canyon to Upper Salt Wash and Wolfe Ranch—

This hike is recommended only for experienced hikers who are comfortable with finding their own way through tangled thickets and across steep slickrock. It begins at the Sand Dune/Broken Arch Trailhead, follows down Clover Canyon, and then strikes for Salt Wash. The 8.5-mile hike ends at Wolfe Ranch, where you will need to be picked up.

Lower Courthouse Wash—

If you can arrange a shuttle, this interesting hike, a little over 5 miles long, can be completed in half a day. Hikers can be dropped off at the bridge where the paved road crosses Courthouse Wash 4.5 miles from the visitors center. Arrange a pickup where Courthouse Wash intersects with Hwy. 191, just west of the bridge across the Colorado River. There is limited parking at the pullout inside the park, if you prefer to leave a vehicle there. Watch out for flash floods in this section of the wash. The canyon walls grow higher and higher as you descend, and there are a number of side canyons worthy of exploration if you have the time. An excellent rock art panel is located along the northeastern side of the canyon wall, at the mouth of the wash. Unfortunately, the panel was vandalized; attempts to repair it have been partially successful.

Lower Salt Wash to the Colorado River—

Two major drainages of the Colorado River bisect Arches: Courthouse Wash and Salt Wash. A hike down the lower portion of Salt Wash from Wolfe Ranch to the Colorado River is 13.4 miles round-trip and takes you through one of the most remote sections of the park. There is no trail; hikers simply follow the wash. The canyon walls rise as much as 1,200 feet above the floor of the wash, and a series of salt springs gush from cracks in the rock. The upper section of the hike is through thickets of greasewood, sagebrush, and rabbitbrush. Farther down the wash, boulders and rocks are the major obstacles. When you reach the Colorado River, you cannot cross the river to Hwy. 128, so turn around and go back the way you came. This hike can be excruciatingly hot during the summer and is more fatiguing than other hikes. Take plenty of water and plan for a full day to complete the hike.

SCENIC DRIVES

At the visitors center you can purchase the booklet *Road Guide: Arches National Park*. This is an excellent guide to the scenic road that winds for 18 miles through the center of Arches National Park from its entrance to the end of the paved road at Devils Garden. Most of the arches, scenic views, and historic sites are readily accessible by auto or by a short hike from convenient parking areas. A companion booklet is *Hiking Guide: Arches National Park*, which has summaries and outline maps for 13 short hiking trails in the park.

WILDLIFE

There is a rich assortment of wildlife within Arches, although many animals are nocturnal, seeking food and water at night to avoid the searing heat of summer day. The largest mammals are bighorn sheep, deer, coyotes (whose eerie howl can be heard at night), and bobcats. Smaller mammals, such as porcupines, cottontail rabbits, jackrabbits, gray foxes, mice, and squirrels, form the diet of coyotes, which range widely throughout the park. Lizards and snakes that have adapted to an arid environment are common, with the midget faded rattlesnake the only poisonous snake found within the park. Bats and a good variety of birds can be seen, both resident and migratory. Some common species include piñon jays, canyon wrens, ravens, eagles, hawks, and waterfowl along the Colorado River.

WHERE TO STAY

CAMPING

There are no lodging facilities within the park, but you can find plenty of accommodations in nearby Moab. **Devils Garden Campground** is the only campground in the park. It has 52 sites and is located near the north end of the park road, about 18 miles from the visitors center. Open year-round. Recreational vehicles and tents share the 53 sites. The campground has drinking water and flush toilets in season (the water is turned off in winter) and handicap facilities. Stays are limited to seven days, and a fee is charged. Campsites fill up quickly, so arrive early at the visitors center to get a space.

Canyonlands National Park

In Canyonlands lies the heart and soul of the Colorado Plateau. A vast, rugged land of remarkable beauty, the expanses of rocks under an even more expansive sky, this is a land of paradox. There is something quite eternal about this land, yet it continues to change in response to the ongoing but seldom-seen forces of erosion. The delicateness of the wind-sculpted pinnacles stands against a backdrop of monumental buttes and mesas. Majesty, durability, and fragility are all linked in a panorama of beauty. The landscape is a three-dimensional divine work of art. A multitude of elements are perfectly placed and masterfully combined in this tapestry of the gods.

The best way to approach Canyonlands National Park is to consider it three national parks combined under one administrative jurisdiction. (You can consider the rivers a fourth district—the park service does.) The park is known for its canyons, mesas, pillars, standing rocks, grabens, arches, and two of the West's most important rivers: the Colorado and the Green, whose confluence takes place in the heart of Canyonlands National Park. The three sections of Canyonlands—**Island in the Sky, The Maze,** and **Needles**—are distinct units, separated by natural boundaries formed by the Green and Colorado rivers and their canyons. Each requires a separate access, and it is impossible to see more than one section in a day. Much of the park remains undeveloped, and the best way to really see it is by hiking. The largest of Utah's five national parks, with 337,570 acres Canyonlands is nearly 10 times larger than Bryce Canyon, 5 times larger than Arches, 3 times as large as Zion, and half again as large as Capitol Reef. Even so, it receives far fewer visitors than most of the other national parks in Utah. Located northeast of the park, Moab is the gateway city to the park, although as you will learn, there is really no "gateway" to the Maze District. Monticello also provides good access to the Needles District. The newest of Utah's national parks, Canyonlands was created on September 12, 1964, when President Lyndon Johnson signed the act making Canyonlands the 32nd national park.

HISTORY

The history of Canyonlands is nearly as complex as the geography and geology that make up the park. Prehistoric use dates back more than 11,000 years ago, as evidenced by the discovery of a Clovis projectile point near Canyonlands. These Paleo-Indians lived in the region from about 11,000 BC to around 5000 BC. As the culture of the Paleo-Indians changed from a reliance on big game such as giant bison, elk, and possibly mammoths, to one that emphasized using plants as well as animals and a greater variety of methods and weapons, such as nets, snares, and atlatls, to hunt animals, the early inhabitants became known as the Archaic culture. The Archaic people lived in the area until about 500 BC and left outstanding examples of rock art known as the Barrier Canyon style, characterized by large, trapezoidal, ghostlike anthropomorphic figures.

While the Paleo-Indians and their descendants, the Archaic people, were nomadic, the next groups of people were basically sedentary. As the Archaic people turned more and more to planting and farming instead of hunting, they developed into two related but somewhat different cultures, known today as the Fremont and the Anasazi. While the Fremont tended to occupy the region to the west and north, and the Anasazi lands to the south and east, the Canyonlands area, became an important point of contact between the two groups. Both peoples seem to have left a rich treasure of millions of artifacts, dwellings, kivas, pit houses, granaries, and rock art. Archaeologists continue to research and debate the extent of both cultures in the Canyonlands area, and current scholarship holds that the Anasazi presence was greater than that of the Fremont. Both cultures flourished from about the time of Christ until around AD 1250, at which time a particularly long drought and the invasion of other peoples—notably the Utes and Navajos from the north—may have caused them to flee. The Anasazi moved to the south and east and intermingled with the Pueblo Indians of Arizona and New Mexico; no one is sure what happened to the Fremont.

Fur trapper Denis Julien was probably the first Euro-American to see what is now Canyonlands National Park, although it is possible that Spanish traders, including members of the 1765 Juan Maria Antonio Rivera expedition, visited the area before Julien left his engraved signature in the canyons in 1836.

But it was not until 1859 that an organized expedition under Captain John N. Macomb was sent out to locate the confluence of the Green and Colorado rivers. This was the first systematic exploration of Canyonlands. Macomb was not impressed with what he found, penning in his final report, "I cannot conceive of a more worthless and impracticable region than the one we now found ourselves in." But another member of the expedition, Dr. John S. Newberry, offered a dissenting opinion, describing the towers of the Needles District as a "forest of Gothic spires," without parallel in nature or art.

Ten years later, Major John Wesley Powell passed through the heart of Canyonlands as he floated down the Green River, through its confluence with the Colorado, and into the fury of Cataract Canyon. At the end of the next decade, cattlemen began to move into southeastern Utah, and they too began to note many of the formations and sites in Canyonlands. These cowboys were joined by lonely prospectors and gold miners who ventured into Canyonlands but did not tap any significant sources of wealth. During the 1950s, uranium miners scoured the region for radioactive "gold," blazing jeep trails across this convoluted canyon landscape. They, along with an ever-increasing number of river runners, stirred a dormant interest in the area by outsiders.

In 1936, Harold Ickes, Secretary of the Interior under Franklin D. Roosevelt, proposed the creation of 7,000-square-mile Escalante National Monument that would encompass nearly all of southeastern Utah west of Hwy. 160, between Bluff and Moab, and a large chunk of real estate west of the Colorado River. World War II and the opposition from state commercial interests doomed the Escalante proposal. But in 1961, Utah's US senator Frank E. "Ted" Moss introduced legislation to establish Canyonlands National Park. This proposal met with resistance, delays, counterproposals, indifference if not hostility from many of his constituents, and criticism from environmentalists when he offered compromise in their behalf. Nevertheless, Canyonlands was given a huge boost by the support of then–Secretary of the Interior Stewart Udall. He flew over the area and decided then and there that such a place must be a national park. Superintendent Bates Wilson of Arches National Park was also very involved in having the park established. Sen. Moss persisted in spearheading the initiative and on September 12, 1964, Canyonlands National Park was created. Sen. Moss took unrestrained pride in being labeled the "Father of Canyonlands National Park."

GEOLOGY

Canyonlands is geology, and the sculpted rocks and mile-deep canyons trace their history back 300 million years when movements along ancient faults formed the Uncompahgre Uplift—a range of lofty mountains to the northwest. At the same time the mountains were being formed, the area that encompasses Canyonlands, known as the Paradox Basin, dropped. Over millions of years the Paradox Basin was covered by ancient seas which left salt deposits that are thousands of feet thick. Added to the salt deposits were layers of dark shale which washed down from the 15,000-foot mountains formed by the Uncompahgre Uplift. On top of these deposits were added layers of silt, sand, mud, and lime from the shells of dying marine creatures. The seas receded and were replaced by vast sand dunes covering thousands of square miles over almost all of the Colorado Plateau. This happened several times, the result of all of this being a multilayered geology thousands of feet thick. These layers hardened into stone and caused the salt layers underneath to flow away.

As the salt layers flowed and shifted, forces inside the earth began pushing upward, intensifying the cracking and fracturing and leaving a broken landscape that was intensified through the forces of erosion acting on layers of differing hardness and thickness. These layers range from the Navajo sandstone on top to the Honeker Trail and Paradox formations, the latter visible only in the depths of the canyon of the Colorado River. As you travel Utah's Canyonlands, you will see black streaks formed on the canyon walls. They come mostly from windblown soil. The clay particles in the soil adhere to moist rock surfaces to which very small amounts of iron and manganese are attracted. Over time, a thin veneer of minerals builds up, creating what is called desert varnish.

PLANT AND ANIMAL LIFE

Rock and sky dominate the view throughout Canyonlands, but the varied plant and animal life should not go unnoticed. The way plants have adapted to a nearly waterless environment and the way wildlife survives in the seemingly hostile desert are an exciting part of the Canyonlands story. Part of the story is the elevation of Canyonlands, which ranges from 4,000 feet along the Colorado River to nearly 7,000 feet atop Cedar Mesa in the Needles District. Cottonwood trees, willows, and tamarisk are found along the rivers and some canyon bottoms. Hanging gardens of maidenhair fern and columbine are clustered around seeps in the rocks. Indian ricegrass, cactus, narrow-leafed yucca, sagebrush, rabbitbrush, blackbrush, Mormon tea, and piñon-juniper woodlands are found in the broad valleys and on top of the mesas that are the backdrop for the canyons and stone formations.

Animal life ranges from tiny biting midges that can be very bothersome to visitors, to the curious inhabitants of potholes—tadpoles, toads, and horsehair worms, to countless lizards, kangaroo rats, piñon mice, chipmunks, ground squirrels, sage sparrows, scrub jays, cliff swallows (which build their nests of mud and plant materials under the protection of overhanging ledges), ravens, hawks, peregrine falcons, turkey vultures, golden eagles, beaver, bobcats, deer, coyotes, foxes, and bighorn sheep.

GETTING THERE

Headquarters for **Canyonlands National Park** is located in Moab at **2282 Southwest Resource Blvd., Moab, UT 84532; (801) 259-7164.** However, unless you have business with park officials, visitors are urged to use the **Moab Visitors Center at Main St. and Center St.** This is an interagency information center and is staffed by national park employees and representatives of other agencies as well. The interagency visitors center in Monticello is located in the **San Juan County Courthouse at 117 South Main.** These three locations are all outside the national park boundaries. Because a visit to the three sections of the park requires three trips, each district has been discussed separately below. Park entrance fees collected at one location are good for the other sections of the park within a seven-day period.

SAFETY AND REGULATIONS

The National Park Service is concerned about safety and proper conduct inside the national parks, with points that apply to all activities in the region. Keep these points in mind. To ignore them can result in fines or placing yourself and companions in life-threatening situations.

- Be prepared for the heat. Carry and drink at least 1 gallon of water per person per day.

- Rest occasionally to avoid overexerting yourself.

- Watch yourself at overlooks and other cliff edges. Walk carefully on slickrock surfaces. It is easy to get stranded, and both adults and unsupervised children have been killed or injured in falls.

- Stay with companions in the backcountry; separation can mean getting lost. If you become lost, stay where you are. Wandering will endanger your life and make finding you more difficult.

- Dogs must be leashed at all times. They are not permitted on park trails or overlooks.

- Help preserve Indian ruins, rock art, historic sites, and other artifacts. Leave them undisturbed; simply entering a ruin or touching rock art can cause damage.

- All park features are protected. Do not pick flowers or collect rocks.

- Flash floods can occur without warning. Never camp in a dry wash or drive across a flooded area.

- Stay off fragile cryptobiotic crust. This black, crunchy soil is actually a delicate, living community of lichens and cyanobacteria that plays a vital ecological role.

- Avoid overexposure to cold, wet conditions—especially on the rivers—that can lead to hypothermia.

- Lightning is a serious threat. When a thunderstorm is near, avoid overlooks, return to your vehicle, and close the windows.

ISLAND IN THE SKY DISTRICT

The northernmost district within Canyonlands, the Island in the Sky District, is a 6,000-foot-high mesa, wedged between the Colorado River on the east and the Green River on the west, with its southern tip towering above the confluence of the two rivers. It is located about 35 miles from Moab and is the most accessible of all the park's units. To get there, drive northwest from Moab on Hwy. 191 for 10 miles to the junction with Hwy. 313, then turn west onto Hwy. 313 and follow it southwest. A **visitors center,** located about 25 miles from Hwy. 191, is open from 8:00 am–4:30 pm in winter, with extended hours spring–fall, and provides information, books, maps, a schedule of interpretive activities, and backcountry permits.

Visitors to Island in the Sky generally spend the day driving the scenic park road, stopping at the overlooks, and perhaps hiking some of the shorter trails. Most visitors also combine a visit to Island in the Sky with a stop at Dead Horse Point State Park, just before you reach the park boundary. (See the **Moab** chapter.) The island road is paved and, unlike many other sections of the park, is user-friendly for automobiles. If you only have a day, this is the best unit of the park to visit.

About 6 miles southwest of the visitors center, the road branches. The southern branch continues on for 6 miles to its terminus at **Grand View Point,** the breathtaking climax to the drive. The western branch heads to **Upheaval Dome Overlook** about 6 miles away, for a look at the park's geological origins.

HIKING

The park road provides access to a dozen or more trailheads that lead to walks and hikes over smooth slickrock of less than a mile to 20 miles in length. Here are some of the most popular and easy-to-hike trails.

Grand View Trail—

One of the most popular trails in Canyonlands, the Grand View Trail is located at the southern end of the scenic drive and provides a stunning view over at least 100 miles of canyons, mesas, rivers, and distant mountains. After studying the display at the Grand View Overlook to become familiar with the landmarks in the distance, hike the 2-mile round-trip trail and drink in this remarkable desert landscape.

Mesa Arch Loop Trail—

About 5.5 miles from the visitors center, the Mesa Arch Loop Trail is another short trail that offers a magnificent view of Mesa Arch. A self-guiding trail pamphlet, available at the trailhead, offers a good introduction to the plant life of Canyonlands. The loop trail, which begins on the east side of the road, is .5 mile long. It winds through piñon and juniper for a magnificent view of the La Sal Mountains as framed through Mesa Arch hanging precariously on the edge of the cliff.

Murphy Point Overlook Trail—

Three miles beyond the Mesa Arch Loop Trailhead, the Murphy Point Overlook Trail offers superb views of the Green River below and a panorama that takes in the Needles District and Blue Mountains to the southeast, the Maze District and Henry Mountains to the southwest, and the San Rafael Swell to the west. The 2.4-mile round-trip hike is mostly across unmarked slickrock, but it is not difficult to negotiate or to keep your orientation.

Neck Spring Loop Trail—

From the same trailhead that takes you to the Shafer Canyon Overlook, you can start west instead of east and follow the 5-mile-long Neck Spring Loop Trail, which offers magnificent views of Canyonlands and a more intimate perspective on the early cattle-ranching activities in the region. The remains of an old corral, water trough, and drift fence are visible. The trail follows paths used by animals to reach the springs. On occasion mule deer, bobcats, and bighorn sheep have been spotted, more likely will be the ground squirrels and chipmunks.

Shafer Canyon Overlook Trail—

Located .5 mile south of the visitor center, the Shafer Canyon Overlook Trail is only .25 mile in length and the .5-mile-round-trip has little elevation gain and can be made by most visitors. From the viewpoint you can see the canyon of the Colorado River, the beginning of the 100-mile-long White Rim Rd., and the switchbacks of the Shafer Trail Rd. winding 1,000 feet into the canyon.

Upheaval Dome Overlook Trail—

Located at the end of the Upheaval Dome Rd. or the western branch of the park road, this 2-mile round-trip hike offers sensational close-up views of 1,500-foot Upheaval Dome, described by geologists as among the most peculiar geological features in the world. The dome is thought by many geologists to be either a collapsed salt dome or a meteorite impact crater. The salt dome theory is based on the fact that a salt layer, thousands of feet thick, underlies the entire area. Because the salt is less dense than the sandstone covering it, the salt moved upward into the sandstone at this location, forming a "salt bubble"; when the overlying sandstone eroded away, the salt was exposed. It also eroded away, leaving the sandstone, which separated the bubble from the rest of the salt layer. The meteor theory, a more recent theory proposed by some geologists, holds that this was the site of impact for a meteor approximately .33 mile in diameter, which struck around 60 million years ago. Erosion has washed away any evidence of meteorite debris. The Upheaval Dome viewpoint offers a panorama of the western Canyonlands stretching from the Henry Mountains north to Thousand Lake Mountain, the San Rafael Swell, and the Book Cliffs. The trail is a geology enthusiast's dream. The "Upheaval Dome View Trail Guide," available at the trailhead, describes the theories of crater origin.

White Rim Overlook Trail—

For the best view in the Island in the Sky District of the 2,000-foot-deep canyon of the Colorado River, you will want to take the White Rim Overlook. The trail is 1.5 miles round-trip and begins about 11 miles south of the visitors center, after turning off the park road into a picnic area.

CAMPING

Willow Flat Campground—

Twelve sites. No fee. Available on a first-come, first-served basis. No water available at the campground or anywhere on the Island—bring all the water you will need. Arrive very early to secure a site. The campground is located on the Island in the Sky Mesa just off the Upheaval Dome Rd. near its junction with the road to Grand View Point. Camping is not allowed anywhere else in the district, except backcountry vehicle sites by permit only.

———————— NEEDLES DISTRICT ————————

The southeastern district of Canyonlands, the Needles District, is accessed from Hwy. 191, south of Moab. Follow the highway south for 40 miles to its junction with Hwy. 211, a Scenic Byway. Turn west and follow 211 and follow the 38-mile paved Scenic Byway through Indian Creek Canyon to Squaw Flat, where many trails into the Needles begin. The **Needles Visitors Center** is 35 miles from Hwy. 191. Four-wheel-drive trails take you to overlooks, Anasazi ruins, and rock art.

BIKING

Within the Needles District, there are two excellent mountain bike trails which are also used by backpackers and four-wheel-drivers. The 14-mile round-trip, moderately difficult Colorado River Overlook Rd. offers beautiful scenery all along the trail. The view from the Colorado River Overlook, more than 1,000 feet down, is one not soon to be forgotten. Bikers in good shape can make the ride in a couple of hours, but with so much scenery on this ride, it is best to take your time. The trail begins from the southwestern end of the visitors center parking area and heads north along a signed dirt road. The Elephant Hill Rd. is more difficult because of the sandy and rocky sections that bikers will need to walk, but it is also a good ride of 9.6 miles over a semiloop which can be expanded to 28.5 miles by taking a couple of side trips. The trail begins at the Elephant Hill Trailhead (see the Hiking section).

HIKING

Always bring water with you no matter what the season. You'll need 1 gallon per person per day and more for summer hiking or extended trips. Wear lightweight hiking boots and protect yourself from the sun, especially your head! Carry a map and know how to use it.

Cave Spring Trail—

This .6-mile loop walk is located 2.5 miles beyond the visitors center. Pick up a trail guide at the trailhead for this hike. The leaflet interprets the vegetation along the trail, which winds past a pictograph panel with ancient handprints and a well-preserved cowboy line camp near Cave Spring that was used from the late 1800s until the 1950s. Because the cattle herds were spread over a vast area, cowboys were required to live away from the ranch to tend the animals. Cowboys often spent six weeks at a time in isolation at the line camps, where they cooked over an open fire and spent their days keeping track of the cattle—an idyllic and adventuresome life that many

have envied. Here you can touch many of the items left by the cowboys, but be sure to leave everything for others to enjoy. The walk requires the use of two ladders to negotiate the steep Cedar Mesa sandstone sections but is still a fairly easy walk. You start out walking along and underneath the cliff, then climb on top of the mesa using the ladders. This is a great trail for families.

Confluence Overlook—

This moderate hike of 11 miles round-trip takes the better part of a day, but the view of the confluence of the Green and Colorado rivers is well worth the effort and the time. The confluence comes into view suddenly and is one of the most impressive sights in all of southeastern Utah. The trail begins at the end of the north branch of the paved road, 5.5 miles past the visitors center.

Elephant Hill Trailhead—

This trailhead offers three excellent day hikes of 10 to 11 miles round-trip. The most popular hike is the 10.8-mile round-trip Druid Arch Trail. One of the most impressive arches anywhere, Druid Arch appears to be southeastern Utah's version of England's Stonehenge. The 10.7-mile semiloop Chesler Park Trail takes you into Chesler Park—a grassy, broad, relatively level area with a cluster of spires jutting up in the middle—and to the east edge of the Grabens—an area of narrow, shallow, grassy valleys which lies between two elevated faults. It is a popular backpacking destination, with three designated camping zones (backcountry permit and fee required) in Chesler Park. The hike also includes the Joint Trail section, one of the most exciting trails within Canyonlands, and one that claustrophobic hikers will not enjoy because of the narrow squeeze (only about 2 feet wide in some sections) between the rocks. The 3rd trail, the Devil's Pocket Trail, is a 10.5-mile semi-loop hike that takes you around the most impressive 500-foot-high pinnacles in the Needles District, through the graben valley known as Devil's Pocket, to the edge of Chesler Park.

Many regard this as the most scenic hike in the Needles District because of the magnificent vistas, balanced rocks, and the 500-foot-high slender needles of stone which you pass. Nevertheless, it is one of the least-used trails in the district. This trailhead is located about 5.5 miles past the visitors center, at the end of the south branch of the park road toward Campground B. Instead of entering the campground, continue straight ahead onto the dirt road after the pavement ends. It is about 2.5 miles from the end of the pavement to the trailhead, but the dirt road is passable for passenger cars. Watch for rocks and sand and pay attention to the sharp curves and narrow stretches.

Pothole Point Trail—

Potholes that have formed in the slickrock are one of the most interesting features of the Canyonlands region. They range in size from a foot or less in diameter to deep depressions that are more like caves turned on their side. Sometimes called "tanks" because they serve as natural reservoirs to store rainwater, they have become the source of legend and folklore in southeastern Utah. One tank (located outside the park) became known as Jailhouse Rock, when a rancher supposedly put his wife into it because she objected to his going to a Moab saloon. You won't pass Jailhouse Rock on this .6-mile semiloop trail since it is many miles away, but with a leaflet available at the trailhead you can learn about potholes and the creatures that inhabit them, including snails, horsehair worms, spade-foot and red-spotted toads, tadpoles, and fairy and clam shrimps. The Pothole Point Trail begins 4.5 miles west of the visitors center.

Roadside Ruin Trail—

This .3-mile walk begins .4 mile west of the visitors center and leads to a well-preserved Anasazi granary. A leaflet keyed to numbered posts along the trail is available at the beginning of the trail which describes native plants, many of which were used by the Anasazi, such as the Utah juniper, the

soft bark of which was used as diapers and cradleboard padding for babies. The seeds of Indian ricegrass were gathered, cooked, and ground into meal. Prickly pear cactus was used as a food and for compresses for wounds. The spines of the narrow-leaf yucca were used as needles and the leaf fibers were made into cord, rope, and woven for sandals and mats.

Slickrock Foot Trail—

This hike may be a little longer than some will want to make. Still, the 3-mile walk is quite easy and offers panoramic views all along its length, plus a good introduction to the slickrock trails marked by rock cairns (small stacks of rocks that mark the way) on the "petrified" sand dunes. A trail guide with a map and brief description interprets the trail. The trailhead is roughly 5 miles past the visitors center, just a short distance before the end of the paved road.

Squaw Flat Trailhead—

Squaw Flat Trailhead offers access to four day hikes, ranging in length from 7.4 miles to 10.7 miles. These trails take you into the heart of the red spires and pinnacles of the Needles themselves and are part of the reason that most campers in the Needles area are hikers. You can spend up to a maximum 14 days in the campground and take a different hike each day. The four trails from Squaw Flat Trailhead are the Squaw Canyon Loop Trail (7.4 miles); Lost Canyon Trail (8.7 miles over a semiloop); Peekaboo Arch Trail (9.4 miles round-trip); and Elephant and Big Spring Canyons Trail (10.7 miles over a semiloop). These hikes are best taken in the spring and early summer or from late Sept.–Nov. to avoid the extreme summer heat. The trailhead is at the end of the middle branch of the paved road, about 3 miles from the visitors center.

FOUR-WHEEL-DRIVE TRIPS

Long before the hikers and mountain bikers discovered the Needles District, and while cowboys from Dugout Ranch were still herding cattle in the region on horseback, the jeepsters, as the early four-wheel-drivers were often called, discovered the unlimited opportunities to test their machines and driving skills over the slickrock, around the pinnacles and ledges, and through the sand of the Needles. Four-wheel-drive vehicles are considered a part of the basic transportation requirements for most residents of southeastern Utah, and four-wheel-drive trips are a popular form of recreation. Rentals and tours can be arranged at the Needles Outpost, located on a spur road near the entrance to Canyonlands, or in several of the surrounding communities. In addition to the Colorado River Overlook and the Elephant Hill Rd. noted above, other four-wheel-drive trips include the following.

Davis Canyon—

Davis Canyon parallels Lavender Canyon to the northwest and it too heads in a southwesterly direction. Watch for the small "Davis Canyon" sign on the left or west side of Hwy. 211 about 24 miles from the junction of Hwy. 211 and Hwy. 191. The round-trip distance is 24 miles and offers plenty of opportunities to explore the side canyons into Davis Canyon at the end of the road.

Lavender Canyon—

If you are inexperienced, this 35-mile round-trip drive is a good choice. The road access is the same as for Davis Canyon, about 24 miles from its junction with Hwy. 191, and heads up Lavender Creek in a southwesterly direction from Hwy. 211. It does not enter Canyonlands National Park until the last couple of miles, near the Cedar Mesa area. Several arches and a labyrinth of narrow canyons make this an interesting area to explore on foot once you get there.

Salt Creek and Horse Canyon Four-Wheel Roads—

These two roads begin 2.3 miles beyond the visitors center and offer a good introduction to four-wheeling within Canyonlands, as well as an up-close look at Indian ruins and rock art. The 20.3-mile road up Salt Creek takes you through the Salt Creek Archaeological District—a 55,000-acre district along Salt Creek and its tributaries, which includes Anasazi sites where arrowheads and other points were made, storage granaries, pictograph and petroglyph panels, and habitation sites ranging from temporary locations to open habitation sites and houses built in alcoves. With an additional 2.6-mile drive you can reach the trailhead to Angel Arch. The hike to Angel Arch is .5 mile. Be sure to make time to hike to the largest, and what many consider the most beautiful, arch in Canyonlands. The Horse Canyon Trail follows the Salt Creek Trail for 2.5 miles before bearing to the left to enter Horse Canyon, a tributary of Salt Creek. The total distance along the Horse Canyon Rd. is just under 9 miles, including a side trip to the Tower Ruin, one of the best-preserved Anasazi cliff dwellings within the park. The trail passes several interesting arches, which can be seen by taking the short hiking trails, each less than .5 mile in length, to Gothic Arch, Castle Arch, and Fortress Arch. Check at the visitors center for specific information since draft management plans call for closing some of the roads to four-wheel vehicles.

CAMPING

Squaw Flat Campground—

Campground A has 16 sites; **Campground B** has 10 sites. Chemical toilets are provided in each campground. Water is available Apr.–Oct. The rest of the year, it must be either brought in or obtained in other locations within the park. Fees are charged for the campsites, and stays are limited to seven days. A private campground, **Needles Outpost,** is located just outside the park. It has a general store with maps and books, gasoline, snack bar, showers, and a campground with water. A fee is charged for camping.

MAZE DISTRICT

Even though it is visible from both the Island in the Sky and Needles districts, you have to really want to go into the Maze District to get there. But the pure experience that the Maze District offers, the desert and the rocks at their finest, make the effort to get there all the more worthwhile. Located west of the Green and Colorado rivers, it is accessible only by four-wheel-drive roads and hiking trails, and it is the intent of the National Park Service to keep it this way. This primitive area has no facilities. Its primary users are hikers wishing to see the spectacular Barrier Canyon–style rock art in Horseshoe Canyon and backpackers who spend several days hiking and exploring the deep canyons and strange rock landmarks that begin west of the river confluence.

Getting There

About 25 miles south of the junction with Interstate 70 and 21 miles north of Hanksville, the road into the Maze District leaves Hwy. 24 and heads east. You take a 46-mile unpaved road to **Hans Flat Ranger Station,** which is usually passable to two-wheel-drive vehicles, but from the ranger station you must hike or use a high-clearance four-wheel-drive vehicle.

During the 46-mile drive into Hans Flat you may detour (about 30 miles in) to hike into **Horseshoe Canyon,** a separate unit of Canyonlands National Park in which impressive 2,000-year-old pictographs have been left by the Archaic people. The round-trip hike through Horseshoe Canyon is 6.5 miles long and can take the good part of a day, especially if you count the drive time from Moab, Green River, or Hanksville. The panels of rock art in Horseshoe are arguably the most fascinating and best executed in Utah. They include Archaic and possibly Fremont pictographs, with, in some cases, the more recent red paintings superimposed over the older Archaic panels. The stillness of the canyon, its isolation, and the realization that little has changed in the 2,000 years

since the first paintings were sketched on the canyon walls are an experience not soon forgotten.

From Hans Flat Ranger Station, the four-wheel road continues 14 miles south to the top of the **Flint Trail.** Carefully driving down the narrow switchbacks, the road intersects several jeep trails that eventually make their way to the **Maze Overlook.** Because of the difficult switchbacks, this is a high-clearance four-wheel-drive vehicle trail.

The hiking route into the Maze begins at the Overlook. It is steep and difficult, requiring the use of rope in some places to lower your pack. However, once you enter the Maze, the hiking is along sandy wash bottoms. The trails are marked with rock cairns, but all hikers should carry a compass and topographical maps and know how to use them.

Another area of the Maze District is the **Land of Standing Rocks,** an 8-mile stretch of high plateaus and spires. There are no established trails here, but there are a wide variety of routes that you can follow to **Lizard Rock, The Plug, Chimney Rock,** and **The Wall,** as well as past hundreds of unnamed formations.

Southeast of the Land of Standing Rocks is the **Doll House,** where there are two established trails. The **Spanish Bottoms Trail** is a steep, shadeless, 1.2-mile descent to the Colorado River just above Cataract Canyon. The **Colorado/Green River Overlook Trail** is 5 miles one way and winds up and down over the slickrock, offering wonderful views.

VISITOR INFORMATION

Before venturing into the Maze District, it is best to get outfitted with proper maps and reliable information at the **Moab Information Center,** at the **Needles Visitors Center,** or at **Island in the Sky.** Carry at least 1 gallon of water per person per day (if not more), a towrope (or better yet a winch), a shovel, tire chains, and survival gear. Be prepared in case you get stuck or your vehicle breaks down. The road is rough and slow-going in most sections. About 46 miles from the junction with Hwy. 24 (48 miles if you count the 3.4-mile round-trip detour to Horseshoe Canyon), there is **Hans Flat Ranger Station** that serves both Canyonlands National Park and the northern end of Glen Canyon National Recreation Area, whose eastern boundary is the western boundary of Canyonlands.

Although Canyonlands National Park is five times larger than Arches National Park (pictured above) and three times as large as Zion, it receives far fewer visitors than most of the national parks in Utah. Photo by Brian David.

Index